THE NATIONAL BASEBALL HALL OF FAME ALMANAC

2014 EDITION

National Baseball Hall of Fame and Museum

25 Main Street
Cooperstown, NY 13326
(607) 547-7200

PHOTO CREDITS

All images Baseball Hall of Fame Library, unless otherwise noted

Acknowledgements

Mary Bellew	Sue MacKay
Dan Bennett	Ken Meifert
Bill Francis	Scot Mondore
Sean Gahagan	Craig Muder
Jim Gates	Helen Stiles
Jeff Idelson	Claudette Scrafford
Pat Kelly	Jason Schiellack
Michael Klar	Erik Strohl
Donny Lowe	

The National Baseball Hall of Fame celebrates its 75th anniversary in 2014

Baseball America

4319 S. Alston Avenue, Suite 103
Durham, NC 27713
(919) 682-9635

EDITOR
Will Lingo

PRODUCTION AND DESIGN
Sara Hiatt McDaniel

CONTRIBUTING WRITERS
Ben Badler, Freddy Berowski, Alexis Brudnicki, Teddy
Cahill, Samantha Carr, J.J. Cooper, Kyle Dugan, Matt
Eddy, Aaron Fitt, Bill Francis, Jim Gates, Conor Glassey,
Josh Leventhal, Craig Muder, John Manuel, Nathan Rode,
Jim Shonerd, Tim Wiles

BaseBall america

PRESIDENT/PUBLISHER Lee Folger
DIRECTOR OF EDITORIAL & OPERATIONS Will Lingo

EDITORIAL
EDITOR IN CHIEF John Manuel
MANAGING EDITOR J.J. Cooper
NEWS EDITOR Josh Leventhal
ASSOCIATE EDITOR Matt Eddy
WEB EDITOR Vincent Lara-Cinisomo
NATIONAL WRITERS Ben Badler, Aaron Fitt
ASSISTANT EDITORS Clint Longenecker, Josh Norris, Jim Shonerd

PRODUCTION
DESIGN & PRODUCTION DIRECTOR Sara Hiatt McDaniel
MULTIMEDIA MANAGER Linwood Webb
PRODUCTION MANAGER Jason Jopling

ADVERTISING
ADVERTISING DIRECTOR George Shelton
DIRECT MARKETING MANAGER Ximena Caceres
MARKETPLACE MANAGER Kristopher M. Lull
ADVERTISING ACCOUNT EXECUTIVE Abbey Langdon

BUSINESS
CUSTOMER SERVICE Melissa Hales, Ronnie McCabe
ACCOUNTING/OFFICE MANAGER Hailey Carpenter
TECHNOLOGY MANAGER Brent Lewis
ADMINISTRATIVE ASSISTANT Shannon Tuohey

WHERE TO DIRECT QUESTIONS
ADVERTISING: advertising@baseballamerica.com
BUSINESS BEAT: joshleventhal@baseballamerica.com
COLLEGES: aaronfitt@baseballamerica.com
DESIGN/PRODUCTION: production@baseballamerica.com
DRAFT: johnmanuel@baseballamerica.com
HIGH SCHOOLS: clintlongenecker@baseballamerica.com
INDEPENDENT LEAGUES: jjcooper@baseballamerica.com
MAJOR LEAGUES: matteddy@baseballamerica.com
MINOR LEAGUES: joshleventhal@baseballamerica.com
PHOTOS: photos@baseballamerica.com
PROSPECTS: benbadler@baseballamerica.com
REPRINTS: production@baseballamerica.com
SUBSCRIPTIONS/CUSTOMER SERVICE:
customerservice@baseballamerica.com
WEBSITE: customerservice@baseballamerica.com

GRINDMEDIA MANAGEMENT
SVP, GROUP PUBLISHER Norb Garret
norb.garrett@grindmedia.com
VP, DIGITAL Greg Morrow
greg.morrow@grindmedia.com
PRODUCTION DIRECTOR Kasey Kelley
kasey.kelley@grindmedia.com
EDITORIAL DIRECTOR–DIGITAL Chris Mauro
chris.mauro@grindmedia.com
FINANCE DIRECTOR Adam Miner
adam.miner@grindmedia.com
VP, MANUFACTURING & ADVERTISING OPERATIONS
Greg Parnell greg.parnell@sorc.com
SENIOR DIRECTOR, AD OPERATIONS Pauline Atwood
pauline.atwood@sorc.com
DIRECTOR, PUBLISHING TECHNOLOGIES Dale Bryson
dale.bryson@sorc.com
DIRECTOR OF EVENTS Scott Desiderio
scott.desiderio@transworld.net

ADVERTISING SALES
SALES STRATEGY MGR/PRINT & EVENTS
Chris Engelsman chris.engelsman@grindmedia.com
SALES STRATEGY MGR/DIGITAL Elisabeth Murray
elisabeth.murray@grindmedia.com

DIGITAL
DIRECTOR OF ENGINEERING Jeff Kimmel
jeff.kimmel@grindmedia.com
SENIOR PRODUCT MANAGER Rishi Kumar
rishi.kumar@grindmedia.com
SENIOR PRODUCT MANAGER Marc Bartell
marc.bartell@grindmedia.com
CREATIVE DIRECTOR Peter Tracy peter.tracy@
grindmedia.com

MARKETING & EVENTS
DIRECTOR OF EVENT SALES Sean Nielsen
sean.nielsen@grindmedia.com

FACILITIES
MANAGER Randy Ward randy.ward@grindmedia.com
OFFICE COORDINATOR Ruth Hosea
ruth.hosea@grindmedia.com
ARCHIVIST Thomas Voehringer
thomas.voehringer@sorc.com

SOURCE INTERLINK MEDIA

SOURCE INTERLINK MEDIA, LLC
CEO Scott P. Dickey
PRESIDENT Chris Argentieri
EVP, CHIEF FINANCIAL OFFICER AND TREASURER
Bill Sutman
EVP, GENERAL MANAGER David Algire
EVP, CHIEF CREATIVE OFFICER Alan Alpanian
SVP, FINANCE Dan Bednar
EVP, ENTHUSIAST AUTOMOTIVE Doug Evans
EVP, CHIEF CONTENT OFFICER Angus MacKenzie
EVP, CHIEF ANALYTICS OFFICER John Marriott
EVP, CHIEF PROCUREMENT OFFICER Kevin Mullan
SVP, BUSINESS DEVELOPMENT Tyler Schulze
EVP, SALES AND MARKETING Eric Schwab

DIGITAL MEDIA
CHIEF TECHNOLOGY OFFICER, DIGITAL MEDIA
Raghu Bala
SVP, DIGITAL MARKETING Craig Buccola
SVP, DIGITAL PRODUCT DEVELOPMENT Todd Busby
VP, PRODUCT MANAGEMENT Geoff DeFrance

CONSUMER MARKETING,
ENTHUSIAST MEDIA
SUBSCRIPTION COMPANY, INC.
VP, CONSUMER MARKETING Tom Slater
VP, RETENTION & OPERATIONS FULFILLMENT
Donald T. Robinson III

TABLE OF CONTENTS

Hall of Fame Member Biographies

Appendix

ABOUT THE 2014 NATIONAL BASEBALL HALL OF FAME ALMANAC

Because the historic record of baseball is not perfect, there are many discrepancies and inconsistencies between the multiple sources of historic and statistical data. Researchers are also faced with the fact that baseball data is not static. Playing data and personal data are constantly being updated and corrected as new discoveries are announced. To that end, what is correct today may need to be updated tomorrow.

The National Baseball Hall of Fame follows these protocols in the Almanac:

■ **Basic biographical and statistical data:** Baseball-Reference.com is the standard resource for basic biographical and statistical data.

■ **Negro Leagues data:** The National Baseball Hall of Fame sponsored a major effort with the Negro Leagues Researchers and Authors Group, whose focus was on league-sanctioned games between 1920 and 1954 for which there was either a score sheet or box score. This data is now available at Baseball-Reference.com and serves as the primary source for this Almanac.

Major League Baseball All-Star Game

■ **Selections**: the number of times a player was selected or elected to an All-Star team;

■ **Appearances:** the number of times a player actually appeared in an All-Star Game;

■ **Seasons:** the number of seasons for which a player was selected or elected to an All-Star team.

■ **Please note:** There were two All-Star Games played from 1959 to 1962, with the rosters not being identical.

■ **Major League Baseball Postseason Play:** Postseason appearances refer to an individual actually appearing in at least one postseason game in a given year.

Major League Baseball Awards

■ **Cy Young Award:** Begun in 1956, this Baseball Writers' Association of America award was given to one major league pitcher until 1966, and has been awarded to one pitcher in each league since 1967.

■ **Rookie of the Year Award:** Now called the Jackie Robinson Rookie of the Year Award, it was given to one player in 1947 and 1948, and has since been awarded by the BBWAA to one player in each league.

■ **Most Valuable Player Award:** This BBWAA award has been handed out to one player in each league since 1931.

■ **Manager of the Year Award:** Created in 1983, this BBWAA award is bestowed upon one manager in each league.

■ **Rolaids Relief Man Award:** This award is given to the top closer in each league, and it began in 1976.

■ **Comeback Player of the Year Award:** This recent addition to the awards list began in 2005 and is handed out to one player in each league.

■ **The Sporting News Most Valuable Player Award:** Existing from 1929 to 1945, the TSN handed out this award to one player in each league.

■ **The Chalmers Award:** Sponsored by the Chalmers Motor Company this honor was bestowed upon the player with the highest batting average from 1910 to 1914.

The 2014
INDUCTEES

Bobby Cox

Bobby Cox always preferred the shadows of his office, puffing on cigars and talking baseball. His unparalleled three decades as a big league manager, however, kept dragging him into the spotlight.

"Of the men in my life, after my father, Bobby Cox would be right there," Leo Mazzone once said with moisture in his eyes during his tenure as Cox's long-time pitching coach with the Braves. "He has been the biggest influence on my career out of anybody I've been around."

It was an influence that turned players into teams and the Braves into a model franchise. It was an influence that resulted in15 division championships, five pennants and the 1995 World Series title.

It was an influence that changed everyone Cox met.

Born May 21, 1941 in Tulsa, Okla., Cox grew up in Fresno, Calif., and signed with the Dodgers following his high school graduation and worked his way through the minor leagues for a decade. The New York Yankees gave Cox his chance to play in the majors for two seasons in 1968 and 1969. And when he couldn't play third base anymore due to wobbly knees, the Yankees gave Cox a chance to manage in their farm system in 1971.

Cox coached first base for the Yankees during their 1977 World Championship season, then joined the Braves to manage owner Ted Turner's team in 1978. Turner reluctantly dismissed Cox following the strike-affected 1981 season, then talked Cox into leaving the Blue Jays as their manager after they won their division in 1985 and into joining the Braves as general manager.

Soon afterward, Cox, the GM, became as impressive as Cox, the manager. Under Cox's leadership, the Braves' farm system improved enough to produce the likes of Tom Glavine, David Justice, Steve Avery, Mark Lemke, Jeff Blauser and others who formed the foundation for those championship Braves teams of the 1990s. Those teams eventually began a record streak of 14 consecutive division titles, and they also won five pennants and the 1995 World Series over the Cleveland Indians.

Cox collected four Manager of the Year Awards and is among just four men ever to win that honor in both leagues. He also is the only manager to capture the award in consecutive years.

Nobody not named Connie Mack, John McGraw or Tony La Russa has more career victories as a manager than Cox.

"It's the players," Cox said. "You have to have the players."

Elected To The Hall Of Fame: *2014.*
Born: *May 21, 1941 at Tulsa, Okla.*
Teams: *Manager, Atlanta N.L. 1978-81, 1990-2010; Toronto A.L.1982-85.*

TEAM	LEAGUE	YEARS	W	L	PCT.	CHAMPIONSHIPS
ATLANTA	NL	25 (1978-81, 1990-2010)	2149	1709	.557	5 PENNANTS, 1 WORLD SERIES TITLE
TORONTO	AL	4 (1982-85)	355	292	.549	
CAREER TOTALS		29	2504	2001	.556	

TOM GLAVINE

Tom Glavine never looked the part of an intimidating two-time Cy Young Award winner.

Physically, that is. And yet Glavine always appeared thicker and taller than his 6-foot, 175-pound frame whenever he took the pitcher's mound in the big leagues. That's because everybody – from the hitters to the fans to the man himself – sensed his unwavering confidence.

"Anybody who knows me knows that, if I'm going to do something, I'm going to do it as well as I can," Glavine said.

What Glavine did was carve out one of the greatest careers of any left-handed pitcher. During his 17 seasons with the Braves and five with the New York Mets, Glavine used a potent combination of talent, longevity and guts to fashion his journey to Cooperstown. He won two Cy Young Awards (in 1991 and 1998), and finished second twice and third twice. There were his five seasons with 20 or more victories. Only three left-handers – Warren Spahn, Steve Carlton and Eddie Plank – ever posted more victories than Glavine's 305.

Drafted by the Braves in 1984, Glavine was also taken by the National Hockey League's Los Angeles Kings in the NHL Draft that year but chose to focus on baseball. After a rocky start that saw him go 31-37 in his first three full seasons, Glavine evolved into the face of a Braves franchise that finished in first place in 14 straight completed seasons.

It wasn't a coincidence the soft-spoken man with the even softer pitches won the clinching game in 1995 when the Braves captured their only World Series during their record-setting run. With David Justice slamming a solo home run, and with Glavine limiting a heavy-hitting Cleveland Indians team to no runs and one hit for eight innings in Game 6, the Braves captured a 1-0 victory.

"Being around guys like John (Smoltz) and Greg (Maddux) and so many other guys that were here over the years – people always talk about that competition we had on the pitching staff, and we had it," Glavine said. "But it was always in a fun way, always in a respectful way, always in a way that we honestly drove each other to be better."

Elected To The Hall Of Fame: 2014.
Born: March 25, 1966 in Concord, Mass.
Height: 6-0. **Weight:** 175.
Threw: Left. **Batted:** Left.
Debut: Aug. 17, 1987.
Final Game: Aug. 14, 2008.
Teams: Atlanta N.L. (1987-2002, 2008);
New York N.L. (2003-07)
Postseason: World Series Champion (1995);
5 N.L. Pennants (1991-92, 1995-96, 1999);
12-Time Playoff Qualifier (1991-93, 1995-2002, 2006).
Awards: 10-Time All-Star (1991-93, 1996-98, 2000, 2002, 2004, 2006); 2-Time N.L. Cy Young Award Winner (1991, 1998).

YEAR	TEAM	LEAGUE	G	W	L	SV	SHO	IP	H	BB	SO	ERA
1987	ATLANTA	NL	9	2	4	0	0	50	55	33	20	5.54
1988	ATLANTA	NL	34	7	17	0	0	195	201	63	84	4.56
1989	ATLANTA	NL	29	14	8	0	4	186	172	40	90	3.68
1990	ATLANTA	NL	33	10	12	0	0	214	232	78	129	4.28
1991	ATLANTA	NL	34	20	11	0	1	247	201	69	192	2.55
1992	ATLANTA	NL	33	20	8	0	5	225	197	70	129	2.76
1993	ATLANTA	NL	36	22	6	0	2	239	236	90	120	3.2
1994	ATLANTA	NL	25	13	9	0	0	165	173	70	140	3.97
1995	ATLANTA	NL	29	16	7	0	1	199	182	66	127	3.08
1996	ATLANTA	NL	36	15	10	0	0	235	222	85	181	2.98
1997	ATLANTA	NL	33	14	7	0	2	240	197	79	152	2.96
1998	ATLANTA	NL	33	20	6	0	3	229	202	74	157	2.47
1999	ATLANTA	NL	35	14	11	0	0	234	259	83	138	4.12
2000	ATLANTA	NL	35	21	9	0	2	241	222	65	152	3.4
2001	ATLANTA	NL	35	16	7	0	1	219	213	97	116	3.57
2002	ATLANTA	NL	36	18	11	0	1	225	210	78	127	2.96
2003	NEW YORK	NL	32	9	14	0	0	183	205	66	82	4.52
2004	NEW YORK	NL	33	11	14	0	1	212	204	70	109	3.6
2005	NEW YORK	NL	33	13	13	0	1	211	227	61	105	3.53
2006	NEW YORK	NL	32	15	7	0	0	198	202	62	131	3.82
2007	NEW YORK	NL	34	13	8	0	1	200	219	64	89	4.45
2008	ATLANTA	NL	13	2	4	0	0	63	67	37	37	5.54
CAREER TOTALS			**682**	**305**	**203**	**0**	**25**	**4413**	**4298**	**1500**	**2607**	**3.54**

TONY LA RUSSA

Tony La Russa always seemed two steps ahead of other managers. He did it by working twice as hard as nearly everyone else.

"Hope to be great," La Russa said. "But always prepare for the worst."

La Russa prepared as well as any manager in history. Born Oct. 4, 1944 in Tampa, Fla., La Russa was a $100,000 bonus player when he signed with the Kansas City Athletics in 1962. Though he had a long and prosperous minor league career, he hurt his throwing arm early in his career and never really stuck in the big leagues.

In infrequent play, he collected just 35 big league hits – none of them home runs – in 176 at-bats. So it was that more than one instructor along the way recommended he should try to become a coach or a manager.

After earning a law degree from Florida State University in the 1970s, La Russa appeared headed for a career as a lawyer. But after giving managing a try in the minors, he quickly ascended to the majors and was named the White Sox manager by Bill Veeck in August of 1979 at the age of 34.

By 1983, La Russa had led the White Sox to the American League West title and won the first of his four career Manager of the Year crowns. He was dismissed by the Sox during the 1986 season before landing with the A's just weeks later. By 1988, La Russa had turned the A's into AL champions. From 1988-92, Oakland won four AL West titles, three AL pennants and the 1989 World Series title.

La Russa left the A's following the 1995 season and headed for St. Louis, where he managed the Cardinals from 1996-2011. In those 16 seasons, his teams won 1,408 games (an average of 88 games a year), including seven National League Central titles, three NL pennants and World Series titles in 2006 and 2011.

Along the way, La Russa established himself as one of the game's most respected managers – and one willing to adapt to changing conditions.

"The first concession you have to make," said La Russa, "is that if you're part of a solid organization, the influence of you as a manager or staff is going to be affected in a very important way – the way I had it in Chicago, Oakland and St. Louis, starting from the top. That's not just being politically correct. It's the truth.

"I always looked at it as a responsibility. Not only was it our staff but it was the trainers, the equipment guys and the video people. Everybody who made an impact on the major league – we were part of the responsibility."

Elected To The Hall Of Fame: 2014.
Born: Oct. 4 1944 in Tampa, Fla.
Teams: Manager, Chicago A.L. 1979-86; Oakland A.L. 1986-95; St. Louis N.L. 1996-2011.

TEAM	LEAGUE	YEARS	W	L	PCT.	CHAMPIONSHIPS
CHICAGO	AL	8 (1979-86)	522	510	.506	
OAKLAND	AL	10 (1986-95)	798	673	.542	3 PENNANTS, 1 WORLD SERIES TITLE
ST. LOUIS	NL	16 (1996-2011)	1408	1182	.544	3 PENNANTS, 2 WORLD SERIES TITLES
CAREER TOTALS		**33**	**2728**	**2365**	**.536**	

GREG MADDUX

Growing up, Greg Maddux and his brother played a game they called Home Run Derby.

"It was one strike and you're out," said Mike Maddux, a former big league pitcher himself and now a respected pitching coach for the Texas Rangers. "Home plate was a wicker lawn chair, and we used a Wiffle ball. A swing and a miss or a foul ball was an out. If you didn't swing and the pitch hit the chair, you were out. So we had a target for every single pitch. We learned as boys the importance of location."

Greg Maddux parlayed that Home Run Derby experience and pinpoint pitching accuracy into a pitching career that frustrated the best hitters in the game and took him to Cooperstown.

"It was the most fun we had growing up," Greg says. "Yes, it was great practice, but it never for a minute felt like work."

The statistics Maddux compiled in 23 years in the major leagues present a picture of one of the game's best pitchers: A 3.16 career ERA, 355 wins, 3,371 strikeouts with only 999 walks, an unmatched 17 straight seasons of 15 or more wins, 18 Gold Glove Awards, four Cy Young Awards (1992-95) and one of the aces of an Atlanta Braves staff that won 10 straight divisional crowns, three NL pennants and the 1995 World Series.

But there are other, less-noticed attributes that solidify his credentials, including being a great teammate.

"Greg kept everything lighthearted in the locker room," rotation-mate John Smoltz said. "But even with all the joking and needling that went on, Greg was always willing to help other guys on the team when they might be struggling with their motion, or wondering how to get a hitter out. Here was a guy on top of his profession, and there was a lot of pressure for him year after year to perform to his own high standards, yet he handled it with remarkable ease."

Elected To The Hall Of Fame: 2014.
Born: April 14, 1966 in San Angelo, Texas.
Height: 6-0. **Weight:** 170.
Threw: Right. **Batted:** Right.
Debut: Sept. 2, 1986. **Final Game:** Sept. 27, 2008.
Teams: Chicago N.L. 1986-92, 2004-06; Atlanta N.L. 1993-2003; Los Angeles N.L. 2006, 2008; San Diego N.L. 2007-08.
Postseason: World Series Champion (1995); 3 N.L. Pennants (1995-96, 1999); 13-Time Playoff Qualifier (1989, 1993, 1995-2003, 2006, 2008).
Awards: 8-Time All-Star (1988, '92, '94-98, 2000); 4-Time Cy Young Award Winner (1992-95).

YEAR	TEAM	LEAGUE	G	W	L	SV	SHO	IP	H	BB	SO	ERA
1986	CHICAGO	NL	6	2	4	0	0	31	44	11	20	5.52
1987	CHICAGO	NL	30	6	14	0	1	156	181	74	101	5.61
1988	CHICAGO	NL	34	18	8	0	3	249	230	81	140	3.18
1989	CHICAGO	NL	35	19	12	0	1	238	222	82	135	2.95
1990	CHICAGO	NL	35	15	15	0	2	237	242	71	144	3.46
1991	CHICAGO	NL	37	15	11	0	2	263	232	66	198	3.35
1992	CHICAGO	NL	35	20	11	0	4	268	201	70	199	2.18
1993	ATLANTA	NL	36	20	10	0	1	267	228	52	197	2.36
1994	ATLANTA	NL	25	16	6	0	3	202	150	31	156	1.56
1995	ATLANTA	NL	28	19	2	0	3	210	147	23	181	1.63
1996	ATLANTA	NL	35	15	11	0	1	245	225	28	172	2.72
1997	ATLANTA	NL	33	19	4	0	2	233	200	20	177	2.2
1998	ATLANTA	NL	34	18	9	0	5	251	201	45	204	2.22
1999	ATLANTA	NL	33	19	9	0	0	219	258	37	136	3.57
2000	ATLANTA	NL	35	19	9	0	3	249	225	42	190	3
2001	ATLANTA	NL	34	17	11	0	3	233	220	27	173	3.05
2002	ATLANTA	NL	34	16	6	0	0	199	194	45	118	2.62
2003	ATLANTA	NL	36	16	11	0	0	218	225	33	124	3.96
2004	CHICAGO	NL	33	16	11	0	1	213	218	33	151	4.02
2005	CHICAGO	NL	35	13	15	0	0	225	239	36	136	4.24
2006	CHICAGO	NL	22	9	11	0	0	136	153	23	81	4.69
	LOS ANGELES	NL	12	6	3	0	0	74	66	14	36	3.3
2007	SAN DIEGO	NL	34	14	11	0	0	198	221	25	104	4.14
2008	SAN DIEGO	NL	26	6	9	0	0	153	161	26	80	3.99
	LOS ANGELES	NL	7	2	4	0	0	41	43	4	18	5.09
CAREER TOTALS			**744**	**355**	**227**	**0**	**35**	**5008**	**4726**	**999**	**3371**	**3.16**

FRANK THOMAS

Frank Thomas had Cooperstown on his mind from his earliest days as a big leaguer. "I've never understood why players say they don't think of the Hall of Fame," Thomas said during his playing days. "I want it. I'm not embarrassed to say that. I want to be the best."

Mission accomplished for a man who accomplished almost everything else on the baseball diamond. The player dubbed "The Big Hurt" set standards for power and on-base percentage to win back-to-back American League Most Valuable Player awards in 1993 and 1994 with the White Sox.

At 6-foot-5 and 240 pounds, Thomas, a former tight end at Auburn University before injuries pushed him full-time to baseball, was both imposing for his power and almost impossible to get out because of his batting eye.

"Every day I felt I was supposed to do something special out on the field," Thomas said. "Some people thought it was arrogant, but it wasn't arrogance. It was me wanting to accomplish something every day for this organization, to win, and I put that upon myself. I thought I was supposed to go 3-for-4 every night, 4-for-4 every night, hit a home run every night. That was just me."

Thomas is still the only player in history to log seven straight seasons (1991-97) with a .300 average, 20 home runs, 100 RBI and 100 walks. In 1997, he won the American League batting title. Yet his best season may have been 1994, when the season-ending strike may have cost him a Triple Crown. His statistics were mind-boggling: a major league-leading .487 on-base percentage, a league-leading .729 slugging percentage, an OPS of 1.217, and a .353 batting average with 38 home runs and 101 RBI. Even with the shortened season, Thomas became the only player in major league history to hit .300 or better with 100 RBI, 20 homers, 100 walks and 100 runs in each of his first four full seasons.

Most of Thomas' early career was spent as a first baseman, but as time wore on and injuries wore him down, he began to DH more. He is the first player elected to the Hall of Fame who played the majority of his big league games as a designated hitter.

The Big Hurt

Elected To The Hall Of Fame: *2014.*
Born: *May 27, 1968 in Columbus, Ga.*
Height: *6-5.* **Weight:** *240.*
Threw: *Right.* **Batted:** *Right.*
Debut: *Aug. 2, 1990.*
Final Game: *Aug. 29, 2008.*
Teams: *Chicago A.L. 1990-2005; Oakland A.L. 2006, 2008; Toronto A.L. 2007-08.*
Postseason: *3-Time Playoff Qualifier (1993, 2000, 2006).*
Awards: *5-Time All-Star (1993-97); 2-Time A.L. Most Valuable Player (1993-94).*

YEAR	TEAM	LEAGUE	G	AB	R	H	2B	3B	HR	RBI	SB	AVG
1990	CHICAGO	AL	60	191	39	63	11	3	7	31	0	.330
1991	CHICAGO	AL	158	559	104	178	31	2	32	109	1	.318
1992	CHICAGO	AL	160	573	108	185	46	2	24	115	6	.323
1993	CHICAGO	AL	153	549	106	174	36	0	41	128	4	.317
1994	CHICAGO	AL	113	399	106	141	34	1	38	101	2	.353
1995	CHICAGO	AL	145	493	102	152	27	0	40	111	3	.308
1996	CHICAGO	AL	141	527	110	184	26	0	40	134	1	.349
1997	CHICAGO	AL	146	530	110	184	35	0	35	125	1	.347
1998	CHICAGO	AL	160	585	109	155	35	2	29	109	7	.265
1999	CHICAGO	AL	135	486	74	148	36	0	15	77	3	.305
2000	CHICAGO	AL	159	582	115	191	44	0	43	143	1	.328
2001	CHICAGO	AL	20	68	8	15	3	0	4	10	0	.221
2002	CHICAGO	AL	148	523	77	132	29	1	28	92	3	.252
2003	CHICAGO	AL	153	546	87	146	35	0	42	105	0	.267
2004	CHICAGO	AL	74	240	53	65	16	0	18	49	0	.271
2005	CHICAGO	AL	34	105	19	23	3	0	12	26	0	.219
2006	OAKLAND	AL	137	466	77	126	11	0	39	114	0	.270
2007	TORONTO	AL	155	531	63	147	30	0	26	95	0	.277
2008	TORONTO	AL	71	246	27	59	7	1	8	30	0	.240
2008	TORONTO	AL	16	60	7	10	1	0	3	11	0	.167
2008	OAKLAND	AL	55	186	20	49	6	1	5	19	0	.263
CAREER TOTALS			**2322**	**8199**	**1494**	**2468**	**495**	**12**	**521**	**1704**	**32**	**.301**

JOE TORRE

Joe Torre and the Yankees were a curious match in 1996, as neither had experienced the success they yearned for in the previous 15 years.

Twelve seasons later, Torre and the Yankees had compiled 12 straight winning seasons, 12 straight playoff berths, six American League pennants and four World Series titles. And Torre's place in baseball history was secure.

"Joe let us enjoy the game," said Mariano Rivera, the closer whose consistency was reflected in Torre's steady hand. "When you have a manager like that, you play with love and good things happen. As a player, that's all you can ever ask for."

Joseph Paul Torre grew up in the Marine Park section of Brooklyn. Torre was a Giants fan but was in the stands at Yankee Stadium the day Don Larsen pitched a perfect game over the Dodgers in Game Five of the 1956 World Series. He was there again for the World Series games in 1957 and '58 cheering for his brother, Frank, a first baseman on the Milwaukee Braves clubs that opposed the Yanks.

Torre made it to the big leagues with the Braves as well, originally as a catcher. In 18 seasons, Torre he made nine All-Star Games, won the 1971 National League Most Valuable Player Award with the Cardinals and finished with 252 home runs, 1,185 RBI and a .297 batting average.

As he wound down his playing career with the Mets, Torre became the team's manager midway through the 1977 season. The Mets struggled under Torre during a rebuilding stage, but he landed in Atlanta in 1982 and led the Braves to their first NL West title since 1969. He managed the Braves for two more seasons before heading into broadcasting for the remainder of the 1980s, then returned to the dugout from 1990-95 with the Cardinals.

When he joined the Yankees, Torre had played or managed in 4,113 regular-season and postseason games without reaching the World Series, and the Yankees had not been to the World Series for 14 seasons. But in 1996, Torre led the Yankees to the AL pennant and then back from an 0-2 deficit to defeat the Braves in the Fall Classic.

With the Yankees, Torre won 1,173 games against 767 losses, and their run of three straight World Series titles from 1998-2000 was matched only by the 1936-39 Yankees, 1949-53 Yankees and the 1972-74 Athletics.

"Once you get into the competition, it never gets old," Torre said. "After we won in '96, because that is really what I wanted, I realized it wasn't enough. And you just keep driving. You never really look back at what you did, because once you start looking back, you stop doing what you're trying to do."

Torre completed his managerial career with three seasons with the Dodgers, before going to work in the commissioner's office.

Elected To The Hall Of Fame: 2014.
Born: July 18, 1940 in Brooklyn, N.Y.
Teams: New York N.L. 1977-81; Atlanta N.L. 1982-84; St. Louis N.L. 1990-95; New York A.L. 1996-2007; Los Angeles N.L. 2008-10

TEAM	LEAGUE	YEARS	W	L	PCT.	CHAMPIONSHIPS
NEW YORK	NL	5 (1977-81)	286	420	.405	
ATLANTA	NL	3 (1982-84)	257	229	.529	
ST. LOUIS	NL	6 (1990-95)	351	354	.498	
NEW YORK	AL	12 (1996-2007)	1173	767	.605	6 PENNANTS, 4 WORLD SERIES TITLES
LOS ANGELES	NL	3 (2008-10)	259	227	.533	
CAREER TOTALS		29	2326	1997	.538	

Gifts That Keep On Giving

ARTIFACT GIFTS FROM GENEROUS DONORS TELL THE STORY OF 2013 SEASON

They were the heroes of 2013, setting new standards for greatness on the diamond. Their gifts of artifacts to the National Baseball Hall of Fame and Museum ensure their stories will be preserved forever in Cooperstown. The Museum's permanent collection now totals more than 40,000 three-dimensional artifacts, dozens of which were accessioned in 2013. Of those, many were pieces from the most recent big league season, including:

Trio of no-nos

Three pitchers tossed no-hitters in 2013: The Reds' Homer Bailey on July 2, the Giants' Tim Lincecum on July 13 and the Marlins' Henderson Alvarez on the season's final day on Sept. 29.

Bailey donated his spikes, Lincecum sent the Museum his cap and Alvarez donated his spikes from the no-hitter that ended in walk-off fashion when Giancarlo Stanton scored on a wild pitch.

Spikes worn by the Reds' Homer Bailey in his July 2 no-hitter.

Cap and ball from Tim Lincecum's no-hitter on July 13.

He wore it well

Max Scherzer went 21-3 for the Tigers in 2013, one of only four modern-era pitchers to win 20 games and post a winning percentage of at least .875 in one season.

Scherzer donated the jersey he wore on Sept. 20, when he notched his 20th victory of the season.

Tigers jersey worn by Max Scherzer when he won his 20th game of the season.

Kings of the World

The Museum documented the 2013 World Baseball Classic with several artifacts, including: the cap worn by Team USA manager Joe Torre; the ball hit by Dai-Kang Yang of Chinese Taipei for the first hit of the 2013 Classic; the batting helmet from Team Puerto Rico's Angel Pagan; the cap worn by Team Italy coach Mike Piazza; the jersey worn by Team USA's Brandon Phillips in Round One games; a jersey worn by Team Dominican Republic pitcher Fernando Rodney; and the ball Rodney threw to record the final out of the WBC.

Artifacts from the 2013 World Baseball Classic, including (from top left): Batting helmet worn by Team Puerto Rico's Angel Pagan; cap worn by Team Italy coach Mike Piazza; cap worn by Team USA manager Joe Torre; ball hit by Dai-Kang Yang of Chinese Taipei for the first hit of the WBC; jersey worn by Team Dominican Republic's Fernando Rodney; and ball thrown by Fernando Rodney to record the final out and clinch the title for Team Dominican Republic.

Capping it off

Mariano Rivera wrapped up his unparalleled career in 2013 with 44 saves, pushing his career total to 652 – the most ever.

Rivera donated the cap he wore during the 2013 All-Star Game, his 13th selection to the Mid-Summer Classic. Rivera – if he remains retired – will become eligible for the Hall of Fame in 2019.

Cap worn by the Yankees' Mariano Rivera during the 2013 All-Star Game.

Glove of the game

Andy Pettitte retired at the end of the 2013 season, wrapping up an 18-year career that featured 256 wins and five World Series rings.

Pettitte donated the glove he used on July 1 when he set a new Yankees record for strikeouts for a pitcher.

Glove worn by the Yankees' Andy Pettitte when he set a new team career strike-out record for pitchers on July 1.

End of the streak

The Pittsburgh Pirates won 94 regular season games in 2013, snapping a 20-year losing streak from 1993-2012 – the longest in baseball history.

Pirates rookie pitcher Gerrit Cole wore this cap when he defeated the Rangers on Sept. 9, giving the Pirates their 82 win of the year and clinching a winning season.

Cap worn by Pirates pitcher Gerrit Cole when he beat the Rangers on Sept. 9, notching the Pirates their 82nd win of the year to snap their 20-year losing streak.

HENRY LOUIS GEHRIG
NEW YORK YANKEES · 1923-1939

The
HALL of FAME
MEMBERS

HENRY AARON

Boxing legend Muhammad Ali once called Hank Aaron "The only man I idolize more than myself."

In 1970, Hall of Famer Mickey Mantle said "As far as I'm concerned, Aaron is the best baseball player of my era. He is to baseball the last 15 years what Joe DiMaggio was before him. He's never received the credit he's due."

Hank Aaron grew from humble beginnings in Mobile, Alabama, passed through the sandlots with brief stops in the negro leagues and the minor leagues before he settled in with the Braves where he ultimately became one of baseball's most iconic figures. He was a consistent producer both at the plate and in the field, reaching the .300 mark in batting 14 times, 30 home runs 15 times, 90 RBI 16 times and captured three Gold Glove Awards en route to 25 All-Star Game selections (and 24 appearances). Phillies and Cardinals pitcher Curt Simmons said "Trying to sneak a pitch past Hank Aaron is like trying to sneak a sunrise past a rooster."

1957 was arguably Hank Aaron's best season. He hit .322 that year with 44 home runs and 132 RBI, captured the National League MVP Award and led the Braves to their first World Series Championship since 1914.

Despite his consistent production, it wasn't until 1973 that Aaron was thrust into the national spotlight as he neared the finish of a successful assault on one of sport's most cherished records: Babe Ruth's mark of 714 home runs. It was on April 8, 1974, that Hammerin' Hank sent a 1-0 pitch from Dodgers hurler Al Downing into the leftfield bullpen. Aaron was recognized for thirty years as baseball's all-time home run king until his record of 755 home runs was passed in 2007.

Hank Aaron's humility and grace was never more evident than at his Hall of Fame induction speech in 1982, where he proclaimed "I never want them to forget Babe Ruth. I just want them to remember Henry Aaron."

Hank

Elected To The Hall Of Fame: Class of 1982.
Born: Feb. 5, 1934 in Mobile, Ala.
Height: 6-0. **Weight:** 180.
Batted: Right. **Threw:** Right.
Debut: Apr. 13, 1954.
Final Game: Oct. 3, 1976.
Teams: Milwaukee N.L. 1954-1965 Atlanta N.L. 1966-1974; Milwaukee A.L. 1975-1976
Postseason: World Series Champion (1957); 2 N.L. Pennants (1957-1958).
Awards: 25-time All-Star (1955-1975); 1957 N.L. Most Valuable Player.

YEAR	TEAM	LEAGUE	G	AB	R	H	2B	3B	HR	RBI	SB	AVG
1954	MILWAUKEE	NL	122	468	58	131	27	6	13	69	2	.280
1955	MILWAUKEE	NL	153	602	105	189	37	9	27	106	3	.314
1956	MILWAUKEE	NL	153	609	106	200	34	14	26	92	2	.328
1957	MILWAUKEE	NL	151	615	118	198	27	6	44	132	1	.322
1958	MILWAUKEE	NL	153	601	109	196	34	4	30	95	4	.326
1959	MILWAUKEE	NL	154	629	116	223	46	7	39	123	8	.355
1960	MILWAUKEE	NL	153	590	102	172	20	11	40	126	16	.292
1961	MILWAUKEE	NL	155	603	115	197	39	10	34	120	21	.327
1962	MILWAUKEE	NL	156	592	127	191	28	6	45	128	15	.323
1963	MILWAUKEE	NL	161	631	121	201	29	4	44	130	31	.319
1964	MILWAUKEE	NL	145	570	103	187	30	2	24	95	22	.328
1965	MILWAUKEE	NL	150	570	109	181	40	1	32	89	24	.318
1966	ATLANTA	NL	158	603	117	168	23	1	44	127	21	.279
1967	ATLANTA	NL	155	600	113	184	37	3	39	109	17	.307
1968	ATLANTA	NL	160	606	84	174	33	4	29	86	28	.287
1969	ATLANTA	NL	147	547	100	164	30	3	44	97	9	.300
1970	ATLANTA	NL	150	516	103	154	26	1	38	118	9	.298
1971	ATLANTA	NL	139	495	95	162	22	3	47	118	1	.327
1972	ATLANTA	NL	129	449	75	119	10	0	34	77	4	.265
1973	ATLANTA	NL	120	392	84	118	12	1	40	96	1	.301
1974	ATLANTA	NL	112	340	47	91	16	0	20	69	1	.268
1975	MILWAUKEE	AL	137	465	45	109	16	2	12	60	0	.234
1976	MILWAUKEE	AL	85	271	22	62	8	0	10	35	0	.229
CAREER TOTALS			**3298**	**12364**	**2174**	**3771**	**624**	**98**	**755**	**2297**	**240**	**.305**

PETE ALEXANDER

A rawboned right-handed hurler straight off a Nebraska farm, Grover Cleveland Alexander broke into the big leagues with a flourish in 1911 with the Philadelphia Phillies, setting a rookie record with 28 wins. Using a wide variety of breaking pitches, deceptive speed and pinpoint control, Alexander soon found himself being compared to the top pitchers of his era.

And why not? He averaged 27 wins per season during his seven years in Philadelphia, including one three-year span in which he won 31, 33 and 30.

"He made me want to throw my bat away when I went to the plate," said Hall of Fame second baseman Johnny Evers. "He fed me pitches I couldn't hit. If I let them go, they were strikes. He made you hit bad balls. He could throw into a tin can all day long."

A stint in the military during World War I preceded Alexander's trade to the Chicago Cubs in 1918, where he soon established himself as the ace of the staff. There were some good years with the Cubs, including a 27-win campaign in 1920, but eventually the St. Louis Cardinals claimed him off waivers midway through the 1926 season.

Though he looked every bit of his 39 years of age, "Old Pete," as he was nicknamed, had some life left in his arm. He won nine games down the stretch, helping the Cards get to the World Series against the famed New York Yankees of Babe Ruth and Lou Gehrig. This grizzled veteran would soon find himself with one of the most famous strikeouts in baseball history.

After complete game victories in the second and sixth games, Alexander was called upon to close out the Series. St. Louis was ahead 3-2 in the bottom of the seventh, and Alexander came in to face rookie second baseman Tony Lazzeri. After nearly giving up a grand slam homer down the left field line that went foul at the last moment, Alexander would strike out Lazzeri and then toss two more hitless innings to lock down the title.

Upon Alexander's death in 1950, sportswriter Grantland Rice penned that the winner of 373 big league games was the most cunning pitcher that baseball had ever seen, adding, "Above everything else, Alex had one terrific feature to his pitching – he knew just what the batter didn't want – and he put it there to the half-inch."

GROVER CLEVELAND ALEXANDER

GREAT NATIONAL LEAGUE PITCHER FOR TWO DECADES WITH PHILLIES, CUBS AND CARDINALS STARTING IN 1911. WON 1926 WORLD CHAMPIONSHIP FOR CARDINALS BY STRIKING OUT LAZZERI WITH BASES FULL IN FINAL CRISIS AT YANKEE STADIUM.

Old Pete

Elected To The Hall Of Fame: Class of 1938.
Born: Feb. 26, 1887 in Elba, Neb.
Died: Nov. 4, 1950 in St. Paul, Neb.
Height: 6-1. **Weight:** 185.
Threw: Right. **Batted:** Right.
Debut: Apr. 15, 1911.
Final Game: May 28, 1930.
Teams: Philadelphia N.L. 1911-1917, 1930; Chicago N.L. 1918-1926; St. Louis N.L. 1926-1929.
Postseason: World Series Champion (1926); 3 N.L. Pennants (1915, 1926, 1928).

YEAR	TEAM	LEAGUE	G	W	L	SV	SH	IP	H	BB	SO	ERA
1911	PHILADELPHIA	NL	48	28	13	3	7	367	285	129	227	2.57
1912	PHILADELPHIA	NL	46	19	17	3	3	310.3	289	105	195	2.81
1913	PHILADELPHIA	NL	47	22	8	2	9	306.3	288	75	159	2.79
1914	PHILADELPHIA	NL	46	27	15	1	6	355	327	76	214	2.38
1915	PHILADELPHIA	NL	49	31	10	3	12	376.3	253	64	241	1.22
1916	PHILADELPHIA	NL	48	33	12	3	16	389	323	50	167	1.55
1917	PHILADELPHIA	NL	45	30	13	0	8	388	336	56	200	1.83
1918	CHICAGO	NL	3	2	1	0	0	26	19	3	15	1.73
1919	CHICAGO	NL	30	16	11	1	9	235	180	38	121	1.72
1920	CHICAGO	NL	46	27	14	5	7	363.3	335	69	173	1.91
1921	CHICAGO	NL	31	15	13	1	3	252	286	33	77	3.39
1922	CHICAGO	NL	33	16	13	1	1	245.7	283	34	48	3.63
1923	CHICAGO	NL	39	22	12	2	3	305	308	30	72	3.19
1924	CHICAGO	NL	21	12	5	0	0	169.3	183	25	33	3.03
1925	CHICAGO	NL	32	15	11	0	1	236	270	29	63	3.39
1926	CHICAGO	NL	7	3	3	0	0	52	55	7	12	3.46
1926	ST. LOUIS	NL	23	9	7	2	2	148.3	136	24	35	2.91
1927	ST. LOUIS	NL	37	21	10	3	2	268	261	38	48	2.52
1928	ST. LOUIS	NL	34	16	9	2	1	243.7	262	37	59	3.36
1929	ST. LOUIS	NL	22	9	8	0	0	132	149	23	33	3.89
1930	PHILADELPHIA	NL	9	0	3	0	0	21.7	40	6	6	9.14
CAREER TOTALS			**696**	**373**	**208**	**32**	**90**	**5190**	**4868**	**951**	**2198**	**2.56**

ROBERTO ALOMAR

For most of his career, the only time the word "second" appeared in the same sentence as Roberto Alomar was when someone was describing his position in the field. At the plate, with the leather or in the final standings, Alomar was usually on top.

Alomar had baseball in his blood. His father, Sandy Alomar Sr., was an All-Star second baseman in his 15-year major league career. Like his father, Roberto played second, threw right-handed and switch-hit. Alomar's brother, Sandy, Jr., also made it to the big leagues as a catcher.

At 18, Roberto Alomar signed with the San Diego Padres and won the California League batting title in his second year in the minors with a .346 batting average. By 1988, he was with the parent club, making a splash with his defense and speed and finishing fifth in National League Rookie of the Year voting. He earned his first All-Star selection in 1990.

Following that season, Alomar was traded to Toronto – where his offense took off. Alomar raised his average over .300, helping the Blue Jays to back-to-back World Series titles in 1992-1993 while finishing third in the AL batting title race in 1993. He hit a combined .354 in four postseason series in those seasons.

Following the 1995 season, Alomar signed with the Baltimore Orioles. Forming a Hall of Fame double-play combination with Cal Ripken Jr., helped his team get back to the playoffs – advancing to the ALCS in 1996 and 1997. Following the 1998 season, Alomar signed with the Cleveland Indians and played with his brother Sandy for the first time.

"He reminds me of some of the great players that I've played with, who seem like they write their own script," said Davey Johnson, who managed Alomar with the Orioles. "Frank Robinson's one, Henry Aaron was the other."

It was in Cleveland that Alomar had two of his best seasons. In 1999, he hit .323 with 24 homers, 120 RBI and 37 stolen bases. Teamed with Omar Vizquel, the double-play combo won three consecutive Gold Gloves together. The Indians advanced to the postseason in both 1999 and 2001. Alomar was traded to the Mets in 2002 before later stops with the White Sox and Diamondbacks. He retired after the 2004 season.

ROBERTO ALOMAR VELAZQUEZ
"ROBBIE"
SAN DIEGO, N.L., 1988-90; TORONTO, A.L., 1991-95;
BALTIMORE, A.L., 1996-98; CLEVELAND, A.L., 1999-2001;
NEW YORK, N.L., 2002-03; CHICAGO, A.L., 2003-04;
ARIZONA, N.L., 2004

SET THE STANDARD FOR A GENERATION OF SECOND BASEMEN WITH A QUICK, POWERFUL BAT, A SMOOTH, STEADY GLOVE AND SEEMINGLY ENDLESS RANGE. MEMBER OF A PUERTO RICAN FAMILY OF BASEBALL STARS, HIS GRACE, TIRELESS PREPARATION AND POISED PRESENCE RESULTED IN A .300 BATTING AVERAGE, 2,724 HITS, 210 HOME RUNS, 474 STOLEN BASES, AND 12 ALL-STAR GAME APPEARANCES. HIS 10 GOLD GLOVE AWARDS ARE A POSITION RECORD. A MODEL OF CONSISTENCY, HIT .300 OR BETTER NINE TIMES. SPURRED BLUE JAYS TO CONSECUTIVE WORLD SERIES TITLES IN 1992-1993.

Elected To The Hall Of Fame: *Class of 2011.*

Born: *Feb. 5, 1968 in Ponce, Puerto Rico*

Height: *6-0.* **Weight:** *184.*

Threw: *Right.* **Batted:** *Both.*

Debut: *Apr. 22, 1988.*

Final Game: *Sept. 5, 2004.*

Teams: *San Diego N.L. 1988-1990; Toronto A.L. 1991-1995; Baltimore A.L. 1996-1998; Cleveland A.L. 1999-2001; New York N.L. 2002-2003; Chicago A.L. 2003-2004; Arizona N.L. 2004 .*

Postseason: *2-Time World Series Champion (1992, 1993); 3 A.L. Pennants (1991-1993); 7-Time Playoff Qualifier (1991-1993, 1996-1997, 1999, 2001).*

Awards: *12-time All Star (1990-2001).*

YEAR	TEAM	LEAGUE	G	AB	R	H	2B	3B	HR	RBI	SB	AVG
1988	SAN DIEGO	NL	143	545	84	145	24	6	9	41	24	.266
1989	SAN DIEGO	NL	158	623	82	184	27	1	7	56	42	.295
1990	SAN DIEGO	NL	147	586	80	168	27	5	6	60	24	.287
1991	TORONTO	AL	161	637	88	188	41	11	9	69	53	.295
1992	TORONTO	AL	152	571	105	177	27	8	8	76	49	.310
1993	TORONTO	AL	153	589	109	192	35	6	17	93	55	.326
1994	TORONTO	AL	107	392	78	120	25	4	8	38	19	.306
1995	TORONTO	AL	130	517	71	155	24	7	13	66	30	.300
1996	BALTIMORE	AL	153	588	132	193	43	4	22	94	17	.328
1997	BALTIMORE	AL	112	412	64	137	23	2	14	60	9	.333
1998	BALTIMORE	AL	147	588	86	166	36	1	14	56	18	.282
1999	CLEVELAND	AL	159	563	138	182	40	3	24	120	37	.323
2000	CLEVELAND	AL	155	610	111	189	40	2	19	89	39	.310
2001	CLEVELAND	AL	157	575	113	193	34	12	20	100	30	.336
2002	NEW YORK	NL	149	590	73	157	24	4	11	53	16	.266
2003	NY/CHICAGO	NL/AL	140	516	76	133	28	2	5	39	12	.258
2004	CHICAGO/ARIZONA	AL/NL	56	171	18	45	6	2	4	24	0	.263
CAREER TOTALS			**2379**	**9073**	**1508**	**2724**	**504**	**80**	**210**	**1134**	**474**	**.300**

CAP ANSON

H e never played a game in baseball's "modern" era, but Adrian Constantine "Cap" Anson was one of the great modernizers of the game, bringing strategy and leadership to the National Pastime.

Anson was a 19-year-old third baseman for the Rockford Forest Citys in 1871, and the 6-foot, 227-pound strapping right-hander hit .325 with a league-leading 11 doubles. The next season, Anson hit .415 for the Philadelphia Athletics, also of the National Association, driving in 48 runs in just 46 games.

In 1876, Chicago White Stockings president William Hulbert, looking to add talent to his club, negotiated a deal with Anson and other stars. Hulbert then helped form the National League, and that summer Anson hit .356 to lead Chicago to a 52-14 record and the first championship title.

Anson would play 22 seasons for the team that became the Cubs, hitting at least .300 in 19 of those years. He moved across the diamond to first base in 1879, and led the league in RBI eight times between 1880 and 1891, winning batting titles in 1881 and 1888.

When he retired after the 1897 season at the age of 45, Anson owned big league records for games, hits, at-bats, doubles and runs. He finished with more than 3,000 hits, becoming the first player to cross that threshold.

Anson also managed Chicago for 19 seasons, winning five National League pennants as a player/manager while accumulating almost 1,300 career victories. He helped usher in popular strategies such as the hit-and-run and the pitching rotation.

After leaving the Cubs following the 1897 season, Anson managed the New York Giants for 22 games in 1898 before ending his big league career. In his later years, he ran several semi-pro teams and ventured into the vaudeville circuit.

Elected To The Hall Of Fame: *1939.*
Born: *Apr. 17, 1852 in Marshalltown, Iowa.*
Died: *Apr. 14, 1922 in Chicago, Ill.*
Height: *6-0.* **Weight:** *227.*
Threw: *Right.* **Batted:** *Right.*
Debut: *May 6, 1871.*
Final Game: *Oct. 3, 1897.*
Teams: *Rockford, National Association 1871;*
Philadelphia, National Association 1872-1875;
Chicago N.L. 1876-1897.
Postseason: *World Series Champion (1885); 2*
N.L. Pennants (1885-1886).

YEAR	TEAM	LEAGUE	G	AB	R	H	2B	3B	HR	RBI	SB	AVG
1871	ROCKFORD	NA	25	120	29	39	11	3	0	16	6	.325
1872	PHILADELPHIA	NA	46	217	60	90	10	7	0	48	6	.415
1873	PHILADELPHIA	NA	52	254	53	101	9	2	0	36	1	.398
1874	PHILADELPHIA	NA	55	260	51	87	8	3	0	37	6	.335
1875	PHILADELPHIA	NA	69	326	84	106	15	3	0	58	11	.325
1876	CHICAGO	NL	66	309	63	110	9	7	2	59	—	.356
1877	CHICAGO	NL	59	255	52	86	19	1	0	32	—	.337
1878	CHICAGO	NL	60	261	55	89	12	2	0	40	—	.341
1879	CHICAGO	NL	51	227	40	72	20	1	0	34	—	.317
1880	CHICAGO	NL	86	356	54	120	24	1	1	74	—	.337
1881	CHICAGO	NL	84	343	67	137	21	7	1	82	—	.399
1882	CHICAGO	NL	82	348	69	126	29	8	1	83	—	.362
1883	CHICAGO	NL	98	413	70	127	36	5	0	68	—	.308
1884	CHICAGO	NL	112	475	108	159	30	3	21	102	—	.335
1885	CHICAGO	NL	112	464	100	144	35	7	7	108	—	.310
1886	CHICAGO	NL	125	504	117	187	35	11	10	147	29	.371
1887	CHICAGO	NL	122	472	107	164	33	13	7	102	27	.347
1888	CHICAGO	NL	134	515	101	177	20	12	12	84	28	.344
1889	CHICAGO	NL	134	518	100	177	32	7	7	117	27	.342
1890	CHICAGO	NL	139	504	95	157	14	5	7	107	29	.312
1891	CHICAGO	NL	136	540	81	157	24	8	8	120	17	.291
1892	CHICAGO	NL	146	559	62	152	25	9	1	74	13	.272
1893	CHICAGO	NL	103	398	70	125	24	2	0	91	13	.314
1894	CHICAGO	NL	84	343	85	133	29	4	5	100	17	.388
1895	CHICAGO	NL	122	474	87	159	23	6	2	91	12	.335
1896	CHICAGO	NL	108	402	72	133	18	2	2	90	24	.331
1897	CHICAGO	NL	114	424	67	121	17	3	3	75	11	.285
CAREER TOTALS			**2524**	**10281**	**1999**	**3435**	**582**	**142**	**97**	**2075**	**277**	**.334**

LUIS APARICIO

Few men Luis Aparicio's size have starred at the big league level. Even fewer have controlled the diamond like the slick-fielding Venezuelan shortstop.

Signed as an amateur free agent by the White Sox in 1954, Aparicio spent two years in the minors before making his major league debut on April 17, 1956. The 5-foot-9, 160-pound Aparicio quickly made a name for himself as the starting shortstop, leading the league with 21 stolen bases and 14 sacrifice hits in his first season. His efforts earned him the American League Rookie of the Year award.

It marked the first of nine straight seasons where Aparico led the American League in stolen bases. No other player has ever led his league in steals more than six years in a row.

In 1959, "Little Louie" propelled the White Sox to the World Series with stellar regular season numbers, scoring 98 runs while stealing 56 bases – finishing second that year in AL MVP voting. Although his team lost to the Los Angeles Dodgers in the Fall Classic, Aparicio batted .308 with eight hits.

Aparicio led AL shortstops in fielding percentage from 1959-66 and racked up nine Gold Glove Awards over the span of his career.

The White Sox traded Aparicio to the Baltimore Orioles on Jan. 14, 1963. In his five years with the Orioles, he led the AL in stolen bases twice. Aparicio also made his second World Series appearance in 1966. This time, his Orioles swept the Dodgers to win it all. Aparicio was traded back to the White Sox after the 1967 season, and he spent three more years with Chicago before moving to the Boston Red Sox. Aparicio spent his last three seasons in the major leagues in Boston.

Aparicio played his final game on Sept. 28, 1973 at the age of 39 and officially retired after he was released by the Red Sox in March of 1974. At the time of his retirement, he held the record for shortstops in games played, double plays turned and assists. He finished his career with 2,677 hits and a .311 on-base-percentage. He appeared in 13 All-Star Games.

In 1984, Aparicio was inducted into the Hall of Fame— becoming the first Venezuela native to earn enshrinement in Cooperstown.

LUIS ERNESTO APARICIO
CHICAGO A.L. 1956-1962, 1968-1970
BALTIMORE A.L. 1963-1967
BOSTON A.L. 1971-1973
REGULAR SHORTSTOP FOR ALL OF HIS 18 SEASONS. SET MAJOR LEAGUE CAREER RECORDS FOR MOST GAMES (2,581), ASSISTS (8,016), CHANCES ACCEPTED (12,564) AND DOUBLE PLAYS (1,553) BY A SHORTSTOP; AND HAS MOST A.L. PUTOUTS (4,548). LED A.L. IN FIELDING 8 TIMES. TOPPED LEAGUE IN STEALS HIS FIRST 9 SEASONS, BEGINNING STOLEN BASE RENAISSANCE. A.L. ROOKIE OF THE YEAR IN 1956.

Little Louie

Elected To The Hall Of Fame: *1984.*
Born: *Apr. 29, 1934 in Maracaibo, Ven.*
Height: *5-9.* **Weight:** *160.*
Threw: *Right.* **Batted:** *Right.*
Debut: *Apr. 17, 1956.*
Final Game: *Sept. 28, 1973.*
Teams: *Chicago A.L. 1956-1962, 1968-1970; Baltimore A.L. 1963-1967; Boston A.L. 1971-1973.*
Postseason: *World Series Champion (1966); 2 A.L. Pennants (1959, 1966).*
Awards: *13-time All Star (1958-1964, 1970-1972); 1956 A.L. Rookie of the Year.*

YEAR	TEAM	LEAGUE	G	AB	R	H	2B	3B	HR	RBI	SB	AVG
1956	CHICAGO	AL	152	533	69	142	19	6	3	56	21	.266
1957	CHICAGO	AL	143	575	82	148	22	6	3	41	28	.257
1958	CHICAGO	AL	145	557	76	148	20	9	2	40	29	.266
1959	CHICAGO	AL	152	612	98	157	18	5	6	51	56	.257
1960	CHICAGO	AL	153	600	86	166	20	7	2	61	51	.277
1961	CHICAGO	AL	156	625	90	170	24	4	6	45	53	.272
1962	CHICAGO	AL	153	581	72	140	23	5	7	40	31	.241
1963	BALTIMORE	AL	146	601	73	150	18	8	5	45	40	.250
1964	BALTIMORE	AL	146	578	93	154	20	3	10	37	57	.266
1965	BALTIMORE	AL	144	564	67	127	20	10	8	40	26	.225
1966	BALTIMORE	AL	151	659	97	182	25	8	6	41	25	.276
1967	BALTIMORE	AL	134	546	55	127	22	5	4	31	18	.233
1968	CHICAGO	AL	155	622	55	164	24	4	4	36	17	.264
1969	CHICAGO	AL	156	599	77	168	24	5	5	51	24	.280
1970	CHICAGO	AL	146	552	86	173	29	3	5	43	8	.313
1971	BOSTON	AL	125	491	56	114	23	0	4	45	6	.232
1972	BOSTON	AL	110	436	47	112	26	3	3	39	3	.257
1973	BOSTON	AL	132	499	56	135	17	1	0	49	13	.271
CAREER TOTALS			**2599**	**10230**	**1335**	**2677**	**394**	**92**	**83**	**791**	**506**	**.262**

LUKE APPLING

He was a line-drive machine for 20 seasons, a man who had more career extra-base hits (587) than strikeouts (528). Luke Appling retired as one of the most consistent and durable shortstops in big league history—a seemingly improbable reputation for a player known as "Old Aches and Pains." But underneath Appling's physical complaints lay a fierce competitor who battled American League pitchers for two decades.

Appling grew up in Georgia and attended Oglethorpe University before the White Sox purchased his contract from Atlanta of the Southern Association in 1930. He debuted with the White Sox that same season and became entrenched at shortstop the following year. By 1936, Appling won his first All-Star Game selection en route to a .388 batting average – the top single-season mark ever by a modern-era shortstop. That same season, Appling drove in 128 runs while hitting just six homers. Appling also had one of the best batting eyes in the game, averaging 87 walks and just 35 strikeouts a season en route to a career on-base percentage of .399. All this came despite a myriad of injuries that kept Appling bemoaning his physical status but rarely out of the lineup.

"Few were better or more deadly with two strikes then Appling," wrote Arthur Daley of the *New York Times*. "He just waited for the pitch he wanted and lashed into it. If there was a good pitch he didn't want, he artistically spoiled it by fouling it off."

Appling was also one of the top fielding shortstops in baseball, consistently ranking in the top five in fielding percentage while leading the American League in assists seven times and putouts twice. He played in at least 141 games at shortstop – in an era where the season only lasted 154 games – 10 times. Appling finished his career in 1950 with a .310 career batting average, two batting titles (he hit .328 in 1943 to win his second), seven All-Star Game selections and 2,749 hits. He played each of his 20 big league seasons with the White Sox and was named the Sox's greatest player by Chicago fans in 1969. In 1964, Appling won a winner-take-all Baseball Writers' Association of America runoff election to earn Hall of Fame enshrinement.

LUCIUS BENJAMIN APPLING
CHICAGO A.L. 1930-1950
A.L. BATTING CHAMPION IN 1936 AND 1943.
PLAYED 2,218 GAMES AT SHORTSTOP
FOR MAJOR LEAGUE MARK.
HAD 2,749 HITS.
LIFETIME BATTING AVERAGE OF .310.
LED A.L. IN ASSIST 7 YEARS.
HOLDS A.L. RECORD FOR CHANCES
ACCEPTED BY SHORTSTOP 11,569.

Old Aches and Pains

Elected To The Hall Of Fame: *1964.*
Born: *Apr. 2, 1907 in High Point, N.C.*
Died: *Jan. 3, 1991 in Cumming, Ga.*
Height: *5-10.* **Weight:** *183.*
Threw: *Right.* **Batted:** *Right.*
Debut: *Sept. 10, 1930.*
Final Game: *Oct. 1, 1950.*
Teams: *Chicago A.L. 1930-1943, 1945-1950.*
Awards: *7-Time All-Star (1936, 1939-1941, 1943, 1946-1947).*

YEAR	TEAM	LEAGUE	G	AB	R	H	2B	3B	HR	RBI	SB	AVG
1930	CHICAGO	AL	6	26	2	8	2	0	0	2	2	.308
1931	CHICAGO	AL	96	297	36	69	13	4	1	28	9	.232
1932	CHICAGO	AL	139	489	66	134	20	10	3	63	9	.274
1933	CHICAGO	AL	151	612	90	197	36	10	6	85	6	.322
1934	CHICAGO	AL	118	452	75	137	28	6	2	61	3	.303
1935	CHICAGO	AL	153	525	94	161	28	6	1	71	12	.307
1936	CHICAGO	AL	138	526	111	204	31	7	6	128	10	.388
1937	CHICAGO	AL	154	574	98	182	42	8	4	77	18	.317
1938	CHICAGO	AL	81	294	41	89	14	0	0	44	1	.303
1939	CHICAGO	AL	148	516	82	162	16	6	0	56	16	.314
1940	CHICAGO	AL	150	566	96	197	27	13	0	79	3	.348
1941	CHICAGO	AL	154	592	93	186	26	8	1	57	12	.314
1942	CHICAGO	AL	142	543	78	142	26	4	3	53	17	.262
1943	CHICAGO	AL	155	585	63	192	33	2	3	80	27	.328
1945	CHICAGO	AL	18	57	12	21	2	2	1	10	1	.368
1946	CHICAGO	AL	149	582	59	180	27	5	1	55	6	.309
1947	CHICAGO	AL	139	503	67	154	29	0	8	49	8	.306
1948	CHICAGO	AL	139	497	63	156	16	2	0	47	10	.314
1949	CHICAGO	AL	142	492	82	148	21	5	5	58	7	.301
1950	CHICAGO	AL	50	128	11	30	3	4	0	13	2	.234
CAREER TOTALS			**2422**	**8856**	**1319**	**2749**	**440**	**102**	**45**	**1116**	**179**	**.310**

RICHIE ASHBURN

A fleet-footed baseball player who used his athletic gifts to get on base and chase down fly balls in the field, then a broadcaster who used his oratory skills to become a much beloved voice off the field, Richie Ashburn would become a fixture on the Philadelphia sports scene for a half century.

Because he played in an era that featured such stalwart center fielders as Willie Mays, Mickey Mantle and Duke Snider, Ashburn was sometimes overlooked by fans of the game. But during a 15-year big league career, the lefty swinging Ashburn twice won the National League batting title, finished second twice and nine times batted over .300. A lifetime .308 hitter, he also finished with a .396 on-base percentage.

"Ashburn is the fastest man I've ever seen getting down to first base," said Brooklyn Dodgers manager Leo Durocher in 1948. "He's even faster than Pete Reiser in his prime. Anybody who's faster than Ashburn isn't running. He's flying."

Short and slight, the 5-foot-10, 170 pound Ashburn excelled from 1948 to 1959 as the prototypical leadoff hitter and center fielder with the Phillies. In possession of an excellent eye at the plate, he led the league in walks on four separate occasions and his 1958 season marked the first time a leadoff hitter paced the league in both batting average and bases on balls. Defensively, Ashburn set outfield marks with 10 years of 400 or more putouts and six years with 500 or more.

"Richie was very serious when it came to playing the game," said longtime Phillies teammate and Hall of Fame pitcher Robin Roberts. "He would play cards and was a fun guy off the field, but on the field he really teed it up."

After spending two seasons (1960-61) with the Chicago Cubs, Ashburn ended his playing career as a member of the expansion New York Mets for their inaugural 1962 season. Despite hitting .306 and being the lone All-Star representative for a team that lost a record 120 games, he become one of the few regulars to ever retire following a season in which they batted at least .300.

Ashburn soon began a second career when he returned to Philadelphia as a member of the Phillies' television-radio broadcasting team in 1963, where he would combine perceptive commentary with a wry sense of humor for 35 years.

DON RICHARD ASHBURN
(RICHIE)
PHILADELPHIA, N.L. 1948-1959
CHICAGO, N.L. 1960-1961
NEW YORK, N.L. 1962
DURABLE, HUSTLING LEAD-OFF HITTER AND CLUTCH PERFORMER WITH SUPERB KNOWLEDGE OF STRIKE ZONE. BATTED .308 LIFETIME WITH NINE .300 SEASONS AND 2,574 HITS IN 2,189 GAMES. WINNING BATTING CHAMPIONSHIPS IN 1955 AND 1958. AS A CENTER FIELDER, ESTABLISHED MAJOR LEAGUE RECORDS FOR MOST YEARS LEADING LEAGUE IN CHANCES (9), MOST YEARS 500 OR MORE PUTOUTS (4) AND MOST SEASONS 400 OR MORE PUTOUTS (9).

Whitey

Elected To The Hall Of Fame: *1995.*
Born: *Mar. 19, 1927 in Tilden, Neb.*
Died: *Sept. 9, 1997 in New York, N.Y.*
Height: *5-10.* **Weight:** *170.*
Threw: *Right.* **Batted:** *Left.*
Debut: *Apr. 20, 1948.*
Final Game: *Sept. 30, 1962.*
Teams: *Philadelphia N.L. 1948-1959; Chicago N.L. 1960-1961; New York N.L. 1962.*
Postseason: *N.L. Pennant (1950).*

YEAR	TEAM	LEAGUE	G	AB	R	H	2B	3B	HR	RBI	SB	AVG
1948	PHILADELPHIA	NL	117	463	78	154	17	4	2	40	32	.333
1949	PHILADELPHIA	NL	154	662	84	188	18	11	1	37	9	.284
1950	PHILADELPHIA	NL	151	594	84	180	25	14	2	41	14	.303
1951	PHILADELPHIA	NL	154	643	92	221	31	5	4	63	29	.344
1952	PHILADELPHIA	NL	154	613	93	173	31	6	1	42	16	.282
1953	PHILADELPHIA	NL	156	622	110	205	25	9	2	57	14	.330
1954	PHILADELPHIA	NL	153	559	111	175	16	8	1	41	11	.313
1955	PHILADELPHIA	NL	140	533	91	180	32	9	3	42	12	.338
1956	PHILADELPHIA	NL	154	628	94	190	26	8	3	50	10	.303
1957	PHILADELPHIA	NL	156	626	93	186	26	8	0	33	13	.297
1958	PHILADELPHIA	NL	152	615	98	215	24	13	2	33	30	.350
1959	PHILADELPHIA	NL	153	564	86	150	16	2	1	20	9	.266
1960	CHICAGO	NL	151	547	99	159	16	5	0	40	16	.291
1961	CHICAGO	NL	109	307	49	79	7	4	0	19	7	.257
1962	NEW YORK	NL	135	389	60	119	7	3	7	28	12	.306
CAREER TOTALS			**2189**	**8365**	**1322**	**2574**	**317**	**109**	**29**	**586**	**234**	**.308**

EARL AVERILL

Howard Earl Averill burst onto the big league scene with a rookie season many would consider their best. However, Averill was just getting started, and by the time he was finished, the Washington State native dubbed the Earl of Snohomish had crafted a career worthy of Cooperstown.

Born May 21, 1902, in Snohomish, Washington, Averill broke into the majors in 1929 at the relatively late age of 26. He quickly made up for lost time during his rookie year, starting the season as the center fielder and number three batter for the Cleveland Indians.

The compact 5-foot-9, 172-pound Averill quickly proved to be a line-drive machine, pounding out 198 hits that season en route to a .332 batting average, 18 homers, 96 RBI and 110 runs scored.

Averill posted similar numbers in 1930 with 19 homers, 119 RBI and a .339 average, then found his power stroke in 1931 with 32 homers, 143 RBI and 140 runs scored. During his first 10 big league seasons, he averaged 22 home runs, 108 RBI and 115 runs scored a season and hit .323.

"I thank the good Lord he wasn't twins," said Hall of Fame pitcher Lefty Gomez, whose Yankees battled the Indians in the American League throughout the 1930s. "One more like him probably would have kept me out of the Hall of Fame."

Averill was traded to the Tigers on June 14, 1939, and the next year as a bench player he helped Detroit win the American League pennant. He retired after spending part of the 1941 season with the Boston Braves.

For his 13-year career, Averill hit .318 with 238 home runs (his 226 homers was a Cleveland Indians record for 58 years), 2,019 hits and 1,224 runs scored. He hit over .300 in eight of his 12 full big league seasons, topping out at .378 in 1936 when he led the American League with 232 hits and 15 triples. Averill finished in the top four of the American League Most Valuable Player voting in three seasons and was named to six All-Star teams.

He was elected to the Hall of Fame in 1975.

"I could have gotten in sooner," said Averill of his Hall of Fame election. "But it's sure better late than never."

HOWARD EARL AVERILL
"ROCK".
CLEVELAND A.L.   DETROIT A.L.
BOSTON N.L.   1929-1941
COMPILED .318 CAREER BATTING AVERAGE
AND HIT 238 HOME RUNS. TWICE MADE
MORE THAN 200 HITS IN SEASON, PACING
LEAGUE WITH 232 IN 1936. DROVE IN
100 OR MORE RUNS FIVE TIMES. RAPPED
FOUR HOMERS, THREE CONSECUTIVELY
IN FIRST GAME AND BATTED IN 11 RUNS
IN 1930 TWIN-BILL.

The Earl of Snohomish

Elected To The Hall Of Fame: *1975.*
Born: *May 21, 1902 in Snohomish, Wash.*
Died: *Aug. 16, 1983 in Everett, Wash.*
Height: *5-9.* **Weight:** *172.*
Threw: *Right.* **Batted:** *Left.*
Debut: *Apr. 16, 1929.*
Final Game: *Apr. 25, 1941.*
Teams: *Cleveland A.L. 1929-1939; Detroit A.L. 1939-1940; Boston N.L. 1941.*
Postseason: *A.L. Pennant (1940).*
Awards: *Six-time All-Star (1933-38).*

YEAR	TEAM	LEAGUE	G	AB	R	H	2B	3B	HR	RBI	SB	AVG
1929	CLEVELAND	AL	152	597	110	198	43	13	18	96	13	.332
1930	CLEVELAND	AL	139	534	102	181	33	8	19	119	10	.339
1931	CLEVELAND	AL	155	627	140	209	36	10	32	143	9	.333
1932	CLEVELAND	AL	153	631	116	198	37	14	32	124	5	.314
1933	CLEVELAND	AL	151	599	83	180	39	16	11	92	3	.301
1934	CLEVELAND	AL	154	598	128	187	48	6	31	113	5	.313
1935	CLEVELAND	AL	140	563	109	162	34	13	19	79	8	.288
1936	CLEVELAND	AL	152	614	136	232	39	15	28	126	3	.378
1937	CLEVELAND	AL	156	609	121	182	33	11	21	92	5	.299
1938	CLEVELAND	AL	134	482	101	159	37	15	14	93	5	.330
1939	CLE/DET	AL	111	364	66	96	28	6	11	65	4	.264
1940	DETROIT	AL	64	118	10	33	4	1	2	20	0	.280
1941	BOSTON	NL	8	17	2	2	0	0	0	2	0	.118
CAREER TOTALS			**1669**	**6353**	**1224**	**2019**	**401**	**128**	**238**	**1164**	**70**	**.318**

FRANK BAKER

By today's standards, his nickname seems less than appropriate. But in his time, John Franklin "Home Run" Baker – author of 96 big league round trippers – was the symbol of power on the diamond. And more than 100 years after earning his nickname, Baker remains a part of baseball lore.

Born March 13, 1886, in Trappe, Md., Baker grew up on a farm and later used his exceptional strength playing for semi-pro teams around Maryland's Eastern Shore. Baker hooked on with Reading, Pa., of the Tri-State League in 1908 – and that September he debuted with Connie Mack's Philadelphia Athletics.

The next season, the 23-year-old Baker took over as the A's third baseman, leading the American League in triples with 19 while hitting .305 with 85 RBI – but hitting only four home runs. In 1910, Baker's homer total dropped to two – but he more than made up for it by hitting .409 in the World Series against the Cubs, leading the A's past the Cubs in five games with six runs scored and four RBI.

Then in 1911, Baker – who used an unusually heavy bat weighing 46 ounces – hit an AL-best 11 home runs and drove in 115 runs. In that year's World Series, Baker crafted his legend with game-winning home runs in Game 2 off future Hall of Famer Rube Marquard and in Game 3 against future Hall of Famer Christy Mathewson – the final blast handing Mathewson his first World Series defeat.

Thereafter, the press referred to him as Home Run Baker.

Baker led the AL in home runs and RBI in both 1912 and 1913, helping the A's win a third World Championship in four seasons in the latter season. But Baker sat out the 1915 season during a contract dispute with A's manager Connie Mack—announcing that he would retire. Prior to the 1916 season, Mack sold Baker's contract to the Yankees for $37,500.

Baker spent the next four seasons as New York's third baseman, averaging eight home runs a year. He retired prior to the 1920 season following the death of his first wife, but returned to the Yankees in 1921 and 1922 before ending his big league career.

His final totals: 13 big league seasons, a .307 batting average, 103 triples, 96 home runs and three World Championships.

JOHN FRANKLIN BAKER
PHILADELPHIA A.L.1908-1914
NEW YORK A.L.1916-1922
MEMBER OF CONNIE MACK'S FAMOUS
$100,000 INFIELD. LED AMERICAN LEAGUE
IN HOME-RUNS 1911-12-13, TIED IN 1914.
WON TWO WORLD SERIES GAMES FROM
GIANTS IN 1911 WITH HOME-RUNS THUS
GETTING NAME "HOME RUN" BAKER. PLAYED
IN SIX WORLD SERIES 1910-11-13-14-21-22.

Home Run

Elected To The Hall Of Fame: 1955.
Born: Mar. 13, 1886 in Trappe, MD.
Died: June 28, 1963 in Trappe, MD.
Height: 5-11. **Weight:** 173.
Threw: Right. **Batted:** Left.
Debut: Sept. 21, 1908.
Final Game: Sept. 29, 1922.
Teams: Philadelphia A.L. 1908-1914; New York A.L. 1916-1919, 1921-1922.
Postseason: 3-time World Series Champion (1910-1911, 1913); 6 A.L. Pennants (1910-1911, 1913-1914, 1921-1922).

YEAR	TEAM	LEAGUE	G	AB	R	H	2B	3B	HR	RBI	SB	AVG
1908	PHILADELPHIA	AL	9	31	5	9	3	0	0	2	0	.290
1909	PHILADELPHIA	AL	148	541	73	165	27	19	4	85	20	.305
1910	PHILADELPHIA	AL	146	561	83	159	25	15	2	74	21	.283
1911	PHILADELPHIA	AL	148	592	96	198	42	14	11	115	38	.334
1912	PHILADELPHIA	AL	149	577	116	200	40	21	10	130	40	.347
1913	PHILADELPHIA	AL	149	564	116	190	34	9	12	117	34	.337
1914	PHILADELPHIA	AL	150	570	84	182	23	10	9	89	19	.319
1916	NEW YORK	AL	100	360	46	97	23	2	10	52	15	.269
1917	NEW YORK	AL	146	553	57	156	24	2	6	71	18	.282
1918	NEW YORK	AL	126	504	65	154	24	5	6	62	8	.306
1919	NEW YORK	AL	141	567	70	166	22	1	10	83	13	.293
1921	NEW YORK	AL	94	330	46	97	16	2	9	71	8	.294
1922	NEW YORK	AL	69	234	30	65	12	3	7	36	1	.278
CAREER TOTALS			1575	5984	887	1838	315	103	96	987	235	.307

DAVE BANCROFT

A graceful, quick-handed shortstop for several National League squads, Dave Bancroft developed a reputation as a solid leadoff hitter. The switch-hitting Bancroft was also known for his intelligence on the field and fiery leadership in the dugout. He earned the nickname "Beauty" for his habit of shouting the term on each good pitch to the opposition as a minor league player and throughout his major league career.

As a rookie, Dave Bancroft helped bring the Philadelphia Phillies their first National League pennant. From there, the slick-fielding shortstop was well on his way to the Hall of Fame.

Bancroft made his professional baseball debut in 1909 with Duluth of the Minnesota-Wisconsin League, then quickly joined Superior of the same league. In 1912, Bancroft was drafted by Portland of the Pacific Coast League – and after three seasons was sold to the Phillies before the 1915 campaign.

Bancroft quickly solidified Philadelphia's infield, accepting an incredible 892 chances at shortstop in that 1915 season to lead the Phillies into the World Series. Bancroft hit .294 in the Fall Classic, but the Phillies fell to the Red Sox in five games.

Over the next four years, Bancroft established himself as one of the National League's best-fielding shortstops – and also as a consistently effective hitter. But in 1920, a contract dispute resulted in Bancroft's trade to the Giants for Art Fletcher in a swap of shortstops. Bancroft thrived in New York, hitting .299 in 108 games with the Giants in 1920. In 150 total games that year, Bancroft led all shortstops with 598 assists and 362 putouts.

The next season, Bancroft hit .300 for the first time (.318) while scoring a career-best 121 runs for the World Champion Giants. New York repeated as Fall Classic champions in 1922, with Bancroft hitting .321 with 209 hits and 117 runs scored. In the field that year, Bancroft accepted 1,046 total chances, including 405 putouts – the fourth-best total of all modern-era shortstops. His 984 total chances are the most for any shortstop in any one season.

Injuries limited Bancroft to 107 games in 1923, and after that season he was traded to the Braves. In Boston, Bancroft took over as player-manager, and he finished his career with the Giants.

DAVID JAMES BANCROFT
"BEAUTY"
PHILADELPHIA N.L., NEW YORK N.L.,
BOSTON N.L., BROOKLYN N.L.
1915-1930
SET MAJOR LEAGUE RECORD FOR CHANCES
HANDLED BY A SHORTSTOP IN A SEASON-984
IN 1922. LED LEAGUE IN PUTOUTS FOR SHORT-
STOPS IN 1918·1920·1921·1922. HIT .319 IN 1921,
.521 IN 1922 AND .304 IN 1925 WITH
NEW YORK GIANTS. HIT .319 IN 1925 AND
.311 IN 1926 WITH BOSTON.
PLAYER·MANAGER OF BRAVES, 1924-1927.

Beauty

Elected To The Hall Of Fame: *1971.*
Born: *Apr. 20, 1891 in Sioux City, Iowa.*
Died: *Oct. 9, 1972 in Superior, Wis.*
Height: *5-9.* **Weight:** *160.*
Threw: *Right.* **Batted:** *Both.*
Debut: *Apr. 14, 1915.*
Final Game: *May 31, 1930.*
Teams: *Philadelphia N.L. 1915-1920; New York N.L. 1920-1923, 1930; Boston N.L. 1924-1927; Brooklyn N.L. 1928-1929.*
Postseason: *2-Time World Series Champion (1921-1922); 4 N.L. Pennants (1915, 1921-1923).*

YEAR	TEAM	LEAGUE	G	AB	R	H	2B	3B	HR	RBI	SB	AVG
1915	PHILADELPHIA	NL	153	563	85	143	18	2	7	30	15	.254
1916	PHILADELPHIA	NL	142	477	53	101	10	0	3	33	15	.212
1917	PHILADELPHIA	NL	127	478	56	116	22	5	4	43	14	.243
1918	PHILADELPHIA	NL	125	499	69	132	19	4	0	26	11	.265
1919	PHILADELPHIA	NL	92	335	45	91	13	7	0	25	8	.272
1920	PHIL./NEW YORK	NL	150	613	102	183	36	9	0	36	8	.299
1921	NEW YORK	NL	153	606	121	193	26	15	6	67	17	.318
1922	NEW YORK	NL	156	651	117	209	41	5	4	60	16	.321
1923	NEW YORK	NL	107	444	80	135	33	3	1	31	8	.304
1924	BOSTON	NL	79	319	49	89	11	1	2	21	4	.279
1925	BOSTON	NL	128	479	75	153	29	8	2	49	7	.319
1926	BOSTON	NL	127	453	70	141	18	6	1	44	3	.311
1927	BOSTON	NL	111	375	44	91	13	4	1	31	5	.243
1928	BROOKLYN	NL	149	515	47	127	19	5	0	51	7	.247
1929	BROOKLYN	NL	104	358	35	99	11	3	1	44	7	.277
1930	NEW YORK	NL	10	17	0	1	1	0	0	0	0	.059
CAREER TOTALS			**1913**	**7182**	**1048**	**2004**	**320**	**77**	**32**	**591**	**145**	**.279**

ERNIE BANKS

"There's sunshine, fresh air, and the team's behind us. Let's play two."

Ernie Banks reprised his signature line at his Hall of Fame induction speech in 1977. His sunny disposition was perfect for the Friendly Confines of Wrigley Field, last outpost of exclusively day baseball. Perhaps no player defines his team as thoroughly as "Mr. Cub," who played with joy and immense talent for the Cubs from 1953-71, though never making a postseason appearance.

A native of Dallas, 19-year-old Ernie Banks debuted for the Kansas City Monarchs of the Negro leagues in 1950. After two years in the Army, Banks returned to the Monarchs, who sold his contract to the Chicago Cubs in 1953. His debut marked the first appearance of an African-American player for the franchise.

Banks started every game at shortstop for the Cubs in 1954, and would go on to win National League Most Valuable Player Awards in 1958 and '59.

Banks was an excellent defensive player at two positions, shortstop from 1953-61, and first base from 1962-71. At the former position, he led the league in fielding percentage three times, picking up a Gold Glove Award in 1960, when he led all NL shortstops in fielding percentage, double plays, games, putouts, and assists. As a first baseman, he led the league in putouts five times, assists three times, and double plays and fielding percentage once, compiling a .994 fielding percentage at the first sack.

It was with the bat that Banks really shone, hitting over 40 homers five times and leading the league twice in homers and twice in RBI. He was a three-time .300 hitter who compiled a lifetime batting average of .274, along with 2,583 hits, 1,305 runs scored, and 1,636 runs batted in. On May 12, 1970, he hit the 500th home run of his career, becoming just the ninth player and first shortstop to reach the plateau. He finished with 512. Banks played in 14 All-Star Games, and in a 1969 *Chicago Sun-Times* fan poll, he was voted the "Greatest Cub Ever."

ERNEST BANKS
"MR. CUB"
CHICAGO N. L., 1953·1971
HIT 512 CAREER HOMERS WITH MORE THAN 40 IN A SEASON FIVE TIMES. HAD RECORD FIVE GRAND-SLAMS IN 1955. FIRST TO BE ELECTED N.L. MOST VALUABLE PLAYER TWO SUCCESSIVE YEARS, 1958-59. LED LEAGUE IN HOME RUNS AND RUNS BATTED IN TWICE AND SLUGGING PCT. ONCE. ESTABLISHED RECORDS FOR MOST HOMERS IN SEASON BY SHORTSTOP (47 IN 1958) AND FOR FEWEST ERRORS (12) AND BEST FIELDING AVERAGE (.985) BY A SHORTSTOP IN 1959.

Mr. Cub

Elected To The Hall Of Fame: *1977.*

Born: *Jan. 31, 1931 in Dallas, Texas.*

Height: *6-1.* **Weight:** *180.*

Threw: *Right.* **Batted:** *Right.*

Debut: *Sept. 17, 1953.*

Final Game: *Sept. 26, 1971.*

Teams: *Chicago N.L. 1953-1971.*

Awards: *14-Time All-Star (1955-1962, 1965, 1967, 1969); 2-Time N.L. Most Valuable Player (1958-1959).*

YEAR	TEAM	LEAGUE	G	AB	R	H	2B	3B	HR	RBI	SB	AVG
1953	CHICAGO	NL	10	35	3	11	1	1	2	6	0	.314
1954	CHICAGO	NL	154	593	70	163	19	7	19	79	6	.275
1955	CHICAGO	NL	154	596	98	176	29	9	44	117	9	.295
1956	CHICAGO	NL	139	538	82	160	25	8	28	85	6	.297
1957	CHICAGO	NL	156	594	113	169	34	6	43	102	8	.285
1958	CHICAGO	NL	154	617	119	193	23	11	47	129	4	.313
1959	CHICAGO	NL	155	589	97	179	25	6	45	143	2	.304
1960	CHICAGO	NL	156	597	94	162	32	7	41	117	1	.271
1961	CHICAGO	NL	138	511	75	142	22	4	29	80	1	.278
1962	CHICAGO	NL	154	610	87	164	20	6	37	104	5	.269
1963	CHICAGO	NL	130	432	41	98	20	1	18	64	0	.227
1964	CHICAGO	NL	157	591	67	156	29	6	23	95	1	.264
1965	CHICAGO	NL	163	612	79	162	25	3	28	106	3	.265
1966	CHICAGO	NL	141	511	52	139	23	7	15	75	0	.272
1967	CHICAGO	NL	151	573	68	158	26	4	23	95	2	.276
1968	CHICAGO	NL	150	552	71	136	27	0	32	83	2	.246
1969	CHICAGO	NL	155	565	60	143	19	2	23	106	0	.253
1970	CHICAGO	NL	72	222	25	56	6	2	12	44	0	.252
1971	CHICAGO	NL	39	83	4	16	2	0	3	6	0	.193
CAREER TOTALS			**2528**	**9421**	**1305**	**2583**	**407**	**90**	**512**	**1636**	**50**	**.274**

JAKE BECKLEY

His durability was so impressive that almost 90 years after his death, Jake Beckley's name appeared on the computer screens of baseball writers across the world. But Beckley's ability to play every day is only part of the story of the powerful first baseman whose standards still top the record books.

Beckley played 19 National League seasons with the Pirates, Giants, Reds and Cardinals and one season with Pittsburgh in the Players' League from 1888-1907. He played 2,380 of his 2,389 games at first base, setting a big league standard that was not eclipsed until 1994.

Born Aug. 4, 1867 in the town Mark Twain made famous – Hannibal, Mo. – Beckley began his career in semipro leagues before St. Louis of the Western Association sold him to the NL's Pittsburgh Alleghenys in June of 1888 for $4,000. Beckley immediately won the first base job and batted .343 that season.

Beckley hit .301 and drove in 97 runs in 1889, then jumped to Pittsburgh of the Players' League the following year, leading the league with 22 triples and driving in 120 runs. Beckley returned to the NL after the Players' League folded following the 1890 season, averaging 102 RBI and 106 runs scored with Pittsburgh during the next five seasons.

Beckley was traded to the Giants in 1896, but did not hit well in New York and was released in 1897. Given another chance by the Reds, Beckley's batting form returned with a .345 average in 97 games in Cincinnati. For the next seven seasons, Beckley hit at least .300 six times – establishing himself as one the best contact hitters and earning the nickname "Eagle Eye." His skills as a bunter were well known – he could drop a sacrifice with the handle of the bat, holding the thicker end – and he continued to thrive at the plate even after he was beaned by a Christy Mathewson fastball in 1901.

Sold to the Cardinals before the 1904 season, Beckley left the big leagues following the 1907 season but continued to play and manage in the minor leagues.

JACOB PETER BECKLEY
"OLD EAGLE EYE"
1888 - 1907
FAMED NATIONAL LEAGUE SLUGGER
MADE 2,930 HITS FOR LIFETIME .309 BATTING
AVERAGE. HOLDS RECORD IN MAJORS FOR
FIRST BASE: FOR CHANCES ACCEPTED 25,000
MOST PUTOUTS 23,696, MOST GAMES 2,368,
PLAYED 20 SEASONS WITH PITTSBURGH,
NEW YORK, CINCINNATI AND ST. LOUIS.

Eagle Eye

Elected To The Hall Of Fame: 1971.
Born: Aug. 4, 1867 in Hannibal, Mo.
Died: June 25, 1918 in Kansas City, Mo.
Height: 5-10. **Weight:** 200.
Threw: Left. **Batted:** Left.
Debut: June 20, 1888.
Final Game: June 15, 1907.
Teams: Pittsburgh N.L. 1888-1889, 1891-1896; Pittsburgh, Players' League 1890; New York N.L. 1896-1897; Cincinnati N.L. 1897-1903; St. Louis N.L. 1904-1907.

YEAR	TEAM	LEAGUE	G	AB	R	H	2B	3B	HR	RBI	SB	AVG
1888	PITTSBURGH	NL	71	283	35	97	15	3	0	27	20	.343
1889	PITTSBURGH	NL	123	522	91	157	24	10	9	97	11	.301
1890	PITTSBURGH	PL	121	516	109	167	38	22	9	120	18	.324
1891	PITTSBURGH	NL	133	554	94	162	20	19	4	73	13	.292
1892	PITTSBURGH	NL	151	614	102	145	21	19	10	96	30	.236
1893	PITTSBURGH	NL	131	542	108	164	32	19	5	106	15	.303
1894	PITTSBURGH	NL	132	537	123	185	36	19	7	122	21	.345
1895	PITTSBURGH	NL	130	534	104	175	31	19	5	111	20	.328
1896	PITT/NEW YORK	NL	105	399	81	110	15	9	9	70	19	.276
1897	NEW YORK/CINCINNATI	NL	114	433	84	143	19	12	8	87	25	.330
1898	CINCINNATI	NL	118	459	86	135	20	12	4	72	6	.294
1899	CINCINNATI	NL	135	517	87	172	27	16	3	99	20	.333
1900	CINCINNATI	NL	141	558	98	190	26	10	2	94	23	.341
1901	CINCINNATI	NL	140	580	78	178	36	13	3	79	4	.307
1902	CINCINNATI	NL	129	531	82	175	23	7	5	69	15	.330
1903	CINCINNATI	NL	120	459	85	150	29	10	2	81	23	.327
1904	ST. LOUIS	NL	142	551	72	179	22	9	1	67	17	.325
1905	ST. LOUIS	NL	134	514	48	147	20	10	1	57	12	.286
1906	ST. LOUIS	NL	87	320	29	79	16	6	0	44	3	.247
1907	ST. LOUIS	NL	32	115	6	24	3	0	0	7	0	.209
CAREER TOTALS			**2389**	**9538**	**1602**	**2934**	**473**	**244**	**87**	**1578**	**315**	**.308**

COOL PAPA BELL

"One time he hit a line drive right past my ear. I turned around and saw the ball hit him sliding into second." Many of the stories, such as that one told by Satchel Paige, are apocryphal, but Cool Papa Bell may well have been the fastest man ever to play the game. We'll never know for sure, mostly because the Negro Leagues were not well covered in the press, and Bell, who played from 1922-46, never got the chance to show what he could do in the major leagues.

"I remember one time I got five hits and stole five bases, but none of it was written down because they forgot to bring the scorebook to the game that day," he told the Hall in 1981. But the stories of his speed are legendary. The most colorful was told by former roommate Josh Gibson, who said that Bell was so fast he could flip the light switch and be in bed before the room got dark. Stories of his baserunning speed are legion, advancing two and even three bases on a bunt, beating out tappers back to the pitcher, and also playing a shallow center field, because his speed allowed him to catch up to just about anything out there.

His nickname derived from his youthful stint as a pitcher. At age 19 he joined the St. Louis Stars as a left-handed pitcher, with an assortment of curves, knucklers and screwballs thrown from any of three release points. His calm demeanor on the mound, especially after a pressure-packed strikeout of Oscar Charleston, earned him the colorful sobriquet. Once he moved off the mound, Bell was a switch-hitter and a contact hitter, with great bat control, bunting ability, and speed.

He was a member of three of the greatest Negro League teams in history, winning three championships each with the Stars, the Pittsburgh Crawfords, and the Homestead Grays. The 1935 Crawfords featured four future Hall of Famers: Bell, Charleston, Gibson and Judy Johnson. In addition to the Negro Leagues, Bell played several seasons in the Mexican League, having great success and enjoying the more relaxed racial atmosphere. He also played 21 seasons of winter ball in Cuba, Mexico, and California. Late in his career he became a player-manager, and later, a scout in the early 1950s for the St. Louis Browns.

JAMES THOMAS BELL
"COOL PAPA"
NEGRO LEAGUES 1922-1950
COMBINED SPEED, DARING AND BATTING SKILL TO RANK AMONG BEST PLAYERS IN NEGRO LEAGUES. CONTEMPORARIES RATED HIM FASTEST MAN ON BASE PATHS. HIT OVER .300 REGULARLY, TOPPING .400 ON OCCASION. PLAYED 29 SUMMERS AND 21 WINTERS OF PROFESSIONAL BASEBALL.

Elected To The Hall Of Fame: *1974.*
Born: *May 17, 1903 in Starkville, Miss.*
Died: *Mar. 7, 1991 in St. Louis, Mo.*
Height: *6-0.* **Weight:** *150.*
Threw: *Left.* **Batted:** *Both.*
Debut: *1922.*
Final Game:*1946.*
Teams: *Negro Leagues 1922-1946; St. Louis 1922-1931; Chicago 1929, 1942; Kansas City 1932; Homestead 1932, 1943-1946; Detroit 1932.*

YEAR	TEAM	LEAGUE	G	AB	R	H	2B	3B	HR	RBI	SB	AVG
1922	ST. LOUIS	NNL	—	31	5	10	3	0	1	—	0	.323
1923	ST. LOUIS	NNL	—	108	24	26	5	1	2	—	1	.241
1924	ST. LOUIS	NNL	—	209	42	60	11	2	0	—	7	.287
1925	ST. LOUIS	NNL	—	304	55	94	19	2	5	—	13	.309
1926	ST. LOUIS	NNL	—	238	59	80	14	4	7	—	4	.336
1927	ST. LOUIS	NNL	—	270	50	84	12	2	3	—	10	.311
1928	ST. LOUIS	NNL	—	353	83	113	21	7	4	—	16	.320
1929	CHCAGO/ST. LOUIS	NNL	—	279	60	79	13	5	1	—	21	.283
1930	ST. LOUIS	NNL	—	179	46	62	8	2	4	—	5	.346
1931	ST. LOUIS	NNL	—	30	5	5	0	0	0	—	4	.167
1932	K.C/DET./HOMESTEAD	INDP/EWL	—	153	37	57	9	6	0	—	7	.373
1933	PITTSBURGH	NNL	—	170	33	48	5	3	1	—	8	.282
1934	PITTSBURGH	NNL	—	200	42	63	6	1	1	—	12	.315
1935	PITTSBURGH	NNL	—	170	46	53	3	5	2	—	7	.312
1936	PITTSBURGH	NNL	—	92	23	29	4	2	0	—	1	.315
1937	PITTSBURGH	NNL	—	20	5	10	1	0	2	—	0	.500
1942	CHICAGO	NAL	—	59	8	21	2	0	0	—	0	.356
1943	HOMESTEAD	NNL	—	200	33	64	6	4	0	—	8	.320
1944	HOMESTEAD	NNL	—	155	26	46	6	4	0	—	4	.297
1945	HOMESTEAD	NNL	—	71	15	27	2	0	0	—	0	.380
1946	HOMESTEAD	NNL	—	87	20	35	2	1	0	—	4	.402
CAREER TOTALS			**—**	**3378**	**717**	**1066**	**152**	**51**	**33**	**—**	**132**	**.316**

JOHNNY BENCH

"The way I see it, the first thing you want in a catcher is the ability to handle the pitchers. Then you want defensive skill, and, of course, the good arm. Last of all, if he can hit with power, well, then you've got a Johnny Bench," said longtime front office executive Frank Cashen. Reds manager Sparky Anderson was more succinct: "I don't want to embarrass any other catchers by comparing him with Johnny Bench."

Bench, raised in the tiny town of Binger, Okla., was taught catching at an early age by his father. Making his major league debut in 1967 at the age of 19, he would go on to play his entire 17-year big league career (1967-83) with the Reds, providing everything you could ask of from a backstop.

As the leader of Cincinnati's Big Red Machine team of the 1970s, in which he helped the franchise to four National League pennants and two World Series titles, the rugged and durable Bench was a 10-time Gold Glove Award winner as the result of his skilled handling of pitchers, unparalleled defensive skills and a lightning quick throwing arm that would intimidate would-be base runners. Bench also provided a potent bat, knocking out 389 home runs and leading the league in RBI three times and homers twice. Highly honored during his career, Bench won the 1968 NL Rookie of the Year, was a two-time NL MVP (1970 and 1972) and 14-time All-Star. When Ted Williams once autographed a baseball for Bench, he wrote, "To Johnny, a Hall of Famer for sure."

Bench received the game's ultimate honor when he was elected to the National Baseball Hall of Fame in 1989. "Johnny Bench's desire to succeed and his excellent work habits were two of the reasons why he was elected to the Hall of Fame on the first ballot," said longtime Orioles manager and fellow Hall of Famer Earl Weaver.

Bench spent part of his Hall of Fame induction speech putting the honor in perspective. "I had no idea that the Hall of Fame was waiting for me. I don't think that any youngster ever dreams of that or ever thinks that's possible. You might think of All-Star games and World Series but certainly you wouldn't think of the Hall of Fame because that is a place for the fantasies."

Elected To The Hall Of Fame: *1989.*

Born: *Dec. 7, 1947 at Oklahoma City, Okla.*

Height: *6-1.* **Weight:** *197.*

Threw: *Right.* **Batted:** *Right.*

Debut: *Aug. 28, 1967.*

Final Game: *Sept. 29, 1983.*

Teams: *Cincinnati N.L. 1967-1983.*

Postseason: *2-Time World Series Champion (1975-1976); 4 N.L. Pennants (1970, 1972, 1975, 1976); 6-Time Playoff Qualifier.*

Awards: *14-Time All-Star (1968-1980, 1983); N.L. Rookie of the Year (1968); 2-Time N.L. Most Valuable Player (1970, 1972); World Series MVP (1976).*

YEAR	TEAM	LEAGUE	G	AB	R	H	2B	3B	HR	RBI	SB	AVG
1967	CINCINNATI	NL	26	86	7	14	3	1	1	6	0	.163
1968	CINCINNATI	NL	154	564	67	155	40	2	15	82	1	.275
1969	CINCINNATI	NL	148	532	83	156	23	1	26	90	6	.293
1970	CINCINNATI	NL	158	605	97	177	35	4	45	148	5	.293
1971	CINCINNATI	NL	149	562	80	134	19	2	27	61	2	.238
1972	CINCINNATI	NL	147	538	87	145	22	2	40	125	6	.270
1973	CINCINNATI	NL	152	557	83	141	17	3	25	104	4	.253
1974	CINCINNATI	NL	160	621	108	174	38	2	33	129	5	.280
1975	CINCINNATI	NL	142	530	83	150	39	1	28	110	11	.283
1976	CINCINNATI	NL	135	465	62	109	24	1	16	74	13	.234
1977	CINCINNATI	NL	142	494	67	136	34	2	31	109	2	.275
1978	CINCINNATI	NL	120	393	52	102	17	1	23	73	4	.260
1979	CINCINNATI	NL	130	464	73	128	19	0	22	80	4	.276
1980	CINCINNATI	NL	114	360	52	90	12	0	24	68	4	.250
1981	CINCINNATI	NL	52	178	14	55	8	0	8	25	0	.309
1982	CINCINNATI	NL	119	399	44	103	16	0	13	38	1	.258
1983	CINCINNATI	NL	110	310	32	79	15	2	12	54	0	.255
CAREER TOTALS			**2158**	**7658**	**1091**	**2048**	**381**	**24**	**389**	**1376**	**68**	**.267**

CHIEF BENDER

CHARLES ALBERT BENDER
"CHIEF"
PHILADELPHIA A.L. 1903 - 1914
PHILADELPHIA N.L. 1916 - 1917
CHICAGO A.L. 1925
FAMOUS CHIPPEWA INDIAN, WON OVER 200
GAMES, PITCHED FOR ATHLETICS IN 1905-
1910 - 1911 - 1913 - 1914 WORLD SERIES.
DEFEATED N.Y. GIANTS 3-0 FOR A'S ONLY
VICTORY IN 1905. FIRST PITCHER IN
WORLD SERIES OF 6 GAMES (1911) TO PITCH
3 COMPLETE GAMES. PITCHED NO-HIT GAME
AGAINST CLEVELAND IN 1910.
HIGHEST A.L. PERCENTAGES IN
1910 - 1911 - 1914.

The winningest manager in history saw his share of outstanding big-game pitchers. But when Connie Mack had everything on the line, Chief Bender was his guy. "If everything depended on one game, I just used Albert – the greatest money pitcher of all time," said Mack of Charles Albert Bender, a full-blooded Ojibwa Indian who pitched for Mack for the Philadelphia Athletics from 1903-14. "I'd tell Albert when I planned to use him in a crucial series. Then I relaxed. He never let me down."

Born Charles Albert Bender on May 5, 1884 in Crow Wing County, Minn., while pitching indoor batting practice at the age of 16, he caught the eye of Glenn "Pop" Warner, an innovative coach in the young sport of football. Warner was also Carlisle's baseball coach – and upon witnessing Bender's talent immediately assigned the lanky right-hander to the varsity squad.

In 1902 while playing for a semi-pro team down the road from Carlisle in Harrisburg, Pa., Bender caught Mack's eye after beating the Chicago Cubs in an exhibition game. By 1903, Bender was in the major leagues.

An 18-year-old rookie, Bender went 17-14 with 29 complete games and a 3.07 earned-run average. Two years later, Bender was 18-11 with the pennant-winning A's, capturing Philadelphia's only victory in that year's World Series while losing his other start in the Fall Classic to Christy Mathewson.

Bender continued to improve over the next few years, peaking in 1910 with a 23-5 record and 1.58 ERA – the seventh season in a row where he lowered his ERA from the previous campaign. The A's won the World Series in 1910, 1911 and 1913, with Bender winning five of his seven Fall Classic starts in that stretch.

In 1914, Bender went 17-3 – leading the AL in winning percentage for the third time in five seasons. But the A's lost to the Boston Braves in that World Series, and soon after Mack dismantled his dynasty in the face of surging salaries brought on by competition with the new Federal League.

Bender jumped to the Baltimore Terrapins of the FL in 1915, but went 4-16 with a 3.99 ERA. He returned to Philadelphia to pitch for the Phillies in 1916 and 1917, then made his last big league appearance in 1925 with the White Sox.

Elected To The Hall Of Fame: *1953.*
Born: *May 5, 1884 in Crow Wing County, Minn.*
Died: *May 22, 1954 in Philadelphia, Pa.*
Height: *6-2.* **Weight:** *185.*
Threw: *Right.* **Batted:** *Right.*
Debut: *Apr. 20, 1903.*
Final Game: *July 21, 1925.*
Teams: *Philadelphia A.L. 1903-1914; Baltimore, Federal League 1915; Philadelphia N.L. 1916-1917; Chicago A.L. 1925.*
Postseason: *3-Time World Series Champion (1910-1911, 1913); 5 A.L. Pennants (1905, 1910-1911, 1913-1914).*

YEAR	TEAM	LEAGUE	G	W	L	SV	SH	IP	H	BB	SO	ERA
1903	PHILADELPHIA	AL	36	17	14	0	2	270	239	65	127	3.07
1904	PHILADELPHIA	AL	29	10	11	0	4	203.7	167	59	149	2.87
1905	PHILADELPHIA	AL	35	18	11	0	4	229	193	90	142	2.83
1906	PHILADELPHIA	AL	36	15	10	3	0	238.3	208	48	159	2.53
1907	PHILADELPHIA	AL	33	16	8	3	4	219.3	185	34	112	2.05
1908	PHILADELPHIA	AL	18	8	9	1	2	138.7	121	21	85	1.75
1909	PHILADELPHIA	AL	34	18	8	1	5	250	196	45	161	1.66
1910	PHILADELPHIA	AL	30	23	5	0	3	250	182	47	155	1.58
1911	PHILADELPHIA	AL	31	17	5	3	2	216.3	198	58	114	2.16
1912	PHILADELPHIA	AL	27	13	8	2	1	171	169	33	90	2.74
1913	PHILADELPHIA	AL	48	21	10	13	2	236.7	208	59	135	2.21
1914	PHILADELPHIA	AL	28	17	3	2	7	179	159	55	107	2.26
1915	BALTIMORE	FL	26	4	16	1	0	178.3	198	37	89	3.99
1916	PHILADELPHIA	NL	27	7	7	3	0	122.7	137	34	43	3.74
1917	PHILADELPHIA	NL	20	8	2	2	4	113	84	26	43	1.67
1925	CHICAGO	AL	1	0	0	0	0	1	1	1	0	18.00
CAREER TOTALS			**459**	**212**	**127**	**34**	**40**	**3017**	**2645**	**712**	**1711**	**2.46**

YOGI BERRA

Yogi Berra is a cultural icon whose fame transcended the baseball diamond. "Yogi-isms" such as "it ain't over till its over" and "a nickel ain't worth a dime anymore" have found there way into the vernacular.

People think Yogi is funny, but as his old manager Casey Stengel once put it: "They say he's funny. Well, he has a lovely wife and family, a beautiful home, money in the bank, and he plays golf with millionaires. What's funny about that?"

Lawrence Peter Berra got the nickname Yogi during his teenage years, when he was playing American Legion Baseball. One afternoon, after attending a movie that had a short piece on India, a friend Jack McGuire Jr. noticed a resemblance between him and the "yogi", or person who practiced yoga, on the screen. McGuire said "I'm going to call you Yogi" and from that moment on, the name stuck.

One thing is clear: As colorful as Yogi's stories were and as popular as his star shined off of the field, he was also quite the character behind home plate. He had a reputation as a talker, attempting to take opposing batters off their game. In the 1958 World Series, Yogi kept telling Hank Aaron to "hit with the label up on the bat." Finally Aaron turned and said "Yogi, I came up here to hit, not to read."

In addition to his colorful persona, what made Yogi so great was that he was one of the most feared hitters the game had ever seen. Teammate Hector Lopez said "Yogi had the fastest bat I ever saw. He could hit a ball late, that was already past him, and take it out of the park. The pitchers were afraid of him because he'd hit anything, so they didn't know what to throw. Yogi had them psyched out and he wasn't even trying to psych them out."

What was even more amazing was that when he donned the "tools of ignorance", he had a reputation as being one of the best in the business behind the plate as well, as his manager Casey Stengel often said as well. "Why has our pitching been so great?" Stengel said. "Our catcher that's why. He looks cumbersome but he's quick as a cat."

LAWRENCE PETER BERRA
"YOGI"
NEW YORK, A.L. 1946-1963
NEW YORK, N.L. 1965
PLAYED ON MORE PENNANT-WINNERS (14) AND
WORLD CHAMPIONS (10) THAN ANY PLAYER IN
HISTORY. HAD 358 HOME RUNS AND LIFETIME
.285 BATTING AVERAGE. SET MANY RECORDS
FOR CATCHERS, INCLUDING 148 CONSECUTIVE
GAMES WITHOUT AN ERROR. VOTED A.L. MOST
VALUABLE PLAYER 1951-54-55. MANAGED
YANKEES TO PENNANT IN 1964.

Elected To The Hall Of Fame: 1972.
Born: May 12, 1925 in St. Louis, Mo.
Height: 5-7. **Weight:** 185.
Threw: Right. **Batted:** Left.
Debut: Sept. 22, 1946.
Final Game: May 9, 1965.
Teams: New York A.L. 1946-1963; New York N.L. 1965.
Postseason: 10-Time World Series Champion (1947, 1949-1953, 1956, 1958, 1961-1962); 14 A.L. Pennants (1947, 1949-1953, 1955-1958, 1960-1963).
Awards: 18-Time All-Star (1948-1962); 3-Time A.L. Most Valuable Player (1951, 1954-1955).

YEAR	TEAM	LEAGUE	G	AB	R	H	2B	3B	HR	RBI	SB	AVG
1946	NEW YORK	AL	7	22	3	8	1	0	2	4	0	.364
1947	NEW YORK	AL	83	293	41	82	15	3	11	54	0	.280
1948	NEW YORK	AL	125	469	70	143	24	10	14	98	3	.305
1949	NEW YORK	AL	116	415	59	115	20	2	20	91	2	.277
1950	NEW YORK	AL	151	597	116	192	30	6	28	124	4	.322
1951	NEW YORK	AL	141	547	92	161	19	4	27	88	5	.294
1952	NEW YORK	AL	142	534	97	146	17	1	30	98	2	.273
1953	NEW YORK	AL	137	503	80	149	23	5	27	108	0	.296
1954	NEW YORK	AL	151	584	88	179	28	6	22	125	0	.307
1955	NEW YORK	AL	147	541	84	147	20	3	27	108	1	.272
1956	NEW YORK	AL	140	521	93	155	29	2	30	105	3	.298
1957	NEW YORK	AL	134	482	74	121	14	2	24	82	1	.251
1958	NEW YORK	AL	122	433	60	115	17	3	22	90	3	.266
1959	NEW YORK	AL	131	472	64	134	25	1	19	69	1	.284
1960	NEW YORK	AL	120	359	46	99	14	1	15	62	2	.276
1961	NEW YORK	AL	119	395	62	107	11	0	22	61	2	.271
1962	NEW YORK	AL	86	232	25	52	8	0	10	35	0	.224
1963	NEW YORK	AL	64	147	20	43	6	0	8	28	1	.293
1965	NEW YORK	NL	4	9	1	2	0	0	0	0	0	.222
CAREER TOTALS			**2120**	**7555**	**1175**	**2150**	**321**	**49**	**358**	**1430**	**30**	**.285**

Bert Blyleven

RIK AALBERT BLYLEVEN
"BERT"
MINNESOTA, A.L. 1970-76, 1985-88;
TEXAS, A.L. 1976-77; PITTSBURGH, N.L., 1978-80;
CLEVELAND, A.L., 1981-85; CALIFORNIA, A.L., 1989-90, 1992
DETERMINED, DURABLE AND FUN-LOVING DUTCHMAN WHO BAFFLED
BIG-LEAGUE BATTERS WITH A CRUEL AND KNEE-BUCKLING BREAKING
BALL. PITCHED 22 MAJOR LEAGUE SEASONS, RECORDING 287 CAREER
WINS, 242 COMPLETE GAMES, 4,970 INNINGS PITCHED, AND AN
ASTOUNDING 60 CAREER SHUTOUTS. RECORDED 3,701 STRIKEOUTS,
THIRD MOST ALL-TIME WHEN HE RETIRED. FANNED AT LEAST 200
BATTERS EIGHT TIMES. A TWO-TIME WORLD SERIES CHAMPION WITH THE
1979 PIRATES AND 1987 TWINS, POSTED A 5-1 MARK IN EIGHT CAREER
POSTSEASON GAMES.

B ert Blyleven didn't play baseball until well into his childhood years. He quickly, however, made up for lost time.

Rik Aalbert Blyleven was born in Zeist, Netherlands, on April 6, 1951, and was raised in Southern California. He became interested in baseball when his father took him to see Sandy Koufax pitch for the Dodgers. Later, he was drafted by the Minnesota Twins in the third round of the 1969 amateur draft.

He became the youngest pitcher in the majors when he was called up to the Twins on June 2, 1970 after just 30 minor league starts. He gave up a home run to the first batter he faced, Lee Maye of the Senators, but got the win that day and nine more that season – and was eventually named A.L. Rookie Pitcher of the Year by the *Sporting News*. In 1973, Blyleven won 20 games and threw 325 innings. After five years with 200-plus innings pitched and 15-plus wins for the Twins, he was sent to the Texas Rangers. Blyleven threw a no-hitter for his last start of his first full year with the Rangers against California on Sept. 22, 1977.

Often considered to have the toughest curveball of his time, Blyleven threw two different types: The "roundhouse" and the "overhand drop." He gripped both like a fastball and used a balanced, full follow-through to get movement.

"It (his curveball) was nasty, I'll tell you that," said Hall of Famer Brooks Robinson. "Enough to make your knees buckle. Bert (Blyleven) was a terrific pitcher – a dominating pitcher."

After the 1977 season, he was traded to the Pirates, who won the World Series in 1979 while Blyleven went 1-0 with a 1.80 ERA in the Series. He was traded to Cleveland after the 1980 season, and in 1985 went back to Minnesota. The following year, he established a league record with eight seasons with 200 or more strikeouts. In 1987 he led the Twins to the World Series with two ALCS wins and another in the World Series. At age 38, he went to the Angels where he went 17-5 with a 2.73 ERA, and he pitched three seasons there before retiring in 1992.

Elected To The Hall Of Fame: *2011.*

Born: *Apr. 6, 1951 in Zeist, Netherlands.*

Height: *6'3.* **Weight:** *200.*

Threw: *Right.* **Batted:** *Right.*

Debut: *June 5, 1970.*

Final Game: *Oct. 4, 1992.*

Teams: *Minnesota A.L. (1970-1976, 1985-1988); Texas A.L. (1976-1977); Pittsburgh N.L. (1978-1980); Cleveland A.L. (1981-1985); California A.L. (1989-1990, 1992).*

Postseason: *2-Time World Series Champion (1979, 1987); A.L. Pennant (1987); N.L. Pennant (1979); 3-Time Playoff Qualifier.*

Awards: *2-Time All-Star (1973, 1985).*

YEAR	TEAM	LEAGUE	G	W	L	SV	SH	IP	H	BB	SO	ERA
1970	MINNESOTA	AL	27	10	9	0	1	164	143	47	135	3.18
1971	MINNESOTA	AL	38	16	15	0	5	278.3	267	59	224	2.81
1972	MINNESOTA	AL	39	17	17	0	3	287.3	247	69	228	2.73
1973	MINNESOTA	AL	40	20	17	0	9	325	296	67	258	2.52
1974	MINNESOTA	AL	37	17	17	0	3	281	244	77	249	2.66
1975	MINNESOTA	AL	35	15	10	0	3	275.7	219	84	233	3.00
1976	MINN/TEXAS	AL	36	13	16	0	6	297.7	283	81	219	2.87
1977	TEXAS	AL	30	14	12	0	5	234.7	181	69	182	2.72
1978	PITTSBURGH	NL	34	14	10	0	4	243.7	217	66	182	3.03
1979	PITTSBURGH	NL	37	12	5	0	0	237.3	238	92	172	3.60
1980	PITTSBURGH	NL	34	8	13	0	2	216.7	219	59	168	3.82
1981	CLEVELAND	AL	20	11	7	0	1	159.3	145	40	107	2.88
1982	CLEVELAND	AL	4	2	2	0	0	20.3	16	11	19	4.87
1983	CLEVELAND	AL	24	7	10	0	0	156.3	160	44	123	3.91
1984	CLEVELAND	AL	33	19	7	0	4	245	204	74	170	2.87
1985	CLE/MINNESOTA	AL	37	17	16	0	5	293.7	264	75	206	3.16
1986	MINNESOTA	AL	36	17	14	0	3	271.7	262	58	215	4.01
1987	MINNESOTA	AL	37	15	12	0	1	267	249	101	196	4.01
1988	MINNESOTA	AL	33	10	17	0	0	207.3	240	51	145	5.43
1989	CALIFORNIA	AL	33	17	5	0	5	241	225	44	131	2.73
1990	CALIFORNIA	AL	23	8	7	0	0	134	163	25	69	5.24
1992	CALIFORNIA	AL	25	8	12	0	0	133	150	29	70	4.74
CAREER TOTALS			**692**	**287**	**250**	**0**	**60**	**4970**	**4632**	**1322**	**3701**	**3.31**

WADE BOGGS

Wade Boggs was an artist whose medium was the national pastime, whose tool of choice was a bat, and whose canvas was a ball field. His mother may have summed it up best when she said, "It seemed like he was born to hit just like some kids are born to play the piano."

A 12-time All-Star third baseman, Boggs ended his 18-year (1982-99) major league career with 3,010 hits, a .328 batting average and a .415 on-base percentage. In his 2,440 career games, Boggs reached base safely in 80 percent of them.

Drafted by the Boston Red Sox in 1976, the left-handed-hitting Boggs soon was able to showcase the inside-out swing taught to him by his father. Ensconced as an everyday player by 1983, Boggs rewarded Boston's faith in him by batting a league-leading .361.

"Can that guy hit ropes?" said Detroit Tigers manager Sparky Anderson. "He's one of the best-looking young hitters I've ever seen."

Boggs continued to spray line drives to all fields throughout every American League park. In 1985, he hit a career-best .368, the highest mark by a Red Sox player since Ted Williams hit .388 in 1957. His 240 hits were the most in baseball in 55 years.

After the 1985 season, Williams was quoted as saying "Boggs is as smart a hitter as I've ever seen. The next five or six years will tell the tale, but if he keeps up like he's going now, he stands to be one of the greatest hitters of all time."

Boggs would remain with the Red Sox for 11 seasons (1982-92), winning five batting titles, finishing second once, and third twice.

Next for Boggs was a five-year stint with the New York Yankees, where he not only batted .313 during his stay in the Bronx but won Gold Glove Awards at third base in 1994 and '95, at 36 years of age becoming the oldest first-time winner among non-pitchers. It was with the Tampa Bay Devil Rays, where he signed prior to the expansion franchise's first season in 1998, that Boggs would not only play his final two seasons but also become the 23rd member of the 3,000-hit club.

WADE ANTHONY BOGGS
BOSTON, A.L., 1982-1992
NEW YORK, A.L., 1993-1997
TAMPA BAY, A.L., 1998-1999

A DISCIPLINED HITTER WHOSE COMMANDING KNOWLEDGE OF THE STRIKE ZONE MADE HIM ONE OF BASEBALL'S TOUGHEST OUTS. ONLY 20TH CENTURY PLAYER WITH SEVEN STRAIGHT 200-HIT SEASONS. REACHED BASE SAFELY IN 80 PERCENT OF GAMES PLAYED. BEGAN CAREER WITH 10 CONSECUTIVE SEASONS HITTING ABOVE .300. A FIVE-TIME BATTING CHAMPION WHO ALSO LED THE LEAGUE IN ON-BASE PERCENTAGE AND INTENTIONAL WALKS SIX TIMES EACH. A 12-TIME ALL-STAR. HIT .328 WITH 3,010 HITS AND 1,412 WALKS. MEMBER OF THE 1996 WORLD SERIES CHAMPION YANKEES AND WON TWO GOLD GLOVES. LEGENDARY FOR HIS SUPERSTITIONS.

Elected To The Hall Of Fame: 2005.
Born: June 15, 1958 in Omaha, Neb.
Height: 6-2. **Weight:** 190.
Threw: Right. **Batted:** Left.
Debut: Apr. 10, 1982.
Final Game: Aug. 27, 1999.
Teams: Boston A.L. 1982-1992; New York A.L. 1993-1997; Tampa Bay A.L. 1998-1999.
Postseason: World Series Champion (1996); 2 A.L. Pennants (1986, 1996); 6-Time Playoff Qualifier (1986, 1988, 1990, 1995-1997).
Awards: 12-Time All-Star (1985-1996).

YEAR	TEAM	LEAGUE	G	AB	R	H	2B	3B	HR	RBI	SB	AVG
1982	BOSTON	AL	104	338	51	118	14	1	5	44	1	.349
1983	BOSTON	AL	153	582	100	210	44	7	5	74	3	.361
1984	BOSTON	AL	158	625	109	203	31	4	6	55	3	.325
1985	BOSTON	AL	161	653	107	240	42	3	8	78	2	.368
1986	BOSTON	AL	149	580	107	207	47	2	8	71	0	.357
1987	BOSTON	AL	147	551	108	200	40	6	24	89	1	.363
1988	BOSTON	AL	155	584	128	214	45	6	5	58	2	.366
1989	BOSTON	AL	156	621	113	205	51	7	3	54	2	.330
1990	BOSTON	AL	155	619	89	187	44	5	6	63	0	.302
1991	BOSTON	AL	144	546	93	181	42	2	8	51	1	.332
1992	BOSTON	AL	143	514	62	133	22	4	7	50	1	.259
1993	NEW YORK	AL	143	560	83	169	26	1	2	59	0	.302
1994	NEW YORK	AL	97	366	61	125	19	1	11	55	2	.342
1995	NEW YORK	AL	126	460	76	149	22	4	5	63	1	.324
1996	NEW YORK	AL	132	501	80	156	29	2	2	41	1	.311
1997	NEW YORK	AL	104	353	55	103	23	1	4	28	0	.292
1998	TAMPA BAY	AL	123	435	51	122	23	4	7	52	3	.280
1999	TAMPA BAY	AL	90	292	40	88	14	1	2	29	1	.301
CAREER TOTALS			**2440**	**9180**	**1513**	**3010**	**578**	**61**	**118**	**1014**	**24**	**.328**

JIM BOTTOMLEY

When scout Charley Barrett invited Jim Bottomley to try out with the Cardinals in 1920, there was just one problem. Bottomley, an Illinois native, didn't know where the old Cardinal Field was located. So his taxi driver – sensing Bottomley's uncertainty in the unfamiliar city – took him for a joy ride around St. Louis and watched as his cab fare climbed. From that moment on, it was smoother sailing for Bottomley as he adjusted to life in the Gateway City.

In his 11-year tenure with the Cardinals organization, he made an indelible mark on the team, city and their fans – with one of his most memorable moments coming in 1928, when he was named the National League's Most Valuable Player.

In 1928, Bottomley batted .325 and posted league-leading numbers in home runs (31), RBI (136) and triples (20). His efforts propelled the Cardinals to the World Series, where they were ultimately swept by the New York Yankees.

From 1926-31, "Sunny Jim," as he was often referred to for his light-hearted disposition, led the Cardinals to the World Series four times (1926, 1928, 1930-31) with his stellar regular season stats. From 1924-29, he posted 100 or more regular season RBI and batted .300 or better from 1927-31.

Of the four World Series appearances, the Cardinals won it all twice: in 1926 against the Yankees and in 1931 against the Philadelphia Athletics, creating a mini-dynasty.

"Jim Bottomley was a morale man, a winner, the guy who held early St. Louis championship clubs together," Hall of Famer Bill Terry said in an interview with the *St. Louis Post-Dispatch*.

Another notable moment in Bottomley's career came on Sept. 16, 1924, when he established a major league record for driving in 12 runs in a nine inning game against the Brooklyn Dodgers. The record would stand alone for 69 years before being matched by fellow Cardinal Mark Whiten in 1993.

And his talent didn't end at the plate.

"I noticed one thing that day, and that was that Bottomley could field," former St. Louis manager and Hall of Famer Branch Rickey said of the first time he saw Bottomley play. "By the sinews of Joshua how he could field! His reach from wrist to ankle was sublime."

JAMES LE ROY BOTTOMLEY
"SUNNY JIM"
ST. LOUIS N.L., CINCINNATI N.L.,
ST. LOUIS A.L. 1922-1937
SUPERB CLUTCH HITTER. DROVE IN
100 OR MORE RUNS SIX YEARS IN ROW,
1924-1929, LEADING LEAGUE TWICE.
ESTABLISHED RECORD BY BATTING IN
12 RUNS IN ONE GAME. MOST VALUABLE
PLAYER 1928. HIT SEVEN HOMERS
IN SPAN OF FIVE GAMES IN 1929. HAD
LIFETIME .310 BATTING AVERAGE.

Sunny Jim

Elected To The Hall Of Fame: *1974.*
Born: *Apr. 23, 1900 in Oglesby, Ill.*
Died: *Dec. 11, 1959 in St. Louis, Mo.*
Height: *6-0.* **Weight:** *180.*
Threw: *Left.* **Batted:** *Left.*
Debut: *Aug. 18, 1922.*
Final Game: *Sept. 16, 1937.*
Teams: *St. Louis N.L. 1922-1932;*
Cincinnati N.L. 1933-1935; St. Louis A.L. 1936-1937.
Postseason: *Two-time World Series Champion (1926, 1931); 4 N.L. Pennants (1926, 1928, 1930-1931).*
Awards: *N.L. Most Valuable Player (1928).*

YEAR	TEAM	LEAGUE	G	AB	R	H	2B	3B	HR	RBI	SB	AVG
1922	ST. LOUIS	NL	37	151	29	49	8	5	5	35	3	.325
1923	ST. LOUIS	NL	134	523	79	194	34	14	8	94	4	.371
1924	ST. LOUIS	NL	137	528	87	167	31	12	14	111	5	.316
1925	ST. LOUIS	NL	153	619	92	227	44	12	21	128	3	.367
1926	ST. LOUIS	NL	154	603	98	180	40	14	19	120	4	.299
1927	ST. LOUIS	NL	152	574	95	174	31	15	19	124	8	.303
1928	ST. LOUIS	NL	149	576	123	187	42	20	31	136	10	.325
1929	ST. LOUIS	NL	146	560	108	176	31	12	29	137	3	.314
1930	ST. LOUIS	NL	131	487	92	148	33	7	15	97	5	.304
1931	ST. LOUIS	NL	108	382	73	133	34	5	9	75	3	.348
1932	ST. LOUIS	NL	91	311	45	92	16	3	11	48	2	.296
1933	CINCINNATI	NL	145	549	57	137	23	9	13	83	3	.250
1934	CINCINNATI	NL	142	556	72	158	31	11	11	78	1	.284
1935	CINCINNATI	NL	107	399	44	103	21	1	1	49	3	.258
1936	ST. LOUIS	AL	140	544	72	162	39	11	12	95	0	.298
1937	ST. LOUIS	AL	65	109	11	26	7	0	1	12	1	.239
CAREER TOTALS			1991	7471	1177	2313	465	151	219	1422	58	.310

LOU BOUDREAU

"This is reaching the top. That's what we all strive for no matter what profession we're in. I feel that my life is fulfilled now." Lou Boudreau did it all in baseball – he played, managed, and broadcast. He was an excellent defensive shortstop and a line-drive hitter, and it landed him in the Hall of Fame.

After one game in 1938 and 53 games in 1939, Boudreau became the Indians regular shortstop in 1940, hitting .295, driving in 101 runs, and leading the AL in fielding percentage for the first of 10 consecutive seasons.

In 1942, the Indians shocked the baseball world by hiring their 24-year-old shortstop as a player-manager. Boudreau would continue in that role through 1950. In 1946, he devised the "Williams Shift," sometimes known as the "Boudreau Shift," placing all of the infielders on the right side of second base and leaving only the left-fielder across the diamond, in an attempt to stop the pull-hitting Ted Williams. Williams continued to pull the ball, and acknowledged that the shift hurt him.

Few players (or managers) ever had a better season than Boudreau did in 1948. "That year, Lou Boudreau was the greatest shortstop and leader I have ever seen," said Hall of Famer Bill McKechnie, a coach with the club. The Indians went 97-58, while Boudreau hit .355 with 106 RBI, a career-high 18 home runs, and struck out only nine times in 560 at-bats.

The Indians and the Red Sox finished the regular season tied, necessitating a one-game playoff at Fenway Park, in which Boudreau went 4 for 4—homering twice. The Indians went on to beat the Braves in the World Series, and Boudreau picked up the AL Most Valuable Player Award.

Boudreau moved to the Red Sox for the 1951 season, and was a player-manager for the club in 1952, his final season as a player. He managed the Sox for two more seasons, before taking over the Kansas City Athletics from 1955-57.

In 1958, he moved to the broadcast booth for WGN and the Chicago Cubs. In 1960, he was involved in a most unusual trade, switching placed with Cubs manager Charlie Grimm. Grimm went up to the radio booth, while Boudreau took over as manager. In 1961, he was back on the airwaves, where he remained with the Cubs until 1987.

LOUIS BOUDREAU
CLEVELAND A. L. 1938-1950
BOSTON A. L. 1951-1952

LED A L. SHORTSTOPS IN FIELDING EIGHT SEASONS. SET MAJOR LOOP MARK FOR DOUBLE PLAYS BY SHORTSTOP (134) AND WON BATTING TITLE,1944, PACED A. L. IN DOUBLES THREE TIMES. MOST VALUABLE PLAYER,1948, WHEN HE BATTED .355 TO LEAD INDIANS TO PENNANT AS PLAYER-PILOT. LIFETIME BATTING AVERAGE .295

Elected To The Hall Of Fame: 1970.

Born: July 17, 1917 in Harvey, Ill.

Died: Aug. 10, 2001 in Olympia Fields, Ill.

Height: 5-11. **Weight:** 185.

Threw: Right. **Batted:** Right.

Debut: Sept. 9, 1938.

Final Game: Aug. 24, 1952.

Teams: Cleveland A.L. 1938-1950; Boston A.L. 1951-1952.

Postseason: World Series Champion (1948); A.L. Pennant (1948).

Awards: 8-Time All-Star (1940-1945, 1947-1948); A.L. Most Valuable Player (1948).

YEAR	TEAM	LEAGUE	G	AB	R	H	2B	3B	HR	RBI	SB	AVG
1938	CLEVELAND	AL	1	1	0	0	0	0	0	0	0	.000
1939	CLEVELAND	AL	53	225	42	58	15	4	0	19	2	.258
1940	CLEVELAND	AL	155	627	97	185	46	10	9	101	6	.295
1941	CLEVELAND	AL	148	579	95	149	45	8	10	56	9	.257
1942	CLEVELAND	AL	147	506	57	143	18	10	2	58	7	.283
1943	CLEVELAND	AL	152	539	69	154	32	7	3	67	4	.286
1944	CLEVELAND	AL	150	584	91	191	45	5	3	67	11	.327
1945	CLEVELAND	AL	97	345	50	106	24	1	3	48	0	.307
1946	CLEVELAND	AL	140	515	51	151	30	6	6	62	6	.293
1947	CLEVELAND	AL	150	538	79	165	45	3	4	67	1	.307
1948	CLEVELAND	AL	152	560	116	199	34	6	18	106	3	.355
1949	CLEVELAND	AL	134	475	53	135	20	3	4	60	0	.284
1950	CLEVELAND	AL	81	260	23	70	13	2	1	29	1	.269
1951	BOSTON	AL	82	273	37	73	18	1	5	47	1	.267
1952	BOSTON	AL	4	2	1	0	0	0	0	2	0	.000
CAREER TOTALS			**1646**	**6029**	**861**	**1779**	**385**	**66**	**68**	**789**	**51**	**.295**

ROGER BRESNAHAN

His mark on the game is seen in every contest at every level, whenever a catcher dons shin guards.
Roger Bresnahan, however, did more than revolutionize how catchers dressed. He changed the way the position was played.

Born June 11, 1879 in Toledo, Ohio, Bresnahan – known as "The Duke of Tralee" due to his Irish roots – began his big league career as a pitcher in 1897 with the National League's Washington Senators. By 1901, Bresnahan found himself with the Baltimore Orioles of the new American League. The Orioles catcher, future Hall of Fame manager Wilbert Robinson, was sidelined with an injury.

As a pitcher, Bresnahan was displeased with the Orioles' backup receivers, leading manager John McGraw to ask if Bresnahan wanted to catch. From that day on, Bresnahan was a catcher.

"I never thought catching was hard," Bresnahan said. "I liked it."

Bresnahan hit .268 that year as a first-year receiver, then jumped to the National League along with McGraw in 1902 to play for the Giants. In 1903, Bresnahan hit .350, then led the Giants to NL pennants in 1904 and 1905. He hit .313 with three runs scored in the Giants' 1905 World Series win over the Philadelphia Athletics.

In 1907, became the first catcher to wear shin guards – another in a long line of protective gear innovations, including a rudimentary batting helmet, that Bresnahan brought to the game.

"Boy, they sure called me lots of names when I tried on those shin guards," Bresnahan said. "They must have been a good idea at that, though, because they tell me catchers still wear them."

Bresnahan retired as an active big league ballplayer after the 1915 season having played 17 big league seasons. He compiled a .279 career batting average with 1,252 hits. He also managed four full seasons with the Cardinals (1909-12) and one with the Cubs (1915).

"Roger is a fighter," wrote Fred Lieb in *Baseball Magazine*. "He was a fighter when he was a pupil of (John) McGraw's, and he instilled this fighting spirit into his team."

The Duke of Tralee

Elected To The Hall Of Fame: 1945.
Born: June 11, 1879 in Toledo, Ohio.
Died: Dec. 4, 1944 in Toledo, Ohio.
Height: 5-9. **Weight:** 200.
Threw: Right. **Batted:** Right.
Debut: Aug. 27,1897.
Final Game: Oct. 3, 1915.
Teams: Washington N.L. 1897; Chicago N.L. 1900, 1913-1915; Baltimore A.L. 1901-1902; New York N.L. 1902-1908; St. Louis N.L. 1909-1912.
Postseason: World Series Champion (1905); N.L. Pennant (1904).

YEAR	TEAM	LEAGUE	G	AB	R	H	2B	3B	HR	RBI	SB	AVG
1897	WASHINGTON	NL	6	16	1	6	0	0	0	3	0	.375
1900	CHICAGO	NL	2	2	0	0	0	0	0	0	0	.000
1901	BALTIMORE	AL	86	295	40	79	9	9	1	32	10	.268
1902	BAL/NEW YORK	AL/NL	116	413	46	115	17	9	5	56	18	.278
1903	NEW YORK	NL	113	406	87	142	30	8	4	55	34	.350
1904	NEW YORK	NL	109	402	81	114	22	7	5	33	13	.284
1905	NEW YORK	NL	104	331	58	100	18	3	0	46	11	.302
1906	NEW YORK	NL	124	405	69	114	22	4	0	43	25	.281
1907	NEW YORK	NL	110	328	57	83	9	7	4	38	15	.253
1908	NEW YORK	NL	140	449	70	127	25	3	1	54	14	.283
1909	ST. LOUIS	NL	72	234	27	57	4	1	0	23	11	.244
1910	ST. LOUIS	NL	88	234	35	65	15	3	0	27	13	.278
1911	ST. LOUIS	NL	81	227	22	63	17	8	3	41	4	.278
1912	ST. LOUIS	NL	48	108	8	36	7	2	1	15	4	.333
1913	CHICAGO	NL	69	162	20	37	5	2	1	21	7	.228
1914	CHICAGO	NL	101	248	42	69	10	4	0	24	14	.278
1915	CHICAGO	NL	77	221	19	45	8	1	1	19	19	.204
CAREER TOTALS			**1446**	**4481**	**682**	**1252**	**218**	**71**	**26**	**530**	**212**	**.279**

GEORGE BRETT

For three decades, he was the standard by which other hitters were judged, mastering the art of hitting line drives. In the simplest terms, George Brett was hitting royalty.

Brett was the youngest of four brothers who all played pro ball, including older brother Ken, who pitched in the majors. George grew up in Southern California and was taken in the second round of the 1971 draft by the Kansas City Royals. He shot through the minor leagues, but after winning the big league third base job in 1974, Brett struggled. He came under the tutelage of Royals hitting instructor Charlie Lau, who taught his pupil how to keep his weight back and cover more of home plate with his swing. Brett applied the advice and finished the season batting .282 – his lowest average during the next 17 seasons.

Brett hit .308 with an American League-best 195 hits in 1975, then won his first batting title the next year with a .333 average.

Then in 1980, Brett made a run at the magic .400 mark – a number that hadn't been reached since Ted Williams hit .406 in 1941. Brett kept his average over .400 deep into the summer, but a late slump left him at .390. It was a good enough performance, however, to merit the AL Most Valuable Player Award.

The Royals advanced to the World Series that year after three losses in the American League Championship Series from 1976-78. But Kansas City lost to the Phillies despite Brett's .375 average. Brett continued his hitting excellence into the 1980s, and in 1985 he led the Royals back to the World Series – where this time they came out on top in seven games against the Cardinals. Brett hit .335 with 30 homers and 112 RBI that season, winning his first Gold Glove Award at third base and finishing second in the AL MVP vote.

In 1990 at the age of 37, Brett won his third batting title with a .329 mark – the first player to win a batting title in three decades. Two years later, Brett recorded his 3,000th career hit. He retired after 21 seasons with the Royals as one of only four players with 3,000 hits, 300 home runs and a .300 batting average.

GEORGE HOWARD BRETT
KANSAS CITY, A.L., 1973 – 1993

PLAYED EACH GAME WITH CEASELESS INTENSITY AND UNBRIDLED PASSION. LIFETIME MARKS INCLUDE .305 BA, .317 HR, 1,595 RBI AND 3,154 HITS. ELEVEN .300 SEASONS. A 13-TIME ALL-STAR AND THE FIRST PLAYER TO WIN BATTING TITLES IN THREE DECADES (1976, '80, '90). HIT .390 IN 1980 MVP SEASON AND LED ROYALS TO FIRST WORLD SERIES TITLE IN 1985. RANKS AMONG ALL-TIME LEADERS IN HITS, DOUBLES, LONG HITS AND TOTAL BASES. A.L. CAREER RECORD, MOST INTENTIONAL WALKS. A CLUTCH HITTER WHOSE PROFOUND RESPECT FOR THE GAME LED TO UNIVERSAL REVERENCE.

Elected To The Hall Of Fame: *1999.*
Born: *May 15, 1953 in Glen Dale, W. Va.*
Height: *6-0.* **Weight:** *185.*
Threw: *Right.* **Batted:** *Left.*
Debut: *Aug. 2, 1973.*
Final Game: *Oct. 3, 1993.*
Teams: *Kansas City A.L. 1973-1993*
Postseason: *World Series Champion (1985); 2 A.L. Pennants (1980, 1985); 7-Time Playoff Qualifier (1976-1978, 1980-1981, 1984-1985).*
Awards: *13-Time All-Star (1976-1988); A.L. Most Valuable Player (1980).*

YEAR	TEAM	LEAGUE	G	AB	R	H	2B	3B	HR	RBI	SB	AVG
1973	KANSAS CITY	AL	13	40	2	5	2	0	0	0	0	.125
1974	KANSAS CITY	AL	133	457	49	129	21	5	2	47	8	.282
1975	KANSAS CITY	AL	159	634	84	195	35	13	11	90	13	.308
1976	KANSAS CITY	AL	159	645	94	215	34	14	7	67	21	.333
1977	KANSAS CITY	AL	139	564	105	176	32	13	22	88	14	.312
1978	KANSAS CITY	AL	128	510	79	150	45	8	9	62	23	.294
1979	KANSAS CITY	AL	154	645	119	212	42	20	23	107	17	.329
1980	KANSAS CITY	AL	117	449	87	175	33	9	24	118	15	.390
1981	KANSAS CITY	AL	89	347	42	109	27	7	6	43	14	.314
1982	KANSAS CITY	AL	144	552	101	166	32	9	21	82	6	.301
1983	KANSAS CITY	AL	123	464	90	144	38	2	25	93	0	.310
1984	KANSAS CITY	AL	104	377	42	107	21	3	13	69	0	.284
1985	KANSAS CITY	AL	155	550	108	184	38	5	30	112	9	.335
1986	KANSAS CITY	AL	124	441	70	128	28	4	16	73	1	.290
1987	KANSAS CITY	AL	115	427	71	124	18	2	22	78	6	.290
1988	KANSAS CITY	AL	157	589	90	180	42	3	24	103	14	.306
1989	KANSAS CITY	AL	124	457	67	129	26	3	12	80	14	.282
1990	KANSAS CITY	AL	142	544	82	179	45	7	14	87	9	.329
1991	KANSAS CITY	AL	131	505	77	129	40	2	10	61	2	.255
1992	KANSAS CITY	AL	152	592	55	169	35	5	7	61	8	.285
1993	KANSAS CITY	AL	145	560	69	149	31	3	19	75	7	.266
CAREER TOTALS			**2707**	**10349**	**1583**	**3154**	**665**	**137**	**317**	**1596**	**201**	**.305**

LOU BROCK

He was baseball's most dangerous base stealer for more than a decade, pressuring opponents with speed and daring on the basepaths.

But Lou Brock was much more than a stolen base specialist. And by the end of his spectacular 19-year big league career, Brock was recognized as one of baseball's most complete – and clutch – players of the 20th Century.

Brock played college baseball at Southern University before signing as an amateur free agent with the Cubs in 1960. After tearing up the minors in 1961, Brock surfaced in Chicago at the end of the 1961 season, becoming the Cubs' regular center fielder in 1962. The following year, the 24-year-old Brock played 148 games as Chicago's right fielder, scoring 79 runs while stealing 24 bases and hitting .258. But on June 15, 1964, the Cubs – desperate for pitching – dealt Brock to the Cardinals as part of a trade for Ernie Broglio, an 18-game winner in 1963.

"I guess that fewer than two percent of the people in baseball thought it was a good trade for us," said Cardinals third baseman Ken Boyer.

Brock proved the doubters wrong, hitting .348 with 81 runs scored and 33 stolen bases in just 103 games for St. Louis while leading the Cardinals to the National League pennant. In the World Series, the Cardinals' new left fielder hit .300 with five RBI to help St. Louis beat the Yankees in seven games.

The next year, Brock began a stretch of 12 seasons when he averaged 65 steals and 99 runs scored a year. He led the Cardinals to back-to-back NL pennants in 1967 and 1968 and the World Series title in 1967, hitting .439 in the Fall Classics, including a record 13 hits in the 1968 World Series and 12 the year before.

In 1974, the 35-year-old Brock mounted a successful challenge to Maury Wills' 12-year-old stolen base record, amassing 118 steals while finishing second in the NL Most Valuable Player voting. Brock surpassed Ty Cobb's all-time stolen base mark of 892 during the 1977 season. He led the NL in steals every year but one between 1966 and 1974.

LOUIS CLARK BROCK
CHICAGO N.L., 1961-1964
ST. LOUIS N.L., 1964-1979
BASEBALL'S ALL-TIME LEADER IN STOLEN BASES WITH 938. SET MAJOR LEAGUE RECORD BY STEALING OVER 50 BASES 12 TIMES AND N.L. RECORD WITH 118 STEALS IN 1974. LED N.L. IN STOLEN BASES 8 TIMES. COLLECTED 3,023 HITS DURING 19 YEAR CAREER AND HOLDS WORLD SERIES RECORD WITH .391 BATTING AVERAGE IN 21 POST-SEASON GAMES.

Elected To The Hall Of Fame: 1985.

Born: June 18, 1939 in El Dorado, Ariz.

Height: 5-11. Weight: 170.

Threw: Left. Batted: Left.

Debut: Sept. 10, 1961.

Final Game: Sept. 30, 1979.

Teams: Chicago N.L. 1961-1964; St. Louis N.L. 1964-1979.

Postseason: 2-Time World Series Champion (1964, 1967); 3 N.L. Pennants (1964, 1967-1968).

Awards: 6-Time All-Star (1967, 1971-1972, 1974-1975, 1979).

YEAR	TEAM	LEAGUE	G	AB	R	H	2B	3B	HR	RBI	SB	AVG
1961	CHICAGO	NL	4	11	1	1	0	0	0	0	0	.091
1962	CHICAGO	NL	123	434	73	114	24	7	9	35	16	.263
1963	CHICAGO	NL	148	547	79	141	19	11	9	37	24	.258
1964	CHICAGO/ST. LOUIS	NL	155	634	111	200	30	11	14	58	43	.315
1965	ST. LOUIS	NL	155	631	107	182	35	8	16	69	63	.288
1966	ST. LOUIS	NL	156	643	94	183	24	12	15	46	74	.285
1967	ST. LOUIS	NL	159	689	113	206	32	12	21	76	52	.299
1968	ST. LOUIS	NL	159	660	92	184	46	14	6	51	62	.279
1969	ST. LOUIS	NL	157	655	97	195	33	10	12	47	53	.298
1970	ST. LOUIS	NL	155	664	114	202	29	5	13	57	51	.304
1971	ST. LOUIS	NL	157	640	126	200	37	7	7	61	64	.313
1972	ST. LOUIS	NL	153	621	81	193	26	8	3	42	63	.311
1973	ST. LOUIS	NL	160	650	110	193	29	8	7	63	70	.297
1974	ST. LOUIS	NL	153	635	105	194	25	7	3	48	118	.306
1975	ST. LOUIS	NL	136	528	78	163	27	6	3	47	56	.309
1976	ST. LOUIS	NL	133	498	73	150	24	5	4	67	56	.301
1977	ST. LOUIS	NL	141	489	69	133	22	6	2	46	35	.272
1978	ST. LOUIS	NL	92	298	31	66	9	0	0	12	17	.221
1979	ST. LOUIS	NL	120	405	56	123	15	4	5	38	21	.304
CAREER TOTALS			**2616**	**10332**	**1610**	**3023**	**486**	**141**	**149**	**900**	**938**	**.293**

DAN BROUTHERS

He was a power hitter in an era built for speed and contact at the plate. Dan Brouthers, however, was strong enough – and smart enough – to become one of baseball's first great long-ball hitters.

Born May 8, 1858 in Sylvan Lake, N.Y., Brouthers became an amateur star in upstate New York thanks to a 6-foot-2, 207-pound build that made him one of the larger players of his era. He made his big league debut in 1879 with the Troy Trojans of the National League, but was released after just 39 games.

After playing in the minors for most of the 1880 season, Brouthers appeared in three more games with Troy, then hooked on with the National League's Buffalo Bisons in 1881.

Over the next five seasons, Brouthers led the league in batting average twice, hits twice, triples once and runs batted in once.

From 1886 through 1894, Brouthers starred for NL teams in Detroit, Boston, Brooklyn and Baltimore – and also made stops with teams in the Players League and the American Association.

"He was a great hitter, one of the most powerful batters of all time," said future Hall of Fame manager John McGraw, who was a teammate of Brouthers with the 1894 Baltimore team that scored 1,171 runs in just 128 games. "Big Dan in his prime, against (modern) pitching and the modern lively ball, would have hit as many home runs as anybody."

Brouthers was a part-time player in his final three big league seasons, retiring for good after the 1904 campaign. He won five batting titles and led the league in slugging percentage seven times. The powerful lefty batter never hit worse than .300 in a full season, compiling a .342 career average. He drove in at least 100 runs in five different seasons and scored 100-or-more runs in eight seasons.

Brouthers' total of 106 career home runs ranks fourth among players who were active in the 19th Century.

"Brouthers meant little to the younger generation," wrote baseball historian Si Goodfriend. "But he was a great player among great players in his day."

Elected To The Hall Of Fame: 1945.
Born: May 8, 1858 in Sylvan Lake, N.Y.
Died: Aug. 2, 1932 in East Orange, N.J.
Height: 6-2. **Weight:** 207.
Threw: Left. **Batted:** Left.
Debut: June 23, 1879.
Final Game: Oct. 4, 1904.
Teams: Troy N.L. (1879-1880); Buffalo N.L. (1881-1885); Detroit N.L. (1886-1888); Boston, Players League (1890); Boston, American Association (1891); Brooklyn N.L. (1892-1893). Boston N.L. (1889); Baltimore N.L. (1894-95); Louisville (N.L.) 1895; Philadelphia N.L. (1896); New York N.L. (1904).
Postseason: World Champion (1887); N.L. Pennant (1887).

YEAR	TEAM	LEAGUE	G	AB	R	H	2B	3B	HR	RBI	SB	AVG
1879	TROY	NL	39	168	17	46	12	1	4	17	0	.274
1880	TROY	NL	3	12	0	2	0	0	0	1	0	.167
1881	BUFFALO	NL	65	270	60	86	18	9	8	45	0	.319
1882	BUFFALO	NL	84	351	71	129	23	11	6	63	0	.368
1883	BUFFALO	NL	98	425	85	159	41	17	3	97	0	.374
1884	BUFFALO	NL	94	398	82	130	22	15	14	79	0	.327
1885	BUFFALO	NL	98	407	87	146	32	11	7	59	0	.359
1886	DETROIT	NL	121	489	139	181	40	15	11	72	21	.370
1887	DETROIT	NL	123	500	153	169	36	20	12	101	34	.338
1888	DETROIT	NL	129	522	118	160	33	11	9	66	34	.307
1889	BOSTON	NL	126	485	105	181	26	9	7	118	22	.373
1890	BOSTON	PL	123	460	117	152	36	9	1	97	28	.330
1891	BOSTON	AA	130	486	117	170	26	19	5	109	31	.350
1892	BROOKLYN	NL	152	588	121	197	30	20	5	124	31	.335
1893	BROOKLYN	NL	77	282	57	95	21	11	2	59	9	.337
1894	BALTIMORE	NL	123	525	137	182	39	23	9	128	38	.347
1895	BALTIMORE/LOUISVILLE	NL	29	120	15	36	12	1	2	20	1	.300
1896	PHILADELPHIA	NL	57	218	42	75	13	3	1	41	7	.344
1904	NEW YORK	NL	2	5	0	0	0	0	0	0	0	.000
CAREER TOTALS			**1673**	**6711**	**1523**	**2296**	**460**	**205**	**106**	**1296**	**256**	**.342**

MORDECAI BROWN

"I always felt if I had had a normal hand, I would have been a greater pitcher." For any other pitcher, a right hand mangled in a childhood accident might have derailed a career before it started

But for Mordecai "Three Finger" Brown, the incident on a local farm became the genesis of a Hall of Fame career.

"It was a great ball, that downward curve of his," said Ty Cobb, owner of the game's best career batting average, of the curveball that evolved from Brown's misshapen fingers. "I can't talk about all of baseball, but I can say this: It was the most deceiving, the most devastating pitch I ever faced."

Born Mordecai Peter Centennial Brown on Oct. 19, 1876 in Nyesville, Ind., Brown's life changed when – as a five year old – he got his right index finger caught in a machine designed to separate grain from stalks and husks. The digit was sliced off, leaving only a stump. The next year, Brown damaged the hand again in a fall – breaking the remaining fingers. The bones healed, but the fingers were left at permanently odd angles.

Brown, however, showed baseball aptitude into his teen years and hooked on with semi-pro teams near his home. By 1901, Brown was dominating hitters with Terre Haute in the Three-I League. He surfaced in the big leagues with the Cardinals in 1903, but struggled to a 9-13 record while trying to harness his movement-laden pitches.

The Cubs acquired Brown following the 1903 season, and the next year – at the age of 27 – Brown found success with a 15-10 record and 1.86 earned-run average. Over the next seven seasons, Brown averaged almost 24 wins a season while leading the Cubs to the World Series title in 1907 and 1908. In 1906, Brown posted a 1.04 ERA for a Cubs team that won a record 116 games – the lowest National League figure of the modern era among qualifying pitchers.

In 1908, Brown won the replayed game against the Giants following the "Merkle Boner" game, giving the Cubs the pennant. In nine career World Series games, Brown was 5-4 with a 2.97 ERA. He pitched for the Cubs through 1912 before moving to Cincinnati. Brown then jumped to the upstart Federal League in for the 1914 and 1915 seasons before ending his career back with the Cubs in 1916.

MORDECAI PETER BROWN
(THREE-FINGERED AND MINER)
MEMBER OF CHICAGO N.L. CHAMPIONSHIP TEAM OF 1906,'07,'08,'10. A RIGHT HANDED PITCHER, WON 239 GAMES DURING MAJOR LEAGUE CAREER THAT ALSO INCLUDED ST. LOUIS AND CINCINNATI N.L. AND CLUBS IN F.L. FIRST MAJOR LEAGUER TO PITCH FOUR CONSECUTIVE SHUTOUTS, ACHIEVING THIS FEAT ON JUNE 13, JUNE 25, JULY 2 AND JULY 4 IN 1908.

Three Finger

Elected To The Hall Of Fame: 1949.
Born: Oct. 19, 1876 in Nyesville, Ind.
Died: Feb. 14, 1948 in Terre Haute, Ind.
Height: 5-10. **Weight:** 175.
Threw: Right. **Batted:** Both.
Debut: Apr. 19, 1903.
Final Game: Sept. 4, 1916.
Teams: St. Louis N.L. 1903; Chicago N.L. 1904-1912, 1916; Cincinnati N.L. 1913; St. Louis, Federal League 1914; Brooklyn, Federal League 1914; Chicago, Federal League 1915
Postseason: 2-Time World Series Champion (1907-1908); 4 N.L. Pennants (1906-1908, 1910).

YEAR	TEAM	LEAGUE	G	W	L	SV	SH	IP	H	BB	SO	ERA
1903	ST. LOUIS	NL	26	9	13	0	1	201	231	59	83	2.60
1904	CHICAGO	NL	26	15	10	1	4	212.3	155	50	81	1.86
1905	CHICAGO	NL	30	18	12	0	4	249	219	44	89	2.17
1906	CHICAGO	NL	36	26	6	3	9	277.3	198	61	144	1.04
1907	CHICAGO	NL	34	20	6	3	6	233	180	40	107	1.39
1908	CHICAGO	NL	44	29	9	5	9	312.3	214	49	123	1.47
1909	CHICAGO	NL	50	27	9	7	8	342.7	246	53	172	1.31
1910	CHICAGO	NL	46	25	14	7	6	295.3	256	64	143	1.86
1911	CHICAGO	NL	53	21	11	13	0	270	267	55	129	2.80
1912	CHICAGO	NL	15	5	6	0	2	88.7	92	20	34	2.64
1913	CINCINNATI	NL	39	11	12	6	1	173.3	174	44	41	2.91
1914	ST. LOUIS/BROOKLYN	FL	35	14	11	0	2	232.7	235	61	113	3.52
1915	CHICAGO	FL	35	17	8	4	3	236.3	189	64	95	2.09
1916	CHICAGO	NL	12	2	3	0	0	48.3	52	9	21	3.91
CAREER TOTALS			**481**	**239**	**130**	**49**	**55**	**3172.1**	**2708**	**673**	**1375**	**2.06**

RAYMOND BROWN

In an era when every ticket sold meant job security, Raymond Brown was the pitcher of choice in the Negro Leagues.

"He's what they called their Sunday Pitcher," said Negro leagues historian James Riley. "They'd pitch their best on Sunday to draw a crowd, and nobody was better."

Born Feb. 23, 1908 in Alger, Ohio, the 6-foot-1, 195-pound Brown developed a reputation while still an amateur as an all-around star on the diamond. After short stints with pro teams in Indianapolis and Detroit, Brown hooked on with Cum Posey's Homestead Grays – a blossoming Negro Leagues powerhouse.

In 14 seasons with the Grays, Brown became one of the great stars of African-American baseball, leading the team to eight pennants in one nine-year span. His vast repertoire of pitches included sinkers, sliders and even knuckleballs, but his curve was his go-to offering.

"So confident was Ray in all of his pitches that he would throw a curve with a 3-0 count on the batter," Riley said. "He had good control of all of his pitches."

In 1938, the *Pittsburgh Courier* newspaper listed Brown as one of five Negro leagues stars who would be certain major leaguers if allowed to play. The others: Cool Papa Bell, Josh Gibson, Buck Leonard and Satchel Paige. All have been enshrined in the Hall of Fame.

Brown threw a one-hitter in the 1944 Negro League World Series – leading the Grays to the title – and pitched a perfect game in 1945.

Brown also starred in winter league play during this era, posting an incredible 21-4 record with Santa Clara of the Cuban Winter League in 1936 while hitting .311 at the plate. He completed 23 of his 26 starts that season.

In the Negro Leagues, Brown appeared in two East-West All-Star Games, compiled a 3-2 record in seven Negro League World Series games and finished his Negro Leagues career with a record of 105-44.

Brown pitched in the Mexican League and the Canadian Provincial League before retiring following the 1953 season.

RAYMOND BROWN
"RAY"
NEGRO LEAGUES, 1930-1948

A MAINSTAY OF THE HOMESTEAD GRAYS PITCHING STAFF FOR 14 SEASONS, UTILIZING A VARIETY OF BREAKING BALLS, INCLUDING A DEVASTATING CURVEBALL, TO HELP LEAD THEM TO EIGHT PENNANTS IN NINE YEARS FROM 1937-1945. RANKS AMONG ALL-TIME NEGRO LEAGUES LEADERS IN WINS, WINNING PERCENTAGE AND SHUTOUTS. SELECTED TO THREE EAST-WEST ALL-STAR GAMES. TOSSED ONE-HITTER AGAINST BIRMINGHAM BLACK BARONS IN 1944 NEGRO LEAGUES WORLD SERIES. SPENT SEVERAL STANDOUT SEASONS PITCHING IN CUBA, PUERTO RICO AND MEXICO.

The Sunday Pitcher

Elected To The Hall Of Fame: 2006.
Born: Feb. 23, 1908 in Alger, Ohio.
Died: Feb. 8, 1965 in Dayton, Ohio.
Height: 6-1. **Weight:** 195.
Threw: Right. **Batted:** Both.
Teams: Negro Leagues 1930-1948. Indianapolis 1931; Detroit 1932; Homestead 1932-1945.

YEAR	TEAM	LEAGUE	G	W	L	SV	SH	IP	H	BB	SO	RAVG
1931	INDIANAPOLIS	NNL	—	1	0	—	0	9	7	0	0	1.00
1932	DET./HOMESTEAD	EWL	—	4	6	—	1	90.7	96	21	30	4.47
1933	HOMESTEAD	NNL	—	1	0	—	0	11	14	1	8	7.36
1934	HOMESTEAD	INDP	—	2	2	—	0	30.7	35	4	15	5.28
1935	HOMESTEAD	NNL	—	8	4	—	1	100.7	95	31	30	4.92
1936	HOMESTEAD	NNL	—	2	1	—	0	31	34	5	7	6.68
1937	HOMESTEAD	NNL	—	7	4	—	0	77	73	20	40	5.38
1938	HOMESTEAD	NNL	—	5	0	—	1	33.7	28	0	3	1.34
1939	HOMESTEAD	NNL	—	6	1	—	1	64.7	65	12	17	4.18
1940	HOMESTEAD	NNL	—	15	4	—	3	169	136	30	62	2.61
1941	HOMESTEAD	NNL	—	10	6	—	1	143.3	140	25	43	4.40
1942	HOMESTEAD	NNL	—	11	5	—	1	151.7	140	36	59	3.44
1943	HOMESTEAD	NNL	—	7	0	—	1	64.7	61	20	27	3.48
1944	HOMESTEAD	NNL	—	11	4	—	3	128	131	14	49	3.87
1945	HOMESTEAD	NNL	—	2	4	—	0	45	60	6	19	8.00
CAREER TOTALS			—	92	41	—	13	1150	1115	225	409	4.14

WILLARD BROWN

WILLARD JESSE BROWN
"ESE HOMBRE" "HOME RUN"
NEGRO LEAGUES, 1935-1952, 1958
ST. LOUIS A.L., 1947
A POWER-HITTING CENTER FIELDER WHO HELPED LEAD THE
KANSAS CITY MONARCHS TO SIX PENNANTS IN 10 SEASONS
FROM 1937-1946, INCLUDING A NEGRO LEAGUES CHAMPIONSHIP
IN 1942. A FREE-SWINGER WHOSE AVERAGE REGULARLY
TOPPED .300. PLAYED IN EIGHT EAST-WEST ALL-STAR GAMES.
FIRST BLACK PLAYER TO BELT A HOME RUN IN THE AMERICAN
LEAGUE, DURING A BRIEF STINT WITH THE ST. LOUIS BROWNS
IN 1947. TWO-TIME TRIPLE CROWN WINNER IN PUERTO RICAN
WINTER LEAGUE.

His big league statistics – 21 games, a .179 batting average – tell the most incomplete story possible of the player who was Willard Brown.

His Hall of Fame plaque, however, speaks volumes about the pioneer who was one of the Negro leagues' greatest power hitters.

"He was the most natural ballplayer I ever saw," said Negro leagues legend Buck O'Neil. "He'd steal second base standing up. He was a great talent."

"Home Run" Brown – named by future Hall of Famer Josh Gibson – began his pro baseball career with the Negro minor league Monroe Monarchs before being called up to the Kansas City Monarchs of Negro American League in 1935. Brown quickly became one of the league's most formidable hitters, leading the loop home runs in 1937 and 1938. He helped lead the Monarchs to five pennants between 1937 and 1942, also playing in the Mexican League in 1940, where he hit .354.

A speedy outfielder who usually played center field, the 5-foot-11, 200-pound Brown again led the Negro Leagues in home runs in 1942 and 1943 before serving in the Army the next two years during World War II. He was among those on 5,000 ships that crossed the English Channel during the D-Day Invasion of 1944.

In 1946, Brown returned to baseball and the Monarchs and again began hitting prodigious numbers of home runs. The next season, Hank Thompson and Brown became the second and third black players in American League history when they signed with the St. Louis Browns. The adjustment proved difficult as Willard Brown played in just 21 games before he was released.

During his time in the majors, however, Brown became the first African-American to homer in the AL when he connected off future Hall of Famer Hal Newhouser of the Tigers on Aug. 13. Brown returned to the Monarchs, then played two more years in Kansas City, leading the league in home runs in 1949. Then he hit .432 with 27 homers in just 234 at-bats for Santurce of the Puerto Rican Winter League. He won two Triple Crowns in the PRWL. Brown continued to play through the 1958 season, hitting 35 home runs and driving in 120 runs in the Texas League in 1954. He finished his Negro leagues career with a .339 average.

Home Run

Elected To The Hall Of Fame: 2006.
Born: June 26, 1915 in Shreveport, La.
Died: Aug. 4, 1996 in Houston, Texas.
Height: 5-11. **Weight:** 200.
Threw: Right. **Batted:** Right.
Debut: July 19, 1947.
Final Game: Aug. 17, 1947.
Teams: Negro Leagues 1935-1944, 1946-1952; Kansas City 1935-1944; 1946-1948; St. Louis A.L. 1947

YEAR	TEAM	LEAGUE	G	AB	R	H	2B	3B	HR	RBI	SB	AVG
1935	KANSAS CITY	INDP	—	25	5	13	3	0	3	—	1	.520
1937	KANSAS CITY	NAL	—	174	36	58	2	7	6	—	6	.333
1938	KANSAS CITY	NAL	—	78	14	27	5	1	3	—	9	.346
1939	KANSAS CITY	NAL	—	70	10	22	5	2	1	—	5	.314
1940	KANSAS CITY	NAL	—	4	0	0	0	0	0	—	0	.000
1941	KANSAS CITY	NAL	—	87	19	30	3	3	2	—	4	.345
1942	KANSAS CITY	NAL	—	127	28	47	7	2	5	—	3	.370
1943	KANSAS CITY	NAL	—	79	15	27	3	0	3	—	2	.342
1944	KANSAS CITY	NAL	—	4	0	1	0	0	0	—	0	.250
1946	KANSAS CITY	NAL	—	106	15	27	6	4	2	—	8	.255
1947	KANSAS CITY	NAL	—	57	12	21	3	5	2	—	0	.368
1948	KANSAS CITY	NAL	—	86	18	31	5	1	3	—	4	.360
NEGRO LEAGUE TOTALS			**—**	**897**	**172**	**304**	**42**	**25**	**30**	**—**	**42**	**.339**

YEAR	TEAM	LEAGUE	G	AB	R	H	2B	3B	HR	RBI	SB	AVG
1947	ST. LOUIS	AL	21	67	4	12	3	0	1	6	2	.179

JIM BUNNING

JAMES PAUL DAVID BUNNING
DETROIT, A.L. 1955-1963
PHILADELPHIA, N.L. 1964-1967, 1970-1971
PITTSBURGH, N.L. 1968-1969
LOS ANGELES, N.L. 1969
MAINTAINED DEDICATION AND CONSISTENCY
THROUGHOUT 17 SEASONS WHILE POSTING CAREER
RECORD OF 224-184 WITH 3.27 ERA. INTIMIDATING
RIGHT-HANDED SIDEARMER WON 100 GAMES, PITCHED
NO-HITTER AND STRUCK OUT 1,000 IN BOTH LEAGUES.
1964 PERFECT GAME WAS FIRST IN N.L. IN 20TH
CENTURY. SECOND ALL-TIME IN STRIKEOUTS (2,855).
UPON RETIREMENT IN 1971, ENJOYED SECOND CAREER
AS MULTI-TERM U.S. CONGRESSMAN

Jim Bunning was a tough right-handed sidearm pitcher during his 17-year big league career, but consistency was what he craved, once stating, "I am most proud of the fact I went through nearly 11 years without missing a start. They wrote my name down, and I went to the post."

From 1955 to 1971, in a playing career spent mostly with the Detroit Tigers and Philadelphia Phillies, Bunning would be triumphant in 224 games.

Though the nine-time All-Star would have only one 20-win season, Bunning won 19 games four times. Often pitching with tough luck, he lost a major league-record five 1-0 decisions in a season. When Bunning retired, he was second on the all-time strikeouts list to Walter Johnson.

Bunning's most memorable performance may have come on June 21, 1964 when, on Father's Day, the father of nine tossed the seventh perfect game in major league history and the first no-hitter by a Phillies pitcher in more than 58 years in a 6-0 victory at the New York Mets. He also pitched a no-hitter for Detroit on July 20, 1958, against Boston, winning 3-0.

"For most pitchers like me, who aren't overpowering supermen with extraordinary stuff like Sandy Koufax or Nolan Ryan, a no-hitter is a freaky thing," Bunning said. "You can't plan it. It's not something you can try to do. It just happens.

"Everything has to come together – good control, outstanding plays from your teammates, a whole lot of good fortune on your side and a lot of bad luck for the other guys. A million things could go wrong – but on this one particular day of your life none of them do."

Besides throwing no-hitters in the American and National leagues, Bunning was also the second pitcher, behind Hall of Famer Cy Young, to win 100 games and collect 1,000 strikeouts in both circuits.

Allen Lewis, a 1981 Ford C. Frick Award honoree who covered Bunning while writing for *The Philadelphia Inquirer*, said, "He's the only pitcher I ever saw who never threw a pitch that he didn't know exactly what he was trying to do with it. He had purpose with every pitch."

Elected To The Hall Of Fame: *1996.*
Born: *Oct. 23, 1931 at Southgate, Ky.*
Height: *6-3.* **Weight:** *190.*
Threw: *Right.* **Batted:** *Right.*
Debut: *July 20, 1955.*
Final Game: *Sept. 3, 1971.*
Teams: *Detroit A.L. 1955-1963; Philadelphia N.L. 1964-1967, 1970-1971; Pittsburgh N.L. 1968-1969; Los Angeles N.L. 1969*
Awards: *9-Time All-Star (1957, 1959-1964, 1966).*

YEAR	TEAM	LEAGUE	G	W	L	SV	SH	IP	H	BB	SO	ERA
1955	DETROIT	AL	15	3	5	1	0	51	59	32	37	6.35
1956	DETROIT	AL	15	5	1	1	0	53.3	55	28	34	3.71
1957	DETROIT	AL	45	20	8	1	1	267.3	214	72	182	2.69
1958	DETROIT	AL	35	14	12	0	3	219.7	188	79	177	3.52
1959	DETROIT	AL	40	17	13	1	1	249.7	220	75	201	3.89
1960	DETROIT	AL	36	11	14	0	3	252	217	64	201	2.79
1961	DETROIT	AL	38	17	11	1	4	268	232	71	194	3.19
1962	DETROIT	AL	41	19	10	6	2	258	262	74	184	3.59
1963	DETROIT	AL	39	12	13	1	2	248.3	245	69	196	3.88
1964	PHILADELPHIA	NL	41	19	8	2	5	284.3	248	46	219	2.63
1965	PHILADELPHIA	NL	39	19	9	0	7	291	253	62	268	2.60
1966	PHILADELPHIA	NL	43	19	14	1	5	314	260	55	252	2.41
1967	PHILADELPHIA	NL	40	17	15	0	6	302.3	241	73	253	2.29
1968	PITTSBURGH	NL	27	4	14	0	1	160	168	48	95	3.88
1969	PITTSBURGH/LOS ANGELES	NL	34	13	10	0	0	212.3	212	59	157	3.69
1970	PHILADELPHIA	NL	34	10	15	0	0	219	233	56	147	4.11
1971	PHILADELPHIA	NL	29	5	12	1	0	110	126	37	58	5.48
CAREER TOTALS			**591**	**224**	**184**	**16**	**40**	**3760.1**	**3433**	**1000**	**2855**	**3.27**

JESSE BURKETT

The .400 batting average remains the domain of only the greatest hitters baseball has known.

Jesse Burkett visited that rarified air twice in his career, helping him lay claim to the title as one of baseball's best hitters.

Born Dec. 4, 1868, in Wheeling, W.Va., Burkett made his pro baseball debut in 1888 as a pitcher, winning 27 games for a minor league team in Scranton, Pa. The next season, Burkett went 39-6 for a team in Worcester, Mass., then surfaced in the big leagues in 1890 with the New York Giants.

On the mound, the 5-foot-8, 155-pound Burkett was 3-10 that season. But at the plate, the lefty hit .309 in 101 games – and his transformation from pitcher to outfielder began.

Burkett's contract was purchased by the National League's Cleveland Spiders before the 1891 season, and he honed his skills for most of that year in the minors in Lincoln, Neb. By 1893, he was hitting .348 as an everyday outfielder for the Spiders. In 1895 and 1896, Burkett batted .405 and .410, respectively, becoming just the second player to reach the .400 mark twice.

Burkett was nicknamed "The Crab" by his Cleveland teammates – a reflection of his disposition between the lines.

"You've got to be a battler," Burkett said. "If you don't, they'll walk all over you."

"Once the bell rang, I had no friends on the other team."

Burkett was transferred to the St. Louis Cardinals in 1899 by the Spiders' owner Frank Robison, who owned both teams. That year, Burkett hit .396 – a figure that was revised down from .402 in future years. After two more seasons with the Cardinals – which included a .376 average in 1901 that was good for his third National League batting crown – Burkett jumped to the St. Louis Browns of the American League for three years. He finished his big league career in 1905 with the AL's Boston franchise.

For his career, Burkett compiled a .338 batting average on the strength of 2,850 hits. He scored 1,720 runs and notched 320 doubles. Following his big league debut as a pitcher in 1890, Burkett pitched only two more games in the major leagues.

Burkett returned to Worcester following his retirement and later scouted and coached for John McGraw's Giants as well as coaching at Holy Cross.

JESSE C. BURKETT
BATTING STAR WHO PLAYED OUTFIELD FOR THE NEW YORK, CLEVELAND AND ST. LOUIS N.L. TEAMS AND THE ST. LOUIS AND BOSTON A.L. TEAMS. SHARES WITH ROGERS HORNSBY AND TY COBB THE RECORD OF HITTING .400 OR BETTER THE MOST TIMES. ACCOMPLISHED THIS ON THREE OCCASIONS. TOPPED THE N.L. IN HITTING THREE TIMES, BATTING OVER .400 TO GAIN THE CHAMPIONSHIP IN 1895 AND 1896.

The Crab

Elected To The Hall Of Fame: 1946.
Born: Dec. 4, 1868 in Wheeling, W. Va.
Died: May 27, 1953 in Worcester, Mass.
Height: 5-8. **Weight:** 155.
Threw: Left. **Batted:** Left.
Debut: Apr. 22, 1890.
Final Game: Oct. 7, 1905.
Teams: New York N.L. 1890; Cleveland N.L. 1891-1898; St. Louis N.L. 1899-1901; St. Louis A.L. 1902-1904; Boston A.L. 1905.
Postseason: Championship League Pennant (1892).

YEAR	TEAM	LEAGUE	G	AB	R	H	2B	3B	HR	RBI	SB	AVG
1890	NEW YORK	NL	101	401	67	124	23	13	4	60	14	.309
1891	CLEVELAND	NL	40	167	29	45	7	4	0	13	1	.269
1892	CLEVELAND	NL	145	608	119	167	15	14	6	66	36	.275
1893	CLEVELAND	NL	125	511	145	178	25	15	6	82	39	.348
1894	CLEVELAND	NL	125	523	138	187	27	14	8	94	28	.358
1895	CLEVELAND	NL	132	555	153	225	22	13	5	83	41	.405
1896	CLEVELAND	NL	133	586	160	240	27	16	6	72	34	.410
1897	CLEVELAND	NL	127	517	129	198	28	7	2	60	28	.383
1898	CLEVELAND	NL	150	624	114	213	18	9	0	42	19	.341
1899	ST. LOUIS	NL	141	558	116	221	21	8	7	71	25	.396
1900	ST. LOUIS	NL	141	559	88	203	11	15	7	68	32	.363
1901	ST. LOUIS	NL	142	601	142	226	20	15	10	75	27	.376
1902	ST. LOUIS	AL	138	553	97	169	29	9	5	52	23	.306
1903	ST. LOUIS	AL	132	515	73	151	20	7	3	40	17	.293
1904	ST. LOUIS	AL	147	575	72	156	15	10	2	27	12	.271
1905	BOSTON	AL	148	573	78	147	12	13	4	47	13	.257
CAREER TOTALS			**2067**	**8426**	**1720**	**2850**	**320**	**182**	**75**	**952**	**389**	**.338**

Roy Campanella

"To play this game good, a lot of you has to be a little boy." Roy Campanella's career started late due to the color of his skin, and ended early after a tragic auto accident. In between, he blazed across the baseball landscape with 10 years of catching perfection.

"Nobody discovered Campanella," said Dodgers scout Clyde Sukeforth, who recommended Campanella to the Dodgers. "We looked at him and there he was. There was never any question about his ability."

Campanella began playing professional baseball at the age of 15 and went on to star for the Baltimore Elite Giants of the Negro National League. He spent eight years in the Negro Leagues before the Dodgers signed him in 1946, after Jackie Robinson had broken the color barrier in Organized Baseball. He played for Nashua in the Class B New England League, then made the jump to Triple-A Montreal in 1947. In 1948, Campanella began the season in the American Association with St. Paul, hitting 11 home runs in his first 24 games. By midseason, he was the Dodgers' regular catcher.

"More than one observer has likened Campanella's quickness behind the plate to that of a cat," wrote Tom Meany of the *New York World-Telegram*. "He can pounce on bunts placed far out in front of the plate and he gets his throws away with no wasted motion."

At the plate, Campanella established himself as one of the best hitting catchers in baseball. In his first full big league season in 1949, Campanella hit 22 home runs and drove in 82 runs en route to the first of eight straight All-Star Game selections. In 1951, Campanella won the National League Most Valuable Player Award while hitting .325 with 33 home runs and 108 RBI. He won his second MVP in 1953 while driving in a record (since broken) 142 runs as a catcher, then grabbed a third MVP award in 1955 while leading the Dodgers to their first World Series title.

His production dropped during the 1956 and 1957 seasons, but Campanella appeared energized by the Dodgers' move to Los Angeles before the 1958 season. Shortly after 1:30 a.m. on Jan. 28 of that year, however, Campanella lost control of a rented car on a patch of ice on an S-curve in Long Island, N.Y. Campanella suffered a broken fifth vertebra in his back, costing him almost complete use of his body below the shoulders.

Elected To The Hall Of Fame: *1969.*

Born: *Nov. 19, 1921 in Philadelphia, Pa.*

Died: *June 26, 1993 in Woodland Hills, Calif.*

Height: *5-9.* **Weight:** *190.*

Threw: *Right.* **Batted:** *Right.*

Debut: *Apr. 20, 1948*

Final Game: *Sept. 29, 1957*

Teams: *Brooklyn N.L. 1948-1957.*

Postseason: *World Series Champion (1955); 5 N.L. Pennants (1949, 1952-1953, 1955-1956).*

Awards: *8-Time All-Star (1949-1956); 3-Time N.L. Most Valuable Player (1951, 1953, 1955).*

YEAR	TEAM	LEAGUE	G	AB	R	H	2B	3B	HR	RBI	SB	AVG
1948	BROOKLYN	NL	83	279	32	72	11	3	9	45	3	.258
1949	BROOKLYN	NL	130	436	65	125	22	2	22	82	3	.287
1950	BROOKLYN	NL	126	437	70	123	19	3	31	89	1	.281
1951	BROOKLYN	NL	143	505	90	164	33	1	33	108	1	.325
1952	BROOKLYN	NL	128	468	73	126	18	1	22	97	8	.269
1953	BROOKLYN	NL	144	519	103	162	26	3	41	142	4	.312
1954	BROOKLYN	NL	111	397	43	82	14	3	19	51	1	.207
1955	BROOKLYN	NL	123	446	81	142	20	1	32	107	2	.318
1956	BROOKLYN	NL	124	388	39	85	6	1	20	73	1	.219
1957	BROOKLYN	NL	103	330	31	80	9	0	13	62	1	.242
CAREER TOTALS			**1215**	**4205**	**627**	**1161**	**178**	**18**	**242**	**856**	**25**	**.276**

ROD CAREW

"He has no weakness as a hitter. Anything you throw he can handle." – Catfish Hunter

For a generation of American League baseball fans, Rod Carew was the definition of "batting champion." The owner of a .328 career average and 3,053 hits to go along with seven batting titles and 18 All-Star Game selections, Carew tormented pitchers with a smooth swing from a crouched stance, using incredible hand-eye coordination developed as a youth in Panama.

Born Oct. 1, 1945, on a train in the Canal Zone and named for the doctor who delivered him, Rodney Cline Carew used a broomstick and bottle caps as his first bat and balls before moving to New York City as a teenager. Carew did not play high school baseball, but was spotted by Minnesota Twins scouts on a semi-pro team and was signed as an amateur free agent in 1964.

In 1967, Carew hit .292 with 51 RBI, earning an All-Star Game selection and winning the AL Rookie of the Year Award. The next season, Carew hit .273 – the last season Carew would finish under .300 for 15 years. Carew hit .332 in 1969 en route to his first batting title, helping Minnesota win the inaugural AL West crown. He was hitting .366 in 51 games in 1970 before a knee injury sidelined him for three months. After hitting .307 in 1971, Carew reeled off four straight batting titles – missing a fifth in 1976 by .002. The next year, Carew had his best season – flirting with the magic .400 mark for most of the year before ending up at .388 with 239 hits, 128 runs scored, 100 RBI and the AL Most Valuable Player Award.

Carew hit .333 in 1978 to win his seventh and final batting crown, then left via free agency for the California Angels. In seven years in California, Carew – who moved to first base in 1976 – led the Angels to their first two AL West titles in 1979 and 1982, batting .294 in the ALCS for California.

Carew retired following the 1985 season after reaching the 3,000-hit milestone that summer, becoming the 16th player to join that exclusive club. In 1990, he became the 27th player elected to the Hall of Fame in his first year of eligibility.

RODNEY CLINE CAREW
MINNESOTA, A.L., 1967-1978
CALIFORNIA, A.L., 1979-1985
BATTING WIZARD WHO LINED, CHOPPED AND BUNTED HIS WAY TO 3,053 HITS. 7 BATTING TITLES SURPASSED ONLY BY COBB AND WAGNER. USED VARIETY OF RELAXED, CROUCHED BATTING STANCES TO HIT OVER .300 15 CONSECUTIVE SEASONS, ACHIEVING .328 LIFETIME. A.L. ROOKIE OF YEAR IN 1967 AND A.L. MVP 10 YEARS LATER WHEN HE BATTED .388 WITH 239 HITS. NAMED TO 18 STRAIGHT ALL-STAR TEAMS. NATIONAL HERO IN PANAMA.

Elected To The Hall Of Fame: 1991.

Born: Oct. 1, 1945 in Gatun, Panama.

Height: 6-0. **Weight:** 170.

Threw: Right. **Batted:** Left.

Debut: Apr. 11, 1967.

Final Game: Oct. 5, 1985.

Teams: Minnesota A.L. 1967-1978; California A.L. 1979-1985.

Postseason: 4-Time Playoff Qualifier (1969-1970, 1979, 1982).

Awards: 18-Time All-Star (1967-1984); A.L. Rookie of the Year (1967); A.L. Most Valuable Player (1977).

YEAR	TEAM	LEAGUE	G	AB	R	H	2B	3B	HR	RBI	SB	AVG
1967	MINNESOTA	AL	137	514	66	150	22	7	8	51	5	.292
1968	MINNESOTA	AL	127	461	46	126	27	2	1	42	12	.273
1969	MINNESOTA	AL	123	458	79	152	30	4	8	56	19	.332
1970	MINNESOTA	AL	51	191	27	70	12	3	4	28	4	.366
1971	MINNESOTA	AI	147	577	88	177	16	10	2	48	6	.307
1972	MINNESOTA	AL	142	535	61	170	21	6	0	51	12	.318
1973	MINNESOTA	AL	149	580	98	203	30	11	6	62	41	.350
1974	MINNESOTA	AL	153	599	86	218	30	5	3	55	38	.364
1975	MINNESOTA	AL	143	535	89	192	24	4	14	80	35	.359
1976	MINNESOTA	AL	156	605	97	200	29	12	9	90	49	.331
1977	MINNESOTA	AL	155	616	128	239	38	16	14	100	23	.388
1978	MINNESOTA	AL	152	564	85	188	26	10	5	70	27	.333
1979	CALIFORNIA	AL	110	409	78	130	15	3	3	44	18	.318
1980	CALIFORNIA	AL	144	540	74	179	34	7	3	59	23	.331
1981	CALIFORNIA	AL	93	364	57	111	17	1	2	21	16	.305
1982	CALIFORNIA	AL	138	523	88	167	25	5	3	44	10	.319
1983	CALIFORNIA	AL	129	472	66	160	24	2	2	44	6	.339
1984	CALIFORNIA	AL	93	329	42	97	8	1	3	31	4	.295
1985	CALIFORNIA	AL	127	443	69	124	17	3	2	39	5	.280
CAREER TOTALS			**2469**	**9315**	**1424**	**3053**	**445**	**112**	**92**	**1015**	**353**	**.328**

MAX CAREY

Many Hall of Famers made it to the big leagues with their bats or their arms. Max Carey did it with his legs. Carey, nicknamed "Scoops", set a National League record with 738 career stolen bases and led the NL in steals 10 times.

Carey was on track to become a minister at Concordia Seminary in St. Louis, but after playing baseball in college, he signed with South Bend of the Central League in 1909. He became a switch-hitter and joined the Pittsburgh Pirates in 1910. By 1913, at age 23, Carey led the NL in plate appearances (692), at bats (620), runs (99) and (61) stolen bases while hitting .277. It was the first of six seasons Carey would steal over 50 bases.

"The secret is getting a good jump," said Carey. "I'd watch the pitcher's motion and then be at full speed after two steps. I think stealing third can sometimes be easier than stealing second. It all depends on the pitcher."

In 1922, Carey stole 51 bases in 53 attempts. He kept his legs in good shape in the off season and believed it took a smart man to steal bases.

In 1926, Carey had an argument with management and was waived by the Pirates. He joined the Brooklyn Dodgers, where he finished his career in 1929.

Carey not only excelled on the basepaths, but led the National League in outfield putouts nine times and established a then-career record of 6,363. He hit over .300 six times for a lifetime batting average of .285. He also posted 2,665 hits, 159 triples and 1,545 runs scored.

In 1930, Carey returned as a coach for the Pirates and also managed the Brooklyn Dodgers from 1932-33. He stayed active in baseball as a scout for the Orioles and managed several minor league teams. In 1944, he became a skipper in a different league. He managed the Milwaukee Chicks of the All-American Girls Professional Baseball League. And from 1950-52 he managed the Fort Wayne Daisies.

MAX GEORGE CAREY
PITTSBURGH N.L. 1910-1926, 1930
BROOKLYN N.L. 1926-1929, 1932-1933
HOLDS NATIONAL LEAGUE RECORDS FOR OUT-
FIELDERS: GAMES PLAYED, 2421; PUT OUTS,
6363; ASSISTS, 339; TOTAL CHANCES,
6702. MODERN LEAGUE RECORD FOR MOST
STOLEN BASES, 738. MAJOR LEAGUE RECORD
MOST YEARS LEADING LEAGUE IN STOLEN
BASES, 10. BATTING AVERAGE .285 FOR
20 SEASONS. IN 1922 51 STOLEN BASES
IN 53 ATTEMPTS.

Scoops

Elected To The Hall Of Fame: *1961.*

Born: *Jan. 11, 1890 in Terre Haute, Ind.*

Died: *May 30, 1976 in Miami, Fla.*

Height: *5-11.* **Weight:** *170.*

Threw: *Right.* **Batted:** *Both.*

Debut: *Oct. 3, 1910.*

Final Game: *Sept. 29, 1929.*

Teams: *Pittsburgh N.L. 1910-1926; Brooklyn N.L. 1926-1929.*

Postseason: *World Series Champion (1925); N.L. Pennant (1925).*

YEAR	TEAM	LEAGUE	G	AB	R	H	2B	3B	HR	RBI	SB	AVG
1910	PITTSBURGH	NL	2	6	2	3	0	1	0	2	0	.500
1911	PITTSBURGH	NL	129	427	77	110	15	10	5	43	27	.258
1912	PITTSBURGH	NL	150	587	114	177	23	8	5	66	45	.302
1913	PITTSBURGH	NL	154	620	99	172	23	10	5	49	61	.277
1914	PITTSBURGH	NL	156	593	76	144	25	17	1	31	38	.243
1915	PITTSBURGH	NL	140	564	76	143	26	5	3	27	36	.254
1916	PITTSBURGH	NL	154	599	90	158	23	11	7	42	63	.264
1917	PITTSBURGH	NL	155	588	82	174	21	12	1	51	46	.296
1918	PITTSBURGH	NL	126	468	70	128	14	6	3	48	58	.274
1919	PITTSBURGH	NL	66	244	41	75	10	2	0	9	18	.307
1920	PITTSBURGH	NL	130	485	74	140	18	4	1	35	52	.289
1921	PITTSBURGH	NL	140	521	85	161	34	4	7	56	37	.309
1922	PITTSBURGH	NL	155	629	140	207	28	12	10	70	51	.329
1923	PITTSBURGH	NL	153	610	120	188	32	19	6	63	51	.308
1924	PITTSBURGH	NL	149	599	113	178	30	9	8	55	49	.297
1925	PITTSBURGH	NL	133	542	109	186	39	13	5	44	46	.343
1926	PITTSBURGH/BROOKLYN	NL	113	424	64	98	17	6	0	35	10	.231
1927	BROOKLYN	NL	144	538	70	143	30	10	1	54	32	.266
1928	BROOKLYN	NL	108	296	41	73	11	0	2	19	18	.247
1929	BROOKLYN	NL	19	23	2	7	0	0	0	1	0	.304
CAREER TOTALS			**2476**	**9363**	**1545**	**2665**	**419**	**159**	**70**	**800**	**738**	**.285**

STEVE CARLTON

Baseball players, especially pitchers, work hard to stay in shape during the off-season with cardio conditioning. But running just wasn't for Steve Carlton.

Instead, Carlton, nicknamed "Lefty", used martial arts and weight lifting as part of his conditioning program and got himself to a fitness level that allowed him to throw for 24 seasons in the big leagues. A focused competitor, Carlton used his biting slider and a great fastball to achieve excellence on the mound.

Born on Dec. 22, 1944 in Miami, Fla., Carlton signed with the St. Louis Cardinals in 1963. He made the big league club in 1965. He appeared in both World Series appearances for the Cardinals in 1967 and 1968, earning a ring in 1967. In 1971, he had his first 20-win season and requested a contract of $60,000 for the following year.

"Auggie Busch traded me to the last-place Phillies over a salary dispute," said Carlton. "I was mentally committed to winning 25 games with the Cardinals and now I had to re-think my goals. I decided to stay with the 25-win goal and won 27 of the Phillies 59 victories. I consider that season my finest individual achievement."

His first season in Philadelphia, Carlton led the league in wins, ERA, innings pitched and strikeouts. It earned him his first Cy Young Award. In 14-plus seasons with the Phillies, Carlton led the league in wins four times, winning 20 or more games four times. The 10-time All-Star would go on to win three more Cy Young Awards and a Gold Glove Award in 1981. On Sept. 24, 1983, he became just the 16th pitcher to win 300 games.

He signed with the San Francisco Giants in 1986 and finished out his career with the Cleveland Indians and Minnesota Twins. He finished his career with 329 wins – second to only Warren Spahn among lefties – and 4,136 strikeouts.

STEVEN NORMAN CARLTON
"LEFTY"
ST. LOUIS, N.L., 1965-1971
PHILADELPHIA, N.L., 1972-1986
SAN FRANCISCO, N.L., 1986
CHICAGO, A.L., 1986
CLEVELAND, A.L., 1987
MINNESOTA, A.L., 1987-1988
EXTREMELY FOCUSED COMPETITOR WITH COMPLETE DEDICATION
TO EXCELLENCE. THRIVED ON MOUND BY PHYSICALLY AND MENTALLY
CHALLENGING HIMSELF OFF THE FIELD. OUT PITCH WAS HARD,
BITING SLIDER. 329 VICTORIES SECOND ONLY TO SPAHN AMONG
LEFTIES AND 4,136 STRIKEOUTS EXCEEDED ONLY BY RYAN. SHARES
N.L. RECORD WITH 19 STRIKEOUTS IN GAME. SIX 20 WIN SEASONS.
ONLY HURLER TO WIN 4 CY YOUNG AWARDS.

Lefty

Elected To The Hall Of Fame: 1994.
Born: Dec. 22, 1944 in Miami, Fla.
Height: 6-4. **Weight:** 210.
Threw: Left. **Batted:** Left.
Debut: Apr. 12, 1965. **Final Game:** Apr. 23, 1988.
Teams: St. Louis N.L. 1965-1971; Philadelphia N.L. 1972-1986; San Francisco N.L. 1986; Chicago A.L. 1986; Cleveland A.L. 1987; Minnesota A.L. 1987-1988.
Postseason: 2-time World Series Champion (1967, 1980); 4 N.L. Pennants (1967-1968, 1980, 1983).
Awards: 10-Time All-Star (1968-1969, 1971-1972, 1974, 1977, 1979-1982); 4-Time N.L. Cy Young (1972, 1977, 1980, 1982).

YEAR	TEAM	LEAGUE	G	W	L	SV	SH	IP	H	BB	SO	ERA
1965	ST. LOUIS	NL	15	0	0	0	0	25	27	8	21	2.52
1966	ST. LOUIS	NL	9	3	3	0	1	52	56	18	25	3.12
1967	ST. LOUIS	NL	30	14	9	1	2	193	173	62	168	2.98
1968	ST. LOUIS	NL	34	13	11	0	5	232	214	61	162	2.99
1969	ST. LOUIS	NL	31	17	11	0	2	236.3	185	93	210	2.17
1970	ST. LOUIS	NL	34	10	19	0	2	253.7	239	109	193	3.73
1971	ST. LOUIS	NL	37	20	9	0	4	273.3	275	98	172	3.56
1972	PHILADELPHIA	NL	41	27	10	0	8	346.3	257	87	310	1.97
1973	PHILADELPHIA	NI	40	13	20	0	3	293.3	293	113	223	3.90
1974	PHILADELPHIA	NL	39	16	13	0	1	291	249	136	240	3.22
1975	PHILADELPHIA	NL	37	15	14	0	3	255.3	217	104	192	3.56
1976	PHILADELPHIA	NL	35	20	7	0	2	252.7	224	72	195	3.13
1977	PHILADELPHIA	NL	36	23	10	0	2	283	229	89	198	2.64
1978	PHILADELPHIA	NL	34	16	13	0	3	247.3	228	63	161	2.84
1979	PHILADELPHIA	NL	35	18	11	0	4	251	202	89	213	3.62
1980	PHILADELPHIA	NL	38	24	9	0	3	304	243	90	286	2.34
1981	PHILADELPHIA	NL	24	13	4	0	1	190	152	62	179	2.42
1982	PHILADELPHIA	NL	38	23	11	0	6	295.7	253	86	286	3.10
1983	PHILADELPHIA	NL	37	15	16	0	3	283.7	277	84	275	3.11
1984	PHILADELPHIA	NL	33	13	7	0	0	229	214	79	163	3.58
1985	PHILADELPHIA	NL	16	1	8	0	0	92	84	53	48	3.33
1986	PHI/SF/CHICAGO	AL	32	9	14	0	0	176.3	196	86	120	5.10
1987	CLEVELAND/MINNESOTA	AL	32	6	14	1	0	152	165	86	91	5.74
1988	MINNESOTA	AL	4	0	1	0	0	9.7	20	5	5	16.76
CAREER TOTALS			741	329	244	2	55	5217.2	4672	1833	4136	3.22

GARY CARTER

G ary Carter earned the nickname "The Kid" at Expos training camp in 1973 at the age of 19.

"I tried to impress everybody that spring, you know, being the first in line for sprints," Carter said. "Running hard to first base all the time." The nickname as well as the style of play stuck with him throughout his 19-year career. The 11-time All-Star was an enthusiastic and resilient backstop for the Expos, Mets, Giants and Dodgers who helped his teams behind the plate and in the batter's box.

Carter played baseball, basketball and football in high school, but rejected dozens of college scholarships to sign with the Montreal Expos. Used primarily as an outfielder during his 1975 rookie season, Carter came in second in Rookie of the Year voting before earning the full-time catching job in 1977.

"I was out of position. I was running into walls and hurting myself," said Carter about his experience in the outfield.

A three-time Gold Glove Award winner, Carter set a record for fewest passed balls in 1978 and paced all National League catchers in total chances (1977-82), putouts (1977-80, 1982), assists (1977, 1979-80, 1982) and double plays (1978-79, 1983).

"He was a human backstop back there," said former teammate Keith Hernandez. "Early, before his knees went bad, you couldn't steal on him in Montreal. When he wasn't able to throw because of his knees, that never affected his performance. He was running on and off the field after three outs. This guy played in some pain and it was hustle, hustle, hustle."

Carter was traded to the Mets in 1985. He led his team to a World Series championship, hitting .276 with two home runs and nine RBI in the 1986 Fall Classic. His two-out, 10th-inning single ignited a three-run rally that resulted in a Mets' win to even the series. New York went onto win the Series in seven games.

Slowed by injuries, Carter played for the Giants and Dodgers before returning to Montreal to end his career in 1992. He had a career .262 batting average, belted 324 home runs and knocked in 1,225 runs to earn five Silver Slugger Awards.

GARY EDMUND CARTER
"KID"
MONTREAL, N.L., 1974-1984, 1992
NEW YORK, N.L., 1985-1989
SAN FRANCISCO, N.L., 1990
LOS ANGELES, N.L., 1991
AN EXUBERANT ON-FIELD GENERAL WITH A SIGNATURE SMILE WHO WAS KNOWN FOR CLUTCH HITTING AND ROCK-SOLID DEFENSE OVER 19 SEASONS. HIS TIRELESS WORK ETHIC AND DURABILITY LED TO THE ALL-TIME RECORD FOR TOTAL CHANCES BY A CATCHER, AND NATIONAL LEAGUE RECORDS FOR GAMES CAUGHT, PUTOUTS, AND YEARS LEADING THE LEAGUE IN PUTOUTS. AN 11-TIME ALL STAR, TWICE THE GAME MVP, EARNED THREE GOLD GLOVE AWARDS AND CLUBBED 324 HOME RUNS. A CATALYST FOR THE EXPOS FIRST POSTSEASON BERTH IN 1981 AND A KEY TO THE METS 1986 WORLD CHAMPIONSHIP.

The Kid

Elected To The Hall Of Fame: *2003.*

Born: *Apr. 8, 1954 in Culver City, Calif.*

Died: *Feb. 16, 2012 in West Palm Beach, Fla.*

Height: *6-2.* **Weight:** *205.*

Threw: *Right.* **Batted:** *Right.*

Debut: *Sept. 16, 1974.*

Final Game: *Sept. 27, 1992.*

Teams: *Montreal N.L. 1974-1984, 1992; New York N.L. 1985-1989; San Francisco N.L. 1990; Los Angeles N.L. 1991.*

Postseason: *World Series Champion (1986); N.L. Pennant (1986); 3-Time Playoff Qualifier (1981, 1986, 1988).*

Awards: *11-Time All-Star (1975, 1979-1988).*

YEAR	TEAM	LEAGUE	G	AB	R	H	2B	3B	HR	RBI	SB	AVG
1974	MONTREAL	NL	9	27	5	11	0	1	1	6	2	.407
1975	MONTREAL	NL	144	503	58	136	20	1	17	68	5	.270
1976	MONTREAL	NL	91	311	31	68	8	1	6	38	0	.219
1977	MONTREAL	NL	154	522	86	148	29	7	31	84	5	.284
1978	MONTREAL	NL	157	533	76	136	27	1	20	72	10	.255
1979	MONTREAL	NL	141	505	74	143	26	5	22	75	3	.283
1980	MONTREAL	NL	154	549	76	145	25	5	29	101	3	.264
1981	MONTREAL	NL	100	374	48	94	20	2	16	68	1	.251
1982	MONTREAL	NL	154	557	91	163	32	1	29	97	2	.293
1983	MONTREAL	NL	145	541	63	146	37	3	17	79	1	.270
1984	MONTREAL	NL	159	596	75	175	32	1	27	106	2	.294
1985	NEW YORK	NL	149	555	83	156	17	1	32	100	1	.281
1986	NEW YORK	NL	132	490	81	125	14	2	24	105	1	.255
1987	NEW YORK	NL	139	523	55	123	18	2	20	83	0	.235
1988	NEW YORK	NL	130	455	39	110	16	2	11	46	0	.242
1989	NEW YORK	NL	50	153	14	28	8	0	2	15	0	.183
1990	SAN FRANCISCO	NL	92	244	24	62	10	0	9	27	1	.254
1991	LOS ANGELES	NL	101	248	22	61	14	0	6	26	2	.246
1992	MONTREAL	NL	95	285	24	62	18	1	5	29	0	.218
CAREER TOTALS			**2296**	**7971**	**1025**	**2092**	**371**	**31**	**324**	**1225**	**39**	**.262**

ORLANDO CEPEDA

Orlando Cepeda's father Pedro was a well-known baseball hero in his native Puerto Rico, where he was called "Perucho" or "the Bull". So naturally, when Orlando came on the baseball scene, his countrymen began calling him "Baby Bull."

But Cepeda quickly set himself apart and made a name for himself as a powerful slugger in the major leagues. Becoming interested in the game because of his dad, Cepeda participated in a baseball tournament for paperboys at the age of 10. That was the beginning for an 11-time All-Star who spent 17 seasons with the Giants, Cardinals, Braves, Athletics, Red Sox and Royals.

Born on Sept.17, 1937 in Ponce, Puerto Rico, Cepeda signed with the San Francisco Giants in 1955 at age 17. He joined the team in 1958, hitting .312 with 25 home runs and was unanimously named National League Rookie of the Year.

"He is annoying every pitcher in the league," said fellow Hall of Famer Willie Mays. "He is strong, he hits to all fields and he makes all the plays. He's the most relaxed first-year man I ever saw."

In 1961, Cepeda led the league in home runs (46) and RBI (142) and finished second in MVP voting. Six years later, while playing for the Cardinals, Cepeda took home the MVP Award in a unanimous vote after leading the league with 111 RBI and 25 home runs. He was the first player born in Latin America to win the home run and RBI titles.

"He was the toughest hitter I ever faced," said All-Star pitcher Lew Burdette.

In 1963, Cepeda suffered a knee injury and played the whole season in pain. Despite his discomfort, he finished fifth in the race for the batting title.

Cepeda won a World Series with St. Louis in addition to his MVP in 1967 and finished his career with 2,351 hits, 1,365 RBI, 379 home runs and nine seasons with better than a .300 average. Cepeda struggled with chronic knee injuries throughout his career, but was known for his legendary strength and ability to hammer the ball.

ORLANDO MANUEL CEPEDA PENNES
"BABY BULL" "CHA-CHA"
SAN FRANCISCO, N.L., 1958 – 1966, ST. LOUIS, N.L., 1966 – 1968
ATLANTA, N.L., 1969 – 1972, OAKLAND, A.L., 1972
BOSTON, A.L., 1973, KANSAS CITY, A.L., 1974

A POWERFUL FIRST BASEMAN AND CONSISTENT RUN PRODUCER FOR 17 MAJOR LEAGUE SEASONS, NOTWITHSTANDING CHRONIC KNEE PROBLEMS. HIS ABILITY TO DRIVE THE BALL WITH AUTHORITY WAS RESPECTED AND FEARED BY THE OPPOSITION. UNANIMOUS SELECTION FOR BOTH THE 1958 N.L. ROOKIE OF THE YEAR AWARD AND 1967 MVP HONORS. THE 11-TIME ALL-STAR LED THE N.L. IN HOME RUNS (46) AND RBI (142) IN 1961. BATTED .300 NINE TIMES AND SLUGGED 379 HOME RUNS. HIS STALWART LEADERSHIP PROPELLED HIS CLUBS TO THREE WORLD SERIES.

Cha-Cha, Baby Bull

Elected To The Hall Of Fame: 1999.
Born: Sept.17, 1937 in Ponce, Puerto Rico.
Height: 6-2. **Weight:** 210.
Threw: Right. **Batted:** Right.
Debut: Apr. 15, 1958.
Final Game: Sept. 19, 1974.
Teams: San Francisco N.L. 1958-1966; St. Louis N.L. 1966-1968; Atlanta N.L. 1969-1972; Oakland A.L. 1972; Boston A.L. 1973; Kansas City A.L. 1974.
Postseason: World Series Champion (1967); 3 N.L. Pennants (1962, 1967-68).
Awards: 11-Time All-Star (1959-1964, 1967); N.L. Rookie of the Year (1958); N.L. Most Valuable Player (1967).

YEAR	TEAM	LEAGUE	G	AB	R	H	2B	3B	HR	RBI	SB	AVG
1958	SAN FRANCISCO	NL	148	603	88	188	38	4	25	96	15	.312
1959	SAN FRANCISCO	NL	151	605	92	192	35	4	27	105	23	.317
1960	SAN FRANCISCO	NL	151	569	81	169	36	3	24	96	15	.297
1961	SAN FRANCISCO	NL	152	585	105	182	28	4	46	142	12	.311
1962	SAN FRANCISCO	NL	162	625	105	191	26	1	35	114	10	.306
1963	SAN FRANCISCO	NL	156	579	100	183	33	4	34	97	8	.316
1964	SAN FRANCISCO	NL	142	529	75	161	27	2	31	97	9	.304
1965	SAN FRANCISCO	NL	33	34	1	6	1	0	1	5	0	.176
1966	SAN FRAN/ST. LOUIS	NL	142	501	70	151	26	0	20	73	9	.301
1967	ST. LOUIS	NL	151	563	91	183	37	0	25	111	11	.325
1968	ST. LOUIS	NL	157	600	71	149	26	2	16	73	8	.248
1969	ATLANTA	NL	154	573	74	147	28	2	22	88	12	.257
1970	ATLANTA	NL	148	567	87	173	33	0	34	111	6	.305
1971	ATLANTA	NL	71	250	31	69	10	1	14	44	3	.276
1972	ATLANTA/OAKLAND	NL/AL	31	87	6	25	3	0	4	9	0	.287
1973	BOSTON	AL	142	550	51	159	25	0	20	86	0	.289
1974	KANSAS CITY	AL	33	107	3	23	5	0	1	18	1	.215
CAREER TOTALS			**2124**	**7927**	**1131**	**2351**	**417**	**27**	**379**	**1365**	**142**	**.297**

FRANK CHANCE

Few men in the history of baseball have seen great success as a player and as a manager. Frank Chance was one of them.

But Chance's most enduring legacy – despite his success on the field and in the dugout – has been as the subject of the most celebrated baseball poem ever written.

"Baseball's Sad Lexicon" uses the refrain "Tinkers to Evers to Chance" as a description of the Chicago Cubs double-play combination in the early 1900s. After mostly catching and playing outfield for his first four years in the big leagues, Chance played the majority of his games at first base beginning in 1902, leading to his place in the poem.

Born on Sept. 9, 1876 in Fresno, Calif., Chance played 17 seasons in the big leagues, 10 of those as a player/manager, earning the nickname "Peerless Leader." He signed with the Chicago Orphans (the team name changed to the Cubs in 1903) in 1898 at age 21 and was moved to first base in 1902 by manager Frank Selee.

"Here's the most promising player I ever saw," said Bill Lange, former Chicago Colts outfielder who discovered Chance. "Some day he'll be a wonder."

Chance led the National League in stolen bases in 1903 with 67 and again in 1906 with 57. He also led the league in runs scored in 1906 with 103. As a first baseman, Chance had a .983 fielding percentage and was involved in 470 double plays.

"Chance is one great artist and to my mind ranks with Lajoie and Wagner," said former major leaguer Danny Shay. "He is everything they are – a great hitter, splendid fielder, fast base-runner and has a head full of brains."

He led the Cubs to four pennants in five years (1906-08, 1910), helping set a long-standing team record for wins in 1906 with 116, matched only by the 2001 Seattle Mariners. The Cubs lost the 1906 World Series to the White Sox, but won back-to-back championships in 1907-08. He posted a .300 career average in the Fall Classic with 10 stolen bases and 21 hits.

Chance played for the Yankees in 1913-14, but appeared in considerably less games from 1912 on after suffering chronic headaches caused by several beanings. He finished his career with a .296 batting average, 1,274 hits, 403 stolen bases and 798 runs.

FRANK LEROY CHANCE
FAMOUS LEADER OF CHICAGO CUBS, WON PENNANT WITH CUBS IN FIRST FULL SEASON AS MANAGER IN 1906 · THAT TEAM COMPILED 116 VICTORIES UNEQUALLED IN MAJOR LEAGUE HISTORY · ALSO WON PENNANTS IN 1907, 08 AND 1910 AND WORLD SERIES WINNER IN 07 AND 08. STARTED WITH CHICAGO IN 1898. ALSO MANAGER NEW YORK A.L. AND BOSTON A.L.

Elected To The Hall Of Fame: *1946.*
Born: *Sept. 9, 1876 in Fresno, Calif.*
Died: *Sept. 15, 1924 in Los Angeles, Calif.*
Height: *6-0.* ***Weight:*** *190.*
Threw: *Right.* ***Batted:*** *Right.*
Debut: *Apr. 29, 1898.*
Final Game: *Apr. 21, 1914.*
Teams: *Chicago N.L. 1898-1912; New York A.L. 1913-1914.*
Postseason: *2-Time World Series Champion (1907-1908); 4 N.L. Pennants (1906-1908, 1910).*

YEAR	TEAM	LEAGUE	G	AB	R	H	2B	3B	HR	RBI	SB	AVG
1898	CHICAGO	NL	53	147	32	41	4	3	1	14	7	.279
1899	CHICAGO	NL	64	192	37	55	6	2	1	22	10	.286
1900	CHICAGO	NL	56	149	26	44	9	3	0	13	8	.295
1901	CHICAGO	NL	69	241	38	67	12	4	0	36	27	.278
1902	CHICAGO	NL	76	242	40	70	9	4	1	31	29	.289
1903	CHICAGO	NL	125	441	83	144	24	10	2	81	67	.327
1904	CHICAGO	NL	124	451	89	140	16	10	6	49	42	.310
1905	CHICAGO	NL	118	392	92	124	16	12	2	70	38	.316
1906	CHICAGO	NL	136	474	103	151	24	10	3	71	57	.319
1907	CHICAGO	NL	111	382	58	112	19	2	1	49	35	.293
1908	CHICAGO	NL	129	452	65	123	27	4	2	55	27	.272
1909	CHICAGO	NL	93	324	53	88	16	4	0	46	29	.272
1910	CHICAGO	NL	88	295	54	88	12	8	0	36	16	.298
1911	CHICAGO	NL	31	88	23	21	6	3	1	17	9	.239
1912	CHICAGO	NL	2	5	2	1	0	0	0	0	1	.200
1913	NEW YORK	AL	12	24	3	5	0	0	0	6	1	.208
1914	NEW YORK	AL	1	0	0	0	0	0	0	0	0	—
CAREER TOTALS			**1288**	**4299**	**798**	**1274**	**200**	**79**	**20**	**596**	**403**	**.296**

OSCAR CHARLESTON

"Charlie was a tremendous left-handed hitter who could also bunt, steal a hundred bases a year, and cover center field as well as anyone before him or since," said Buck O'Neil. "He was like Ty Cobb, Babe Ruth and Tris Speaker rolled into one."

A powerful hitter who could hit to all fields and bunt, Charleston was also extremely fast on the base paths and in center field. He played a very shallow center, almost behind second base, and his great speed and instincts helped him outrun many batted balls. He had a powerful arm. Coupled with this great natural ability was a Cobb-like aggressive demeanor and will to win. His temper flared on and off the field, and a story is told in which Charleston ripped the mask off a Ku Klux Klan member and confronted him face-to-face.

His finest season was likely 1921, when he hit well over .400 and led the Negro National League in doubles, triples, and homers. He won batting titles in the Eastern Colored League in 1924 and '25, and led the American Negro League in hitting in 1928. From the mid-1920s on, he was a player-manager for several clubs. In 1932, he joined the Pittsburgh Crawfords and managed the club many consider the finest Negro League team of all time, featuring five future Hall of Famers including himself, Cool Papa Bell, Josh Gibson, Judy Johnson, and Satchel Paige. Charleston hit three home runs in leading the Crawfords to victory in the seven-game championship in 1935 against the New York Cubans.

He played nine seasons of winter ball in Cuba, amassing statistics quite similar to his Negro league achievements. He is thought to have hit .326 lifetime in exhibition games against white major leaguers. In the 1940s, Charleston scouted for Branch Rickey, making recommendations on the best players to consider for the job of integrating the major leagues. He managed as late as 1954, when he led the Indianapolis Clowns to a league championship.

OSCAR McKINLEY CHARLESTON
NEGRO LEAGUES 1915·1944

RATED AMONG ALL-TIME GREATS OF NEGRO LEAGUES. VERSATILE STAR BATTED WELL OVER .300 MOST YEARS. SPEED, STRONG ARM AND FIELDING INSTINCTS MADE HIM STANDOUT CENTER FIELDER. LATER MOVED TO FIRST BASE. ALSO MANAGED SEVERAL TEAMS DURING 40 YEARS IN NEGRO BASEBALL.

Elected To The Hall Of Fame: *1976.*
Born: *Oct. 14, 1896 in Indianapolis, Ind.*
Died: *Oct. 5, 1954 in Philadelphia, Pa.*
Height: *6-0.* **Weight:** *200.*
Threw: *Left.* **Batted:** *Left.*
Teams: *Negro Leagues 1915-1944. Indianapolis 1915-1918, 1920, 1922-1923, 1940; New York 1916; Chicago 1919; Detroit 1919; St. Louis 1921-1922; Harrisburg 1924-1927; Hilldale 1926, 1928-1929; Homestead 1929-1931; Pittsburgh 1932-1937; Toledo 1939-1940; Philadelphia 1941.*

YEAR	TEAM	LEAGUE	G	AB	R	H	2B	3B	HR	RBI	SB	AVG
1915	INDIANAPOLIS	INDP/CNCS	76	289	38	70	10	6	2	37	16	.242
1916	NEW YORK/IND.	INDP	32	118	25	38	1	3	0	13	7	.322
1917	INDIANAPOLIS	INDP	48	178	26	52	6	4	1	19	3	.292
1918	INDIANAPOLIS	INDP	38	147	37	56	7	7	3	43	11	.381
1919	CHICAGO/DET.	INDP	45	176	48	70	9	6	8	44	14	.398
1920	IND./ST. LOUIS	NNL	—	180	24	51	5	4	4	—	12	.283
1921	ST. LOUIS	NNL	—	169	51	75	9	8	6	—	22	.444
1922	INDIANAPOLIS	NNL	—	215	48	85	14	9	11	—	15	.395
1923	INDIANAPOLIS	NNL	—	308	68	112	25	6	11	—	26	.364
1924	HARRISBURG	ECOL	—	192	57	73	16	3	13	—	13	.380
1925	HARRISBURG	ECOL	—	235	95	106	22	3	20	—	17	.451
1926	H'BURG/HILLDALE	ECOL	—	272	52	67	18	1	13	—	23	.302
1927	HARRISBURG	ECOL	—	126	32	45	9	4	8	—	1	.357
1928	HILLDALE	ECOL	—	217	59	74	7	5	10	—	12	.341
1929	HOMESTEAD/HILL.	ANL	—	213	40	69	9	4	4	—	5	.324
1930	HOMESTEAD	INDP	—	113	25	33	8	4	4	—	3	.292
1931	HOMESTEAD	INDP	—	130	24	45	5	3	2	—	1	.346
1932	PITTSBURGH	INDP	—	184	36	58	12	3	4	—	13	.315
1933	PITTSBURGH	NNL	—	158	32	47	7	2	5	—	3	.297
1934	PITTSBURGH	NNL	—	165	25	55	6	3	5	—	2	.333
1935	PITTSBURGH	NNL	—	132	23	39	7	1	5	—	7	.295
1936	PITTSBURGH	NNL	—	46	8	14	4	0	2	—	0	.304
1937	PITTSBURGH	NNL	—	34	1	4	1	0	0	—	0	.118
1939	TOLEDO	NAL	—	30	4	9	2	0	0	—	0	.300
1940	TOLEDO/IND.	NAL	—	4	0	3	0	0	0	—	0	.750
1941	PHILADELPHIA	NNL	—	0	1	0	0	0	0	—	—	—
CAREER TOTALS			—	3981	879	1350	219	89	141	—	226	.339

JACK CHESBRO

A 20-win season remains the standard for big league pitchers. But in 1904, Hall of Famer Jack Chesbro more than doubled that number by himself when he won a modern era record 41 games during one of the finest seasons of any pitcher in the history of the game. It was the crowning season of a pitcher whose career numbers added up to a place in Cooperstown.

Chesbro began playing baseball on sandlot teams and earned the nickname "Happy Jack" because of his pleasant disposition. His professional career began in Albany, N.Y., of the New York State League in 1895. At a time when baseball leagues were struggling to get off the ground, Chesbro bounced around and even spent time in 1896 as a semi-pro in Cooperstown, N.Y.

In July 1899, Chesbro was sold to the Pittsburgh Pirates. He won 21 games in 1901 as Pittsburgh captured its first National League pennant. In 1902, Chesbro changed his approach and began throwing a then-legal spitball. He described the spitball as the "most effective ball that possibly could be used." With his new pitch, Chesbro led the league in wins with 28 and shutouts with eight and the Pirates won their second pennant.

Before the 1903 season, Chesbro jumped to the American League and joined the newly formed New York Highlanders. He went 21-15 with a 2.77 ERA in his first season with the club. But it was in his second year that Chesbro had his personal best season on the mound. En route to 41 victories, Chesbro also led the league in winning percentage (.774), games (55), games started (51), complete games (48), and innings pitched (454.2).

Going into the last two games of the season, Chesbro's Highlanders trailed the Boston Red Sox by one and a half games. He took the mound with confidence but Boston's Bill Dinneen pitched well, and the score was tied 2-2 in the top of the ninth with the Red Sox's Lou Criger on third base and Fred Parent at the plate. "It was a passed ball," said Highlanders manager Clark Griffith of the spitball from Chesbro, officially scored as a wild pitch. "(Catcher Jack) Kleinow let the pitch get away from him."

New York won the second game, but lost the pennant. Chesbro spent six more seasons in New York, but was slowed by an ankle injury. He pitched his final game in 1909 for Boston.

JOHN DWIGHT CHESBRO
"HAPPY JACK"
FAMED PITCHER WHO LED BOTH LEAGUES IN PERCENTAGE-NATIONAL LEAGUE IN 1902; AMERICAN LEAGUE IN 1904. SERVED WITH PITTSBURGH N.L. AND THE NEW YORK AND BOSTON A.L. WON 41 GAMES, TOPS IN MAJORS, IN 1904 AND DURING BIG LEAGUE CAREER COMPILED 192 VICTORIES WHILE LOSING ONLY 128.

Happy Jack

Elected To The Hall Of Fame: *1946.*
Born: *June 5, 1874 in North Adams, Mass.*
Died: *Nov. 6, 1931 in Conway, Mass.*
Height: *5-9.* **Weight:** *180.*
Threw: *Right.* **Batted:** *Right.*
Debut: *July 12, 1899.*
Final Game: *Oct. 2, 1909.*
Teams: *Pittsburgh N.L. 1899-1902; New York A.L. 1903-1909; Boston A.L. 1909.*

YEAR	TEAM	LEAGUE	G	W	L	SV	SH	IP	H	BB	SO	ERA
1899	PITTSBURGH	NL	19	6	9	0	0	149	165	59	28	4.11
1900	PITTSBURGH	NL	32	15	13	1	3	215.7	220	79	56	3.67
1901	PITTSBURGH	NL	36	21	10	1	6	287.7	261	52	129	2.38
1902	PITTSBURGH	NL	35	28	6	1	8	286.3	242	62	136	2.17
1903	NEW YORK	AL	40	21	15	0	1	324.7	300	74	147	2.77
1904	NEW YORK	AL	55	41	12	0	6	454.7	338	88	239	1.82
1905	NEW YORK	AL	41	19	15	0	3	303.3	262	71	156	2.20
1906	NEW YORK	AL	49	23	17	1	4	325	314	75	152	2.96
1907	NEW YORK	AL	30	10	10	0	1	206	192	46	78	2.53
1908	NEW YORK	AL	45	14	20	1	3	288.7	276	67	124	2.93
1909	NEW YORK/BOSTON	AL	10	0	5	0	0	55.7	77	17	20	6.14
CAREER TOTALS			**392**	**198**	**132**	**5**	**35**	**2896.2**	**2647**	**690**	**1265**	**2.68**

FRED CLARKE

Twenty-four year-olds are not often found in leadership positions, but at that age, Fred Clarke fit right in as a player and skipper of a major league club.

As one of the first "boy-managers," Clarke starred in left field and led his teams to win from the field and the dugout.

"I tell you managing a team from the bench is far different from directing from the field," he said. "I would much rather be a playing manager not only because I like to play ball, but because when I am in there playing my mind is on the game, and not filled with the perplexities and troubles of the manager."

Clarke spent a lot of time on a ball diamond as a youngster. His first professional experience came in 1892 with the Nebraska State League in Hastings. "I thought I was pretty good if I caught half the fly balls that came to me," said Clarke.

He signed with the Louisville Colonels in 1894. He saw immediate success, recording four singles and a triple by using a light bat in his five plate appearances. Winning over fans and fellow players alike, he was named manager in 1897 and saw limited success leading the team. Hall of Fame executive Barney Dreyfuss purchased the Pittsburgh Pirates in 1899 and brought Clarke and other players from the Colonels to his new club.

Dreyfuss named Clarke captain/manager. The team went from a seventh place finish in 1899 to second place in Clarke's first season in 1900. Clarke led the Pirates to pennants from 1901-1903 and 1909 and a World Series championship in 1909.

"You've got to love baseball and want to play it above all else," said Clarke. "You have to take every opportunity to practice and play. And not be discouraged. The most important thing is desire."

Clarke batted over .300 eleven times, stole over 30 bases seven times and led NL left fielders in fielding percentage nine times. As a manager, Clarke won 1,602 games with a .576 winning percentage.

FRED CLARKE
THE FIRST OF THE SUCCESSFUL
"BOY MANAGERS," AT TWENTY-FOUR HE
PILOTED LOUISVILLE'S COLONELS IN
THE NATIONAL LEAGUE. WON 4 PENNANTS
FOR PITTSBURGH AND A WORLD
CHAMPIONSHIP IN 1909. STARRED AS
AN OUTFIELDER FOR 22 SEASONS.

Elected To The Hall Of Fame: 1945.
Born: Oct. 3, 1872 in Winterset, Iowa.
Died: Aug. 14, 1960 in Winfield, Kan.
Height: 5-10. **Weight:** 165.
Threw: Right. **Batted:** Left
Debut: June 30, 1894.
Final Game: Sept. 23, 1915.
Teams: Louisville N.L. 1894-1899; Pittsburgh N.L. 1900-1911, 1913-1915.
Postseason: World Series Champion (1909); 4 N.L. Pennants (1901-03, 1909).

YEAR	TEAM	LEAGUE	G	AB	R	H	2B	3B	HR	RBI	SB	AVG
1894	LOUISVILLE	NL	76	314	55	86	11	7	7	48	26	.274
1895	LOUISVILLE	NL	132	550	96	191	21	5	4	82	40	.347
1896	LOUISVILLE	NL	131	517	96	168	15	18	9	79	34	.325
1897	LOUISVILLE	NL	130	526	122	205	30	13	6	67	59	.390
1898	LOUISVILLE	NL	149	599	116	184	23	12	3	47	40	.307
1899	LOUISVILLE	NL	149	606	122	206	23	9	5	70	49	.340
1900	PITTSBURGH	NL	106	399	84	110	15	12	3	32	21	.276
1901	PITTSBURGH	NL	129	527	118	171	24	15	6	60	23	.324
1902	PITTSBURGH	NL	113	459	103	145	27	14	2	53	29	.316
1903	PITTSBURGH	NL	104	427	88	150	32	15	5	70	21	.351
1904	PITTSBURGH	NL	72	278	51	85	7	11	0	25	11	.306
1905	PITTSBURGH	NL	141	525	95	157	18	15	2	51	24	.299
1906	PITTSBURGH	NL	118	417	69	129	14	13	1	39	18	.309
1907	PITTSBURGH	NL	148	501	97	145	18	13	2	59	37	.289
1908	PITTSBURGH	NL	151	551	83	146	18	15	2	53	24	.265
1909	PITTSBURGH	NL	152	550	97	158	16	11	3	68	31	.287
1910	PITTSBURGH	NL	123	429	57	113	23	9	2	63	12	.263
1911	PITTSBURGH	NL	110	392	73	127	25	13	5	49	10	.324
1913	PITTSBURGH	NL	9	13	0	1	1	0	0	0	0	.077
1914	PITTSBURGH	NL	2	2	0	0	0	0	0	0	0	.000
1915	PITTSBURGH	NL	1	2	0	1	0	0	0	0	0	.500
CAREER TOTALS			2246	8584	1622	2678	361	220	67	1015	509	.312

JOHN CLARKSON

John Clarkson's pitching statistics belong to his era: Baseball's infancy during the 1880s.

His dominance on the mound, however, has stood the test of time.

Born July 1, 1861 in Cambridge, Mass., Clarkson began his big league journey at the age of 20 with the Worcester Ruby Legs of the National League. After only three games, however, shoulder problems forced the 5-foot-10, 155-pound right-hander back home to Cambridge.

Two years later, Clarkson emerged from the minors with Cap Anson's Chicago White Stockings. This time, thanks to a strong curveball and a unique "drop" that would now be called a sinker, Clarkson found regular work – posting a 10-3 record in 14 games.

The next year, 1885, Clarkson improved his win total by 43 games – winning an astounding 53 contests against only 16 losses. He completed 68 of the 70 games he started, logged 623 innings pitched, struck out 308 batters and pitched a no-hitter against the Providence Grays on July 27, 1885.

He went 36-17 in 1886, then led the National League in victories for a second time in 1887 with a mark of 38-21.

"I have stood behind him day-in and day-out and watched his magnificent control," said White Stockings second baseman Fred Pfeffer. "I believe he could put a ball where he wanted it nine times out of ten."

Apparently, the other clubs in the National League believed Pfeffer's assessment. Before the 1888 season, Clarkson was sold to the Boston Beaneaters for the then-astronomical sum of $10,000. He spent the next four full seasons in Boston, averaging 35 wins per season. In 1889, he went 49-19 with a league-best 2.73 earned-run average in 620 innings of work.

The Beaneaters released Clarkson midway through the 1892 season, but he hooked on with the Cleveland Spiders for another three years before retiring after the 1894 season. His final totals: a 328-178 record, a 2.81 ERA and 485 complete games in 518 starts. For eight seasons from 1885 through 1892, Clarkson averaged better than 36 victories per year.

JOHN GIBSON CLARKSON
WORCESTER, N.L. 1882
CHICAGO, N.L. 1884-87
BOSTON, N.L. 1888-92
CLEVELAND, N.L. 1892-94
PITCHED 4 TO 0 NO-HIT GAME AGAINST
PROVIDENCE IN 1885. WON 328 LOST 175
PCT.652 LED LEAGUE WITH 55 VICTORIES
IN 1885 (INCLUDING 10 SHUTOUTS) 38 IN
1887, 49 IN 1888 AND 49 IN 1889. HAD
2015 STRIKEOUTS IN 4514 INNINGS.

Elected To The Hall Of Fame: *1963.*
Born: *July 1, 1861 in Cambridge, Mass.*
Died: *Feb. 4, 1909 in Belmont, Mass.*
Height: *5-10.* ***Weight:*** *155.*
Threw: *Right.* ***Batted:*** *Right.*
Debut: *May 2, 1882.*
Final Game: *July 12, 1894.*
Teams: *Worcester N.L. 1882; Chicago N.L. 1884-1887; Boston N.L. 1888-1892; Cleveland N.L. 1892-1894.*
Postseason: *3 N.L. Pennants (1885-1886, 1892).*

YEAR	TEAM	LEAGUE	G	W	L	SV	SH	IP	H	BB	SO	ERA
1882	WORCESTER	NL	3	1	2	0	0	24	49	2	3	4.50
1884	CHICAGO	NL	14	10	3	0	0	118	94	25	102	2.14
1885	CHICAGO	NL	70	53	16	0	10	623	497	97	308	1.85
1886	CHICAGO	NL	55	36	17	0	3	466.7	419	86	313	2.41
1887	CHICAGO	NL	60	38	21	0	2	523	513	92	237	3.08
1888	BOSTON	NL	54	33	20	0	3	483.3	448	119	223	2.76
1889	BOSTON	NL	73	49	19	1	8	620	589	203	284	2.73
1890	BOSTON	NL	44	26	18	0	2	383	370	140	138	3.27
1891	BOSTON	NL	55	33	19	3	3	460.7	435	154	141	2.79
1892	BOSTON/CLEVELAND	NL	45	25	16	1	5	389	350	132	139	2.48
1893	CLEVELAND	NL	36	16	17	0	0	295	358	95	62	4.45
1894	CLEVELAND	NL	22	8	10	0	1	150.7	173	46	28	4.42
CAREER TOTALS			**531**	**328**	**178**	**5**	**37**	**4536.1**	**4295**	**1191**	**1978**	**2.81**

CLARKSON, P. BOSTON'S.

Copyright 1888
Goodwin & Co.
N.Y.

C

ROBERTO CLEMENTE

"He played a kind of baseball that none of us had ever seen before . . . As if it were a form of punishment for everyone else on the field." – Roger Angell

The numbers he assembled over 18 big league seasons tell the story of a complete ballplayer. The story of Roberto Clemente, however, goes beyond mere numbers.

Clemente excelled in athletics as a youngster – and at the age of 18 was playing for the Santurce Crabbers of the Puerto Rican League. The Dodgers signed him the following year, and by 1954 he was playing for their Triple-A team in Montreal. Following the 1954 season, however, the Dodgers tried to slip Clemente through the offseason without putting him on the big league roster. He was taken by the Pirates in the Rule 5 draft for $4,000.

Clemente, a native of Puerto Rico, worked to find his stride during the next five seasons, battling injuries and a language barrier in a country where he was a citizen but had no home. But in 1960, the Pirates and Clemente came of age as the limber right fielder batted .314 with a team-high 94 RBI to lead the Pirates to the World Series. In the Fall Classic, Clemente hit .310 to help the Pirates defeat the Yankees in seven games. During the next seven years, Clemente won four National League batting titles, the 1966 NL Most Valuable Player Award and began a string of 12 straight Gold Glove Award seasons in right field.

In 1971, the 37-year-old Clemente led the Pirates back to the World Series, where he hit .414 to power Pittsburgh to another world title en route to the Series' Most Valuable Player Award.

Clemente recorded his 3,000th career hit late in the 1972 season, becoming just the 11th player to reach the milestone. The Pirates won the NL East that year, but lost to the Reds in five games in the National League Championship Series.

On Dec. 31, 1972, Clemente boarded a small plane en route from Puerto Rico to Nicaragua to assist with earthquake relief. The heavily loaded plane crashed just off the Puerto Rican coast, and Clemente's body was never recovered.

He was elected to the Hall of Fame in 1973 in a special election that waived the mandatory five-year waiting period.

Elected To The Hall Of Fame: 1973.
Born: Aug. 18, 1934 in Carolina, Puerto Rico.
Died: Dec. 31, 1972 in San Juan, Puerto Rico.
Height: 5-11. **Weight:** 175.
Threw: Right. **Batted:** Right.
Debut: Apr. 17, 1955.
Final Game: Oct. 3, 1972.
Teams: Pittsburgh N.L. 1955-1972.
Postseason: 2-Time World Series Champion (1960, 1971); 2 N.L. Pennants (1960, 1971).
Awards: 15-Time All-Star (1960-1967, 1969-1972); N.L. Most Valuable Player (1966); World Series Most Valuable Player (1971).

YEAR	TEAM	LEAGUE	G	AB	R	H	2B	3B	HR	RBI	SB	AVG
1955	PITTSBURGH	NL	124	474	48	121	23	11	5	47	2	.255
1956	PITTSBURGH	NL	147	543	66	169	30	7	7	60	6	.311
1957	PITTSBURGH	NL	111	451	42	114	17	7	4	30	0	.253
1958	PITTSBURGH	NL	140	519	69	150	24	10	6	50	8	.289
1959	PITTSBURGH	NL	105	432	60	128	17	7	4	50	2	.296
1960	PITTSBURGH	NL	144	570	89	179	22	6	16	94	4	.314
1961	PITTSBURGH	NL	146	572	100	201	30	10	23	89	4	.351
1962	PITTSBURGH	NL	144	538	95	168	28	9	10	74	6	.312
1963	PITTSBURGH	NL	152	600	77	192	23	8	17	76	12	.320
1964	PITTSBURGH	NL	155	622	95	211	40	7	12	87	5	.339
1965	PITTSBURGH	NL	152	589	91	194	21	14	10	65	8	.329
1966	PITTSBURGH	NL	154	638	105	202	31	11	29	119	7	.317
1967	PITTSBURGH	NL	147	585	103	209	26	10	23	110	9	.357
1968	PITTSBURGH	NL	132	502	74	146	18	12	18	57	2	.291
1969	PITTSBURGH	NL	138	507	87	175	20	12	19	91	4	.345
1970	PITTSBURGH	NL	108	412	65	145	22	10	14	60	3	.352
1971	PITTSBURGH	NL	132	522	82	178	29	8	13	86	1	.341
1972	PITTSBURGH	NL	102	378	68	118	19	7	10	60	0	.312
CAREER TOTALS			**2433**	**9454**	**1416**	**3000**	**440**	**166**	**240**	**1305**	**83**	**.317**

Ty Cobb

Ty Cobb may have been the best all-around baseball player that ever lived. But one thing is for sure: Cobb had a burning desire to win.

"I never could stand losing," he said. "Second place didn't interest me. I had a fire in my belly."

After spending time in the South Atlantic League and with semipro teams, Cobb joined the Detroit Tigers in 1905. He spent 22 seasons in Detroit and another two in Philadelphia, before retiring as the holder of 43 career records.

Cobb was known for his aggressive baserunning style and his ability to hit to all fields. He won eight AL batting titles from 1907 to 1915 and three more in his career. He hit .320 or better for 22 consecutive seasons including over .400 three times.

In 1909, he led the league in home runs for the only time in his career and won the Triple Crown. Cobb's best offensive season was 1911 when he led the AL in every major offensive category except home runs including hits, runs, RBI, batting average and slugging percentage and was named AL MVP.

"He didn't outhit and he didn't outrun them, he out thought them," said Hall of Fame teammate Sam Crawford.

Spending most of his career in the outfield, Cobb also spent time in the infield and pitched in three games. He served as player-manager of the Tigers from 1921-1926.

"I never saw anyone like Ty Cobb. No one even close to him. He was the greatest all time ballplayer. That guy was superhuman, amazing," said Hall of Fame manager Casey Stengel.

In 1936, the first balloting was held for election to the Hall of Fame. Cobb received the most votes of the five electees and came within four votes of unanimity.

The Georgia Peach

Elected To The Hall Of Fame: 1936.
Born: Dec. 18, 1886 in Narrows, Ga.
Died: July 17, 1961 in Atlanta, Ga.
Height: 6-1. **Weight:** 175.
Threw: Right. **Batted:** Left.
Debut: Aug. 30, 1905.
Final Game: Sept. 11, 1928.
Teams: Detroit A.L. 1905-1926; Philadelphia A.L. 1927-1928.
Postseason: 3 A.L. Pennants (1907-1909).
Awards: A.L. Most Valuable Player (1911).

YEAR	TEAM	LEAGUE	G	AB	R	H	2B	3B	HR	RBI	SB	AVG
1905	DETROIT	AL	41	150	19	36	6	0	1	15	2	.240
1906	DETROIT	AL	98	358	45	113	15	5	1	34	23	.316
1907	DETROIT	AL	150	605	97	212	28	14	5	119	53	.350
1908	DETROIT	AL	150	581	88	188	36	20	4	108	39	.324
1909	DETROIT	AL	156	573	116	216	33	10	9	107	76	.377
1910	DETROIT	AL	140	506	106	194	35	13	8	91	65	.383
1911	DETROIT	AL	146	591	147	248	47	24	8	127	83	.420
1912	DETROIT	AL	140	553	120	226	30	23	7	83	61	.409
1913	DETROIT	AL	122	428	70	167	18	16	4	67	51	.390
1914	DETROIT	AL	98	345	69	127	22	11	2	57	35	.368
1915	DETROIT	AL	156	563	144	208	31	13	3	99	96	.369
1916	DETROIT	AL	145	542	113	201	31	10	5	68	68	.371
1917	DETROIT	AL	152	588	107	225	44	24	6	102	55	.383
1918	DETROIT	AL	111	421	83	161	19	14	3	64	34	.382
1919	DETROIT	AL	124	497	92	191	36	13	1	70	28	.384
1920	DETROIT	AL	112	428	86	143	28	8	2	63	15	.334
1921	DETROIT	AL	128	507	124	197	37	16	12	101	22	.389
1922	DETROIT	AL	137	526	99	211	42	16	4	99	9	.401
1923	DETROIT	AL	145	556	103	189	40	7	6	88	9	.340
1924	DETROIT	AL	155	625	115	211	38	10	4	79	23	.338
1925	DETROIT	AL	121	415	97	157	31	12	12	102	13	.378
1926	DETROIT	AL	79	233	48	79	18	5	4	62	9	.339
1927	PHILADELPHIA	AL	133	490	104	175	32	7	5	93	22	.357
1928	PHILADELPHIA	AL	95	353	54	114	27	4	1	40	6	.323
CAREER TOTALS			**3034**	**11434**	**2246**	**4189**	**724**	**295**	**117**	**1938**	**897**	**.366**

MICKEY COCHRANE

"**G**reatest catcher of them all, (Mickey) Cochrane was," said Hall of Fame pitcher Lefty Grove of his longtime Philadelphia Athletics batterymate. Gordon "Mickey" Cochrane was a fiery catcher, nicknamed "Black Mike" for his fierce competitive spirit, who helped lead his teams to five pennants and three World Series crowns during his 13 big league seasons. He spent his first nine years with the Connie Mack's A's, capturing American League flags from 1929 to 1931, with Fall Classic titles coming in 1929 and '30.

The Tigers acquired Cochrane for Johnny Pasek and $100,000 after the 1933 campaign to become the team's player-manager, and he promptly lead his new team to the top of the Junior Circuit his first two seasons and a World Championship in 1935.

"He showed us how to get a man on first, move him over to third and then get him in. We needed somebody to take charge and show us how to win and that's what Mickey did," said Tigers slugger Hank Greenberg.

"Cochrane was a great inspirational leader," said Tigers Hall of Fame second baseman Charlie Gehringer. "Boy, he was a hard loser, the hardest loser I think I ever saw. He wouldn't stand for any tomfoolery. He wanted everybody to put out as hard as they could and he set the example himself. Always hustling, always battling. Cochrane was in charge out there."

Winner of the American League's Most Valuable Player Award in 1928 and 1934, Cochrane finished with a .320 career batting average, a career-best .357 coming in 1930. But it was his handling of pitchers which impressed those around him.

"Hardly ever shook him off," Grove said. "If Mickey was living today, he'd tell you I only shook him off about five or six times all the years he caught me. Funny, before I'd even look at him, I had in my mind what I was going to pitch and I'd look up and there'd be Mickey's signal, just what I was thinking. Like he was reading my mind. That's the kind of catcher he was."

Cochrane's career came to an abrupt halt at the age of 34 when he was hit in the head by a fastball from Yankees' pitcher Bump Hadley on May 25, 1937. Cochrane survived the fractured skull, of which one doctor reported, "The X-rays looked like a road map," but was never the same afterward.

Black Mike

Elected To The Hall Of Fame: *1947.*
Born: *Apr. 6, 1903 in Bridgewater, Mass.*
Died: *June 28, 1962 in Lake Forest, Ill.*
Height: *5-10.* **Weight:** *180.*
Threw: *Right.* **Batted:** *Left.*
Debut: *Apr. 14, 1925.*
Final Game: *May 25, 1937.*
Teams: *Philadelphia A.L. 1925-1933; Detroit A.L. 1934-1937.*
Postseason: *3-Time World Series Champion (1929-1930, 1935); 5 A.L. Pennants (1929-1931, 1934-1935).*
Awards: *A.L. MVP (1928, 1934).*

YEAR	TEAM	LEAGUE	G	AB	R	H	2B	3B	HR	RBI	SB	AVG
1925	PHILADELPHIA	AL	134	420	69	139	21	5	6	55	7	.331
1926	PHILADELPHIA	AL	120	370	50	101	8	9	8	47	5	.273
1927	PHILADELPHIA	AL	126	432	80	146	20	6	12	80	9	.338
1928	PHILADELPHIA	AL	131	468	92	137	26	12	10	57	7	.293
1929	PHILADELPHIA	AL	135	514	113	170	37	8	7	95	7	.331
1930	PHILADELPHIA	AL	130	487	110	174	42	5	10	85	5	.357
1931	PHILADELPHIA	AL	122	459	87	160	31	6	17	89	2	.349
1932	PHILADELPHIA	AL	139	518	118	152	35	4	23	112	0	.293
1933	PHILADELPHIA	AL	130	429	104	138	30	4	15	60	8	.322
1934	DETROIT	AL	129	437	74	140	32	1	2	76	8	.320
1935	DETROIT	AL	115	411	93	131	33	3	5	47	5	.319
1936	DETROIT	AL	44	126	24	34	8	0	2	17	1	.270
1937	DETROIT	AL	27	98	27	30	10	1	2	12	0	.306
CAREER TOTALS			1482	5169	1041	1652	333	64	119	832	64	.320

EDDIE COLLINS

"Eddie Collins is the best ballplayer I have seen during my career on the diamond." – John McGraw
In the second decade of the 20th Century, Eddie Collins thrived in the "small ball" environment the game demanded. In the third decade he starred in a "go for broke" era as one of the game's most productive catalysts. In any baseball environment, Collins' skills and savvy were nearly without peer.

Collins graduated from Columbia University before establishing himself in the majors with manager Connie Mack's Philadelphia A's in 1908. The next year, Collins became the A's regular second baseman. From 1911-14, Collins finished third, sixth, third and first in the Chalmers Award voting – the de facto MVP – helping the Athletics win World Series titles in 1911 and 1913 and another American League pennant in 1914.

But following his team's shocking 1914 Fall Classic loss to the Braves and in the face of a national recession, Mack broke up his A's and their legendary "$100,000 infield." Mack sold the 27-year-old Collins to the Chicago White Sox for a record $50,000.

Collins continued his outstanding all-around play in Chicago, leading the White Sox to the 1917 World Series title despite batting under .300 for a full season (at .289) for the first time. In 1919, Collins hit .319 and stole a league-best 33 bases in leading the White Sox back to the World Series. Collins was never implicated in the Black Sox scandal.

Collins thrived with the introduction of the lively ball in 1920, recording career-bests of 224 hits and a .372 batting average. He continued to post batting averages well over .300 and managed the White Sox from the end of the 1924 season through the 1926 season – finishing with records better than .500 in each season.

EDWARD TROWBRIDGE COLLINS
PHILADELPHIA - CHICAGO
PHILADELPHIA, A.L. -1906 -1930
FAMED AS BATSMAN, BASE RUNNER
AND SECOND BASEMAN AND ALSO AS
FIELD CAPTAIN. BATTED .333 DURING
MAJOR LEAGUE CAREER. SECOND ONLY
TO TY COBB IN MODERN BASE STEALING.
MADE 3313 HITS IN 2826 GAMES.

Elected To The Hall Of Fame: 1939.
Born: May 2, 1887 in Millerton, NY.
Died: Mar. 25, 1951 in Boston, Mass.
Height: 5-9. **Weight:** 175.
Threw: Right. **Batted:** Left.
Debut: Sept. 17, 1906.
Final Game: Aug. 2, 1930.
Teams: Philadelphia A.L. 1906-1914, 1927-1930; Chicago A.L. 1915-1926.
Postseason: 4-Time World Series Champion (1910-1911, 1913, 1917); 6 A.L. Pennants (1910-1911, 1913-1914, 1917, 1919).
Awards: A.L. Most Valuable Player (1914).

YEAR	TEAM	LEAGUE	G	AB	R	H	2B	3B	HR	RBI	SB	AVG
1906	PHILADELPHIA	AL	6	15	2	3	0	0	0	0	1	.200
1907	PHILADELPHIA	AL	14	23	0	8	0	1	0	2	0	.348
1908	PHILADELPHIA	AL	102	330	39	90	18	7	1	40	8	.273
1909	PHILADELPHIA	AL	153	571	104	198	30	10	3	56	63	.347
1910	PHILADELPHIA	AL	153	581	81	188	16	15	3	81	81	.324
1911	PHILADELPHIA	AL	132	493	92	180	22	13	3	73	38	.365
1912	PHILADELPHIA	AL	153	543	137	189	25	11	0	64	63	.348
1913	PHILADELPHIA	AL	148	534	125	184	23	13	3	73	55	.345
1914	PHILADELPHIA	AL	152	526	122	181	23	14	2	85	58	.344
1915	CHICAGO	AL	155	521	118	173	22	10	4	77	46	.332
1916	CHICAGO	AL	155	545	87	168	14	17	0	52	40	.308
1917	CHICAGO	AL	156	564	91	163	18	12	0	67	53	.289
1918	CHICAGO	AL	97	330	51	91	8	2	2	30	22	.276
1919	CHICAGO	AL	140	518	87	165	19	7	4	80	33	.319
1920	CHICAGO	AL	153	602	117	224	38	13	3	76	20	.372
1921	CHICAGO	AL	139	526	79	177	20	10	2	58	12	.337
1922	CHICAGO	AL	154	598	92	194	20	12	1	69	20	.324
1923	CHICAGO	AL	145	505	89	182	22	5	5	67	48	.360
1924	CHICAGO	AL	152	556	108	194	27	7	6	86	42	.349
1925	CHICAGO	AL	118	425	80	147	26	3	3	80	19	.346
1926	CHICAGO	AL	106	375	66	129	32	4	1	62	13	.344
1927	PHILADELPHIA	AL	95	226	50	76	12	1	1	15	6	.336
1928	PHILADELPHIA	AL	36	33	3	10	3	0	0	7	0	.303
1929	PHILADELPHIA	AL	9	7	0	0	0	0	0	0	0	.000
1930	PHILADELPHIA	AL	3	2	1	1	0	0	0	0	0	.500
CAREER TOTALS			2826	9949	1821	3315	438	187	47	1300	741	.333

JIMMY COLLINS

"Third base was put into baseball for (Jimmy) Collins," said fellow big leaguer Bill Coughlin, also a veteran of the hot corner.

Collins was a star as baseball entered the 20th Century, acclaimed by many as the "king of the third basemen." And while he was a good hitter, finishing with a .294 lifetime average, it was as a fielder he won the headlines.

"Collins was a model for all third basemen, the king of trappers and footworkers," commented 1978 J.G. Taylor Spink Award winner Tim Murnane. "Collins was always graceful. Bill Bradley, another great third baseman, would get twice the applause on the same play Collins made easy."

"The two best third basemen I ever saw, defensively, until Ossie Bluege came along, were Collins and Bill Bradley of Cleveland," said Washington Senators owner Clark Griffith, a former player and Hall of Fame executive. "But Collins, with the Red Sox, was a shade the better. He was a cat on bunts."

As the toast of Boston, Collins, having spent the majority of his 14-year big league career with either the Braves or Red Sox, is credited with revolutionizing third base play, whether in setting up defensively away from the bag or mastering the art of defense against the bunt, a famous tactic of the Baltimore Orioles of John McGraw, Hughie Jennings and Willie Keeler.

Collins also spent a six-year stint (1901-06) as player-manager of the Red Sox in the fledging American League, skippering his team to two pennants and a triumph over the Pittsburgh Pirates in the first modern World Series in 1903.

At the time of his death in 1943, Collins, only 5-foot-9 and 178 pounds, was considered by many baseball observers as the best player at his position of all time.

"They say I was the greatest third baseman, and I would like to believe it," Collins said. "But I don't know. There were many great third basemen in my day.

"I gave baseball everything I had and when I quit, I was like the guy who died with his boots on. My arches had broken down, my legs ached, I had charley horses and I could hardly lift my right arm."

JAMES COLLINS
CONSIDERED BY MANY THE GAME'S GREATEST THIRD BASEMAN. HE REVOLUTIONIZED STYLE OF PLAY AT THAT BAG. LED BOSTON RED SOX TO FIRST WORLD CHAMPIONSHIP IN 1903. A CONSISTENT BATTER. HIS DEFENSIVE PLAY THRILLED FANS OF BOTH MAJOR LEAGUES.

Elected To The Hall Of Fame: 1945.
Born: Jan. 16, 1870 in Buffalo, NY.
Died: Mar. 6, 1943 in Buffalo, NY.
Height: 5-9. **Weight:** 178.
Threw: Right. **Batted:** Right.
Debut: Apr. 19, 1895.
Final Game: Aug. 29, 1908.
Teams: Louisville N.L. 1895; Boston N.L. 1895-1900; Boston A.L. 1901-1907; Philadelphia A.L. 1907-1908.
Postseason: World Series Champion (1903); A.L. Pennant (1903).

YEAR	TEAM	LEAGUE	G	AB	R	H	2B	3B	HR	RBI	SB	AVG
1895	LOUISVILLE/BOSTON	NL	107	411	75	112	20	5	7	57	12	.273
1896	BOSTON	NL	84	304	48	90	10	9	1	46	10	.296
1897	BOSTON	NL	134	529	103	183	28	13	6	132	14	.346
1898	BOSTON	NL	152	597	107	196	35	5	15	111	12	.328
1899	BOSTON	NL	151	599	98	166	28	11	5	92	12	.277
1900	BOSTON	NL	142	586	104	178	25	5	6	95	23	.304
1901	BOSTON	AL	138	564	108	187	42	16	6	94	19	.332
1902	BOSTON	AL	108	429	71	138	21	10	6	61	18	.322
1903	BOSTON	AL	130	540	88	160	33	17	5	72	23	.296
1904	BOSTON	AL	156	631	85	171	33	13	3	67	19	.271
1905	BOSTON	AL	131	508	66	140	26	5	4	65	18	.276
1906	BOSTON	AL	37	142	17	39	8	4	1	16	1	.275
1907	BOSTON/PHILADELPHIA	AL	140	522	51	145	29	0	0	45	8	.278
1908	PHILADELPHIA	AL	115	433	34	94	14	3	0	30	5	.217
CAREER TOTALS			**1725**	**6795**	**1055**	**1999**	**352**	**116**	**65**	**983**	**194**	**.294**

Horner
Photo

EARLE COMBS

Though Earle Combs may have been overshadowed by more celebrated teammates Babe Ruth and Lou Gehrig, the center fielder and leadoff hitter on some of the most successful Yankees teams of the 1920s and '30s was held in high regard by those in the game.

"He was a table-setter for Ruth and Gehrig," said fellow Hall of Fame player Joe Cronin. "He was always on base, it seemed, when they'd hit a homer. He was an important cog in that Yankee team of 1927 that a lot of people consider the best of all time. He was a great fielder, a great leadoff hitter and fast as the devil – he could really get to the ball."

A line drive hitter, a deadly ballhawk in center field and a speed demon in the field and on the bases, Combs was part of four pennant-winning teams and three World Series championships during his 12 seasons with the Yankees.

Included in Combs' legendary run was the famed 1927 team, nicknamed Murderers' Row and considered by many as the best team in baseball history. It also produced one of the great outfields, with left fielder Bob Meusel hitting .337, Combs .356, and Ruth .356 - with 60 home runs.

Surrounded by such a powerful lineup, Combs' ability to showcase his speed on the basepaths was negated. But this didn't stop a young Combs from one day broaching the subject with manager Miller Huggins.

"Down in Louisville," Combs said, "they called me the 'The Mail Carrier.'"

"Up here," Huggins said, "we'll call you the 'The Waiter.' When you get on first base, you just wait there for Ruth or Gehrig, or one of the other fellows, to send you the rest of the way around."

Huggins, a fellow Hall of Famer, would later remark, "If you had nine Combses on your ball club, you could go to bed every night and sleep like a baby."

Combs finished with 1,866 hits and a .325 batting average during a career cut short by injuries. Despite the hardships, he collected more than 200 hits in a season three times, scored more than 100 runs eight straight years, from 1925 through 1932, and hit at least .300 nine times with a high of .356 in 1927.

EARLE BRYAN COMBS
NEW YORK YANKEES 1924-1935

LEAD-OFF HITTER AND CENTER FIELDER OF YANKEE CHAMPIONS OF 1926·27·28·32. LIFETIME BATTING AVERAGE .325. 200 OR MORE HITS THREE SEASONS. LED LEAGUE WITH 231 HITS IN 1927 WHILE BATTING .356. PACED A.L. IN TRIPLES THREE TIMES AND TWICE LED OUTFIELDERS IN PUTOUTS. BATTED .350 IN FOUR WORLD SERIES

The Kentucky Colonel

Elected To The Hall Of Fame: *1970.*

Born: *May 14, 1899 in Pebworth, Ky.*

Died: *July 21, 1976 in Richmond, Ky.*

Height: *6-0.* **Weight:** *185.*

Threw: *Right.* **Batted:** *Left.*

Debut: *Apr. 16, 1924.*

Final Game: *Sept. 29, 1935.*

Teams: *New York A.L. 1924-1935.*

Postseason: *3-Time World Series Champion (1927-1928, 1932); 4 A.L. Pennants (1926-1928, 1932).*

YEAR	TEAM	LEAGUE	G	AB	R	H	2B	3B	HR	RBI	SB	AVG
1924	NEW YORK	AL	24	35	10	14	5	0	0	2	0	.400
1925	NEW YORK	AL	150	593	117	203	36	13	3	61	12	.342
1926	NEW YORK	AL	145	606	113	181	31	12	8	55	8	.299
1927	NEW YORK	AL	152	648	137	231	36	23	6	64	15	.356
1928	NEW YORK	AL	149	626	118	194	33	21	7	56	11	.310
1929	NEW YORK	AL	142	586	119	202	33	15	3	65	12	.345
1930	NEW YORK	AL	137	532	129	183	30	22	7	82	16	.344
1931	NEW YORK	AL	138	563	120	179	31	13	5	58	11	.318
1932	NEW YORK	AL	144	591	143	190	32	10	9	65	3	.321
1933	NEW YORK	AL	122	417	86	125	22	16	5	64	6	.300
1934	NEW YORK	AL	63	251	47	80	13	5	2	25	3	.319
1935	NEW YORK	AL	89	298	47	84	7	4	3	35	1	.282
CAREER TOTALS			**1455**	**5746**	**1186**	**1866**	**309**	**154**	**58**	**632**	**98**	**.325**

ROGER CONNOR

W hen 19th-century baseball star Roger Connor passed away in 1931 at the age of 73, the first line of his obituary called him "The Babe Ruth of the '80s." But Connor was much more than just a slugger.

Connor spent 18 seasons in the big leagues, breaking in with the Troy Trojans in 1880 before finding a longtime home with the New York Giants. The broad-shouldered first baseman with the distinctive moustache would eventually become the national pastime's first power hitter as well as one of the most popular players of his time. When he retired in 1897, his 138 career home runs were more than anybody had ever hit until Ruth surpassed it in 1921.

"He is as fine a specimen of physical development as any in the profession, being a few inches over six feet in height, weighing over two hundred pounds, without an ounce of superfluous flesh, and being admirably proportioned," read a profile in *The New York Clipper*. "Not withstanding his great size, he is endowed with more than the average amount of activity, and evidently possesses extraordinary powers of endurance."

An offensive marvel, the lefty-swinging Connor would hit more than 10 home runs in a season seven times, a 19th-century record, and on 11 occasions topped a .300 batting average. On Sept. 10, 1881, he also hit the National League's first grand slam home run.

One of Connor's more memorable feats occurred on Sept. 11, 1886. Playing at the old Polo Grounds at 110th Street and Fifth Avenue, he hit a ball that landed on 112th Street on the other side of the right field wall. So impressed were members of the New York Stock Exchange that they passed around a black top hat and took up a collection that eventually led to a $500 gold watch being presented to Connor a few games later.

According to *The New York Times*, "He met it squarely and it soared up with the speed of a carrier pigeon. All eyes were turned on the tiny sphere as it soared over the head of Charlie Buffington in right field."

ROGER CONNOR
TROY N. L., NEW YORK N. L.,
NEW YORK P. L., PHILADELPHIA N. L.,
ST. LOUIS N. L. 1880-1897
POWER-HITTING STAR OF DEAD-BALL ERA.
SET CAREER HOME RUN RECORD FOR 19TH
CENTURY PLAYERS. WON LEAGUE BATTING
CHAMPIONSHIP IN 1885 AND HIT .300 OR
BETTER 12 TIMES. HIT THREE HOMERS
IN A GAME IN 1886 AND MADE SIX HITS IN
SIX AT-BATS IN A GAME IN 1895.

Dear Old Roger

Elected To The Hall Of Fame: *1976.*

Born: *July 1, 1857 in Waterbury, Conn.*

Died: *Jan. 4, 1931 in Waterbury, Conn.*

Height: *6-3.* **Weight:** *220.*

Threw: *Left.* **Batted:** *Left.*

Debut: *May 1, 1880.*

Final Game: *May 18, 1897.*

Teams: *Troy N.L. 1880-1882; New York N.L. 1883-1889, 1891, 1893-1894; New York, Players' League 1890; Philadelphia N.L. 1892; St. Louis N.L. 1894-1897.*

Postseason: *2-Time World Champion (1888-1889).*

YEAR	TEAM	LEAGUE	G	AB	R	H	2B	3B	HR	RBI	SB	AVG
1880	TROY	NL	83	340	53	113	18	8	3	47	—	.332
1881	TROY	NL	85	367	55	107	17	6	2	31	—	.292
1882	TROY	NL	81	349	65	115	22	18	4	42	—	.330
1883	NEW YORK	NL	98	409	80	146	28	15	1	50	—	.357
1884	NEW YORK	NL	116	477	98	151	28	4	4	82	—	.317
1885	NEW YORK	NL	110	455	102	169	23	15	1	65	—	.371
1886	NEW YORK	NL	118	485	105	172	29	20	7	71	17	.355
1887	NEW YORK	NL	127	471	113	134	26	22	17	104	43	.285
1888	NEW YORK	NL	134	481	98	140	15	17	14	71	27	.291
1889	NEW YORK	NL	131	496	117	157	32	17	13	130	21	.317
1890	NEW YORK	PL	123	484	133	169	24	15	14	103	22	.349
1891	NEW YORK	NL	129	479	112	139	29	13	7	94	27	.290
1892	PHILADELPHIA	NL	155	564	123	166	37	11	12	73	22	.294
1893	NEW YORK	NL	135	511	111	156	25	8	11	105	24	.305
1894	NEW YORK/ST. LOUIS	NL	121	462	93	146	35	25	8	93	19	.316
1895	ST. LOUIS	NL	104	401	78	131	29	9	8	78	9	.327
1896	ST. LOUIS	NL	126	483	71	137	21	9	11	72	10	.284
1897	ST. LOUIS	NL	22	83	13	19	3	1	1	12	3	.229
CAREER TOTALS			**1998**	**7797**	**1620**	**2467**	**441**	**233**	**138**	**1323**	**244**	**.316**

ANDY COOPER

A baseball player who spent the entirety of his playing career in the shadows of the major leagues due to the color of his skin, Andy Cooper made a name for himself in black baseball due to his mound mastery.

Negro leagues historian Dick Clark once said of Cooper, "In my estimation, the greatest black pitcher ever to pitch for Detroit – that's for the Stars or the Tigers."

Cooper, all 6-foot-2 and roughly 220 pounds of him, spent the majority of his Negro Leagues career as a durable and consistent left-handed hurler with the Detroit Stars and Kansas City Monarchs over a career that spanned the 1920s and '30s.

Included among Cooper's many accomplishments was a 43-inning stretch with the Stars in which he didn't issue a base on balls, winning twice as many games as he lost with both the Stars and Monarchs, helping lead Kansas City to the Negro National League pennant in 1929, once pitching 17 innings in a 1937 playoff game against the Chicago American Giants, and taking the mound in the 1936 East-West All-Star Game at the age of 38.

According to a scouting report prepared by famed Negro leagues player and manager Buck O'Neil, Cooper had a live arm with a total command of all of his pitches, which included a running fastball, tight curveball and biting screwball.

"Andy never possessed the fine assortment of curves held in the supple arms of other pitchers. However, he did have what so many pitchers lack – sterling control," wrote Russ J. Cowans in 1941 in *The Chicago Defender*. "Cooper could almost put the ball any place he wanted it to go.

"In addition, Cooper had a keen knowledge of batters. He knew the weakness of every batter in the league and would pitch to that weakness when he was on the mound."

A top starting pitcher early in his career who became a valuable reliever near the end, Cooper would also turn to managing, leading the Monarchs to three pennants between 1937 and 1940.

"Cooper was a smart manager and a great, great teacher," said Monarchs pitcher and fellow Hall of Famer Hilton Smith.

After Cooper's death in 1941, the *Defender* wrote, "he not only won glory on the hurling mound but also won the respect and praise of the fans through his deportment off the field."

ANDREW LEWIS COOPER
"ANDY" "LEFTY"
NEGRO LEAGUES, 1920-1941

A SUPERB LEFT-HANDED CONTROL PITCHER WHOSE REPERTOIRE INCLUDED A WIDE ARRAY OF PITCHES AND SPEEDS WHICH CONFUSED HITTERS FOR TWO DECADES. EXCELLED WITH DETROIT STARS FROM 1920-1927, BEFORE TRADE TO KANSAS CITY. MONARCHS FOR FIVE PLAYERS. PITCHED MONARCHS TO A NEGRO NATIONAL LEAGUE CHAMPIONSHIP IN 1929. AS PLAYER-MANAGER, ADDED THREE MORE TITLES IN 1937, 1939 AND 1940. OFTEN PITCHED IN RELIEF BETWEEN STARTING ASSIGNMENTS. RANKS AMONG NEGRO LEAGUES LEADERS IN VIRTUALLY EVERY CAREER PITCHING CATEGORY AND WON MORE THAN TWO-THIRDS OF HIS DECISIONS.

Elected To The Hall Of Fame: *2006.*
Born: *April 24, 1898 in Waco, Texas.*
Died: *June 3, 1941 in Waco, Texas.*
Height: *6-2.* **Weight:** *220.*
Threw: *Left.* **Batted:** *Right.*
Teams: *Negro Leagues 1920-1939. Detroit 1920-1927, 1930; Kansas City 1928-1929, 1931-1939.*

YEAR	TEAM	LEAGUE	G	W	L	SV	SH	IP	H	BB	SO	ERA
1920	DETROIT	NNL	8	1	1	1	0	37	30	13	9	4.38
1921	DETROIT	NNL	19	3	5	1	2	102	116	12	24	3.44
1922	DETROIT	NNL	17	8	3	0	1	116	112	16	45	2.87
1923	DETROIT	NNL	36	15	7	6	1	183.3	168	44	68	3.93
1924	DETROIT	NNL	30	11	6	4	1	152.3	151	31	76	3.37
1925	DETROIT	NNL	29	11	2	4	1	141	125	25	47	2.81
1926	DETROIT	NNL	36	13	9	3	1	184	189	34	59	3.33
1927	DETROIT	NNL	8	4	1	1	0	49	58	4	21	3.86
1928	KANSAS CITY	NNL	21	11	6	1	2	126	119	9	48	2.86
1929	KANSAS CITY	NNL	15	13	3	6	2	148	150	20	50	2.86
1930	DETROIT	NNL	25	13	6	2	2	164	176	8	43	3.40
1931	KANSAS CITY	NNL	3	1	2	0	0	20.3	17	8	6	5.31
1933	KANSAS CITY	INDP	4	3	1	0	0	25	25	2	13	2.16
1934	KANSAS CITY	INDP	2	0	2	0	0	10	11	3	3	2.70
1935	KANSAS CITY	INDP	4	1	0	0	0	18.7	22	0	2	4.82
1936	KANSAS CITY	INDP	1	0	0	0	0	1	1	0	0	0.00
1937	KANSAS CITY	NAL	8	4	2	0	0	67.7	49	8	39	2.13
1938	KANSAS CITY	NAL	4	2	0	0	0	24.3	22	6	13	3.33
1939	KANSAS CITY	NAL	3	2	1	0	0	23	23	1	12	1.96
CAREER TOTALS			**284**	**116**	**57**	**29**	**14**	**1592.7**	**1564**	**244**	**578**	**3.24**

STAN COVELESKI

"The pressure never lets up. Don't matter what you did yesterday. That's history. It's tomorrow that counts. So you worry all the time. It never ends. Lord, baseball is a worrying thing," Stan Coveleski said.

Coveleski took his baseball seriously — after all, it was his ticket out of the coal mines around his birthplace of Shamokin, Pa. At age 12, he quit school to work 12 hours a day, seven days a week in the mines, bringing home $3.75 to his large family. Amazingly, he still found time to practice at baseball, after work, in the dark.

The youngest of five ballplaying brothers — his brother Harry also had a lengthy big league pitching career — Stan signed into pro ball in 1908 after playing just five amateur games. He surfaced briefly with the Philadelphia Athletics in 1912, going 2-1, before returning to a lengthy minor league apprenticeship.

Coveleski hit the big leagues for good with the Cleveland Indians in 1916, winning 15 games in his first full big league season. The following year, he led the league with nine shutouts, while winning 19 games and posting an ERA of 1.81. He won 22 games the following season, the first of four consecutive 20-plus victory seasons.

His high water mark in the big leagues was 1920, when he went 24-14, leading the league in strikeouts and leading the Indians to the AL pennant. In the World Series, Coveleski shone like few others ever have, winning Games One, Four and Seven. Each game was a complete game five-hitter, and Game Seven was a shutout. As he gave up just one earned run in each of the other games, his World Series ERA was a sparkling 0.67.

In December, 1924, he was traded to the Washington Senators and enjoyed another fantastic season, winning 13 consecutive games and leading the Senators to the World Series by going 20-5, leading the league in ERA (2.84), and winning percentage (.800).

Released in midseason 1927 by the Senators, Coveleski signed as a free agent with the Yankees in December and helped the 1928 World Champions with a 5-1 record in 12 games.

STANLEY ANTHONY COVELESKI

PHILADELPHIA A.L. 1912
CLEVELAND A.L. 1916-1924
WASHINGTON A.L. 1925-1927
NEW YORK A.L. 1928
STAR PITCHER WITH A RECORD OF 214 WINS,
141 LOSSES, AVERAGE .603, E.R.A. 2.88.
WON 20 OR MORE GAMES IN 5 SEASONS. WON
13 STRAIGHT GAMES IN 1925. PITCHED AND
WON 3 GAMES FOR CLEVELAND IN 1920
WORLD SERIES WITH E.R.A. 0.67.

Elected To The Hall Of Fame: 1969.
Born: July 13, 1889 in Shamokin, Pa.
Died: March 20, 1984 in South Bend, Ind.
Height: 5-11. **Weight:** 166.
Threw: Right. **Batted:** Right.
Debut: Sept. 10, 1912.
Final Game: Aug. 3, 1928.
Teams: Philadelphia A.L. 1912; Cleveland A.L. 1916-1924; Washington A.L. 1925-1927; New York A.L. 1928.
Postseason: World Series Champion (1920). 2 A.L. Pennants (1920, 1925).

YEAR	TEAM	LEAGUE	G	W	L	SV	SH	IP	H	BB	SO	ERA
1912	PHILADELPHIA	AL	5	2	1	0	1	21	18	4	9	3.43
1916	CLEVELAND	AL	45	15	13	3	1	232	247	58	76	3.41
1917	CLEVELAND	AL	45	19	14	4	9	298.3	202	94	133	1.81
1918	CLEVELAND	AL	38	22	13	1	2	311	261	76	87	1.82
1919	CLEVELAND	AL	43	24	12	4	4	286	286	60	118	2.61
1920	CLEVELAND	AL	41	24	14	2	3	315	284	65	133	2.49
1921	CLEVELAND	AL	43	23	13	2	7	315	341	84	99	3.37
1922	CLEVELAND	AL	35	17	14	2	3	276.7	292	64	98	3.32
1923	CLEVELAND	AL	33	13	14	2	5	228	251	42	54	2.76
1924	CLEVELAND	AL	37	15	16	0	2	240.3	286	73	58	4.04
1925	WASHINGTON	AL	32	20	5	0	3	241	230	73	58	2.84
1926	WASHINGTON	AL	36	14	11	1	3	245.3	272	81	50	3.12
1927	WASHINGTON	AL	5	2	1	0	0	14.3	13	8	3	3.14
1928	NEW YORK	AL	12	5	1	0	0	58	72	20	5	5.74
CAREER TOTALS			**450**	**215**	**142**	**21**	**38**	**3082**	**3055**	**802**	**981**	**2.89**

SAM CRAWFORD

"If we were looking for a model for a statue of a slugger, we would choose Sam Crawford," *Baseball Magazine* wrote in 1916.

"Wahoo Sam" Crawford began his baseball career playing semi-pro ball around his birthplace of Wahoo, Neb. He rose quickly through the minors, debuting at age 19 with the Cincinnati Reds in September 1899, batting .307 in 31 games. After moderate success in 1900, he emerged the next season, hitting .330 and leading the National League with 16 home runs.

The consistent Crawford hit .333 the following year, and .335 in 1903, when he jumped to the Detroit Tigers. It was his second consecutive year leading his league in triples, with 25, and the triple was a specialty of Crawford's. He finished his career with a big league record 309 three-baggers, legged out in the cavernous ballparks of the dead ball era.

With outfield contributions from Crawford and the young Ty Cobb, the Tigers broke out in 1907 to the first of three consecutive pennants. Crawford led the league in runs in 1907, while hitting .323. The next year he led in home runs, with seven, batting .311. In the third straight pennant year, 1909, he hit .314, leading the league in doubles, with 35. The Tigers lost all three World Series, the first two to the Cubs and the 1909 Series to Honus Wagner and the Pirates. Crawford hit three doubles and a homer in the 1909 Series.

Though there would be no more World Series for the Tigers with Crawford, he continued to pace the club and the league. In 1910, he led the league in triples and runs batted in, the first of three times he would lead the league in that vital category. In 1911, he batted .378, the highest mark of his career. He led the league in triples three consecutive years, beginning in 1913, and in runs batted in in 1914 and 1915. 1917 was the final big league season for Crawford, who led the league in triples six times, home runs twice, runs batted in three times, total bases twice, and once each in runs and doubles. For his career, he batted .309 over 19 seasons.

SAMUEL EARL CRAWFORD
"WAHOO SAM"
CINCINNATI N.L. 1899-1902
DETROIT A.L. 1903-1917
HAD LIFETIME RECORD OF 2964 HITS,
BATTING AVERAGE OF .309. PLAYED 2505
GAMES. HOLDS MAJOR LEAGUE RECORD
FOR MOST TRIPLES, 312. LEAGUE LEADER
ONE OR MORE SEASONS IN DOUBLES, TRIPLES,
RUNS BATTED IN, RUNS SCORED, CHANCES
ACCEPTED, HOME RUNS (N.L. 1901-A.L. 1908)
AND TOTAL BASES (N.L. 1902-A.L. 1915).

Wahoo Sam

Elected To The Hall Of Fame: *1957.*
Born: *Apr. 18, 1880 in Wahoo, Neb.*
Died: *June 15, 1968 in Hollywood, Calif.*
Height: *6-0.* **Weight:** *190.*
Threw: *Left.* **Batted:** *Left.*
Debut: *Sept. 10, 1899.*
Final Game: *Sept. 16, 1917.*
Teams: *Cincinnati N.L. 1899-1902; Detroit A.L. 1903-1917.*
Postseason: *3 A.L. Pennants (1907-1909).*

YEAR	TEAM	LEAGUE	G	AB	R	H	2B	3B	HR	RBI	SB	AVG
1899	CINCINNATI	NL	31	127	25	39	3	7	1	20	6	.307
1900	CINCINNATI	NL	101	389	68	101	15	15	7	59	14	.260
1901	CINCINNATI	NL	131	515	91	170	20	16	16	104	13	.330
1902	CINCINNATI	NL	140	555	92	185	18	22	3	78	16	.333
1903	DETROIT	AL	137	550	88	184	23	25	4	89	18	.335
1904	DETROIT	AL	150	562	49	143	22	16	2	73	20	.254
1905	DETROIT	AL	154	575	73	171	38	10	6	75	22	.297
1906	DETROIT	AL	145	563	65	166	25	16	2	72	24	.295
1907	DETROIT	AL	144	582	102	188	34	17	4	81	18	.323
1908	DETROIT	AL	152	591	102	184	33	16	7	80	15	.311
1909	DETROIT	AL	156	589	83	185	35	14	6	97	30	.314
1910	DETROIT	AL	154	588	83	170	26	19	5	120	20	.289
1911	DETROIT	AL	146	574	109	217	36	14	7	115	37	.378
1912	DETROIT	AL	149	581	81	189	30	21	4	109	42	.325
1913	DETROIT	AL	153	609	78	193	32	23	9	83	13	.317
1914	DETROIT	AL	157	582	74	183	22	26	8	104	25	.314
1915	DETROIT	AL	156	612	81	183	31	19	4	112	24	.299
1916	DETROIT	AL	100	322	41	92	11	13	0	42	10	.286
1917	DETROIT	AL	61	104	6	18	4	0	2	12	0	.173
CAREER TOTALS			**2517**	**9570**	**1391**	**2961**	**458**	**309**	**97**	**1525**	**367**	**.309**

JOE CRONIN

"Every day I put on a uniform was a thrill. Just to be a part of the show was a real thrill for me. Every day could have been my first big league game," Joe Cronin once said of playing in the major leagues.

Cronin had one of the most interesting, multifaceted careers in baseball. He was a player, manager, general manager, American League President, and a member of the Hall of Fame's board of directors and Veterans Committee.

A fine-fielding shortstop who hit for power and average, he played briefly for the Pittsburgh Pirates in 1926 and 1927. The Washington Senators purchased his contract in 1928 for $7,500, a whopping sum at the time. The following year he became the Senators regular shortstop. He played for the Senators through 1934. During his time there, he led the league twice in games played, and once each in doubles and triples. He became player-manager in 1933, winning the pennant in his first season. Though the Senators lost the Series to the Giants, Cronin hit .318.

In October of 1934, the Boston Red Sox traded for Cronin, sending Lyn Lary and $225,000 to Washington. Cronin played shortstop for the Red Sox until 1945, and managed the club until 1947. Cronin hit over .300 for the Red Sox six times, and managed the team to the 1946 pennant, losing to the St. Louis Cardinals in the World Series.

A fine fielder, Cronin led the league in putouts and assists three times each, and twice in fielding percentage. He was a 7-time All-Star and finished in the top 10 of American League Most Valuable Player voting five times.

He was a leader as a player, as a manager, and as an executive, and was lauded for the leadership and other intangibles he brought to his ball clubs. His managerial winning percentage was .540. From 1948 through 1959, Cronin served in the Red Sox front office in several capacities: general manager, treasurer, and vice president. He was the first former player to become President of the American League in 1959, a position he held through 1973. He was elected to the Hall of Fame in 1956.

Elected To The Hall Of Fame: 1956.
Born: Oct. 12, 1906 in San Francisco, Calif.
Died: Sept. 7, 1984 in Barnstable, Mass.
Height: 5-11. **Weight:** 180.
Threw: Right. **Batted:** Right.
Debut: Apr. 29, 1926.
Final Game: Apr. 19, 1945.
Teams: Pittsburgh N.L. 1926-1927; Washington A.L. 1928-1934; Boston A.L. 1935-1945.
Postseason: A.L. Pennant (1933).
Awards: 7-Time All-Star (1933-1935, 1937-1939, 1941).

YEAR	TEAM	LEAGUE	G	AB	R	H	2B	3B	HR	RBI	SB	AVG
1926	PITTSBURGH	NL	38	83	9	22	2	2	0	11	0	.265
1927	PITTSBURGH	NL	12	22	2	5	1	0	0	3	0	.227
1928	WASHINGTON	AL	63	227	23	55	10	4	0	25	4	.242
1929	WASHINGTON	AL	145	494	72	139	29	8	8	61	5	.281
1930	WASHINGTON	AL	154	587	127	203	41	9	13	126	17	.346
1931	WASHINGTON	AL	156	611	103	187	44	13	12	126	10	.306
1932	WASHINGTON	AL	143	557	95	177	43	18	6	116	7	.318
1933	WASHINGTON	AL	152	602	89	186	45	11	5	118	5	.309
1934	WASHINGTON	AL	127	504	68	143	30	9	7	101	8	.284
1935	BOSTON	AL	144	556	70	164	37	14	9	95	3	.295
1936	BOSTON	AL	81	295	36	83	22	4	2	43	1	.281
1937	BOSTON	AL	148	570	102	175	40	4	18	110	5	.307
1938	BOSTON	AL	143	530	98	172	51	5	17	94	7	.325
1939	BOSTON	AL	143	520	97	160	33	3	19	107	6	.308
1940	BOSTON	AL	149	548	104	156	35	6	24	111	7	.285
1941	BOSTON	AL	143	518	98	161	38	8	16	95	1	.311
1942	BOSTON	AL	45	79	7	24	3	0	4	24	0	.304
1943	BOSTON	AL	59	77	8	24	4	0	5	29	0	.312
1944	BOSTON	AL	76	191	24	46	7	0	5	28	1	.241
1945	BOSTON	AL	3	8	1	3	0	0	0	1	0	.375
CAREER TOTALS			**2124**	**7579**	**1233**	**2285**	**515**	**118**	**170**	**1424**	**87**	**.301**

KIKI CUYLER

Hazen Shirley Cuyler died 18 years before his election to the Baseball Hall of Fame, but the player nick-named "Kiki" posted achievements on the diamond far too great to be obscured by history.

Cuyler was born Aug. 30, 1898, in Harrisville, Mich. He died on Feb. 11, 1950. And for nearly half of his 51 years, Cuyler was one of Major League Baseball's greatest hitters.

"Cuyler can hit, run, field and throw with the best of 'em," said broadcaster Fred Hoey.

His nickname rhymes with "sky" and was derived from the first syllable of his surname, and few had trouble remembering the strapping right-handed hitter after he posted a .354 batting average in 1924 as a Pittsburgh Pirates rookie. During his first eight big league seasons, Cuyler hit .336 with three 200-hit seasons (and another in which he finished three short). He also averaged 110 runs scored per year (despite missing half of the 1927 season in a contract dispute) and 32 steals.

Cuyler led the Pirates to a World Series victory in 1925, but was benched for the 1927 World Series – in which the Bucs were swept by the New York Yankees. That offseason, Cuyler was traded to the Chicago Cubs for infielder Sparky Adams (who hit .286 in his 13 big league seasons) and reserve outfielder Pete Scott (whose 1928 season with Pittsburgh was his last of three years in the majors). Over the next seven seasons, Cuyler batted .328, helping the Cubs win National League pennants in 1929 and 1932. He spent four more seasons in the Majors, finishing his 18-year career with 2,299 hits, 1,305 runs scored and a .321 batting average. His 155 runs scored in 1930 is tied for 24th on the all-time single-season list and has been surpassed only by Lou Gehrig (163 runs in 1931 and 167 in '36) in all the seasons since.

For many years, Cuyler spent his off-seasons touring with an All-Star basketball team. He also served as a minor league manager and major league coach following his playing career.

Cuyler received votes in 12 of the writers' Hall of Fame ballots, reaching a peak of 33.8 percent of the vote in 1958. He was elected to the Hall of Fame by the Veterans Committee in 1968.

Elected To The Hall Of Fame: *1968.*

Born: *Aug. 30, 1898 in Harrisville, Mich.*

Died: *Feb. 11, 1950 in Ann Arbor, Mich.*

Height: *5-10.* **Weight:** *180.*

Threw: *Right.* **Batted:** *Right.*

Debut: *Sept. 29, 1921.*

Final Game: *Sept. 14, 1938.*

Teams: *Pittsburgh N.L. 1921-1927; Chicago N.L. 1928-1935; Cincinnati N.L. 1935-1937; Brooklyn N.L. 1938.*

Postseason: *World Series Champion (1925); 3 N.L. Pennants (1925, 1929, 1932).*

Awards: *All-Star (1934).*

YEAR	TEAM	LEAGUE	G	AB	R	H	2B	3B	HR	RBI	SB	AVG
1921	PITTSBURGH	NL	1	3	0	0	0	0	0	0	0	.000
1922	PITTSBURGH	NL	1	0	0	0	0	0	0	0	0	—
1923	PITTSBURGH	NL	11	40	4	10	1	1	0	2	2	.250
1924	PITTSBURGH	NL	117	466	94	165	27	16	9	85	32	.354
1925	PITTSBURGH	NL	153	617	144	220	43	26	18	102	41	.357
1926	PITTSBURGH	NL	157	614	113	197	31	15	8	92	35	.321
1927	PITTSBURGH	NL	85	285	60	88	13	7	3	31	20	.309
1928	CHICAGO	NL	133	499	92	142	25	9	17	79	37	.285
1929	CHICAGO	NL	139	509	111	183	29	7	15	102	43	.360
1930	CHICAGO	NL	156	642	155	228	50	17	13	134	37	.355
1931	CHICAGO	NL	154	613	110	202	37	12	9	88	13	.330
1932	CHICAGO	NL	110	446	58	130	19	9	10	77	9	.291
1933	CHICAGO	NL	70	262	37	83	13	3	5	35	4	.317
1934	CHICAGO	NL	142	559	80	189	42	8	6	69	15	.338
1935	CHI./CINCINNATI	NL	107	380	58	98	13	4	6	40	8	.258
1936	CINCINNATI	NL	144	567	96	185	29	11	7	74	16	.326
1937	CINCINNATI	NL	117	406	48	110	12	4	0	32	10	.271
1938	BROOKLYN	NL	82	253	45	69	10	8	2	23	6	.273
CAREER TOTALS			**1879**	**7161**	**1305**	**2299**	**394**	**157**	**128**	**1065**	**328**	**.321**

RAY DANDRIDGE

"There never was a smoother-functioning master at third base than Dandridge, and he can hit that apple too," Hall of Famer Cumberland Posey said.

Ray Dandridge and Judy Johnson were probably the two best third basemen in the history of Negro Leagues baseball. Dandridge was signed off a Buffalo, N.Y., sandlot in 1933 by the Detroit Stars of the Negro National League, at the age of 19. He was a contact hitter who could hit to all fields, and a fancy fielder at third base who could also play shortstop, second base, and the outfield.

Dandridge moved the following season to Newark, N.J., where he played for both the Dodgers and the Eagles. He also played for the New York Cubans and spent off seasons playing and managing in Cuba, Mexico, Puerto Rico, and Venezuela. In 1949 he was named player-manager of the New York Cubans. Former player Lenny Pearson recalled that as a manager, "He wanted perfection. Complete perfection. That's the way he played baseball."

The Cubans sold him mid-year to the Minneapolis Millers of the American Association, a farm club for the major league New York Giants. Though he was 36 years old, and told the Giants that he was considerably younger, he was selected as the league's Rookie of the Year. In 99 games for the Millers that year, he hit .362, with 144 hits including 33 extra base hits, and 64 runs batted in. The following season he was named league MVP after leading the Millers to the championship, hitting .311 with 195 hits, 80 RBI, and 106 runs scored. Such numbers presumably would have earned a player a promotion to the Giants, but his advanced age may have worked against him.

In 1951, the aging Dandridge briefly mentored 20-year-old teammate Willie Mays, who spent just 35 games at the highest level of the Giants organization before moving up. Dandridge and Mays sought relief from the summer heat at a cool movie theater one afternoon, and the usher came and told Mays his manager wanted him back at the hotel – the call to the big leagues had come. Dandridge, who hit .324 that season, his third straight in the high minors, was not included in the call-up.

RAYMOND EMMETT DANDRIDGE
NEGRO AND MEXICAN LEAGUES
1933 - 1948
FLASHY BUT SMOOTH THIRD BASEMAN, DEFENSIVELY,
A BRILLIANT FIELDER WITH POWERFUL ARM.
OFFENSIVELY, A SPRAY HITTER WITH OUTSTANDING
BAT CONTROL. PLAYED FOR DETROIT STARS, NEWARK
DODGERS, NEWARK EAGLES AND NEW YORK CUBANS
IN NEGRO LEAGUES AND FOR VERACRUZ AND MEXICO
CITY IN MEXICAN LEAGUES. AMERICAN ASSOCIATION
MVP IN 1950 WITH .311, 11 HOME RUNS AND
80 RBI'S PLAYING FOR MINNEAPOLIS MILLERS.

Elected To The Hall Of Fame: 1987.
Born: Aug. 31, 1913 in Richmond, Va.
Died: Feb. 12, 1994 in Palm Bay, Fla.
Height: 5-7. *Weight:* 170.
Threw: Right. *Batted:* Right.
Teams: Negro and Mexican Leagues 1933-1949.
Nashville 1933; Detroit 1933; Newark 1934-1944; Homestead 1937.

YEAR	TEAM	LEAGUE	G	AB	R	H	2B	3B	HR	RBI	SB	AVG
1933	NASHVILLE/DET.	NNL	—	48	4	9	0	2	0	—	0	.188
1934	NEWARK	INDP	—	119	20	48	8	3	0	—	0	.403
1935	NEWARK	NNL	—	112	11	29	7	3	0	—	5	.259
1936	NEWARK	NNL	—	48	7	11	0	0	1	—	4	.229
1937	HOMESTEAD/NWK.	NNL	—	94	16	35	3	0	0	—	1	.372
1938	NEWARK	NNL	—	97	21	33	1	0	0	—	0	.340
1942	NEWARK	NNL	—	81	8	15	1	1	0	—	0	.185
1944	NEWARK	NNL	—	92	15	34	8	2	1	—	3	.370
CAREER TOTALS			—	**691**	**102**	**214**	**28**	**11**	**2**	—	**13**	**.310**

GEORGE DAVIS

"**M**any ball players regard him as the best short-stop in the business; batting, base running and fielding considered," the *Sporting News Supplements* wrote in 1899.

When he was inducted into the Hall of Fame in 1998, George Davis was likely the best ballplayer you'd never heard of. But due to the dogged efforts of historians, he finally received his due, a century after he made a name for himself as one of the greatest shortstops in baseball history.

Davis was an outfielder and a solid, dependable hitter for the Cleveland Spiders from 1890-92. The following February, he was traded to the New York Giants for future Hall of Famer Buck Ewing. He began with the Giants as a third base-man, eventually transitioning to shortstop. In his initial season with the Giants, his batting average jumped 114 points to .355, kicking off a string of nine consecutive seasons in which he would hit at better than a .300 clip. The switch-hitting run producer was named manager of the Giants in 1895, and returned to that capacity in 1900-01.

He jumped to the Chicago White Sox in 1902, return-ing to the Giants in 1903, in violation of the peace treaty between the American and National Leagues. The AL and the White Sox kept him out of all but four Giants games that year, and the following season, he returned to Chicago.

A career highlight was his performance as a member of the White Sox "Hitless Wonders" team of 1906. They won the American League pennant while the crosstown Cubs set an all-time mark with a record of 116-36. If they were in the same league, the Cubs would have finished 22.5 games ahead of the White Sox, and few gave them any chance in the first intra-city World Series. The upstart Sox beat the Cubs in six games, with Davis batting .308 and driving in six runs.

He scouted and coached briefly after his playing days.

GEORGE STACEY DAVIS
CLEVELAND, N.L., 1890-1892
NEW YORK, N.L., 1893-1901, 1903
CHICAGO, A.L. 1902, 1904-1909
A SHORTSTOP OF SHINING PROMINENCE WHOSE OFFENSIVE PROWESS GREATLY SURPASSED HIS PEERS IN THE DEAD BALL ERA. A PROLIFIC SWITCH-HITTER, HIS IMPRESSIVE CAREER TOTALS INCLUDE A .295 BATTING AVERAGE, 2,660 HITS, 451 DOUBLES, 1437 RBI, 616 STOLEN BASES AND 163 TRIPLES. A RECORD AMONG SWITCH-HITTERS, HIT 300 OR BETTER NINE TIMES AND HIS 136 RBI IN 1897 LED THE NATIONAL LEAGUE. PACED THE 1906 CHICAGO "HITLESS WONDERS" TO A WORLD SERIES CHAMPIONSHIP. SERVED AS PLAYER-MANAGER FOR THE 1895, 1900 AND 1901 GIANTS.

Elected To The Hall Of Fame: 1998.

Born: Aug. 23, 1870 in Cohoes, N.Y.

Died: Oct. 17, 1940 in Philadelphia, Pa.

Height: 5-9. **Weight:** 180.

Threw: Right. **Batted:** Both.

Debut: Apr. 19,1890.

Final Game: Aug. 15, 1909.

Teams: Cleveland N.L. 1890-1892; New York N.L. 1893-1901, 1903; Chicago A.L. 1902, 1904-1909.

Postseason: N.L. Championship Series (1892); World Series Champion (1906).

YEAR	TEAM	LEAGUE	G	AB	R	H	2B	3B	HR	RBI	SB	AVG
1890	CLEVELAND	NL	136	526	98	139	22	9	6	73	22	.264
1891	CLEVELAND	NL	136	570	115	165	35	12	3	89	42	.289
1892	CLEVELAND	NL	144	597	95	144	27	12	5	82	36	.241
1893	NEW YORK	NL	133	549	112	195	22	27	11	119	37	.355
1894	NEW YORK	NL	124	486	125	171	27	19	9	93	42	.352
1895	NEW YORK	NL	110	430	108	146	36	9	5	101	48	.340
1896	NEW YORK	NL	124	494	98	158	25	12	5	99	48	.320
1897	NEW YORK	NL	131	521	112	184	31	10	10	135	65	.353
1898	NEW YORK	NL	121	486	80	149	20	5	2	86	26	.307
1899	NEW YORK	NL	109	419	69	141	22	5	1	59	35	.337
1900	NEW YORK	NL	114	426	69	136	20	4	3	61	29	.319
1901	NEW YORK	NI	130	491	69	148	26	7	7	65	27	.301
1902	CHICAGO	AL	132	485	76	145	27	7	3	93	31	.299
1903	NEW YORK	NL	4	15	2	4	0	0	0	1	0	.267
1904	CHICAGO	AL	152	563	75	142	27	15	1	69	32	.252
1905	CHICAGO	AL	151	550	74	153	29	1	1	55	31	.278
1906	CHICAGO	AL	133	484	63	134	26	6	0	80	27	.277
1907	CHICAGO	AL	132	466	59	111	16	2	1	52	15	.238
1908	CHICAGO	AL	128	419	41	91	14	1	0	26	22	.217
1909	CHICAGO	AL	28	68	5	9	1	0	0	2	4	.132
CAREER TOTALS			2372	9045	1545	2665	453	163	73	1440	619	.295

ANDRE DAWSON

Just one knee surgery can derail a baseball player from his major league career. Andre Dawson had 12 knee surgeries and finished his career in Cooperstown.

Dawson, known as the "Hawk", was only the second player in baseball history to reach 400 home runs and 300 stolen bases.

"If Andre didn't have bad knees, he would have finished with 600 home runs and 500 stolen bases," said former teammate Shawon Dunston.

The eight-time All-Star outfielder battled constant rehab and treatment on his knees to survive 21 seasons in the big leagues. Born on July 10, 1954 in Miami, Fla., Dawson was drafted by the Montreal Expos in 1975 and played only 186 minor league games before joining the parent club. In June of 1977, Future Hall of Fame manager Dick Williams made Dawson the Expos starting centerfielder. He responded by winning the National League Rookie of the Year Award.

With Montreal, Dawson won six straight Gold Glove Awards and twice finished second in MVP balloting (1981 and 1983). He led the league in hits and total bases in 1983. "I took pride in being a four- or five-tool player, and being consistent," said Dawson.

The artificial turf at Montreal's Olympic Stadium took a toll on Dawson's knees and his stolen base totals began to decline after 1982. By 1987, he left Montreal as a free agent and signed a blank contract with Chicago. He asked the Cubs to pay him what he was worth. In his first year with the new club, Dawson led the league in home runs with 49, RBI with 137, batted .287, won a Gold Glove Award and was named National League MVP despite the fact that the Cubs finished last in the National League East.

"I don't think I ever managed a greater player or a human being," said Don Zimmer, who managed Dawson in Chicago.

Dawson would go on to win his eighth Gold Glove Award in 1988 to add to his four Silver Slugger Awards.

Hawk

Elected To The Hall Of Fame: 2010.
Born: July 10, 1954 in Miami, Fla.
Height: 6-3. **Weight:** 180.
Threw: Right. **Batted:** Right.
Debut: Sept. 11, 1976.
Final Game: Sept. 29, 1996.
Teams: Montreal N.L. 1976-1986; Chicago N.L. 1987-1992; Boston A.L. 1993-1994; Florida A.L. 1995-1996.
Postseason: 2-Time Playoff Qualifier (1981, 1989).
Awards: 8-Time All-Star (1981-1983, 1987-1991); N.L. Rookie of the Year (1977); N.L. Most Valuable Player (1987).

YEAR	TEAM	LEAGUE	G	AB	R	H	2B	3B	HR	RBI	SB	AVG
1976	MONTREAL	NL	24	85	9	20	4	1	0	7	1	.235
1977	MONTREAL	NL	139	525	64	148	26	9	19	65	21	.282
1978	MONTREAL	NL	157	609	84	154	24	8	25	72	28	.253
1979	MONTREAL	NL	155	639	90	176	24	12	25	92	35	.275
1980	MONTREAL	NL	151	577	96	178	41	7	17	87	34	.308
1981	MONTREAL	NL	103	394	71	119	21	3	24	64	26	.302
1982	MONTREAL	NL	148	608	107	183	37	7	23	83	39	.301
1983	MONTREAL	NL	159	633	104	189	36	10	32	113	25	.299
1984	MONTREAL	NL	138	533	73	132	23	6	17	86	13	.248
1985	MONTREAL	NL	139	529	65	135	27	2	23	91	13	.255
1986	MONTREAL	NL	130	496	65	141	32	2	20	78	18	.284
1987	CHICAGO	NL	153	621	90	178	24	2	49	137	11	.287
1988	CHICAGO	NL	157	591	78	179	31	8	24	79	12	.303
1989	CHICAGO	NL	118	416	62	105	18	6	21	77	8	.252
1990	CHICAGO	NL	147	529	72	164	28	5	27	100	16	.310
1991	CHICAGO	NL	149	563	69	153	21	4	31	104	4	.272
1992	CHICAGO	NL	143	542	60	150	27	2	22	90	6	.277
1993	BOSTON	AL	121	461	44	126	29	1	13	67	2	.273
1994	BOSTON	AL	75	292	34	70	18	0	16	48	2	.240
1995	FLORIDA	NL	79	226	30	58	10	3	8	37	0	.257
1996	FLORIDA	NL	42	58	6	16	2	0	2	14	0	.276
CAREER TOTALS			2627	9927	1373	2774	503	98	438	1591	314	.279

LEON DAY

Monte Irvin recalled, "People don't know what a great pitcher Leon Day was. He was as good or better than Bob Gibson. He was a better fielder, a better hitter, could run like a deer. When he pitched against Satchel, Satchel didn't have an edge. You thought Don Newcombe could pitch. You should have seen Day! One of the best complete athletes I've ever seen."

The quiet, soft-spoken and modest right-hander had a deceptive fastball and a sharp curve. He was the opposite of Satchel Paige, but just as good.

Day pitched in six East-West All-Star Games, recording 14 strikeouts. In the 1942 East-West Game, with the West threatening in the seventh inning, the Eagles ace entered the game in relief and shut down the rally retiring the last seven batters of the game, five of them on strikes.

Although his Newark Eagles missed out on the Negro National League pennant that year, Day still had the opportunity to shine in the Negro World Series. On loan from the Eagles to the Homestead Grays, Day pitched a gem against the Monarchs, striking out 12 and besting Satchel Paige, a victory that was ultimately overturned when Kansas City protested after the game. The game was replayed without Day on the hill and the Monarchs won that contest and the series.

Following the season, Gray's owner Cumberland Posey, who also wrote a column for one of the leading black newspapers, the *Pittsburgh Courier*, named his annual All-American team for Negro baseball leagues. At the top of that list was Leon Day, whom Posey rated higher than Satchel Paige, "Leon was the best pitcher in Negro Baseball… despite the fact that he was used daily, either as a pitcher, outfielder, or infielder."

Around that time rumors swirled about the Pittsburgh Pirates possibly giving tryouts to black ballplayers. At the time, the *Pittsburgh Courier* speculated who might be given such tryouts: "Leon Day is the type of hurler the Pirates need . . . He has all the qualities necessary for the majors. We believe he could do much better than the Pirates' leading hurler, Rip Sewell." Although the tryouts never took place, this was high praise nonetheless for the talented right-hander.

LEON DAY
NEGRO LEAGUES 1934-1949

USED DECEPTIVE, NO-WIND UP, SHORT-ARM DELIVERY TO COMPILE IMPRESSIVE SINGLE-SEASON AND CAREER STATISTICS DURING 10 YEARS IN NEGRO LEAGUES. ALSO PLAYED BALL IN PUERTO RICO, CUBA, VENEZUELA, MEXICO AND CANADA. SET NEGRO NATIONAL LEAGUE RECORD IN 1942 WITH 18 STRIKEOUTS IN GAME. HURLED NO-HITTER ON OPENING DAY 1946 FOR NEWARK EAGLES VS. PHILADELPHIA STARS. PITCHED IN RECORD 7 NEGRO LEAGUE ALL-STAR GAMES.

Elected To The Hall Of Fame: 1995.
Born: Oct. 30, 1916 in Alexandria, Va.
Died: March 14, 1995 in Baltimore, Md.
Height: 5-9. **Weight:** 170.
Threw: Right. **Batted:** Right.
Teams: Negro Leagues 1934-1946. Baltimore 1934; Brooklyn 1935; Newark 1936-1939, 1941-1943, 1946; Homestead 1937; Philadelphia 1943.

YEAR	TEAM	LEAGUE	G	W	L	SV	SH	IP	H	BB	SO	RAVG
1934	BALTIMORE	NNL	—	0	0	—	0	1.3	8	1	1	47.25
1935	BROOKLYN	NNL	—	7	3	—	0	102.7	89	23	39	4.03
1936	NEWARK	NNL	—	1	2	—	0	20.7	27	8	14	7.40
1937	NEWARK/H'STEAD	NNL	—	5	0	—	0	46.3	43	5	27	4.47
1938	NEWARK	NNL	—	0	2	—	0	6	9	0	0	9.00
1939	NEWARK	NNL	—	2	1	—	0	34	36	19	9	6.62
1941	NEWARK	NNL	—	1	1	—	0	13.3	16	6	4	7.42
1942	NEWARK	NNL	—	6	3	—	1	68	31	16	59	2.25
1943	NEWARK	NNL	—	2	2	—	0	28.7	33	12	11	7.53
1946	NEWARK	NNL	—	9	2	—	2	106	84	20	73	3.23
CAREER TOTALS			**—**	**33**	**16**	**—**	**3**	**427**	**376**	**110**	**237**	**4.51**

DIZZY DEAN

Every ballplayer can remember the passion they had for the game as a kid. Dizzy Dean kept that passion and excitement all the way through his major league career. "When ole Diz was out there pitching it was more than just another ballgame," said teammate Pepper Martin. "It was a regular three-ring circus and everybody was wide awake and enjoying being alive."

Born Jay Hanna Dean, he attended public school only through second grade. His colorful personality and eccentric behavior earned him the nickname "Dizzy."

"Nobody ever taught him baseball and he never had to learn," said sportswriter Red Smith. "He was just doing what came naturally when a scout named Don Curtis discovered him on a Texas sandlot and gave him his first contract."

Dean made his professional debut in 1930 and worked his way up to the major leagues that same year, throwing a complete game three-hitter for a win with the Cardinals. Dean became a regular starter for St. Louis in 1932, leading the league in shutouts and innings pitched. It was also the first of four straight seasons he led the league in strikeouts. In 1934, Dean went 30-7, leading the league in wins with a 2.66 ERA to win the National League MVP Award. Dean was thought of as a leader of the "Gashouse Gang," a nickname given to the '34 Cardinals.

Along with his younger brother Paul, also a pitcher on the team and often referred to as "Daffy", the Cardinals were hardworking, gritty players during the Great Depression. The team captured the 1934 National League pennant and beat the Tigers in the World Series. Dean won 28 and 24 games in 1935 and 1936 respectively, finishing second in MVP voting in both seasons. In 1937, Dean suffered an injury after being hit in the toe by a line drive. Trying to return from the injury too quickly, Dean hurt his arm and largely lost his effectiveness.

Traded to the Cubs in 1938, Dean spent four seasons in Chicago, including appearing in the 1938 World Series, which the Cubs lost to the Yankees. He appeared again for the St. Louis Browns in 1947 as a promotional stunt, pitching just four innings before retiring.

Elected To The Hall Of Fame: 1953.
Born: Jan. 16, 1910 in Lucas, Ark.
Died: July 17, 1974 in Reno, Nev.
Height: 6-2. **Weight:** 182.
Threw: Right. **Batted:** Right.
Debut: Sept. 28, 1930.
Final Game: Sept. 28, 1947.
Teams: St. Louis N.L. 1930, 1932-1937; Chicago N.L. 1938-1941; St. Louis A.L. 1947.
Postseason: World Series Champion (1934); Two N.L. Pennants (1934, 1938).
Awards: 4-Time All-Star (1934-1937); N.L. Most Valuable Player (1934).

YEAR	TEAM	LEAGUE	G	W	L	SV	SH	IP	H	BB	SO	ERA
1930	ST. LOUIS	NL	1	1	0	0	0	9	3	3	5	1.00
1932	ST. LOUIS	NL	46	18	15	2	4	286	280	102	191	3.30
1933	ST. LOUIS	NL	48	20	18	4	3	293	279	64	199	3.04
1934	ST. LOUIS	NL	50	30	7	7	7	311.7	288	75	195	2.66
1935	ST. LOUIS	NL	50	28	12	5	3	325.3	324	77	190	3.04
1936	ST. LOUIS	NL	51	24	13	11	2	315	310	53	195	3.17
1937	ST. LOUIS	NL	27	13	10	1	4	197.3	200	33	120	2.69
1938	CHICAGO	NL	13	7	1	0	1	74.7	63	8	22	1.81
1939	CHICAGO	NL	19	6	4	0	2	96.3	98	17	27	3.36
1940	CHICAGO	NL	10	3	3	0	0	54	68	20	18	5.17
1941	CHICAGO	NL	1	0	0	0	0	1	3	0	1	18.00
1947	ST. LOUIS	AL	1	0	0	0	0	4	3	1	0	0.00
CAREER TOTALS			**317**	**150**	**83**	**30**	**26**	**1967.1**	**1919**	**453**	**1163**	**3.02**

ED DELAHANTY

ED DELAHANTY

ONE OF THE GAME'S GREATEST SLUGGERS. LED NATIONAL LEAGUE HITTERS IN 1899 WITH AN AVERAGE OF .408 FOR PHILADELPHIA; AMERICAN LEAGUE BATTERS IN 1902 WITH A MARK OF .376 FOR WASHINGTON. MADE 6 HITS IN 6 TIMES AT BAT TWICE DURING CAREER AND ONCE HIT 4 HOME RUNS IN A GAME.

Arguably one of the best players of the 19th Century, Ed Delahanty was the first player in National League history to hit over .400 three times. The eldest of five brothers to play in the big leagues, Big Ed was a five-tool player- he could hit for power and average, was a terrific fielder with a strong arm and was quick on the basepaths leading the league in stolen bases with 58 in 1898.

The Sporting Life, the prominent sports publication of the 19th Century said, "Delahanty is an awfully even, well balanced player all around . . . You look at his batting and say well, that chap is valuable if he couldn't catch the measles, and then you look at his fielding and conclude that it wouldn't pay to let him go if he couldn't hit a bat bag."

Not only could the big left fielder slug doubles and home runs, but he could hit the ball all over the field depending on the situation. If the outfielders played deep he would drop one in front of them, at normal depth he would slug away and try to put one over their heads. Reds hurler Philip "Red" Ehret said Delahanty was "The hardest man in the league for pitchers to puzzle" and Sam Crawford called him "The best right-handed hitter I ever saw."

In his 16 years in the big leagues, Delahanty led the league in home runs twice, RBI three times, doubles five times, and hits and triples once each. Twice, Big Ed went 6 for 6 in a game and he once went 9 for 9 in a doubleheader. Twenty-year veteran backstop Jack O'Connor recalled, "If Del had a weakness at the bat, I never could discover it."

Delahanty was one of baseball's first superstars. Conscious of his star power, Delahanty jumped teams several times in search of a bigger pay day; first in 1890 to the Player's League and then again in 1902 to the American League. An agreement between the two leagues in 1903 prevented Delahanty from jumping to the National League's New York Giants. At age 35, Delahanty's life came to a tragic end when he exited a train and fell off the International Railway Bridge that crossed over Niagara Falls.

Years after his death, the *Sporting News* wrote of Delahanty: "He was among the greatest batters the game ever produced. Great batters, like poets, are born, not made."

Big Ed

Elected To The Hall Of Fame: *1945.*
Born: *Oct. 30, 1867 in Cleveland, Ohio.*
Died: *July 2, 1903 in Niagara Falls, Ont., Canada.*
Height: *6-1.* **Weight:** *170.*
Threw: *Right.* **Batted:** *Right.*
Debut: *May 22, 1888.*
Final Game: *June 25, 1903.*
Teams: *Philadelphia N.L. 1888-1889, 1891-1901; Cleveland, Player's League 1890; Washington A.L. 1902-1903.*

YEAR	TEAM	LEAGUE	G	AB	R	H	2B	3B	HR	RBI	SB	AVG
1888	PHILADELPHIA	NL	74	290	40	66	12	2	1	31	38	.228
1889	PHILADELPHIA	NL	56	246	37	72	13	3	0	27	19	.293
1890	CLEVELAND	PL	115	517	107	153	26	13	3	64	25	.296
1891	PHILADELPHIA	NL	128	543	92	132	19	9	5	86	25	.243
1892	PHILADELPHIA	NL	123	477	79	146	30	21	6	91	29	.306
1893	PHILADELPHIA	NL	132	595	145	219	35	18	19	146	37	.368
1894	PHILADELPHIA	NL	116	495	148	200	39	19	4	133	21	.404
1895	PHILADELPHIA	NL	116	480	149	194	49	10	11	106	46	.404
1896	PHILADELPHIA	NL	123	499	131	198	44	17	13	126	37	.397
1897	PHILADELPHIA	NL	129	530	109	200	40	15	5	96	26	.377
1898	PHILADELPHIA	NL	144	548	115	183	36	9	4	92	58	.334
1899	PHILADELPHIA	NL	146	581	135	238	55	9	9	137	30	.410
1900	PHILADELPHIA	NL	131	539	82	174	32	10	2	109	16	.323
1901	PHILADELPHIA	NL	139	542	106	192	38	16	8	108	29	.354
1902	WASHINGTON	AL	123	473	103	178	43	14	10	93	16	.376
1903	WASHINGTON	AL	42	156	22	52	11	1	1	21	3	.333
CAREER TOTALS			**1837**	**7511**	**1600**	**2597**	**522**	**186**	**101**	**1466**	**455**	**.346**

D

BILL DICKEY

Hall of Famer Bob Feller said, "Bill Dickey is the best (catcher) I ever saw… He was as good as anyone behind the plate, and better with the bat. I believe I could have won 35 games if Bill Dickey was my catcher."

In 1928, Bill Dickey was claimed on waivers from the Class D Jackson, Miss., team. Yankee scout Johnny Nee thought so highly of Dickey that he told Yankee GM Ed Barrow "I will quit scouting if this boy does not make good." Needless to say, the Yankees scooped him up and Nee didn't need to quit scouting.

Dickey made his big league debut that year and became the Yankees regular backstop the following season. Playing alongside Babe Ruth, Dickey tried to model his game on the Bambino's. Manager Miller Huggins told Dickey "We pay one player here for hitting home runs and that's Babe Ruth. So choke up and drill the ball. That way, you'll be around here longer." Dickey took his skipper's advice and started driving the ball all over the field. He soon became a force in the Bronx Bombers' line-up.

An 11-time All-Star and seven-time World Series champion, Dickey reached double digits in home runs nine times, the 100 RBI mark four times, and batted better than .300 11 times.

And his defense, arm and game-calling ability were spectacular too. Yankee hurler Charlie Devens recalled "I was lucky to work with Hall of Fame catcher Bill Dickey, who was always one pitch ahead of the batters. He not only called a great game, but had the best arm I'd ever seen."

On the field Dickey was all business but off the field he was mild-mannered and well liked by all. As his career wound down he mentored young Yankee backstops. Yogi Berra said "I owe everything I did in baseball to Bill Dickey. He was a great man," and Elston Howard recalled "You've got to have Bill work with you to understand how much he can help you . . . The year I came to the Yankees from Toronto, I wasn't as good as a lot of semipro catchers. Bill took me over and he talked to me. Then he worked with me. We'd go off in a corner and practice. Without Bill, I'm nobody. Nobody at all. He made me a catcher. Now when I start to slip and get careless, there's old Bill to give me a hand."

WILLIAM MALCOLM DICKEY
NEW YORK A.L. 1928-1946

SET RECORD BY CATCHING 100 OR MORE
GAMES 13 SUCCESSIVE SEASONS. PLAYED
WITH YANKEES, CHAMPIONS OF 1932-36-37-
38-39-41-42-43, WHEN CLUB WON 7 WORLD
SERIES TITLES. HOLDS NUMEROUS WORLD
SERIES RECORDS FOR CATCHERS, INCLUDING
MOST GAMES, 38. PLAYED ON 8 ALL-STAR
TEAMS FROM 1932 TO 1946. LIFETIME
BATTING AVERAGE OF .313 IN 1789 GAMES.

Elected To The Hall Of Fame: *1954.*
Born: *June 6, 1907 in Bastrop, La.*
Died: *Nov. 12, 1993 in Little Rock, Ark.*
Height: *6-1.* **Weight:** *185.*
Threw: *Right.* **Batted:** *Left.*
Debut: *Aug. 15, 1928.*
Final Game: *Sept. 8, 1946.*
Teams: *New York A.L. 1928-1943, 1946.*
Postseason: *7-Time World Series Champion (1932, 1936-1939, 1941,1943); 8 A.L. Pennants (1932, 1936-1939, 1941-1943).*
Awards: *11-Time All-Star (1933-1934, 1936-1943, 1946).*

YEAR	TEAM	LEAGUE	G	AB	R	H	2B	3B	HR	RBI	SB	AVG
1928	NEW YORK	AL	10	15	1	3	1	1	0	2	0	.200
1929	NEW YORK	AL	130	447	60	145	30	6	10	65	4	.324
1930	NEW YORK	AL	109	366	55	124	25	7	5	65	7	.339
1931	NEW YORK	AL	130	477	65	156	17	10	6	78	2	.327
1932	NEW YORK	AL	108	423	66	131	20	4	15	84	2	.310
1933	NEW YORK	AL	130	478	58	152	24	8	14	97	3	.318
1934	NEW YORK	AL	104	395	56	127	24	4	12	72	0	.322
1935	NEW YORK	AL	120	448	54	125	26	6	14	81	1	.279
1936	NEW YORK	AL	112	423	99	153	26	8	22	107	0	.362
1937	NEW YORK	AL	140	530	87	176	35	2	29	133	3	.332
1938	NEW YORK	AL	132	454	84	142	27	4	27	115	3	.313
1939	NEW YORK	AL	128	480	98	145	23	3	24	105	5	.302
1940	NEW YORK	AL	106	372	45	92	11	1	9	54	0	.247
1941	NEW YORK	AL	109	348	35	99	15	5	7	71	2	.284
1942	NEW YORK	AL	82	268	28	79	13	1	2	37	2	.295
1943	NEW YORK	AL	85	242	29	85	18	2	4	33	2	.351
1946	NEW YORK	AL	54	134	10	35	8	0	2	10	0	.261
CAREER TOTALS			**1789**	**6300**	**930**	**1969**	**343**	**72**	**202**	**1209**	**36**	**.313**

MARTÍN DIHIGO

"He was the best ballplayer of all time, black or white," Hall of Famer Buck Leonard said.

Martín Dihigo's nickname said it all, in both English and his native Spanish. El Maestro. The Cuban-born Dihigo (pronounced dee-EE-go) debuted with the Cuban Stars of the Eastern Colored League in 1923 as an 18-year-old, light-hitting second baseman. Tall and thin, Dihigo evoked comparisons with Joe DiMaggio for the style and grace he displayed on the ballfield.

Playing year-round, summers in the U.S. and winters in the Caribbean, Dihigo developed into a feared fastball hitter, but one with a weakness for curveballs. "Don't throw me any more fastballs," he soon told his batting practice pitcher. "I can hit them like anything. Throw me curves." With the determination that marked his entire career, Dihigo made himself into one of the game's premier curveball hitters.

As he filled out, his natural athletic ability became increasingly obvious. Dihigo began playing more positions on the field. He eased over to shortstop, where his quickness made him a natural. With his cannon of a right arm, El Maestro also excelled in the outfield, where he delighted in throwing out players at the plate. He outperformed most third basemen, but he truly excelled as a pitcher. On the mound, Dihigo possessed both speed and control. In 1938, he threw the first no-hitter in the history of the Mexican League, hit over .300, and led the league in strikeouts.

The easygoing Dihigo became popular with his teammates, at least in part because of his fluent English. He was knowledgeable and willingly shared his vast store of baseball knowledge. He was soon called upon to be a player-manager; his feel for the game and understanding of players made him a star in that venue as well.

In 1943, at the age of 38, Dihigo managed a team in the Dominican Republic that featured Johnny Mize, then a star for the New York Giants. Evaluating Dihigo, even at that age, Mize called him the greatest player he had ever seen. Finally, at 41, Dihigo hung up his spikes and retired to his native Cuba. By then, he had earned another nickname: El Inmortal—the Immortal One.

El Maestro

Elected To The Hall Of Fame: 1977.
Born: May 25, 1905 in Matanzas, Cuba.
Died: May 20, 1971 in Cienfuegos, Cuba.
Height: 6-2. **Weight:** 190.
Threw: Right. **Batted:** Right.
Teams: Negro Leagues 1923-1945. Cuban Stars East 1923-1927, 1930; Homestead 1928; Hilldale 1929-1931; New York 1935; New York Cubans 1936, 1945.

YEAR	TEAM	LEAGUE	G	AB	R	H	2B	3B	HR	RBI	SB	AVG
1923	CUBAN EAST STARS	ECOL	—	59	9	14	2	1	0	—	0	.237
1924	CUBAN EAST STARS	ECOL	—	189	30	46	7	3	2	—	3	.243
1925	CUBAN EAST STARS	ECOL	—	88	11	31	5	1	1	—	2	.352
1926	CUBAN EAST STARS	ECOL	—	111	29	41	9	0	9	—	6	.369
1927	CUBAN EAST STARS	ECOL	—	152	39	54	8	1	10	—	2	.355
1928	HOMESTEAD	ECOL	—	69	15	23	1	1	4	—	0	.333
1929	HILLDALE	ANL	—	194	48	62	6	3	11	—	7	.320
1930	HILLDALE/CUBAN E.S.	INDP	—	57	13	22	4	1	4	—	1	.386
1931	HILLDALE	INDP	—	145	27	35	0	3	2	—	0	.241
1935	NEW YORK	NNL	—	160	30	41	9	1	7	—	8	.256
1936	N.Y. CUBANS	NNL	—	97	23	32	6	1	6	—	2	.330
1945	N.Y. CUBANS	NNL	—	33	5	11	1	1	1	—	1	.333
CAREER TOTALS			**—**	**1354**	**279**	**412**	**58**	**17**	**57**	**—**	**32**	**.304**

JOE DIMAGGIO

Joe DiMaggio was a cultural icon. He married Hollywood starlets Marilyn Monroe and Dorothy Arnold. He was immortalized in Simon and Garfunkel's hit song "Mrs. Robinson." To a generation he was the face of Mr. Coffee – and he was regarded as one of the greatest players who ever played the game.

Hall of Fame teammate Phil Rizzuto recalled: "There was an aura about him. He walked like no one else walked. He did things so easily. He was immaculate in everything he did. Kings of State wanted to meet him and be with him. He carried himself so well. He could fit in any place in the world."

On the ball field, Joe DiMaggio could do it all. He could hit for average and power and patrolled centerfield in Yankee Stadium so gracefully that he earned the nickname "The Yankee Clipper," a reference to the great sailing ship. Hall of Famer owner and manager Connie Mack called him "the best player that ever lived," and longtime teammate Yogi Berra said "I wish everybody had the drive he had. He never did anything wrong on the field."

The son of a San Francisco fisherman, Joe was the eighth of nine children and his brothers Vince and Dom were also major league All-Stars. Of his on-field accomplishments, perhaps none are more notable than his 56-game hitting streak in 1941, a streak many pundits say will never be broken. However, that streak was not the longest of his professional career. In 1933, as a member of the San Francisco Seals of the Pacific Coast League, DiMaggio put together a 61-game hitting streak.

By the 1970's broadcasters and writers began simply to call him "Joe D." and because he was so ingrained in American culture, everyone knew who they were talking about. His rival Ted Williams recalled, "DiMaggio was the greatest all-around player I ever saw. His career cannot be summed up in numbers and awards. It might sound corny, but he had a profound and lasting impact on the country."

His successor in center field at Yankee Stadium, Mickey Mantle, described how he viewed the Yankee Clipper: "Heroes are people who are all good with no bad in them. That's the way I always saw Joe DiMaggio. He was beyond question one of the greatest players of the century."

The Yankee Clipper

Elected To The Hall Of Fame: *1955.*
Born: *Nov. 25, 1914 in Martinez, Calif.*
Died: *Mar. 8, 1999 in Hollywood, Fla.*
Height: *6-2.* **Weight:** *193.*
Threw: *Right.* **Batted:** *Right.*
Debut: *May 3, 1936.*
Final Game: *Sept. 30, 1951.*
Teams: *New York A.L. 1936-1942, 1946-1951.*
Postseason: *9-Time World Series Champion (1936-1939, 1941, 1947, 1949-1951); 10 A.L. Pennants (1936-1939, 1941-1942, 1947, 1949-1951).*
Awards: *13-Time All-Star (1936-1942, 1946-1951); 3-Time A.L. Most Valuable Player (1939, 1941, 1947).*

YEAR	TEAM	LEAGUE	G	AB	R	H	2B	3B	HR	RBI	SB	AVG
1936	NEW YORK	AL	138	637	132	206	44	15	29	125	4	.323
1937	NEW YORK	AL	151	621	151	215	35	15	46	167	3	.346
1938	NEW YORK	AL	145	599	129	194	32	13	32	140	6	.324
1939	NEW YORK	AL	120	462	108	176	32	6	30	126	3	.381
1940	NEW YORK	AL	132	508	93	179	28	9	31	133	1	.352
1941	NEW YORK	AL	139	541	122	193	43	11	30	125	4	.357
1942	NEW YORK	AL	154	610	123	186	29	13	21	114	4	.305
1946	NEW YORK	AL	132	503	81	146	20	8	25	95	1	.290
1947	NEW YORK	AL	141	534	97	168	31	10	20	97	3	.315
1948	NEW YORK	AL	153	594	110	190	26	11	39	155	1	.320
1949	NEW YORK	AL	76	272	58	94	14	6	14	67	0	.346
1950	NEW YORK	AL	139	525	114	158	33	10	32	122	0	.301
1951	NEW YORK	AL	116	415	72	109	22	4	12	71	0	.263
CAREER TOTALS			**1736**	**6821**	**1390**	**2214**	**389**	**131**	**361**	**1537**	**30**	**.325**

LARRY DOBY

Perhaps no one is more remembered for being second than Larry Doby. He was the second African-American to play Major League Baseball in the modern era after Jackie Robinson. He was the second African-American manager of a major league club after Frank Robinson. He may have been second in those two regards, but Larry Doby was so much more.

Larry Doby began his baseball career as a star infielder for the Newark Eagles of the Negro National League and was also the first African-American player to play professional basketball in the ABL, a precursor to the NBA. After taking time out from professional sports to serve in the United States Navy during WWII, Doby returned to the NNL and led the Eagles to the Negro Leagues championship in 1946.

In 1947, only a few months after Jackie Robinson's major league debut, Cleveland Indians owner Bill Veeck signed Doby and he became the first African-American player in the American League. Doby suffered the same indignities as Jackie Robinson, but his struggles did not get the media attention Robinson's received. Whether it was being forced to stay in separate hotels or eat in separate restaurants on the road, or not being accepted by some of his teammates, Doby persevered. Teammate Mel Harder recalled "it may have (bothered Doby), but he never complained to the players, when he joined, naturally it was a tough time. But after he was with us a while he got along pretty good."

His first major league manager Lou Boudreau recalled: "Larry proved to them that he was a major leaguer in handling himself in more ways than one – on the field and off the field." In 1948, his sophomore campaign in the big leagues, Doby became the first African American to hit a home run in World Series play. On April 12, 1950, Doby hit the first home run of the decade in the major leagues. In 1952, the slugging centerfielder became the first African-American to lead either league in home runs.

During his time in the major leagues, Doby was a seven-time All-Star and put together five 100-RBI and eight 20-home run seasons. In 1978, the same man who gave him his shot as a player in the major leagues in 1947, Bill Veeck, hired him to manage his Chicago White Sox.

LAWRENCE EUGENE DOBY
CLEVELAND, A.L. 1947-55, 1958
CHICAGO, A.L. 1956-57, 1959
DETROIT, A.L., 1959
EXCEPTIONAL ATHLETIC PROWESS AND A STAUNCH CONSTITUTION LED TO A SUCCESSFUL PLAYING CAREER AFTER INTEGRATING THE AMERICAN LEAGUE IN 1947. A SEVEN-TIME ALL-STAR WHO BATTED .283 WITH 253 HOME RUNS AND 970 RBI IN 13 MAJOR LEAGUE SEASONS. THE POWER-HITTING CENTER FIELDER PACED THE A.L. IN HOME RUNS TWICE AND COLLECTED 100 RBI FIVE TIMES, WHILE LEADING THE INDIANS TO PENNANTS IN 1948 AND 1954. APPOINTED MANAGER OF THE WHITE SOX IN 1978. THE SECOND AFRICAN-AMERICAN TO LEAD A MAJOR LEAGUE CLUB. PLAYED FOUR SEASONS WITH NEWARK IN THE NEGRO NATIONAL LEAGUE. FOLLOWING PLAYER CAREER WORKED AS A SCOUT AND MAJOR LEAGUE BASEBALL EXECUTIVE.

Elected To The Hall Of Fame: *1998.*
Born: *Dec.13, 1923 in Camden, S.C.*
Died: *June 18, 2003 in Montclair, N.J.*
Height: *6-1.* **Weight:** *180.*
Threw: *Right.* **Batted:** *Left.*
Debut: *July 5, 1947.*
Final Game: *July 26, 1959.*
Teams: *Cleveland A.L. 1947-1955, 1958;*
Chicago A.L. 1956-1957, 1959; Detroit A.L. 1959.
Postseason: *World Series Champion (1948); 2*
A.L. Pennants (1948, 1954).
Awards: *7-Time All-Star (1949-1955).*

YEAR	TEAM	LEAGUE	G	AB	R	H	2B	3B	HR	RBI	SB	AVG
1947	CLEVELAND	AL	29	32	3	5	1	0	0	2	0	.156
1948	CLEVELAND	AL	121	439	83	132	23	9	14	66	9	.301
1949	CLEVELAND	AL	147	547	106	153	25	3	24	85	10	.280
1950	CLEVELAND	AL	142	503	110	164	25	5	25	102	8	.326
1951	CLEVELAND	AL	134	447	84	132	27	5	20	69	4	.295
1952	CLEVELAND	AL	140	519	104	143	26	8	32	104	5	.276
1953	CLEVELAND	AL	149	513	92	135	18	5	29	102	3	.263
1954	CLEVELAND	AL	153	577	94	157	18	4	32	126	3	.272
1955	CLEVELAND	AL	131	491	91	143	17	5	26	75	2	.291
1956	CHICAGO	AL	140	504	89	135	22	3	24	102	0	.268
1957	CHICAGO	AL	119	416	57	120	27	2	14	79	2	.288
1958	CLEVELAND	AL	89	247	41	70	10	1	13	45	0	.283
1959	DETROIT/CHICAGO	AL	39	113	6	26	4	2	0	13	1	.230
CAREER TOTALS			**1533**	**5348**	**960**	**1515**	**243**	**52**	**253**	**970**	**47**	**.283**

BOBBY DOERR

"Bobby Doerr was an absolutely outstanding player. He was an exceptional second baseman, he rarely booted ground balls, he was a good clutch hitter and a good all-around hitter who could bat third, fourth, or fifth in a lineup of good hitters. We never had a captain, but he was the silent captain of the team," said Ted Williams.

Bobby Doerr was the second baseman for the Boston Red Sox from 1937-1951. He and teammate Ted Williams were both scouted on the same trip by Eddie Collins from the 1936 San Diego Padres of the Pacific Coast League.

Named to nine all-star teams, Doerr was steady, consistent, and showed leadership on and off the field. Defensively, he led the AL in fielding percentage four times and in double plays five times. He once held the AL record for most consecutive chances at second base without an error: 414. "I never saw him misplay a ball, and he had the best backhand of any second baseman I ever saw," said Red Sox teammate Johnny Pesky.

Offensively, Doerr hit .288 for his career, with 2,042 hits, 381 doubles, 89 triples, and 223 home runs, which at the time of his retirement, was the third-highest total ever amassed by a second baseman. He racked up 1,094 runs scored and 1,247 runs batted in.

He missed the 1945 season in order to serve in the military, but returned to lead the team to the 1946 pennant with 18 home runs and 116 runs batted in. He hit .409 and drove in three more runs in the World Series loss to the St. Louis Cardinals.

He retired in his early thirties due to back problems. He scouted for the Red Sox from 1957-66, and coached there from 1967-69. He served as the hitting coach for the Toronto Blue Jays from 1977-81. In 1969, Red Sox fans voted him the team's all-time best second baseman. He was elected to the Hall of Fame in 1986.

An all-around gentleman with a great reputation in the game, New York Yankees rival Tommy Henrich said: "Bobby Doerr is one of the very few who played the game hard and retired with no enemies."

Elected To The Hall Of Fame: *1986.*
Born: *Apr. 7, 1918 in Los Angeles, Calif.*
Height: *5-11.* **Weight:** *175.*
Threw: *Right.* **Batted:** *Right.*
Debut: *Apr. 20, 1937.*
Final Game: *Sept. 7, 1951.*
Teams: *Boston A.L. 1937-1944, 1946-1951.*
Postseason: *A.L. Pennant (1946).*
Awards: *9-Time All-Star (1941-1944, 1946-1948, 1950-1951).*

YEAR	TEAM	LEAGUE	G	AB	R	H	2B	3B	HR	RBI	SB	AVG
1937	BOSTON	AL	55	147	22	33	5	1	2	14	2	.224
1938	BOSTON	AL	145	509	70	147	26	7	5	80	5	.289
1939	BOSTON	AL	127	525	75	167	28	2	12	73	1	.318
1940	BOSTON	AL	151	595	87	173	37	10	22	105	10	.291
1941	BOSTON	AL	132	500	74	141	28	4	16	93	1	.282
1942	BOSTON	AL	144	545	71	158	35	5	15	102	4	.290
1943	BOSTON	AL	155	604	78	163	32	3	16	75	8	.270
1944	BOSTON	AL	125	468	95	152	30	10	15	81	5	.325
1946	BOSTON	AL	151	583	95	158	34	9	18	116	5	.271
1947	BOSTON	AL	146	561	79	145	23	10	17	95	3	.258
1948	BOSTON	AL	140	527	94	150	23	6	27	111	3	.285
1949	BOSTON	AL	139	541	91	167	30	9	18	109	2	.309
1950	BOSTON	AL	149	586	103	172	29	11	27	120	3	.294
1951	BOSTON	AL	106	402	60	116	21	2	13	73	2	.289
CAREER TOTALS			1865	7093	1094	2042	381	89	223	1247	54	.288

DON DRYSDALE

Pirates shortstop Dick Groat once said, "Batting against Don Drysdale is the same as making a date with a dentist." Drysdale was a tough pitcher, who along with Sandy Koufax, formed the most dominant pitching tandem of the 1960s.

The hard throwing righthander had a reputation for owning the plate. Sportswriter Dave Anderson wrote: "Home plate is 17 inches wide. But to Don Drysdale it is divided into three parts – the inside four inches, the middle nine inches and the outside four inches. To him only the middle part belongs to the hitter; the inside and the outside part belong to the pitcher."

Drysdale used a sidearm fastball and brushback pitches to intimidate hitters, and was not afraid to throw inside, as Orlando Cepeda described: "The trick against Drysdale is to hit him before he hits you." Upon his retirement from the game, Drysdale's 154 batters hit by a pitch were a modern National League record. As he put it, "My own little rule was two for one – if one of my teammates got knocked down, then I knocked down two on the other team."

Although he had better peripheral stats in other seasons, Drysdale took home the Cy Young Award in 1962 when he won 25 games, at a time when there was only one Award given in the major leagues. In 1968, he pitched 58 straight scoreless innings, a record that would stand for 20 years. During that stretch of consecutive scoreless innings was a record six straight shutouts.

A terrific all around athlete, Drysdale could swing the bat as well as throw the ball. In his career he hit 29 home runs, including seven in each of the 1958 and 1965 seasons, a record for home runs in a season by a National League hurler. In his major league career he batted as high as sixth in the lineup and was used as a pinch-hitter from time to time. He was the only .300 hitter in the lineup for the 1965 World Series champion Dodgers.

Drysdale's 14-year career ended in 1969 at the age of 33. After his playing days, he stayed involved in the game as a broadcaster. When his wife, Ann Meyers, was elected to the Basketball Hall of Fame in 1993, it marked the only marriage between Hall of Famers from any of the four major American sports.

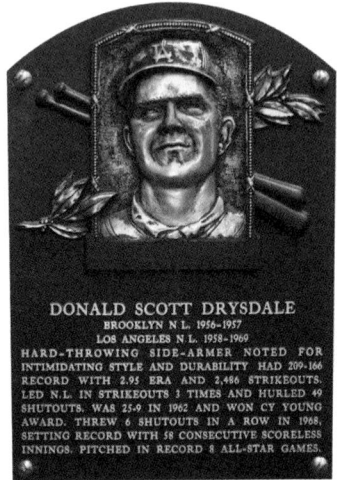

DONALD SCOTT DRYSDALE
BROOKLYN N L. 1956-1957
LOS ANGELES N L. 1958-1969
HARD-THROWING SIDE-ARMER NOTED FOR INTIMIDATING STYLE AND DURABILITY HAD 209-166 RECORD WITH 2.95 ERA AND 2,486 STRIKEOUTS. LED N.L. IN STRIKEOUTS 3 TIMES AND HURLED 49 SHUTOUTS. WAS 25-9 IN 1962 AND WON CY YOUNG AWARD. THREW 6 SHUTOUTS IN A ROW IN 1968, SETTING RECORD WITH 58 CONSECUTIVE SCORELESS INNINGS. PITCHED IN RECORD 8 ALL-STAR GAMES.

Elected To The Hall Of Fame: 1984.
Born: July 23, 1936 in Van Nuys, Calif.
Died: July 3, 1993 in Montreal, Quebec, Canada.
Height: 6-5. **Weight:** 190.
Threw: Right. **Batted:** Right.
Debut: Apr. 17, 1956.
Final Game: Aug. 5, 1969.
Teams: N.L. Brooklyn 1956-1957; N.L. Los Angeles 1958-1969.
Postseason: 3-Time World Series Champion (1959, 1963,1965); 5 N.L. Pennants (1956, 1959, 1963, 1965-1966).
Awards: 9-Time All-Star (1959, 1961-1965, 1967-68); Cy Young (1962).

YEAR	TEAM	LEAGUE	G	W	L	SV	SH	IP	H	BB	SO	ERA
1956	BROOKLYN	NL	25	5	5	0	0	99	95	31	55	2.64
1957	BROOKLYN	NL	34	17	9	0	4	221	197	61	148	2.69
1958	LOS ANGELES	NL	44	12	13	0	1	211.7	214	72	131	4.17
1959	LOS ANGELES	NL	44	17	13	2	4	270.7	237	93	242	3.46
1960	LOS ANGELES	NL	41	15	14	2	5	269	214	72	246	2.84
1961	LOS ANGELES	NL	40	13	10	0	3	244	236	83	182	3.69
1962	LOS ANGELES	NL	43	25	9	1	2	314.3	272	78	232	2.83
1963	LOS ANGELES	NL	42	19	17	0	3	315.3	287	57	251	2.63
1964	LOS ANGELES	NL	40	18	16	0	5	321.3	242	68	237	2.18
1965	LOS ANGELES	NL	44	23	12	1	7	308.3	270	66	210	2.77
1966	LOS ANGELES	NL	40	13	16	0	3	273.7	279	45	177	3.42
1967	LOS ANGELES	NL	38	13	16	0	3	282	269	60	196	2.74
1968	LOS ANGELES	NL	31	14	12	0	8	239	201	56	155	2.15
1969	LOS ANGELES	NL	12	5	4	0	1	62.7	71	13	24	4.45
CAREER TOTALS			**518**	**209**	**166**	**6**	**49**	**3432**	**3084**	**855**	**2486**	**2.95**

HUGH DUFFY

H ugh Duffy was one of the top batsmen of the 1890s recording more hits, home runs and runs batted in during the decade than any other player in the game. He teamed with fellow Hall of Famer Tommy McCarthy to form the "Heavenly Twins" outfield tandem for the Boston Beaneaters that captured two league pennants and a pre-modern World Series Championship in 1892.

A player, coach, manager, executive, and team owner, Hugh Duffy's career in baseball spanned an amazing 68 years.

Scouted by Cap Anson, Duffy was originally signed to play for the Chicago White Stockings in 1888. Not only could Duffy swing the bat, but he had terrific range in the outfield. Fred Clarke recalled: "Duffy was a really great center fielder and an outstanding right-handed hitter. He was a choke hitter, who would rap hits everywhere with good power."

Though diminutive in stature, off the field the powerful Duffy had a grand reputation, always dressing in the finest clothes. But on the field, he was all business.

In 1894, Duffy put together his finest season when he compiled a record .440 batting average on 237 hits, led the league in home runs with 18, knocked in 145 runs, hit 51 doubles, and scored 160 times. On June 18th of that year he established a major league mark when he reached base safely three times in one inning. Duffy commented on his remarkable season years later: "It's very evident that when a batter has a bang-up season he must begin just right, find conditions favorable and go straight ahead through the season full speed. That was what I did back there in '94. I got away to a good start and I held my advantage."

During his time as a coach, Duffy had the opportunity to mentor Ted Williams during William's .406 season, in 1941. Duffy maintained that the Splendid Splinter was the best hitter he'd ever seen.

"Sir Hugh" holds the distinction of being the only player to bat .300 in four major leagues: the Players' League, the American Association, the National League and the American League. As Duffy put it, "it just comes natural . . . You just walk up there and hit it. That's all."

HUGH DUFFY

BRILLIANT AS A DEFENSIVE OUTFIELDER FOR THE BOSTON NATIONALS, HE COMPILED A BATTING AVERAGE IN 1894 WHICH WAS NOT TO BE CHALLENGED IN HIS LIFETIME — .438.

Elected To The Hall Of Fame: 1945.
Born: Nov. 26, 1866 in Cranston, RI.
Died: Oct. 19, 1954 in Boston, Mass.
Height: 5-7. **Weight:** 168.
Threw: Right. **Batted:** Right.
Debut: June 23, 1888.
Final Game: April 13, 1906.
Teams: Chicago N.L. 1888-1889, Chicago, Players' League 1890; Boston, American Association 1891; Boston N.L. 1892-1900; Milwaukee A.L. 1901; Philadelphia N.L. 1904-1906.
Postseason: Champion Series Winner (1892).

YEAR	TEAM	LEAGUE	G	AB	R	H	2B	3B	HR	RBI	SB	AVG
1888	CHICAGO	NL	71	298	60	84	10	4	7	41	13	.282
1889	CHICAGO	NL	136	584	144	182	21	7	12	89	52	.312
1890	CHICAGO	PL	137	596	161	191	36	16	7	82	78	.320
1891	BOSTON	AA	127	536	134	180	20	8	9	110	85	.336
1892	BOSTON	NL	147	612	125	184	28	12	5	81	41	.301
1893	BOSTON	NL	131	560	147	203	23	7	6	118	44	.363
1894	BOSTON	NL	125	539	160	237	51	16	18	145	48	.440
1895	BOSTON	NL	131	533	112	188	30	6	9	100	42	.353
1896	BOSTON	NL	131	527	97	158	16	8	5	113	39	.300
1897	BOSTON	NL	134	550	130	187	25	10	11	129	41	.340
1898	BOSTON	NL	152	568	97	169	13	3	8	108	29	.298
1899	BOSTON	NL	147	588	103	164	29	7	5	102	26	.279
1900	BOSTON	NL	55	181	27	55	5	4	2	31	11	.304
1901	MILWAUKEE	AL	79	285	40	86	15	9	2	45	12	.302
1904	PHILADELPHIA	NL	18	46	10	13	1	1	0	5	3	.283
1905	PHILADELPHIA	NL	15	40	7	12	2	1	0	3	0	.300
1906	PHILADELPHIA	NL	1	1	0	0	0	0	0	0	0	.000
CAREER TOTALS			**1737**	**7044**	**1554**	**2293**	**325**	**119**	**106**	**1302**	**574**	**.326**

DUFFY.

COPYRIGHTED 1888
GOODWIN & CO. NY

S. S. Chicago

DENNIS ECKERSLEY

DENNIS LEE ECKERSLEY
CLEVELAND, A.L., 1975-1977
BOSTON, A.L., 1978-1984, 1998
CHICAGO, N.L., 1984-1986
OAKLAND, A.L., 1987-1995
ST. LOUIS, N.L., 1996-1997
A TOP STARTING PITCHER EARLY IN HIS CAREER WHO BECAME A DOMINANT
CLOSER. COMBINED A BLAZING FASTBALL AND DEVASTATING SLIDER,
PINPOINT CONTROL, AND A DECEPTIVE SIDEARM DELIVERY TO SAVE 390
GAMES. FROM 1988-93, STRUCK OUT 458 WHILE WALKING 51. HIS OAKLAND
ATHLETICS TEAMS APPEARED IN THREE CONSECUTIVE WORLD SERIES FROM
1988-90, WINNING IN 1989. WON AMERICAN LEAGUE MVP AND CY YOUNG
AWARDS IN 1992. AS STARTER, COMPLETED 100 GAMES AND PITCHED A
NO-HITTER FOR CLEVELAND IN 1977. ELECTED TO SIX ALL-STAR TEAMS.

Fellow Hall of Fame hurler Rich "Goose" Gossage once said of Dennis Eckersley's mound skill, "He could hit a gnat in the butt with a pitch if he wanted to."

Eckersley's control helped him blaze a unique path as the only big league pitcher with 100 saves and 100 complete games. He spent the first half of his 24-year career with the Indians, Red Sox and Cubs as one of the game's top starting pitchers, capturing double-figure win totals nine times, including a 20-win season, and tossing a 1977 no-hitter.

"It was obvious to me Eckersley would be an outstanding pitcher," said Bob Quinn, Cleveland's farm director when Eck came through. "He has that extra ingredient that says he will excel. Not necessarily a perfectionist, but he wants nothing but to beat you."

Eckersley was traded to the A's prior to the 1987 season. From 1988 to 1992, he became one of the finest closers in baseball history, averaging 44 saves a season and helping the A's to four American League West titles and a World Series crown in 1989.

"His control is so good, I would be willing to put on the gear and catch any pitch he throws with my eyes closed," said former player, coach and manager Johnny Oates, "because I know he's going to hit some part of the glove with every pitch."

Eckersley's 1992 season may have been his most dominant, finishing with a 7-1 record, a 1.91 ERA, a league-leading 51 saves, and 93 strikeouts with only 11 bases on balls (six intentional) in 80 innings pitched. As a result, he won both the AL Cy Young and MVP awards, becoming the ninth pitcher to capture both prestigious honors in the same season.

Fellow pitcher Jerry Reuss, said, "What he's doing right now is setting new parameters for relief pitchers to come. He's going to be the basis of what everyone else is compared to."

Eck

Elected To The Hall Of Fame: *2004.*
Born: *Oct. 3, 1954 in Oakland, Calif.*
Height: *6-2.* **Weight:** *190.*
Threw: *Right.* **Batted:** *Right.*
Debut: *Apr. 12, 1975.* **Final Game:** *Sept. 26, 1998.*
Teams: *Cleveland A.L. 1975-1977; Boston A.L. 1978-1984, 1998; Chicago N.L. 1984-1986; Oakland A.L. 1987-1995; St. Louis N.L. 1996-97.*
Postseason: *World Series Champion (1989); 3 A.L. Pennants (1988-1990); 7-Time Playoff Qualifier (1984, 1988-1990, 1992, 1996, 1998).*
Awards: *6-Time All-Star (1977, 1982, 1988, 1990-1992); A.L. Cy Young (1992); A.L. Most Valuable Player (1992).*

YEAR	TEAM	LEAGUE	G	W	L	SV	SH	IP	H	BB	SO	ERA
1975	CLEVELAND	AL	34	13	7	2	2	186.7	147	90	152	2.60
1976	CLEVELAND	AL	36	13	12	1	3	199.3	155	78	200	3.43
1977	CLEVELAND	AL	33	14	13	0	3	247.3	214	54	191	3.53
1978	BOSTON	AL	35	20	8	0	3	268.3	258	71	162	2.99
1979	BOSTON	AL	33	17	10	0	2	246.7	234	59	150	2.99
1980	BOSTON	AL	30	12	14	0	0	197.7	188	44	121	4.28
1981	BOSTON	AL	23	9	8	0	2	154	160	35	79	4.27
1982	BOSTON	AL	33	13	13	0	3	224.3	228	43	127	3.73
1983	BOSTON	AL	28	9	13	0	0	176.3	223	39	77	5.61
1984	BOSTON/CHICAGO	AL/NL	33	14	12	0	0	225	223	49	114	3.60
1985	CHICAGO	NL	25	11	7	0	2	169.3	145	19	117	3.08
1986	CHICAGO	NL	33	6	11	0	0	201	226	43	137	4.57
1987	OAKLAND	AL	54	6	8	16	0	115.7	99	17	113	3.03
1988	OAKLAND	AL	60	4	2	45	0	72.7	52	11	70	2.35
1989	OAKLAND	AL	51	4	0	33	0	57.7	32	3	55	1.56
1990	OAKLAND	AL	63	4	2	48	0	73.3	41	4	73	0.61
1991	OAKLAND	AL	67	5	4	43	0	76	60	9	87	2.96
1992	OAKLAND	AL	69	7	1	51	0	80	62	11	93	1.91
1993	OAKLAND	AL	64	2	4	36	0	67	67	13	80	4.16
1994	OAKLAND	AL	45	5	4	19	0	44.3	49	13	47	4.26
1995	OAKLAND	AL	52	4	6	29	0	50.3	53	11	40	4.83
1996	ST. LOUIS	NL	63	0	6	30	0	60	65	6	49	3.30
1997	ST. LOUIS	NL	57	1	5	36	0	53	49	8	45	3.91
1998	BOSTON	AL	50	4	1	1	0	39.7	46	8	22	4.76
CAREER TOTALS			**1071**	**197**	**171**	**390**	**20**	**3285.2**	**3076**	**738**	**2401**	**3.50**

JOHNNY EVERS

At 5-foot-9 and 125 pounds, Johnny Evers wasn't built to hit home runs. Instead, the acrobatic Evers used his savvy and his scrappy, determined style of play to lead his teams to four National League pennants and three World Series titles in the first years of the 20th Century.

Evers made his big league debut at the age of 21 in 1902 and established himself as the Cubs' starting second baseman in 1903 – teaming with shortstop Joe Tinker and first baseman Frank Chance to form one of the best infield combinations of the era.

In 1906, the Cubs dominated the NL from start to finish, winning a record 116 games and posting a record .763 winning percentage.

Evers hit .255 that season, but drove in 51 runs and stole 49 bases. His spectacular infield defense – combined with that of Tinker, Chance and the other members of the Cubs – resulted in Chicago allowing just 381 runs for the entire season.

The Cubs lost the 1906 World Series to the White Sox, but won the Fall Classic in 1907 and 1908. In 1910, Evers – along with Tinker and Chance – was immortalized in the poem: "Baseball's Sad Lexicon," written by newspaper man Franklin P. Adams, a reporter who worked for the *New York Evening Mail* and closely followed the Cubs' main rival, the New York Giants.

After the 1913 season, the Cubs traded Evers to the Boston Braves – who had finished fifth in the NL in 1913. But with Evers as their everyday second baseman in 1914, the Braves caught fire in the second half of the season and stormed to the pennant, earning the nickname "Miracle Braves."

Against the heavily favored Philadelphia Athletics in the 1914 World Series, Evers hit .438 as the Braves swept the series in four games. For his efforts that season, Evers was named the National League winner of the Chalmers Award, which served as a most valuable player award for each league.

Evers played in parts of five more seasons after 1914, ending his career with a .270 batting average, 1,659 hits and 324 stolen bases. He managed the Cubs in 1913 as a player/manager, and also managed the Cubs in 1921 and the White Sox in 1924.

JOHN JOSEPH EVERS
"THE TROJAN"
MIDDLE-MAN OF THE FAMOUS DOUBLE PLAY COMBINATION OF TINKER TO EVERS TO CHANCE. WITH THE PENNANT WINNING CHICAGO CUBS OF 1906, 07-08-10 AND WITH THE BOSTON BRAVES' MIRACLE TEAM OF 1914. VOTED MOST VALUABLE PLAYER IN N.L. IN 1914. SERVED AS PLAYER, COACH AND MANAGER IN BIG LEAGUES AND AS A SCOUT FROM 1902 THROUGH 1934. SHARES RECORD FOR MAKING MOST SINGLES IN FOUR GAME WORLD SERIES.

Elected To The Hall Of Fame: 1946.
Born: July 21, 1881 in Troy, N.Y.
Died: Mar. 28, 1947 in Albany, N.Y.
Height: 5-9. *Weight:* 125.
Threw: Right. *Batted:* Left.
Debut: Sept. 1, 1902.
Final Game: Oct. 6, 1929.
Teams: Chicago N.L. 1902-1913; Boston N.L. 1914-1917, 1929; Philadelphia N.L. 1917; Chicago A.L. 1922.
Postseason: 3-Time World Series Champion (1907-1908, 1914); 4 N.L. Pennants (1906-1908, 1914).
Awards: N.L. Most Valuable Player (1914).

YEAR	TEAM	LEAGUE	G	AB	R	H	2B	3B	HR	RBI	SB	AVG
1902	CHICAGO	NL	26	90	7	20	0	0	0	2	1	.222
1903	CHICAGO	NL	124	464	70	136	27	7	0	52	25	.293
1904	CHICAGO	NL	152	532	49	141	14	7	0	47	26	.265
1905	CHICAGO	NL	99	340	44	94	11	2	1	37	19	.276
1906	CHICAGO	NL	154	533	65	136	17	6	1	51	49	.255
1907	CHICAGO	NL	151	508	66	127	18	4	2	51	46	.250
1908	CHICAGO	NL	126	416	83	125	19	6	0	37	36	.300
1909	CHICAGO	NL	127	463	88	122	19	6	1	24	28	.263
1910	CHICAGO	NL	125	433	87	114	11	7	0	28	28	.263
1911	CHICAGO	NL	46	155	29	35	4	3	0	7	6	.226
1912	CHICAGO	NL	143	478	73	163	23	11	1	63	16	.341
1913	CHICAGO	NL	136	446	81	127	20	5	3	49	11	.285
1914	BOSTON	NL	139	491	81	137	20	3	1	40	12	.279
1915	BOSTON	NL	83	278	38	73	4	1	0	22	7	.263
1916	BOSTON	NL	71	241	33	52	4	1	0	15	5	.216
1917	BOSTON/PHILADELPHIA	NL	80	266	25	57	5	1	1	12	9	.214
1922	CHICAGO	AL	1	3	0	0	0	0	0	1	0	.000
1929	BOSTON	NL	1	0	0	0	0	0	0	0	0	—
CAREER TOTALS			**1784**	**6137**	**919**	**1659**	**216**	**70**	**12**	**538**	**324**	**.270**

BUCK EWING

Catcher is often considered to be the most difficult position on the diamond. A catcher's body often takes a beating from foul balls and wild pitches.

In the 19th century, Buck Ewing earned a reputation as the premier catcher of his era – before catcher's equipment was ever introduced.

Born on Oct. 17, 1859 in Hoagland, Ohio, Ewing was among the first catchers to crouch behind the plate and use larger glove with added padding. He may have worn an early version of a mask, but Ewing played without a chest protector or shin guards that are customary today. His impressive arm allowed him to throw runners out from a squat position behind the plate.

"Ewing is considered by many to have been the greatest all-around player who ever lived," said the 1940 *Official Baseball Guide*. "He could run, bat – and how he could throw! When he was catching he would squat down behind the plate and seemingly hand the ball to whoever was playing second base."

Ewing hit at least .300 in 11 of his 18 major league seasons with the Troy Trojans, New York Gothams, New York Giants, Cleveland Spiders and Cincinnati Reds and compiled a .303 career batting average.

"In his prime, [he was] the greatest player of the game from the standpoint of supreme excellence in all departments: batting, catching, fielding, baserunning, throwing and baseball brains," said the *Reach Guide* in 1919. "A player without a weakness of any kind."

Ewing captained the New York Giants to the club's first postseason wins in 1888 and 1889. A leader on the field, Ewing stole 53 bases in 1888 and exceeded 30 six more times. He played many positions on the field, but caught 636 of the 1,345 games he played in between 1880 and 1897.

Serving as a player-manager for four seasons, Ewing also managed for three seasons after his catching career ended. He became the first catcher elected to the Baseball Hall of Fame in 1939 during the Museum's inaugural year.

Elected To The Hall Of Fame: *1939.*
Born: *Oct. 17, 1859 in Hoagland, Ohio.*
Died: *Oct. 20, 1906 in Cincinnati, Ohio.*
Height: *5-10.* **Weight:** *188.*
Threw: *Right.* **Batted:** *Right.*
Debut: *Sept. 9, 1880.*
Final Game: *May 27, 1897.*
Teams: *Troy N.L. 1880-1882; New York N.L. 1883-1889, 1891-1892; New York, Players' League 1890; Cleveland N.L. 1893-1894; Cincinnati N.L. 1895-1897.*
Postseason: *2-Time World Series Champion (1888-1889); 2 N.L. Pennants (1888-1889).*

YEAR	TEAM	LEAGUE	G	AB	R	H	2B	3B	HR	RBI	SB	AVG
1880	TROY	NL	13	45	1	8	1	0	0	5	0	.178
1881	TROY	NL	67	272	40	68	14	7	0	25	0	.250
1882	TROY	NL	74	328	67	89	16	11	2	29	0	.271
1883	NEW YORK	NL	88	376	90	114	11	13	10	41	0	.303
1884	NEW YORK	NL	94	382	90	106	15	20	3	41	0	.277
1885	NEW YORK	NL	81	342	81	104	15	12	6	63	0	.304
1886	NEW YORK	NL	73	275	59	85	11	7	4	31	18	.309
1887	NEW YORK	NL	77	318	97	17	13	6	44	26	.305
1888	NEW YORK	NL	103	415	83	127	18	15	6	58	53	.306
1889	NEW YORK	NL	99	407	91	133	23	13	4	87	34	.327
1890	NEW YORK	PL	83	352	98	119	19	15	8	72	36	.338
1891	NEW YORK	NL	14	49	8	17	2	1	0	18	5	.347
1892	NEW YORK	NL	105	393	58	122	10	15	8	76	42	.310
1893	CLEVELAND	NL	116	500	117	172	28	15	6	122	47	.344
1894	CLEVELAND	NL	53	211	32	53	12	4	2	39	18	.251
1895	CINCINNATI	NL	105	434	90	138	24	13	5	94	34	.318
1896	CINCINNATI	NL	69	263	41	73	14	4	1	38	41	.278
1897	CINCINNATI	NL	1	1	0	0	0	0	0	0	0	.000
CAREER TOTALS			**1315**	**5363**	**1129**	**1625**	**250**	**178**	**71**	**883**	**354**	**.303**

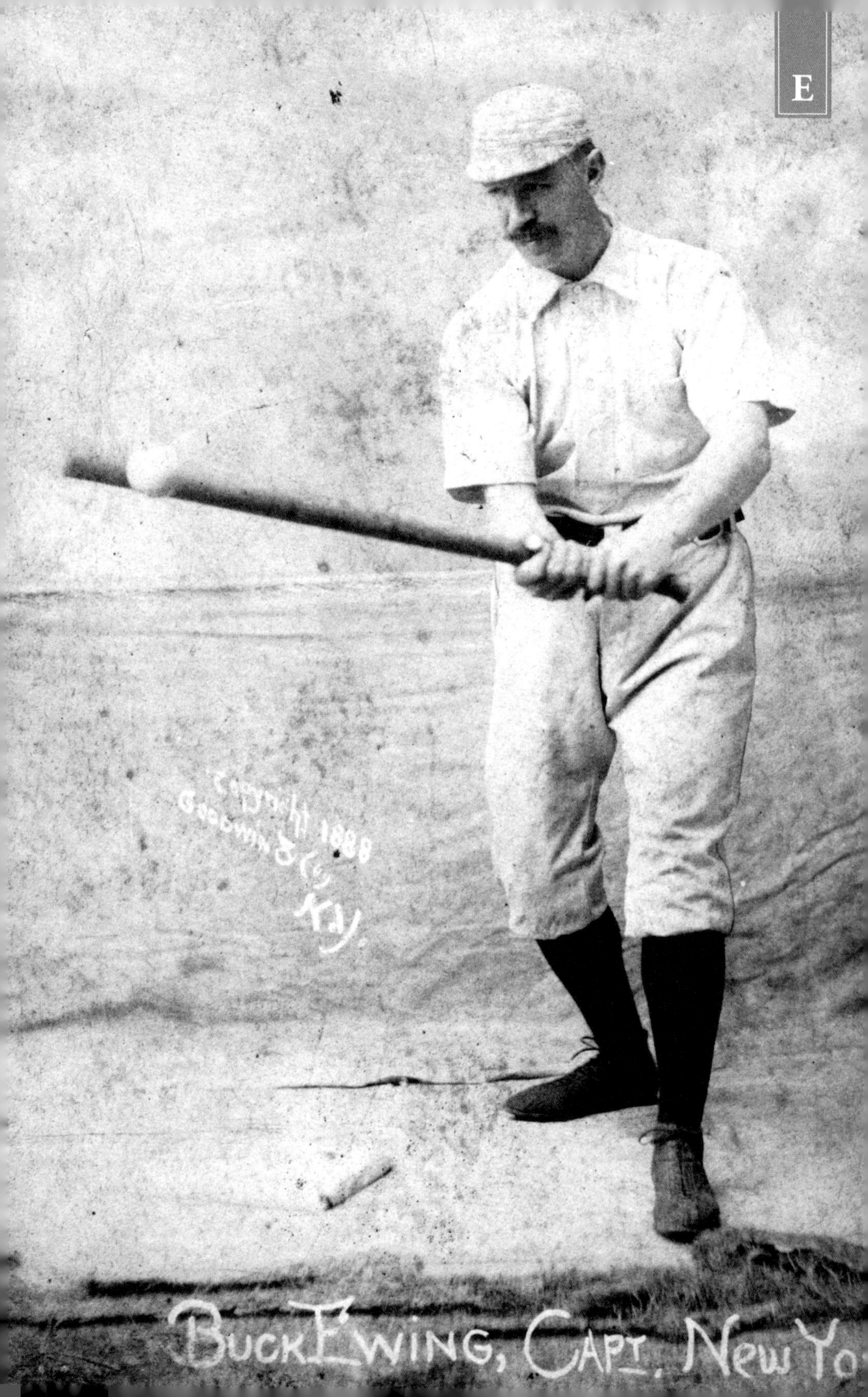
Copyright 1888
Goodwin & Co.
Kay.
BUCK EWING, CAPT. NEW YO

RED FABER

During the 1913 offseason, Red Faber had yet to pitch an inning of major league baseball, but he had made an impression in the minor leagues and the White Sox purchased his contract to take him on a world tour against the New York Giants.

During the tour, the Giants were short pitchers and borrowed Faber for a game in Hong Kong. Faber beat his own team for his first win with a major league club and did it three more times on the trip. When the tour ended, the Giants attempted to purchase Faber, but the White Sox refused and made him a regular in their 1914 rotation. From there, it was a short trip to Cooperstown. Faber spent 20 seasons pitching for the White Sox, utilizing his strong fastball and impressive spitball to record groundball outs.

"That fellow has a lot of stuff," said Giants manager John McGraw. "He's got the best drop curve that I've seen along the line for some time. And his spitter is a pippin', too."

Faber won 254 games during his career, with 273 complete games. His 3.15 ERA and 4,086 innings pitched were products of his low pitch counts. Faber once threw only 67 pitches in a complete game and three times retired the side on three pitches.

Faber won three out of the four decisions to help the White Sox win the 1917 World Series against the Giants, and he won 20 or more games in a season four times. In 1920, the spitball was outlawed by Major League Baseball, but Faber was grandfathered in and was soon the last legal spitballer in the American League.

"The spitball may be a little harder on some pitchers' arms than a straight fastball, but certainly it is not half as bad as throwing a curve, which causes a continual grind at the elbow and in many cases, permanently shortens a pitcher's arm," said Faber.

Faber led the American League in appearances in 1915 with 50, then led the league in earned-run average in both 1921 (2.48) and 1922 (2.81) – pitching more than 330 innings in both seasons. In 1920, Faber was one of four White Sox hurlers who posted 20-win seasons – the first team to pull off the feat.

URBAN CLARENCE FABER
CHICAGO A. L. 1914-1933
DURABLE RIGHTHANDER WHO WON 253,
LOST 211. E.R.A. 3.13 GAMES IN TWO DECADES
WITH WHITE SOX. VICTOR IN 3 GAMES
OF 1917 WORLD'S SERIES AGAINST GIANTS.
WON 20 OR MORE GAMES IN SEASON
FOUR TIMES, THREE IN SUCCESSION.

Elected To The Hall Of Fame: 1964.
Born: Sept. 6, 1888 in Cascade, Iowa.
Died: Sept. 25, 1976 in Chicago, Ill.
Height: 6-2. *Weight:* 180.
Threw: Right. *Batted:* Both.
Debut: Apr. 17, 1914.
Final Game: Sept. 20, 1933.
Teams: Chicago A.L. 1914-1933.
Postseason: World Series Champion (1917); A.L. Pennant (1917).

YEAR	TEAM	LEAGUE	G	W	L	SV	SH	IP	H	BB	SO	ERA
1914	CHICAGO	AL	40	10	9	4	2	181.3	154	64	88	2.68
1915	CHICAGO	AL	50	24	14	2	2	299.7	264	99	182	2.55
1916	CHICAGO	AL	35	17	9	1	3	205.3	167	61	87	2.02
1917	CHICAGO	AL	41	16	13	3	3	248	224	85	84	1.92
1918	CHICAGO	AL	11	4	1	1	1	80.7	70	23	26	1.23
1919	CHICAGO	AL	25	11	9	0	0	162.3	185	45	45	3.83
1920	CHICAGO	AL	40	23	13	1	2	319	332	88	108	2.99
1921	CHICAGO	AL	43	25	15	1	4	330.7	293	87	124	2.48
1922	CHICAGO	AL	43	21	17	2	4	352	334	83	148	2.81
1923	CHICAGO	AL	32	14	11	0	2	232.3	233	62	91	3.41
1924	CHICAGO	AL	21	9	11	0	0	161.3	173	58	47	3.85
1925	CHICAGO	AL	34	12	11	0	1	238	266	59	71	3.78
1926	CHICAGO	AL	27	15	9	0	1	184.7	203	57	65	3.56
1927	CHICAGO	AL	18	4	7	0	0	110.7	131	41	39	4.55
1928	CHICAGO	AL	27	13	9	0	2	201.3	223	68	43	3.75
1929	CHICAGO	AL	31	13	13	0	1	234	241	61	68	3.88
1930	CHICAGO	AL	29	8	13	1	0	169	188	49	62	4.21
1931	CHICAGO	AL	44	10	14	1	1	184	210	57	49	3.82
1932	CHICAGO	AL	42	2	11	6	0	106	123	38	26	3.74
1933	CHICAGO	AL	36	3	4	5	0	86.3	92	28	18	3.44
CAREER TOTALS			669	254	213	28	29	4086.2	4106	1213	1471	3.15

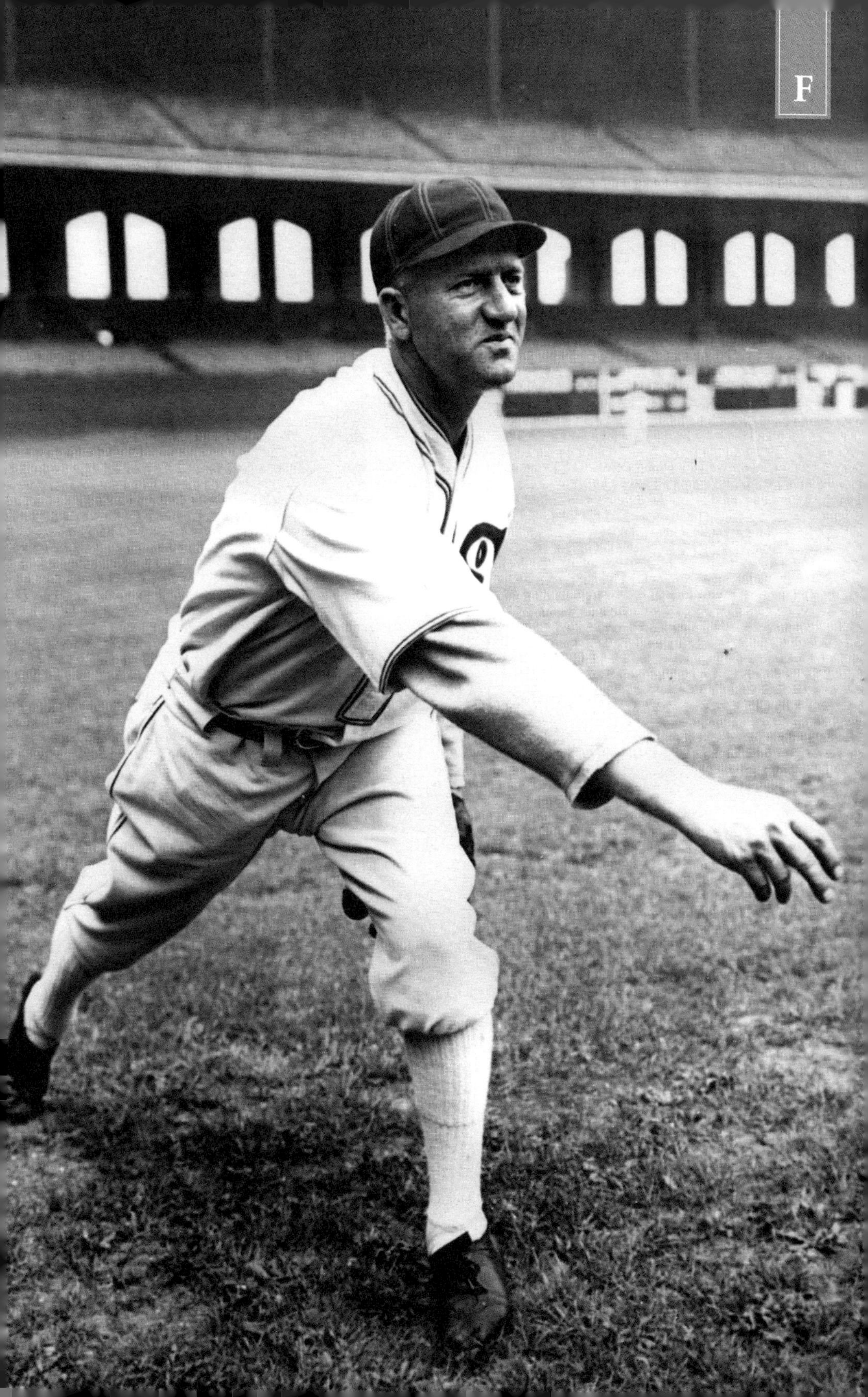

BOB FELLER

ROBERT WILLIAM ANDREW FELLER
CLEVELAND A. L. 1936 TO 1941
1945 TO 1956
PITCHED 3 NO-HIT GAMES IN A.L., 12 ONE HIT GAMES,
SET MODERN STRIKEOUT RECORD WITH 18 IN GAME,
348 FOR SEASON. LED A.L. IN VICTORIES 6 (ONE TIE)
SEASONS, LIFETIME RECORD: WON 266, LOST 162, P.C.
.621, E.R. AVERAGE 3.25, STRUCKOUT 2581.

Hall of Famer Ted Lyons recalled, "It wasn't until you hit against him that you knew how fast he really was, until you saw with your own eyes that ball jumping at you."

Bob Feller began his major league journey in 1936, at age 17, fresh off his family's farm in Van Meter, Iowa. It was during his rookie season that Feller earned the nickname "Rapid Robert" because of his devastating fastball and high strikeout totals.

He made his first major league start in August, striking out 15 St. Louis Browns. A month later, he set an American League rookie record fanning 17 Philadelphia Athletics in a game. Upon completion of his rookie campaign, Feller returned home to Iowa to finish his senior year of high school—his graduation was covered by NBC Radio.

Feller really began to hit his stride after his 19th birthday, rattling off a string of three straight 20-win seasons. It was during this time that Senators' manager Bucky Harris conveyed the following strategy to his players when facing Feller "Go on up there and hit what you see. If you can't see it, come on back."

The day after the bombing of Pearl Harbor, Dec. 8, 1941, Feller put aside his 3-C draft deferment status and enlisted in the Navy. With this selfless act, he became Major League Baseball's first player to enlist in World War II, and in the process gave up nearly four seasons of baseball in the prime of his career. But Feller had no regrets: "I'm proud of that decision to enlist. It was important to serve your country. I didn't worry about losing my baseball career. We needed to win the war. I wanted to do my part."

At the conclusion of the war, Feller returned to the game and picked up right where he left off, averaging more than 19 wins a season over the next six years. Bobby Doerr recalled, "Bob was just a regular, solid person. He was the same guy, all the time. He gave his opinions and he said what he thought. He didn't hedge around anything. He was one of the top pitchers I saw in my time. He was timed at 100 miles per hour and he had a real good curve ball. You had to always be alert with him. He was a real competitor."

Rapid Robert

Elected To The Hall Of Fame: *1962.*
Born: *Nov. 3, 1918 in Van Meter, Iowa.*
Died: *Dec. 15, 2010 in Cleveland, Ohio.*
Height: *6-0.* **Weight:** *185.*
Threw: *Right.* **Batted:** *Right.*
Debut: *July 19, 1936.*
Final Game: *Sept. 30, 1956.*
Teams: *Cleveland A.L. 1936-1941, 1945-1956.*
Postseason: *World Series Champion (1948); 2 A.L. Pennants (1948, 1954).*
Awards: *8-Time All-Star (1938-41, 1946-48, 1950).*

YEAR	TEAM	LEAGUE	G	W	L	SV	SH	IP	H	BB	SO	ERA
1936	CLEVELAND	AL	14	5	3	1	0	62	52	47	76	3.34
1937	CLEVELAND	AL	26	9	7	1	0	148.7	116	106	150	3.39
1938	CLEVELAND	AL	39	17	11	1	2	277.7	225	208	240	4.08
1939	CLEVELAND	AL	39	24	9	1	4	296.7	227	142	246	2.85
1940	CLEVELAND	AL	43	27	11	4	4	320.3	245	118	261	2.61
1941	CLEVELAND	AL	44	25	13	2	6	343	284	194	260	3.15
1945	CLEVELAND	AL	9	5	3	0	1	72	50	35	59	2.50
1946	CLEVELAND	AL	48	26	15	4	10	371.3	277	153	348	2.18
1947	CLEVELAND	AL	42	20	11	3	5	299	230	127	196	2.68
1948	CLEVELAND	AL	44	19	15	3	2	280.3	255	116	164	3.56
1949	CLEVELAND	AL	36	15	14	0	0	211	198	84	108	3.75
1950	CLEVELAND	AL	35	16	11	0	3	247	230	103	119	3.43
1951	CLEVELAND	AL	33	22	8	0	4	249.7	239	95	111	3.50
1952	CLEVELAND	AL	30	9	13	0	0	191.7	219	83	81	4.74
1953	CLEVELAND	AL	25	10	7	0	1	175.7	163	60	60	3.59
1954	CLEVELAND	AL	19	13	3	0	1	140	127	39	59	3.09
1955	CLEVELAND	AL	25	4	4	0	1	83	71	31	25	3.47
1956	CLEVELAND	AL	19	0	4	1	0	58	63	23	18	4.97
CAREER TOTALS			**570**	**266**	**162**	**21**	**44**	**3827**	**3271**	**1764**	**2581**	**3.25**

RICK FERRELL

A strong-armed and durable catcher who could also handle the bat, Rick Ferrell spent nearly two decades working with pitching staffs throughout the Junior Circuit.

A seven-time All-Star, Ferrell played for the St. Louis Browns, Boston Red Sox and Washington Senators between 1929 and 1947. He retired with the American League record for most games caught, at 1,806, until fellow Hall of Famer Carlton Fisk passed him in 1988.

Though it has been decades since he left the game, Ferrell may still be remembered best today for the two seasons in the mid-1940s in which he handled a quartet of unique hurlers.

"When I was catching for the Washington Senators, every game was an adventure because our four best pitchers (in 1944 and '45) were knuckleballers," said Ferrell, referring to the two seasons in which he led the league in passed balls. "When they released the ball, they didn't know where it was going and neither did I. But I struggled through two seasons with Roger Wolff, Dutch Leonard, Mickey Haefner and Johnny Niggeling."

According to longtime scout Joe Mathes, "Even if Rick hadn't been a good hitter and a durable catcher, clever with the glove, he would have deserved the Hall of Fame for catching four knuckleball pitchers at one time."

"The mental heat catching those things with a big run on third base was worse than physically strapping on the harness for a hot summer doubleheader in St. Louis," Ferrell said. "I guess having to handle those four flutter pitchers at one time was just the law of averages catching up with me."

Ferrell's brother, Wes, won 193 games over 15 major league seasons, the two spending time as teammates with the Red Sox and Senators. Rick and Wes Ferrell are two of six brothers, and two of four to play professional baseball.

"I had five brothers and I was the only one with a mitt," Ferrell said. "Anyway, they all thought they were pitchers, especially Wes, who wouldn't put a mitt on. If he couldn't pitch, he wouldn't play. I was stuck with the catcher's mitt, and I'm glad I was."

RICHARD BENJAMIN FERRELL
ST. LOUIS A.L. 1929-1933, 1941-1943
BOSTON A.L. 1933-1937
WASHINGTON A.L. 1937-1941, 1944-1947
CAUGHT MORE GAMES (1,806) THAN ANY OTHER
AMERICAN LEAGUER. DURABLE DEFENSIVE STAND-OUT
WITH FINE ARM. EXPERT AT HANDLING PITCHERS.
MET CHALLENGE OF 4 KNUCKLE-BALLERS IN SENATORS'
STARTING ROTATION. OFTEN FORMED BATTERY WITH
BROTHER, WES. HIT OVER .300 4 TIMES. SECOND
ONLY TO DICKEY IN A.L. CAREER PUTOUTS AT
RETIREMENT.

Elected To The Hall Of Fame: *1984.*
Born: *Oct. 12, 1905 in Durham, N.C.*
Died: *July 27, 1995 in Bloomfield Hills, Mich.*
Height: *5-10.* ***Weight:*** *160.*
Threw: *Right.* ***Batted:*** *Right.*
Debut: *Apr. 19, 1929.*
Final Game: *Sept. 14, 1947.*
Teams: *St. Louis A.L. 1929-1933, 1941-1943; Boston A.L. 1933-1937; Washington A.L. 1937-1941, 1944-1945, 1947*
Awards: *8-Time All-Star (1933-1938, 1944-1945).*

YEAR	TEAM	LEAGUE	G	AB	R	H	2B	3B	HR	RBI	SB	AVG
1929	ST. LOUIS	AL	64	144	21	33	6	1	0	20	1	.229
1930	ST. LOUIS	AL	101	314	43	84	18	4	1	41	1	.268
1931	ST. LOUIS	AL	117	386	47	118	30	4	3	57	2	.306
1932	ST. LOUIS	AL	126	438	67	138	30	5	2	65	5	.315
1933	ST. LOUIS/BOSTON	AL	140	493	58	143	21	4	4	77	4	.290
1934	BOSTON	AL	132	437	50	130	29	4	1	48	0	.297
1935	BOSTON	AL	133	458	54	138	34	4	3	61	5	.301
1936	BOSTON	AL	121	410	59	128	27	5	8	55	0	.312
1937	BOSTON/WASHINGTON	AL	104	344	39	84	8	0	2	36	1	.244
1938	WASHINGTON	AL	135	411	55	120	24	5	1	58	1	.292
1939	WASHINGTON	AL	87	274	32	77	13	1	0	31	1	.281
1940	WASHINGTON	AL	103	326	35	89	18	2	0	28	1	.273
1941	WASHINGTON/ST. LOUIS	AL	121	387	38	99	19	3	2	36	3	.256
1942	ST. LOUIS	AL	99	273	20	61	6	1	0	26	0	.223
1943	ST. LOUIS	AL	74	209	12	50	7	0	0	20	0	.239
1944	WASHINGTON	AL	99	339	14	94	11	1	0	25	2	.277
1945	WASHINGTON	AL	91	286	33	76	12	1	1	38	2	.266
1947	WASHINGTON	AL	37	99	10	30	11	0	0	12	0	.303
CAREER TOTALS			**1884**	**6028**	**687**	**1692**	**324**	**45**	**28**	**734**	**29**	**.281**

ROLLIE FINGERS

Rollie Fingers had quite possibly the most famous mustache in baseball. But fans didn't come to the ballpark to see just that. They came to see him close out games with his sinking fastball night after night.

"When he came in, you took a deep sigh of relief," said former teammate Sal Bando. "You knew the game was in control."

The 1981 American League MVP and Cy Young Award winner spent 17 years in the big leagues with the Athletics, Padres and Brewers. He set the record for career saves – since broken – with 341. The handlebar mustache was first grown in 1972 because a promotion dreamed up by A's owner Charlie O. Finley offered him a $300 bonus, but it soon became his trademark.

Born on Aug. 25, 1946 in Steubenville, Ohio, Fingers signed with the Kansas City Athletics in 1964. During nine seasons with the A's, Fingers led the league in games twice and finished in the top 10 in the league in saves seven times.

Fingers won three World Series titles while with Oakland from 1972-74 and was the MVP of the 1974 Series, earning a win and two saves in four games. Fingers won or saved eight of the A's 12 World Series victories during their three-year run.

After the 1976 season, the seven-time All-Star went to San Diego, where he led the league in saves during his first two seasons, the second of which he posted 37 saves and tied the National League record. "With Fingers, you know exactly what you're going to get, just about every time out," said Hall of Fame manager Sparky Anderson.

Fingers led the league in saves again in 1981, but this time it was in the American League after a trade to the Brewers. Fingers finished his career with 114 wins, a record 341 saves, 1,299 strikeouts, a 2.90 ERA and 1,701 innings pitched in 944 games.

Fingers began his career as a starter, but found limited success once he reached the big league. He credits manager Dick Williams for moving him to the bullpen and turning him into a closer.

"Every organization realizes the importance of relief pitching now," said Fingers. "Whether I had anything to do with that or not, I'll leave that up to others to determine."

ROLAND GLEN FINGERS
OAKLAND, A.L., 1968-1976
SAN DIEGO, N.L., 1977-1980
MILWAUKEE, A.L., 1981-1985

CAREER EPITOMIZED EMERGENCE OF MODERN-DAY RELIEF ACE AS HE APPROACHED LEGENDARY STATUS WITH CONSISTENT EXCELLENCE COMING OUT OF BULLPEN. RELIED UPON SINKING FAST BALL TO BECOME ALL-TIME MAJOR LEAGUE LEADER WITH 341 CAREER SAVES. APPEARED IN 16 WORLD SERIES GAMES FOR OAKLAND, WINNING 2 AND SAVING 6. A.L. MVP AND CY YOUNG AWARDEE IN 1981.

Elected To The Hall Of Fame: 1992.
Born: Aug. 25, 1946 in Steubenville, Ohio.
Height: 6-4. **Weight:** 190.
Threw: Right. **Batted:** Right.
Debut: Sept. 15, 1968.
Final Game: Sept. 17, 1985.
Teams: Oakland A.L. 1968-1976; San Diego N.L. 1977-1980; Milwaukee A.L. 1981-1982, 1984-1985.
Postseason: 3-Time World Series Champion (1972-1974); 3 A.L. Pennants (1972-1974); 6-Time Playoff Qualifier (1971-1975, 1981).
Awards: 7-Time All-Star (1973-1976, 1978, 1981-1982); World Series Most Valuable Player (1974); A.L. Cy Young (1981); A.L. Most Valuable Player (1981).

YEAR	TEAM	LEAGUE	G	W	L	SV	SH	IP	H	BB	SO	ERA
1968	OAKLAND	AL	1	0	0	0	0	1.3	4	1	0	27.00
1969	OAKLAND	AL	60	6	7	12	1	119	116	41	61	3.71
1970	OAKLAND	AL	45	7	9	2	0	148	137	48	79	3.65
1971	OAKLAND	AL	48	4	6	17	1	129.3	94	30	98	2.99
1972	OAKLAND	AL	65	11	9	21	0	111.3	85	32	113	2.51
1973	OAKLAND	AL	62	7	8	22	0	126.7	107	39	110	1.92
1974	OAKLAND	AL	76	9	5	18	0	119	104	29	95	2.65
1975	OAKLAND	AL	75	10	6	24	0	126.7	95	33	115	2.98
1976	OAKLAND	AL	70	13	11	20	0	134.7	118	40	113	2.47
1977	SAN DIEGO	NL	78	8	9	35	0	132.3	123	36	113	2.99
1978	SAN DIEGO	NL	67	6	13	37	0	107.3	84	29	72	2.52
1979	SAN DIEGO	NL	54	9	9	13	0	83.7	91	37	65	4.52
1980	SAN DIEGO	NL	66	11	9	23	0	103	101	32	69	2.80
1981	MILWAUKEE	AL	47	6	3	28	0	78	55	13	61	1.04
1982	MILWAUKEE	AL	50	5	6	29	0	79.7	63	20	71	2.60
1984	MILWAUKEE	AL	33	1	2	23	0	46	38	13	40	1.96
1985	MILWAUKEE	AL	47	1	6	17	0	55.3	59	19	24	5.04
CAREER TOTALS			**944**	**114**	**118**	**341**	**2**	**1701.1**	**1474**	**492**	**1299**	**2.90**

CARLTON FISK

Carlton Fisk will forever be remembered for one game-winning home run.

But it was durability over the long run that built the Hall of Fame career for a man who retired as the player who spent more games in catcher's gear than any other in history.

Fisk hit a dramatic game-winning home run off the left field foul pole at Fenway Park in the 12th inning of Game 6 of the 1975 World Series against the Cincinnati Reds. The at-bat is still showed on highlight reels of the best moments in baseball.

The 11-time All-Star, known for his pride, work ethic, and ability to handle pitchers, spent 24 years in the big leagues and 2,226 games behind the plate. That hard work earned him the respect of fans, competitors and teammates.

"He played the game the right way," said Hall of Fame teammate Carl Yastrzemski. "Both behind the plate and at the plate."

Born in Bellows Falls, Vt. on Dec. 26, 1947, Fisk attended the University of New Hampshire on a basketball scholarship, but switched games when he was drafted in the first round of the 1967 amateur draft by the Boston Red Sox.

Fisk won the Rookie of the Year Award with Boston in 1972 after leading the league in triples and hitting .293 with 61 RBI and 22 home runs. Pudge had two home runs and three intentional walks in that 1975 World Series and provided the defining moment despite the fact that the Red Sox lost in seven games. In 1980, Fisk signed with the Chicago White Sox after a procedural error made him a free agent.

In 1985, Fisk hit a career-high 37 home runs and set a single-season record for American League catchers. He also recorded a career-high 107 RBI that season. Fisk set the record for most home runs by a catcher with 351 as well as AL records for most seasons, putouts and chances.

CARLTON ERNEST FISK
"PUDGE"
BOSTON, A.L., 1969, 1971-80
CHICAGO, A.L., 1981-93

A COMMANDING FIGURE BEHIND THE PLATE FOR A RECORD 24 SEASONS, HE CAUGHT MORE GAMES (2,226) AND HIT MORE HOME RUNS (351) THAN ANY CATCHER BEFORE HIM. HIS GRITTY RESOLVE AND COMPETITIVE FIRE EARNED HIM THE RESPECT OF TEAMMATES AND OPPOSING PLAYERS ALIKE. A STAUNCH TRAINING REGIMEN EXTENDED HIS DURABILITY AND ENHANCED HIS PRODUCTIVITY—AS EVIDENCED BY A RECORD 72 HOME RUNS AFTER AGE 40. HIS DRAMATIC HOME RUN TO WIN GAME SIX OF THE 1975 WORLD SERIES IS ONE OF BASEBALL'S UNFORGETTABLE MOMENTS. WAS THE 1972 AMERICAN LEAGUE ROOKIE OF THE YEAR AND AN 11-TIME ALL-STAR.

Pudge

Elected To The Hall Of Fame: *2000.*
Born: *Dec. 26, 1947 in Bellows Falls, Vt.*
Height: *6-3.* **Weight:** *200.*
Threw: *Right.* **Batted:** *Right.*
Debut: *Sept. 18, 1969.*
Final Game: *June 22, 1993.*
Teams: *Boston A.L. 1969, 1971-1980; Chicago A.L. 1981-1993.*
Postseason: *A.L. Pennant (1975); 2-Time Playoff Qualifier (1975,1983).*
Awards: *11-Time All-Star (1972-74, '76-78, 1980-82, 1985, 1991); A.L. Rookie of the Year (1972).*

YEAR	TEAM	LEAGUE	G	AB	R	H	2B	3B	HR	RBI	SB	AVG
1969	BOSTON	AL	2	5	0	0	0	0	0	0	0	.000
1971	BOSTON	AL	14	48	7	15	2	1	2	6	0	.313
1972	BOSTON	AL	131	457	74	134	28	9	22	61	5	.293
1973	BOSTON	AL	135	508	65	125	21	0	26	71	7	.246
1974	BOSTON	AL	52	187	36	56	12	1	11	26	5	.299
1975	BOSTON	AL	79	263	47	87	14	4	10	52	4	.331
1976	BOSTON	AL	134	487	76	124	17	5	17	58	12	.255
1977	BOSTON	AL	152	536	106	169	26	3	26	102	7	.315
1978	BOSTON	AL	157	571	94	162	39	5	20	88	7	.284
1979	BOSTON	AL	91	320	49	87	23	2	10	42	3	.272
1980	BOSTON	AL	131	478	73	138	25	3	18	62	11	.289
1981	CHICAGO	AL	96	338	44	89	12	0	7	45	3	.263
1982	CHICAGO	AL	135	476	66	127	17	3	14	65	17	.267
1983	CHICAGO	AL	138	488	85	141	26	4	26	86	9	.289
1984	CHICAGO	AL	102	359	54	83	20	1	21	43	6	.231
1985	CHICAGO	AL	153	543	85	129	23	1	37	107	17	.238
1986	CHICAGO	AL	125	457	42	101	11	0	14	63	2	.221
1987	CHICAGO	AL	135	454	68	116	22	1	23	71	1	.256
1988	CHICAGO	AL	76	253	37	70	8	1	19	50	0	.277
1989	CHICAGO	AL	103	375	47	110	25	2	13	68	1	.293
1990	CHICAGO	AL	137	452	65	129	21	0	18	65	7	.285
1991	CHICAGO	AL	134	460	42	111	25	0	18	74	1	.241
1992	CHICAGO	AL	62	188	12	43	4	1	3	21	3	.229
1993	CHICAGO	AL	25	53	2	10	0	0	1	4	0	.189
CAREER TOTALS			**2499**	**8756**	**1276**	**2356**	**421**	**47**	**376**	**1330**	**128**	**.269**

ELMER FLICK

In 1891, a 15-year old Elmer Flick went down to the train station to give his hometown semi-professional baseball team in Bedford, Ohio a send-off. With the train ready to leave and only eight players present, someone asked the youngster to join them. Despite being barefoot, Flick jumped at the opportunity – and a Hall of Fame career began.

Flick starred as a catcher for his high school team, but didn't join organized baseball until he made his debut with Youngstown, Ohio, in 1896. "In my first game for Youngstown, I hit a ninth-inning homer with one on to win, 2-1," said Flick. "That's when they first started to call me 'Elmer Flick, the demon of the stick'."

After one more season in the minor leagues, Flick was brought up to the Phillies in 1898, but was largely expected to come off the bench because of Philadelphia's veteran outfield. "Flick is going to make the outfielders hustle to hold their positions," said Francis Richter, a Philadelphia writer. "He is the fastest and most promising youngster the Phillies have ever had."

On April 26, future Hall of Fame outfielder Sam Thompson went down with an injury. Flick entered the game, recorded two hits and began his 13-year career. In four full seasons with the Phillies, Flick hit .338 with a career best .367 in 1900.

Following the 1901 season, Flick was one of several National League players who jumped to the year-old American League. He appeared in 11 games for the Philadelphia Athletics that spring, but was prohibited from playing any more when the Pennsylvania Supreme Court ruled that any players under contract to the Phillies could not play for another team.

Flick, however – along with teammate and future Hall of Famer Nap Lajoie – circumvented the order by signing with the AL's Cleveland Naps. The court order could not be enforced outside of Pennsylvania, so Flick and Lajoie were eligible to play for the Naps except when Cleveland traveled to Philadelphia. During those games, Flick and Lajoie took a paid vacation.

Flick played the rest of his career in Cleveland, where he led the league in stolen bases twice and triples three times. He also won the batting title in 1905. Illness slowed Flick's career from 1908-1910 and he played his last two seasons of professional ball in Toledo, Ohio, in 1911 and 1912.

ELMER HARRISON FLICK
PHILADELPHIA, N.L. 1898-1902
CLEVELAND, A.L. 1902-1910
OUTFIELDER WHO BATTED .378 FOR
1900 PHILLIES. LEFT LIFETIME MARK
OF .315 FOR 13 SEASONS. A.L. BATTING
CHAMPION IN 1905. LED A.L. IN TRIPLES,
1905-06-07, AND IN STEALS, 1904, TYING
FOR LEADERSHIP AGAIN IN 1906.

The Demon of the Stick

Elected To The Hall Of Fame: 1963.
Born: Jan. 11, 1876 in Bedford, Ohio.
Died: Jan. 9, 1971 in Bedford, Ohio.
Height: 5-9. **Weight:** 168.
Threw: Right. **Batted:** Left.
Debut: Apr. 26, 1898.
Final Game: July 4, 1910.
Teams: Philadelphia N.L. 1898-1901;
Philadelphia A.L. 1902; Cleveland A.L. 1902-10.

YEAR	TEAM	LEAGUE	G	AB	R	H	2B	3B	HR	RBI	SB	AVG
1898	PHILADELPHIA	NL	134	453	84	137	16	13	8	81	23	.302
1899	PHILADELPHIA	NL	127	485	98	166	22	11	2	98	31	.342
1900	PHILADELPHIA	NL	138	545	106	200	32	16	11	110	35	.367
1901	PHILADELPHIA	NL	138	540	112	180	32	17	8	88	30	.333
1902	PHILADELPHIA/CLEVELAND	NL/AL	121	461	85	137	21	12	2	64	24	.297
1903	CLEVELAND	AL	140	523	81	155	23	16	2	51	38	.296
1904	CLEVELAND	AL	150	579	97	177	31	17	6	56	35	.306
1905	CLEVELAND	AL	132	500	72	154	29	18	4	64	39	.308
1906	CLEVELAND	AL	157	624	98	194	34	22	1	62	41	.311
1907	CLEVELAND	AL	147	549	80	166	15	18	3	58	0	.302
1908	CLEVELAND	AL	9	35	4	8	1	1	0	2	0	.229
1909	CLEVELAND	AL	66	235	28	60	10	2	0	15	9	.255
1910	CLEVELAND	AL	24	68	5	18	2	1	1	7	1	.265
CAREER TOTALS			**1483**	**5597**	**950**	**1752**	**268**	**164**	**48**	**756**	**330**	**.313**

WHITEY FORD

At the heart of baseball is great pitching, the most indispensable part of any team.

At the heart of baseball's greatest dynasty was Whitey Ford, who won a higher percentage of his decisions than any other modern pitcher.

Since his Hall of Fame election in 1974 following his 16-year big league career, Ford became the embodiment of the New York Yankees team that was baseball for the postwar generation. "I don't care what the situation was, how high the stakes were – the bases could be loaded and the pennant riding on every pitch, it never bothered Whitey," said Mickey Mantle, who along with Ford and Yogi Berra powered Yankee Dynasty III that produced 14 American League pennants and nine World Series titles from 1949-64. "He pitched his game."

Signed to an amateur free contract by the Yankees prior to the 1947 season, Ford quickly rose through the minor leagues – surfacing in New York in the summer of 1950. The 5-foot-10, 178-pound Ford quickly established himself in a Yankee rotation filled with veterans like Vic Raschi, Eddie Lopat and Allie Reynolds. In 20 games, Ford went 9-1with a 2.81 earned-run average and finished second in the AL Rookie of the Year voting.

In the World Series, Ford started Game 4 and pitched for 26 of the 27 outs, recording a 5-2 victory against the Philadelphia Phillies that clinched the Series for the Bronx Bombers.

Ford spent the next two seasons in the Army, returning in 1953 after two more Fall Classic wins by the Yankees. Ford picked up where he left off, going 18-6 while helping New York win its fifth straight World Series championship – a record that has not been approached since.

Over the next seven seasons, Ford averaged 15 wins per year despite manager Casey Stengel's cautious use. Ford never pitched in more than 255 innings a season during that span but did appear in 11 World Series games, winning six en route to a record 10 Fall Classic wins.

Stengel was fired following the Yankees' 1960 World Series loss to Pittsburgh. The next season, new manager Ralph Houk began pitching Ford every fourth day – and the little lefty thrived on the extra work, going 25-4 to win his first Cy Young Award.

Chairman of the Board, Slick

Elected To The Hall Of Fame: *1974.*

Born: *Oct. 21, 1928 in New York, N.Y.*

Height: *5-10.* **Weight:** *178.*

Threw: *Left.* **Batted:** *Left.*

Debut: *July 1, 1950.*

Final Game: *May 21, 1967.*

Teams: *New York A.L. 1950, 1953-1967.*

Postseason: *6-Time World Series Champion (1950, 1953, 1956, 1958, 1961-1962); 11 A.L. Pennants (1950, 1953, 1955-1958, 1960-1964).*

Awards: *10-Time All-Star (1954-1956, 1958-1961, 1964); Major League Cy Young (1961); World Series Most Valuable Player (1961).*

YEAR	TEAM	LEAGUE	G	W	L	SV	SH	IP	H	BB	SO	ERA
1950	NEW YORK	AL	20	9	1	1	2	112	87	52	59	2.81
1953	NEW YORK	AL	32	18	6	0	3	207	187	110	110	3.00
1954	NEW YORK	AL	34	16	8	1	3	210.7	170	101	125	2.82
1955	NEW YORK	AL	39	18	7	2	5	253.7	188	113	137	2.63
1956	NEW YORK	AL	31	19	6	1	2	225.7	187	84	141	2.47
1957	NEW YORK	AL	24	11	5	0	0	129.3	114	53	84	2.57
1958	NEW YORK	AL	30	14	7	1	7	219.3	174	62	145	2.01
1959	NEW YORK	AL	35	16	10	1	2	204	194	89	114	3.04
1960	NEW YORK	AL	33	12	9	0	4	192.7	168	65	85	3.08
1961	NEW YORK	AL	39	25	4	0	3	283	242	92	209	3.21
1962	NEW YORK	AL	38	17	8	0	0	257.7	243	69	160	2.90
1963	NEW YORK	AL	38	24	7	1	3	269.3	240	56	189	2.74
1964	NEW YORK	AL	39	17	6	1	8	244.7	212	57	172	2.13
1965	NEW YORK	AL	37	16	13	1	2	244.3	241	50	162	3.24
1966	NEW YORK	AL	22	2	5	0	0	73	79	24	43	2.47
1967	NEW YORK	AL	7	2	4	0	1	44	40	9	21	1.64
CAREER TOTALS			**498**	**236**	**106**	**10**	**45**	**3170.1**	**2766**	**1086**	**1956**	**2.75**

BILL FOSTER

"Bill Foster was my star pitcher, not even barring Satchel Paige," manager Dave Malarcher said.
The younger half-brother of Negro League legend and founder Andrew "Rube" Foster, Bill Foster was a tall left-handed pitcher who played from 1923-37. For much of that time, he was considered the best lefty in the Negro Leagues. According to Hall of Fame umpire Jocko Conlan, "Foster had the same perfect delivery of Herb Pennock, but was faster by far, with a sharp curve, and had what all great pitchers have: control."

Foster could throw hard, but he was a pitcher, not just a thrower. His repertoire included the fastball, curve, slider, a drop ball, and most importantly, a phenomenal change-of-pace. Malarcher called him "the greatest exponent of the change-of-pace. He could throw you a fast ball with maybe six or eight changes of speed." According to Hall of Famer Hilton Smith, Foster would throw his high curve for a called strike: "Then when he got ready for you to swing, he'd start it 'round your waist and the catcher would catch it in the dirt. You couldn't hit it with anything."

Foster starred for his brother's Chicago American Giants through much of the twenties, helping the team to pennants in 1926, '27, and '33. The 1926 season and postseason may have been his greatest. He won 26 consecutive games (both league and non-league games) during the season. In the play-off between the Giants and the first-half winners the Kansas City Monarchs, the Giants needed to win both games to take the pennant. Foster started and won both games of the doubleheader, both against future Hall of Famer Bullet Joe Rogan. The American Giants then advanced to the World Series, defeating the Bacharach Giants while Foster won two games, pitched in two others, and posted an ERA of 1.27.

Foster was the winning pitcher for the West in the first East-West All-Star Game, going the distance against a formidable lineup. He briefly served as a player-manager in 1931 for the American Giants, but resigned in order to concentrate on pitching. He played winter ball in Cuba and California. After retiring from baseball, Foster was dean of men and baseball coach at Alcorn State College from 1960 until his death in 1978.

WILLIAM HENDRICK FOSTER
NEGRO LEAGUES, 1923-1937
REGARDED AS ONE OF THE BEST LEFT-HANDED PITCHERS IN NEGRO LEAGUE HISTORY AND ALSO MANAGED SEVERAL CLUBS. DEVASTATING SIDEARM DELIVERY MADE HIM CONSISTENT WINNER INSTRUMENTAL IN CHICAGO AMERICAN GIANTS' NEGRO LEAGUE PENNANT AND WORLD SERIES SUCCESS IN 1926, 1927, 1928 AND 1933. WON 26 STRAIGHT IN 1926 AND HAD 32-3 MARK IN 1927. COACHED BASEBALL AT ALMA MATER, ALCORN A & M COLLEGE IN MISSISSIPPI, 1960-1978

Elected To The Hall Of Fame: *1996.*
Born: *June 12, 1904 in Calvert, Texas.*
Died: *Sept. 16, 1978 in Lorman, Miss.*
Height: *6-1.* **Weight:** *195.*
Threw: *Left.* **Batted:** *Both.*
Teams: *Negro Leagues 1923-1937. Memphis 1923-1924; Chicago 1923-1930, 1932-1935, 1937; Birmingham 1925; Homestead 1931; Kansas City 1931; Pittsburgh 1936.*

YEAR	TEAM	LEAGUE	G	W	L	SV	SH	IP	H	BB	SO	RAVG
1923	MEMPHIS/CHI.	INDP/NNL	—	4	2	—	1	51.7	32	14	38	3.48
1924	CHI./MEMPHIS	NNL	—	6	1	—	3	51	39	17	36	3.00
1925	BIRM./CHICAGO	NNL	—	6	0	—	2	78	57	21	49	2.31
1926	CHICAGO	NNL	—	16	6	—	5	226.3	171	84	134	2.62
1927	CHICAGO	NNL	—	17	5	—	4	178	148	65	94	2.78
1928	CHICAGO	NNL	—	15	10	—	3	231	217	73	136	3.55
1929	CHICAGO	NNL	—	12	7	—	3	163.3	136	47	87	3.69
1930	CHICAGO	NNL	—	12	7	—	2	162.7	144	55	139	3.32
1931	HOMESTEAD/K.C.	NNL	—	8	1	—	0	79	56	22	64	3.08
1932	CHICAGO	NSL	—	10	6	—	2	134.3	119	25	84	2.95
CAREER TOTALS			**—**	**128**	**63**	**—**	**30**	**1675**	**1348**	**511**	**987**	**3.27**

NELLIE FOX

"Fox is what you'd call a manager's ballplayer. He does his job expertly and he does it every day. He's the type of player you can count on. He's an old pro. A great many times, he is hurting pretty badly from the dumpings he's taken on the field, but he's always ready to play," Hall of Fame manager Al Lopez said.

Jacob Nelson Fox, or Nellie as he would come to be known, was born in St. Thomas, Pa., on Christmas Day 1927. Less than 20 years later, he would make his debut in the Major Leagues at the ripe age of 19 for the Philadelphia Athletics. Trade winds carried him to the Chicago White Sox after the 1949 season, and here truly begins the story of Nellie Fox.

In 1951, after his uninspiring debut season for the Sox in which he hit only .247, Nellie began an eleven season stretch of All-Star selections, playing in a total of 1,691 games. This period also included a 798 consecutive game streak, the 11th longest of its kind in major league history. Over these years, Fox batted .299 and had 561 walks while striking out only 146 times. This would come to be one of Nellie's defining traits: a refusal to give in at the plate. Fox is one of the toughest outs in Major League Baseball history, recording only 216 strikeouts in over 10,000 plate appearances. In addition to his solidarity at the plate, Nellie was also one of the best defenders to ever play second base.

The Gold Glove Awards were first handed out in 1957 and Fox was the inaugural American League second base recipient. Long lauded for his defensive prowess, Fox would go on to win two more Gold Gloves in 1959 and 1960.

Nellie Fox had arguably the best year of his career in 1959, a season in which he hit .306, and captured the American League MVP award, narrowly edging out his double play partner, Luis Aparicio. This would be the only year Fox tasted the postseason and while the White Sox would lose to the Los Angeles Dodgers in the World Series, Nellie rose to the occasion, leading the Sox with a .375 batting average.

In 1975, skin cancer claimed Nellie Fox; he was 47 years old. Twenty-two years later, he entered the Hall of Fame.

Elected To The Hall Of Fame: 1997.
Born: Dec. 25, 1927 in St. Thomas, Pa.
Died: Dec. 1, 1975 at Baltimore, Md.
Height: 5-10. **Weight:** 160.
Threw: Right. **Batted:** Left.
Debut: June 8, 1947.
Final Game: July 25, 1965.
Teams: Philadelphia A.L. 1947-1949; Chicago A.L. 1950-1963; Houston N.L. 1964-1965
Postseason: A.L. Pennant (1959).
Awards: 15-Time All-Star (1951-1961, 1963); A.L. Most Valuable Player (1959).

YEAR	TEAM	LEAGUE	G	AB	R	H	2B	3B	HR	RBI	SB	AVG
1947	PHILADELPHIA	AL	7	3	2	0	0	0	0	0	0	.000
1948	PHILADELPHIA	AL	3	13	0	2	0	0	0	0	1	.154
1949	PHILADELPHIA	AL	88	247	42	63	6	2	0	21	2	.255
1950	CHICAGO	AL	130	457	45	113	12	7	0	30	4	.247
1951	CHICAGO	AL	147	604	93	189	32	12	4	55	9	.313
1952	CHICAGO	AL	152	648	76	192	25	10	0	39	5	.296
1953	CHICAGO	AL	154	624	92	178	31	8	3	72	4	.285
1954	CHICAGO	AL	155	631	111	201	24	8	2	47	16	.319
1955	CHICAGO	AL	154	636	100	198	28	7	6	59	7	.311
1956	CHICAGO	AL	154	649	109	192	20	10	4	52	8	.296
1957	CHICAGO	AL	155	619	110	196	27	8	6	61	5	.317
1958	CHICAGO	AL	155	623	82	187	21	6	0	49	5	.300
1959	CHICAGO	AL	156	624	84	191	34	6	2	70	5	.306
1960	CHICAGO	AL	150	605	85	175	24	10	2	59	2	.289
1961	CHICAGO	AL	159	606	67	152	11	5	2	51	2	.251
1962	CHICAGO	AL	157	621	79	166	27	7	2	54	1	.267
1963	CHICAGO	AL	137	539	54	140	19	0	2	42	0	.260
1964	HOUSTON	NL	133	442	45	117	12	6	0	28	0	.265
1965	HOUSTON	NL	21	41	3	11	2	0	0	1	0	.268
CAREER TOTALS			**2367**	**9232**	**1279**	**2663**	**355**	**112**	**35**	**790**	**76**	**.288**

JIMMIE FOXX

Hall of Famer Bill Dickey said, "If I were catching blindfolded, I'd always know when it was (Jimmie) Foxx who connected. He hit the ball harder than anyone else."

The powerful Sudlersville, Md., farm boy signed his first professional contract with the nearby Easton minor league club at age 16, and made his major league debut before the end of his junior year in high school.

Foxx played sparingly during his first few years in the big leagues, blocked at his regular position, catcher, by another future Hall of Famer, Mickey Cochrane. Hall of Fame backstop Rick Ferrell said of Foxx's ability behind the plate "If it wasn't for Cochrane, Foxx would have developed into a great catcher. He was the greatest all-around athlete I ever saw play Major League Baseball." Foxx finally broke out and earned regular playing time at a new position, first base, in 1929 and led the Athletics to the first of two consecutive World Series titles.

During his career, he was one of the most dominant offensive forces in the majors as he put together 12 30-home run seasons and 13 100-RBI seasons. When he retired in 1945, his 534 career home runs were second to only Babe Ruth and the most by any right-handed batter in big league history.

Fox was dubbed "The Beast" because of his powerful right-handed swing and the distance of the blasts he hit, and Hall of Famer Ted Lyons recalled "He had great powerful arms, and he used to wear his sleeves cut off way up, and when he dug in and raised that bat, his muscles would bulge and ripple." The nickname is also a little bit deceiving as Foxx had a reputation for being one of the kindest, most generous men in the game.

Hall of Fame hurler Lefty Gomez, who had the misfortune of facing Jimmie Foxx many times in his career, proclaimed, "When Neil Armstrong first set foot on the moon, he and all the space scientists were puzzled by an unidentifiable white object. I knew immediately what it was. That was a home-run ball hit off me in 1937 by Jimmie Foxx."

The Beast

Elected To The Hall Of Fame: 1951.
Born: Oct. 22, 1907 in Sudlersville, Md.
Died: July 21, 1967 in Miami, Fla.
Height: 6-0. **Weight:** 195.
Threw: Right. **Batted:** Right.
Debut: May 1, 1925.
Final Game: Sept. 23, 1945.
Teams: Philadelphia A.L. 1925-1935; Boston A.L. 1936-1942; Chicago N.L. 1942, 1944; Philadelphia N.L. 1945.
Postseason: 2-Time World Series Champion (1929-1930); 3 A.L. Pennants (1929-1931).
Awards: 9-Time All-Star (1933-1941); 3-Time Most Valuable Player (1932-1933, 1938).

YEAR	TEAM	LEAGUE	G	AB	R	H	2B	3B	HR	RBI	SB	AVG
1925	PHILADELPHIA	AL	10	9	2	6	1	0	0	0	0	.667
1926	PHILADELPHIA	AL	26	32	8	10	2	1	0	5	1	.313
1927	PHILADELPHIA	AL	61	130	23	42	6	5	3	20	2	.323
1928	PHILADELPHIA	AL	118	400	85	131	29	10	13	79	3	.328
1929	PHILADELPHIA	AL	149	517	123	183	23	9	33	118	9	.354
1930	PHILADELPHIA	AL	153	562	127	188	33	13	37	156	7	.335
1931	PHILADELPHIA	AL	139	515	93	150	32	10	30	120	4	.291
1932	PHILADELPHIA	AL	154	585	151	213	33	9	58	169	3	.364
1933	PHILADELPHIA	AL	149	573	125	204	37	9	48	163	2	.356
1934	PHILADELPHIA	AL	150	539	120	180	28	6	44	130	11	.334
1935	PHILADELPHIA	AL	147	535	118	185	33	7	36	115	6	.346
1936	BOSTON	AL	155	585	130	198	32	8	41	143	13	.338
1937	BOSTON	AL	150	569	111	162	24	6	36	127	10	.285
1938	BOSTON	AL	149	565	139	197	33	9	50	175	5	.349
1939	BOSTON	AL	124	467	130	168	31	10	35	105	4	.360
1940	BOSTON	AL	144	515	106	153	30	4	36	119	4	.297
1941	BOSTON	AL	135	487	87	146	27	8	19	105	2	.300
1942	BOSTON/CHICAGO	NL/AL	100	305	43	69	12	0	8	33	1	.226
1944	CHICAGO	NL	15	20	0	1	1	0	0	2	0	.050
1945	PHILADELPHIA	NL	89	224	30	60	11	1	7	38	0	.268
CAREER TOTALS			**2317**	**8134**	**1751**	**2646**	**458**	**125**	**534**	**1922**	**87**	**.325**

FRANKIE FRISCH

"If I needed one player to do the job of winning the game I needed to win, that player would be Frank Frisch," Yankees manager Joe McCarthy said.

Frankie Frisch was a collegiate sports superstar, playing for Fordham University's baseball, basketball, football and track teams. His remarkable speed would earn him the nickname of the "Fordham Flash." Frisch would not finish his undergraduate career at Fordham, however, instead choosing to sign a contract with the New York Giants in 1919.

The Giants wasted no time with Frisch, placing him directly on the major league squad instead of seasoning him in the minors. At first glance the effort seemed to be a failure; Frisch hit only .226 in an abbreviated season, but in 1920, Frankie rewarded the Giants' investment. In his first full season, Frisch hit .280 and drove in 77 runs to go along with 34 stolen bases. His effort in 1921 would prove even better, as Frisch batted .341 and stole 49 bases to lead the National League. He would capture two more stolen base titles in 1927 and 1931, but not with the New York Giants.

Despite winning back to back World Series with the Giants (1921, 1922) and being named captain by manager John McGraw, Frisch's time in New York would come to an unceremonious end. After a Giants loss in the latter half of the 1926 season, McGraw berated Frisch in front of his teammates. Frisch responded by leaving the team and heading to New York. He would eventually return to the Giants, but McGraw and Frisch's relationship was finished, as was Frankie's tenure in New York.

The Giants would trade Frisch along with pitcher Jimmy Ring to the St. Louis Cardinals for Rogers Hornsby after the 1926 season. In 1927, Frisch, always known for his stellar glove work, posted one of the best defensive efforts ever, setting the record for most assists in a single season (643). He also won an MVP award with the Cardinals in 1931 while helping them capture the World Series both that year and in 1934. In 1935 Frisch was selected as an All-Star for the third consecutive year.

The Fordham Flash

Elected To The Hall Of Fame: 1947.
Born: Sept. 9, 1898 in Bronx, N.Y.
Died: Mar. 12, 1973 in Wilmington, Del.
Height: 5-11. **Weight:** 165.
Threw: Right. **Batted:** Both.
Debut: June 17, 1919.
Final Game: Aug. 5, 1937.
Teams: New York N.L. 1919-1926; St. Louis N.L. 1927-1937.
Postseason: 4-Time World Series Champion (1921-1922, 1931, 1934); 8-Time N.L. Pennants (1921-1924, 1928, 1930-1931, 1934).
Awards: 3-Time All-Star (1933-1935); N.L. Most Valuable Player (1931).

YEAR	TEAM	LEAGUE	G	AB	R	H	2B	3B	HR	RBI	SB	AVG
1919	NEW YORK	NL	54	190	21	43	3	2	2	24	15	.226
1920	NEW YORK	NL	110	440	57	123	10	10	4	77	34	.280
1921	NEW YORK	NL	153	618	121	211	31	17	8	100	49	.341
1922	NEW YORK	NL	132	514	101	168	16	13	5	51	31	.327
1923	NEW YORK	NL	151	641	116	223	32	10	12	111	29	.348
1924	NEW YORK	NL	145	603	121	198	33	15	7	69	22	.328
1925	NEW YORK	NL	120	502	89	166	26	6	11	48	21	.331
1926	NEW YORK	NL	135	545	75	171	29	4	5	44	23	.314
1927	ST. LOUIS	NL	153	617	112	208	31	11	10	78	48	.337
1928	ST. LOUIS	NL	141	547	107	164	29	9	10	86	29	.300
1929	ST. LOUIS	NL	138	527	93	176	40	12	5	74	24	.334
1930	ST. LOUIS	NL	133	540	121	187	46	9	10	114	15	.346
1931	ST. LOUIS	NL	131	518	96	161	24	4	4	82	28	.311
1932	ST. LOUIS	NL	115	486	59	142	26	2	3	60	18	.292
1933	ST. LOUIS	NL	147	585	74	177	32	6	4	66	18	.303
1934	ST. LOUIS	NL	140	550	74	168	30	6	3	75	11	.305
1935	ST. LOUIS	NL	103	354	52	104	16	2	1	55	2	.294
1936	ST. LOUIS	NL	93	303	40	83	10	0	1	26	2	.274
1937	ST. LOUIS	NL	17	32	3	7	2	0	0	4	0	.219
CAREER TOTALS			**2311**	**9112**	**1532**	**2880**	**466**	**138**	**105**	**1244**	**419**	**.316**

PUD GALVIN

JAMES F. (PUD) GALVIN
ST. LOUIS N.A. 1875
BUFFALO N.L. 1879-1885
PITTSBURGH A.A. 1885-1886
PITTSBURGH N.L. 1887-1889 1891-1892
PITTSBURGH P.L. 1890
ST. LOUIS N.L. 1892
WON 365 GAMES, LOST 311.
WHEN ELECTED ONLY FOUR PITCHERS
HAD WON MORE GAMES.
PITCHED NO-HIT GAMES IN 1880 AND 1884.
PITCHED 649 COMPLETE GAMES.

"If I had Galvin to catch, no one would ever steal a base on me. That fellow keeps them glued to the bag," Hall of Fame catcher Buck Ewing said.

James Francis Galvin would earn the nickname "Pud" over the course of his baseball career for his uncanny ability to make hitters look like "pudding." Born on Christmas Day 1856 in St. Louis, Galvin would go on to make his debut as a teenager in the National Association for his hometown Brown Stockings in 1875. Four years later, Pud would surface in the National League pitching for the Buffalo Bisons and begin one of the most workmanlike careers baseball has ever seen.

Galvin was renowned for his durability, even in an era of baseball where two-man pitching rotations were commonplace. Galvin's strong constitution allowed him to regularly take the mound and pitch deep into the game.

Over a two-year period spanning the 1883 and 1884 seasons, Pud would win 92 games, nearly a quarter of his career total, while twirling 143 complete games en route to nearly 1,300 innings. Galvin also paced the NL in shutouts in both years, with five and 12 in 1883 and 1884, respectively. This stretch represents the height of Pud's career and his performance would end up drawing interest from other baseball organizations.

The Pittsburgh Alleghenys purchased Pud Galvin from the Bisons on July 13, 1885, and in 1888, Pud Galvin became the first player in history to win 300 games, a number many now use as a benchmark for greatness. Unfortunately, the tremendous mileage Galvin's arm accrued in the previous decade would begin to catch up to him. Pud's games pitched and innings totals began to fall year after year until his retirement following the 1892 season.

Pud Galvin would live out the rest of his days in the suburbs of Pittsburgh, for a time working as a National League umpire and later opening a bar. On March 7, 1902, Galvin died; some sixty years later, the Veterans Committee elected Pud Galvin to the Baseball Hall of Fame in 1965.

Elected To The Hall Of Fame: 1965.
Born: Dec. 25, 1856 in St. Louis, Mo.
Died: Mar. 7, 1902 in Pittsburgh, Pa.
Height: 5-8. **Weight:** 190.
Threw: Right. **Batted:** Right.
Debut: May 22, 1875.
Final Game: Aug. 2, 1892.
Teams: St. Louis, National Association 1875; Buffalo N.L. 1879-1885; Pittsburgh, American Association 1885-1886; Pittsburgh N.L. 1887-1889, 1891-1892; Pittsburgh, Player's League 1890; St. Louis N.L. 1892.

YEAR	TEAM	LEAGUE	G	W	L	SV	SH	IP	H	BB	SO	ERA
1875	ST. LOUIS	NA	8	4	2	1	0	62	53	1	8	1.16
1879	BUFFALO	NL	66	37	27	0	6	593	585	31	136	2.28
1880	BUFFALO	NL	58	20	35	0	5	458.7	528	32	128	2.71
1881	BUFFALO	NL	56	28	24	0	5	474	546	46	136	2.37
1882	BUFFALO	NL	52	28	23	0	3	445.3	476	40	162	3.17
1883	BUFFALO	NL	76	46	29	0	5	656.3	676	50	279	2.72
1884	BUFFALO	NL	72	46	22	0	12	636.3	566	63	369	1.99
1885	BUFFALO/PITTSBURGH	NL/AA	44	16	26	1	3	372.3	453	44	120	3.99
1886	PITTSBURGH	AA	50	29	21	0	2	434.7	457	75	72	2.67
1887	PITTSBURGH	NL	49	28	21	0	3	440.7	490	67	76	3.29
1888	PITTSBURGH	NL	50	23	25	0	6	437.3	446	53	107	2.63
1889	PITTSBURGH	NL	41	23	16	0	4	341	392	78	77	4.17
1890	PITTSBURGH	PL	26	12	13	0	1	217	275	49	35	4.35
1891	PITTSBURGH	NL	33	15	14	0	2	246.7	256	62	46	2.88
1892	PITTSBURGH/ST. LOUIS	NL	24	10	12	0	0	188	206	54	56	2.92
CAREER TOTALS			705	365	310	2	57	6003.1	6405	745	1807	2.85

LOU GEHRIG

HENRY LOUIS GEHRIG
NEW YORK YANKEES·1923·1939
HOLDER OF MORE THAN A SCORE OF
MAJOR AND AMERICAN LEAGUE RECORDS,
INCLUDING THAT OF PLAYING 2130
CONSECUTIVE GAMES. WHEN HE RETIRED
IN 1939, HE HAD A LIFE TIME BATTING
AVERAGE OF 340.

"I took the two most expensive aspirins in history," said Yankee first baseman Wally Pipp, who sat out a 1925 game with a headache and lost his position to Lou Gehrig, who would play every game there for the Yankees until his retirement in 1939.

If you look up the word ballplayer in the dictionary, it is likely they'll have a picture of Lou Gehrig, stalwart New York Yankee first baseman. Gehrig is chiefly known for playing in 2,130 consecutive games for the Yankees, a magnificent streak long thought to have been unbreakable, until Cal Ripken, Jr. came along.

Gehrig wore uniform No. 4 because he hit behind Babe Ruth, who was No. 3. One of the most magnificent hitters and run producers in history, Gehrig was always overshadowed by Ruth, who was not only an unparalleled hitter, but was as outgoing and flamboyant as Gehrig was reserved and quiet. "He just went out and did his job every day," said his teammate, Bill Dickey.

Gehrig scored over 100 runs and drove in over 100 runs for 13 straight seasons. He led the American League in runs four times, home runs three times, RBI five times, on-base percentage five times, and batting average once. He finished among the league's top three hitters seven times. He racked up eight 200-plus hit seasons.

In 1931, he set the AL single-season RBI mark with 184–hitting behind Ruth, who knocked in 163 of his own. One wonders who was left on base for Gehrig to bring home. His 1934 Triple-Crown season was remarkable, as he hit .363, knocked 49 home runs, and drove in 165 runs.

He was the All-Star first baseman for the first seven All-Star teams, from 1933-39, though he retired just shy of the 1939 game. During his 17 seasons, the Yankees won seven pennants and six World Series. Gehrig's World Series contributions include a .361 batting average, 10 home runs, and 35 RBI in 34 games.

Gehrig's consecutive games streak came to an end on May 2, 1939, when he removed himself from the lineup after a dismal start caused by his mysterious neuromuscular disease, amyotrophic lateral sclerosis, or ALS, later known as "Lou Gehrig's Disease."

The Iron Horse

Elected To The Hall Of Fame: 1939.
Born: June 19, 1903 in New York, N.Y.
Died: June 2, 1941 in Riverdale, N.Y.
Height: 6-0. **Weight:** 200.
Threw: Left. **Batted:** Left.
Debut: June 15, 1923.
Final Game: Apr. 30, 1939.
Teams: New York A.L. 1923-1939.
Postseason: 6-Time World Series Champion (1927-1928, 1932, 1936-1938); 7 A.L. Pennants (1926-1928, 1932, 1936-1938).
Awards: 7-Time All-Star (1933-1939); Two-Time A.L. Most Valuable Player (1927, 1936).

YEAR	TEAM	LEAGUE	G	AB	R	H	2B	3B	HR	RBI	SB	AVG
1923	NEW YORK	AL	13	26	6	11	4	1	1	9	0	.423
1924	NEW YORK	AL	10	12	2	6	1	0	0	5	0	.500
1925	NEW YORK	AL	126	437	73	129	23	10	20	68	6	.295
1926	NEW YORK	AL	155	572	135	179	47	20	16	112	6	.313
1927	NEW YORK	AL	155	584	149	218	52	18	47	175	10	.373
1928	NEW YORK	AL	154	562	139	210	47	13	27	142	4	.374
1929	NEW YORK	AL	154	553	127	166	32	10	35	126	4	.300
1930	NEW YORK	AL	154	581	143	220	42	17	41	174	12	.379
1931	NEW YORK	AL	155	619	163	211	31	15	46	184	17	.341
1932	NEW YORK	AL	156	596	138	208	42	9	34	151	4	.349
1933	NEW YORK	AL	152	593	138	198	41	12	32	139	9	.334
1934	NEW YORK	AL	154	579	128	210	40	6	49	165	9	.363
1935	NEW YORK	AL	149	535	125	176	26	10	30	119	8	.329
1936	NEW YORK	AL	155	579	167	205	37	7	49	152	3	.354
1937	NEW YORK	AL	157	569	138	200	37	9	37	159	4	.351
1938	NEW YORK	AL	157	576	115	170	32	6	29	114	6	.295
1939	NEW YORK	AL	8	28	2	4	0	0	0	1	0	.143
CAREER TOTALS			**2164**	**8001**	**1888**	**2721**	**534**	**163**	**493**	**1995**	**102**	**.340**

CHARLIE GEHRINGER

He was The Mechanical Man, a player whose remarkable consistency was equaled only by his self-effacing demeanor.

He was so consistent he even played in every inning of the first six All-Star games as the starting second baseman for the American League and hit .500 in 20 at-bats. "Charlie says 'hello' on Opening Day, 'goodbye' on closing day, and in between hits .350," said Hall of Fame player-manager Mickey Cochrane.

Gehringer played his entire 19-year big league career with the Detroit Tigers, breaking into the majors at age 21 in 1924 and retiring after the 1942 season. Of his 2,221 games in the field, only 15 came at a position other than second base.

"I tell you, I used to cuss him – I couldn't hit a ball past him," said Hall of Fame shortstop Joe Sewell. "I'm left-handed and I just couldn't get one through there on the ground. He'd just coast around that infield, just like somebody skating."

At the plate, Gehringer was even better. He batted better than .300 in 13 full seasons, had more than 200 hits seven times, drove in more than 100 runs seven times and won the 1937 American League batting title with an average of .371. He was also the league's MVP that season – a year when runner-up Joe DiMaggio had 46 home runs, 167 RBI and scored 151 runs.

"I always thought that Charlie was one of the great hitters of my time," said Hall of Fame catcher Rick Ferrell. "He didn't have the tremendous power of Jimmie Foxx, Ruth or Gehrig or those guys, but he was tough to strike out and he hit more line drives and met the ball more solidly than any hitter."

When Gehringer retired, he had scored 1,774 runs (still 20th all-time), batted .320 and thumped 574 doubles. His 60 doubles in 1936 mark one of only six times in baseball history a batter has cracked the 60-double barrier in one season.

"You wind him up in the spring, turn him loose, he hits .330 or .340, and you shut him off at the end of the season," said Hall of Fame pitcher Lefty Gomez, whose Yankees battled Gehringer's Tigers for the AL pennant almost yearly during the 1930s.

The Mechanical Man

Elected To The Hall Of Fame: 1949.
Born: May 11, 1903 in Fowlerville, Mich.
Died: Jan. 21, 1993 in Bloomfield Hills, Mich.
Height: 5-11. **Weight:** 180.
Threw: Right. **Batted:** Left.
Debut: Sept. 22, 1924.
Final Game: Sept. 27, 1942.
Teams: Detroit A.L. 1924-1942.
Postseason: World Series Champion (1935); 3 A.L. Pennants (1934-1935, 1940).
Awards: 6-Time All-Star (1933-1938); A.L. Most Valuable Player (1937).

YEAR	TEAM	LEAGUE	G	AB	R	H	2B	3B	HR	RBI	SB	AVG
1924	DETROIT	AL	5	13	2	6	0	0	0	1	1	.462
1925	DETROIT	AL	8	18	3	3	0	0	0	0	0	.167
1926	DETROIT	AL	123	459	62	127	19	17	1	48	9	.277
1927	DETROIT	AL	133	508	110	161	29	11	4	61	17	.317
1928	DETROIT	AL	154	603	108	193	29	16	6	74	15	.320
1929	DETROIT	AL	155	634	131	215	45	19	13	106	27	.339
1930	DETROIT	AL	154	610	144	201	47	15	16	98	19	.330
1931	DETROIT	AL	101	383	67	119	24	5	4	53	13	.311
1932	DETROIT	AL	152	618	112	184	44	11	19	107	9	.298
1933	DETROIT	AL	155	628	103	204	42	6	12	105	5	.325
1934	DETROIT	AL	154	601	134	214	50	7	11	127	11	.356
1935	DETROIT	AL	150	610	123	201	32	8	19	108	11	.330
1936	DETROIT	AL	154	641	144	227	60	12	15	116	4	.354
1937	DETROIT	AL	144	564	133	209	40	1	14	96	11	.371
1938	DETROIT	AL	152	568	133	174	32	5	20	107	14	.306
1939	DETROIT	AL	118	406	86	132	29	6	16	86	4	.325
1940	DETROIT	AL	139	515	108	161	33	3	10	81	10	.313
1941	DETROIT	AL	127	436	65	96	19	4	3	46	1	.220
1942	DETROIT	AL	45	45	6	12	0	0	1	7	0	.267
CAREER TOTALS			**2323**	**8860**	**1774**	**2839**	**574**	**146**	**184**	**1427**	**181**	**.320**

BOB GIBSON

ROBERT GIBSON
ST. LOUIS N. L., 1959-1975
FIVE-TIME 20-GAME WINNER. HIS 3,117
STRIKEOUTS MADE HIM ONLY 2ND PITCHER TO
REACH 3,000. FIRST TO FAN 200 OR MORE IN
A SEASON 9 TIMES, SET N. L. MARK WITH 1.12
ERA IN 1968; HURLING 13 SHUTOUTS. TWICE
WORLD SERIES MVP; SETTING RECORDS FOR
CONSECUTIVE VICTORIES (7), CONSECUTIVE
COMPLETE GAMES (8), AND STRIKEOUTS IN A
GAME (17) AND A SERIES (35). VOTED N. L.
MVP IN 1968 AND CY YOUNG AWARD WINNER IN
1968 AND 1970. WON NINE GOLD GLOVE AWARDS.

"Gibby is one of baseball's greatest competitors." Hall of Famer Stan Musial said.

Bob Gibson may well have been the most intimidating pitcher in history. He was certainly one of the most successful. The Omaha, Neb., native excelled at baseball and basketball in high school, and played college hoops for Creighton before a brief stint with the Harlem Globetrotters. In 1957, he signed with the Cardinals, and made his big-league debut in 1959.

A 15-game winner by 1962, Gibson began to take flight soon after. He won 18 games in 1963, and 19 in the Cardinals' pennant-winning season of 1964, when he went 9-2 down the stretch. In the World Series against the Yankees, he went 2-1, winning Game Five at Yankee Stadium and then Game Seven at home on two days rest. He was named World Series MVP.

He was a 20-game winner in 1965 and '66, winning the first of nine consecutive Gold Gloves in '65. A broken ankle in July of 1967 slowed him down to a 13-7 record, including three wins late in the season to help the Cards clinch another pennant. He went 3-0 with an ERA of 1.00 in the Cardinals' victory over the Red Sox, winning games 1, 4, and 7, and picking up his second World Series MVP award in two tries.

The 1968 season has come to be known as "The Year of the Pitcher," and Bob Gibson was certainly the pitcher of the year. He went 22-9 with a sparkling 1.12 ERA, to go along with 268 strikeouts, 13 shutouts, and a stretch of 92 innings in which he gave up just two runs. He was again 2-1 in the World Series, beating the Tigers in Games One and Four before going the distance in a Game Seven loss.

Gibson brought home both the 1968 Cy Young Award and the NL Most Valuable Player awards, and, in the ultimate compliment, baseball actually lowered the mound the following season, because pitchers, led by Gibson, were dominating hitters and games were historically low-scoring. Gibson bagged a second Cy Young Award in 1970, and pitched a no-hitter against the Pirates in 1971. Injuries were beginning to take their toll, however, and Gibson wound down with double-figure victory totals in 1973 and '74, before retiring in 1975.

Gibby, Hoot

Elected To The Hall Of Fame: 1981.
Born: Nov. 9, 1935 in Omaha, Neb.
Height: 6-1. **Weight:** 189.
Threw: Right. **Batted:** Right.
Debut: Apr. 15, 1959.
Final Game: Sept. 3, 1975.
Teams: St. Louis N.L. 1959-1975.
Postseason: 2-Time World Series Champion (1964, 1967); 3 N.L. Pennants (1964, 1967-1968).
Awards: 9-time All-Star (1962-two games, 1965-70, 1972); 2-Time World Series Most Valuable Player (1964, 1967); 2-Time N.L. Cy Young (1968, 1970); N.L. Most Valuable Player (1968).

YEAR	TEAM	LEAGUE	G	W	L	SV	SH	IP	H	BB	SO	ERA
1959	ST. LOUIS	NL	13	3	5	0	1	75.7	77	39	48	3.33
1960	ST. LOUIS	NL	27	3	6	0	0	86.7	97	48	69	5.61
1961	ST. LOUIS	NL	35	13	12	1	2	211.3	186	119	166	3.24
1962	ST. LOUIS	NL	32	15	13	1	5	233.7	174	95	208	2.85
1963	ST. LOUIS	NL	36	18	9	0	2	254.7	224	96	204	3.39
1964	ST. LOUIS	NL	40	19	12	1	2	287.3	250	86	245	3.01
1965	ST. LOUIS	NL	38	20	12	1	6	299	243	103	270	3.07
1966	ST. LOUIS	NL	35	21	12	0	5	280.3	210	78	225	2.44
1967	ST. LOUIS	NL	24	13	7	0	2	175.3	151	40	147	2.98
1968	ST. LOUIS	NL	34	22	9	0	13	304.7	198	62	268	1.12
1969	ST. LOUIS	NL	35	20	13	0	4	314	251	95	269	2.18
1970	ST. LOUIS	NL	34	23	7	0	3	294	262	88	274	3.12
1971	ST. LOUIS	NL	31	16	13	0	5	245.7	215	76	185	3.04
1972	ST. LOUIS	NL	34	19	11	0	4	278	226	88	208	2.46
1973	ST. LOUIS	NL	25	12	10	0	1	195	159	57	142	2.77
1974	ST. LOUIS	NL	33	11	13	0	1	240	236	104	129	3.83
1975	ST. LOUIS	NL	22	3	10	2	0	109	120	62	60	5.04
CAREER TOTALS			**528**	**251**	**174**	**6**	**56**	**3884.1**	**3279**	**1336**	**3117**	**2.91**

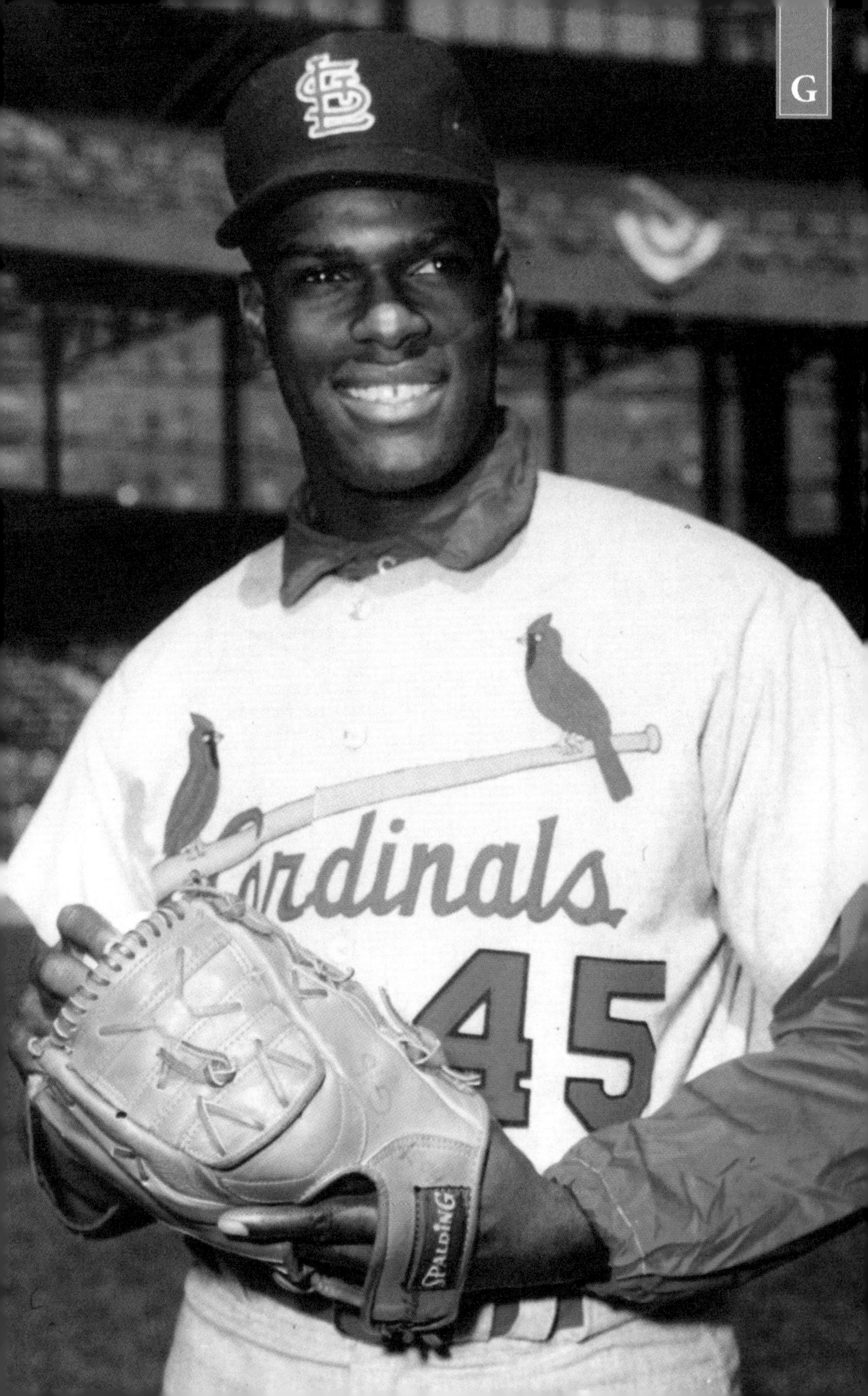
45
SPALDING

JOSH GIBSON

"Yes sir, I've seen a lot of colored boys who should have been playing in the majors. First of all I'd name this guy Josh Gibson for a place. He's one of the greatest backstops in history, I think. Any team in the big leagues could use him right now," said Carl Hubbell.

Josh Gibson is widely regarded as the best power hitter in Negro League history, with some estimates crediting him with over 800 home runs. Gibson was born in Buena Vista, Ga., on Dec. 21, 1911, but he would move to Pittsburgh in 1923 when his father landed a job working for the Carnegie-Illinois Steel Company. Gibson had planned to be an electrician, but a natural ability to crush a baseball quickly shaped his future plans.

The career of Gibson in the Negro Leagues was spent with two teams: the Homestead Grays and the Pittsburgh Crawfords. In his first season with the Grays as an 18 year old, Gibson would hit the first ball to clear the center field fence in Forbes Field, which sat at a mammoth 457 feet from home plate. This was not an isolated incident of strength and hitting prowess; over his 17-year career, Gibson would amass 12 home run titles while hitting for a high average.

In 1940, Gibson's baseball career would take him to Mexico, where he would exercise his typical level of dominance. Gibson set a Mexican League home run record in 1941 playing for the Veracruz Blues when he belted 33 long balls, more than double the standing mark. That record would stand for two decades.

Gibson returned to the states and to his original team, the Homestead Grays, in 1942, continuing to post unheard of power numbers for the time. In 1943, Gibson entered a coma and was diagnosed with a brain tumor. While he would awaken, Gibson opted not to have surgery and would endure frequent headaches in the following years. His last season would come in 1946 and on Jan. 20, 1947, Gibson died of a stroke only three months before Jackie Robinson would break the color barrier in baseball.

JOSHUA (JOSH) GIBSON
NEGRO LEAGUES 1930-1946

CONSIDERED GREATEST SLUGGER IN NEGRO BASEBALL LEAGUES. POWER-HITTING CATCHER WHO HIT ALMOST 800 HOME RUNS IN LEAGUE AND INDEPENDENT BASEBALL DURING HIS 17-YEAR CAREER. CREDITED WITH HAVING BEEN NEGRO NATIONAL LEAGUE BATTING CHAMPION IN 1936-38-42-45.

Elected To The Hall of Fame: *1972.*
Born: *Dec. 21, 1911 in Buena Vista, Ga.*
Died: *Jan. 20, 1947 in Pittsburgh, Pa.*
Height: *6-1.* **Weight:** *210*
Threw: *Right.* **Batted:** *Right.*
Teams: *Negro Leagues 1930-1946. Homestead 1930-1931, 1937-1940, 1942-1944; Pittsburgh 1932-1936.*

YEAR	TEAM	LEAGUE	G	AB	R	H	2B	3B	HR	RBI	SB	AVG
1930	HOMESTEAD	INDP	—	71	13	24	2	0	5	—	0	.338
1931	HOMESTEAD	INDP	—	132	27	38	6	5	6	—	0	.288
1932	PITTSBURGH	INDP	—	187	33	61	10	5	7	—	0	.326
1933	PITTSBURGH	NNL	—	129	27	44	3	1	6	—	1	.341
1934	PITTSBURGH	NNL	—	190	38	61	14	3	11	—	2	.321
1935	PITTSBURGH	NNL	—	145	37	54	10	2	8	—	7	.372
1936	PITTSBURGH	NNL	—	82	27	37	3	2	6	—	1	.451
1937	HOMESTEAD	NNL	—	97	39	38	6	4	12	—	1	.392
1938	HOMESTEAD	NNL	—	91	25	28	3	1	0	—	0	.308
1939	HOMESTEAD	NNL	—	74	22	27	3	2	10	—	3	.365
1940	HOMESTEAD	NNL	—	6	2	1	0	0	1	—	0	.167
1942	HOMESTEAD	NNL	—	138	37	41	6	1	7	—	3	.297
1943	HOMESTEAD	NNL	—	181	64	88	22	5	12	—	5	.486
1944	HOMESTEAD	NNL	—	126	27	46	4	3	9	—	3	.365
CAREER TOTALS			**—**	**1825**	**453**	**638**	**100**	**40**	**107**	**—**	**26**	**.350**

Joshua Gi
Dec 21, 19
Gibson
Gibb

LEFTY GOMEZ

"I'd rather be lucky than good," Lefty Gomez once said. Vernon Louis Gomez, or "Lefty" as he'd come to be known, was far more talented than he'd ever give himself credit for. Notorious for an overpowering fastball as he was for his razor sharp wit, Gomez's lighthearted nature belied a ferocious ability to get hitters out. Born in Rodeo, Calif., on Nov. 26, 1908, Gomez attended Richmond High School. He came to the San Francisco Seals' attention around this time and was brought into their organization, but he wasn't long for it. On Aug. 17, 1929, the New York Yankees purchased Gomez from the San Francisco Seals for the sum of $45,000.

Gomez was used primarily in relief during his first season with the Yankees in 1930, making only a handful of starts. Lefty went on to win over 20 games his sophomore season, firmly entrenching himself in the Yankee rotation. The next year would hold more of the same for Gomez, as he posted another 24 wins, but Lefty's best was still yet to come.

In 1933, Gomez led the majors in strikeouts and was selected to the first All-Star Game. It would be the first of seven consecutive All-Star appearances for him. Gomez's 1934 season stands out as his best; he dominated the MLB pitching leaderboard that year, pacing the league in wins (26), win percentage (.839), ERA (2.33), complete games (25), shutouts (6), innings pitched (281.2) and one again in strikeouts (158). Lefty would go on to win another pitcher's Triple Crown in 1937. While Gomez received more than his fair share of individual accolades, he was also a vital cog in the Yankee machine that dominated the late 1930s.

Lefty's postseason legacy is virtually without flaw: he won every game he started in each of the 1936 and 1937 World Series (both versus the New York Giants). In total, Gomez started seven games and was awarded six victories with zero losses. At the end of his career, Lefty would have enough championships to fully decorate a hand ('32, '36, '37, '38, '39).

The Veterans Committee elected Gomez into the National Baseball Hall of Fame on Feb. 2, 1972. After spending his final years in Novato, Calif., Gomez died in 1989.

VERNON LOUIS GOMEZ
"LEFTY"
NEW YORK A.L. 1930-1942
WASHINGTON A.L. 1943
WON 20 OR MORE GAMES FOUR TIMES IN HELPING YANKEES TO WIN SEVEN PENNANTS. LED A.L. WITH 26-5 RECORD, 2.33 EARNED RUN AVERAGE IN 1934 AND WITH 21 VICTORIES AND 2.33 ERA IN 1937. PACED A.L. IN WINNING PCT. TWICE, STRIKEOUTS THREE TIMES. SET WORLD SERIES MARK BY WINNING 6 GAMES WITHOUT A LOSS.

Goofy

Elected To The Hall Of Fame: *1972.*

Born: *Nov. 26, 1908 in Rodeo, Calif.*

Died: *Feb. 17, 1989 in Greenbrae, Calif.*

Height: *6-2.* **Weight:** *173.*

Threw: *Left.* **Batted:** *Left.*

Debut: *Apr. 29, 1930.*

Final Game: *May 30, 1943.*

Teams: *New York A.L. 1930-1942; Washington A.L. 1943.*

Postseason: *5-Time World Series Champion (1932, 1936-1939); 5 A.L. Pennants (1932, 1936-1939).*

Awards: *7-Time All-Star (1933-1939).*

YEAR	TEAM	LEAGUE	G	W	L	SV	SH	IP	H	BB	SO	ERA
1930	NEW YORK	AL	15	2	5	1	0	60	66	28	22	5.55
1931	NEW YORK	AL	40	21	9	3	1	243	206	85	150	2.67
1932	NEW YORK	AL	37	24	7	1	1	265.3	266	105	176	4.21
1933	NEW YORK	AL	35	16	10	2	4	234.7	218	106	163	3.18
1934	NEW YORK	AL	38	26	5	1	6	281.7	223	96	158	2.33
1935	NEW YORK	AL	34	12	15	1	2	246	223	86	138	3.18
1936	NEW YORK	AL	31	13	7	0	0	188.7	184	122	105	4.39
1937	NEW YORK	AL	34	21	11	0	6	278.3	233	93	194	2.33
1938	NEW YORK	AL	32	18	12	0	4	239	239	99	129	3.35
1939	NEW YORK	AL	26	12	8	0	2	198	173	84	102	3.41
1940	NEW YORK	AL	9	3	3	0	0	27.3	37	18	14	6.59
1941	NEW YORK	AL	23	15	5	0	2	156.3	151	103	76	3.74
1942	NEW YORK	AL	13	6	4	0	0	80	67	65	41	4.28
1943	WASHINGTON	AL	1	0	1	0	0	4.7	4	5	0	5.79
CAREER TOTALS			**368**	**189**	**102**	**9**	**28**	**2503**	**2290**	**1095**	**1468**	**3.34**

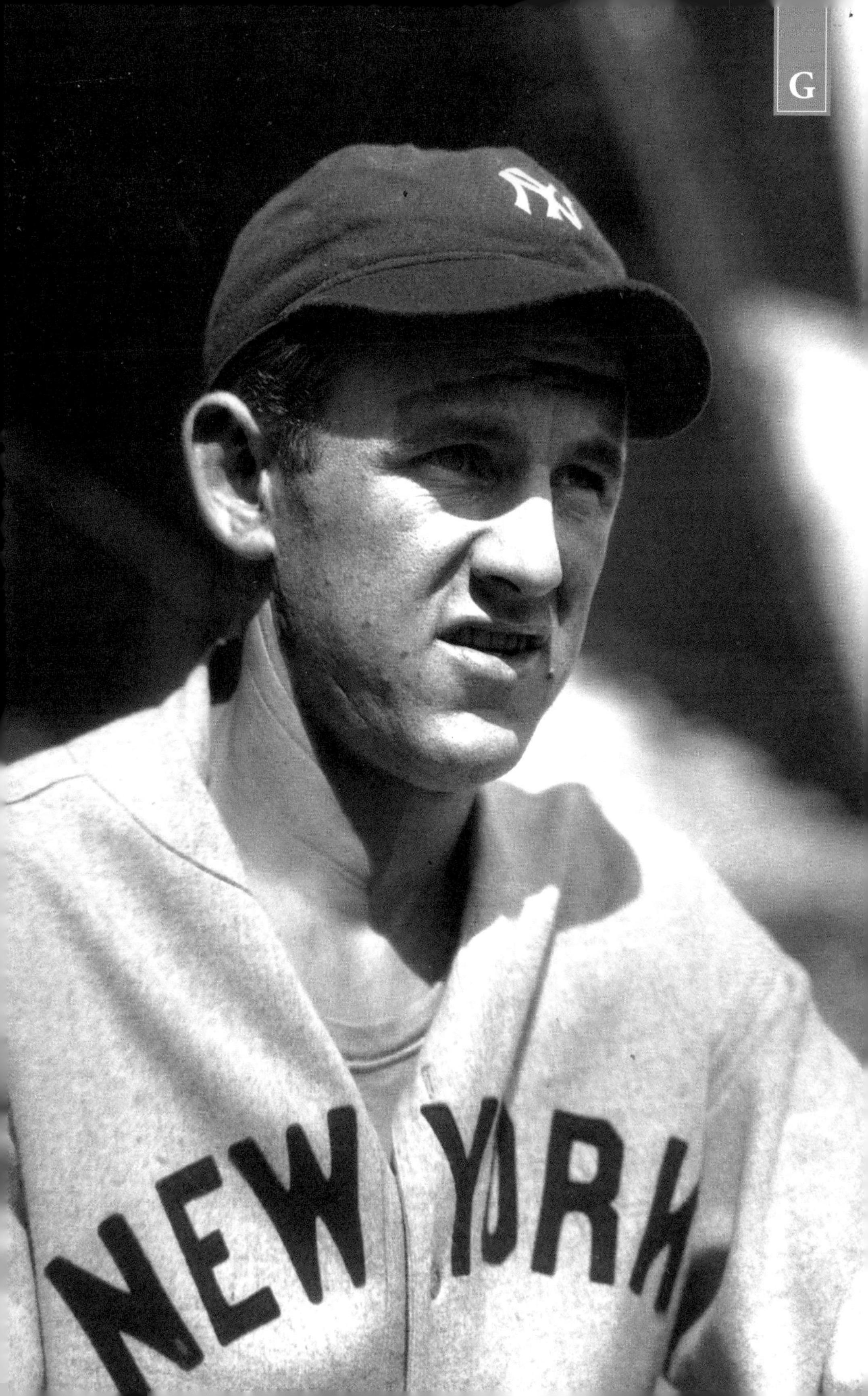
NEW YORK

JOE GORDON

"We're not afraid of DiMaggio or Keller. The man we fear is Gordon," Dodgers manager Leo Durocher said before the 1941 World Series.

He redefined the tools necessary for middle infielders, adding power to the mix while setting the bar even higher for acrobatic play in the field. In the final analysis, however, one word has always defined Joe Gordon: Winner.

Gordon, nicknamed "Flash" in reference to the popular comic book figure of the 1930s and his quick feet, combined hitting and fielding skills as few other second basemen ever have. He played for the New York Yankees (1938-1943; 1946) and the Cleveland Indians (1947-1950) and won five World Series rings despite losing two seasons while he served his country in World War II in the Army Air Corps.

Gordon won the 1942 American League MVP Award – beating out Boston's Ted Williams despite the fact that Williams won the AL's Triple Crown. He was traded to the Indians following the 1946 season, and two years later led the Tribe to the World Series title. He appeared in the postseason in six of his 11 big league seasons.

Gordon was selected to play in the All-Star Game in nine of his 11 seasons. Of the Hall of Famers who played their entire career in the All-Star Game era, only nine — Joe DiMaggio, Cal Ripken Jr., Rod Carew, Kirby Puckett, Stan Musial, Willie Mays, Mickey Mantle, Hank Aaron and Ted Williams — appeared in a higher percentage of Mid-Summer Classics (nine All-Star Games in 11 seasons, 82 percent) during their career than Gordon.

Gordon was the first AL second baseman to hit 20 home runs in a season, which he did seven times in his 11-year career, and holds the league mark for career HRs at second base (246). He led the AL in assists four times and double plays three times.

Gordon also managed the Cleveland Indians starting in 1958, and led Cleveland to a second-place finish in 1959. In 1960, he was involved in the first manager-for-manager trade when the Indians and Tigers swapped skippers, with Jimmy Dykes going to Cleveland. He finished the season managing the Tigers, then signed to manage the Kansas City Athletics in 1961 and the Kansas City Royals in 1969.

JOSEPH LOWELL GORDON
"JOE" "FLASH"
NEW YORK, A.L., 1938-1943, 1946
CLEVELAND, A.L., 1947-1950

AN ACROBATIC SECOND BASEMAN WITH TREMENDOUS POWER WHO HELPED LEAD HIS TEAMS TO SIX PENNANTS IN 11 SEASONS, WINNING FIVE WORLD SERIES TITLES. RENOWNED FOR SUPERB DEFENSIVE RANGE. THE NINE-TIME ALL-STAR AND 1942 A.L. MVP LED THE LEAGUE IN ASSISTS FOUR TIMES AND DOUBLE PLAYS THREE TIMES. SET CAREER A.L. HOME RUN RECORD FOR SECOND BASEMEN. DROVE IN MORE THAN 100 RUNS FOUR TIMES AND HIT 20 OR MORE HOME RUNS SEVEN TIMES. ALSO MANAGED PARTS OF FIVE SEASONS WITH CLEVELAND, DETROIT AND KANSAS CITY ATHLETICS AND ROYALS.

Flash

Elected To The Hall Of Fame: *2009.*
Born: *Feb. 18, 1915 in Los Angeles, Calif.*
Died: *Apr. 14,1978 in Sacramento, Calif.*
Height: *5-10.* **Weight:** *180.*
Threw: *Right.* **Batted:** *Right.*
Debut: *Apri. 18, 1938.*
Final Game: *Sept. 30, 1950.*
Teams: *New York A.L. 1938-1943, 1946;*
Cleveland A.L. 1947-1950.
Postseason: *5-Time World Series Champion*
(1938-1939, 1941,1943, 1948); 6 A.L. Pennants
(1938-1939, 1941-1943, 1948).
Awards: *9-Time All-Star (1939-1943, 1946-*
1949); A.L. Most Valuable Player (1942).

YEAR	TEAM	LEAGUE	G	AB	R	H	2B	3B	HR	RBI	SB	AVG
1938	NEW YORK	AL	127	458	83	117	24	7	25	97	11	.255
1939	NEW YORK	AL	151	567	92	161	32	5	28	111	11	.284
1940	NEW YORK	AL	155	616	112	173	32	10	30	103	18	.281
1941	NEW YORK	AL	156	588	104	162	26	7	24	87	10	.276
1942	NEW YORK	AL	147	538	88	173	29	4	18	103	12	.322
1943	NEW YORK	AL	152	543	82	135	28	5	17	69	4	.249
1946	NEW YORK	AL	112	376	35	79	15	0	11	47	2	.210
1947	CLEVELAND	AL	155	562	89	153	27	6	29	93	7	.272
1948	CLEVELAND	AL	144	550	96	154	21	4	32	124	5	.280
1949	CLEVELAND	AL	148	541	74	136	18	3	20	84	5	.251
1950	CLEVELAND	AL	119	368	59	87	12	1	19	57	4	.236
CAREER TOTALS			**1566**	**5707**	**914**	**1530**	**264**	**52**	**253**	**975**	**89**	**.268**

Goose Goslin

"For the country at large the eagle may remain the national bird, but for the National Capital the greatest bird that flies is the Goose," sportswriter W.O. McGeehan once wrote.

While he was a gifted slugger, Leon Allen Goslin's outfield play was questionable. A penchant for flapping his arms as he tracked down fly balls, a task he had no small amount of difficulty with, as well as a general awkwardness about his mannerisms earned him the title of "Goose." The story of Goose Goslin begins many years before he would acquire that nickname, however.

Goslin's early playing career would take him to the Sally League in South Carolina. A move to the outfield in 1921 and a high batting average attracted the attention of bigger clubs. Two owners, the Baltimore Orioles' Jack Dunn (whose minor league team was one of the strongest in the country) and the Washington Senators' Clark Griffith, both tendered offers to Goslin, but the latter rushed to deliver the offer. The move would pay off, as Goslin would go on to become one of the best position players in Senators history.

Goslin's second full season in the majors, 1923, would see him lead the league in triples, while driving in 99 runs and batting .300. In 1924, Goslin led the American League in RBIs (129) and helped the Senators to their first and only World Series title. He would go on to capture an American League batting title in 1928, hitting .379 and beating out the St. Louis Browns' Heinie Manush by a single point. On June 13, 1930, the Senators traded Goose to the St. Louis Browns for General Crowder and Manush. Goslin responded by clubbing 30 home runs for the Browns, setting a career-high of 37. Goose would spend the next couple years on the move, as the Senators would re-acquire him in 1933, then turn around and move him to the Detroit the following season. Goose's lone All-Star selection would come with the Tigers in 1936, when at age 35, he hit .315 with 24 home runs. The 1938 season would be Goslin's last in the majors.

Goose Goslin would go on to become a player-manager for the Trenton Senators from 1939 to 1941; he would officially retire from baseball after the '41 season.

LEON ALLEN GOSLIN
"GOOSE"
WASHINGTON A.L. 1921 TO 1930, 1933, 1938
ST. LOUIS A.L. 1930 TO 1932
DETROIT A.L. 1934 TO 1937
BATTED .344 IN 1924, .334 IN 1925,
.354 IN 1926, .334 IN 1927. LED A.L.
IN BATTING IN 1928 WITH .379 AVERAGE.
RUNS BATTED IN FOR 1924=129.
HIT .300 OR BETTER 11 YEARS.
LIFETIME TOTAL OF 2735 HITS,
BATTING AVERAGE .316.
MADE 37 HITS IN 5 WORLD SERIES.

Elected To The Hall Of Fame: *1968.*

Born: *Oct. 16, 1900 in Salem, N.J.*

Died: *May 15, 1971 in Bridgeton, N.J.*

Height: *5-11.* **Weight:** *185.*

Threw: *Right.* **Batted:** *Left.*

Debut: *Sept. 16, 1921.*

Final Game: *Sept. 25, 1938.*

Teams: *Washington A.L. 1921-1930, 1933, 1938; St. Louis A.L. 1930-1932; Detroit A.L. 1934-1937.*

Postseason: *2-Time World Series Champion (1924, 1935); 5 A.L. Pennants (1924-1925, 1933-1935).*

Awards: *All-Star (1936).*

YEAR	TEAM	LEAGUE	G	AB	R	H	2B	3B	HR	RBI	SB	AVG
1921	WASHINGTON	AL	14	50	8	13	1	1	1	6	0	.260
1922	WASHINGTON	AL	101	358	44	116	19	7	3	53	4	.324
1923	WASHINGTON	AL	150	600	86	180	29	18	9	99	7	.300
1924	WASHINGTON	AL	154	579	100	199	30	17	12	129	15	.344
1925	WASHINGTON	AL	150	601	116	201	34	20	18	113	27	.334
1926	WASHINGTON	AL	147	568	105	201	26	15	17	108	8	.354
1927	WASHINGTON	AL	148	581	96	194	37	15	13	120	21	.334
1928	WASHINGTON	AL	135	456	80	173	36	10	17	102	16	.379
1929	WASHINGTON	AL	145	553	82	159	28	7	18	91	11	.288
1930	WASHINGTON/ST. LOUIS	AL	148	584	115	180	36	12	37	138	17	.308
1931	ST. LOUIS	AL	151	591	114	194	42	10	24	105	9	.328
1932	ST. LOUIS	AL	150	572	88	171	28	9	17	104	12	.299
1933	WASHINGTON	AL	132	549	97	163	35	10	10	64	5	.297
1934	DETROIT	AL	151	614	106	187	38	7	13	100	5	.305
1935	DETROIT	AL	147	590	88	172	34	6	9	109	5	.292
1936	DETROIT	AL	147	572	122	180	33	8	24	125	14	.315
1937	DETROIT	AL	79	181	30	43	11	1	4	35	0	.238
1938	WASHINGTON	AL	38	57	6	9	3	0	2	8	0	.158
CAREER TOTALS			**2287**	**8656**	**1483**	**2735**	**500**	**173**	**248**	**1609**	**176**	**.316**

RICH GOSSAGE

Bob Watson, both an opponent and teammate of Rich "Goose" Gossage, once said of the fireballing pitcher, "He's all arms and legs and he's not looking at you. That doesn't make you feel good when he's throwing 100 miles an hour. I don't mind a guy throwing 100 miles an hour if he's looking at you. I'll tell you it's a lot better playing behind him."

Gossage could be an intimidating presence on the mound, standing 6-feet-3 and solidly built with a deathly scowl. But of all his attributes, it was his overpowering fastball, which could reach 100 miles per hour, which made him one of the top relief pitchers throughout the 1970s and '80s.

A rookie relief pitcher with the White Sox in 1972, Gossage established himself as a premier closer by the mid-1970s. After spending 1976 as a starting pitcher, he was traded to the Pirates, where he began a 12-year streak of double-figure save totals.

Free agency followed and Gossage signed a contract with the Yankees in November 1977. His six years as the New York closer included four All-Star teams, 150 saves and a 2.10 ERA. He was also on the mound to finish the 1978 playoff game against the Red Sox.

"We know before the game starts that he'll be coming in in the eighth or ninth if the game is close," said fellow Hall of Famer Carl Yastrzemski. "There's nothing you can do.

"Well, there is. You can try to have a big lead."

Signing a free agent deal with the Padres prior to the 1984 season provided immediate dividends for Gossage's new ball club, as his 10 wins and 25 saves helped San Diego to its first-ever World Series.

When Gossage, a nine-time All-Star, finally retired after the 1994 season, he had built up quite a resume, finishing a 22-year big league career with nine different big league clubs. His lifetime statistics included a 124-107 record, 3.01 ERA, 1,002 games, 310 saves, 1,809 innings pitched and 1,502 strikeouts.

RICHARD MICHAEL GOSSAGE
"RICH" "GOOSE"
CHICAGO, A.L., 1972-1976; PITTSBURGH, N.L., 1977
NEW YORK, A.L., 1978-1983, 1989; SAN DIEGO, N.L., 1984-1987
CHICAGO, N.L., 1988; SAN FRANCISCO, N.L., 1989
TEXAS, A.L., 1991; OAKLAND, A.L., 1992-1993; SEATTLE, A.L., 1994
A DOMINANT RELIEF PITCHER WITH A TRADEMARK MOUSTACHE,
WHOSE MENACING GLARE AND EXPLODING FASTBALL INTIMIDATED
BATTERS FOR MORE THAN TWO DECADES. POSTED A 124-107 RECORD
WITH 310 SAVES, 1,502 STRIKEOUTS AND A 3.01 ERA IN 1,002 GAMES,
CLOSING OUT VICTORIES CONVINCINGLY. INCREDIBLY DURABLE,
POSTED 52 SAVES OF AT LEAST SEVEN OUTS. A NINE-TIME ALL-STAR
WHO LED THE A.L. IN SAVES THREE TIMES. PITCHED IN THREE WORLD
SERIES, CLINCHING VICTORY FOR NEW YORK IN 1978.

Goose

Elected To The Hall Of Fame: 2008.

Born: July 5, 1951 in Colorado Springs, Colo.

Height: 6-3. **Weight:** 180.

Threw: Right. **Batted:** Right.

Debut: Apr. 16, 1972. **Final Game:** Aug. 8, 1994.

Teams: Chicago A.L. 1972-76; Pittsburgh N.L. 1977; New York A.L. 1978-83, 1989; San Diego N.L. 1984-87; Chicago N.L. 1988; San Francisco N.L. 1989; Texas A.L. 1991; Oakland A.L. 1992-93; Seattle A.L. 1994.

Postseason: World Series Champion (1978); A.L. Pennant (1981); N.L. Pennant (1984); 4-Time Playoff Qualifier (1978, 1980-81, 1984).

Awards: 9-Time All-Star (1975-1978, 1980-1982, 1984-1985).

YEAR	TEAM	LEAGUE	G	W	L	SV	SH	IP	H	BB	SO	ERA
1972	CHICAGO	AL	36	7	1	2	0	80	72	44	57	4.28
1973	CHICAGO	AL	20	0	4	0	0	49.7	57	37	33	7.43
1974	CHICAGO	AL	39	4	6	1	0	89.3	92	47	64	4.13
1975	CHICAGO	AL	62	9	8	26	0	141.7	99	70	130	1.84
1976	CHICAGO	AL	31	9	17	1	0	224	214	90	135	3.94
1977	PITTSBURGH	NL	72	11	9	26	0	133	78	49	151	1.62
1978	NEW YORK	AL	63	10	11	27	0	134.3	87	59	122	2.01
1979	NEW YORK	AL	36	5	3	18	0	58.3	48	19	41	2.62
1980	NEW YORK	AL	64	6	2	33	0	99	74	37	103	2.27
1981	NEW YORK	AL	32	3	2	20	0	46.7	22	14	48	0.77
1982	NEW YORK	AL	56	4	5	30	0	93	63	28	102	2.23
1983	NEW YORK	AL	57	13	5	22	0	87.3	82	25	90	2.27
1984	SAN DIEGO	NL	62	10	6	25	0	102.3	75	36	84	2.90
1985	SAN DIEGO	NL	50	5	3	26	0	79	64	17	52	1.82
1986	SAN DIEGO	NL	45	5	7	21	0	64.7	69	20	63	4.45
1987	SAN DIEGO	NL	40	5	4	11	0	52	47	19	44	3.12
1988	CHICAGO	NL	46	4	4	13	0	43.7	50	15	30	4.33
1989	SAN FRANCISCO/NEW YORK	AL/NL	42	3	1	5	0	58	46	30	30	2.95
1991	TEXAS	AL	44	4	2	1	0	40.3	33	16	28	3.57
1992	OAKLAND	AL	30	0	2	0	0	38	32	19	26	2.84
1993	OAKLAND	AL	39	4	5	1	0	47.7	49	26	40	4.53
1994	SEATTLE	AL	36	3	0	1	0	47.3	44	15	29	4.18
CAREER TOTALS			**1002**	**124**	**107**	**310**	**0**	**1809.1**	**1497**	**732**	**1502**	**3.01**

FRANK GRANT

"Were it not for the fact that he is a colored man, he would without a doubt be at the top notch of the records among the finest teams in the country."

So begins a contemporary press account on Ulysses "Frank" Grant, perhaps the best of the African-American players who played in white organized baseball in the 1880s, before the color line was drawn. Grant was a quick, agile, skilled second baseman, and also a pitcher at the very beginning of his career. He was known as "The Black Dunlap," a reference to Frank Dunlap, one of the best fielding white second basemen of the decade.

After playing with local semi-pro teams in his native Pittsfield, Mass., and in Plattsburgh, N.Y, Grant joined the Meriden, Conn., team in the Eastern League in 1886. Grant led the team with a batting average of .331. When the team folded in July, he and two teammates, both former major leaguers, reported to Buffalo of the International League, one step below the majors. Grant led the team with a .344 batting average and drew strong press throughout the league for his play in the field. The following year, he again led the Bisons with a .353 batting average, hit for the cycle in one game, and stole home twice in another.

The 1887 season was pivotal for African-American players in organized baseball, and at mid-season, the International League banned teams from signing new contracts with black players. Grant, like other African-American players, faced discrimination on and off the field, from teammates and opponents. He would wear improvised wooden shin guards at second base to protect himself from spikings. He was thrown at by pitchers repeatedly, and on several occasions, his own teammates threatened to strike if he continued to play—and refused to pose for team portraits if he was included.

However, he continued to lead his team in hitting, batting .346 in 1888. The following season, he relented to the changing environment and the pressure coming from his team, his teammates, fans and the media and switched to the Cuban Giants, one of the leading African-American clubs at the time. He played through the 1903 season, with several of the leading black clubs, including the Page Fence Giants and the Philadelphia Giants.

ULYSSES F. GRANT
"FRANK"
PRE-NEGRO LEAGUES, 1886-1903

ONE OF BASEBALL'S EARLY STARS WHO BECAME AN INSPIRATION FOR FUTURE GENERATIONS OF AFRICAN-AMERICAN BALLPLAYERS. BEGAN CAREER AS SECOND BASEMAN IN INTEGRATED MINOR LEAGUES FROM 1886-1891. A SLICK FIELDER WITH A STRONG ARM, WHO HIT FOR AVERAGE AND HAD SURPRISING POWER DESPITE SLIGHT 5'7" FRAME. SEGREGATION EVENTUALLY FORCED HIM TO PLAY FOR TOP TOURING BLACK TEAMS, MOST NOTABLY THE CUBAN GIANTS, WHERE HE SERVED AS TEAM CAPTAIN AND OFTEN MENTORED YOUNGER PLAYERS.

The Black Dunlap

Elected To The Hall Of Fame: 2006.
Born: Aug. 1, 1865 in Pittsfield, Mass.
Died: May 27, 1937 in New York, N.Y.
Height: 5-7. **Weight:** 155.
Threw: Right. **Batted:** Right.
Teams: Pre-Negro Leagues 1886-1903.

YEAR	TEAM	LEAGUE	G	W	L	SV	SH	IP	H	BB	SO	ERA
1886	MERIDEN/BUFFALO	EL/IL	7	2	2	0	0	44.7	58	11	16	3.02

YEAR	TEAM	LEAGUE	G	AB	R	H	2B	3B	HR	RBI	SB	AVG
1886	MERIDEN/BUFFALO	EL/IL	93	369	61	122	30	8	3	—	15	.331
1887	BUFFALO	INTA	—	—	—	—	—	—	—	—	—	—
1888	BUFFALO	INTA	84	347	95	120	19	6	11	—	23	.346
1889	TRENTON	MIDS	—	—	—	—	—	—	—	—	—	—
1890	HARRISBURG/HARRISBURG	EISL/ATLA	106	439	99	146	25	8	5	—	32	.333
1891	ANSONIA	CTST	—	—	—	—	—	—	—	—	—	—

EDITOR'S NOTE: Frank Grant played when barnstorming and travel teams were the norm. His available statistics are limited to a number of higher-level Triple-A teams. He also played on some high-level African-American teams for which there are no reliable statistics available.

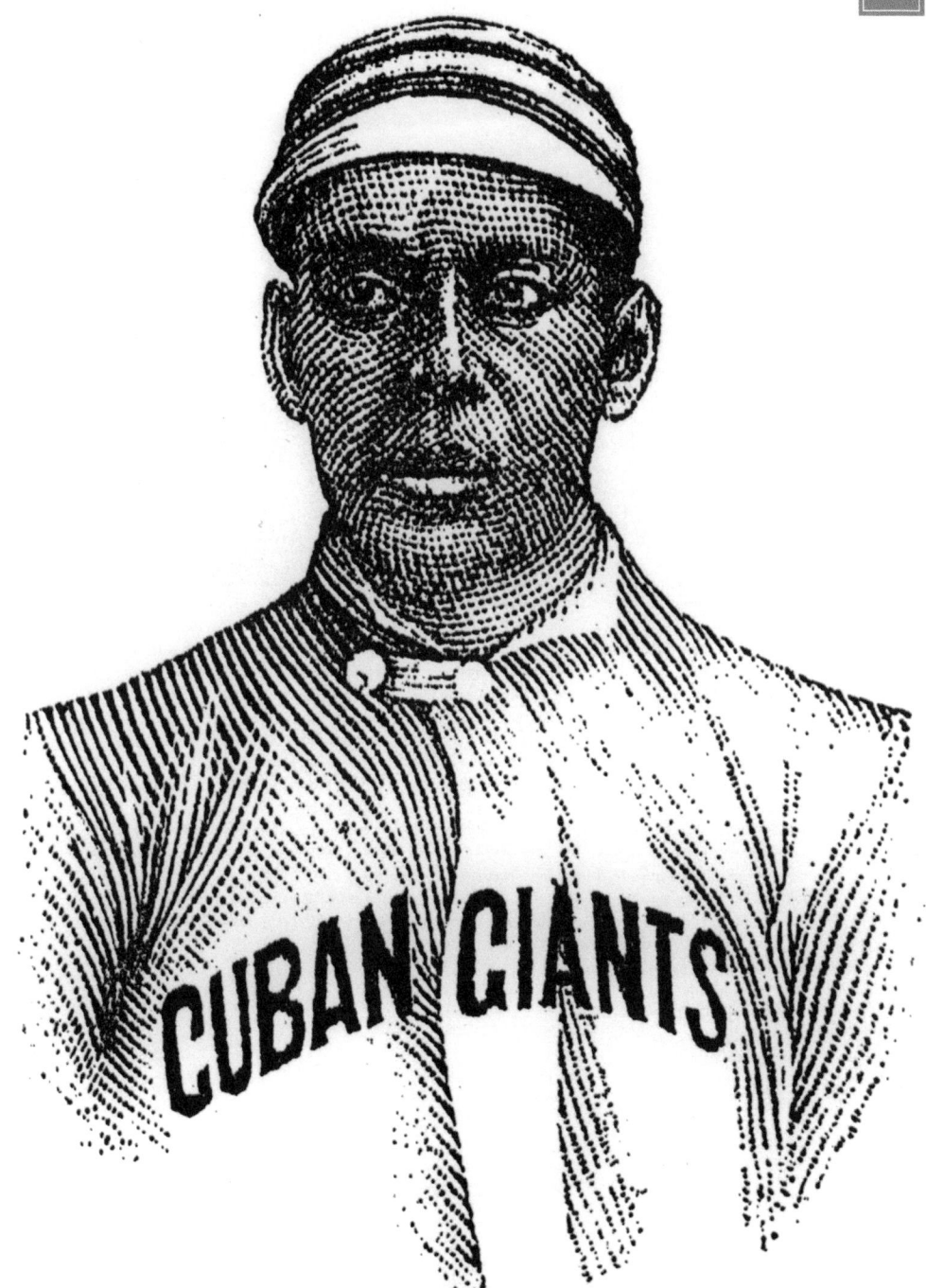

SECOND BASEMAN GRANT

HANK GREENBERG

"He was one of the truly great hitters, and when I first saw him at bat, he made my eyes pop out," Joe DiMaggio said.

Hank Greenberg is widely regarded as one of the best hitters ever. Born Hyman Greenberg on Jan. 1, 1911, in New York City, his hometown Yankees would offer him a contract, but he would spurn them, instead choosing to join the Detroit Tigers.

Greenberg would win two MVP awards in his career with Detroit. The first came in 1935 when playing first base he hit .328 and led the league in both home runs (36) and RBI (170). Greenberg's Detroit Tigers would win the World Series that year, though he missed the majority of it after breaking his wrist in the second game. Greenberg acquired his second MVP in 1940 as an outfielder; he batted .340 and again paced the American League in homers (41) while driving in the most runs (150). This would be the first time in MLB history that a player won an MVP award at two different positions.

War spreading across the globe in the 1940s would cut out a significant portion of Greenberg's playing career. Hank was initially brought into military service in May 1941, only to be honorably discharged on Dec. 5 of that year, a mere two days before the attacks at Pearl Harbor. Greenberg would immediately re-enlist. In June 1945, his military service concluded and the Hammer jumped right back into baseball.

Even though he had been out of baseball for a number of years, Greenberg's skills hadn't waned. His return in the latter half of the 1945 season helped drive the Tigers to another World Series appearance. Greenberg's performance was spectacular, as he drove in seven runs in seven games while hitting .304, propelling the Tigers to victory.

In 1946, the Hammer put on a vintage performance, once again leading the league in home runs (44) and RBI (127). That would be his final year as a member of the Detroit Tigers, however, as the Pittsburgh Pirates purchased Greenberg's contract before the 1947 season. He would play only one season with the Pirates before retiring to take over direction of the Indians' farm system. Greenberg would shortly become their General Manager and would later serve the White Sox in that same capacity.

Elected To The Hall Of Fame: *1956.*
Born: *Jan. 1, 1911 in New York, N.Y.*
Died: *Sept. 4, 1986 in Beverly Hills, Calif.*
Height: *6-3.* **Weight:** *210.*
Threw: *Right.* **Batted:** *Right.*
Debut: *Sept. 14, 1930.*
Final Game: *Sept. 18, 1947.*
Teams: *Detroit A.L. 1930, 1933-1941, 1945-1946; Pittsburgh N.L. 1947.*
Postseason: *2-Time World Series Champion (1935, 1945); 4 A.L. Pennants (1934-1935, 1940, 1945).*
Awards: *5-Time All-Star (1937-1940, 1945); 2-Time A.L. Most Valuable Player (1935, 1940).*

YEAR	TEAM	LEAGUE	G	AB	R	H	2B	3B	HR	RBI	SB	AVG
1930	DETROIT	AL	1	1	0	0	0	0	0	0	0	.000
1933	DETROIT	AL	117	449	59	135	33	3	12	87	6	.301
1934	DETROIT	AL	153	593	118	201	63	7	26	139	9	.339
1935	DETROIT	AL	152	619	121	203	46	16	36	170	4	.328
1936	DETROIT	AL	12	46	10	16	6	2	1	16	1	.348
1937	DETROIT	AL	154	594	137	200	49	14	40	183	8	.337
1938	DETROIT	AL	155	556	144	175	23	4	58	146	7	.315
1939	DETROIT	AL	138	500	112	156	42	7	33	112	8	.312
1940	DETROIT	AL	148	573	129	195	50	8	41	150	6	.340
1941	DETROIT	AL	19	67	12	18	5	1	2	12	1	.269
1945	DETROIT	AL	78	270	47	84	20	2	13	60	3	.311
1946	DETROIT	AL	142	523	91	145	29	5	44	127	5	.277
1947	PITTSBURGH	NL	125	402	71	100	13	2	25	74	0	.249
CAREER TOTALS			**1394**	**5193**	**1051**	**1628**	**379**	**71**	**331**	**1276**	**58**	**.313**

BURLEIGH GRIMES

"I used to chew slippery elm – the bark, right off the tree. Come spring the bark would get nice and loose and you could slice it free without any trouble. What I checked was the fiber from inside, and that's what I put on the ball. The ball would break like hell, away from right-handed hitters and in on lefties," Burleigh Grimes once said.

A noted spitballer, Grimes' career began in 1916 with the Pittsburgh Pirates. In two seasons with the Pirates, Grimes would accumulate a 5-19 record. That led to a departure from the Steel City. The Pirates traded Grimes to the Brooklyn Robins (which would late become the Brooklyn Dodgers) and he immediately dispelled any doubts about his ability to pitch.

Grimes' first season with the Robins was impressive as he racked up a 19-9 record. He would play eight more seasons in Brooklyn, racking up an additional 139 wins while leading the National League in complete games three times (1921, 1923, 1924), innings twice (1923, 1924) and both wins (1921) and strikeouts (1921) once. It was during this period that MLB banned the spitball, but continued to allow Grimes and 16 other pitchers to continue utilizing the pitch.

The next eight years of Grimes' career was spent on the move, as he would end up playing for the New York Giants, Pittsburgh Pirates, Boston Braves, St. Louis Cardinals, Chicago Cubs and New York Yankees. His most noteworthy effort came in his second stint with the Pirates in 1928 when he again paced the NL in wins (25), games (48), complete games (28), and innings pitched (330.2). In 1931 as a member of the St. Louis Cardinals, Grimes claimed his first and only championship, as he won both of his starts in the World Series versus the Philadelphia Athletics.

After his playing career ended in 1934, Grimes would go on to manage in the major leagues. In 1937 and 1938, he was the manager of the Brooklyn Dodgers. Grimes would continue his managing career primarily in the International League with the Toronto Maple Leafs.

Ol' Stubblebeard

Elected To The Hall Of Fame: 1964.
Born: Aug. 18, 1893 in Emerald, Wis.
Died: Dec. 6, 1985 in Clear Lake, Wis.
Height: 5-10. **Weight:** 175.
Threw: Right. **Batted:** Right.
Debut: Sept. 10, 1916.
Final Game: Sept. 20, 1934.
Teams: Pittsburgh N.L. 1916-1917, 1928-1929, 1934; Brooklyn N.L. 1918-1926; New York N.L. 1927; Boston N.L. 1930; St. Louis N.L. 1930-1931, 1933-1934; Chicago N.L. 1932-1933; New York A.L. 1934.
Postseason: World Series Champion (1931); 4 N.L. Pennants (1920, 1930-1932).

YEAR	TEAM	LEAGUE	G	W	L	SV	SH	IP	H	BB	SO	ERA
1916	PITTSBURGH	NL	6	2	3	0	0	45.7	40	10	20	2.36
1917	PITTSBURGH	NL	37	3	16	0	1	194	186	70	72	3.53
1918	BROOKLYN	NL	40	19	9	1	7	270	210	76	113	2.13
1919	BROOKLYN	NL	25	10	11	0	1	181.3	179	60	82	3.47
1920	BROOKLYN	NL	40	23	11	2	5	303.7	271	67	131	2.22
1921	BROOKLYN	NL	37	22	13	0	2	302.3	313	76	136	2.83
1922	BROOKLYN	NL	36	17	14	1	1	259	324	84	99	4.76
1923	BROOKLYN	NL	39	21	18	0	2	327	356	100	119	3.58
1924	BROOKLYN	NL	38	22	13	1	1	310.7	351	91	135	3.82
1925	BROOKLYN	NL	33	12	19	0	0	246.7	305	102	73	5.04
1926	BROOKLYN	NL	30	12	13	0	1	225.3	238	88	64	3.71
1927	NEW YORK	NL	39	19	8	2	2	259.7	274	87	102	3.54
1928	PITTSBURGH	NL	48	25	14	3	4	330.7	311	77	97	2.99
1929	PITTSBURGH	NL	33	17	7	2	2	232.7	245	70	62	3.13
1930	BOSTON/ST. LOUIS	NL	33	16	11	0	1	201.3	246	65	73	4.07
1931	ST. LOUIS	NL	29	17	9	0	3	212.3	240	59	67	3.65
1932	CHICAGO	NL	30	6	11	1	1	141.3	174	50	36	4.78
1933	CHICAGO/ST. LOUIS	NL	21	3	7	4	1	83.3	86	37	16	3.78
1934	NEW YORK/PITTSBURGH	AL/NL	22	4	5	1	0	53	63	26	15	6.11
CAREER TOTALS			**616**	**270**	**212**	**18**	**35**	**4180**	**4412**	**1295**	**1512**	**3.53**

LEFTY GROVE

"Lefty Grove didn't have a curve. All he had was a fastball. Everybody knew what they were going to hit at, but they still couldn't hit him. He was fabulous," former teammate Doc Cramer said.

Robert "Lefty" Grove was born in Lonaconing, Md., and would become a regional star. Blessed with an exceptional fastball, Grove caught the attention of the then minor league Baltimore Orioles' owner Jack Dunn and joined his organization in 1920. Dunn would refuse multiple offers for Grove over the following years, until 1925 when the Philadelphia Athletics offered him $100,000, an unprecedented amount for the young left hander.

While Grove's first year with the Athletics saw him lead the league in strikeouts, it also saw him lead the league in walks and consequently post a 10-12 record. It would be the last time he finished under .500. In 1926, Lefty cut his walk rate dramatically while again leading the American League in strikeouts and managing his first of nine ERA titles. Grove would pace the league in strikeouts for the next five years, establishing a seven-season streak of dominance.

Grove's most prolific season came in 1931, when he led the majors in wins (31), ERA (2.06), strikeouts (175) and tied for the lead in complete games (27). For his efforts that season, Grove was awarded the AL MVP and he was the first pitcher to capture it since Walter Johnson in 1924. Unfortunately for Grove, his team would lose the World Series that year to the St. Louis Cardinals, though he would pitch to his normal level of excellence as he posted a 2-1 record with a 2.42 ERA. While disappointing, Grove had already taken home two championship rings with the Athletics from the previous years (1929, 1930).

After the 1933 season and despite the fact that he was an All-Star who had led the A.L. once again in wins, the Athletics felt motivated to move Grove and traded him to the Boston Red Sox. Grove won 105 games as a member of the Red Sox while being selected as an All-Star five consecutive times (1935-1939). Grove's career would come to an end following the 1941 season.

The Baseball Writers' Association of America voted to induct Lefty Grove into the Hall of Fame in 1947.

Elected To The Hall Of Fame: 1947.
Born: Mar. 6, 1900 in Lonaconing, Md.
Died: May 22, 1975 in Norwalk, Ohio.
Height: 6-3. **Weight:** 190.
Threw: Left. **Batted:** Left.
Debut: Apr. 14, 1925.
Final Game: Sept. 28, 1941.
Teams: Philadelphia A.L. 1925-1933; Boston A.L. 1934-1941.
Postseason: 2-Time World Series (1929-1930); 3 A.L. Pennants (1929-1931).
Awards: 6-Time All-Star (1933, 1935-1939); A.L. Most Valuable Player (1931).

YEAR	TEAM	LEAGUE	G	W	L	SV	SH	IP	H	BB	SO	ERA
1925	PHILADELPHIA	AL	45	10	12	1	0	197	207	131	116	4.75
1926	PHILADELPHIA	AL	45	13	13	6	1	258	227	101	194	2.51
1927	PHILADELPHIA	AL	51	20	13	9	1	262.3	251	79	174	3.19
1928	PHILADELPHIA	AL	39	24	8	4	4	261.7	228	64	183	2.58
1929	PHILADELPHIA	AL	42	20	6	4	2	275.3	278	81	170	2.81
1930	PHILADELPHIA	AL	50	28	5	9	2	291	273	60	209	2.54
1931	PHILADELPHIA	AL	41	31	4	5	4	288.7	249	62	175	2.06
1932	PHILADELPHIA	AL	44	25	10	7	4	291.7	269	79	188	2.84
1933	PHILADELPHIA	AL	45	24	8	6	2	275.3	280	83	114	3.20
1934	BOSTON	AL	22	8	8	0	0	109.3	149	32	43	6.50
1935	BOSTON	AL	35	20	12	1	2	273	269	65	121	2.70
1936	BOSTON	AL	35	17	12	2	6	253.3	237	65	130	2.81
1937	BOSTON	AL	32	17	9	0	3	262	269	83	153	3.02
1938	BOSTON	AL	24	14	4	1	1	163.7	169	52	99	3.08
1939	BOSTON	AL	23	15	4	0	2	191	180	58	81	2.54
1940	BOSTON	AL	22	7	6	0	1	153.3	159	50	62	3.99
1941	BOSTON	AL	21	7	7	0	0	134	155	42	54	4.37
CAREER TOTALS			**616**	**300**	**141**	**55**	**35**	**3940.2**	**3849**	**1187**	**2266**	**3.06**

TONY GWYNN

At one point it looked as if Tony Gwynn's path to athletic greatness would be on a basketball court, as he would prove adept at passing the ball. But Gwynn could not pass up baseball, a game where the left-handed batter with the natural inside-out swing would shine.

A highly recruited point guard, Gwynn would attend San Diego State University on a basketball scholarship. Although he didn't play baseball for the Aztecs as a freshman, he was back on the diamond by his second year.

"Baseball was just something to do in the spring and summer," Gwynn once said. "I told my mom I didn't think I would try baseball in college. She and my dad told me it was something I might want to fall back on."

Drafted by both the San Diego Padres (third round) and the National Basketball Association's San Diego Clippers (10th round) in 1981, it wasn't long before the lefty-swinging Gwynn's mastery with a bat in his hand became evident, especially with his ability to slap the ball between third base and shortstop.

"How do you defense a hitter who hits the ball down the left-field line, the right-field line and up the middle," said Los Angeles Dodgers manager Tommy Lasorda in 1984.

Gwynn, an early advocate of using videotape to study his swing, once said, "I love to hit. I can't wait until it's my turn. Sometimes, I think that's all baseball is. I root for the other team to go down 1-2-3 so I can hit again."

A 15-time All-Star and five-time Gold Glove Award winner in right field, Gwynn spent his entire 20-season big league career with the Padres, one of only 17 players to play to have played at least 20 seasons and spent their entire careers with one team.

With his eighth and final batting crown in 1997, Gwynn tied Honus Wagner, the great Pittsburgh Pirates shortstop, for the most in National League history. In addition to his .338 career batting average, he earned seven Silver Slugger awards for offense and batted .371 in his two World Series appearances.

ANTHONY KEITH GWYNN
"TONY" "MR. PADRE"
SAN DIEGO, N.L., 1982-2001

AN ARTISAN WITH A BAT WHOSE DAILY PURSUIT OF EXCELLENCE PRODUCED A .338 LIFETIME BATTING AVERAGE, 3,141 HITS AND A NATIONAL LEAGUE RECORD-TYING EIGHT BATTING TITLES. CONSISTENCY WAS HIS HALLMARK, HITTING ABOVE .300 IN 19 OF 20 MAJOR LEAGUE SEASONS, INCLUDING .394 IN 1994. RENOWNED FOR ABILITY TO HIT TO ALL FIELDS, FREQUENTLY COLLECTING OPPOSITE-FIELD BASE HITS BETWEEN THIRD BASE AND SHORTSTOP. STRUCK OUT JUST ONCE EVERY 21 AT BATS. A 15-TIME ALL-STAR AND FIVE-TIME GOLD GLOVE AWARD WINNER. HIT .371 IN TWO WORLD SERIES - 1984 AND 1998.

Mr. Padre

Elected To The Hall Of Fame: *2007.*
Born: *May 9, 1960 in Los Angeles, Calif.*
Height: *5-11.* **Weight:** *185.*
Threw: *Left.* **Batted:** *Left.*
Debut: *July 19, 1982.*
Final Game: *Oct. 7, 2001.*
Teams: *San Diego N.L. 1982-2001.*
Postseason: *2 N.L. Pennants (1984, 1998); 3-Time Playoff Qualifier (1984, 1996, 1998).*
Awards: *15-Time All-Star (1984-1987, 1989-1999).*

YEAR	TEAM	LEAGUE	G	AB	R	H	2B	3B	HR	RBI	SB	AVG
1982	SAN DIEGO	NL	54	190	33	55	12	2	1	17	8	.289
1983	SAN DIEGO	NL	86	304	34	94	12	2	1	37	7	.309
1984	SAN DIEGO	NL	158	606	88	213	21	10	5	71	33	.351
1985	SAN DIEGO	NL	154	622	90	197	29	5	6	46	14	.317
1986	SAN DIEGO	NL	160	642	107	211	33	7	14	59	37	.329
1987	SAN DIEGO	NL	157	589	119	218	36	13	7	54	56	.370
1988	SAN DIEGO	NL	133	521	64	163	22	5	7	70	26	.313
1989	SAN DIEGO	NL	158	604	82	203	27	7	4	62	40	.336
1990	SAN DIEGO	NL	141	573	79	177	29	10	4	72	17	.309
1991	SAN DIEGO	NL	134	530	69	168	27	11	4	62	8	.317
1992	SAN DIEGO	NL	128	520	77	165	27	3	6	41	3	.317
1993	SAN DIEGO	NL	122	489	70	175	41	3	7	59	14	.358
1994	SAN DIEGO	NL	110	419	79	165	35	1	12	64	5	.394
1995	SAN DIEGO	NL	135	535	82	197	33	1	9	90	17	.368
1996	SAN DIEGO	NL	116	451	67	159	27	2	3	50	11	.353
1997	SAN DIEGO	NL	149	592	97	220	49	2	17	119	12	.372
1998	SAN DIEGO	NL	127	461	65	148	35	0	16	69	3	.321
1999	SAN DIEGO	NL	111	411	59	139	27	0	10	62	7	.338
2000	SAN DIEGO	NL	36	127	17	41	12	0	1	17	0	.323
2001	SAN DIEGO	NL	71	102	5	33	9	1	1	17	1	.324
CAREER TOTALS			**2440**	**9288**	**1383**	**3141**	**543**	**85**	**135**	**1138**	**319**	**.338**

CHICK HAFEY

"I always thought that if Hafey had been blessed with normal eyesight and good health, he might have been the best right-handed hitter baseball had ever known," Hall of Fame general manager Branch Rickey said.

Hampered by poor eyesight and severe sinus problems, Hafey played just 1,283 games but still managed to amass 1,466 hits and a career batting average of .317. Hafey won one batting title and was named to the inaugural All-Star Game, where he collected the first ever hit in All-Star Game history.

Hafey was one of the first products of Rickey's farm system, arriving in St. Louis as a rookie in 1924. He was a part of the 1926 Cardinals team that won the World Series, but was limited after suffering several beanings that season. It is believed his health problems were a result of the beanings, and he would become the most prominent player to wear glasses at the time. Hafey continued to wear glasses throughout his career and is one of two players depicted wearing glasses on their Hall of Fame plaques, joined by Reggie Jackson.

Hafey bounced back to play more than 100 games in a season for the first time in 1927. That year, Hafey led the National League in slugging percentage with a .590 mark and received MVP votes for the first time in his career.

From 1927 until his time with the Cardinals came to an end after the 1931 season, Hafey played the best baseball of his career. From 1928-1930, Hafey hit at least 26 home runs and drove in more than 100 runs. Then in 1931, Hafey won one of the closest batting titles ever, beating Bill Terry and Jim Bottomley with a hit in his final at-bat of the season. Hafey then faced Al Simmons, the AL batting champion, in the World Series. The Cardinals beat the Athletics in seven games for Hafey's second World Series title in four appearances.

Hafey played his final five seasons in Cincinnati, his career coming to a close in 1937 at the age of 34. He played more than 100 games just twice in five years with the Reds, but made All-Star Game history with his hit in 1933. Hafey led off the second inning with a single against Lefty Gomez and finished the game 1-for-4.

CHARLES JAMES HAFEY
"CHICK"
ST. LOUIS N.L. 1924 - 1931
CINCINNATI N.L. 1932 - 1937
GREAT OUTFIELDER WHO COMPILED .317
LIFETIME BATTING AVERAGE. LEADING
HITTER OF N.L. WITH .349 IN 1931.
BATTED .329 OR BETTER SIX CONSECUTIVE
YEARS. EQUALLED LEAGUE RECORD OF TEN
HITS IN SUCCESSION, 1929. LIFETIME
FIELDING AVERAGE .971.

Elected To The Hall Of Fame: *1971.*
Born: *Feb. 12, 1903 in Berkeley, Calif.*
Died: *July 2, 1973 in Calistoga, Calif.*
Height: *6-0.* **Weight:** *185.*
Threw: *Right.* **Batted:** *Right.*
Debut: *Aug. 28, 1924.*
Final Game: *Sept. 30, 1937.*
Teams: *St. Louis N.L. 1924-1931; Cincinnati N.L. 1932-1935, 1937.*
Postseason: *2-Time World Series Champion (1926, 1931). 4 N.L. Pennants (1926, 1928, 1930-1931).*
Awards: *All-Star (1933).*

YEAR	TEAM	LEAGUE	G	AB	R	H	2B	3B	HR	RBI	SB	AVG
1924	ST. LOUIS	NL	24	91	10	23	5	2	2	22	1	.253
1925	ST. LOUIS	NL	93	358	36	108	25	2	5	57	3	.302
1926	ST. LOUIS	NL	78	225	30	61	19	2	4	38	2	.271
1927	ST. LOUIS	NL	103	346	62	114	26	5	18	63	12	.329
1928	ST. LOUIS	NL	138	520	101	175	46	6	27	111	8	.337
1929	ST. LOUIS	NL	134	517	101	175	47	9	29	125	7	.338
1930	ST. LOUIS	NL	120	446	108	150	39	12	26	107	12	.336
1931	ST. LOUIS	NL	122	450	94	157	35	8	16	95	11	.349
1932	CINCINNATI	NL	83	253	34	87	19	3	2	36	4	.344
1933	CINCINNATI	NL	144	568	77	172	34	6	7	62	3	.303
1934	CINCINNATI	NL	140	535	75	157	29	6	18	67	4	.293
1935	CINCINNATI	NL	15	59	10	20	6	1	1	9	1	.339
1937	CINCINNATI	NL	89	257	39	67	11	5	9	41	2	.261
CAREER TOTALS			**1283**	**4625**	**777**	**1466**	**341**	**67**	**164**	**833**	**70**	**.317**

JESSE HAINES

"**M**y favorite ball is the knuckler," Jesse Haines said. "I don't believe any batter in uniform likes to face a good knuckleball when it's sweeping in with a lot of zip and breaking right."

Haines played his first full season in the major leagues as a 26-year old in 1920. Despite his late start, Haines would pitch for the next 18 years for the Cardinals thanks to his knuckleball. He finished his career with 210 wins and a 3.64 ERA.

After some initial struggles to break into the big leagues, Haines quickly became a stalwart in St. Louis. In his rookie season, Haines pitched 301 2/3 innings and led the National League in appearances with 47. Though he finished the season with a 13-20 record, he did have a 2.98 ERA.

Haines pitched in four World Series, helping the Cardinals to two championships. The first of those titles came in 1926. He beat the Yankees twice in the Fall Classic, including shutting them out once. Haines built on the momentum from the World Series to have the best season of his career in 1927. That year he went 24-10 with a 2.72 ERA and led the National League in complete games (25) and shutouts (six).

Haines won 20 games for the third and final time of his career in 1928 at the age of 34. From there, however, Haines' career began to go into decline. He pitched for nine more years, winning 70 more games, but never more than 13 in a season. He appeared in two more World Series, including in 1934, when the Cardinals' "Gashouse Gang" topped Detroit.

Haines retired after the 1937 season at the age of 44. He was elected to the Hall of Fame in 1970 by the Veteran's Committee. Haines died in 1978 at the age of 85.

"When I saw how hard a nice old man like Pop could take it after losing a game, I realized why he'd been such a consistent winner and the Cardinals, too," St. Louis center fielder Terry Moore said. "I never forgot how much Haines expected of himself and of others."

JESSE JOSEPH (POP) HAINES
CINCINNATI N. L. 1918
ST. LOUIS N. L. 1920-1937

DURABLE RIGHT-HANDER WON 210 GAMES, LOST 158--ALL IN HIS 18 YEARS WITH CARDINALS. GAINED 20-VICTORY CLASS THREE TIMES. TOSSED 5-0 NO-HITTER VS. BOSTON, 1924. DEFEATED YANKEES TWICE IN 1926 WORLD SERIES. LED N. L. IN COMPLETE GAMES (25), SHUTOUTS (6) WHILE POSTING 24-10 RECORD, 1927.

Pop

Elected To The Hall Of Fame: 1970.
Born: July 22 1893 in Clayton, Ohio.
Died: Aug. 5, 1978 in Dayton, Ohio.
Height: 6-0. **Weight:** 190.
Threw: Right. **Batted:** Right.
Debut: July 20, 1918.
Final Game: Sept. 10, 1937.
Teams: Cincinnati N.L. 1918; St. Louis N.L. 1920-1937.
Postseason: 2-Time World Series Champion (1926, 1934); 4 N.L. Pennants (1926, 1928, 1930, 1934).

YEAR	TEAM	LEAGUE	G	W	L	SV	SH	IP	H	BB	SO	ERA
1918	CINCINNATI	NL	1	0	0	0	0	5	5	1	2	1.80
1920	ST. LOUIS	NL	47	13	20	2	4	301.7	303	80	120	2.98
1921	ST. LOUIS	NL	37	18	12	0	2	244.3	261	56	84	3.50
1922	ST. LOUIS	NL	29	11	9	0	2	183	207	45	62	3.84
1923	ST. LOUIS	NL	37	20	13	0	1	266	283	75	73	3.11
1924	ST. LOUIS	NL	35	8	19	0	1	222.7	275	66	69	4.41
1925	ST. LOUIS	NL	29	13	14	0	0	207	234	52	63	4.57
1926	ST. LOUIS	NL	33	13	4	1	3	183	186	48	46	3.25
1927	ST. LOUIS	NL	38	24	10	1	6	300.7	273	77	89	2.72
1928	ST. LOUIS	NL	33	20	8	0	1	240.3	238	72	77	3.18
1929	ST. LOUIS	NL	28	13	10	0	0	179.7	230	73	59	5.71
1930	ST. LOUIS	NL	29	13	8	1	0	182	215	54	68	4.30
1931	ST. LOUIS	NL	19	12	3	0	2	122.3	134	28	27	3.02
1932	ST. LOUIS	NL	20	3	5	0	1	85.3	116	16	27	4.75
1933	ST. LOUIS	NL	32	9	6	1	0	115.3	113	37	37	2.50
1934	ST. LOUIS	NL	37	4	4	1	0	90	86	19	17	3.50
1935	ST. LOUIS	NL	30	6	5	2	0	115.3	110	28	24	3.59
1936	ST. LOUIS	NL	25	7	5	1	0	99.3	110	21	19	3.90
1937	ST. LOUIS	NL	16	3	3	0	0	65.7	81	23	18	4.52
CAREER TOTALS			**555**	**210**	**158**	**10**	**23**	**3208.2**	**3460**	**871**	**981**	**3.64**

BILLY HAMILTON

"I never saw a runner get a lead off first base like Billy," Handsome Jack Carney said.

Throughout Hamilton's career he made good use of his good leads. Hamilton amassed 914 career stolen bases and led the major leagues five times in his 14-year career. He retired with the career stolen base record, which stood until Lou Brock broke it.

Hamilton began his career with the Kansas City Cowboys of the American Association. He played in Kansas City for two seasons, stealing 111 bases in 1889.Though he jumped to Philadelphia the next year, 1889 began a three-year streak that saw Hamilton stole more than 100 bases each season.

Hamilton's best year came in 1894 when he set the Major League record for runs scored in a season with 198, a mark that still stands. He also tied the record for stolen bases in a game with seven on August 31, which also still stands. Hamilton hit .403, stole 100 bases for the last time in his career that season and led baseball with a .521 on-base percentage.

Hamilton played one more year in Philadelphia, again leading baseball in stolen bases and runs scored, before moving to the Boston Beaneaters in 1896. Though Hamilton's stolen base totals began to decline in Boston as he entered his 30s, he continued to contribute offensively. In six years with the Beaneaters, Hamilton never had an on-base percentage below .400 and led baseball with a .480 mark in 1898.

Hamilton retired in 1901 with a career batting average of .344 and 1,697 runs. After retiring, Hamilton was a minor league manager and scout. Hamilton died in 1940 at the age of 74. He was inducted to the Hall of Fame in 1961 by the Veteran's Committee, becoming the first player from New Jersey in Cooperstown.

"[Jesse] Burkett was one of the greatest hitters I've ever seen," Hall of Fame outfielder Hugh Duffy said. "But Hamilton was one of the very best ballplayers."

Sliding Billy

Elected To The Hall Of Fame: 1961.
Born: Feb. 15, 1866 in Newark, N.J.
Died: Dec. 15, 1940 in Worcester, Mass.
Height: 5-6. **Weight:** 165.
Threw: Right. **Batted:** Left.
Debut: July 31, 1888.
Final Game: Sept. 16, 1901.
Teams: Kansas City, American Association 1888-1889; Philadelphia N.L. 1890-1895; Boston N.L. 1896-1901.

YEAR	TEAM	LEAGUE	G	AB	R	H	2B	3B	HR	RBI	SB	AVG
1888	KANSAS CITY	AA	35	129	21	34	4	4	0	11	19	.264
1889	KANSAS CITY	AA	137	534	144	161	17	12	3	77	111	.301
1890	PHILADELPHIA	NL	123	496	133	161	13	9	2	49	102	.325
1891	PHILADELPHIA	NL	133	527	141	179	23	7	2	60	111	.340
1892	PHILADELPHIA	NL	139	554	132	183	21	7	3	53	57	.330
1893	PHILADELPHIA	NL	82	355	110	135	22	7	5	44	43	.380
1894	PHILADELPHIA	NL	132	558	198	225	25	15	4	90	100	.403
1895	PHILADELPHIA	NL	123	517	166	201	22	6	7	74	97	.389
1896	BOSTON	NL	131	524	153	192	24	10	3	55	83	.366
1897	BOSTON	NL	127	507	152	174	17	5	3	61	66	.343
1898	BOSTON	NL	110	417	110	154	16	5	3	50	54	.369
1899	BOSTON	NL	84	297	63	92	7	1	1	33	19	.310
1900	BOSTON	NL	136	520	103	173	20	5	1	47	32	.333
1901	BOSTON	NL	102	348	71	100	11	2	3	38	20	.287
CAREER TOTALS			**1594**	**6283**	**1697**	**2164**	**242**	**95**	**40**	**742**	**914**	**.344**

GABBY HARTNETT

"I rated Gabby [Hartnett] the perfect catcher," Hall of Fame manager Joe McCarthy said. "He was super smart and nobody could throw with him. And he also was an outstanding clutch hitter."

Hartnett first played in the big leagues at age 21 for the Chicago Cubs in 1922. Two years later he was already one of the best players in the National League, a position he would hold for much of the next two decades. Hartnett was known as an exceptional defensive catcher, and was perhaps the best catcher in National League history before Johnny Bench.

In 1925, he set a record for home runs by a catcher with 24, the second highest total in the National League behind only Rogers Hornsby. He also developed a reputation for having a strong throwing arm.

Though injured for much of the Cubs' pennant-winning season in 1929, Hartnett rebounded with his best offensive season up to that point in 1930, hitting .339 with career-highs in home runs (37) and RBI (122). Hartnett showed his prowess for handling a pitching staff in 1932, when he guided the Cubs to a 3.44 ERA, the lowest in the National League. The Cubs reached the World Series, where Hartnett hit .313 and was next to Babe Ruth for his famous called shot.

Hartnett was a member of the National League roster in the inaugural All-Star Game in 1933, and became an All-Star regular in the game's infancy. In 1935, Hartnett was named NL MVP after hitting .344 with 13 home runs and 91 RBI. He came in second in the MVP voting in 1937, when he hit .354. That batting average proved to be the best mark by a catcher for 60 years until Mike Piazza hit .362 in 1997.

Hartnett became player-manager in July 1938 and guided the Cubs to the World Series, where they lost to the Yankees. Hartnett remained player-manager through 1940 when he was fired after a fifth-place finish. He played one final season with the New York Giants as a player-coach before retiring in 1941.

Elected To The Hall Of Fame: 1955.
Born: Dec. 20, 1900 in Woonsocket, R.I.
Died: Dec. 20, 1972 in Park Ridge, Ill.
Height: 6-1. *Weight:* 195.
Threw: Right. *Batted:* Right.
Debut: Apr. 12, 1922.
Final Game: Sept. 24, 1941.
Teams: Chicago N.L. 1922-1940; New York N.L. 1941.
Postseason: 4 N.L. Pennants (1929, 1932, 1935, 1938).
Awards: 6-Time All-Star (1933-1938); N.L. Most Valuable Player (1935).

YEAR	TEAM	LEAGUE	G	AB	R	H	2B	3B	HR	RBI	SB	AVG
1922	CHICAGO	NL	31	72	4	14	1	1	0	4	1	.194
1923	CHICAGO	NL	85	231	28	62	12	2	8	39	4	.268
1924	CHICAGO	NL	111	354	56	106	17	7	16	67	10	.299
1925	CHICAGO	NL	117	398	61	115	28	3	24	67	1	.289
1926	CHICAGO	NL	93	284	35	78	25	3	8	41	0	.275
1927	CHICAGO	NL	127	449	56	132	32	5	10	80	2	.294
1928	CHICAGO	NL	120	388	61	117	26	9	14	57	3	.302
1929	CHICAGO	NL	25	22	2	6	2	1	1	9	1	.273
1930	CHICAGO	NL	141	508	84	172	31	3	37	122	0	.339
1931	CHICAGO	NL	116	380	53	107	32	1	8	70	3	.282
1932	CHICAGO	NL	121	406	52	110	25	3	12	52	0	.271
1933	CHICAGO	NL	140	490	55	135	21	4	16	88	1	.276
1934	CHICAGO	NL	130	438	58	131	21	1	22	90	0	.299
1935	CHICAGO	NL	116	413	67	142	32	6	13	91	1	.344
1936	CHICAGO	NL	121	424	49	130	25	6	7	64	0	.307
1937	CHICAGO	NL	110	356	47	126	21	6	12	82	0	.354
1938	CHICAGO	NL	88	299	40	82	19	1	10	59	1	.274
1939	CHICAGO	NL	97	306	36	85	18	2	12	59	0	.278
1940	CHICAGO	NL	37	64	3	17	3	0	1	12	0	.266
1941	NEW YORK	NL	64	150	20	45	5	0	5	26	0	.300
CAREER TOTALS			**1990**	**6432**	**867**	**1912**	**396**	**64**	**236**	**1179**	**28**	**.297**

HARRY HEILMANN

"People nowadays just don't realize how great a hitter Harry was," Hall of Famer Ty Cobb said. "Next to Rogers Hornsby, he was the best right-handed hitter of them all."

Though somewhat overshadowed because he shared the outfield in Detroit with Ty Cobb, Heilmann was one of the greatest players of his generation. He played 17 years in the big leagues, ending his career with a .342 batting average, surpassed only by Rogers Hornsby and Ed Delahanty for the right-handed career batting average record. Heilmann won four batting titles and hit .403 in 1923 to lead all of baseball.

Heilmann struggled to hit at first and then took half of 1918 off because he entered the Navy in World War I. Upon returning to baseball in 1919, Heilmann found his swing, hitting .300 for the first time in his career. Heilmann would take advantage of the end of the dead ball era and truly break out in 1921, however. With Ty Cobb taking over as manager, Heilmann moved from first base to right field and his hitting took off. Heilmann won his first batting title that season, hitting .394 with a career-high 139 RBI. Heilmann became the first righthander to win the American League batting title since Napoleon Lajoie in 1910.

As Heilmann established himself as one of the game's biggest stars, the Tigers' outfield became one of the best in the history of the game. Heilmann and Cobb were joined at first by Bobby Veach, who led the AL in RBI three times, and later by Hall of Famer Heinie Manush.

Heilmann made a habit of winning batting titles every other year, taking the crown in 1921, 1923, 1925 and 1927. But as quickly as it had started for Heilmann, it was over. Arthritis in his wrists hampered him, though he continued to post good statistics, the pain became too much. He didn't play in 1931 before attempting a failed comeback in 1932.

Heilmann retired for good after 17 seasons in the big leagues. He died believing he was already in the Hall of Fame. While Heilmann was on his deathbed, Cobb told his former teammate that he had been inducted into Cooperstown, but he wasn't. Heilmann died in 1951 at the age of 56 and was elected to the Hall of Fame in 1952.

Elected To The Hall Of Fame: 1952.
Born: Aug. 3, 1894 in San Francisco, Calif.
Died: July 9, 1951 in Southfield, Mich.
Height: 6-1. **Weight:** 195.
Threw: Right. **Batted:** Right.
Debut: May 16, 1914.
Final Game: May 31, 1932.
Teams: Detroit A.L. 1914, 1916-1929; Cincinnati N.L. 1930, 1932.

YEAR	TEAM	LEAGUE	G	AB	R	H	2B	3B	HR	RBI	SB	AVG
1914	DETROIT	AL	68	182	25	41	8	1	2	18	1	.225
1916	DETROIT	AL	136	451	57	127	30	11	2	73	9	.282
1917	DETROIT	AL	150	556	57	156	22	11	5	86	11	.281
1918	DETROIT	AL	79	286	34	79	10	6	5	39	13	.276
1919	DETROIT	AL	140	537	74	172	30	15	8	93	7	.320
1920	DETROIT	AL	145	543	66	168	28	5	9	89	3	.309
1921	DETROIT	AL	149	602	114	237	43	14	19	139	2	.394
1922	DETROIT	AL	118	455	92	162	27	10	21	92	8	.356
1923	DETROIT	AL	144	524	121	211	44	11	18	115	9	.403
1924	DETROIT	AL	153	570	107	197	45	16	10	114	13	.346
1925	DETROIT	AL	150	573	97	225	40	11	13	134	6	.393
1926	DETROIT	AL	141	502	90	184	41	8	9	103	6	.367
1927	DETROIT	AL	141	505	106	201	50	9	14	120	11	.398
1928	DETROIT	AL	151	558	83	183	38	10	14	107	7	.328
1929	DETROIT	AL	125	453	86	156	41	7	15	120	5	.344
1930	CINCINNATI	NL	142	459	79	153	43	6	19	91	2	.333
1932	CINCINNATI	NL	15	31	3	8	2	0	0	6	0	.258
CAREER TOTALS			2147	7787	1291	2660	542	151	183	1539	113	.342

RICKEY HENDERSON

Rickey Henderson used the ultimate combination of power and speed to break numerous major league records during his career. But what solidified his place in baseball history was his love for the game.

"If my uniform doesn't get dirty, I haven't done anything in the baseball game," said Henderson.

Born on Christmas Day 1958 in Chicago, Henderson spent most of his childhood in Oakland. An All-America running back in high school, Henderson turned down multiple football scholarships to sign with the Oakland Athletics out of the draft in 1976.

In his first full major league season in 1980, Henderson broke Hall of Famer Ty Cobb's 65-year-old American League stolen base record of 96 with 100 swipes. In 1982, he stole 130 bases, breaking Hall of Famer Lou Brock's major league single-season record of 118.

"He's the greatest leadoff hitter of all time, and I'm not sure there's a close second," said Billy Beane, Athletics general manager.

He played for nine teams over his 25-year career, including the Athletics, Yankees, Padres, Mets, Red Sox, Dodgers, Angels, Mariners and Blue Jays. He led the American League in steals 12 times and went on to be the all-time record holder with 1,406, earning him the nickname "Man of Steal."

"It wasn't until I saw Rickey that I understood what baseball was about. Rickey Henderson is a run, man," said Athletics teammate Mitchell Page. "That's it. When you see Rickey Henderson, I don't care when, the score's already 1-0. If he's with you, that's great. If he's not, you won't like it."

Henderson also set all-time records for runs scored (2,295) and unintentional walks (2,129). The 10-time All-Star won the AL MVP Award in 1990, leading the league in runs, stolen bases and on-base percentage. He finished in the top 10 in MVP voting five other times. "He was one of the best players that I ever played with and obviously the best leadoff hitter in baseball," said Hall of Famer Dave Winfield.

RICKEY NELSON HENLEY HENDERSON
"MAN OF STEAL."
OAKLAND, A.L., 1979-1984, 1989-1995, 1998; NEW YORK, A.L., 1985-1989; TORONTO,
A.L., 1993; SAN DIEGO, N.L., 1996-1997, 2001; ANAHEIM, A.L., 1997; NEW YORK,
N.L., 1999-2000; SEATTLE, A.L., 2000; BOSTON, A.L., 2002; LOS ANGELES, N.L., 2003
FASTER THAN A SPEEDING BULLET, SCORED MORE RUNS (2,295) AND
STOLE MORE BASES (1,406) THAN ANY PLAYER IN HISTORY. COMBINED
POWER, PLATE DISCIPLINE, FLAIR AND AN UNCANNY ABILITY TO
ELECTRIFY CROWDS. HIT .279 WITH 3,055 HITS, 297 HOME RUNS AND
1,115 RBI. SET RECORDS FOR HOME RUNS TO LEAD OFF GAME (81) AND
UNINTENTIONAL WALKS (2,129). A TEN-TIME ALL-STAR AND THE 1990
A.L. MVP, LED LEAGUE IN STEALS 12 TIMES, INCLUDING THREE 100-
PLUS SEASONS AND A MODERN-DAY RECORD 130 THEFTS IN 1982.
WON WORLD SERIES WITH OAKLAND AND TORONTO.

The Man of Steal

Elected To The Hall Of Fame: 2009.
Born: Dec. 25, 1958 in Chicago, Ill.
Height: 5-10. **Weight:** 195.
Threw: Left. **Batted:** Right.
Debut: June 24, 1979. **Final Game:** Sept. 19, 2003.
Teams: Oakland A.L. 1979-84, 1989-93, 1994-95, 1998;
New York A.L. 1985-89; Toronto A.L. 1993; San Diego
N.L. 1996-97, 2001; Anaheim A.L. 1997; New York N.L.
1999-2000; Seattle A.L. 2000; Boston A.L. 2002; Los
Angeles N.L. 2003. **Postseason:** 2-Time World Series
Champion (1989, 1993); 3 A.L. Pennants (1989-1990,
1993); 8-Time Playoff Qualifier (1981, 1989-1990, 1992-
1993, 1996, 1999-2000). **Awards:** 10-Time All-Star
(1980, 1982-88, 1990-91); A.L. MVP (1990).

YEAR	TEAM	LEAGUE	G	AB	R	H	2B	3B	HR	RBI	SB	AVG
1979	OAKLAND	AL	89	351	49	96	13	3	1	26	33	.274
1980	OAKLAND	AL	158	591	111	179	22	4	9	53	100	.303
1981	OAKLAND	AL	108	423	89	135	18	7	6	35	56	.319
1982	OAKLAND	AL	149	536	119	143	24	4	10	51	130	.267
1983	OAKLAND	AL	145	513	105	150	25	7	9	48	108	.292
1984	OAKLAND	AL	142	502	113	147	27	4	16	58	66	.293
1985	NEW YORK	AL	143	547	146	172	28	5	24	72	80	.314
1986	NEW YORK	AL	153	608	130	160	31	5	28	74	87	.263
1987	NEW YORK	AL	95	358	78	104	17	3	17	37	41	.291
1988	NEW YORK	AL	140	554	118	169	30	2	6	50	93	.305
1989	NEW YORK/OAKLAND	AL	150	541	113	148	26	3	12	57	77	.274
1990	OAKLAND	AL	136	489	119	159	33	3	28	61	65	.325
1991	OAKLAND	AL	134	470	105	126	17	1	18	57	58	.268
1992	OAKLAND	AL	117	396	77	112	18	3	15	46	48	.283
1993	OAKLAND/TORONTO	AL	134	481	114	139	22	2	21	59	53	.289
1994	OAKLAND	AL	87	296	66	77	13	0	6	20	22	.260
1995	OAKLAND	AL	112	407	67	122	31	1	9	54	32	.300
1996	SAN DIEGO	NL	148	465	110	112	17	2	9	29	37	.241
1997	SAN DIEGO/ANAHEIM	NL/AL	120	403	84	100	14	0	8	34	45	.248
1998	OAKLAND	AL	152	542	101	128	16	1	14	57	66	.236
1999	NEW YORK	NL	121	438	89	138	30	0	12	42	37	.315
2000	NEW YORK/SEATTLE	NL/AL	123	420	75	98	14	2	4	32	36	.233
2001	SAN DIEGO	NL	123	379	70	86	17	3	8	42	25	.227
2002	BOSTON	AL	72	179	40	40	6	1	5	16	8	.223
2003	LOS ANGELES	NL	30	72	7	15	1	0	2	5	3	.208
CAREER TOTALS			3081	10961	2295	3055	510	66	297	1115	1406	.279

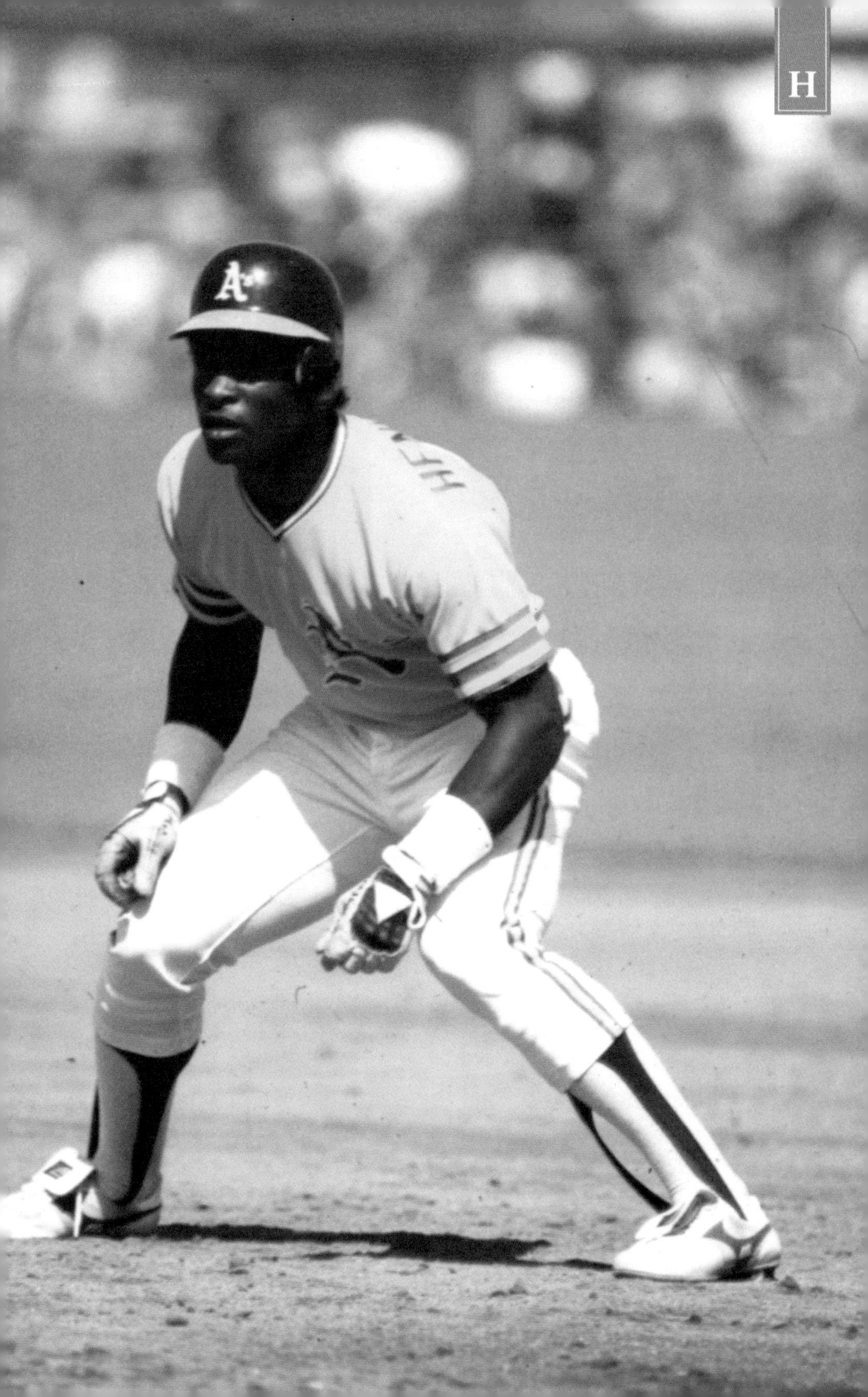

BILLY HERMAN

"Baseball was always kind of a struggle for me," Billy Herman said. "I guess maybe I was doing all right and didn't realize it, but it always seemed like a struggle to me."

Any evidence of Herman's struggles as a player is difficult to find. From the time he spent his first full season in the big league as a 22-year old in 1932, Herman was one of the best players in baseball. A 10-time All-Star, Herman finished his career with a .304 batting average and 2,345 hits, despite serving in the Navy for two years during World War II.

In Herman's first full season in the big leagues, he led the National League in games played with 154 as he helped the Chicago Cubs to the World Series. He finished ninth in MVP balloting after hitting .314. Though Herman missed the inaugural All-Star Game in 1933, he was named to the next 10 in a row.

Herman's best season came in 1935 when he helped lead the Cubs to the National League pennant. He led baseball with 227 hits and 57 doubles and hit a career-high .341. 1935 was one of three seasons when Herman had more than 200 hits and earned him a fourth place finish in the MVP voting, which was won by his teammate Gabby Hartnett.

Herman's tenure in Chicago ended in 1941 when he was traded to the Brooklyn Dodgers. He helped the Dodgers reach the World Series that year, the last of his four trips to the Fall Classic as a player. But it ended like the previous three, with a loss for Herman's team.

World War II interrupted Herman's career, and his swing never regained its previous form after he returned to baseball from the Navy. In his final two years, Herman hit .290 in just 137 games for the Dodgers, the Boston Braves and the Pittsburgh Pirates.

Herman retired in 1947 after playing just 15 games as Pittsburgh's player manager. He holds the single-season N.L. record for putouts by a second baseman (466). He coached in the big leagues until 1964, when he began a three-year stint as the manager of the Red Sox.

Elected To The Hall Of Fame: 1975.

Born: July 7, 1909 in New Albany, Ind.

Died: Sept. 5, 1992 in West Palm Beach, Fla.

Height: 5-11. **Weight:** 180.

Threw: Right. **Batted:** Right.

Debut: Aug. 29, 1931.

Final Game: Aug. 1, 1947.

Teams: Chicago N.L. 1931-1941; Brooklyn N.L. 1941-1943, 1946; Boston N.L. 1946; Pittsburgh N.L. 1947.

Postseason: 4 N.L. Pennants (1932, 1935, 1938, 1941).

Awards: 10-Time All-Star (1934-1943).

YEAR	TEAM	LEAGUE	G	AB	R	H	2B	3B	HR	RBI	SB	AVG
1931	CHICAGO	NL	25	98	14	32	7	0	0	16	2	.327
1932	CHICAGO	NL	154	656	102	206	42	7	1	51	14	.314
1933	CHICAGO	NL	153	619	82	173	35	2	0	44	5	.279
1934	CHICAGO	NL	113	456	79	138	21	6	3	42	6	.303
1935	CHICAGO	NL	154	666	113	227	57	6	7	83	6	.341
1936	CHICAGO	NL	153	632	101	211	57	7	5	93	5	.334
1937	CHICAGO	NL	138	564	106	189	35	11	8	65	2	.335
1938	CHICAGO	NL	152	624	86	173	34	7	1	56	3	.277
1939	CHICAGO	NL	156	623	111	191	34	18	7	70	9	.307
1940	CHICAGO	NL	135	558	77	163	24	4	5	57	1	.292
1941	CHICAGO/BROOKLYN	NL	144	572	81	163	30	5	3	41	1	.285
1942	BROOKLYN	NL	155	571	76	146	34	2	2	65	6	.256
1943	BROOKLYN	NL	153	585	76	193	41	2	2	100	4	.330
1946	BROOKLYN/BOSTON	NL	122	436	56	130	31	5	3	50	3	.298
1947	PITTSBURGH	NL	15	47	3	10	4	0	0	6	0	.213
CAREER TOTALS			**1922**	**7707**	**1163**	**2345**	**486**	**82**	**47**	**839**	**67**	**.304**

PETE HILL

Playing most of his career in the pre-Negro Leagues era, Pete Hill emerged from the backwoods of Culpeper County, Va., to become one of the most feared line-drive hitters in the game. His baseball years run roughly from 1905 to the mid-1920s and involve some of the pioneer programs of black baseball.

Hill is considered to be a great center fielder with a rocket arm and excellent glove. His talents also extended to the batter's box, where he was a consistent line-drive hitter with outstanding speed on the base paths. One quote from the book *Shades of Glory: The Negro Leagues and the Story of African-American Baseball* describes Hill as a "restless type, always in motion, jumping back and forth, trying to draw a throw from the pitcher."

Baseball historian Jim Riley has said that if an all-star outfield was created from the pre-1920 era, it would include Ty Cobb, Tris Speaker and Pete Hill. *The Chicago Defender* supports this, as noted from an article in 1910, Hill can "do anything a white player can do. He can hit, run, throw and is what is termed a wise, heady ballplayer."

He played for some legendary teams, including the Pittsburgh Keystones, Cuban X Giants, Philadelphia Giants, Leland Giants and the Chicago American Giants. His knowledge of the game was also noted as he closed his career by serving as the player-manager for the Detroit Stars, Milwaukee Bears and the Baltimore Black Sox. After retiring from baseball and moving to Buffalo, he also helped form the Buffalo Red Caps. There was no part of the game in which he was not involved.

In 1944, Hall of Famer Cumberland Posey selected Pete Hill to his All-Time All-Star team and referred to him as "the most consistent hitter of his lifetime." "A lot of people forget about the baseball players who were pioneers of the game. They're forgotten like they never existed, but they were part of American history," said Hill's great nephew, Ron Hill, "How can you talk about baseball without talking about Pete Hill."

As for his final legacy, perhaps *The Chicago Defender* summed it up best in 1951 when sportswriter Fay Young said that Hill "helped put Negro baseball on the map."

JOHN PRESTON HILL
"PETE"
PRE-NEGRO LEAGUES, 1899-1919
NEGRO LEAGUES, 1920-1921, 1923-1925
THE CATALYST AND CAPTAIN OF THE GREAT CHICAGO AMERICAN GIANTS CLUBS OF THE 1910s. LEFT-HANDED LINE DRIVE HITTER WITH EXCEPTIONAL BAT CONTROL WHO HIT TO ALL FIELDS. GRACEFULLY ROAMED CENTER FIELD WITH COMBINATION OF SPEED, RANGE AND A RIFLE ARM. RATTLED OPPOSING PITCHERS, CATCHERS AND INFIELDERS WITH HIS CONSTANT MOTION ON THE BASE PATHS. RESPECTED LEADER WHO SERVED AS PLAYER-MANAGER OF THE DETROIT STARS (1919-1921) AND BALTIMORE BLACK SOX (1924-1925). ALSO STARRED IN CUBAN WINTER LEAGUE.

Elected To The Hall Of Fame: 2006.
Born: Oct. 12, 1882 in Culpeper County, Va.
Died: Nov. 19, 1951 in Buffalo, N.Y.
Height: 5-9. **Weight:** 170.
Threw: Right. **Batted:** Left.
Teams: Pre-Negro Leagues 1905-19; Negro Leagues 1920-1921, 1923-1925. Cuban X Giants 1905-1906; Fe 1906; Habana 1907-1911; Philadelphia 1907; Brooklyn 1908; Chicago 1910; Chicago American Giants 1914-1918; Detroit 1919-1921; Toledo 1923; Milwaukee 1923; Baltimore 1924-1925.

YEAR	TEAM	LEAGUE	G	AB	R	H	2B	3B	HR	RBI	SB	AVG
1905	CUBAN X GIANTS	CNCS	9	37	6	12	1	0	0	4	4	.324
1906	FE/CUBAN X GIANTS	CUGL/CNCS	32	127	24	37	3	3	0	14	11	.291
1907	HABANA/PHILADELPHIA	CUGL/CNCS	46	162	46	51	1	6	2	24	22	.315
1908	HABANA/BROOKLYN	CUGL/CNCS	56	205	51	57	2	7	2	13	22	.278
1909	HABANA	CMLS	6	19	4	7	0	1	0	3	1	.368
1910	HABANA/CHICAGO	CUGL/CNCS	50	181	27	62	5	5	0	19	15	.343
1911	HABANA	CUNL	32	108	27	30	1	1	0	14	12	.278
1914	CHICAGO AM. GIANTS	INDP	44	172	35	53	12	4	2	29	2	.308
1915	CHICAGO AM. GIANTS	INDP	54	204	40	52	13	2	6	33	2	.255
1916	CHICAGO AM. GIANTS	INDP	56	184	41	56	7	2	2	23	8	.304
1917	CHICAGO AM. GIANTS	INDP	54	178	27	45	8	3	0	25	9	.253
1918	CHICAGO AM. GIANTS	INDP	25	86	22	24	4	2	0	14	5	.279
1919	DETROIT	INDP	38	139	40	55	9	6	16	52	6	.396
1920	DETROIT	NNL	—	92	13	26	4	1	3	—	5	.283
1921	DETROIT	NNL	—	143	17	44	8	4	2	—	3	.308
1923	TOLEDO/MILWAUKEE	NNL	—	90	8	27	5	1	0	—	1	.300
1924	BALTIMORE	ECOL	—	62	9	12	1	1	0	—	1	.194
1925	BALTIMORE	ECOL	—	17	1	6	0	0	1	—	0	.353
CAREER TOTALS			—	2206	438	656	84	49	36	—	129	.297

HARRY HOOPER

"The best outfield trio I ever saw? That's easy," former Red Sox manager Bill Carrigan said. "[Tris] Speaker, [Duffy] Lewis and Hooper – and the greatest of those was Hooper."

Hooper arrived in Boston for his first full season in 1910, joining Speaker and Lewis in the outfield for a six-year run. The trio was dubbed the "Million-Dollar Outfield" and won two World Series together. Hooper added two more after Speaker and then Lewis left, making him one of two players in the organization's history to win four championships.

While Speaker was clearly the outfield's headliner, Hooper proved to be an outstanding player as well. He was known for his defense in right field and for being one of the better leadoff hitters of his time. Hooper hit .311 in 1911, the first of five times in his career he would hit better than .300. He took a step back at the plate in 1912, hitting .242 when the Red Sox won their first AL pennant in his time with Boston, but made up for it with a .290 average in the World Series.

Hooper bounced back in 1913, hitting .288 and scoring 100 runs for the first time in his career. Then in the 1915 World Series, Hooper hit .350 with two home runs as Boston defeated Philadelphia in five games.

Despite Speaker's departure for Cleveland in 1916, Boston was able to defend its World Series championship. Hooper hit .333 in five games against the Brooklyn Robins. Hooper's one poor World Series came in 1918 when he hit just .200 in six games against the Cubs. Still, Hooper finished his World Series career with a .293 batting average.

Like the other two members of the Million-Dollar Outfield, Hooper eventually departed Boston. He joined the White Sox for the 1921 season, playing the final five years of his career in Chicago. Hooper retired in 1925 with a career .281 batting average and 1,429 runs.

In 1931, Hooper became Princeton's baseball coach, a position he held for two years. He also served as the postmaster for Capitola, Calif., for more than 20 years.

HARRY BARTHOLOMEW HOOPER
BOSTON A.L. 1909-1920
CHICAGO A.L. 1921-1925
LEADOFF HITTER AND RIGHT FIELDER OF
1912-15-16-18 WORLD CHAMPION RED SOX.
NOTED FOR SPEED AND STRONG ARM.
COLLECTED 2,466 HITS FOR .281 CAREER
AVERAGE. HAD 3,981 PUTOUTS AND 344
ASSISTS, LIFETIME FIELDING AVERAGE .966.

Elected To The Hall Of Fame: 1971.
Born: Aug. 24, 1887 in Bell Station, Calif.
Died: Dec. 18, 1974 in Santa Cruz, Calif.
Height: 5-10. **Weight:** 168.
Threw: Right. **Batted:** Left.
Debut: Apr. 16, 1909.
Final Game: Oct. 4, 1925.
Teams: Boston A.L. 1909-1920; Chicago A.L. 1921-1925.
Postseason: 4-Time World Series Champion (1912, 1915-1916, 1918).

YEAR	TEAM	LEAGUE	G	AB	R	H	2B	3B	HR	RBI	SB	AVG
1909	BOSTON	AL	81	255	29	72	3	4	0	12	15	.282
1910	BOSTON	AL	155	584	81	156	9	10	2	27	40	.267
1911	BOSTON	AL	130	524	93	163	20	6	4	45	38	.311
1912	BOSTON	AL	147	590	98	143	20	12	2	53	29	.242
1913	BOSTON	AL	148	586	100	169	29	12	4	40	26	.288
1914	BOSTON	AL	142	530	85	137	23	15	1	41	19	.258
1915	BOSTON	AL	149	566	90	133	20	13	2	51	22	.235
1916	BOSTON	AL	151	575	75	156	20	11	1	37	27	.271
1917	BOSTON	AL	151	559	89	143	21	11	3	45	21	.256
1918	BOSTON	AL	126	474	81	137	26	13	1	44	24	.289
1919	BOSTON	AL	128	491	76	131	25	6	3	49	23	.267
1920	BOSTON	AL	139	536	91	167	30	17	7	53	16	.312
1921	CHICAGO	AL	108	419	74	137	26	5	8	58	13	.327
1922	CHICAGO	AL	152	602	111	183	35	8	11	80	16	.304
1923	CHICAGO	AL	145	576	87	166	32	4	10	65	18	.288
1924	CHICAGO	AL	130	476	107	156	27	8	10	62	16	.328
1925	CHICAGO	AL	127	442	62	117	23	5	6	55	12	.265
CAREER TOTALS			2309	8785	1429	2466	389	160	75	817	375	.281

ROGERS HORNSBY

"I don't like to sound egotistical," Rogers Hornsby said. "But every time I stepped up to the plate with a bat in my hands, I couldn't help but feel sorry for the pitcher."

Hornsby arrived in the major leagues as a 19-year-old with only one year of minor league experience, which came at Class D. Twenty-three years later, Hornsby retired as one of the greatest hitters in the history of the game with the best batting average for a righthander. Along the way he won two MVPs, two Triple Crowns, seven batting titles and became the only player ever to hit more than .400 with 40 home runs in a season.

Inserted into the starting lineup as a 20-year old in 1916, Hornsby hit .313 while playing all four infield positions. He would find a home at second base for the Cardinals in 1920 and his offense reached another level. He hit .370 in 1920 to win his first National League batting title while driving in a league-leading 94 runs. Two years later, Hornsby won his first Triple Crown and hit .401 to top .400 for the first time in his career. His 42 home runs were a career-high and led all of baseball. He drove in 152 runs and had 250 hits, both career highs. Unfortunately for Hornsby, the National League did not start giving out MVP awards regularly until 1924, likely costing him the honor.

Hornsby became the Cardinals' player-manager in 1925 and again won the Triple Crown, hitting .403 with 39 home runs and 143 RBI.

The Cardinals won the World Series in 1926, the only championship of Hornsby's career. Hornsby was 30 that year and hit just .317, so he was traded to the New York Giants that December for future Hall of Famer Frankie Frisch, who was younger.

Hornsby moved to the Boston Braves in 1928 and regained his form in the process. He won his last batting title that season, hitting .387. He went to the Chicago Cubs the next season and won his second MVP, hitting .380 with 39 home runs and 149 RBI.

Rajah

Elected To The Hall Of Fame: 1942.
Born: Apr. 27, 1896 in Winters, Texas.
Died: Jan. 5, 1963 in Chicago, Ill.
Height: 5-11. **Weight:** 175.
Threw: Right. **Batted:** Right.
Debut: Sept. 10, 1915.
Final Game: July 20, 1937.
Teams: St. Louis N.L. 1915-1926, 1933; New York N.L. 1927; Boston N.L. 1928; Chicago N.L. 1929-1932; St. Louis A.L. 1933-1937.
Postseason: World Series Champion (1926); 2 N.L. Pennants (1926, 1929).
Awards: 2-Time N.L. Most Valuable Player (1925, 1929).

YEAR	TEAM	LEAGUE	G	AB	R	H	2B	3B	HR	RBI	SB	AVG
1915	ST. LOUIS	NL	18	57	5	14	2	0	0	4	0	.246
1916	ST. LOUIS	NL	139	495	63	155	17	15	6	65	17	.313
1917	ST. LOUIS	NL	145	523	86	171	24	17	8	66	17	.327
1918	ST. LOUIS	NL	115	416	51	117	19	11	5	60	8	.281
1919	ST. LOUIS	NL	138	512	68	163	15	9	8	71	17	.318
1920	ST. LOUIS	NL	149	589	96	218	44	20	9	94	12	.370
1921	ST. LOUIS	NL	154	592	131	235	44	18	21	126	13	.397
1922	ST. LOUIS	NL	154	623	141	250	46	14	42	152	17	.401
1923	ST. LOUIS	NL	107	424	89	163	32	10	17	83	3	.384
1924	ST. LOUIS	NL	143	536	121	227	43	14	25	94	5	.424
1925	ST. LOUIS	NL	138	504	133	203	41	10	39	143	5	.403
1926	ST. LOUIS	NL	134	527	96	167	34	5	11	93	3	.317
1927	NEW YORK	NL	155	568	133	205	32	9	26	125	9	.361
1928	BOSTON	NL	140	486	99	188	42	7	21	94	5	.387
1929	CHICAGO	NL	156	602	156	229	47	8	39	149	2	.380
1930	CHICAGO	NL	42	104	15	32	5	1	2	18	0	.308
1931	CHICAGO	NL	100	357	64	118	37	1	16	90	1	.331
1932	CHICAGO	NL	19	58	10	13	2	0	1	7	0	.224
1933	ST. LOUIS/ST. LOUIS	NL/AL	57	92	11	30	7	0	3	23	1	.326
1934	ST. LOUIS	AL	24	23	2	7	2	0	1	11	0	.304
1935	ST. LOUIS	AL	10	24	1	5	3	0	0	3	0	.208
1936	ST. LOUIS	AL	2	5	1	2	0	0	0	2	0	.400
1937	ST. LOUIS	AL	20	56	7	18	3	0	1	11	0	.321
CAREER TOTALS			**2259**	**8173**	**1579**	**2930**	**541**	**169**	**301**	**1584**	**135**	**.358**

WAITE HOYT

"He appeared almost casual on the mound, never creating the impression that he was bearing down with any great amount of sweat or strain," Tom Meany wrote. "Games when the chips were down brought out the best in him."

Waite Hoyt first signed a professional contract with the New York Giants as a 15-year old at Erasmus High School in Brooklyn. But Hoyt played just one game for the Giants before embarking on a 21-year career with seven teams. Hoyt made his name with the Yankees, helping to win three World Series titles in the 1920s.

The Yankees acquired Hoyt from the Red Sox before the 1921 season, when he was 21. He immediately validated the move by winning 19 games in each of his first two seasons in the Bronx. In the 1921 World Series against the Giants, Hoyt didn't allow an earned run in 27 innings, but still only went 2-1.

Hoyt continued to be a key contributor for the Yankees throughout the decade, peaking with the Yankees' World Series championship teams in 1923, 1927 and 1928. His 22-7 mark was the best winning percentage in baseball in 1927, and he earned MVP votes in 1928 after going 23-7. Hoyt was the ace of the 1927 Yankees, often considered the best team in baseball history.

Hoyt left New York during the 1930 season and would play for five teams before retiring in 1938. His best year after leaving the Yankees came in Pittsburgh in 1934, when he went 15-6 with a 2.93 ERA. Hoyt finished his career with a 237-182 record and a 3.59 ERA.

During retirement, Hoyt became a popular broadcaster for the Cincinnati Reds, where he did play-by-play for 24 years. Perhaps his most famous moment as a broadcaster came when he spoke impromptu about Babe Ruth for two hours on air after a game when his death was announced. He was inducted into the Hall of Fame by the Veteran's Committee in 1969, 31 years after he retired.

Schoolboy

Elected To The Hall Of Fame: 1969.
Born: Sept. 9, 1899 in Brooklyn, N.Y.
Died: Aug. 25, 1984 in Cincinnati, Ohio.
Height: 6-0. **Weight:** 180.
Threw: Right. **Batted:** Right.
Debut: July 24, 1918.
Final Game: May 15, 1938.
Teams: New York N.L. 1918, 1932; Boston A.L. 1919-1920; New York A.L. 1921-1930; Detroit A.L. 1930-1931; Philadelphia A.L. 1931; Brooklyn N.L. 1932, 1937-1938; Pittsburgh N.L. 1933-1937.
Postseason: 3-Time World Series Champion (1923, 1927-1928); 7-A.L. Pennants (1921-1923, 1926-1928, 1931).

YEAR	TEAM	LEAGUE	G	W	L	SV	SH	IP	H	BB	SO	ERA
1918	NEW YORK	NL	1	0	0	0	0	1	0	0	2	0.00
1919	BOSTON	AL	13	4	6	0	1	105.3	99	22	28	3.25
1920	BOSTON	AL	22	6	6	1	2	121.3	123	47	45	4.38
1921	NEW YORK	AL	43	19	13	3	1	282.3	301	81	102	3.09
1922	NEW YORK	AL	37	19	12	0	3	265	271	76	95	3.43
1923	NEW YORK	AL	37	17	9	1	1	238.7	227	66	60	3.02
1924	NEW YORK	AL	46	18	13	4	2	247	295	76	71	3.79
1925	NEW YORK	AL	46	11	14	6	1	243	283	78	86	4.00
1926	NEW YORK	AL	40	16	12	4	1	217.7	224	62	79	3.85
1927	NEW YORK	AL	36	22	7	1	3	256.3	242	54	86	2.63
1928	NEW YORK	AL	42	23	7	8	3	273	279	60	67	3.36
1929	NEW YORK	AL	30	10	9	1	0	201.7	219	69	57	4.24
1930	NEW YORK/DETROIT	AL	34	11	10	4	1	183.3	240	56	35	4.71
1931	DETROIT/PHILADELPHIA	AL	32	13	13	0	2	203	254	69	40	4.97
1932	BROOKLYN/NEW YORK	NL	26	6	10	1	0	124	141	37	36	4.35
1933	PITTSBURGH	NL	36	5	7	4	1	117	118	19	44	2.92
1934	PITTSBURGH	NL	48	15	6	5	3	190.7	184	43	105	2.93
1935	PITTSBURGH	NL	39	7	11	6	0	164	187	27	63	3.40
1936	PITTSBURGH	NL	22	7	5	1	0	116.7	115	20	37	2.70
1937	PITTSBURGH/BROOKLYN	NL	38	8	9	2	1	195	211	36	65	3.42
1938	BROOKLYN	NL	6	0	3	0	0	16.3	24	5	3	4.96
CAREER TOTALS			**674**	**237**	**182**	**52**	**26**	**3762.1**	**4037**	**1003**	**1206**	**3.59**

CARL HUBBELL

"He could throw strikes at midnight. I never saw another pitcher who could so fascinate the opposition the way Hubbell did." Hall of Famer Billy Herman said.

Carl Hubbell is best known for his standout single-game performances, the most memorable being during the three innings he spent on the mound in the 1934 All-Star game.

"In terms of All-Star Game pitching feats, there is one standing far, far apart from all others," sportswriter Bob Ryan said in the *Boston Globe*. "On July 10, 1934, in the Polo Grounds, the National League's Carl Hubbell wrote himself some baseball history by striking out the final three men of the first inning and the first two of the second. Any self-respecting baseball historian knows the names by heart, and almost invariably rattles them off so quickly it's as if the five men had one name – Ruthgehrigfoxxsimmonscronin."

After giving up a single and a walk, the left-hander struck out five future Hall of Famers in succession. Hubbell cited the feat as one of his best days.

Prior to that game, though, the southpaw had another single-game stunner. On July 2, 1933, he threw 18 scoreless innings and allowed only six hits to beat the Cardinals 1-0 at the Polo Grounds. He threw a perfect game for 12 of the innings, striking out 12 along the way without giving up a walk.

Nicknamed the Meal Ticket, Hubbell threw a devastating screwball that led to 253 career wins and a 2.98 ERA in 3,590 innings pitched. From 1933 to 1937 he had five straight 20-win seasons, helping his team to three pennants and a World Series championship. In the 1933 Fall Classic, Hubbell pitched two complete-game victories, one of them an 11-inning, 2-1 win. The run against him was unearned. In his six career World Series starts, the lefty was 4-2 with 32 strikeouts and a 1.79 ERA.

In 1936, Hubbell was the first-ever unanimous pick for the NL MVP Award, with a 26-6 record. Hubbell finished the regular season with 16 straight victories, leading the Giants to the World Series.

When his playing days were done, Hubbell remained in the game as a farm director in the Giants organization for more than 30 years.

CARL HUBBELL
NEW YORK N.L. 1928-1943
HAILED FOR IMPRESSIVE PERFORMANCE IN 1934 ALL-STAR GAME WHEN HE STRUCK OUT RUTH, GEHRIG, FOXX, SIMMONS AND CRONIN IN SUCCESSION. NICKNAMED GIANTS' MEAL-TICKET. WON 253 GAMES IN MAJORS. SCORING 16 STRAIGHT IN 1936, COMPILED STREAK OF 46 1/3 SCORELESS INNINGS IN 1933. HOLDER OF MANY RECORDS.

King Carl, The Meal Ticket

Elected To The Hall Of Fame: 1947.
Born: June 22, 1903 in Carthage, Mo.
Died: Nov. 21, 1988 in Scottsdale, Ariz.
Height: 6-0. **Weight:** 170.
Threw: Left. **Batted:** Right.
Debut: July 26, 1928.
Final Game: Aug. 24, 1943.
Teams: New York N.L. 1928-1943.
Postseason: World Series Champion (1933); 3 N.L. Pennants (1933,1936-1937).
Awards: 9-Time All-Star (1933-1938, 1940-1942); 2-Time N.L. Most Valuable Player (1933, 1936).

YEAR	TEAM	LEAGUE	G	W	L	SV	SH	IP	H	BB	SO	ERA
1928	NEW YORK	NL	20	10	6	1	1	124	117	21	37	2.83
1929	NEW YORK	NL	39	18	11	1	1	268	273	67	106	3.69
1930	NEW YORK	NL	37	17	12	2	3	241.7	263	58	117	3.87
1931	NEW YORK	NL	36	14	12	3	4	248	211	67	155	2.65
1932	NEW YORK	NL	40	18	11	2	0	284	260	40	137	2.50
1933	NEW YORK	NL	45	23	12	5	10	308.7	256	47	156	1.66
1934	NEW YORK	NL	49	21	12	8	5	313	286	37	118	2.30
1935	NEW YORK	NL	42	23	12	0	1	302.7	314	49	150	3.27
1936	NEW YORK	NL	42	26	6	3	3	304	265	57	123	2.31
1937	NEW YORK	NL	39	22	8	4	4	261.7	261	55	159	3.20
1938	NEW YORK	NL	24	13	10	1	1	179	171	33	104	3.07
1939	NEW YORK	NL	29	11	9	2	0	154	150	24	62	2.75
1940	NEW YORK	NL	31	11	12	0	2	214.3	220	59	86	3.65
1941	NEW YORK	NL	26	11	9	1	1	164	169	53	75	3.57
1942	NEW YORK	NL	24	11	8	0	0	157.3	158	34	61	3.95
1943	NEW YORK	NL	12	4	4	0	0	66	87	24	31	4.91
CAREER TOTALS			535	253	154	33	36	3590.1	3461	725	1677	2.98

CATFISH HUNTER

"He was a fabulous human being. He was a man of honor. He was a man of loyalty," said Reggie Jackson of his teammate.

James Augustus "Catfish" Hunter played for championship teams in both Oakland and New York, finding success wherever he went. Though his career ended when he was just 33 years old, he still managed to win 224 games and five World Series championships along the way.

After three seasons in Kansas City, the right-hander started his career off in Oakland with a perfect game on May 8, 1968, just the ninth such game in baseball history. It was the first in the American League since 1922.

With the Athletics, he not only earned his nickname, but he had four consecutive years with 20 or more wins, and won four World Series games and lost none. The name "Catfish" was invented by A's owner Charlie Finley, to garner attention from the media.

In Hunter's final season in Oakland he was named the A.L. Pitcher of the Year by the *Sporting News* and also earned the A.L. Cy Young Award for compiling a 25-12 record with a league-leading 2.49 ERA. Following that great campaign, Catfish signed with the Yankees for $3.75 million over five years, becoming the highest-paid pitcher in baseball after a contract dispute made him a free agent.

During the 1975 season, he led the league in wins for the second year in a row, this time with 23. The hurler also led with 328 innings pitched and 30 complete games.

"Catfish Hunter was the cornerstone of the Yankees success over the last quarter century," Yankees owner George Steinbrenner said. "We were not winning before Catfish arrived...He exemplified class and dignity and he taught us how to win."

With Hunter, New York won three straight pennants from 1976 to 1978, and he joined Cy Young, Christy Mathewson and Walter Johnson as the only pitchers in major league history to win 200 games by the age of 31.

The righty was forced into early retirement in 1979 because of the effects of diabetes and early onset ALS, appearing in the form of arm strain. He lived 20 more years, dying in 1999 at the age of 53.

JAMES AUGUSTUS HUNTER
"CATFISH"
KANSAS CITY, A.L., 1965 – 1967
OAKLAND, A.L., 1968 – 1974
NEW YORK, A.L., 1975 – 1979
THE BIGGER THE GAME, THE BETTER HE PITCHED.
ONE OF BASEBALL'S MOST DOMINANT PITCHERS FROM
1970-76, WINNING OVER 20 FIVE STRAIGHT TIMES. COMPILED
224-166 MARK WITH 3.26 ERA BEFORE ARM TROUBLE
ENDED CAREER AT AGE 33. HURLED PERFECT GAME
VS. TWINS IN 1968. 1974 A.L. CY YOUNG AWARD WINNER.
5-3 IN 12 WORLD SERIES GAMES.

Elected To The Hall Of Fame: 1987.
Born: Apr. 8, 1946 in Hertford, N.C.
Died: Sept. 9, 1999 in Hertford, N.C.
Height: 6-0. **Weight:** 190.
Threw: Right. **Batted:** Right.
Debut: May 13, 1965.
Final Game: Sept. 17, 1979.
Teams: Kansas City A.L. 1965-1967; Oakland A.L. 1968-1974; New York A.L. 1975-1979.
Postseason: 5-Time World Series Champion (1972-1974, 1977-1978); 6 A.L. Pennants (1972-1974, 1976-1978); 7-Time Postseason Qualifier (1971-1974, 1976-1978).
Awards: 8-Time All-Star (1966-1967, 1970, 1972-1976); A.L. Cy Young (1974).

YEAR	TEAM	LEAGUE	G	W	L	SV	SH	IP	H	BB	SO	ERA
1965	KANSAS CITY	AL	32	8	8	0	2	133	124	46	82	4.26
1966	KANSAS CITY	AL	30	9	11	0	0	176.7	158	64	103	4.02
1967	KANSAS CITY	AL	35	13	17	0	5	259.7	209	84	196	2.81
1968	OAKLAND	AL	36	13	13	1	2	234	210	69	172	3.35
1969	OAKLAND	AL	38	12	15	0	3	247	210	85	150	3.35
1970	OAKLAND	AL	40	18	14	0	1	262.3	253	74	178	3.81
1971	OAKLAND	AL	37	21	11	0	4	273.7	225	80	181	2.96
1972	OAKLAND	AL	38	21	7	0	5	295.3	200	70	191	2.04
1973	OAKLAND	AL	36	21	5	0	3	256.3	222	69	124	3.34
1974	OAKLAND	AL	41	25	12	0	6	318.3	268	46	143	2.49
1975	NEW YORK	AL	39	23	14	0	7	328	248	83	177	2.58
1976	NEW YORK	AL	36	17	15	0	2	298.7	268	68	173	3.53
1977	NEW YORK	AL	22	9	9	0	1	143.3	137	47	52	4.71
1978	NEW YORK	AL	21	12	6	0	1	118	98	35	56	3.58
1979	NEW YORK	AL	19	2	9	0	0	105	128	34	34	5.31
CAREER TOTALS			**500**	**224**	**166**	**1**	**42**	**3449.1**	**2958**	**954**	**2012**	**3.26**

MONTE IRVIN

MONFORD (MONTE) IRVIN
NEGRO LEAGUES 1937-1948
NEW YORK N.L., CHICAGO N.L.,
1949-1956
REGARDED AS ONE OF NEGRO LEAGUES' BEST
HITTERS, STAR SLUGGER OF NEWARK EAGLES
WON 1946 NEGRO LEAGUE BATTING TITLE,
LED N.L. IN RUNS BATTED IN AND PACED
"MIRACLE" GIANTS IN HITTING IN 1951
DRIVE TO PENNANT. BATTED .458 AND
STOLE HOME IN 1951 WORLD SERIES.

Monte Irvin was not the first African-American player in the modern major leagues, but of all the talented players who made the perilous trip from the Negro leagues to the big leagues in the late 1940s, Irvin may have been the best.

"Monte was the choice of all Negro National and American League club owners to serve as the No. 1 player to join a white major league team," said Hall of Famer Effa Manley, owner of the Newark Eagles. "We all agreed, in meeting, he was the best qualified by temperament, character, ability, sense of loyalty, morals, age, experiences and physique to represent us as the first black player to enter the white majors since the Walker brothers back in the 1880s. Of course, Branch Rickey lifted Jackie Robinson out of Negro ball and made him the first, and it turned out just fine."

It also turned out fine for Irvin, who starred for eight seasons in the majors with the Giants and the Cubs before being elected to the Hall of Fame in 1973. Irvin, born Feb. 25, 1919 in Haleburg, Ala., was a four-sport athlete in high school and began playing professional baseball in college under an assumed name to keep his amateur status. He joined the Newark Eagles and quickly became an outstanding all-around player. He could hit for power, was a strong fielder at shortstop and could steal bases. One of the league's biggest stars, he was elected to five East-West All-Star games. After asking for a raise and being denied, Irvin left for Mexico and starred for three years south of the border.

He returned to the Eagles in 1946 where he won his second batting title and helped win the Negro World Series. In 1949, the New York Giants bought Irvin's contract from the Eagles. In 1951, as New York's regular left fielder, he sparked the Giants to win the pennant, hitting .312 with 24 home runs and a National League-best 121 RBI, en route to a third-place finish in the MVP voting. Although the Giants lost to the Yankees in the World Series, Irvin batted .458 in the six-game series.

He played for the Giants for seven seasons, was elected to the 1952 All-Star Game and won a World Series with them in 1954. After an ankle injury, he spent his final season with the Cubs in 1956. Irvin became a scout for the New York Mets and later spent 17 years in the commissioner's office under Bowie Kuhn.

Elected To The Hall Of Fame: 1973.
Born: Feb. 25, 1919 in Haleburg, Ala.
Height: 6-1. **Weight:** 195.
Threw: Right. **Batted:** Right.
Debut: July 8, 1949.
Final Game: Sept. 30, 1956.
Teams: Negro Leagues 1938-1948 Newark 1938-1942, 1945-1948; New York N.L. 1949-1955; Chicago N.L. 1956.
Postseason: World Series Champion (1954); 2 N.L. Pennants (1951, 1954).
Awards: All-Star (1952).

YEAR	TEAM	LEAGUE	G	AB	R	H	2B	3B	HR	RBI	SB	AVG
1938	NEWARK	NNL	—	4	0	0	0	0	0	—	0	.000
1939	NEWARK	NNL	—	52	3	10	0	0	0	—	0	.192
1940	NEWARK	NNL	—	131	26	46	8	4	3	—	2	.351
1941	NEWARK	NNL	—	130	30	52	10	1	4	—	7	.400
1942	NEWARK	NNL	—	12	3	9	1	1	1	—	2	.750
1945	NEWARK	NNL	—	13	2	5	1	0	0	—	0	.385
1946	NEWARK	NNL	—	152	34	57	6	1	6	—	3	.375
1947	NEWARK	NNL	—	46	13	16	1	0	4	—	1	.348
1948	NEWARK	NNL	—	30	6	7	0	0	2	—	2	.233
NEGRO LEAGUE TOTALS			—	**570**	**117**	**202**	**27**	**7**	**20**	—	**17**	**.354**
1949	NEW YORK	NL	36	76	7	17	3	2	0	7	0	.224
1950	NEW YORK	NL	110	374	61	112	19	5	15	66	3	.299
1951	NEW YORK	NL	151	558	94	174	19	11	24	121	12	.312
1952	NEW YORK	NL	46	126	10	39	2	1	4	21	0	.310
1953	NEW YORK	NL	124	444	72	146	21	5	21	97	2	.329
1954	NEW YORK	NL	135	432	62	113	13	3	19	64	7	.262
1955	NEW YORK	NL	51	150	16	38	7	1	1	17	3	.253
1956	CHICAGO	NL	111	339	44	92	13	3	15	50	1	.271
MAJOR LEAGUE TOTALS			**764**	**2499**	**366**	**731**	**97**	**31**	**99**	**443**	**28**	**.293**

REGGIE JACKSON

ob Marshall said, "Just as nature fills a vacuum, Reggie fills a spotlight." Outspoken and charismatic, Reggie Jackson was never afraid to speak his mind. He was good – very good, and he knew it.

One of the biggest sports stars of a generation, Reggie called himself "the straw that stirs the drink." In 1973, as a member of the Oakland Athletics, Jackson said if he played in New York they would name a candy bar after him – and within five years, those words came true.

Jackson could have been in New York sooner, had the New York Mets not passed on him and taken high school catcher Steve Chilcott with the No. 1 overall pick of the 1966 draft. Jackson went second to the Athletics. But it was Jackson's dream to play in New York. When he finally got there in 1977, always the showman, he said, "I didn't come to New York to be a star, I brought my star with me."

Named the World Series MVP in 1973 and 1977, Jackson's star seemed to shine its brightest on baseball's grandest stage. In five World Series, Jackson hit 10 home runs while batting .357. His most memorable moment in the Fall Classic came in Game Six of the 1977 series when Reggie hit three home runs on three pitches, earning the nickname "Mr. October." Dodgers first baseman Steve Garvey later said, "I must admit, when Reggie hit his third home run and I was sure nobody was looking, I applauded in my glove."

Reggie was also a star off the field, invading pop culture and appearing in movies and television programs such as "MacGyver," "Malcom in the Middle," "BASEketball" and "The Naked Gun."

Jackson was a 14-time American League All-Star, a member of five World Series teams and won the American League MVP Award in 1973, when he led the junior circuit in home runs, RBI and runs scored.

After five tumultuous years in New York, Reggie moved back out west, joining the California Angels. During his first season there, Reggie once again led the league in home runs. Jackson finished his career back where he started, as a member of the Athletics.

REGINALD MARTINEZ JACKSON
"MR. OCTOBER"
KANSAS CITY, A.L., 1967
OAKLAND, A.L., 1968-1975, 1987
BALTIMORE, A.L., 1976
NEW YORK, A.L., 1977-1981
CALIFORNIA, A.L., 1982-1986

EXCITING PERFORMER WHO PLAYED FOR 11 DIVISION WINNERS AND FOUND SPECIAL SUCCESS IN WORLD SERIES SPOTLIGHT WITH 10 HOME RUNS, 24 RBI'S AND .357 BATTING AVERAGE IN 27 GAMES. IN 1977 SERIES, HIT RECORD 5 HOMERS, 4 OF THEM CONSECUTIVE, INCLUDING 3 IN ONE GAME ON 3 FIRST PITCHES OFF 3 DIFFERENT HURLERS. MAMMOTH CLOUT MARKED 1971 ALL STAR GAME. 563 HOMERS RANK 6TH ON ALL-TIME LIST. A.L. MVP, 1973.

Mr. October

Elected To The Hall Of Fame: 1993.
Born: May 18, 1946 in Abington, Pa.
Height: 6-0. **Weight:** 195.
Threw: Left. **Batted:** Left.
Debut: June 9, 1967. **Final Game:** Oct. 4, 1987.
Teams: Kansas City A.L. 1967; Oakland A.L. 1968-1975, 1987; Baltimore A.L. 1976; New York A.L. 1977-1981; California A.L. 1982-1986.)
Postseason: 5-Time World Series Champion (1972 – did not play in World Series due to injury; 1973-1974, 1977-1978); 6 A.L. Pennants (1972-1974, 1977-1978, 1981); 11-Time Playoff Qualifier (1971-1975, 1977-1978, 1980-1982, 1986).
Awards: 14-Time All- Star (1969, 1971-75, 1977-1984); A.L. Most Valuable Player (1973); 2-Time World Series Most Valuable Player (1973, 1977).

YEAR	TEAM	LEAGUE	G	AB	R	H	2B	3B	HR	RBI	SB	AVG
1967	KANSAS CITY	AL	35	118	13	21	4	4	1	6	1	.178
1968	OAKLAND	AL	154	553	82	138	13	6	29	74	14	.250
1969	OAKLAND	AL	152	549	123	151	36	3	47	118	13	.275
1970	OAKLAND	AL	149	426	57	101	21	2	23	66	26	.237
1971	OAKLAND	AL	150	567	87	157	29	3	32	80	16	.277
1972	OAKLAND	AL	135	499	72	132	25	2	25	75	9	.265
1973	OAKLAND	AL	151	539	99	158	28	2	32	117	22	.293
1974	OAKLAND	AL	148	506	90	146	25	1	29	93	25	.289
1975	OAKLAND	AL	157	593	91	150	39	3	36	104	17	.253
1976	BALTIMORE	AL	134	498	84	138	27	2	27	91	28	.277
1977	NEW YORK	AL	146	525	93	150	39	2	32	110	17	.286
1978	NEW YORK	AL	139	511	82	140	13	5	27	97	14	.274
1979	NEW YORK	AL	131	465	78	138	24	2	29	89	9	.297
1980	NEW YORK	AL	143	514	94	154	22	4	41	111	1	.300
1981	NEW YORK	AL	94	334	33	79	17	1	15	54	0	.237
1982	CALIFORNIA	AL	153	530	92	146	17	1	39	101	4	.275
1983	CALIFORNIA	AL	116	397	43	77	14	1	14	49	0	.194
1984	CALIFORNIA	AL	143	525	67	117	17	2	25	81	8	.223
1985	CALIFORNIA	AL	143	460	64	116	27	0	27	85	1	.252
1986	CALIFORNIA	AL	132	419	65	101	12	2	18	58	1	.241
1987	OAKLAND	AL	115	336	42	74	14	1	15	43	2	.220
CAREER TOTALS			**2820**	**9864**	**1551**	**2584**	**463**	**49**	**563**	**1702**	**228**	**.262**

TRAVIS JACKSON

"In all the years I watched him, playing with him and against him, I never saw him make a mistake," said Rogers Hornsby.

Travis Jackson was a standout shortstop for the Giants from 1922 to 1936, spending his entire career in New York. His exceptional range earned him the nickname "Stonewall," and his leadership earned him the role of team captain.

Not known for his power hitting, Jackson established himself as an everyday player in 1924. In 151 games, he batted .302 with 11 home runs, finishing the season with two grand slams and helping the Giants win a pennant by a game and a half.

The slick-fielding shortstop was on four National League pennant-winning teams and won one World Series Championship in 1933. During the Fall Classic, Jackson scored three runs and drove in two, helping the Giants win in five games over the Washington Senators.

In Game Four of the Series, Jackson led off the 11th inning in a 1-1 game with a drag-bunt single and scored the winning run to give the Giants a 3-1 series advantage. The clutch-hitter cited it at his greatest accomplishment at the time.

"I've punched out quite a few hits in my time, but none that have given me greater gladness than the one I punched out yesterday in the 11th to start our rally."

Jackson batted .300-or-more six times, hitting a career-high 21 home runs in 1929 and driving in a career-best 101 runs in 1934. In 1928 he had eight RBI in one game and in 1929 he had a double, a triple and two home runs in one game.

Regularly among the league leaders in assists and double plays, he was voted the Most Outstanding Shortstop by the *Sporting News* in 1927, 1928 and 1929. His throwing arm and quick release were among the best in the majors. Jackson led the league in fielding average and double plays each twice, and led in assists four times.

In 1930, he hit a career-high .339. The Arkansas Sports Hall of Fame member became a coach when his playing days were over, helping out the Giants, and then lending a hand to several minor league clubs.

Stonewall

Elected To The Hall Of Fame: *1982.*
Born: *Nov. 2, 1903 in Waldo, Ark.*
Died: *July 27, 1987 in Waldo, Ark.*
Height: *5-10.* **Weight:** *160.*
Threw: *Right.* **Batted:** *Right.*
Debut: *Sept. 27, 1922.*
Final Game: *Sept. 24, 1936.*
Teams: *New York N.L. 1922-1936.*
Postseason: *World Series Champion (1933); 4 N.L. Pennants (1923-1924, 1933, 1936).*
Awards: *All-Star (1934).*

YEAR	TEAM	LEAGUE	G	AB	R	H	2B	3B	HR	RBI	SB	AVG
1922	NEW YORK	NL	3	8	1	0	0	0	0	0	0	.000
1923	NEW YORK	NL	96	327	45	90	12	7	4	37	3	.275
1924	NEW YORK	NL	151	596	81	180	26	8	11	76	6	.302
1925	NEW YORK	NL	112	411	51	117	15	2	9	59	8	.285
1926	NEW YORK	NL	111	385	64	126	24	8	8	51	2	.327
1927	NEW YORK	NL	127	469	67	149	29	4	14	98	8	.318
1928	NEW YORK	NL	150	537	73	145	35	6	14	77	8	.270
1929	NEW YORK	NL	149	551	92	162	21	12	21	94	10	.294
1930	NEW YORK	NL	116	431	70	146	27	8	13	82	6	.339
1931	NEW YORK	NL	145	555	65	172	26	10	5	71	13	.310
1932	NEW YORK	NL	52	195	23	50	17	1	4	38	1	.256
1933	NEW YORK	NL	53	122	11	30	5	0	0	12	2	.246
1934	NEW YORK	NL	137	523	75	140	26	7	16	101	1	.268
1935	NEW YORK	NL	128	511	74	154	20	12	9	80	3	.301
1936	NEW YORK	NL	126	465	41	107	8	1	7	53	0	.230
CAREER TOTALS			**1656**	**6086**	**833**	**1768**	**291**	**86**	**135**	**929**	**71**	**.291**

FERGUSON JENKINS

"One of the best pitchers in baseball, ever," said Cubs manager Leo Durocher.

Ferguson "Fergie" Jenkins originally signed with the Philadelphia Phillies in 1962, but didn't find great success until the Chicago Cubs took him out of the bullpen and converted him into a starting pitcher five years later.

In his first year as a starter in 1967, the right-hander notched 20 wins to go with a 2.80 ERA and 236 strikeouts. He tied for second place in the voting for the Cy Young Award. The following year, he again won 20 games, had an ERA of 2.63 and struck out 260. From 1967-72, Jenkins won 20 or more games each year, striking out more than 200 in every season, averaging 314 innings pitched. He also threw 97 complete games over that span.

Fergie's best single-game performance came in the 1967 All-Star Game, when he struck out six of the top sluggers in American League: Harmon Killebrew, Tony Conigliaro, Mickey Mantle, Jim Fregosi, Rod Carew and Tony Oliva.

His best year came in 1971, when Jenkins was the National League Cy Young Award winner. He went 24-13, throwing a complete game in 30 of his 39 starts, walked 37 and struck out 263 in 325 innings. Jenkins also became the first Cubs pitcher and the first Canadian to ever win the Cy Young.

In 1974 with the Texas Rangers, he had a career-high 25 wins, and became the first baseball player to win the Lou Marsh Trophy, an award given each year to Canada's top athlete. He was inducted into the Canadian Baseball Hall of Fame in 1987.

Jenkins led the NL in wins two times, complete games four times and had the fewest walks per nine innings in the league five times. The right-hander is one of only four pitchers in major league history to record more than 3,000 strikeouts with fewer than 1,000 walks.

As a hockey, basketball and baseball player growing up, Jenkins eventually found a focus, but never completely gave up other sports. In fact, he played with the Harlem Globetrotters during the baseball off-season on multiple occasions.

Fergie

Elected To The Hall Of Fame: *1991.*

Born: *Dec. 13, 1942 in Chatham, Ontario, Canada.*

Height: *6-5.* **Weight:** *205.*

Threw: *Right.* **Batted:** *Right.*

Debut: *Sept. 10, 1965.*

Final Game: *Sept. 26, 1983.*

Teams: *Philadelphia N.L. 1965-1966; Chicago N.L. 1966-1973, 1982-1983; Texas A.L. 1974-1975, 1978-1981; Boston A.L. 1976-1977.*

Awards: *3-Time All-Star (1967, 1971-1972); N.L. Cy Young (1971).*

YEAR	TEAM	LEAGUE	G	W	L	SV	SH	IP	H	BB	SO	ERA
1965	PHILADELPHIA	NL	7	2	1	1	0	12.3	7	2	10	2.19
1966	PHILADELPHIA/CHICAGO	NL	61	6	8	5	1	184.3	150	52	150	3.32
1967	CHICAGO	NL	38	20	13	0	3	289.3	230	83	236	2.80
1968	CHICAGO	NL	40	20	15	0	3	308	255	65	260	2.63
1969	CHICAGO	NL	43	21	15	1	7	311.3	284	71	273	3.21
1970	CHICAGO	NL	40	22	16	0	3	313	265	60	274	3.39
1971	CHICAGO	NL	39	24	13	0	3	325	304	37	263	2.77
1972	CHICAGO	NL	36	20	12	0	5	289.3	253	62	184	3.20
1973	CHICAGO	NL	38	14	16	0	2	271	267	57	170	3.89
1974	TEXAS	AL	41	25	12	0	6	328.3	286	45	225	2.82
1975	TEXAS	AL	37	17	18	0	4	270	261	56	157	3.93
1976	BOSTON	AL	30	12	11	0	2	209	201	43	142	3.27
1977	BOSTON	AL	28	10	10	0	1	193	190	36	105	3.68
1978	TEXAS	AL	34	18	8	0	4	249	228	41	157	3.04
1979	TEXAS	AL	37	16	14	0	3	259	252	81	164	4.07
1980	TEXAS	AL	29	12	12	0	0	198	190	52	129	3.77
1981	TEXAS	AL	19	5	8	0	0	106	122	40	63	4.50
1982	CHICAGO	NL	34	14	15	0	1	217.3	221	68	134	3.15
1983	CHICAGO	NL	33	6	9	0	1	167.3	176	46	96	4.30
CAREER TOTALS			**664**	**284**	**226**	**7**	**49**	**4500.2**	**4142**	**997**	**3192**	**3.34**

HUGHIE JENNINGS

"Jennings in his prime was the greatest shortstop in baseball," said Joe Vila of the *New York Sun*.

Inducted into the Hall of Fame as a player, Hughie Jennings was also a leader on the field, which propelled him to a successful career as a manager after his playing days were over.

Jennings played with Baltimore teams that won National League championships for three consecutive years from 1894-1896. Over those three seasons, Jennings had 355 RBI and hit .335, .386 and .401. In 1895, to go with his .386 average, he had 204 hits, scored 159 runs, drove in 125 and stole 53 bases. During the following season, he had 209 hits and 70 stolen bases, also setting a major league record by being hit by a pitch 51 times.

For his career, Jennings batted .312 with 1,526 hits, scored 992 runs and stole 359 bases. He also led all shortstops in the league in fielding average three times.

The shortstop was hit by a pitch an astounding 287 times in his career. In one game in particular, he was hit in the head by a pitch in the third inning and remarkably, he continued to play the rest of the game. But, as soon as it finished, he collapsed and remained unconscious for the three days that followed.

After the 1899 season, in which he played for the pennant-winning Brooklyn Superbas, Jennings went to Cornell Law School and began his managerial career with the university baseball team while also completing his studies. He left campus before finishing his degree in the 1904 season to manage the Eastern League Orioles, and was hired as the manager of the Detroit Tigers in 1907. He later passed the bar and enjoyed a long career practicing law.

Jennings led the Tigers to three consecutive pennants in his first three seasons with the team, and stayed with them until 1920. He compiled 1,131 wins in his 14 years as Detroit's manager.

The Detroit manager became known for yelling "Ee-yah!" from the coaching box, as a form of encouragement for his players. It became his nickname, and fans would yell the word whenever he came on the field.

HUGHIE JENNINGS
OF BALTIMORE'S FAMOUS OLD ORIOLES,
HE WAS ONE OF THE GAME'S MIGHTY
MITES. A STAR SHORTSTOP HE WAS A
CONSTANT THREAT AT THE PLATE.
ONCE HIT .397. PILOTED DETROIT
TO THREE CHAMPIONSHIPS.

Elected To The Hall Of Fame: 1945.
Born: April 2, 1869 in Pittston, Pa.
Died: Feb. 1, 1928 in Scranton, Pa.
Height: 5-8. **Weight:** 165.
Threw: Right. **Batted:** Right.
Debut: June 1, 1891.
Final Game: Sept. 2, 1918.
Teams: Louisville, American Association 1891; Louisville N.L. 1892-1893; Baltimore N.L. 1893-1899; Brooklyn N.L. 1899-1900, 1903; Philadelphia N.L. 1901-1902; Detroit A.L. 1907, 1909-10, 1912, 1918.

YEAR	TEAM	LEAGUE	G	AB	R	H	2B	3B	HR	RBI	SB	AVG
1891	LOUISVILLE	AA	88	351	51	103	10	8	1	58	12	.293
1892	LOUISVILLE	NL	152	594	65	133	16	4	2	61	28	.224
1893	LOUISVILLE/BALTIMORE	NL	39	143	12	26	3	0	1	15	0	.182
1894	BALTIMORE	NL	128	501	134	168	28	16	4	109	37	.335
1895	BALTIMORE	NL	131	529	159	204	41	7	4	125	53	.386
1896	BALTIMORE	NL	130	521	125	209	27	9	0	121	70	.401
1897	BALTIMORE	NL	117	439	133	156	26	9	2	79	60	.355
1898	BALTIMORE	NL	143	534	135	175	25	11	1	87	28	.328
1899	BROOKLYN/BALTIMORE	NL	69	224	44	67	3	12	0	42	18	.299
1900	BROOKLYN	NL	115	441	61	120	18	6	1	69	31	.272
1901	PHILADELPHIA	NL	82	302	38	79	21	2	1	39	13	.262
1902	PHILADELPHIA	NL	78	290	32	79	13	4	1	32	8	.272
1903	BROOKLYN	NL	6	17	2	4	0	0	0	1	1	.235
1907	DETROIT	AL	1	4	0	1	1	0	0	0	0	.250
1909	DETROIT	AL	2	4	1	2	0	0	0	2	0	.500
1910	DETROIT	AL	1	0	0	0	0	0	0	0	0	.500"
1912	DETROIT	AL	1	1	0	0	0	0	0	0	0	.000
1918	DETROIT	AL	1	0	0	0	0	0	0	0	0	.000"
CAREER TOTALS			**1284**	**4895**	**992**	**1526**	**232**	**88**	**18**	**840**	**359**	**.312**

JUDY JOHNSON

"Judy could do all that is required to make up a sterling third baseman and do it better than the rest of the field. He hit the ball hard to all corners of the lot. Slight of build, this Hilldale luminary was a fielding gem, whose breathtaking plays on bunts and hard smashes are treasured among many fans' memoirs," opined writer and official scorekeeper Lloyd Thompson.

Considered one of the best third basemen to play in the Negro leagues, along with fellow Hall of Famers Ray Dandridge and Jud Wilson, William "Judy" Johnson was a slick-fielding, spray-hitting, clutch performer, and later a manager, scout and coach.

Johnson was born in Snow Hill, Md., in 1899. At age 18, he began playing semipro baseball for five dollars a game. He quickly moved up to the Hilldale Stars, joining the club full time in 1921. It was there that he acquired his nickname, after a veteran Negro Leagues player named "Judy" Gans. His mentor as a young player was Hall of Famer John Henry "Pop" Lloyd. Johnson, a smart ballplayer with a skill for recognizing and developing talent, would later serve as a mentor for Hall-of-Famer Josh Gibson.

Johnson led the Hilldales to three pennants in a row from 1923-25. He played in the first Negro World Series in 1924, losing to the Kansas City Monarchs. The Hilldales turned the table on the Monarchs the following year.

In 1929, Johnson was named the Negro Leagues Most Valuable Player by the *Chicago Defender* and the *Pittsburgh Courier*, two of the leading black newspapers. The following season, he became player-manager of the Homestead Grays. In 1932, he and most of the club jumped to the Pittsburgh Crawfords. He was captain of the 1935 club that featured five future Hall of Famers: himself, Cool Papa Bell, Oscar Charleston, Josh Gibson, and Satchel Paige. He retired as a player in 1937.

In 1951, Johnson scouted for the Philadelphia Athletics, later scouting for the Braves, Phillies, and Dodgers. He signed Richie Allen and Bill Bruton, and could have signed Hank Aaron for the A's, who reportedly balked at the price. In 1954, he was hired as a spring training coach for the A's.

WILLIAM JULIUS JOHNSON
"JUDY"
NEGRO LEAGUES 1923-1937
CONSIDERED BEST THIRD BASEMAN OF HIS DAY IN NEGRO LEAGUES, OUTSTANDING AS FIELDER AND EXCELLENT CLUTCH HITTER WHO BATTED OVER .300 MOST OF CAREER. HELPED HILLDALE TEAM WIN THREE FLAGS IN ROW, 1923-24-25. ALSO PLAYED FOR 1935 CHAMPION PITTSBURGH CRAWFORDS.

Elected To The Hall Of Fame: *1975.*
Born: *Dec. 26. 1899 in Snow Hill, Md.*
Died: *June 15, 1989 in Wilmington, Del.*
Height: *5-11.* **Weight:** *150.*
Threw: *Right.* **Batted:** *Right.*
Teams: *Negro Leagues 1918-1936. Hilldale 1918, 1921-1929, 1931-1932; Atlantic City 1918; Homestead 1929-1930; Pittsburgh 1932-1936.*

YEAR	TEAM	LEAGUE	G	AB	R	H	2B	3B	HR	RBI	SB	AVG
1918	HILLDALE/ATLANTIC CITY	INDP	3	8	0	3	1	0	0	0	0	.375
1921	HILLDALE	INDP	—	108	13	28	2	5	1	—	1	.259
1922	HILLDALE	INDP	—	31	3	5	0	1	0	—	2	.161
1923	HILLDALE	ECOL	—	214	28	62	4	1	2	—	3	.290
1924	HILLDALE	ECOL	—	325	60	111	28	6	5	—	11	.342
1925	HILLDALE	ECOL	—	252	48	98	13	10	5	—	7	.389
1926	HILLDALE	ECOL	—	367	67	117	22	7	2	—	13	.319
1927	HILLDALE	ECOL	—	217	26	55	4	2	1	—	0	.253
1928	HILLDALE	ECOL	—	230	26	56	8	4	1	—	2	.243
1929	HILLDALE/HOMESTEAD	ANL	—	226	55	85	11	1	5	—	10	.376
1930	HOMESTEAD	INDP	—	121	23	38	3	3	0	—	1	.314
1931	HILLDALE	INDP	—	160	18	38	2	2	0	—	1	.238
1932	PITTSBURGH/HILLDALE	INDP/EWL	—	157	25	50	2	1	1	—	1	.318
1933	PITTSBURGH	NNL	—	154	18	35	4	0	0	—	1	.227
1934	PITTSBURGH	NNL	—	189	22	48	11	1	1	—	3	.254
1935	PITTSBURGH	NNL	—	130	19	30	6	1	2	—	1	.231
1936	PITTSBURGH	NNL	—	101	15	17	0	1	0	—	2	.168
CAREER TOTALS			—	2990	466	876	121	46	26	—	59	.293

WALTER JOHNSON

Addie Joss could not have been more right when he predicted, "That young fellow is another Cy Young. I never saw a kid with more than he displayed. Of course, he is still green, but when he has a little experience he should be one of the greatest pitchers that ever broke into the game."

Walter Johnson came from humble beginnings, the son of a Kansas farmer. It wasn't until his parents moved the family out west that he began to pick up the trade that would make him a star. Johnson was a natural from the moment he stepped on to the Southern California sandlots.

Labor Day Weekend of 1908, Johnson's sophomore campaign in the junior circuit, saw one of the most dominating performances of his career. He started three consecutive games, September 4, 5 and 7, and shut out the New York Highlanders in each of those contests giving up six, four and two hits respectively—truly one of the most remarkable pitching performances of any generation.

In 1911, famed sportswriter Grantland Rice popularized the nickname "The Big Train" in referring to Johnson. At a time when trains were the fastest things known to man, Ty Cobb recalled Johnson's fastball as "just speed, raw speed, blinding speed, too much speed." "The Big Train" added to his arsenal when he developed a curveball in the early 1910s and put together a string of 10 straight 20-win seasons. During his career, Johnson amassed 11 seasons with a sub 2.00 ERA and completed 531 of his 666 career starts.

In 1924, the Senators made the World Series for the first time. After playing on very poor teams for nearly two decades, Johnson finally got the opportunity to shine on baseball's grandest stage. In the ninth inning of Game 7, Senators skipper Bucky Harris called on Johnson in relief "You're the best we've got, Walter, We've got to win or lose with you"- and win they did. Johnson blanked the Giants for four innings and earned the victory and Washington's only World Series championship.

The Big Train

Elected To The Hall Of Fame: *1936.*
Born: *Nov. 6, 1887 in Humboldt, Kan.*
Died: *Dec. 10, 1946 in Washington, D.C.*
Height: *6-1.* **Weight:** *200.*
Threw: *Right.* **Batted:** *Right.*
Debut: *Aug. 2, 1907.*
Final Game: *Sept. 30, 1927.*
Teams: *Washington A.L. 1907-1927.*
Postseason: *World Series Champion (1924); 2 A.L. Pennants (1924-1925).*
Awards: *2-Time Most Valuable Player (1913, 1924).*

YEAR	TEAM	LEAGUE	G	W	L	SV	SH	IP	H	BB	SO	ERA
1907	WASHINGTON	AL	14	5	9	0	2	110.3	100	20	71	1.88
1908	WASHINGTON	AL	36	14	14	1	6	256.3	194	53	160	1.65
1909	WASHINGTON	AL	40	13	25	1	4	296.3	247	84	164	2.22
1910	WASHINGTON	AL	45	25	17	1	8	370	262	76	313	1.36
1911	WASHINGTON	AL	40	25	13	1	6	322.3	292	70	207	1.90
1912	WASHINGTON	AL	50	33	12	2	7	369	259	76	303	1.39
1913	WASHINGTON	AL	48	36	7	2	11	346	232	38	243	1.14
1914	WASHINGTON	AL	51	28	18	1	9	371.7	287	74	225	1.72
1915	WASHINGTON	AL	47	27	13	4	7	336.7	258	56	203	1.55
1916	WASHINGTON	AL	48	25	20	1	3	369.7	290	82	228	1.90
1917	WASHINGTON	AL	47	23	16	3	8	326	248	68	188	2.21
1918	WASHINGTON	AL	39	23	13	3	8	326	241	70	162	1.27
1919	WASHINGTON	AL	39	20	14	2	7	290.3	235	51	147	1.49
1920	WASHINGTON	AL	21	8	10	3	4	143.7	135	27	78	3.13
1921	WASHINGTON	AL	35	17	14	1	1	264	265	92	143	3.51
1922	WASHINGTON	AL	41	15	16	4	4	280	283	99	105	2.99
1923	WASHINGTON	AL	42	17	12	4	3	261	263	73	130	3.48
1924	WASHINGTON	AL	38	23	7	0	6	277.7	233	77	158	2.72
1925	WASHINGTON	AL	30	20	7	0	3	229	217	78	108	3.07
1926	WASHINGTON	AL	33	15	16	0	2	260.7	259	73	125	3.63
1927	WASHINGTON	AL	18	5	6	0	1	107.7	113	26	48	5.10
CAREER TOTALS			**802**	**417**	**279**	**34**	**110**	**5914.1**	**4913**	**1363**	**3509**	**2.17**

ADDIE JOSS

Though time couldn't tell the full effect Addie Joss might have had on the game of baseball, he left a legacy large enough to remember.

With his unconventional corkscrew delivery, he was able to get the ball across the plate before most batters even had a chance at seeing it, let alone making contact.

"Joss sort of hid the ball on you," Hall of Famer Bobby Wallace said. "One moment, you'd be squinting at a long, graceful windup and the next instant, out of nowhere, the ball was hopping across the plate – and a lot of us standing flat-footed with our bat glued to our shoulders."

The right-hander would turn his back to the batter to begin his windup motion, hiding the ball the whole time before whipping back around to fire it across the plate. His technique found him great success, including a 1.89 lifetime ERA and four seasons in a row of 20 or more wins.

Joss never experienced a losing season in the nine years he pitched in the major leagues. His biggest accomplishments came in 1908, when he was 24-11 with a 1.16 ERA and nine shutouts. In his 11 losses, his team scored a total of only 11 runs in support of him.

Joss gave his club a chance to win every time he stepped on the mound, keeping them in every game he pitched. He had incredible control over his pitches, and in 1908, he walked only 30 batters in the 325 innings he threw.

On Oct. 2, 1908, Joss threw the fourth perfect game in baseball history, a victory over future Hall of Famer Ed Walsh. He accomplished the feat with just 74 pitches. It was the first of two no-hitters he would throw, the second coming in 1910. Both games were against the Chicago White Sox, and he is the only pitcher to no-hit the same team twice.

Of his 160 career wins, 45 of them were shutouts. His career ERA is ranked second all-time and he led the American League twice in the same category while he was playing.

Joss' dominance as a pitcher was cut short when tubercular meningitis ended his life at the age of 31, in April 1911. His death was a shock to the baseball world and Cleveland's game in Detroit was postponed for the funeral in Toledo.

ADRIAN (ADDIE) JOSS
CLEVELAND A.L., 1902-1910
ONE OF PREMIER PITCHERS OF AMERICAN LEAGUE'S FIRST DECADE. SPEED, SHARP CONTROL HELPED HIM TO WIN 20 OR MORE GAMES FOUR SEASONS IN A ROW. POSTED LEAGUE-LEADING 27 VICTORIES AND THREE ONE-HITTERS IN 1907. HURLED PERFECT GAME IN 1908. HAD ANOTHER NO-HITTER IN 1910. CREDITED WITH 45 SHUTOUTS AMONG HIS 160 CAREER VICTORIES.

Elected To The Hall Of Fame: 1978.
Born: April 12, 1880 in Woodland, Wis.
Died: April 14, 1911 in Toledo, Ohio.
Height: 6-3. **Weight:** 185.
Threw: Right. **Batted:** Right.
Debut: April 26, 1902.
Final Game: July 11, 1910.
Teams: Cleveland A.L. 1902-1910.

YEAR	TEAM	LEAGUE	G	W	L	SV	SH	IP	H	BB	SO	ERA
1902	CLEVELAND	AL	32	17	13	0	5	269.3	225	75	106	2.77
1903	CLEVELAND	AL	32	18	13	0	3	283.7	232	37	120	2.19
1904	CLEVELAND	AL	25	14	10	0	5	192.3	160	30	83	1.59
1905	CLEVELAND	AL	33	20	12	0	3	286	246	46	132	2.01
1906	CLEVELAND	AL	34	21	9	1	9	282	220	43	106	1.72
1907	CLEVELAND	AL	42	27	11	2	6	338.7	279	54	127	1.83
1908	CLEVELAND	AL	42	24	11	2	9	325	232	30	130	1.16
1909	CLEVELAND	AL	33	14	13	0	4	242.7	198	31	67	1.71
1910	CLEVELAND	AL	13	5	5	0	1	107.3	96	18	49	2.26
CAREER TOTALS			**286**	**160**	**97**	**5**	**45**	**2327**	**1888**	**364**	**920**	**1.89**

AL KALINE

A l Kaline *was* the Detroit Tigers for more than two decades. Through last place finishes and World Series triumphs, the Motor City knew it had its sweet swinging right fielder to cheer for throughout the summer. Chuck Dressen, a big league skipper for 16 seasons, the last four with the Tigers (1963-66), said Kaline was the best player he had ever managed: "For all-around ability – I mean hitting, fielding, running and throwing – I'll go with Al."

The 18-year-old Kaline came to the Tigers in 1953 directly from high school, having never spent a day in the minors, and by the next season established himself as one of the game's bright new talents. By 1955 he became the youngest player to win a batting title when he hit .340.

"I owe everything to baseball," Kaline once said. "Without it, I'd probably be a bum."

Offensive consistency became Kaline's hallmark over the years, hitting at least 20 home runs and batting .300 or better nine times each. A superb defensive outfielder with a strong throwing arm, he also collected 10 Gold Glove Awards. In the 1968 World Series, Kaline's only appearance in the Fall Classic, he batted .379, hit two home runs and drove in eight to help Detroit knock off the St. Louis Cardinals in seven games.

"You almost have to watch him play every day to appreciate what he does," said veteran pitcher and former Tigers teammate Johnny Podres. "You hear about him, sure, but you really can't understand until you see him. He just never makes a mistake."

By the time Kaline's 22-year big league career ended in 1974, the lifelong Tiger and 18-time All-Star had collected 3,007 hits, 399 home runs and a .297 career batting average.

"People ask me, was it my goal to play in the majors for 20 years? Was it my goal to get 3,000 hits someday? Lord knows, I didn't have any goals," Kaline once said. "I tell them, 'My only desire was to be a baseball player.'"

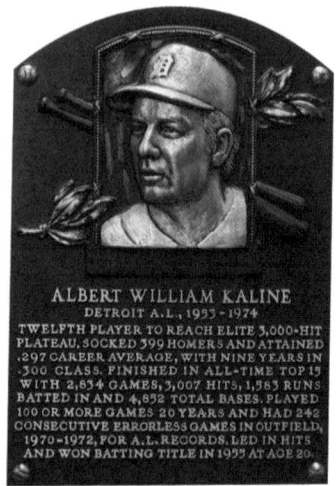

ALBERT WILLIAM KALINE
DETROIT A.L., 1953-1974
TWELFTH PLAYER TO REACH ELITE 3,000-HIT
PLATEAU, SOCKED 399 HOMERS AND ATTAINED
.297 CAREER AVERAGE, WITH NINE YEARS IN
.300 CLASS. FINISHED IN ALL-TIME TOP 15
WITH 2,854 GAMES, 3,007 HITS, 1,583 RUNS
BATTED IN AND 4,852 TOTAL BASES. PLAYED
100 OR MORE GAMES 20 YEARS AND HAD 242
CONSECUTIVE ERRORLESS GAMES IN OUTFIELD,
1970-1972, FOR A.L. RECORDS. LED IN HITS
AND WON BATTING TITLE IN 1955 AT AGE 20.

Elected To The Hall Of Fame: *1980.*
Born: *Dec. 19, 1934 in Baltimore, Md.*
Height: *6-1.* **Weight:** *175.*
Threw: *Right.* **Batted:** *Right.*
Debut: *June 25, 1953.*
Final Game: *Oct. 2, 1974.*
Teams: *Detroit A.L. 1953-1974.*
Postseason: *World Series Champion (1968); 2 A.L. Pennants (1968, 1972).*
Awards: *18-time All-Star (1955-1967, 1971, 1974).*

YEAR	TEAM	LEAGUE	G	AB	R	H	2B	3B	HR	RBI	SB	AVG
1953	DETROIT	AL	30	28	9	7	0	0	1	2	1	.250
1954	DETROIT	AL	138	504	42	139	18	3	4	43	9	.276
1955	DETROIT	AL	152	588	121	200	24	8	27	102	6	.340
1956	DETROIT	AL	153	617	96	194	32	10	27	128	7	.314
1957	DETROIT	AL	149	577	83	170	29	4	23	90	11	.295
1958	DETROIT	AL	146	543	84	170	34	7	16	85	7	.313
1959	DETROIT	AL	136	511	86	167	19	2	27	94	10	.327
1960	DETROIT	AL	147	551	77	153	29	4	15	68	19	.278
1961	DETROIT	AL	153	586	116	190	41	7	19	82	14	.324
1962	DETROIT	AL	100	398	78	121	16	6	29	94	4	.304
1963	DETROIT	AL	145	551	89	172	24	3	27	101	6	.312
1964	DETROIT	AL	146	525	77	154	31	5	17	68	4	.293
1965	DETROIT	AL	125	399	72	112	18	2	18	72	6	.281
1966	DETROIT	AL	142	479	85	138	29	1	29	88	5	.288
1967	DETROIT	AL	131	458	94	141	28	2	25	78	8	.308
1968	DETROIT	AL	102	327	49	94	14	1	10	53	6	.287
1969	DETROIT	AL	131	456	74	124	17	0	21	69	1	.272
1970	DETROIT	AL	131	467	64	130	24	4	16	71	2	.278
1971	DETROIT	AL	133	405	69	119	19	2	15	54	4	.294
1972	DETROIT	AL	106	278	46	87	11	2	10	32	1	.313
1973	DETROIT	AL	91	310	40	79	13	0	10	45	4	.255
1974	DETROIT	AL	147	558	71	146	28	2	13	64	2	.262
CAREER TOTALS			**2834**	**10116**	**1622**	**3007**	**498**	**75**	**399**	**1583**	**137**	**.297**

The Baseball Hall of Fame Almanac

TIMOTHY J. KEEFE

Though Timothy Keefe spent the majority of his baseball career pitching from a distance of 50 feet, he also threw in an era when pitchers worked every other day, and his talent was so great that it withstood the test of time. The submarine pitcher spent his first big league season throwing from 45 feet, and his last from 60 feet, six inches, notching 342 victories along the way.

In his first season, he posted a 0.86 ERA in 105 innings pitched, a record that still stands from when he accomplished the feat in 1880. Over his 14 seasons in the majors, Keefe held many records and teamed up with fellow Hall of Famer Mickey Welch to bring the Giants not only their first pennant, but he also added one more after that one. His teammate saw the dominance Keefe had over batters firsthand.

"I never saw a better pitcher," Welch said. "True, he did his best work from 50 feet, but he still would have had no superior at 60 feet, six inches."

Keefe went to the New York Metropolitans from Troy before the beginning of his fourth season in 1883. He pitched 68 complete games that year in 68 starts for a total of 619 innings. He won 41 games and struck out 359 batters along the way.

Keefe also pitched two complete-game victories on the same day that year for the Mets, surrendering only three hits between them. On July 4, 1883, he first threw a one-hit gem, followed by a two-hit win later that afternoon.

From that first year in New York to 1888, a span of six seasons, Keefe never won less than 32 games a year for his teams. In 1886, he had a 42-20 record with a 2.56 ERA.

His best season came in 1888 with the New York Giants. Keefe was the Triple Crown winner, leading the National League in wins (35), strikeouts (335) and ERA (1.74.) He also had 48 complete games, eight shutouts, a .745 winning percentage and the fewest average hits per nine innings with 6.57.

The right-hander also had 19 consecutive victories in his best season, a record that lasted 24 years. It was also in 1888 when Keefe and Welch brought New York a pennant for the first time.

TIMOTHY J. KEEFE
1880—1893
RIGHTHANDER WHO WON 346 GAMES
FOR TROY, METS, GIANTS AND PHILS
IN ONLY 14 SEASONS.
HIS RECORD STREAK OF 19 STRAIGHT TRIUMPHS
PACED GIANTS TO FLAG IN 1888.
ONE OF FIRST PITCHERS
TO USE A CHANGE OF PACE DELIVERY.

Elected To The Hall Of Fame: 1964.
Born: Jan. 1, 1857 in Cambridge, Mass.
Died: April 23, 1933 in Cambridge, Mass.
Height: 5-10. **Weight:** 185.
Threw: Right. **Batted:** Right.
Debut: Aug. 6, 1880.
Final Game: Aug. 15, 1893.
Teams: Troy N.L.1880-1882; New York, American Association 1883-1884; New York N.L. 1885-1889, 1891; New York, Players League 1890; Philadelphia N.L. 1891-1893.
Postseason: 2-time N.L. Champion (1888-1889); 2 N.L. Pennants (1888-1889); American Association Pennant (1884)

YEAR	TEAM	LEAGUE	G	W	L	SV	SH	IP	H	BB	SO	ERA
1880	TROY	NL	12	6	6	0	0	105	68	16	39	0.86
1881	TROY	NL	45	18	27	0	4	403	434	83	103	3.24
1882	TROY	NL	43	17	26	0	1	376	367	78	111	2.49
1883	NEW YORK	AA	68	41	27	0	5	619	488	108	359	2.41
1884	NEW YORK	AA	58	37	17	0	4	483	380	71	334	2.25
1885	NEW YORK	NL	46	32	13	0	7	400	300	102	227	1.58
1886	NEW YORK	NL	64	42	20	0	2	535	479	102	297	2.56
1887	NEW YORK	NL	56	35	19	0	2	476.7	428	108	189	3.12
1888	NEW YORK	NL	51	35	12	0	8	434.3	317	90	335	1.74
1889	NEW YORK	NL	47	28	13	1	3	364	319	101	225	3.36
1890	NEW YORK	PL	30	17	11	0	1	229	225	89	89	3.38
1891	NEW YORK/PHILADELPHIA	NL	19	5	11	1	0	133.3	152	57	64	4.46
1892	PHILADELPHIA	NL	39	19	16	0	2	313.3	279	98	136	2.36
1893	PHILADELPHIA	NL	22	10	7	0	0	178	202	80	56	4.40
CAREER TOTALS			**600**	**342**	**225**	**2**	**39**	**5049.2**	**4438**	**1233**	**2564**	**2.63**

WILLIE KEELER

illiam Henry "Wee Willie" Keeler was one of the smallest players ever in major league baseball at 5 feet 4, 140 pounds, but he had one of the heaviest bats in the game, both figuratively and literally, weighing up to 46 ounces. His motto was, "Keep your eye on the ball and hit 'em where they ain't," and it certainly worked for the third baseman-turned-outfielder. Keeler had 14 straight seasons in which he batted over .300 and a lifetime average of .341, and for seven straight seasons he also had an on-base percentage that was above .400.

In 1894, he batted .371, scoring 165 runs and notching 94 RBI. He also hit 22 triples in his first year with the Orioles and began his streak of eight consecutive years with 200 or more hits, a record that stood for more than 100 years.

Keeler was the leadoff man for nine seasons in Baltimore and Brooklyn, winning five pennants over that span and seeing his team take second place in the race three times. During those nine years, he averaged 211 hits and 134 runs per season. He hit .373 during his time between the two ball clubs.

Keeler's best season came in 1897 when he batted .424, which is the highest average for a left-handed hitter in baseball history. He led the National League with 239 hits in only 129 games. Keeler also started the season with a 44-game hitting streak, beating the previous record of 42. His new mark stood for 44 years and was broken by Joe DiMaggio. During the 1898 season, Keeler hit 206 singles, a record that stood for more than a century until it was broken by Ichiro Suzuki.

Keeler was known to have handled his bat well, placing hits wherever he wanted and dropping perfect bunts on a whim. He was also smart on the basepaths and had speed to go with it. Of his 33 career home runs, 30 of them were inside-the-park.

When he retired in 1910, Keeler was second only to Cap Anson for the lead in all-time hits with 2,932. Sportscaster Bill Stern called him "the most wonderful hitter that ever lived," and former player Ted Sullivan once commented, "He's the greatest right fielder in the history of baseball."

Wee Willie

Elected To The Hall Of Fame: 1939.
Born: March 3, 1872 in Brooklyn, N.Y.
Died: Jan. 1, 1923 in Brooklyn, N.Y.
Height: 5-4. **Weight:** 140.
Threw: Left. **Batted:** Left.
Debut: Sept. 30, 1892.
Final Game: Sept. 5, 1910.
Teams: New York N.L. 1892-1893, 1910; Brooklyn N.L. 1893, 1899-1902; Baltimore N.L. 1894-1898; New York A.L. 1903-1909.

YEAR	TEAM	LEAGUE	G	AB	R	H	2B	3B	HR	RBI	SB	AVG
1892	NEW YORK	NL	14	53	7	17	3	0	0	6	5	.321
1893	NEW YORK/BROOKLYN	NL	27	104	19	33	3	2	2	16	5	.317
1894	BALTIMORE	NL	129	590	165	219	27	22	5	94	32	.371
1895	BALTIMORE	NL	131	565	162	213	24	15	4	78	47	.377
1896	BALTIMORE	NL	126	544	153	210	22	13	4	82	67	.386
1897	BALTIMORE	NL	129	564	145	239	27	19	0	74	64	.424
1898	BALTIMORE	NL	129	561	126	216	7	2	1	44	28	.385
1899	BROOKLYN	NL	141	570	140	216	12	13	1	61	45	.379
1900	BROOKLYN	NL	136	563	106	204	13	12	4	68	41	.362
1901	BROOKLYN	NL	136	595	123	202	18	12	2	43	23	.339
1902	BROOKLYN	NL	133	559	86	186	20	5	0	38	19	.333
1903	NEW YORK	AL	132	512	95	160	14	7	0	32	24	.313
1904	NEW YORK	AL	143	543	78	186	14	8	2	40	21	.343
1905	NEW YORK	AL	149	560	81	169	14	4	4	38	19	.302
1906	NEW YORK	AL	152	592	96	180	8	3	2	33	23	.304
1907	NEW YORK	AL	107	423	50	99	5	2	0	17	7	.234
1908	NEW YORK	AL	91	323	38	85	3	1	1	14	14	.263
1909	NEW YORK	AL	99	360	44	95	7	5	1	32	10	.264
1910	NEW YORK	NL	19	10	5	3	0	0	0	0	1	.300
CAREER TOTALS			**2123**	**8591**	**1719**	**2932**	**241**	**145**	**33**	**810**	**495**	**.341**

GEORGE KELL

"He's a seven-day-a-week ballplayer." – Red Rolfe. Third base remains baseball's enigmatic position, the one where fielding prowess stands on equal ground with hitting skill. It is the rarest of combinations, and one that has sent just 12 former major leaguers to the Baseball Hall of Fame – the fewest of any category.

George Kell, one of those 12, parlayed his skills with the lumber and the leather into one of baseball's most consistent careers of the middle part of the 20th Century.

Kell broke into the big leagues with the Athletics at the end of the 1943 season, then took over as Philadelphia's every day third baseman the next year at 21 years old. After two get-your-feet wet seasons where he struck out just 38 times out of 1,081 at-bats – and finished 22nd in the American League MVP vote in 1944 – Kell was traded to the Detroit Tigers on May 18, 1946 for Barney McCosky.

It was a trade A's owner Connie Mack would long regret.

Kell hit at least .304 from 1946-53, going to the first of six straight All-Star Games in 1947. He finished fifth in the MVP voting in 1947 with a .320 average and 93 RBIs, then hit .343 in 1949 – winning the batting title by .0002 over Ted Williams and denying Williams his third Triple Crown.

Kell had his greatest season in 1950, hitting .340 with 114 runs scored and 101 RBIs.

Kell was traded to the Red Sox during the 1952 season, and bounced to the White Sox and the Orioles before finishing his career in 1957 with his 10th-and-final All-Star selection. He was selected to the Mid Summer Classic roster in 10 of his final 11 seasons.

"George Kell is a thoroughbred," said Hall of Fame shortstop Lou Boudreau.

Kell wrapped up his career with a .306 average – better than every Hall of Fame third baseman except Frank Baker, Wade Boggs, Fred Lindstrom and Pie Traynor. His ringing right-handed line drives left him with a .300-or-better average in eight straight seasons. He struck out just 287 times.

Following his career, Kell broadcast Tigers games from 1959-63 and 1965-96.

GEORGE CLYDE KELL
PHILADELPHIA A. L. 1943-1946
DETROIT A. L. 1946-1952
BOSTON A. L. 1952-1954
CHICAGO A. L. 1954-1956
BALTIMORE A. L. 1956-1957
PREMIER A. L. THIRD BASEMAN OF 1940'S AND
1950'S. SOLID HITTER AND SURE-HANDED FIELDER
WITH STRONG, ACCURATE ARM. BATTED OVER
.300 9 TIMES, LEADING LEAGUE WITH .343 IN
1949. LED A. L. THIRD BASEMEN IN FIELDING
PCT. 7 TIMES, ASSISTS 4 TIMES AND PUTOUTS
AND DOUBLE PLAYS TWICE.

Elected To The Hall Of Fame: 1983.
Born: Aug. 23, 1922 in Swifton, Ark.
Died: March 24, 2009 in Swifton, Ark.
Height: 5-9. **Weight:** 175.
Threw: Right. **Batted:** Right.
Debut: Sept. 28, 1943.
Final Game: Sept. 14, 1957.
Teams: Philadelphia A.L. 1943-1946;
Detroit A.L. 1946-1952; Boston A.L.
1952-1954; Chicago A.L. 1954-1956;
Baltimore A.L. 1956-1957.
Awards: 10-Time All-Star (1947-1954,
1956-1957).

YEAR	TEAM	LEAGUE	G	AB	R	H	2B	3B	HR	RBI	SB	AVG
1943	PHILADELPHIA	AL	1	5	1	1	0	1	0	1	0	.200
1944	PHILADELPHIA	AL	139	514	51	138	15	3	0	44	5	.268
1945	PHILADELPHIA	AL	147	567	50	154	30	3	4	56	2	.272
1946	PHILADELPHIA/DETROIT	AL	131	521	70	168	25	10	4	52	3	.322
1947	DETROIT	AL	152	588	75	188	29	5	5	93	9	.320
1948	DETROIT	AL	92	368	47	112	24	3	2	44	2	.304
1949	DETROIT	AL	134	522	97	179	38	9	3	59	7	.343
1950	DETROIT	AL	157	641	114	218	56	6	8	101	3	.340
1951	DETROIT	AL	147	598	92	191	36	3	2	59	10	.319
1952	DETROIT/BOSTON	AL	114	428	52	133	23	2	7	57	0	.311
1953	BOSTON	AL	134	460	68	141	41	2	12	73	5	.307
1954	BOSTON/CHICAGO	AL	97	326	40	90	13	0	5	58	1	.276
1955	CHICAGO	AL	128	429	44	134	24	1	8	81	2	.312
1956	CHICAGO/BALTIMORE	AL	123	425	52	115	22	2	9	48	0	.271
1957	BALTIMORE	AL	99	310	28	92	9	0	9	44	2	.297
CAREER TOTALS			1795	6702	881	2054	385	50	78	870	51	.306

JOE KELLEY

"Joe had no prominent weakness. He was fast on the bases, could hit the ball hard and was as graceful an outfielder as one would care to see." –John McGraw
Aside from topping the National League with 87 stolen bases in 1896, Joe Kelley rarely led the league in any categories, but he was a well-rounded outfielder who could run, hit for average, get on base and ranked among the league leaders in various power-hitting categories as well.

Kelley made his major league debut at 19 with the Boston Beaneaters in 1891, but he was released after a brief big league trial. The following season Kelley joined the Pirates, where he appeared in 56 games before Pittsburgh traded him to Baltimore.

By 1893, Kelley had established himself as a regular in the Orioles lineup, hitting .305 to start a string of 11 straight seasons in which he hit over .300. From there on, Kelley became one of the most productive players in baseball during the late 19th century, playing with the Orioles until 1898. From 1894-1898, Kelley drove in at least 100 runs in each season, and his 573 RBIs during that stretch were more than anyone in baseball other than Hugh Duffy. One of the greats of his time at getting on base, Kelley's 401 walks from 1894-1898 ranked fourth in baseball during that span, while his 909 hits ranked eighth.

A last-place team in 1892, Kelley's arrival led to a surge in the standings for the Orioles. After an eighth-place finish in 1893, the Orioles won three straight NL pennants from 1894-1896, then rattled off back-to-back second-place finishes in 1897 and 1898, Kelley's final year with the Orioles.

Kelley joined the Brooklyn Superbas in 1899. While the Orioles dropped to fourth place in the NL, Brooklyn jumped from 54 wins in 1898 to 101 wins and capturing its first of two straight NL pennants with Kelley in 1899 and 1900. After the 1901 season, Kelley joined the Baltimore Orioles of the American League. When new ownership took over for the Orioles during the season, the franchise released Kelley, who hooked on with the Cincinnati Reds. Serving as a player/manager for the Reds from 1902-1905, Kelley led the club to an 88-win season in 1904 as Cincinnati finished third in the NL.

JOSEPH JAMES KELLEY
1891-1908
STANDOUT HITTER AND LEFT FIELDER OF CHAMPION 1894-95-96 BALTIMORE ORIOLES AND 1899-1900 BROOKLYN SUPERBAS. BATTED OVER .300 FOR 11 CONSECUTIVE YEARS WITH HIGH OF .391 IN 1894. EQUALLED RECORD WITH 9 HITS IN 9 AT-BATS IN DOUBLEHEADER. ALSO PLAYED FOR BOSTON, PITTSBURGH AND CINCINNATI OF N.L. AND BALTIMORE OF A.L. MANAGED CINCINNATI 1902 TO 1905 AND BOSTON N. L. IN 1908.

Elected To The Hall Of Fame: *1971.*
Born: *Dec. 9, 1871 in Cambridge, Mass.*
Died: *Aug. 14, 1943 in Baltimore, Md.*
Height: *5-11.* **Weight:** *190.*
Threw: *Right.* **Batted:** *Right.*
Debut: *July 27, 1891.*
Final Game: *Oct. 3, 1908.*
Teams: *Boston N.L. 1891, 1908; Pittsburgh N.L. 1892; Baltimore N.L. 1892-1898; Brooklyn N.L. 1899-1901; Baltimore A.L. 1902; Cincinnati N.L. 1902-1906.*

YEAR	TEAM	LEAGUE	G	AB	R	H	2B	3B	HR	RBI	SB	AVG
1891	BOSTON	NL	12	45	7	11	1	1	0	3	0	.244
1892	PITTSBURGH/BALTIMORE	NL	66	238	29	56	7	7	0	32	10	.235
1893	BALTIMORE	NL	125	502	120	153	27	16	9	76	33	.305
1894	BALTIMORE	NL	129	507	165	199	48	20	6	111	46	.393
1895	BALTIMORE	NL	131	518	148	189	26	19	10	134	54	.365
1896	BALTIMORE	NL	131	519	148	189	31	19	8	100	87	.364
1897	BALTIMORE	NL	131	505	113	183	31	9	5	118	44	.362
1898	BALTIMORE	NL	124	464	71	149	18	15	2	110	24	.321
1899	BROOKLYN	NL	143	538	108	175	21	14	6	93	31	.325
1900	BROOKLYN	NL	121	454	90	145	23	17	6	91	26	.319
1901	BROOKLYN	NL	120	492	77	151	22	12	4	65	18	.307
1902	BALTIMORE/CINCINNATI	AL/NL	100	378	74	119	26	9	2	46	15	.315
1903	CINCINNATI	NL	105	383	85	121	22	4	3	45	18	.316
1904	CINCINNATI	NL	123	449	75	126	21	13	0	63	15	.281
1905	CINCINNATI	NL	90	321	43	89	7	6	1	37	8	.277
1906	CINCINNATI	NL	129	465	43	106	19	11	1	53	9	.228
1908	BOSTON	NL	73	228	25	59	8	2	2	17	5	.259
CAREER TOTALS			**1853**	**7006**	**1421**	**2220**	**358**	**194**	**65**	**1194**	**443**	**.317**

GEORGE KELLY

"They called him 'Highpockets,' but George Kelly was more than just a colorful appellation." —The Asssociated Press, 1973

A gangly 6-foot-4 infielder, George "Highpockets" Kelly reached the major leagues at 19 with the New York Giants in 1915. He established himself as a regular by 1920, when he tied Rogers Hornsby for the National League lead with 94 RBIs.

Kelly spent his prime years with New York, where he became one of baseball's best power hitters of the early 1920s, when the Giants won four consecutive pennants. Kelly led the NL with 23 home runs in 1921, when he won his first World Series, over the Yankees. Kelly won back-to-back rings when the Giants beat the Yankees in four games in the 1922 World Series.

Kelly returned to the World Series against the Yankees again in 1923 and then against the Washington in 1924, but the Giants fell in six games to the Yankees and in seven to the Senators.

Kelly's 1924 season was arguably his most productive, as he drove in 136 runs to capture his second RBI crown and finish sixth in MVP voting.

Kelly spent the majority of his career at first base, but Giants manager John McGraw installed him as the club's primary second baseman for the 1925 season. Well-regarded for his defense at first base, Kelly handled the transition capably. At the plate, he led the Giants in hits and finished third in MVP voting, but the Giants finished second to the Pirates in the NL.

He moved back to first base in 1926 and hit over .300 for the sixth straight year, but the Giants finished under .500 for the first time since Kelly made his debut in 1915.

Traded to the Reds after the 1926 season for Edd Roush, Kelly spent three and a half seasons with Cincinnati. In 1929 he led the Reds in doubles (45) and RBIs (103), his fifth and final season in which he drove in at least 100 runs.

"To Frankie Frisch, he was one of the finest first baseman who ever lived," the AP wrote upon his induction to the Hall of Fame by the Veteran's Committee in 1973. "To Waite Hoyt, he was a dangerous man in the clutch. And to the people who vote for such things, he is a perfect choice for the Baseball Hall of Fame."

Highpockets

Elected To The Hall Of Fame: 1973.
Born: Sept. 10, 1895 in San Francisco, Calif.
Died: Oct. 13, 1984 in Burlingame, Calif.
Height: 6-4. **Weight:** 190.
Threw: Right. **Batted:** Right.
Debut: Aug 18, 1915.
Final Game: July 27, 1932.
Teams: New York N.L. 1915-1917, 1919-1926; Pittsburgh N.L. 1917; Cincinnati N.L. 1927-1930; Chicago N.L. 1930; Brooklyn N.L. 1932.
Postseason: 2-Time World Series Champion (1921-1922); 4 N.L. Pennants (1921-1924).

YEAR	TEAM	LEAGUE	G	AB	R	H	2B	3B	HR	RBI	SB	AVG
1915	NEW YORK	NL	17	38	2	6	0	0	1	4	0	.158
1916	NEW YORK	NL	49	76	4	12	2	1	0	3	1	.158
1917	NEW YORK/PITTSBURGH	NL	19	30	2	2	0	1	0	0	0	.067
1919	NEW YORK	NL	32	107	12	31	6	2	1	14	1	.290
1920	NEW YORK	NL	155	590	69	157	22	11	11	94	6	.266
1921	NEW YORK	NL	149	587	95	181	42	9	23	122	4	.308
1922	NEW YORK	NL	151	592	96	194	33	8	17	107	12	.328
1923	NEW YORK	NL	145	560	82	172	23	5	16	103	14	.307
1924	NEW YORK	NL	144	571	91	185	37	9	21	136	7	.324
1925	NEW YORK	NL	147	586	87	181	29	3	20	99	5	.309
1926	NEW YORK	NL	136	499	70	151	24	4	13	80	4	.303
1927	CINCINNATI	NL	61	222	27	60	16	4	5	21	1	.270
1928	CINCINNATI	NL	116	402	46	119	33	7	3	58	2	.296
1929	CINCINNATI	NL	147	577	73	169	45	9	5	103	7	.293
1930	CINCINNATI/CHICAGO	NL	90	354	40	109	16	2	8	54	1	.308
1932	BROOKLYN	NL	64	202	23	49	9	1	4	22	0	.243
CAREER TOTALS			**1622**	**5993**	**819**	**1778**	**337**	**76**	**148**	**1020**	**65**	**.297**

MIKE KELLY

Mike "King" Kelly was not only one of the top players of his day, but he was also one of the most popular. He played in the late 1870s and into the 1890s, and during that time he was the biggest drawing card in the sport. Kelly helped the Chicago White Stockings to five pennants and was a fan favorite in Chicago before he was sold to the Boston Beaneaters before the 1887 season.

The attendance for the White Stockings' 1887 opener was abysmal, but when the Beaneaters came to Chicago the fans poured through the gates to see their favorite player, even though he was sporting a rival uniform. When Kelly played with the White Stockings, he began to study the rules of baseball, and to figure out ways to get around them. Cap Anson gave Kelly credit for originating the hit-and-run play, and together the two came up with strategies that are now considered commonplace. Some things they worked on were playing off first and third base, adjusting the outfield positions according to the player batting, the double steal and the infield shift.

Kelly's reputation for bending the rules extended beyond the field and into his extracurricular activities. There was even a clause added to his contract that rewarded him for good behavior.

The outfielder started his career in 1878 with the Cincinnati Reds and was soon given the title of the King of Baseball. He led the league in batting for the first time in 1884, hitting .354 for the season. Kelly won the batting crown once again in 1886, a year that could be considered his best. Over the season, he hit .388, with 155 runs scored and a .483 on-base percentage.

Kelly stole at least 50 bases for five consecutive years and swiped a career-high 84 bags for the Beaneaters in 1887. In one game he stole six bases, and on multiple occasions he stole five in a game. Kelly was one of the first players to regularly steal third base and home, something he also often did in succession.

Kelly won nine pennants in his 16 seasons in the game and he also hit better than .300 eight times. He led the league three times in both doubles and runs. Though he primarily played right field with frequent appearances in left, in his career Kelly played every position on the diamond, even trying his hand on the mound.

MIKE J. (KING) KELLY
COLORFUL PLAYER AND AUDACIOUS
BASE-RUNNER. IN 1887 FOR BOSTON
HE HIT .394 AND STOLE 84 BASES.
HIS SALE FOR $10,000 WAS ONE OF
THE BIGGEST DEALS OF BASEBALL'S
EARLY HISTORY.

King

Elected To The Hall Of Fame: *1945.*
Born: *Dec. 31, 1857 in Troy, N.Y.*
Died: *Nov. 8, 1894 in Boston, Mass.*
Height: *5-10.* **Weight:** *170.*
Threw: *Right.* **Batted:** *Right.*
Debut: *May 1, 1878.*
Final Game: *Sept. 2, 1893.*
Teams: *Cincinnati N.L. 1878-1879; Chicago N.L. 1880-1886; Boston N.L. 1887-1889, 1891-1892; Boston, Players League 1890; Cincinnati, American Association 1891; Boston, American Association 1891; New York N.L. 1893.*
Postseason: *2 N.L. Pennants (1885-1886); Championship Series Champion (1892).*

YEAR	TEAM	LEAGUE	G	AB	R	H	2B	3B	HR	RBI	SB	AVG
1878	CINCINNATI	NL	60	237	29	67	7	1	0	27	0	.283
1879	CINCINNATI	NL	77	345	78	120	20	12	2	47	0	.348
1880	CHICAGO	NL	84	344	72	100	17	9	1	60	0	.291
1881	CHICAGO	NL	82	353	84	114	27	3	2	55	0	.323
1882	CHICAGO	NL	84	377	81	115	37	4	1	55	0	.305
1883	CHICAGO	NL	98	428	92	109	28	10	3	61	0	.255
1884	CHICAGO	NL	108	452	120	160	28	5	13	95	0	.354
1885	CHICAGO	NL	107	438	124	126	24	7	9	75	0	.288
1886	CHICAGO	NL	118	451	155	175	32	11	4	79	53	.388
1887	BOSTON	NL	116	484	120	156	34	11	8	63	84	.322
1888	BOSTON	NL	107	440	85	140	22	11	9	71	56	.318
1889	BOSTON	NL	125	507	120	149	41	5	9	78	68	.294
1890	BOSTON	PL	89	340	83	111	18	6	4	66	51	.326
1891	CINCINNATI/BOSTON	AA/NL	102	350	65	100	16	7	2	62	29	.286
1892	BOSTON	NL	78	281	40	53	7	0	2	41	24	.189
1893	NEW YORK	NL	20	67	9	18	1	0	0	15	3	.269
CAREER TOTALS			**1455**	**5894**	**1357**	**1813**	**359**	**102**	**69**	**950**	**368**	**.308**

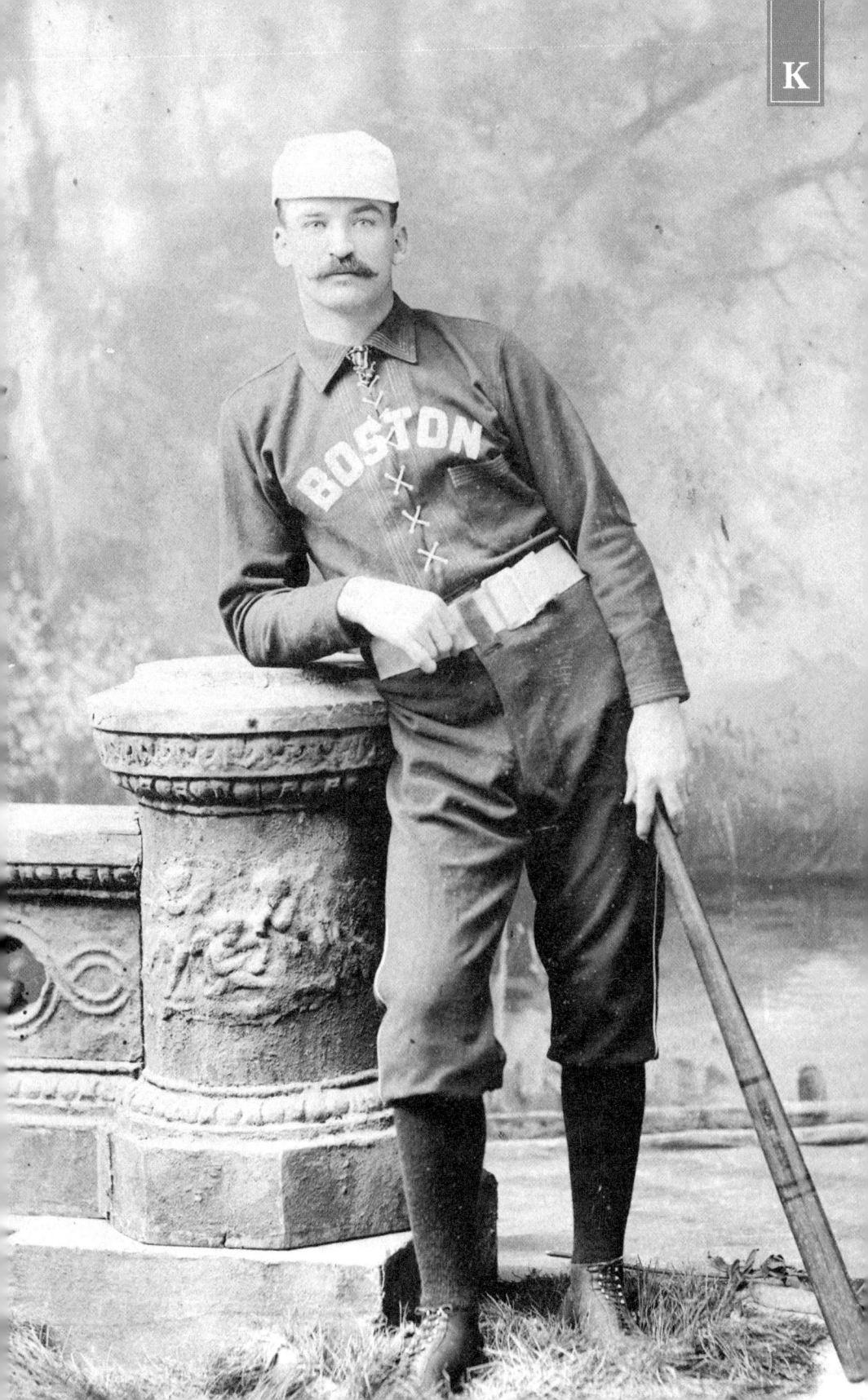

HARMON KILLEBREW

Harmon Killebrew was one of the most feared sluggers of the 1960s and when he retired in 1975, he had accumulated more home runs than any right-handed batter in American League history. Said former Washington Senators player, manager and coach Ossie Bluege "He hit line drives that put the opposition in jeopardy. And I don't mean infielders, I mean outfielders."

It was on the high school ball fields of the small town of Payette, Idaho, where Killebrew was discovered by the Senators in 1954.

The 17-year-old slugger signed on with the club for a relatively large bonus, and the rules of the day dictated that they had to keep the youngster on the Major League roster for two years, or risk losing him to another team, so Killebrew went straight to Washington.

In 1959, at age 23, Killebrew had a breakout year, hitting 42 home runs with 105 RBIs. Orioles manager Paul Richards marveled at his immense power and prestigious blasts: "Killebrew can knock the ball out of any park, including Yellowstone."

His name and tape-measure home runs easily lent themselves to the nickname "Killer," and longtime Senators and Twins owner Calvin Griffith remarked, "He hit home runs like few people can in the category of height and distance . . . He would hit the ball so blooming high in the sky, they were like a rocket ship going up in the air."

Over the course of his 22- year big league career, Killebrew put together eight 40-home run seasons and 46 multiple home run games.

Killebrew was a gentle and quiet man off the field. When asked what he liked to do for fun, he once replied, "Well, I like to wash dishes, I guess." Former Twins public-relations director Tom Mee once said, "He is one of the finest individuals in the major leagues . . . To know Harmon Killebrew is to be a Killebrew fan."

HARMON CLAYTON KILLEBREW
WASHINGTON A.L. 1954-1960
MINNESOTA A.L. 1961-1974
KANSAS CITY A.L. 1975
MUSCULAR SLUGGER WITH MONUMENTAL HOME RUN AND RBI SUCCESS. HIS 573 HOMERS OVER 22 YEARS RANK FIFTH ALL-TIME AND SECOND ONLY TO RUTH AMONG A.L. HITTERS. TIED OR LED A.L. IN HOME RUNS 6 TIMES. BELTED OVER 40 ON 8 OCCASIONS AND IS THIRD IN HOME RUN FREQUENCY. DROVE IN OVER 100 RUNS 9 TIMES. A.L. MVP IN 1969.

Killer

Elected To The Hall Of Fame: 1984.
Born: June 29, 1936 in Payette, Idaho.
Died: May 17, 2011 in Scottsdale, Ariz.
Height: 6-0. **Weight:** 190.
Threw: Right. **Batted:** Right.
Debut: June 23, 1954.
Final Game: Sept. 26, 1975.
Teams: Washington A.L. 1954-1960; Minnesota A.L. 1961-1974; Kansas City A.L. 1975.
Postseason: A.L. Pennant (1965); 3-Time Postseason Qualifier.
Awards: 13-Time All-Star (1959, 1961, 1963-1971); A.L. MVP (1969).

YEAR	TEAM	LEAGUE	G	AB	R	H	2B	3B	HR	RBI	SB	AVG
1954	WASHINGTON	AL	9	13	1	4	1	0	0	3	0	.308
1955	WASHINGTON	AL	38	80	12	16	1	0	4	7	0	.200
1956	WASHINGTON	AL	44	99	10	22	2	0	5	13	0	.222
1957	WASHINGTON	AL	9	31	4	9	2	0	2	5	0	.290
1958	WASHINGTON	AL	13	31	2	6	0	0	0	2	0	.194
1959	WASHINGTON	AL	153	546	98	132	20	2	42	105	3	.242
1960	WASHINGTON	AL	124	442	84	122	19	1	31	80	1	.276
1961	MINNESOTA	AL	150	541	94	156	20	7	46	122	1	.288
1962	MINNESOTA	AL	155	552	85	134	21	1	48	126	1	.243
1963	MINNESOTA	AL	142	515	88	133	18	0	45	96	0	.258
1964	MINNESOTA	AL	158	577	95	156	11	1	49	111	0	.270
1965	MINNESOTA	AL	113	401	78	108	16	1	25	75	0	.269
1966	MINNESOTA	AL	162	569	89	160	27	1	39	110	0	.281
1967	MINNESOTA	AL	163	547	105	147	24	1	44	113	1	.269
1968	MINNESOTA	AL	100	295	40	62	7	2	17	40	0	.210
1969	MINNESOTA	AL	162	555	106	153	20	2	49	140	8	.276
1970	MINNESOTA	AL	157	527	96	143	20	1	41	113	0	.271
1971	MINNESOTA	AL	147	500	61	127	19	1	28	119	3	.254
1972	MINNESOTA	AL	139	433	53	100	13	2	26	74	0	.231
1973	MINNESOTA	AL	69	248	29	60	9	1	5	32	0	.242
1974	MINNESOTA	AL	122	333	28	74	7	0	13	54	0	.222
1975	KANSAS CITY	AL	106	312	25	62	13	0	14	44	1	.199
CAREER TOTALS			2435	8147	1283	2086	290	24	573	1584	19	.256

RALPH KINER

Before Ralph Kiner had played a major league game, Pirates manager Frankie Frisch proclaimed "Kiner looks like he's going to be the best [outfielder] we've ever had." Kiner made his major league debut in 1946, at age 23, having lost three prime years to service of his country in World War II, and wasted no time in making his presence felt as he led the National League in home runs and tied a club record in the process.

For a decade Ralph Kiner was one of the game's premier power hitters. He was the first National Leaguer to hit 50 home runs twice — it had only happened twice in the American League. He became the first major leaguer to hit home runs in four straight at-bats on two separate occasions, and was the first major league player to lead the league in home runs in seven consecutive seasons. Baseball's all-time winningest lefty, Warren Spahn, proclaimed, "Kiner can wipe out your lead with one swing."

Kiner's star shone off the baseball diamond as well. He was well known in Hollywood circles, played golf with James Garner and Jack Lemmon and developed friendships with the likes of Lucille Ball and Desi Arnaz. On the field or off the field, Ralph Kiner was a star.

Back problems forced Kiner off the field for good at age 32. Had he remained healthy, there is no telling what he could have accomplished. Although he was not able to physically compete on the diamond, he didn't leave the game he loved. Ralph Kiner was a baseball lifer.

Upon retirement, Kiner became the general manager of the San Diego Padres, then a Pacific Coast League franchise. It was there that he also developed his skills in the broadcast booth. In 1962, when the expansion New York Mets hired Kiner to do their broadcasts, he jokingly recalled, "The Mets hired me because they looked at my background with the Pirates and saw that I had losing experience." Kiner spent more than 40 years in the booth for the Mets and became known to a whole new generation of baseball fans for his "Kinerisms" such as "Two-thirds of the earth is covered by water. The other third is covered by Garry Maddox."

Elected To The Hall Of Fame: *1975.*
Born: *Oct. 27, 1922 in Santa Rita, N.M.*
Died: *Feb. 6, 2014 in Rancho Mirage, Calif.*
Height: *6-2.* **Weight:** *195.*
Threw: *Right.* **Batted:** *Right.*
Debut: *April 16, 1946.*
Final Game: *Sept. 25, 1955.*
Teams: *Pittsburgh N.L. 1946-1953; Chicago N.L. 1953-1954; Cleveland A.L. 1955.*
Awards: *6-Time All-Star (1948-1953).*

YEAR	TEAM	LEAGUE	G	AB	R	H	2B	3B	HR	RBI	SB	AVG
1946	PITTSBURGH	NL	144	502	63	124	17	3	23	81	3	.247
1947	PITTSBURGH	NL	152	565	118	177	23	4	51	127	1	.313
1948	PITTSBURGH	NL	156	555	104	147	19	5	40	123	1	.265
1949	PITTSBURGH	NL	152	549	116	170	19	5	54	127	6	.310
1950	PITTSBURGH	NL	150	547	112	149	21	6	47	118	2	.272
1951	PITTSBURGH	NL	151	531	124	164	31	6	42	109	2	.309
1952	PITTSBURGH	NL	149	516	90	126	17	2	37	87	3	.244
1953	PITTSBURGH/CHICAGO	NL	158	562	100	157	20	3	35	116	2	.279
1954	CHICAGO	NL	147	557	88	159	36	5	22	73	2	.285
1955	CLEVELAND	AL	113	321	56	78	13	0	18	54	0	.243
CAREER TOTALS			**1472**	**5205**	**971**	**1451**	**216**	**39**	**369**	**1015**	**22**	**.279**

CHUCK KLEIN

Charles Herbert Klein was a powerful hitter who captured the Triple Crown in 1933, also nabbing three other home run titles.

"One of the reasons I've been able to play baseball well is because it's fun for me," Chuck Klein said. "Many players find it work."

For 17 years, Klein excelled at the game he found so much fun. He spent 15 years as the Philadelphia Phillies right fielder where he was an offensive force. He was named National League MVP in 1932 and followed that performance by winning the Triple Crown in 1933. He was also an All-Star in 1933 and 1934.

Throughout his career in Philadelphia, Klein took advantage of the short right field fence in the Baker Bowl. On defense, he would often turn would-be singles into outs at first base by playing very shallow. In 1930, Klein had 44 outfield assists, a record he still holds. The Baker Bowl also likely served to inflate his offensive numbers. But with the Phillies, Klein was one of the most dominant NL hitters of the era. In 1929, his first full season, Klein led the league with 43 home runs. Only Babe Ruth, with 46, hit more home runs in all of baseball.

Though Klein would go on to lead the National League in home runs three more times and finish his career with 300 home runs, he wasn't just a power hitter. Klein was a career .320 hitter and hit .386 in 1930. Had an MVP been awarded in 1930, Klein likely would have been a favorite as he hit 40 home runs, had 170 RBI and led all of baseball with 158 runs scored.

Klein was traded to the Cubs before the 1934 season and was an All-Star that summer. The next year, he would help the Cubs to the World Series, where they lost to the Tigers. In Klein's only trip to the Fall Classic, he hit .333 with a home run.

Klein returned to Philadelphia in 1936 and on July 10 became the first National Leaguer to hit four home runs in a game in the modern era. He remained in Philadelphia for the rest of his career, save for a brief interlude with the Pirates in 1939.

Elected To The Hall Of Fame: 1980.

Born: Oct. 7, 1904 in Indianapolis, Ind.

Died: March 28, 1958 in Indianapolis, Ind.

Height: 6-0. **Weight:** 185.

Threw: Right. **Batted:** Left.

Debut: July 30, 1928.

Final Game: June 11, 1944.

Teams: Philadelphia N.L. 1928-1933, 1936-1944; Chicago N.L. 1934-1936; Pittsburgh N.L. 1939.

Postseason: N.L. Pennant (1935).

Awards: 2-Time All-Star (1933-1934); N.L. Most Valuable Player (1932).

YEAR	TEAM	LEAGUE	G	AB	R	H	2B	3B	HR	RBI	SB	AVG
1928	PHILADELPHIA	NL	64	253	41	91	14	4	11	34	0	.360
1929	PHILADELPHIA	NL	149	616	126	219	45	6	43	145	5	.356
1930	PHILADELPHIA	NL	156	648	158	250	59	8	40	170	4	.386
1931	PHILADELPHIA	NL	148	594	121	200	34	10	31	121	7	.337
1932	PHILADELPHIA	NL	154	650	152	226	50	15	38	137	20	.348
1933	PHILADELPHIA	NL	152	606	101	223	44	7	28	120	15	.368
1934	CHICAGO	NL	115	435	78	131	27	2	20	80	3	.301
1935	CHICAGO	NL	119	434	71	127	14	4	21	73	4	.293
1936	CHICAGO/PHILADELPHIA	NL	146	601	102	184	35	7	25	104	6	.306
1937	PHILADELPHIA	NL	115	406	74	132	20	2	15	57	3	.325
1938	PHILADELPHIA	NL	129	458	53	113	22	2	8	61	7	.247
1939	PHILADELPHIA/PITTSBURGH	NL	110	317	45	90	18	5	12	56	2	.284
1940	PHILADELPHIA	NL	116	354	39	77	16	2	7	37	2	.218
1941	PHILADELPHIA	NL	50	73	6	9	0	0	1	3	0	.123
1942	PHILADELPHIA	NL	14	14	0	1	0	0	0	0	0	.071
1943	PHILADELPHIA	NL	12	20	0	2	0	0	0	3	1	.100
1944	PHILADELPHIA	NL	4	7	1	1	0	0	0	0	0	.143
CAREER TOTALS			1753	6486	1168	2076	398	74	300	1201	79	.320

SANDY KOUFAX

When Sandy Koufax was awarded a basketball scholarship to the University of Cincinnati in 1953, his plans included a career in architecture. Instead, Koufax made a living on a baseball diamond, becoming one of the most dominating left-handers of all time. "Either he throws the fastest ball I've ever seen, or I'm going blind," said Hall of Famer Richie Ashburn.

Born on Dec. 30, 1935 in Brooklyn, N.Y., Koufax impressed a scout who saw him throw for his college baseball team. In 1954, he signed a contract with the Brooklyn Dodgers that required at the time for Koufax to report to the major league team for two years.

"When he (Koufax) first came up he couldn't throw a ball inside the batting cage," said Hall of Fame teammate Duke Snider.

With a limited baseball background, Koufax struggled with control at first, but used his raw talent to begin regularly throwing for the Dodgers in 1958, when the team moved to Los Angeles.

"A foul ball was a moral victory," said Hall of Famer Don Sutton.

In 1959, Koufax struck out 18 Cubs in nine innings and set a major league record for strikeouts in consecutive games with 31. In 1963, Koufax led the league in wins with 25, in ERA with 1.88, in shutouts with 11 and strikeouts with 306. He won both the Cy Young Award and Most Valuable Player Award that season.

"I can see how he won 25 games. What I don't understand is how he lost five," said Hall of Famer Yogi Berra in 1963.

The seven-time All-Star went on to win two more Cy Young Awards in 1965 and 1966, finishing second in MVP voting and leading the league in wins both seasons. He won five straight NL ERA titles from 1962-66 and led the Dodgers to the NL pennant in 1963, 1965 and 1966, winning the World Series in 1963 and 1965.

"He was the greatest pitcher of his time in baseball," said writer Jimmy Cannon.

Traumatic arthritis in his elbow ended Koufax's career early due to a threat of permanent disability. Despite playing only 12 seasons, Koufax became the youngest player ever inducted into the Baseball Hall of Fame, in 1972, at the age of 36.

Elected To The Hall Of Fame: *1972.*
Born: *Dec. 30, 1935 in Brooklyn, N.Y.*
Height: *6-2.* **Weight:** *210.*
Threw: *Left.* **Batted:** *Right.*
Debut: *June 24, 1955.*
Final Game: *Oct. 2, 1966.*
Teams: *Brooklyn N.L. 1955-1957; Los Angeles N.L. 1958-1966.*
Postseason: *4-Time World Series Champion (1955, 1959, 1963, 1965); 6 N.L. Pennants (1955-56, 1959, 1963, 1965-66).*
Awards: *7-Time All-Star (1961-1966); 2-Time World Series Most Valuable Player (1963, 1965); N.L. Most Valuable Player (1963); 3-Time Cy Young (1963, 1965-1966).*

YEAR	TEAM	LEAGUE	G	W	L	SV	SH	IP	H	BB	SO	ERA
1955	BROOKLYN	NL	12	2	2	0	2	41.7	33	28	30	3.02
1956	BROOKLYN	NL	16	2	4	0	0	58.7	66	29	30	4.91
1957	BROOKLYN	NL	34	5	4	0	0	104.3	83	51	122	3.88
1958	LOS ANGELES	NL	40	11	11	1	0	158.7	132	105	131	4.48
1959	LOS ANGELES	NL	35	8	6	2	1	153.3	136	92	173	4.05
1960	LOS ANGELES	NL	37	8	13	1	2	175	133	100	197	3.91
1961	LOS ANGELES	NL	42	18	13	1	2	255.7	212	96	269	3.52
1962	LOS ANGELES	NL	28	14	7	1	2	184.3	134	57	216	2.54
1963	LOS ANGELES	NL	40	25	5	0	11	311	214	58	306	1.88
1964	LOS ANGELES	NL	29	19	5	1	7	223	154	53	223	1.74
1965	LOS ANGELES	NL	43	26	8	2	8	335.7	216	71	382	2.04
1966	LOS ANGELES	NL	41	27	9	0	5	323	241	77	317	1.73
CAREER TOTALS			**397**	**165**	**87**	**9**	**40**	**2324.1**	**1754**	**817**	**2396**	**2.76**

NAPOLEON LAJOIE

NAPOLEON (LARRY) LAJOIE
PHILADELPHIA (N) 1896-1900
PHILADELPHIA (A) 1901
CLEVELAND (A) 1902-14
PHILADELPHIA (A) 1915-16
GREAT HITTER AND MOST GRACEFUL
AND EFFECTIVE SECOND-BASEMAN
OF HIS ERA. MANAGED CLEVELAND 4
YEARS. LEAGUE BATTING CHAMPION
1901-03-04.

"Lajoie was one of the most rugged hitters I ever faced. He'd take your leg off with a line drive, turn the third baseman around like a swinging door, and powder the hand of the left fielder," said Cy Young.

Napoleon Lajoie, hitter extraordinaire, sublime fielder, and manager, has been described as "the first superstar in American League history." And indeed, to concentrate on his hitting or his fielding is to miss his all-around talent as a player.

Lajoie broke in with the Phillies in 1896, hitting .326 in 39 games, and hit over .300 for his first 11 seasons. His best season was 1901, when he signed with the Athletics in apparent violation of the reserve clause. He played one season for the A's before league president Ban Johnson transferred him to Cleveland. But what a season 1901 was! Lajoie won the Triple Crown with a .426 batting average, 14 homers and 125 runs batted in.

In Cleveland, Lajoie became the face of the franchise, when the fledgling club, which had been known as the Bronchos, renamed itself after him – the Naps. Lajoie hit over .300 in 10 of the next 13 seasons, also leading the league in hits, doubles, and batting average three times. Lajoie was a player/manager for the Naps from 1905-09, but resigned to concentrate on playing. He returned to the Athletics at the end of his career for two seasons.

For his career, Lajoie batted .338, topping the .300 mark 16 times and leading the league five times. He cranked out 3,242 hits, 657 doubles, scored 1,504 runs, and drove in 1,599.

As a fielder, Lajoie was special to watch. "Lajoie glides toward the ball and gathers it in nonchalantly, as if picking fruit," commented a New York sportswriter. Connie Mack elaborated: "He plays so naturally and so easily it looks like lack of effort. Larry's reach is so long and and he's fast as lightning."

Following his major league playing career, Lajoie served as a player/manager for Toronto and Indianapolis, and was commissioner of the Ohio-Pennsylvania League.

Nap, Larry

Elected To The Hall Of Fame: 1937.
Born: Sept. 5, 1874 in Woonsocket, R.I.
Died: Feb. 7, 1959 in Daytona Beach, Fla.
Height: 6-1. **Weight:** 195.
Threw: Right. **Batted:** Right.
Debut: Aug. 12, 1896.
Final Game: Aug. 26, 1916.
Teams: Philadelphia N.L. 1896-1900;
Philadelphia A.L. 1901-1902, 1915-1916;
Cleveland A.L. 1902-1914.

YEAR	TEAM	LEAGUE	G	AB	R	H	2B	3B	HR	RBI	SB	AVG
1896	PHILADELPHIA	NL	39	175	36	57	12	7	4	42	7	.326
1897	PHILADELPHIA	NL	127	545	107	197	40	23	9	127	20	.361
1898	PHILADELPHIA	NL	147	608	113	197	43	11	6	127	25	.324
1899	PHILADELPHIA	NL	77	312	70	118	19	9	6	70	13	.378
1900	PHILADELPHIA	NL	102	451	95	152	33	12	7	92	22	.337
1901	PHILADELPHIA	AL	131	544	145	232	48	14	14	125	27	.426
1902	PHILADELPHIA/CLEVELAND	AL	87	352	81	133	35	5	7	65	20	.378
1903	CLEVELAND	AL	125	485	90	167	41	11	7	93	21	.344
1904	CLEVELAND	AL	140	553	92	208	49	15	5	102	29	.376
1905	CLEVELAND	AL	65	249	29	82	12	2	2	41	11	.329
1906	CLEVELAND	AL	152	602	88	214	48	9	0	91	20	.355
1907	CLEVELAND	AL	137	509	53	152	30	6	2	63	24	.299
1908	CLEVELAND	AL	157	581	77	168	32	6	2	74	15	.289
1909	CLEVELAND	AL	128	469	56	152	33	7	1	47	13	.324
1910	CLEVELAND	AL	159	591	94	227	51	7	4	76	26	.384
1911	CLEVELAND	AL	90	315	36	115	20	1	2	60	13	.365
1912	CLEVELAND	AL	117	448	66	165	34	4	0	90	18	.368
1913	CLEVELAND	AL	137	465	66	156	25	2	1	68	17	.335
1914	CLEVELAND	AL	121	419	37	108	14	3	0	50	14	.258
1915	PHILADELPHIA	AL	129	490	40	137	24	5	1	61	10	.280
1916	PHILADELPHIA	AL	113	426	33	105	14	4	2	35	15	.246
CAREER TOTALS			**2480**	**9589**	**1504**	**3242**	**657**	**163**	**82**	**1599**	**380**	**.338**

BARRY LARKIN

BARRY LOUIS LARKIN
CINCINNATI, N.L., 1986-2004

SMOOTH-FIELDING, STEADY-SWINGING SHORTSTOP WHOSE
DYNAMIC DEFENSE AND ALL-AROUND PLAY SPARKED HIS
HOMETOWN REDS. A 12-TIME ALL-STAR, HE TOTALED 2,340
HITS AND 379 STOLEN BASES IN 19 SEASONS. NINE TIMES
BATTING OVER .300, EN ROUTE TO A .295 LIFETIME AVERAGE.
IN 1996, BECAME FIRST SHORTSTOP TO POST 30 HOME RUNS
AND 30 STEALS IN A SINGLE SEASON. CAPTURED NINE SILVER
SLUGGER AWARDS AND THREE GOLD GLOVE AWARDS.
PASSIONATE TEAM CAPTAIN AND COMMANDING CLUBHOUSE
LEADER, HE BATTED .353 IN THE 1990 WORLD SERIES,
GUIDING REDS TO FOUR-GAME SWEEP OF OAKLAND A'S.

His career dawned in the shadow of Ozzie Smith's, peaked at the height of Cal Ripken mania and ended as Derek Jeter and Alex Rodriguez redefined the shortstop position. But check the numbers: 12 All-Star Game selections in 19 seasons for Barry Larkin. It doesn't get much better than that for any shortstop.

Now, Larkin takes his place among baseball's royalty in the Hall of Fame.

Larkin was born in Cincinnati, became an honor student at Cincinnati's Moeller High School and was taken in the second round of the 1982 draft by his hometown Reds. But Larkin decided to attend the University of Michigan, and later earned a spot on the 1984 U.S. Olympic Baseball Team. The Reds took Larkin again with the fourth overall pick in the 1985 draft, and he ended up playing all of his 19 major league seasons for Cincinnati.

Larkin debuted in the majors in 1986 and won the Reds' starting shortstop job the next season, and by 1988 he was a first-time All-Star. In 1990, Larkin hit .301 with 30 steals and 67 RBIs as the Reds went wire-to-wire in winning the NL West, then dispatched the Pirates and the A's in the postseason to win the World Series. In the four-game sweep over Oakland, Larkin hit .353 and scored three runs.

Larkin added power in 1991 when he hit 20 homers, and his all-around play continued to improve. He won the first of three consecutive Gold Glove Awards in 1994, and was named the NL MVP in 1995 after hitting .319 en route to the Reds' NL Central title. In 1996 he became the first shortstop to post a 30-homer/30-steal season.

Larkin was also a role model off the field, winning the Roberto Clemente Award in 1993 for his commitment to community and understanding the value of helping others.

Larkin retired after the 2004 season – after winning his 12th All-Star selection – with a .295 career average, 2,340 hits, 1,329 runs scored and 379 stolen bases. He scored at least 80 runs in a season seven times, hit 30-plus doubles in six seasons and stole 30 or more bases five times. He won his Gold Glove Awards at shortstop en route to a career fielding percentage of .975, and won nine Silver Slugger Awards.

Elected To The Hall Of Fame: 2012.
Born: April 28, 1964 in Cincinnati, Ohio.
Height: 6-0. **Weight:** 185.
Threw: Right. **Batted:** Right.
Debut: Aug. 13, 1986.
Final Game: Oct. 3, 2004.
Teams: Cincinnati N.L. 1986-2004.
Postseason: World Series Champion (1990).
Awards: 12 Time All-Star (1988-91, 1993-97, 1999-2000, 2004), 3 Gold Glove Awards (1994-96); 9 Silver Slugger Awards (1988-92, 1995-96, 1998-99); National League Most Valuable Player Award (1995).

YEAR	TEAM	LEAGUE	G	AB	R	H	2B	3B	HR	RBI	SB	BA
1986	CINCINNATI	NL	41	159	27	45	4	3	3	19	8	.283
1987	CINCINNATI	NL	125	439	64	107	16	2	12	43	21	.244
1988	CINCINNATI	NL	151	588	91	174	32	5	12	56	40	.296
1989	CINCINNATI	NL	97	325	47	111	14	4	4	36	10	.342
1990	CINCINNATI	NL	158	614	85	185	25	6	7	67	30	.301
1991	CINCINNATI	NL	123	464	88	140	27	4	20	69	24	.302
1992	CINCINNATI	NL	140	533	76	162	32	6	12	78	15	.304
1993	CINCINNATI	NL	100	384	57	121	20	3	8	51	14	.315
1994	CINCINNATI	NL	110	427	78	119	23	5	9	52	26	.279
1995	CINCINNATI	NL	131	496	98	158	29	6	15	66	51	.319
1996	CINCINNATI	NL	152	517	117	154	32	4	33	89	36	.298
1997	CINCINNATI	NL	73	224	34	71	17	3	4	20	14	.317
1998	CINCINNATI	NL	145	538	93	166	34	10	17	72	26	.309
1999	CINCINNATI	NL	161	583	108	171	30	4	12	75	30	.293
2000	CINCINNATI	NL	102	396	71	124	26	5	11	41	14	.313
2001	CINCINNATI	NL	45	156	29	40	12	0	2	17	3	.256
2002	CINCINNATI	NL	145	507	72	124	37	2	7	47	13	.245
2003	CINCINNATI	NL	70	241	39	68	16	1	2	18	2	.282
2004	CINCINNATI	NL	111	346	55	100	15	3	8	44	2	.289
CAREER TOTALS			**2180**	**7937**	**1329**	**2340**	**441**	**76**	**198**	**960**	**379**	**.295**

TONY LAZZERI

"Tony not only was a great ballplayer, he was a great man," said Yankees shortstop Frankie Crosetti. "He was a leader. He was like a manager on the field."

Arguably the top second baseman in New York Yankees history, Tony Lazzeri played for the franchise's six American League pennant winners from 1926 through '37, batting .293 with 169 home runs during his 12 seasons in pinstripes. Lazzeri, though, temporarily quit baseball in 1923, when as a 19-year-old he grew disillusioned with being shuttled back and forth between minor league posts.

Lazzeri secured regular play with Salt Lake City of the Pacific Coast League in 1924, and with the same club in '25 the San Francisco native enjoyed a season for the ages, batting a robust .355 while setting PCL records that still stand with 60 home runs, 222 RBI and 202 runs scored. Lazzeri played in 197 games that year.

The Yankees parted with $50,000 (though some accounts go as high as $75,000) and three players to acquire Lazzeri in August 1925, and the 22-year-old rewarded them instantly with a fine rookie season in '26. He belted 18 home runs, a total he would match three other times but never surpass, and finished 10th in MVP balloting. New York lost a taut 1926 World Series to the St. Louis Cardinals in seven games, with Lazzeri batting 5-for-26 (.192) and coming up empty with the bases loaded and two outs in the seventh inning of Game 7. Lazzeri struck out swinging on a 1-2 pitch from future Hall of Fame right-hander Grover Cleveland Alexander, 39 at the time. Alexander's heroics helped the Cardinals clinch the Series with a 3-2 victory, though he just as easily could have found himself on the losing end. One pitch earlier Lazzeri had launched a ball out of Yankee Stadium—but just foul.

Lazzeri secured some measure of redemption by playing well in his next five World Series appearances, batting .291, slugging .494 and belting four home runs in 79 at-bats. The Yankees won all five Series in convincing fashion, dispatching the Pittsburgh Pirates (1927), Cardinals ('28), Chicago Cubs ('32) and New York Giants ('36 and '37.) Lazzeri closed out his career with the Cubs in 1938 and the Brooklyn Dodgers and Giants in '39.

Elected To The Hall Of Fame: *1991.*

Born: *Dec. 6, 1903 in San Francisco, Calif.*

Died: *Aug. 6, 1946 in San Francisco, Calif.*

Height: *5-11.* **Weight:** *170.*

Threw: *Right.* **Batted:** *Right.*

Debut: *April 13, 1926.*

Final Game: *June 7, 1939.*

Teams: *New York A.L. 1926-1937; Chicago N.L. 1938; Brooklyn N.L. 1939; New York N.L. 1939.*

Postseason: *A.L. Pennant (1926). N.L. Pennant (1938). 5-Time World Series Champion (1927-1928, 1932, 1936-1937).*

Awards: *All-Star (1933).*

YEAR	TEAM	LEAGUE	G	AB	R	H	2B	3B	HR	RBI	SB	AVG
1926	NEW YORK	AL	155	589	79	162	28	14	18	114	16	.275
1927	NEW YORK	AL	153	570	92	176	29	8	18	102	22	.309
1928	NEW YORK	AL	116	404	62	134	30	11	10	82	15	.332
1929	NEW YORK	AL	147	545	101	193	37	11	18	106	9	.354
1930	NEW YORK	AL	143	571	109	173	34	15	9	121	4	.303
1931	NEW YORK	AL	135	484	67	129	27	7	8	83	18	.267
1932	NEW YORK	AL	142	510	79	153	28	16	15	113	11	.300
1933	NEW YORK	AL	139	523	94	154	22	12	18	104	15	.294
1934	NEW YORK	AL	123	438	59	117	24	6	14	67	11	.267
1935	NEW YORK	AL	130	477	72	130	18	6	13	83	11	.273
1936	NEW YORK	AL	150	537	82	154	29	6	14	109	8	.287
1937	NEW YORK	AL	126	446	56	109	21	3	14	70	7	.244
1938	CHICAGO	NL	54	120	21	32	5	0	5	23	0	.267
1939	BROOKLYN, NEW YORK	NL	27	83	13	24	2	0	4	14	1	.289
CAREER TOTALS			**1740**	**6297**	**986**	**1840**	**334**	**115**	**178**	**1191**	**148**	**.292**

BOB LEMON

Bob Lemon didn't want to be a pitcher, but thanks to the testimonials of those who faced him early on, he grudgingly became one of the game's best.

"If it hadn't been for baseball," Lemon said, "I'd still be pumping gas back home in Long Beach (Calif.)."

As a minor leaguer, he played the infield and outfield, once leading the Eastern League in runs and hits, but struggled at the major league level with the Cleveland Indians. While serving in the military during World War II, Lemon pitched in service games and so impressed fellow big leaguers with his arm that they advised his big league manager to convert him to a hurler.

Lemon reported to spring training with the Indians in 1946 but his third base skills had deteriorated enough while in the service that he was switched to center field. His switch to the outfield was not a success, so while languishing on the bench, Cleveland manager Lou Boudreau began hearing positive reports from big leaguers that had faced Lemon in the service, players such as Bill Dickey, Birdie Tebbetts and Ted Williams, and gave him a shot on the mound.

Thankfully for Cleveland the experiment worked, and Lemon was soon part of a pitching staff that included such aces as Bob Feller, Early Wynn and Mike Garcia. The right-handed Lemon, who would spend his entire 15-year career with the Indians, would go on to toss a no-hitter in 1948, win 20 games seven times, and lead the American League in complete games five times, innings pitched four times, wins three times, and strikeouts once. When the Tribe won 111 games in 1954, Lemon won 23 of them. Always a good hitter, Lemon's career total of 37 homers is second on the all-time list for pitchers.

"You never know," Lemon said. "If I pitched in the minor leagues, I might've come up with a sore arm."

After his playing career came to an end, Lemon stayed in the game as a scout, managed in the minor leagues, coached in the major leagues, and served as a big league skipper with the Kansas City Royals, Chicago White Sox and New York Yankees. In July 1978, he took over for Billy Martin as manager of the Yankees and led them to a World Series title.

Elected To The Hall Of Fame: *1976.*

Born: *Sept. 22, 1920 in San Bernardino, Calif.*

Died: *Jan. 11, 2000 in Long Beach, Calif.*

Height: *6-0.* **Weight:** *180.*

Threw: *Right.* **Batted:** *Left.*

Debut: *Sept. 9, 1941.*

Final Game: *July 1, 1958.*

Teams: *Cleveland A.L. 1941-1942 (third baseman), 1946-1958 (pitcher).*

Postseason: *World Series Champion (1948); 2 A.L. Pennants (1948, 1954).*

Awards: *7-Time All-Star (1948-1954).*

YEAR	TEAM	LEAGUE	G	W	L	SV	SH	IP	H	BB	SO	ERA
1946	CLEVELAND	AL	32	4	5	1	0	94	77	68	39	2.49
1947	CLEVELAND	AL	37	11	5	3	1	167.3	150	97	65	3.44
1948	CLEVELAND	AL	43	20	14	2	10	293.7	231	129	147	2.82
1949	CLEVELAND	AL	37	22	10	1	2	279.7	211	137	138	2.99
1950	CLEVELAND	AL	44	23	11	3	3	288	281	146	170	3.84
1951	CLEVELAND	AL	42	17	14	2	1	263.3	244	124	132	3.52
1952	CLEVELAND	AL	42	22	11	4	5	309.7	236	105	131	2.50
1953	CLEVELAND	AL	41	21	15	1	5	286.7	283	110	98	3.36
1954	CLEVELAND	AL	36	23	7	0	2	258.3	228	92	110	2.72
1955	CLEVELAND	AL	35	18	10	2	0	211.3	218	74	100	3.88
1956	CLEVELAND	AL	39	20	14	3	2	255.3	230	89	94	3.03
1957	CLEVELAND	AL	21	6	11	0	0	117.3	129	64	45	4.60
1958	CLEVELAND	AL	11	0	1	0	0	25.3	41	16	8	5.33
CAREER TOTALS			**460**	**207**	**128**	**22**	**31**	**2850**	**2559**	**1251**	**1277**	**3.23**

BUCK LEONARD

Walter "Buck" Leonard was one of the best pure hitters to play in the Negro Leagues. He was also a key part of the Homestead Grays dynasty of the 1930s and 1940s.

The first baseman spent his entire 17-year career with the Grays, the longest term of service for a player with one team in Negro league history. He played in a league-record 11 East-West All-Star Games and from 1937 to 1945.

Beginning in 1942, the Grays found themselves in four consecutive Negro World Series, winning in 1943 and 1944.

At the age of 45, with the color barrier broken, he was offered a major league contract, but turned it down. "In 1952, I knew I was over the hill," Leonard said. "I didn't try to fool myself."

League statistics have Leonard batting .320 for his career with a .519 slugging percentage. The number of recorded home runs, runs scored and runs driven in are varied, but there is agreement that Leonard was at the top of his class.

"Buck Leonard was as smooth a first baseman as I ever saw," said booking agent Eddie Gottlieb. "In those days the first baseman on a team in the Negro Leagues often played the clown. They had a funny way of catching the ball so the fans would laugh, but Leonard was strictly baseball – a great glove, a (heck) of a hitter, and drove in runs."

Leonard wasn't able to get a high school diploma until the age of 52, because his hometown didn't have a high school that allowed education for African-Americans. Always an advocate for civil rights, he was an ambassador for Negro League baseball until his death at age 90.

In 1999, the *Sporting News* ranked the slugger No. 47 on its list of the 100 Greatest Baseball Players. He was one of only five men on the list who played most of, or their entire career in the Negro Leagues. Leonard was as a finalist for the Major League Baseball All-Century Team.

Elected To The Hall Of Fame: *1972.*
Born: *Sept. 8, 1907 in Rocky Mount, N.C.*
Died: *Nov. 27, 1997 in Rocky Mount, N.C.*
Height: *5-10.* **Weight:** *185.*
Threw: *Left.* **Batted:** *Left.*
Teams: *Negro Leagues 1933-1950.*
Brooklyn 1933; Homestead 1934-1950.

YEAR	TEAM	LEAGUE	G	AB	R	H	2B	3B	HR	RBI	SB	AVG
1934	HOMESTEAD	INDP	—	82	16	28	4	0	5	—	0	.341
1935	HOMESTEAD	NNL	—	147	26	50	10	1	3	—	3	.340
1936	HOMESTEAD	NNL	—	60	15	15	1	1	2	—	1	.250
1937	HOMESTEAD	NNL	—	124	36	43	9	0	5	—	1	.347
1938	HOMESTEAD	NNL	—	82	19	29	0	0	2	—	0	.354
1939	HOMESTEAD	NNL	—	72	23	30	5	0	5	—	2	.417
1940	HOMESTEAD	NNL	—	162	42	59	12	3	7	—	4	.364
1941	HOMESTEAD	NNL	—	136	46	42	4	5	9	—	7	.309
1942	HOMESTEAD	NNL	—	81	11	17	3	0	0	—	1	.210
1943	HOMESTEAD	NNL	—	193	49	57	11	7	4	—	2	.295
1944	HOMESTEAD	NNL	—	120	31	36	8	6	5	—	2	.300
1945	HOMESTEAD	NNL	—	64	8	18	1	2	0	—	0	.281
1946	HOMESTEAD	NNL	—	102	18	27	3	1	3	—	3	.265
1947	HOMESTEAD	NNL	—	30	7	16	0	0	4	—	1	.533
1948	HOMESTEAD	NNL	—	34	5	9	3	0	3	—	0	.265
CAREER TOTALS			**—**	**1489**	**352**	**476**	**74**	**26**	**57**	**—**	**27**	**.320**

FREDDIE LINDSTROM

Frederick "Freddie" Lindstrom began his professional baseball career at the ripe age of 16.

One of the finest athletes to come out of Chicago, he had tryouts with both the Cubs and the New York Giants. He was signed by the Giants organization, and played for their affiliate Toledo Mud Hens in 1922.

Lindstrom hit .304 in 18 games with the minor league club, making a big impression for such a young player.

Two years later, the third baseman became the youngest ball player ever to take part in a World Series. At 18 years, 10 months and 13 days old, Lindstrom took the field for the Giants in the 1924 Fall Classic against the Washington Senators.

The rookie had four hits in one game off of Hall of Famer Walter Johnson, known for being one of the top pitchers of his time. Lindstrom had 10 total hits in the series, batting .333 over seven games.

His 10 Fall Classic hits were half the number he had reached in the majors to that point. He also had seven assists in Game 2 of the Series, a record that he held for 26 years.

Lindstrom tied another record on July 25, 1928, and that one still stands today. He became the second player in the National League to collect nine hits in a doubleheader.

Lindstrom's best seasons were 1928, when he batted .358 with 14 home runs and 107 RBI, and led the league with 231 hits, and 1930, when he notched 231 hits again and had career highs in average, at .379, and home runs, with 22. He scored 127 runs both years, and drove in 106 during the latter season.

In 1928 he was second in NL MVP voting to Jim Bottomley.

Lindstrom, who eventually became an outfielder, played the majority of his time in New York under manager John McGraw. His best performances came with the Giants, something McGraw acknowledged when naming the greatest players he'd ever had.

"My greatest thrill? That's easy," Lindstrom said. "It came the day Mr. McGraw named his 20 all-time players. I'm ninth on that list and that is thrill enough to last me a lifetime."

FREDERICK CHARLES LINDSTROM
NEW YORK N.L., PITTSBURGH N.L., CHICAGO N.L., BROOKLYN N.L.
1924 · 1936
COMPILED LIFETIME .311 BATTING MARK, INCLUDING SEVEN SEASONS OF .300 OR BETTER. ONE OF ONLY THREE PLAYERS TO AMASS 230 OR MORE HITS A YEAR TWICE. AS YOUNGEST PLAYER (AGE 18) IN WORLD SERIES HISTORY, HE TIED RECORD WITH FOUR HITS IN GAME IN 1924, EQUALLED MAJOR LEAGUE RECORD BY COLLECTING NINE HITS IN 1928 DOUBLEHEADER.

Elected To The Hall Of Fame: 1976.
Born: Nov. 21, 1905 in Chicago, Ill.
Died: Oct. 4, 1981 in Chicago, Ill.
Height: 5-11. **Weight:** 170.
Threw: Right. **Batted:** Right.
Debut: April 15, 1924.
Final Game: May 15, 1936.
Teams: New York N.L. 1924-1932; Pittsburgh N.L. 1933-1934; Chicago N.L. 1935; Brooklyn N.L. 1936.
Postseason: 2 N.L. Pennants (1924, 1935).

YEAR	TEAM	LEAGUE	G	AB	R	H	2B	3B	HR	RBI	SB	AVG
1924	NEW YORK	NL	52	79	19	20	3	1	0	4	3	.253
1925	NEW YORK	NL	104	356	43	102	15	12	4	33	5	.287
1926	NEW YORK	NL	140	543	90	164	19	9	9	76	11	.302
1927	NEW YORK	NL	138	562	107	172	36	8	7	58	10	.306
1928	NEW YORK	NL	153	646	99	231	39	9	14	107	15	.358
1929	NEW YORK	NL	130	549	99	175	23	6	15	91	10	.319
1930	NEW YORK	NL	148	609	127	231	39	7	22	106	15	.379
1931	NEW YORK	NL	78	303	38	91	12	6	5	36	5	.300
1932	NEW YORK	NL	144	595	83	161	26	5	15	92	6	.271
1933	PITTSBURGH	NL	138	538	70	167	39	10	5	55	1	.310
1934	PITTSBURGH	NL	97	383	59	111	24	4	4	49	1	.290
1935	CHICAGO	NL	90	342	49	94	22	4	3	62	1	.275
1936	BROOKLYN	NL	26	106	12	28	4	0	0	10	1	.264
CAREER TOTALS			**1438**	**5611**	**895**	**1747**	**301**	**81**	**103**	**779**	**84**	**.311**

POP LLOYD

Generally considered to be the greatest shortstop in Negro League history, Pop Lloyd enjoyed a 25-year career in which he posted an average of .337 and a .434 slugging percentage, according to league statistics.

In a time when pitchers dominated the game, Lloyd still found a way to score runs. With a great eye for the ball and fantastic bat control, he could drop in hits and bunt with precision. His play also translated to the basepaths and led to many stolen bases. Not only was he known to be the best at fielding his position during his era, but he was also a top run producer for his teams.

As a player, Lloyd spent time with the Philadelphia Giants, Chicago Leland Giants, New York Lincoln Giants, Chicago American Giants, New York Lincoln Stars, Brooklyn Royal Giants, New York Bacharach Giants, Columbus Buckeyes, Atlantic City Bacharach Giants, Hilldale Daisies and New York Black Yankees. Lloyd also managed four of those teams over a span of four years while playing, making his mark both on those who played with him and for him.

"Pop Lloyd was the greatest player, the greatest manager, the greatest teacher," said Bill Yancey, a shortstop who played with him. "He had the ability and knowledge and, above all, patience. I did not know what baseball was until I played under him."

During the four years Lloyd played for the American Giants, they were Western champions three times, and defeated the Eastern champs in the playoffs in both 1914 and 1917.

In Cuba, the shortstop was known as "El Cuchara," "The Tablespoon" or "The Shovel," for how he characteristically scooped up a glove-full of dirt from the ground every time he fielded a ball, similar to the style of Honus Wagner.

While he managed the Hilldale Daisies, the team brought home the first-ever Eastern Colored League pennant, winning the season with a 32-17 record. He earned the nickname "Pop" because he was mild-mannered as a leader with few bad habits, and approached the game as a gentleman.

JOHN HENRY LLOYD
"POP"
NEGRO LEAGUES 1906-1932
REGARDED AS FINEST SHORTSTOP TO PLAY IN NEGRO BASEBALL. SCIENTIFIC HITTER BATTED OVER .400 SEVERAL TIMES DURING HIS 27-YEAR CAREER. PERSONIFIED BEST QUALITIES OF ATHLETE BOTH ON AND OFF FIELD. INSTRUMENTAL IN HELPING OPEN YANKEE STADIUM TO NEGRO BASEBALL IN 1930. MANAGED MORE THAN TEN SEASONS.

Elected To The Hall Of Fame: 1977.
Born: Apr. 25, 1884 in Palatka, Fla.
Died: Mar. 19, 1964 in Atlantic City, N.J.
Height: 5-11. **Weight:** 180.
Threw: Right. **Batted:** Left.
Teams: Negro Leagues 1907-1932.
Philadelphia 1907-1909; Habana 1908-11; Fe 1912; New York 1912, 1915, 1922, 1926-31; Chicago 1914-1917; Brooklyn 1918-1920; Atlantic City 1919; Columbus 1921; Hilldale 1923; Bacharach 1924-1925, 1932.

YEAR	TEAM	LEAGUE	G	AB	R	H	2B	3B	HR	RBI	SB	AVG
1907	PHILADELPHIA	CNCS	23	93	17	26	4	0	0	11	2	.280
1908	HABANA	CUGL	23	96	15	25	2	1	0	16	2	.260
1909	HABANA	CMLS	9	33	4	8	0	1	0	3	2	.242
1910	HAB./CHI./HAB.	CMLS/CNCS/CUNL	24	86	11	29	6	0	0	14	5	.337
1911	HABANA	CUNL	28	103	11	40	3	2	0	28	13	.388
1912	FE/NEW YORK	CUNL/CNCS	45	177	42	64	5	3	0	30	28	.362
1914	CHICAGO	INDP	48	188	36	57	12	5	0	30	7	.303
1915	N.Y./CHICAGO	INDP	47	187	32	70	12	1	1	36	5	.374
1916	CHICAGO	INDP	62	223	38	75	9	2	1	34	6	.336
1917	CHICAGO	INDP	53	188	23	54	11	6	0	34	5	.287
1918	BROOKLYN	INDP	18	71	12	25	3	2	0	13	1	.352
1919	ATL. CITY/BKN.	INDP	22	81	8	31	6	3	0	16	5	.383
1920	BROOKLYN	INDP	—	44	4	14	0	0	1	—	0	.318
1921	COLUMBUS	NNL	—	231	40	77	17	2	0	—	15	.333
1922	N.Y. BACHARACH	INDP	—	100	12	26	6	0	1	—	3	.260
1923	HILLDALE	ECOL	—	147	30	50	10	1	2	—	4	.340
1924	BACHARACH	ECOL	—	216	39	83	8	2	1	—	4	.384
1925	BACHARACH	ECOL	—	139	27	47	4	5	2	—	9	.338
1926	N.Y. LINCOLN	ECOL	—	169	26	61	7	3	1	—	5	.361
1927	N.Y. LINCOLN	ECOL	—	82	13	26	6	0	1	—	0	.317
1928	N.Y. LINCOLN	ECOL	—	157	34	55	4	1	6	—	4	.350
1929	N.Y. LINCOLN	ANL	—	135	29	50	11	3	2	—	2	.370
1930	N.Y. LINCOLN	INDP	—	160	27	59	5	1	1	—	6	.369
1931	NEW YORK	INDP	—	38	4	8	0	0	0	—	0	.211
1932	BACHARACH	INDP	—	15	4	6	0	0	1	—	0	.400
CAREER TOTALS			—	3159	538	1066	151	44	22	—	133	.337

ERNIE LOMBARDI

Catcher Ernie Lombardi would appear to be the kind of tall tale scouts like to invent when they are sitting through a rain delay.

Everything about the longtime Reds star seemed larger than life. He had one of the best arms in baseball, the kind of arm that tempted scouts at times to make him a pitcher. He had hands that seemed to almost make a catcher's mitt superfluous. He swung a 42-ounce bat that made everyone else's bats look like a toothpick, thanks to massive wrists and forearms.

There was his nose, a massive protuberance that earned him the almost inevitable nickname of "Schnozz," and there was his lack of speed. More than anything, Lombardi was one of the biggest, and best, hitters the game has seen.

Lombardi topped .300 on 10 different occasions. He won a pair of batting titles (in 1938 and 1942), becoming the last catcher to win a batting title until Joe Mauer did it in 2006. Lombardi was named the National League MVP in 1938, and was a key member of the Reds' 1939 National League champs and 1940 World Series champs.

Nothing about Lombardi was conventional, from his lack of speed, to his prominent nose, to his batting grip: He held the baseball bat like a golf club, interlocking his hands. There was no real reason to ever change to a more conventional grip, because Lombardi was able to rip line drives like few before or since.

He had to hit scorching line drives, because that was about the only way he could get a hit. Lombardi hit .306 for his career even though teams could play him deeper than anyone else in the game. Infielders knew Lombardi's lack of speed would give them time to get the ball to first from deep in the hole or even from the shallow part of the outfield. Infielders kept moving farther back against Lombardi, buying time to try to handle his line drives.

Because of his size and slowness, Lombardi got a reputation as a poor defensive catcher, but his arm was strong enough to control the running game, and his game-calling skills were exceptional as well — he was the catcher for Johnny Vander Meer's back-to-back no-hitters.

ERNEST NATALI LOMBARDI
BROOKLYN, N.L., 1931
CINCINNATI, N.L., 1932-1941
BOSTON, N.L., 1942
NEW YORK, N.L., 1943-1947
HIT .306 OVER 17 SEASONS DESPITE SLOWNESS AFOOT-TEN TIMES BATTING OVER .300. WON N.L. BATTING TITLE WITH .342 IN 1938 AND AGAIN IN 1942 WITH .330. HELD HANDS LOW, WITH INTERLOCKING GOLF GRIP AND QUICK STROKE. N.L. MVP IN 1938. SKILLED RECEIVER AND HANDLER OF PITCHERS. OUTSTANDING ARM FROM CROUCH POSITION, RIFLING THROWS WITH SIDE-ARM RELEASE.

Schnozz

Elected To The Hall Of Fame: *1986.*

Born: *April 6, 1908 in Oakland, Calif.*

Died: *Sept. 26, 1977 in Santa Cruz, Calif.*

Height: *6-3.* **Weight:** *230.*

Threw: *Right.* **Batted:** *Right.*

Debut: *April 15, 1931.*

Final Game: *Sept. 17, 1947.*

Teams: *Brooklyn N.L. 1931; Cincinnati N.L. 1932-1941; Boston N.L. 1942; New York N.L. 1943-1947.*

Postseason: *World Series Champion (1940); 2 N.L. Pennants (1939-1940).*

Awards: *8-Time All-Star (1936-1940, 1942-1943, 1945); N.L. Most Valuable Player (1938).*

YEAR	TEAM	LEAGUE	G	AB	R	H	2B	3B	HR	RBI	SB	AVG
1931	BROOKLYN	NL	73	182	20	54	7	1	4	23	1	.297
1932	CINCINNATI	NL	118	413	43	125	22	9	11	68	0	.303
1933	CINCINNATI	NL	107	350	30	99	21	1	4	47	2	.283
1934	CINCINNATI	NL	132	417	42	127	19	4	9	62	0	.305
1935	CINCINNATI	NL	120	332	36	114	23	3	12	64	0	.343
1936	CINCINNATI	NL	121	387	42	129	23	2	12	68	1	.333
1937	CINCINNATI	NL	120	368	41	123	22	1	9	59	1	.334
1938	CINCINNATI	NL	129	489	60	167	30	1	19	95	0	.342
1939	CINCINNATI	NL	130	450	43	129	26	2	20	85	0	.287
1940	CINCINNATI	NL	109	376	50	120	22	0	14	74	0	.319
1941	CINCINNATI	NL	117	398	33	105	12	1	10	60	1	.264
1942	BOSTON	NL	105	309	32	102	14	0	11	46	1	.330
1943	NEW YORK	NL	104	295	19	90	7	0	10	51	1	.305
1944	NEW YORK	NL	117	373	37	95	13	0	10	58	0	.255
1945	NEW YORK	NL	115	368	46	113	7	1	19	70	0	.307
1946	NEW YORK	NL	88	238	19	69	4	1	12	39	0	.290
1947	NEW YORK	NL	48	110	8	31	5	0	4	21	0	.282
CAREER TOTALS			**1853**	**5855**	**601**	**1792**	**277**	**27**	**190**	**990**	**8**	**.306**

TED LYONS

"Ted Lyons was one of the toughest I ever hit at. Great stuff, great control," said longtime opponent Doc Cramer.

The first big league game Ted Lyons ever saw, he saw from the pitcher's mound. The 22-year-old Baylor University graduate, who had intended to study law but instead joined the Chicago White Sox, never played a game in the minor leagues.

Lyons spent his entire career with the White Sox, from 1923-42, and again in 1946. At the age of 41 in 1942, Lyons enlisted in the Marines.

As a young right-hander, Lyons primarily threw fastballs. He led the American League in wins in 1925 and 1927. His finest season was perhaps 1930, when he won 20 games for the third time (22-15), led the AL in complete games (29) and innings (297.7). Between 1929 and 1931, Lyons suffered a series of arm and back injuries, and began to throw more slow curves, even slower curves, and knuckleballs. His ability to reinvent his repertoire effectively made a new pitcher out of him.

In 1939, he ran up a streak of 42 consecutive innings without issuing a walk. That year, White Sox manager Jimmy Dykes decided to use Lyons as a Sunday-only pitcher, in part because as one of the few premier players on the Sox, he was an attendance drawing card. Lyons did well in his Sabbath role, going 14-6 that year and making the All-Star team for the first time. In 1942, at the age of 41, he completed each and every one of his 20 starts, going 14-6 and leading the AL in ERA.

Upon his 1946 return from the war, Lyons went 1-4 before retiring and being named manager of the White Sox, a post he held until 1948. He later served as pitching coach for the Tigers and Dodgers, and scouted for the White Sox.

Lyons remains the franchise leader in wins, with 260, and the White Sox retired his number, 16, in 1987. New York Yankees manager Joe McCarthy once said, "If he'd pitched for the Yankees, he would have won over 400 games."

THEODORE AMAR LYONS
CHICAGO A.L. 1923 TO 1946

ENTIRE ACTIVE PITCHING CAREER OF 21 SEASONS WITH CHICAGO A.L. WON 260 GAMES, LOST 230. TIED FOR LEAGUE'S MOST VICTORIES 1925 AND 1927, BEST EARNED RUN AVERAGE, 2.10 IN 1942 WHEN HE STARTED AND FINISHED ALL 20 GAMES. PITCHED NO-HIT GAME, AUG. 21, 1926 AGAINST BOSTON. PITCHED 21-INNING GAME MAY 24, 1929.

Elected To The Hall Of Fame: *1955.*
Born: *Dec. 28, 1900 in Lake Charles, La.*
Died: *July 25, 1986 in Sulphur, La.*
Height: *5-11.* **Weight:** *200.*
Threw: *Right.* **Batted:** *Both.*
Debut: *July 2, 1923.*
Final Game: *May 19, 1946*
Teams: *Chicago A.L. 1923-1942, 1946.*
Awards: *All-Star (1939).*

YEAR	TEAM	LEAGUE	G	W	L	SV	SH	IP	H	BB	SO	ERA
1923	CHICAGO	AL	9	2	1	0	0	22.7	30	15	6	6.35
1924	CHICAGO	AL	41	12	11	3	0	216.3	279	72	52	4.87
1925	CHICAGO	AL	43	21	11	3	5	262.7	274	83	45	3.26
1926	CHICAGO	AL	39	18	16	2	3	283.7	268	106	51	4.87
1927	CHICAGO	AL	39	22	14	2	2	307.7	291	67	71	2.84
1928	CHICAGO	AL	39	15	14	6	0	240	276	68	60	3.98
1929	CHICAGO	AL	37	14	20	2	1	259.3	276	76	57	4.10
1930	CHICAGO	AL	42	22	15	1	1	297.7	331	57	69	3.78
1931	CHICAGO	AL	22	4	6	0	0	101	117	33	16	4.01
1932	CHICAGO	AL	33	10	15	2	1	230.7	243	71	58	3.28
1933	CHICAGO	AL	36	10	21	1	2	228	260	74	74	4.38
1934	CHICAGO	AL	30	11	13	1	0	205.3	249	66	53	4.87
1935	CHICAGO	AL	23	15	8	0	3	190.7	194	56	54	3.02
1936	CHICAGO	AL	26	10	13	0	1	182	227	45	48	5.14
1937	CHICAGO	AL	22	12	7	0	0	169.3	182	45	45	4.15
1938	CHICAGO	AL	23	9	11	0	1	194.7	238	52	54	3.70
1939	CHICAGO	AL	21	14	6	0	0	172.7	162	26	65	2.76
1940	CHICAGO	AL	22	12	8	0	4	186.3	188	37	72	3.24
1941	CHICAGO	AL	22	12	10	0	2	187.3	199	37	63	3.70
1942	CHICAGO	AL	20	14	6	0	1	180.3	167	26	50	2.10
1946	CHICAGO	AL	5	1	4	0	0	42.7	38	9	10	2.32
CAREER TOTALS			**594**	**260**	**230**	**23**	**27**	**4161**	**4489**	**1121**	**1073**	**3.67**

BIZ MACKEY

Though somewhat overshadowed by such legendary names as Josh Gibson and Roy Campanella, when black baseball's top catchers are discussed, Biz Mackey should be considered one of the great players of his era.

"Actually, as much as I admired Campanella as a catcher, all-around, and Gibson as a hitter," said Hall of Famer Cool Papa Bell, a veteran of the Negro leagues, "I believe Biz Mackey was the best catcher I ever saw." In fact, a 1954 *Pittsburgh Courier* poll saw Mackey edge Gibson as the greatest Negro league catcher.

Mackey would don the tools of ignorance in a career that spanned almost 30 years, from the early 1920s to the mid-1940s. Whether while a member of the Hilldale Giants, Philadelphia Stars, Newark Eagles, Indianapolis ABCs or the Baltimore/Washington Elite Giants, he always proved to be a leader behind the plate or later as a manager. Fellow Hall of Famer Cum Posey, a longtime Negro league executive, once said, "For combined hitting, thinking, throwing and physical endowment, there has never been another like Biz Mackey. A tremendous hitter, a fierce competitor . . . he is the standout among catchers."

A line drive hitter whose batting average rarely strayed below .300, Mackey, named to five East-West All-Star teams, was a favorite receiver among pitchers and had a strong throwing arm.

"I've pitched to some great catchers, but my goodness, that Mackey was to my idea the best one I pitched to," said Hall of Fame hurler Hilton Smith. "The way he handled you, the way he just built you up, believing in yourself. He was marvelous."

Mackey has been given credit for furthering the development of a number of Negro leaguers who would go on to success in the major leagues, such as Campanella, Monte Irvin and Larry Doby.

"In my opinion, Biz Mackey was the master of defense of all catchers," Campanella said. "When I was a kid in Philadelphia, I saw both Mackey and Mickey Cochrane in their primes, but for real catching skills, I don't think Cochrane was the master of defense that Mackey was."

JAMES RALEIGH MACKEY
"BIZ"
NEGRO LEAGUES, 1920-1947

A SUPERB DEFENSIVE CATCHER AND NATURAL LEADER WHO COULD PLAY ALL POSITIONS. STARRED IN 1920s WITH HILLDALES OF PHILADELPHIA, LEADING THEM TO 1925 NEGRO LEAGUES WORLD SERIES TITLE. A LINE DRIVE SWITCH-HITTER WHOSE AVERAGE TOPPED .300 MOST SEASONS. PLAYED IN FIVE EAST-WEST ALL-STAR GAMES. AS PLAYER-MANAGER OF BALTIMORE ELITE GIANTS, MENTORED TEENAGE CATCHER ROY CAMPANELLA. MANAGED FIVE OTHER FUTURE HALL OF FAMERS DURING TENURE WITH NEWARK, LEADING EAGLES TO ONLY CHAMPIONSHIP IN 1946.

Elected To The Hall Of Fame: *2006.*
Born: *July 27, 1897 in Eagle Pass, Texas.*
Died: *Sept. 22, 1965 in Los Angeles, Calif.*
Height: *6-0.* **Weight:** *200.*
Threw: *Right.* **Batted:** *Both.*
Teams: *Negro Leagues 1920-1947; St. Louis 1920; Indianapolis 1920-1922; Hilldale 1923-1931; Baltimore 1928, 1930, 1938-1939; Philadelphia 1933-1935, 1937; Washington 1936-1937; Newark 1939-1942, 1945-1947.*

YEAR	TEAM	LEAGUE	G	AB	R	H	2B	3B	HR	RBI	SB	AVG
1920	ST. LOUIS/IND.	NNL	—	78	3	26	2	0	0	—	2	.333
1921	INDIANAPOLIS	NNL	—	168	15	51	6	6	3	—	2	.304
1922	INDIANAPOLIS	NNL	—	158	22	65	14	8	3	—	3	.411
1923	HILLDALE	ECOL	—	189	29	74	6	1	4	—	5	.392
1924	HILLDALE	ECOL	—	323	56	115	21	4	4	—	9	.356
1925	HILLDALE	ECOL	—	204	44	69	15	5	6	—	11	.338
1926	HILLDALE	ECOL	—	330	64	110	20	3	10	—	14	.333
1927	HILLDALE	ECOL	—	81	17	23	0	0	0	—	1	.284
1928	HILLDALE/BALT.	ECOL	—	219	49	78	13	4	4	—	7	.356
1929	HILLDALE	ANL	—	116	19	38	3	2	2	—	2	.328
1930	HILLDALE/BALT.	INDP	—	128	28	52	7	5	4	—	2	.406
1931	HILLDALE	INDP	—	150	28	49	2	1	1	—	0	.327
1933	PHILADELPHIA	INDP	—	90	8	25	2	0	0	—	1	.278
1934	PHILDAELPHJIA	NNL	—	76	7	23	5	0	2	—	0	.303
1935	PHILADELPHIA	NNL	—	156	19	38	5	0	2	—	0	.244
1936	WASHINGTON	NNL	—	107	12	31	6	2	1	—	0	.290
1937	WASH./PHIL.	NNL	—	71	8	18	2	0	0	—	0	.254
1938	BALTIMORE	NNL	—	76	12	19	0	0	0	—	0	.250
1939	BALT./NEWARK	NNL	—	51	5	19	0	0	0	—	1	.373
1940	NEWARK	NNL	—	117	14	35	4	0	1	—	0	.299
1941	NEWARK	NNL	—	56	6	14	1	1	0	—	0	.250
1942	NEWARK	NNL	—	4	0	1	1	0	0	—	0	.250
1945	NEWARK	NNL	—	27	2	5	0	0	1	—	0	.185
1946	NEWARK	NNL	—	6	0	1	0	0	0	—	0	.167
1947	NEWARK	NNL	—	16	0	3	0	0	0	—	0	.188
CAREER TOTALS			—	**2997**	**467**	**982**	**135**	**42**	**48**	**—**	**60**	**.328**

The Baseball Hall of Fame Almanac

MICKEY MANTLE

Whitey Ford refers to him as "a superstar who never acted like one. He was a humble man who was kind and friendly to all his teammates, even the rawest rookie. He was idolized by all the other players."

Mickey Mantle was an iconic baseball player with immense talent. His drive and love for the game pushed him past the injuries he was plagued with and into the record books.

He played his entire 18-year career with the New York Yankees, and the injuries he suffered never allowed him to live up to the potential he displayed to the team when he arrived in 1951.

Despite never quite being at 100 percent, Mantle established himself as the greatest switch-hitter to play the game, and one of the game's best players ever. The outfielder almost had his career cut short when his leg was infected with osteomyelitis after being kicked in the shin playing youth football. Effects of the disease lasted his lifetime and might have been responsible for other injuries that took much of the speed he had early in his career.

A 1951 on-field accident resulted in a serious leg injury, preventing Mantle from ever playing his best again, and he returned to the Yankees in 1952 as the starting center fielder. He batted .311 with 23 home runs, 87 RBI, and 94 runs scored, making the All-Star team for the first of 14 consecutive selections.

From 1953 to 1955, he averaged 28 home runs, 98 RBI and 118 runs per season. He also batted .300 or better in two of the three years. He led the American League in 1954 with 129 runs and in 1955 he topped the AL with 37 home runs, a .431 on-base percentage and a .611 slugging percentage. In 1956 he won the AL Triple Crown, batting .353 with 52 home runs and 130 RBI, and won the first of two consecutive MVP awards. He also led the Yankees to their fifth pennant in six seasons with the team.

In 1962, Mantle missed almost 40 games, but still managed to capture his third MVP title, while bringing New York to their third consecutive pennant and second straight world championship. That season, he batted .321 with 30 home runs, 89 RBI and 96 runs scored. He also led the league with a .486 on-base percentage and a .605 slugging mark.

Elected To The Hall Of Fame: *1974.*
Born: *Oct. 20, 1931 in Spavinaw, Okla.*
Died: *Aug. 13, 1995 in Dallas, Texas.*
Height: *5-11.* ***Weight:*** *195.*
Threw: *Right.* ***Batted:*** *Both.*
Debut: *April 17, 1951.*
Final Game: *Sept. 28, 1968.*
Teams: *New York A.L. 1951-1968.*
Postseason: *7-Time World Series Champion (1951-1953, 1956, 1958, 1961-1962); 12 A.L. Pennants (1951-1953, 1955-1958, 1960-1964).*
Awards: *20-Time All-Star (1952-1965, 1967-1968); 3-Time Most Valuable Player (1956-1957, 1962).*

YEAR	TEAM	LEAGUE	G	AB	R	H	2B	3B	HR	RBI	SB	AVG
1951	NEW YORK	AL	96	341	61	91	11	5	13	65	8	.267
1952	NEW YORK	AL	142	549	94	171	37	7	23	87	4	.311
1953	NEW YORK	AL	127	461	105	136	24	3	21	92	8	.295
1954	NEW YORK	AL	146	543	129	163	17	12	27	102	5	.300
1955	NEW YORK	AL	147	517	121	158	25	11	37	99	8	.306
1956	NEW YORK	AL	150	533	132	188	22	5	52	130	10	.353
1957	NEW YORK	AL	144	474	121	173	28	6	34	94	16	.365
1958	NEW YORK	AL	150	519	127	158	21	1	42	97	18	.304
1959	NEW YORK	AL	144	541	104	154	23	4	31	75	21	.285
1960	NEW YORK	AL	153	527	119	145	17	6	40	94	14	.275
1961	NEW YORK	AL	153	514	131	163	16	6	54	128	12	.317
1962	NEW YORK	AL	123	377	96	121	15	1	30	89	9	.321
1963	NEW YORK	AL	65	172	40	54	8	0	15	35	2	.314
1964	NEW YORK	AL	143	465	92	141	25	2	35	111	6	.303
1965	NEW YORK	AL	122	361	44	92	12	1	19	46	4	.255
1966	NEW YORK	AL	108	333	40	96	12	1	23	56	1	.288
1967	NEW YORK	AL	144	440	63	108	17	0	22	55	1	.245
1968	NEW YORK	AL	144	435	57	103	14	1	18	54	6	.237
CAREER TOTALS			**2401**	**8102**	**1676**	**2415**	**344**	**72**	**536**	**1509**	**153**	**.298**

HEINIE MANUSH

HENRY EMMET MANUSH
1923–1939
SLUGGING OUTFIELDER
FOR 6 MAJOR LEAGUE CLUBS. BATTING
CHAMPION OF A.L. AT .378 WITH 1926 TIGERS.
LIFETIME AVERAGE OF .330 IN 2,009
MAJOR LEAGUE GAMES. HAD 2,524 HITS.

Heinie Manush was a hitting machine who consistently ranked among the game's top batters throughout the 1920s and '30s.

Manush's record included a batting title and four 200-hit seasons in his 17-year career. The left fielder played with six teams after breaking into the majors in 1923 with the Ty Cobb-led Detroit Tigers.

Manush hit .334 in his rookie year, though would struggle to get playing time in a crowded outfield until his breakout year of 1926. He won the batting title that year, hitting .378 with a career-high 14 home runs. To win the batting title, Manush went 6-for-9 in a doubleheader on the last day of the season to pass Babe Ruth and teammates Harry Heilmann and Bob Fothergill. It would be the only batting title Manush would win, but the lefthander finished second in 1928 and 1933 and third in 1929 and 1934. The 1928 batting race also featured late-season drama, with Goose Goslin singling in his final at bat of the year to beat Manush.

Manush made his only trip to the World Series with the Washington Senators in 1933. But he, like the team, had a disappointing result. The New York Giants beat Washington in five games and Manush went just 2-for-18 at the plate after leading the American League with 221 hits in the regular season.

The next season, Manush played in the second ever All-Star Game, the only time he made the game in his career. After his All-Star season, Manush's career began to decline. In his remaining five years in the major leagues, he would hit above .300 only once, in 1937 with the Brooklyn Dodgers.

Manush retired in 1939 at the age of 37 with the Pittsburgh Pirates, ending his career with 2,524 hits, a .330 batting average and 160 triples. He spent six years as a minor league manager after retiring.

Manush's brother Frank also reached the major leagues, playing for the Philadelphia Athletics when Henie was just seven years old. Manush was inducted into the Hall of Fame in 1964.

Elected To The Hall Of Fame: 1964.
Born: July 20, 1901 in Tuscumbia, Ala.
Died: May 12, 1971 in Sarasota, Fla.
Height: 6-1. **Weight:** 200.
Threw: Left. **Batted:** Left.
Debut: April 20, 1923.
Final Game: May 22, 1939.
Teams: Detroit A.L. 1923-1927; St. Louis A.L. 1928-1930; Washington A.L. 1930-1935; Boston A.L. 1936; Brooklyn N.L. 1937-1938; Pittsburgh N.L. 1938-1939.
Postseason: A.L. Pennant (1933).
Awards: All-Star (1934).

YEAR	TEAM	LEAGUE	G	AB	R	H	2B	3B	HR	RBI	SB	AVG
1923	DETROIT	AL	109	308	59	103	20	5	4	54	3	.334
1924	DETROIT	AL	120	422	83	122	24	8	9	68	14	.289
1925	DETROIT	AL	99	278	46	84	14	3	5	47	8	.302
1926	DETROIT	AL	136	498	95	188	35	8	14	86	11	.378
1927	DETROIT	AL	151	593	102	177	31	18	6	90	12	.298
1928	ST. LOUIS	AL	154	638	104	241	47	20	13	108	16	.378
1929	ST. LOUIS	AL	142	574	85	204	45	10	6	81	9	.355
1930	ST. LOUIS/WASHINGTON	AL	137	554	100	194	49	12	9	94	7	.350
1931	WASHINGTON	AL	146	616	110	189	41	11	6	70	3	.307
1932	WASHINGTON	AL	149	625	121	214	41	14	14	116	7	.342
1933	WASHINGTON	AL	153	658	115	221	32	17	5	95	6	.336
1934	WASHINGTON	AL	137	556	88	194	42	11	11	89	7	.349
1935	WASHINGTON	AL	119	479	68	131	26	9	4	56	2	.273
1936	BOSTON	AL	82	313	43	91	15	5	0	45	1	.291
1937	BROOKLYN	NL	132	466	57	155	25	7	4	73	6	.333
1938	BROOKLYN/PITTSBURGH	NL	32	64	11	16	4	2	0	10	1	.250
1939	PITTSBURGH	NL	10	12	0	0	0	0	0	1	0	.000
CAREER TOTALS			**2008**	**7654**	**1287**	**2524**	**491**	**160**	**110**	**1183**	**113**	**.330**

The Baseball Hall of Fame Almanac

RABBIT MARANVILLE

"When I first heard about him, about all the stunts he pulled, I said to myself for a fellow to do all those crazy things and still keep his job, he had to be a damned good ball player," Yankees manager Joe McCarthy said of shortstop Rabbit Maranville. "When I got into the league, I saw that I was right. He was full of fun, but he could play ball."

Maranville stands out in baseball history as one of the game's unique careers and unusual personalities. Any discussion of Maranville must include mention of the stunts he pulled but shouldn't solely focus on the player's colorful side. Indeed, Maranville could play ball, especially defense.

Maranville made his big league debut in 1912, and instantly made the Boston Braves a factor in the National League. He finished third in the Chalmers' Award MVP voting in his rookie season, 1913, despite hitting just .247 for the 69-82 Braves.

Listed at just 5-foot-5 and 155 pounds, Maranville was better suited to the Dead Ball era when his career started, and was peaking as a hitter when World War I hit. He hit .260 in 1917 for Boston and then .267 with a career-best five home runs in 1919, sandwiched around a 1918 season cut to 11 games by his military service. Maranville's numbers picked up in 1920 with the livelier ball, but he never was as valuable offensively as he had been at the end of his tenure with Boston.

Maranville was traded to the Pirates, playing in Pittsburgh from 1921-1924, then was traded to the Cubs for the 1925 season, becoming the team's player/manager. He hit just .233 in Chicago, went 23-30 as skipper and was released at the end of the season; Brooklyn signed him but also released him in August 1926, when he was batting a modest .235. In 1927, after a stint in the minor leagues, Maranville landed one more chance with the Cardinals, and at age 36 became the team's everyday shortstop.

WALTER J. V. MARANVILLE
"RABBIT"
BOSTON, PITTSBURGH, CHICAGO,
BROOKLYN AND ST. LOUIS,
NATIONAL LEAGUE, 1912 - 1935
PLAYED MORE GAMES, 2153, AT SHORTSTOP
THAN ANY OTHER NATIONAL LEAGUE PLAYER.
AT BAT TOTAL, 10078, SURPASSED BY ONLY
ONE NATIONAL LEAGUER, HONUS WAGNER.
MADE 2605 HITS IN 23 SEASONS. MEMBER
OF 1914 BOSTON BRAVES "MIRACLE TEAM"
THAT WON PENNANT, THEN WORLD SERIES
FROM ATHLETICS IN 4 GAMES.

Elected To The Hall Of Fame: *1954.*
Born: *Nov. 11, 1891 in Springfield, Mass.*
Died: *Jan. 5, 1954 in New York, N.Y.*
Height: *5-5.* **Weight:** *155.*
Threw: *Right.* **Batted:** *Right.*
Debut: *Sept. 10, 1912.*
Final Game: *Sept. 29, 1935.*
Teams: *Boston N.L. 1912-1920, 1929-1933, 1935; Pittsburgh N.L. 1921-1924; Chicago N.L. 1925; Brooklyn .N.L. 1926; St. Louis N.L. 1927-1928.*
Postseason: *World Series Champion (1914); 2 N.L. Pennants (1914, 1928).*

YEAR	TEAM	LEAGUE	G	AB	R	H	2B	3B	HR	RBI	SB	AVG
1912	BOSTON	NL	26	86	8	18	2	0	0	8	1	.209
1913	BOSTON	NL	143	571	68	141	13	8	2	48	25	.247
1914	BOSTON	NL	156	586	74	144	23	6	4	78	28	.246
1915	BOSTON	NL	149	509	51	124	23	6	2	43	18	.244
1916	BOSTON	NL	155	604	79	142	16	13	4	38	32	.235
1917	BOSTON	NL	142	561	69	146	19	13	3	43	27	.260
1918	BOSTON	NL	11	38	3	12	0	1	0	3	0	.316
1919	BOSTON	NL	131	480	44	128	18	10	5	43	12	.267
1920	BOSTON	NL	134	493	48	131	19	15	1	43	14	.266
1921	PITTSBURGH	NL	153	612	90	180	25	12	1	70	25	.294
1922	PITTSBURGH	NL	155	672	115	198	26	15	0	63	24	.295
1923	PITTSBURGH	NL	141	581	78	161	19	9	1	41	14	.277
1924	PITTSBURGH	NL	152	594	62	158	33	20	2	71	18	.266
1925	CHICAGO	NL	75	266	37	62	10	3	0	23	6	.233
1926	BROOKLYN	NL	78	234	32	55	8	5	0	24	7	.235
1927	ST. LOUIS	NL	9	29	0	7	1	0	0	0	0	.241
1928	ST. LOUIS	NL	112	366	40	88	14	10	1	34	3	.240
1929	BOSTON	NL	146	560	87	159	26	10	0	55	13	.284
1930	BOSTON	NL	142	558	85	157	26	8	2	43	9	.281
1931	BOSTON	NL	145	562	69	146	22	5	0	33	9	.260
1932	BOSTON	NL	149	571	67	134	20	4	0	37	4	.235
1933	BOSTON	NL	143	478	46	104	15	4	0	38	2	.218
1935	BOSTON	NL	23	67	3	10	2	0	0	5	0	.149
CAREER TOTALS			**2670**	**10078**	**1255**	**2605**	**380**	**177**	**28**	**884**	**291**	**.258**

JUAN MARICHAL

"Put your club a run ahead in the later innings, and Marichal is the greatest pitcher I ever saw," Giants manager Alvin Dark said.

Juan Marichal made his major league debut for the Giants against the Phillies on July 19, 1960. He retired the first 19 batters, and carried a no-hitter two outs into the eighth inning, limiting the Phils to one hit en route to a 2-0, complete game victory with 12 strikeouts and just one walk. The 22-year-old right-hander would go 6-2 that year, with a 2.66 ERA.

In 1962, he went 18-11, helping lead the Giants to the NL pennant, though pitching only briefly in the World Series loss to the Yankees due to an injury. The next season was the first of four consecutive 20-win campaigns for Marichal, who topped that mark of excellence six times, and won 25 or more three times.

Marichal had his breakout season in 1963, going 25-8 and leading the NL in innings with 321.1. June was particularly memorable, as he won five games without a loss, including a shutout of the Dodgers on the road, and a 1-0 no-hitter against the Houston Colt .45s on June 15.

As one of the top hurlers of the pitching-rich 1960s, Marichal in that decade posted all six of his 20-win seasons, leading the NL in wins twice. He also led the league twice in complete games, shutouts, innings, and WHIP (walks and hits per innings pitched). He led the league in winning percentage in 1966 and in ERA in 1969.

For his career, Marichal went 243-142, the second highest win total among Latino pitchers, after Dennis Martinez. Nine times his season ERA was under 3.00, and his career mark was a sparkling 2.89. Six times he struck out more than 200 batters, en route to 2,303 lifetime K's. He recorded 52 career shutouts. He was a 10-time All-Star and was the game's MVP in 1965.

Marichal is remembered for his distinctive, high leg kick, described by sportswriter Ron Bellamy: "The symbol of his artistry … was the windup, with the high, graceful kick that left the San Francisco Giant hurler poised precariously on one leg like a bronzed Nureyev before he swept smoothly forward and propelled the baseball toward the plate."

JUAN ANTONIO
MARICHAL SANCHEZ
SAN FRANCISCO N. L., 1960-1973 BOSTON A L. 1974
LOS ANGELES N. L., 1975
HIGH-KICKING RIGHT-HANDER FROM DOMINICAN
REPUBLIC WON 243 GAMES AND LOST ONLY 142
OVER 16 SEASONS. WON 20 GAMES SIX TIMES AND
NO-HIT HOUSTON IN 1963. LED N.L. IN COMPLETE
GAMES AND SHUTOUTS TWICE AND IN ERA WITH
2.10 IN 1969. COMPLETED 244 GAMES DURING
CAREER, STRIKING OUT 2,303 AND FINISHING
WITH 2.89 ERA.

The Dominican Dandy

Elected To The Hall Of Fame: 1983.
Born: Oct. 20, 1937 in Laguna Verda, Monte Cristi, Dominican Republic.
Height: 6-0. **Weight:** 185.
Threw: Right. **Batted:** Right.
Debut: July 19, 1960.
Final Game: April 16, 1975.
Teams: San Francisco N.L. 1960-1973;
Boston A.L. 1974; Los Angeles N.L. 1975.
Postseason: N.L. Pennant (1962).
Awards: 10-Time All-Star (1962-1969, 1971).

YEAR	TEAM	LEAGUE	G	W	L	SV	SH	IP	H	BB	SO	ERA
1960	SAN FRANCISCO	NL	11	6	2	0	1	81.3	59	28	58	2.66
1961	SAN FRANCISCO	NL	29	13	10	0	3	185	183	48	124	3.89
1962	SAN FRANCISCO	NL	37	18	11	1	3	262.7	233	90	153	3.36
1963	SAN FRANCISCO	NL	41	25	8	0	5	321.3	259	61	248	2.41
1964	SAN FRANCISCO	NL	33	21	8	0	4	269	241	52	206	2.48
1965	SAN FRANCISCO	NL	39	22	13	1	10	295.3	224	46	240	2.13
1966	SAN FRANCISCO	NL	37	25	6	0	4	307.3	228	36	222	2.23
1967	SAN FRANCISCO	NL	26	14	10	0	2	202.3	195	42	166	2.76
1968	SAN FRANCISCO	NL	38	26	9	0	5	325.7	295	46	218	2.43
1969	SAN FRANCISCO	NL	37	21	11	0	8	299.7	244	54	205	2.10
1970	SAN FRANCISCO	NL	34	12	10	0	1	242.7	269	48	123	4.12
1971	SAN FRANCISCO	NL	37	18	11	0	4	279	244	56	159	2.94
1972	SAN FRANCISCO	NL	25	6	16	0	0	165	176	46	72	3.71
1973	SAN FRANCISCO	NL	34	11	15	0	2	207.3	231	37	87	3.82
1974	BOSTON	AL	11	5	1	0	0	57.3	61	14	21	4.87
1975	LOS ANGELES	NL	2	0	1	0	0	6	11	5	1	13.50
CAREER TOTALS			**471**	**243**	**142**	**2**	**52**	**3507**	**3153**	**709**	**2303**	**2.89**

RUBE MARQUARD

"Any hitter can hit a fast one," Rube Marquard said. "But not many can hit slow ones."

It didn't much matter what Marquard threw in his 18-year career, batters had trouble hitting it. He won 201 games and had 1,593 strikeouts, the third most by a left-hander when he retired in 1925.

Marquard's baseball career would never have even happened if his father had gotten his way. Fred Marquard was an engineer for the city of Cleveland and told his son if he played professional baseball he wouldn't be allowed to return home.

Marquard's major league career began in 1908 when the New York Giants purchased his contract from Indianapolis for the then-record price of $11,000. He became known as the "$11,000 Beauty" and made his debut at the age of 21. But Marquard did not live up to the lofty expectations his price placed on him, winning just nine games in his first two full seasons with the Giants and he became known as the "$11,000 Lemon."

In 1911, however, his potential was finally realized, as he won 24 games and led the National League with 237 strikeouts. That season started a three-year run of success for both Marquard and the Giants. He won at least 20 games and helped the team to the World Series each year. Marquard began the 1912 season winning 19-straight decisions, a modern era record. He finished the year with 26 victories and added two more in the World Series, though New York lost to Boston.

With the success came increased fame for Marquard. He married vaudeville star Blossom Seeley, and the two performed their act across the country. He won 23 games in 1913 and in 1915 threw a no-hitter. Later in 1915 he was sold to Brooklyn, where he pitched for the next six years. He posted a career-best 1.58 ERA in 1916 and appeared in two more World Series, though he still was unable to win a championship.

Marquard's career ended in 1925 with the Boston Braves. He was known for his fastball and his control, which made him very difficult to hit when he was at his peak.

RICHARD WILLIAM MARQUARD
"RUBE"
NEW YORK N.L., BROOKLYN N.L.,
CINCINNATI N.L., BOSTON N.L.,
1908 - 1925
THREE-TIME 20-GAME WINNER WITH
GIANT CHAMPIONS OF 1911-12-13. TIED ALL-TIME
RECORD WITH 19 VICTORIES IN A ROW WHILE
WINNING 26 AND LOSING 11 IN 1912. LED
N.L. IN WINNING PERCENTAGE AND
STRIKEOUTS IN 1911. TIED FOR MOST
VICTORIES, 1912. HURLED NO-HIT GAME
AGAINST DODGERS IN 1915.

Elected To The Hall Of Fame: 1971.
Born: Oct. 9, 1886 in Cleveland, Ohio.
Died: June 1, 1980 in Baltimore, Md.
Height: 6-3. **Weight:** 180.
Threw: Left. **Batted:** Both.
Debut: Sept. 25, 1908.
Final Game: Sept. 18, 1925.
Teams: New York N.L. 1908-1915; Brooklyn N.L. 1915-1920; Cincinnati N.L. 1921; Boston N.L. 1922-1925.
Postseason: 5 N.L. Pennants (1911-1913, 1916, 1920).

YEAR	TEAM	LEAGUE	G	W	L	SV	SH	IP	H	BB	SO	ERA
1908	NEW YORK	NL	1	0	1	0	0	5	6	2	2	3.60
1909	NEW YORK	NL	29	5	13	1	0	173	155	73	109	2.60
1910	NEW YORK	NL	13	4	4	0	0	70.7	65	40	52	4.46
1911	NEW YORK	NL	45	24	7	3	5	277.7	221	106	237	2.50
1912	NEW YORK	NL	43	26	11	1	1	294.7	286	80	175	2.57
1913	NEW YORK	NL	42	23	10	3	4	288	248	49	151	2.50
1914	NEW YORK	NL	39	12	22	2	4	268	261	47	92	3.06
1915	NEW YORK/BROOKLYN	NL	33	11	10	3	2	193.7	207	38	92	4.04
1916	BROOKLYN	NL	36	13	6	5	2	205	169	38	107	1.58
1917	BROOKLYN	NL	37	19	12	0	2	232.7	200	60	117	2.55
1918	BROOKLYN	NL	34	9	18	0	4	239	231	59	89	2.64
1919	BROOKLYN	NL	8	3	3	0	0	59	54	10	29	2.29
1920	BROOKLYN	NL	28	10	7	0	1	189.7	181	35	89	3.23
1921	CINCINNATI	NL	39	17	14	0	2	265.7	291	50	88	3.39
1922	BOSTON	NL	39	11	15	1	0	198	255	66	57	5.09
1923	BOSTON	NL	38	11	14	0	3	239	265	65	78	3.73
1924	BOSTON	NL	6	1	2	0	0	36	33	13	10	3.00
1925	BOSTON	NL	26	2	8	0	0	72	105	27	19	5.75
CAREER TOTALS			**536**	**201**	**177**	**19**	**30**	**3306.2**	**3233**	**858**	**1593**	**3.08**

EDDIE MATHEWS

"I've only known three or four perfect swings in my time," said Hall of Famer Ty Cobb. "This lad has one of them."

The "lad" the Georgia Peach was referring to was Eddie Mathews, who became one of the best third baseman the game has ever known. During a 17-year big league career (1952-68), spent mostly with the Braves, the hot corner star not only possessed a rocket arm and a gift for fielding, but the lefty swinger was a feared slugger who became only the seventh player to reach the 500 home run plateau.

"Mathews is the most dangerous hitter in baseball today," was the assessment of Hall of Famer Rogers Hornsby way back in 1954. "And he's going to get better because he wants to learn, because he's always asking questions. He's got power and he's got rhythm, along with a fine level swing. Those big, powerful, awkward guys you see around who can bust a ball a mile are as good now as they'll ever be. Mathews is different. He's loose, limber and coordinated. He'll be a star when most of the guys competing with him now aren't even remembered."

Mathews, the only member of the Braves to have played with the franchise while it called Boston, Milwaukee and Atlanta home, teamed up with Hank Aaron to form one of baseball's most feared pair of homer-hitting teammates (hitting 863 while playing together). The two led the Braves to a pair of classic World Series appearances against the Yankees (1957-58), both going seven games, bringing a title to Milwaukee in 1957.

"At the start, Hank wasn't the home run hitter he ended up to be," Mathews said. "I was two years ahead of him but we were both starry-eyed kids. Later it became a friendly rivalry. It wasn't that we tried to hit home runs because I don't think you can. But we were in our own little competition."

Mathews finished with 512 homers, including a streak of more than 30 nine years in a row, and his 47 in 1953 established a single-season record for third basemen that would last almost 30 years. When he retired he also held the big league third base records for games (2,181), assists (4,322) and chances (6,371).

"The one thing I'm proudest of is that every day I played," Mathews said, "I gave the best I had."

EDWIN LEE MATHEWS
BOSTON N.L., MILWAUKEE N.L., ATLANTA N.L., HOUSTON N.L., DETROIT A.L., 1952-1968
BECAME SEVENTH PLAYER IN MAJOR LEAGUE HISTORY TO HIT 500 HOME RUNS. FINISHED CAREER WITH 512. HIT 30 OR MORE HOMERS NINE YEARS IN ROW, 1953-1961, REACHING 40 MARK FOUR TIMES. ESTABLISHED RECORD FOR HOMERS IN SEASON BY THIRD BASEMAN WITH 47 IN 1953. LED N.L. IN HOME RUNS TWICE AND IN WALKS FOUR TIMES. HAD FIVE SEASONS OF 100 OR MORE RUNS BATTED IN.

Elected To The Hall Of Fame: 1978.

Born: Oct. 13, 1931 in Texarkana, Texas.

Died: Feb. 18, 2001 in La Jolla, Calif.

Height: 6-1. Weight: 190.

Threw: Right. Batted: Left.

Debut: April 15, 1952.

Final Game: Sept. 27, 1968.

Teams: Boston N.L. 1952; Milwaukee N.L. 1953-1965; Atlanta N.L. 1966; Houston N.L. 1967; Detroit A.L. 1967-1968.

Postseason: 2-Time World Series Champion (1957, 1968); 2 N.L. Pennants (1957-1958) 1 A.L. Pennant 1968).

Awards: 9-Time All-Star (1953, 1955-1962).

YEAR	TEAM	LEAGUE	G	AB	R	H	2B	3B	HR	RBI	SB	AVG
1952	BOSTON	NL	145	528	80	128	23	5	25	58	6	.242
1953	MILWAUKEE	NL	157	579	110	175	31	8	47	135	1	.302
1954	MILWAUKEE	NL	138	476	96	138	21	4	40	103	10	.290
1955	MILWAUKEE	NL	141	499	108	144	23	5	41	101	3	.289
1956	MILWAUKEE	NL	151	552	103	150	21	2	37	95	6	.272
1957	MILWAUKEE	NL	148	572	109	167	28	9	32	94	3	.292
1958	MILWAUKEE	NL	149	546	97	137	18	1	31	77	5	.251
1959	MILWAUKEE	NL	148	594	118	182	16	8	46	114	2	.306
1960	MILWAUKEE	NL	153	548	108	152	19	7	39	124	7	.277
1961	MILWAUKEE	NL	152	572	103	175	23	6	32	91	12	.306
1962	MILWAUKEE	NL	152	536	106	142	25	6	29	90	4	.265
1963	MILWAUKEE	NL	158	547	82	144	27	4	23	84	3	.263
1964	MILWAUKEE	NL	141	502	83	117	19	1	23	74	2	.233
1965	MILWAUKEE	NL	156	546	77	137	23	0	32	95	1	.251
1966	ATLANTA	NL	134	452	72	113	21	4	16	53	1	.250
1967	HOUSTON/DETROIT	NL/AL	137	436	53	103	16	2	16	57	2	.236
1968	DETROIT	AL	31	52	4	11	0	0	3	8	0	.212
CAREER TOTALS			**2391**	**8537**	**1509**	**2315**	**354**	**72**	**512**	**1453**	**68**	**.271**

CHRISTY MATHEWSON

"Mathewson was the greatest pitcher who ever lived," said Hall of Fame manager Connie Mack.

Christy Mathewson was the first great pitching star of the modern era, and is still the standard by which greatness is measured. He changed the way people perceived baseball players by his actions on and off the field. His combination of power and poise remains baseball's ideal.

Mathewson attended Bucknell University and played on the basketball, baseball and football teams. He signed in 1899 – a rarity for a college-educated player in that era – and in 1900 went from the New York Giants to the Cincinnati Reds and back to the Giants in a round of deals that included a trade for future Hall of Fame pitcher Amos Rusie.

Using his famous "fadeaway" pitch – what today would be called a screwball – the 6-foot-1, 195-pound right-hander baffled batters with pinpoint control. He won 20 games in his first full big league season in 1901, posted at least 30 wins a season from 1903-1905, and led the National League in strikeouts five times between 1903 and 1908.

He set a modern-era record for wins by an NL pitcher with 37 in 1908, a year when he completed 34 of his 44 starts en route to more than 390 innings pitched. From 1903-14, Mathewson never won fewer than 22 games in a season and led the NL in ERA five times. In the postseason, Mathewson pitched three shutouts in three starts in the 1905 World Series.

"He could pitch into a tin cup," said Hall of Fame second baseman Johnny Evers.

As his career wound down, Mathewson was traded back to the Reds in 1916, finishing his career in a matchup against longtime rival "Three Finger" Brown. Mathewson finished with 373 wins against 188 losses – a figure that leaves him tied with Grover Cleveland Alexander for the most wins in NL history.

In 1918, Mathewson enlisted in the Army during World War I. While serving as a captain in France, he was accidentally gassed during a training exercise. He spent the next seven years battling tuberculosis and died on Oct. 7, 1925.

CHRISTY MATHEWSON
NEW YORK, N.L., 1900-1916,
CINCINNATI, N.L., 1916.
BORN FACTORYVILLE, PA., AUGUST 12, 1880
GREATEST OF ALL THE GREAT PITCHERS
IN THE 20TH CENTURY'S FIRST QUARTER
PITCHED 3 SHUTOUTS IN 1905 WORLD SERIES.
FIRST PITCHER OF THE CENTURY EVER TO
WIN 30 GAMES IN 3 SUCCESSIVE YEARS.
WON 37 GAMES IN 1908
"MATTY WAS MASTER OF THEM ALL"

Big Six

Elected To The Hall Of Fame: 1936.
Born: Aug. 12, 1880 in Factoryville, Pa.
Died: Oct. 7, 1925 in Saranac Lake, N.Y.
Height: 6-1. **Weight:** 195.
Threw: Right. **Batted:** Right.
Debut: July 17, 1900.
Final Game: Sept. 4, 1916.
Teams: New York N.L. 1900-1916;
Cincinnati N.L. 1916.
Postseason: World Series Champion
(1905); 4 N.L. Pennants (1905, 1911-1913).

YEAR	TEAM	LEAGUE	G	W	L	SV	SH	IP	H	BB	SO	ERA
1900	NEW YORK	NL	6	0	3	0	0	33.7	37	20	15	5.08
1901	NEW YORK	NL	40	20	17	0	5	336	288	97	221	2.41
1902	NEW YORK	NL	35	14	17	0	8	284.7	246	77	164	2.12
1903	NEW YORK	NL	45	30	13	2	3	366.3	321	100	267	2.26
1904	NEW YORK	NL	48	33	12	1	4	367.7	306	78	212	2.03
1905	NEW YORK	NL	43	31	9	3	8	338.7	252	64	206	1.28
1906	NEW YORK	NL	38	22	12	1	6	266.7	262	77	128	2.97
1907	NEW YORK	NL	41	24	12	2	8	315	250	53	178	2.00
1908	NEW YORK	NL	56	37	11	5	11	390.7	281	42	259	1.43
1909	NEW YORK	NL	37	25	6	2	8	275.3	192	36	149	1.14
1910	NEW YORK	NL	38	27	9	0	2	318.3	292	60	184	1.89
1911	NEW YORK	NL	45	26	13	3	5	307	303	38	141	1.99
1912	NEW YORK	NL	43	23	12	5	0	310	311	34	134	2.12
1913	NEW YORK	NL	40	25	11	2	4	306	291	21	93	2.06
1914	NEW YORK	NL	41	24	13	2	5	312	314	23	80	3.00
1915	NEW YORK	NL	27	8	14	0	1	186	199	20	57	3.58
1916	NEW YORK/CINCINNATI	NL	13	4	4	2	1	74.7	74	8	19	3.01
CAREER TOTALS			636	373	188	30	79	4788.2	4219	848	2507	2.13

WILLIE MAYS

"If somebody came up and hit .450, stole 100 bases and performed a miracle in the field every day I'd still look you in the eye and say Willie was better. He could do the five things you have to do to be a superstar: hit, hit with power, run, throw, and field. And he had that other magic ingredient that turns a superstar into a super superstar. He lit up the room. He was a joy to be around," said Hall of Famer Leo Durocher of Willie Mays.

At age 16, Mays joined the Birmingham Barons of the Negro American League. The New York Giants purchased his contract in 1950, and he was in center field at the Polo Grounds soon thereafter. Mays started off slowly, but got untracked and won the NL Rookie of the Year award, helping the Giants erase a 13-game deficit to tie the Dodgers at the end of the 1951 regular season.

He spent most of 1952 and all of 1953 in the Army, but in 1954, Mays showed his all-around ability, leading the league with a .345 batting average and 13 triples, while blasting 41 homers and ringing up 110 runs batted in. The Giants again won the pennant, and in the World Series, faced the Cleveland Indians, winners of an AL-record 111 games. With Game 1 tied 2-2 in the top of the eighth, runners on first and second, and no outs, Vic Wertz hit a towering drive that would have been a home run in most parks. Mays, playing shallow, took off and ran with his back to the ball, caught it over the shoulder an estimated 460 feet from the plate, turned, and fired. Larry Doby, who had to turn back and tag up at second base, was forced to stop at third. The Giants went on to win the game and sweep the Series. "The Catch" is considered by many to be the greatest defensive play ever.

Mays played 21 seasons with the Giants, and finished up with the Mets in 1972 and 1973. He hit over .300 10 times, en route to a career .302 mark. He was a two-time NL MVP (1954 and 1965), and a 20-time All-Star. He led the league in home runs four times, finishing with 660 — then the second most ever.

WILLIE HOWARD MAYS, JR.
"THE SAY HEY KID"
NEW YORK N.L., SAN FRANCISCO N.L.,
NEW YORK N.L., 1951 - 1973
ONE OF BASEBALL'S MOST COLORFUL AND EXCITING STARS. EXCELLED IN ALL PHASES OF THE GAME. THIRD IN HOMERS (660), RUNS (2,062) AND TOTAL BASES (6,066); SEVENTH IN HITS (3,283) AND RBI'S (1,903). FIRST IN PUTOUTS BY OUTFIELDER (7,095). FIRST TO TOP BOTH 300 HOMERS AND 300 STEALS. LED LEAGUE IN BATTING ONCE, SLUGGING FIVE TIMES, HOME RUNS AND STEALS FOUR SEASONS. VOTED N.L. MVP IN 1954 AND 1965. PLAYED IN 24 ALL-STAR GAMES - A RECORD.

The Say Hey Kid

Elected To The Hall Of Fame: 1979.
Born: May 6, 1931 in Westfield, Ala.
Height: 5-10. **Weight:** 170.
Threw: Right. **Batted:** Right.
Debut: May 25, 1951. **Final Game:** Sept. 9, 1973.
Teams: Negro Leagues 1948; Birmingham; New York (Giants) N.L. 1951-1952, 1954-1957; San Francisco N.L. 1958-1972; New York (Mets) N.L. 1972-1973.
Postseason: World Series Champion (1954); 4 N.L. Pennants (1951, 1954, 1962, 1973); 5-Time Playoff Qualifier (1951, 1954, 1962, 1971, 1973).
Awards: 20-Time All-Star (1954-1973); N.L. Rookie of the Year (1951); 2-Time N.L. Most Valuable Player (1954,1965).

YEAR	TEAM	LEAGUE	G	AB	R	H	2B	3B	HR	RBI	SB	AVG
1948	BIRMINGHAM	NAL	—	61	9	16	2	0	0	—	0	.262
1951	NEW YORK	NL	121	464	59	127	22	5	20	68	7	.274
1952	NEW YORK	NL	34	127	17	30	2	4	4	23	4	.236
1954	NEW YORK	NL	151	565	119	195	33	13	41	110	8	.345
1955	NEW YORK	NL	152	580	123	185	18	13	51	127	24	.319
1956	NEW YORK	NL	152	578	101	171	27	8	36	84	40	.296
1957	NEW YORK	NL	152	585	112	195	26	20	35	97	38	.333
1958	SAN FRANCISCO	NL	152	600	121	208	33	11	29	96	31	.347
1959	SAN FRANCISCO	NL	151	575	125	180	43	5	34	104	27	.313
1960	SAN FRANCISCO	NL	153	595	107	190	29	12	29	103	25	.319
1961	SAN FRANCISCO	NL	154	572	129	176	32	3	40	123	18	.308
1962	SAN FRANCISCO	NL	162	621	130	189	36	5	49	141	18	.304
1963	SAN FRANCISCO	NL	157	596	115	187	32	7	38	103	8	.314
1964	SAN FRANCISCO	NL	157	578	121	171	21	9	47	111	19	.296
1965	SAN FRANCISCO	NL	157	558	118	177	21	3	52	112	9	.317
1966	SAN FRANCISCO	NL	152	552	99	159	29	4	37	103	5	.288
1967	SAN FRANCISCO	NL	141	486	83	128	22	2	22	70	6	.263
1968	SAN FRANCISCO	NL	148	498	84	144	20	5	23	79	12	.289
1969	SAN FRANCISCO	NL	117	403	64	114	17	3	13	58	6	.283
1970	SAN FRANCISCO	NL	139	478	94	139	15	2	28	83	5	.291
1971	SAN FRANCISCO	NL	136	417	82	113	24	5	18	61	23	.271
1972	SAN FRANCISCO/NEW YORK	NL	88	244	35	61	11	1	8	22	4	.250
1973	NEW YORK	NL	66	209	24	44	10	0	6	25	1	.211
MLB CAREER TOTALS			**2992**	**10881**	**2062**	**3283**	**523**	**140**	**660**	**1903**	**338**	**.302**

BILL MAZEROSKI

Hall of Famer George Sisler said of Bill Mazeroski, "He is one of the greatest second baseman I've ever seen. He has all the tools and he has the desire." Signed by the legendary Branch Rickey as a 17-year-old shortstop in 1954, Mazeroski was moved over to the other side of the second base bag after only one season of pro ball, and by his 20th birthday he was the Pittsburgh Pirates' regular second baseman.

Bill Mazeroski is widely regarded as one of the best fielders the game has ever seen, at any position. Not only could he make the routine plays, but he could make plays no one else could and could make them look routine. Teammate Vern Law said, "Maz would constantly come up with balls we thought were base hits. You're running over to back up a base and here Maz has got the ball and he's throwing that hitter out." Bill Virdon recalled what it was like playing behind him in center field. "The impressive thing about Maz was that he did everything at second base. I backed him up for six years and never got a ball," Virdon said.

Although Mazeroski was never tremendous with the bat, he did enough, and his spectacular defense led him to eight Gold Glove Awards and 10 All-Star Game selections in seven years. Teammate Bob Friend recalled, "He was one of a kind out there. Maz did so many things that never showed up in a box score."

Even though he wasn't a big run producer, Mazeroski's glove saved his team a lot of runs. As Maz put it, "Over 17 years, saving thousands of runs is like driving in thousands of runs. It's the same thing. So, what's the difference?"

For someone known for his glove, it was with his bat that Maz left perhaps his most indelible mark on the game. It was the bottom of the ninth inning of Game 7 of the 1960 World Series, a series in which the Pirates had been outscored in the first six games 46-17. Mazeroski led off the ninth inning of a 9-9 tie and took a 1-0 pitch from Ralph Terry over the left-field wall. That home run won the Pirates their first World Series in 35 years and was the first walk-off series-ending home run in World Series history. Mazeroski recalled years later, "Hell, I thought it would be just another hit to win a ballgame … It's bigger now, I think."

Maz

Elected To The Hall Of Fame: *2001.*
Born: *Sept. 5, 1936 in Wheeling, W. Va.*
Height: *5-11.* **Weight:** *183.*
Threw: *Right.* **Batted:** *Right.*
Debut: *July 7, 1956.*
Final Game: *Oct. 4, 1972.*
Teams: *Pittsburgh N.L. 1956-1972.*
Postseason: *2-Time World Series Champion (1960, 1971); 2 N.L. Pennants (1960, 1971); 4-Time Playoff Qualifier (1960, 1970-1972).*
Awards: *7-Time All-Star (1958-1960, 1962-1964, 1967).*

YEAR	TEAM	LEAGUE	G	AB	R	H	2B	3B	HR	RBI	SB	AVG
1956	PITTSBURGH	NL	81	255	30	62	8	1	3	14	0	.243
1957	PITTSBURGH	NL	148	526	59	149	27	7	8	54	3	.283
1958	PITTSBURGH	NL	152	567	69	156	24	6	19	68	1	.275
1959	PITTSBURGH	NL	135	493	50	119	15	6	7	59	1	.241
1960	PITTSBURGH	NL	151	538	58	147	21	5	11	64	4	.273
1961	PITTSBURGH	NL	152	558	71	148	21	2	13	59	2	.265
1962	PITTSBURGH	NL	159	572	55	155	24	9	14	81	0	.271
1963	PITTSBURGH	NL	142	534	43	131	22	3	8	52	2	.245
1964	PITTSBURGH	NL	162	601	66	161	22	8	10	64	1	.268
1965	PITTSBURGH	NL	130	494	52	134	17	1	6	54	2	.271
1966	PITTSBURGH	NL	162	621	56	163	22	7	16	82	4	.262
1967	PITTSBURGH	NL	163	639	62	167	25	3	9	77	1	.261
1968	PITTSBURGH	NL	143	506	36	127	18	2	3	42	3	.251
1969	PITTSBURGH	NL	67	227	13	52	7	1	3	25	1	.229
1970	PITTSBURGH	NL	112	367	29	84	14	0	7	39	2	.229
1971	PITTSBURGH	NL	70	193	17	49	3	1	1	16	0	.254
1972	PITTSBURGH	NL	34	64	3	12	4	0	0	3	0	.188
CAREER TOTALS			**2163**	**7755**	**769**	**2016**	**294**	**62**	**138**	**853**	**27**	**.260**

TOMMY MCCARTHY

"Until he died, Hugh Duffy charitably deflected praise for his past accomplishments by frequently maintaining that Tommy McCarthy was the best outfielder he ever saw, high praise indeed," Richard Johnson wrote in his dual biography of Hall of Fame teammates McCarthy and Duffy.

McCarthy is most famous for his time with the Boston Beaneaters, when he teamed up with Duffy to form the "Heavenly Twins" from 1892-1895. McCarthy and Duffy were close friends and won two National League titles together.

McCarthy is given credit for developing the hit-and-run while playing with the Beaneaters. He also is heralded as a pioneer in trapping balls in the outfield in an effort to trick opposing base runners and was known as a smart player, helping to change the game into more of a thinking-man's game.

"The best man in the business at the trapped-ball trick was Tommy McCarthy," Giants manager John McGraw said. "He had the play down pat, and on more than one occasion saved his team by resorting to it."

McCarthy is the only member of the Hall of Fame to have played in the short-lived Union Association, where he began his professional career as a 19-year-old with the Boston Reds in 1884. McCarthy moved into the National League with the Beaneaters the next season, but hit just .182 in 40 games.

McCarthy's career began to take off in 1888 when he moved to the St. Louis Browns of the American Association. In four seasons with the Browns, McCarthy hit .306 and twice led baseball in plate appearances.

In 1892, McCarthy returned to his hometown of Boston and the Beaneaters to form the "Heavenly Twins." In the four years he and Duffy played together, McCarthy proved to be one of the game's best players. In 1894 he set career highs for home runs (13), RBI (126) and slugging percentage (.490).

McCarthy finished with the Brooklyn Bridegrooms in 1896. He ended his 13-year career with a .292 batting average and 732 RBI.

THOMAS F. McCARTHY
ONE OF BOSTON'S "HEAVENLY TWINS" UNDER MANAGER FRANK SELEE. OUTSTANDING BASE RUNNER WHO STOLE 109 BASES FOR THE BROWNS IN 1888. PIONEER IN TRAPPING FLY BALLS IN THE OUTFIELD. HOLDS N.L. RECORD FOR ASSISTS IN OUTFIELD-53 WITH BOSTON IN 1893. PLAYED 1268 GAMES IN MAJOR LEAGUES.

Elected To The Hall Of Fame: 1946.
Born: July 24, 1863 in Boston, Mass.
Died: Aug. 5, 1922 in Boston, Mass.
Height: 5-7. **Weight:** 170.
Threw: Right. **Batted:** Right.
Debut: July 10, 1884.
Final Game: Sept. 26, 1896.
Teams: Boston, Union Association 1884; Boston N.L. 1885, 1892-1895; Philadelphia N.L. 1886-1887; St. Louis, American Association 1888-1891; Brooklyn N.L. 1896.
Postseason: American Association Pennant (1888); Championship Series Champion (1892).

YEAR	TEAM	LEAGUE	G	AB	R	H	2B	3B	HR	RBI	SB	AVG
1884	BOSTON	UA	53	209	37	45	2	2	0	0	NA	.215
1885	BOSTON	NL	40	148	16	27	2	0	0	11	NA	.182
1886	PHILADELPHIA	NL	8	27	6	5	2	1	0	3	1	.185
1887	PHILADELPHIA	NL	18	70	7	13	4	0	0	6	15	.186
1888	ST. LOUIS	AA	131	511	107	140	20	3	1	68	93	.274
1889	ST. LOUIS	AA	140	604	136	176	24	7	2	63	57	.291
1890	ST. LOUIS	AA	133	548	137	192	28	9	6	69	83	.350
1891	ST. LOUIS	AA	134	570	124	176	20	6	8	92	37	.309
1892	BOSTON	NL	152	603	119	146	19	5	4	63	53	.242
1893	BOSTON	NL	116	462	107	160	28	6	5	111	46	.346
1894	BOSTON	NL	127	539	118	188	21	8	13	126	43	.349
1895	BOSTON	NL	117	452	90	131	13	2	2	73	18	.290
1896	BROOKLYN	NL	104	377	62	94	8	4	3	47	22	.249
CAREER TOTALS			**1273**	**5120**	**1066**	**1493**	**191**	**53**	**44**	**732**	**468**	**.292**

WILLIE McCOVEY

"Here's a guy who is the most feared in baseball, but everyone pitches around him. If you let him bat 600 times and pitched to him instead of around him, he'd hit 80 home runs," said Hall of Fame manager Sparky Anderson.

The San Francisco Giants gave opponents "The Willies" from 1959-72, when Willie Mays and Willie "Stretch" McCovey comprised the core of their offensive attack. McCovey, a fellow native of the Mobile, Ala., area, joined Mays and the Giants in 1959. Like Mays, McCovey won Rookie of the Year honors, batting .354, hitting 13 home runs and driving in 38 runs in just 52 games.

"He could hit a ball farther than anyone I ever played with," said Mays.

In 1963, McCovey won the first of three NL home run crowns, knocking 44 – the number he wore on his jersey – over the fence. He would belt 521 long balls for his career, and chalk up 18 grand slams, at the time second only to Lou Gehrig's 23. In 1962, the Giants returned to New York to take on the Yankees in a thrilling, seven-game World Series. With the Giants trailing 1-0 in Game 7, McCovey was at bat with two outs in the bottom of the ninth, and runners on second and third. McCovey slashed what looked like a Series-winning hit to the left of Yankee second baseman Bobby Richardson – but he caught the ball. The moment was so stunning it was immortalized in a "Peanuts" comic strip by Charles Schulz.

By the late 1960s, McCovey was one of the premier power hitters in the NL, leading the league in homers and RBI in 1968 and '69, and in slugging percentage from 1968-70. He was the NL MVP in 1969. He spent three seasons with the Padres and had a short stint with Oakland before returning to the Giants from 1977-80. A six-time All-Star and a skilled defensive first baseman, McCovey quietly played most of his career with knee, hip and foot injuries that would hobble many other players.

"I'm not afraid of any pitcher," said McCovey. "I've been pitched almost every way, and I've hit every kind of pitch. There wasn't much else to do in Mobile."

WILLIE LEE MC COVEY
"STRETCH"
SAN FRANCISCO, N.L., 1959 - 1973, 1977 - 1980
SAN DIEGO, N.L., 1974 - 1976
OAKLAND, A.L., 1976
TOP LEFT-HANDED HOME RUN HITTER IN N.L. HISTORY WITH 521. SECOND ONLY TO LOU GEHRIG WITH 18 CAREER GRAND SLAMS. LED N.L. IN HOMERS THREE TIMES AND RBI'S TWICE. N.L. ROOKIE OF YEAR IN 1959, MVP IN 1969 AND COMEBACK PLAYER OF THE YEAR IN '77 TEAMED WITH WILLIE MAYS FOR AWESOME 1-2 PUNCH IN GIANTS' LINEUP.

Stretch

Elected To The Hall Of Fame: 1986.
Born: Jan. 10, 1938 in Mobile, Ala.
Height: 6-4. **Weight:** 198.
Threw: Left. **Batted:** Left.
Debut: July 30, 1959.
Final Game: July 6, 1980.
Teams: San Francisco N.L. 1959-1973, 1977-1980; San Diego N.L. 1974-1976; Oakland A.L. 1976.
Postseason: N.L. Pennant (1962).
Awards: 6-Time All-Star (1963, 1966, 1968-1971); N.L. Rookie of the Year (1959); N.L. Most Valuable Player (1969).

YEAR	TEAM	LEAGUE	G	AB	R	H	2B	3B	HR	RBI	SB	AVG
1959	SAN FRANCISCO	NL	52	192	32	68	9	5	13	38	2	.354
1960	SAN FRANCISCO	NL	101	260	37	62	15	3	13	51	1	.238
1961	SAN FRANCISCO	NL	106	328	59	89	12	3	18	50	1	.271
1962	SAN FRANCISCO	NL	91	229	41	67	6	1	20	54	3	.293
1963	SAN FRANCISCO	NL	152	564	103	158	19	5	44	102	1	.280
1964	SAN FRANCISCO	NL	130	364	55	80	14	1	18	54	2	.220
1965	SAN FRANCISCO	NL	160	540	93	149	17	4	39	92	0	.276
1966	SAN FRANCISCO	NL	150	502	85	148	26	6	36	96	2	.295
1967	SAN FRANCISCO	NL	135	456	73	126	17	4	31	91	3	.276
1968	SAN FRANCISCO	NL	148	523	81	153	16	4	36	105	4	.293
1969	SAN FRANCISCO	NL	149	491	101	157	26	2	45	126	0	.320
1970	SAN FRANCISCO	NL	152	495	98	143	39	2	39	126	0	.289
1971	SAN FRANCISCO	NL	105	329	45	91	13	0	18	70	0	.277
1972	SAN FRANCISCO	NL	81	263	30	56	8	0	14	35	0	.213
1973	SAN FRANCISCO	NL	130	383	52	102	14	3	29	75	1	.266
1974	SAN DIEGO	NL	128	344	53	87	19	1	22	63	1	.253
1975	SAN DIEGO	NL	122	413	43	104	17	0	23	68	1	.252
1976	SAN DIEGO/OAKLAND	NL/AL	82	226	20	46	9	0	7	36	0	.204
1977	SAN FRANCISCO	NL	141	478	54	134	21	0	28	86	3	.280
1978	SAN FRANCISCO	NL	108	351	32	80	19	2	12	64	1	.228
1979	SAN FRANCISCO	NL	117	353	34	88	9	0	15	57	0	.249
1980	SAN FRANCISCO	NL	48	113	8	23	8	0	1	16	0	.204
CAREER TOTALS			**2588**	**8197**	**1229**	**2211**	**353**	**46**	**521**	**1555**	**26**	**.270**

JOE McGINNITY

"**M**cGinnity is the latest find of Manager (John) McCloskey, and to judge of his work in the game he is a jewel of the first order," the *Sporting Life* wrote in 1893. "He is a wonder and pitches a lightning ball."

While Joe McGinnity didn't reach the major leagues until he was 28 years old, once he got there he dominated. In each of his first eight seasons, McGinnity won at least 20 games and twice won more than 30. He led all of baseball in victories five times in his career and lived up to his "Iron Man" nickname as well. McGinnity averaged 344 1/3 innings a season, twice throwing more than 400 innings.

McGinnity won 28 games in each of his first two seasons, leading the National League both times. At the beginning of his career, McGinnity pitched for the Baltimore Orioles and Brooklyn Superbas, before joining the New York Giants midway through 1902.

With the Giants, McGinnity joined with Christy Mathewson to form one of the most dominant 1-2 punches in baseball history. From 1903-1908, McGinnity's last year in the major leagues, either he or Mathewson led the National League in victories.

McGinnity's best season came in 1904. That season, he led the league in wins (35), ERA (1.61), shutouts (nine), innings pitched (408) and WHIP (0.963). While he set many career bests in 1904, his career high in innings had come a year earlier, when he threw 434 innings, the third highest total in the 20th century.

Mathewson and McGinnity's dominance would produce one NL pennant, coming in 1905. McGinnity won 21 games during the regular season and added a shutout in the World Series, helping New York defeat Philadelphia, 4-1.

Though McGinnity's major league career ended when the Giants released him after the 1908 season, he continued pitching in the minor leagues until 1925 when he was 54 years old. He won another 199 games after the end of his major league career, pushing his win total in the majors and minors to more than 450.

McGinnity's "Iron Man" nickname may have come from working in a foundry in the offseason as well as pitching both ends of a doubleheader.

JOSEPH JEROME McGINNITY
"IRONMAN"
DISTINGUISHED AS THE PITCHER WHO HURLED TWO GAMES ON ONE DAY THE MOST TIMES. DID THIS ON FIVE OCCASIONS. WON BOTH GAMES THREE TIMES. PLAYED WITH BALTIMORE, BROOKLYN AND NEW YORK TEAMS IN N.L. AND BALTIMORE IN A.L. GAINED MORE THAN 200 VICTORIES DURING CAREER. RECORDED 20 OR MORE VICTORIES SEVEN TIMES. IN TWO SUCCESSIVE SEASONS WON AT LEAST 30 GAMES

Iron Man

Elected To The Hall Of Fame: 1946.
Born: March 20, 1871 in Cornwall, Ill.
Died: Nov. 14, 1929 in Brooklyn, N.Y.
Height: 5-11. **Weight:** 206.
Threw: Right. **Batted:** Right.
Debut: April 18, 1899.
Final Game: Oct. 5, 1908.
Teams: Baltimore N.L. 1899; Brooklyn N.L. 1900; Baltimore A.L. 1901-02; New York N.L. 1902-1908.
Postseason: World Series Champion (1905); 2 N.L. Pennants (1904-1905).

YEAR	TEAM	LEAGUE	G	W	L	SV	SH	IP	H	BB	SO	ERA
1899	BALTIMORE	NL	48	28	16	2	4	366.3	358	93	74	2.68
1900	BROOKLYN	NL	44	28	8	0	1	343	350	113	93	2.94
1901	BALTIMORE	AL	48	26	20	1	1	382	412	96	75	3.56
1902	BALTIMORE/NEW YORK	AL/NL	44	21	18	0	1	351.7	341	78	106	2.84
1903	NEW YORK	NL	55	31	20	2	3	434	391	109	171	2.43
1904	NEW YORK	NL	51	35	8	5	9	408	307	86	144	1.61
1905	NEW YORK	NL	46	21	15	3	2	320.3	289	71	125	2.87
1906	NEW YORK	NL	45	27	12	2	3	339.7	316	71	105	2.25
1907	NEW YORK	NL	47	18	18	4	3	310.3	320	58	120	3.16
1908	NEW YORK	NL	37	11	7	5	5	186	192	37	55	2.27
CAREER TOTALS			**465**	**246**	**142**	**24**	**32**	**3441.1**	**3276**	**812**	**1068**	**2.66**

BID McPHEE

"This glove business has gone a little too far," Bid McPhee said. "True, hot-hit balls do sting a little at the opening of the season, but after you get used to it there is no trouble on that score."

McPhee is regarded as one of the best defensive second basemen in the 19th century. For almost his entire 18-year career, McPhee took the field without benefit of a glove. He first used a glove in 1896 when he was 36 and promptly set the record for fielding percentage by second basemen.

McPhee played his whole career with the Cincinnati Reds, beginning in 1882 when the organization was a part of the American Association and called the Red Stockings. That season, McPhee helped the Red Stockings to the American Association championship and defeated the National League champions, the Chicago White Stockings, in a postseason series.

Aside from his defense, McPhee was also known for his ability to hit triples. He only once led the league in triples (19 in 1887), but he ranks 11th all-time with 189. He also stole 568 bases and scored 100 runs 10 times.

But McPhee's refusal to wear a glove may be his most remembered quality. When he finally put on a glove for the first time, *The Cincinnati Enquirer* reported it was in an attempt to protect a sore he had developed on his left hand. His fielding percentage jumped from .955 in 1895 to .978 in 1896.

After two seasons as the National League's oldest player, McPhee retired after the 1899 season. He finished with a career .272 batting average, 1,684 runs scored and a .944 fielding percentage. McPhee managed the Reds in 1901 and 1902. He died in 1943. McPhee's exploits were forgotten for much of the 20th century, but he was inducted into the Baseball Hall of Fame in 2000 by the Veterans Committee.

"He was the outstanding player of his time at his position, certainly comparable to Bill Mazeroski," baseball historian Ralph Moses said. "He was breaking records barehanded and when he put on a glove, he set a standard so high that it wasn't broken until 30 years later."

JOHN ALEXANDER McPHEE
"BID"
CINCINNATI, A.A., 1882-89
CINCINNATI, N.L., 1890-99

ONE OF THE 19TH CENTURY'S PREMIER SECOND BASEMEN, HE WAS A STANDOUT FIELDER DESPITE PLAYING BAREHANDED FOR MOST OF HIS 18-YEAR CAREER. THE LAST SECOND BASEMAN TO PLAY WITHOUT A GLOVE, HE REGULARLY LED THE LEAGUE IN DOUBLE PLAYS, FIELDING AVERAGE, ASSISTS AND PUTOUTS. PLAYING WITH A GLOVE FOR THE FIRST TIME IN 1896, HIS FIELDING AVERAGE WAS .982, A MARK THAT STOOD FOR 29 YEARS. A SKILLED LEADOFF HITTER, HE COMPILED 2,250 HITS AND TOPPED THE 100-RUN MARK 10 TIMES, INCLUDING A CAREER-BEST 139 IN 1886. KNOWN FOR HIS SOBER DISPOSITION AND EXEMPLARY SPORTSMANSHIP.

Elected To The Hall Of Fame: *2000.*
Born: *Nov. 1, 1859 in Massena, N.Y.*
Died: *Jan. 3, 1943 in San Diego, Calif.*
Height: *5-8.* **Weight:** *152.*
Threw: *Right.* **Batted:** *Right.*
Debut: *May 2, 1882.*
Final Game: *Oct. 15, 1899.*
Teams: *Cincinnati, American Association 1882-1889; Cincinnati N.L. 1890-1899.*

YEAR	TEAM	LEAGUE	G	AB	R	H	2B	3B	HR	RBI	SB	AVG
1882	CINCINNATI	AA	78	311	43	71	8	7	1	31	NA	.228
1883	CINCINNATI	AA	96	367	61	90	10	10	2	42	NA	.245
1884	CINCINNATI	AA	112	450	107	125	8	7	5	64	NA	.278
1885	CINCINNATI	AA	110	431	78	114	12	4	0	46	NA	.265
1886	CINCINNATI	AA	140	560	139	150	23	12	8	70	40	.268
1887	CINCINNATI	AA	129	540	137	156	20	19	2	87	95	.289
1888	CINCINNATI	AA	111	458	88	110	12	10	4	51	54	.240
1889	CINCINNATI	AA	135	540	109	145	25	7	5	57	63	.269
1890	CINCINNATI	NL	132	528	125	135	16	22	3	39	55	.256
1891	CINCINNATI	NL	138	562	107	144	14	16	6	38	33	.256
1892	CINCINNATI	NL	144	573	111	157	19	12	4	60	44	.274
1893	CINCINNATI	NL	127	491	101	138	17	11	3	68	25	.281
1894	CINCINNATI	NL	128	483	113	151	21	10	5	93	33	.313
1895	CINCINNATI	NL	115	432	107	129	24	12	1	75	30	.299
1896	CINCINNATI	NL	117	433	81	132	18	7	1	87	48	.305
1897	CINCINNATI	NL	81	282	45	85	13	7	1	39	9	.301
1898	CINCINNATI	NL	133	486	72	121	26	9	1	60	21	.249
1899	CINCINNATI	NL	112	377	60	105	17	7	1	65	18	.279
CAREER TOTALS			**2138**	**8304**	**1684**	**2258**	**303**	**189**	**53**	**1072**	**568**	**.272**

JOE MEDWICK

"I never cared where the strike zone was. I wasn't looking to walk. Didn't make no difference to me, high or low, inside or outside. If I liked it, I'd take my riffle. And .324 ain't too bad," said Joe Medwick

In just his second full season in the big leagues in 1934, Joe Medwick had already established himself as one of the National League's best hitters at age 22 and led the Cardinals to the World Series. Medwick opened Game 1 with four straight hits (including a home run) and went on to hit .379 in seven games against the Tigers, winning his first and only World Series ring.

A solid defensive outfielder, Medwick would go on to become one of the National League's most dangerous hitters in the 1930s. After two top-five finishes in the NL MVP race in 1935 and 1936, Medwick received the NL MVP in 1937, when he won the NL Triple Crown and also led the league in hits, runs, doubles, total bases and slugging.

Medwick could hit for average and power, leading the NL in hits twice and extra-base hits three times. He enjoyed his finest years with the Cardinals, earning six of his 10 All-Star selections with the club while playing alongside fellow future Hall of Famers Johnny Mize, Enos Slaughter, Dizzy Dean and Frankie Frisch before St. Louis traded Medwick and righthander Curt Davis to the Dodgers in 1940 in exchange for four players and cash.

Medwick spent four years with Brooklyn, recording more hits than any other Dodgers from 1940-1942 and helping carry the club to the 1941 World Series against the Yankees.

Medwick spent the latter half of his career bouncing between the Giants, Braves and Dodgers (including an All Star campaign with the Giants in 1944) before returning to the Cardinals for his final two seasons. Even as a part-time player at the end of his career, Medwick hit a combined .301 in his last three seasons.

Though Medwick could hit for power, it didn't come at the expense of his ability to put the bat to the ball, as he never struck out more than 100 times in a season. He was a well-rounded hitter, capable of going outside of the strike zone to drive in runs when needed.

JOSEPH MICHAEL MEDWICK
"DUCKY WUCKY"
ST. LOUIS N.L. 1932 TO 1940, 1947, 1948
BROOKLYN N.L. 1940 TO 1943, 1946
NEW YORK N.L. 1943 TO 1945 – BOSTON N.L. 1945
LED N.L. IN BATTING IN 1937 WITH .374
AVERAGE, BATTED .353 IN 1935, .351 IN 1936,
.332 IN 1939. LIFETIME TOTAL 2471 HITS,
BATTING AVERAGE .324. NAMED TO ALL STAR
TEAMS 1935·6·7·8·9. MOST VALUABLE PLAYER
N.L. 1937. LED N.L. IN RUNS BATTED IN
AND TWO BASE HITS 1936·7·8.
BATTED .300 OR MORE 15 TIMES.

Ducky

Elected To The Hall Of Fame: *1968.*

Born: *Nov. 24, 1911 in Carteret, N.J.*

Died: *March 21, 1975 in St. Petersburg, Fla.*

Height: *5-10.* **Weight:** *187.*

Threw: *Right.* **Batted:** *Right.*

Debut: *Sept. 2, 1932.*

Final Game: *July 25, 1948.*

Teams: *St. Louis N.L. 1932-1940, 1947-1948; Brooklyn N.L. 1940-1943, 1946; New York N.L. 1943-1945; Boston N.L. 1945.*

Postseason: *World Series Champion (1934); 2 N.L. Pennants (1934, 1941).*

Awards: *10-Time All-Star (1934-1942, 1944); N.L. Most Valuable Player (1937).*

YEAR	TEAM	LEAGUE	G	AB	R	H	2B	3B	HR	RBI	SB	AVG
1932	ST. LOUIS	NL	26	106	13	37	12	1	2	12	3	.349
1933	ST. LOUIS	NL	148	595	92	182	40	10	18	98	5	.306
1934	ST. LOUIS	NL	149	620	110	198	40	18	18	106	3	.319
1935	ST. LOUIS	NL	154	634	132	224	46	13	23	126	4	.353
1936	ST. LOUIS	NL	155	636	115	223	64	13	18	138	3	.351
1937	ST. LOUIS	NL	156	633	111	237	56	10	31	154	4	.374
1938	ST. LOUIS	NL	146	590	100	190	47	8	21	122	0	.322
1939	ST. LOUIS	NL	150	606	98	201	48	8	14	117	6	.332
1940	ST. LOUIS/BROOKLYN	NL	143	581	83	175	30	12	17	86	2	.301
1941	BROOKLYN	NL	133	538	100	171	33	10	18	88	2	.318
1942	BROOKLYN	NL	142	553	69	166	37	4	4	96	2	.300
1943	BROOKLYN/NEW YORK	NL	126	497	54	138	30	3	5	70	1	.278
1944	NEW YORK	NL	128	490	64	165	24	3	7	85	2	.337
1945	NEW YORK/BOSTON	NL	92	310	31	90	17	0	3	37	5	.290
1946	BROOKLYN	NL	41	77	7	24	4	0	2	18	0	.312
1947	ST. LOUIS	NL	75	150	19	46	12	0	4	28	0	.307
1948	ST. LOUIS	NL	20	19	0	4	0	0	0	2	0	.211
CAREER TOTALS			**1984**	**7635**	**1198**	**2471**	**540**	**113**	**205**	**1383**	**42**	**.324**

The Baseball Hall of Fame Almanac

José Méndez

I n 1912, Hall of Fame manager John McGraw said, "If (José) Mendez was a white man, I would pay $50,000 for his release from Almendares" and that Méndez was "sort of Walter Johnson and Grover Alexander rolled into one."

Although he spent his entire career playing either in Cuba, or in the Negro Leagues of North America, during his prime Méndez faced major league competition in exhibition games besting some of the game's best, including Hall of Fame pitchers Christy Mathewson and Eddie Plank. After a 1911 tour of Cuba, Philadelphia Athletics catcher Ira Thomas said, "More than one big leaguer from the states has faced him and left the plate with a wholesome respect for the great Cuban star. It is not alone my opinion but the opinion of many others who have seen Méndez pitch that he ranks with the best in the game."

Nicknamed "The Black Diamond," the Cuban-born hurler had a lean, wiry frame, with a deceptively hard fastball and a sharp curveball. He was also able to keep hitters off balance because of his ability to change speeds so well.

The high point of Méndez's pitching career may have come in 1911, pitching for Almendares against the New York Lincoln Giants for the "colored championship of the world." The game matched two of the best Negro leagues hurlers of that era — Méndez and Smokey Joe Williams. Through nine innings, Méndez gave up two hits while Williams gave up none. In the 10th inning, the Cubans scored to give Méndez a 1-0 win.

Arm trouble in 1914 forced Méndez to reinvent himself as a shortstop. Over the years Méndez played for several teams and returned to the mound from time-to-time, but it was not until the 1924 Negro Leagues World Series that Méndez's pitching arm would again feature prominently. Then a player-manager for the Kansas City Monarchs, Méndez went 2-0, with a 1.42 ERA in four pitching appearances in the series and led the Monarchs to the Negro Leagues World Series championship.

In her memoirs, Mrs. John McGraw recalled of her husband, whenever Méndez pitched against the Giants, "Without mincing words, John bemoaned the failure of baseball, himself included, to cast aside custom or unwritten law, or whatever it was, and sign a player alone, regardless of race or color."

JOSÉ DE LA CARIDAD MÉNDEZ BAEZ
"EL DIAMANTE NEGRO" "THE BLACK DIAMOND"
PRE-NEGRO LEAGUES, 1908-1919
NEGRO LEAGUES, 1920-1926
A SLENDER RIGHT-HANDED PITCHER WHO WAS ACKNOWLEDGED AS THE FIRST CUBAN-BORN BASEBALL STAR IN THE PRE-NEGRO LEAGUES ERA. UTILIZED A VAST ARRAY OF PITCHES, MAINLY RELYING ON A DECEPTIVE FASTBALL AND SHARP-BREAKING CURVE TO DOMINATE OPPOSING BATTERS. AS PLAYER-MANAGER, LED KANSAS CITY MONARCHS TO THREE CONSECUTIVE NEGRO NATIONAL LEAGUE PENNANTS, 1923-1925. CLINCHED 1924 NEGRO LEAGUES WORLD SERIES TITLE WITH THREE-HIT SHUTOUT. HURLED 25 CONSECUTIVE SHUTOUT INNINGS AGAINST THE CINCINNATI REDS DURING EXHIBITION COMPETITION IN 1908.

The Black Diamond

Elected To The Hall Of Fame: *2006.*
Born: *Jan. 2, 1885 in Cardenas,*
Matanzas, Cuba.
Died: *Nov. 6, 1928 in Havana, Cuba.*
Height: *5-8.* **Weight:** *155.*
Threw: *Right.* **Batted:** *Right.*
Teams: *Pre-Negro Leagues 1908-1919;*
Negro Leagues 1920-1926; Almendares
1907-1915; Kansas City 1917; 1920-
1926; Chicago American Giants 1918;
Detroit 1919.

YEAR	TEAM	LEAGUE	G	W	L	SV	SH	IP	H	BB	SO	RAVG
1907	ALMENDARES	CUGL	13	8	0	—	2	75	38	32	45	1.68
1908	ALMENDARES	CUGL/CMLS/CNCS	32	17	8	—	5	235	141	53	157	2.03
1909	ALMENDARES	CUGL/CMLS	11	9	2	—	1	102	66	22	79	2.91
1910	ALMENDARES	CUGL/CMLS/CNCS	25	16	5	—	5	199	142	56	93	2.44
1911	ALMENDARES	CUNL/CMLS	26	11	9	—	3	194.7	158	58	131	3.33
1912	ALMENDARES	CUNL/CNCS/CMLS	13	1	7	—	0	82.3	90	34	30	6.12
1913	ALMENDARES	CMLS	1	0	1	—	0	9	10	1	5	4.00
1914	ALMENDARES	CNCS	2	1	1	—	0	18	9	6	15	2.00
1915	ALMENDARES	CNCS	1	0	1	—	0	4	4	2	3	6.75
1917	KANSAS CITY	INDP	1	0	0	—	0	1.3	5	2	1	27.00
1918	CHI. AM. GIANTS	INDP	1	1	0	—	0	9	4	2	4	2.00
1919	DETROIT	INDP	7	3	0	—	1	46.3	33	4	21	2.72
1920	KANSAS CITY	NNL	—	3	1	—	0	50.7	44	8	9	4.09
1921	KANSAS CITY	NNL	—	1	0	—	0	15.7	15	1	6	5.17
1922	KANSAS CITY	NNL	—	1	2	—	0	20	30	3	13	7.65
1923	KANSAS CITY	NNL	—	11	4	—	1	129.7	132	29	57	4.51
1924	KANSAS CITY	NNL	—	7	1	—	1	65	50	10	31	3.60
1925	KANSAS CITY	NNL	—	3	2	—	0	26.7	34	5	12	7.09
1926	KANSAS CITY	NNL	—	2	2	—	0	32	36	4	13	3.09
CAREER TOTALS			—	95	46	—	19	1315.3	1041	332	725	3.32

The Baseball Hall of Fame Almanac

JOHNNY MIZE

Johnny Mize entered major league baseball in 1936, and soon took on the nickname "The Big Cat" because of the poise in his stance when he was at bat and his ease in the field.

"Did you ever see a pitcher knock him down at the plate?" Mize's Cardinals teammate Stan Musial said. "Remember how he reacted when brushed back? He'd just lean back and on his left foot, bend his body back and let the pitch go by. Then he'd lean back into the batter's box and resume his stance, as graceful as a big cat."

Mize burst onto the scene with 93 RBI in his rookie season of 1936, and in 1938 he led the National League in slugging percentage with a .614 mark, to go with a .422 on-base percentage. Mize followed it up in 1939 by winning the batting title, with a .349 average. He also led the NL in home runs with 28 and had a .444 on-base mark. In 1940, he was once again the home run leader, this time with 43, and he led the league in RBI, leaving him just one category short of a Triple Crown. He led in RBI twice more, in 1942 and 1947.

The left-handed batter was the runner-up for the NL MVP Award in both 1939 and 1940.

After a leave of absence to defend his country in World War II and a string of injuries, Mize rebounded in a big way in 1947. He launched 51 long balls and tied Ralph Kiner of the Pirates for the league lead. Mize also led the NL in RBI and runs scored, and became the first player to strike out less than 50 times while hitting more than 50 home runs.

He again tied Kiner for the home run title the following year, this time with 40 homers.

Mize joined the Yankees in 1949, winning five consecutive World Series titles with his new team. In the 1952 Fall Classic against the Brooklyn Dodgers he hit three home runs.

Mize set the career record for hitting three homers in a game, at six, a mark Sammy Sosa later tied. Mize completed his career with 359 home runs and a .312 batting average. When Mize's playing career ended, he became part of the Kansas City Athletics coaching staff in 1961.

The Big Cat

Elected To The Hall Of Fame: 1981.
Born: Jan. 7, 1913 in Demorest, Ga.
Died: June 2, 1993 in Demorest, Ga.
Height: 6-2. **Weight:** 215.
Threw: Right. **Batted:** Left.
Debut: Apr. 16, 1936.
Final Game: Sept. 26, 1953.
Teams: St. Louis N.L. 1936-1941; New York N.L. 1942, 1946-1949; New York A.L. 1949-1953.
Postseason: 5-Time World Series Champion (1949-1953); 5 A.L. Pennants (1949-1953).
Awards: 10-Time All-Star (1937, 1939-1942, 1946-1949, 1953).

YEAR	TEAM	LEAGUE	G	AB	R	H	2B	3B	HR	RBI	SB	AVG
1936	ST. LOUIS	NL	126	414	76	136	30	8	19	93	1	.329
1937	ST. LOUIS	NL	145	560	103	204	40	7	25	113	2	.364
1938	ST. LOUIS	NL	149	531	85	179	34	16	27	102	0	.337
1939	ST. LOUIS	NL	153	564	104	197	44	14	28	108	0	.349
1940	ST. LOUIS	NL	155	579	111	182	31	13	43	137	7	.314
1941	ST. LOUIS	NL	126	473	67	150	39	8	16	100	4	.317
1942	NEW YORK	NL	142	541	97	165	25	7	26	110	3	.305
1946	NEW YORK	NL	101	377	70	127	18	3	22	70	3	.337
1947	NEW YORK	NL	154	586	137	177	26	2	51	138	2	.302
1948	NEW YORK	NL	152	560	110	162	26	4	40	125	4	.289
1949	NEW YORK/NEW YORK	NL/AL	119	411	63	108	16	0	19	64	1	.263
1950	NEW YORK	AL	90	274	43	76	12	0	25	72	0	.277
1951	NEW YORK	AL	113	332	37	86	14	1	10	49	1	.259
1952	NEW YORK	AL	78	137	9	36	9	0	4	29	0	.263
1953	NEW YORK	AL	81	104	6	26	3	0	4	27	0	.250
CAREER TOTALS			**1884**	**6443**	**1118**	**2011**	**367**	**83**	**359**	**1337**	**28**	**.312**

PAUL MOLITOR

PAUL LEO MOLITOR
MILWAUKEE, A.L., 1978-1992
TORONTO, A.L., 1993-1995
MINNESOTA, A.L., 1996-1998

A REMARKABLY CONSISTENT CONTACT HITTER AND AGGRESSIVE BASE
RUNNER WITH EXTRAORDINARY INSTINCTS. ONE OF THREE PLAYERS WITH
MORE THAN 3,000 HITS, 600 DOUBLES AND 500 STEALS. A CAREER .306
HITTER, RANKS EIGHTH ALL-TIME WITH 3,319 HITS. HIT SAFELY IN 39
CONSECUTIVE GAMES IN 1987. A GREAT CLUTCH PERFORMER, AS
EVIDENCED BY HIS RECORD FIVE HITS IN GAME ONE OF THE 1982 WORLD
SERIES FOR THE BREWERS, AND WORLD SERIES MVP HONORS FOR THE
CHAMPION BLUE JAYS IN 1993. ELECTED TO SEVEN ALL-STAR TEAMS.

W hen Hall of Famer Ted Williams was asked what he saw when he watched Paul Molitor, the Splendid Splinter's response was, "I see Joe DiMaggio."

As one of the game's most unheralded stars, Paul Molitor played numerous defensive positions on the field in relative obscurity before his short, compact swing vaulted him to baseball's forefront late in his long and illustrious career.

Molitor made his big league debut as a middle infielder with the Brewers in 1978. His manager at the time, George Bamberger, said: "He has tremendous instincts and you could see right away he was a talented athlete. Not only physically, but mentally too. He played the game like he had been up here for years."

"Molly" would remain a Milwaukee fixture for 15 years, though he would switch positions, playing second base third base, outfield and designated hitter, and battle injuries throughout his tenure. In 1982, "The Ignitor" helped the Brewers to their first-ever World Series appearance, leading the league with 136 runs scored while also collecting 201 hits and batting .302.

After signing with Toronto following the 1992 season, the 37-year-old Molitor collected 111 RBI, becoming the oldest player in major league history to post his first 100-RBI season. When Toronto defeated the Phillies in six games in the 1993 World Series, Molitor was named MVP with a .500 batting average (12-for-24), two home runs and 10 runs (tying a Series record.)

After spending two more seasons with the Blue Jays, Molitor signed with his hometown Twins as a free agent. In 1996, at age 40, he batted .341, collected 113 RBI, and led the league with 225 hits, becoming the first 40-year-old since Sam Rice in 1930 to have 200 hits in a season. Molitor, a seven-time All-Star, retired following the 1998 campaign, when he became only the fifth player with at least 3,000 hits and 500 stolen bases, and only the third player (along with Ty Cobb and Honus Wagner) with at least 3,000 hits, 600 doubles and 500 stolen bases.

Molly, The Ignitor

Elected To The Hall Of Fame: *2004.*
Born: *Aug. 22, 1956 in St. Paul, Minn.*
Height: *6-0.* **Weight:** *185.*
Threw: *Right.* **Batted:** *Right.*
Debut: *Apr. 7, 1978.*
Final Game: *Sept. 27, 1998.*
Teams: *Milwaukee A.L. 1978-1992; Toronto A.L. 1993-1995; Minnesota A.L. 1996-1998.*
Postseason: *World Series Champion (1993); 2 A.L. Pennants (1982 1993); 3-Time Playoff Qualifier (1981-1982, 1993).*
Awards: *7-Time All-Star (1980, 1985, 1988, 1991-1994); World Series Most Valuable Player (1993).*

YEAR	TEAM	LEAGUE	G	AB	R	H	2B	3B	HR	RBI	SB	AVG
1978	MILWAUKEE	AL	125	521	73	142	26	4	6	45	30	.273
1979	MILWAUKEE	AL	140	584	88	188	27	16	9	62	33	.322
1980	MILWAUKEE	AL	111	450	81	137	29	2	9	37	34	.304
1981	MILWAUKEE	AL	64	251	45	67	11	0	2	19	10	.267
1982	MILWAUKEE	AL	160	666	136	201	26	8	19	71	41	.302
1983	MILWAUKEE	AL	152	608	95	164	28	6	15	47	41	.270
1984	MILWAUKEE	AL	13	46	3	10	1	0	0	6	1	.217
1985	MILWAUKEE	AL	140	576	93	171	28	3	10	48	21	.297
1986	MILWAUKEE	AL	105	437	62	123	24	6	9	55	20	.281
1987	MILWAUKEE	AL	118	465	114	164	41	5	16	75	45	.353
1988	MILWAUKEE	AL	154	609	115	190	34	6	13	60	41	.312
1989	MILWAUKEE	AL	155	615	84	194	35	4	11	56	27	.315
1990	MILWAUKEE	AL	103	418	64	119	27	6	12	45	18	.285
1991	MILWAUKEE	AL	158	665	133	216	32	13	17	75	19	.325
1992	MILWAUKEE	AL	158	609	89	195	36	7	12	89	31	.320
1993	TORONTO	AL	160	636	121	211	37	5	22	111	22	.332
1994	TORONTO	AL	115	454	86	155	30	4	14	75	20	.341
1995	TORONTO	AL	130	525	63	142	31	2	15	60	12	.270
1996	MINNESOTA	AL	161	660	99	225	41	8	9	113	18	.341
1997	MINNESOTA	AL	135	538	63	164	32	4	10	89	11	.305
1998	MINNESOTA	AL	126	502	75	141	29	5	4	69	9	.281
CAREER TOTALS			**2683**	**10835**	**1782**	**3319**	**605**	**114**	**234**	**1307**	**504**	**.306**

JOE MORGAN

"I have never seen anyone, and I mean anyone, play better than Joe has played this year," Cincinnati Reds manager Sparky Anderson told reporters in 1975.

Comparable in size to Dead Ball era players at 5-foot-7, 160 pounds, Morgan instead was perfectly suited to the artificial surface game of the 1970s, when he emerged as one of the key cogs in Cincinnati's Big Red Machine.

In the Reds' back-to-back World Series championship years in 1975-76, Morgan won back-to-back MVP awards in the National League, as well as two of his five consecutive Gold Glove Awards.

Morgan signed with the expansion Houston Colt .45s in 1962. He reached the majors for the first time in 1963 and became Houston's regular second baseman in 1965. He spent nine seasons with Houston and made two All-Star Game appearances, but became a Hall of Famer after being traded in November 1971 to the Reds and leaving Houston's cavernous Astrodome. He led the league in walks, on-base percentage and runs scored in his first season with Cincinnati and earned All-Star nods in each of his eight seasons with the Reds. In his peak years of 1975 and '76, he led baseball in OPS (on-base plus slugging percentage.)

After leaving the Reds as a 36-year-old free agent in 1980, Morgan remained a key player on winning treams, playing for Houston's division winner in 1980, playing two productive seasons in San Francisco and then belting 16 homers for Philadelphia's pennant-winning "Wheeze Kids" in 1983. He played his final season back home in Oakland in 1984 before embarking on a long career as a broadcaster.

Baseball historian Bill James has called Morgan the best percentages player in baseball history, and indeed Morgan's game was marked by efficiency. He was an ideal hitter early in a batting order, ranking fifth all-time in walks (1,865) and 11th in career stolen bases with 689.

Elected To The Hall Of Fame: 1990.
Born: Sept. 19, 1943 in Bonham, Texas.
Height: 5-7. *Weight:* 160.
Threw: Right. *Batted:* Left.
Debut: Sept. 21, 1963.
Final Game: Sept. 30, 1984.
Teams: Houston N.L. 1963-1971, 1980; Cincinnati N.L. 1972-1979; San Francisco N.L. 1981-1982; Philadelphia N.L. 1983; Oakland A.L. 1984. *Postseason:* 2-Time World Series Champion (1975, 1976); 4 N.L. Pennants (1972, 1975-1976, 1983); 7-Time Playoff Qualifier (1972-1973, 1975-176, 1979-1980, 1983).
Awards: 10-Time All-Star (1966, 1970, 1972-1979); 2-Time Most Valuable Player (1975-1976).

YEAR	TEAM	LEAGUE	G	AB	R	H	2B	3B	HR	RBI	SB	AVG
1963	HOUSTON	NL	8	25	5	6	0	1	0	3	1	.240
1964	HOUSTON	NL	10	37	4	7	0	0	0	0	0	.189
1965	HOUSTON	NL	157	601	100	163	22	12	14	40	20	.271
1966	HOUSTON	NL	122	425	60	121	14	8	5	42	11	.285
1967	HOUSTON	NL	133	494	73	136	27	11	6	42	29	.275
1968	HOUSTON	NL	10	20	6	5	0	1	0	0	3	.250
1969	HOUSTON	NL	147	535	94	126	18	5	15	43	49	.236
1970	HOUSTON	NL	144	548	102	147	28	9	8	52	42	.268
1971	HOUSTON	NL	160	583	87	149	27	11	13	56	40	.256
1972	CINCINNATI	NL	149	552	122	161	23	4	16	73	58	.292
1973	CINCINNATI	NL	157	576	116	167	35	2	26	82	67	.290
1974	CINCINNATI	NL	149	512	107	150	31	3	22	67	58	.293
1975	CINCINNATI	NL	146	498	107	163	27	6	17	94	67	.327
1976	CINCINNATI	NL	141	472	113	151	30	5	27	111	60	.320
1977	CINCINNATI	NL	153	521	113	150	21	6	22	78	49	.288
1978	CINCINNATI	NL	132	441	68	104	27	0	13	75	19	.236
1979	CINCINNATI	NL	127	436	70	109	26	1	9	32	28	.250
1980	HOUSTON	NL	141	461	66	112	17	5	11	49	24	.243
1981	SAN FRANCISCO	NL	90	308	47	74	16	1	8	31	14	.240
1982	SAN FRANCISCO	NL	134	463	68	134	19	4	14	61	24	.289
1983	PHILADELPHIA	NL	123	404	72	93	20	1	16	59	18	.230
1984	OAKLAND	AL	116	365	50	89	21	0	6	43	8	.244
CAREER TOTALS			**2649**	**9277**	**1650**	**2517**	**449**	**96**	**268**	**1133**	**689**	**.271**

EDDIE MURRAY

"When I got to the big leagues, there was a man – Eddie Murray – who showed me how to play this game, day in and day out. I thank him for his example," said Hall of Famer Cal Ripken, Jr.

No one has ever played more major league games at first base. Lou Gehrig played in 2,130, but the steady, consistent, durable and dominant Eddie Murray chalked up 2,413, with almost 600 more as DH. In his 21 big league seasons, Murray averaged 24 home runs and 91 runs-batted-in. He was the third player in history, after Hank Aaron and Willie Mays, to record 3,000 hits and 500 home runs.

The Orioles drafted Murray in 1973, and he made his major league debut in 1977, batting .283 with 27 home runs and 88 runs-batted-in, en route to the Rookie of the Year Award.

Moving to first base full time the following season, Murray grew as a hitter and a fielder, and in 1979, led the Orioles to the AL pennant, batting .295 with 25 home runs and 99 RBI.

The following season, in 1980, Murray posted the first of his six 100-RBI seasons.

In 1982, Murray won the first of three consecutive Gold Glove Awards, and he led the AL in putouts twice, assists twice, and fielding percentage twice. In 1983, he led Baltimore to another pennant, hitting .306 with 33 home runs and 111 runs-batted-in. He clubbed three home runs in the postseason, as the Orioles won the World Series over the Phillies.

Traded to the Dodgers prior to the 1989 season, Murray drove in 279 runs in his hometown over three seasons. He signed with the Mets in 1992, driving in 193 runs in two seasons before signing with Cleveland in 1994.

He led the Indians to their first World Series since 1954, clubbing a home run in each round of the postseason in 1995. He made his final postseason appearance with the Orioles in 1996, hitting .333 in the two playoff rounds. He finished his career at home in 1997, playing for both the Angels and the Dodgers.

Elected To The Hall Of Fame: 2003.
Born: Feb. 24, 1956 in Los Angeles, Calif.
Height: 6-2. Weight: 190.
Threw: Right. Batted: Both.
Debut: April 7, 1977.
Final Game: Sept. 20, 1997.
Teams: Baltimore A.L. 1977-1988, 1996; Los Angeles N.L. 1989-1991, 1997; New York N.L. 1992-1993; Cleveland A.L. 1994-1996; Anaheim A.L. 1997.
Postseason: World Series Champion (1983); 3 A.L. Pennants (1979, 1983, 1995); 4-Time Playoff Qualifier (1979, 1983, 1995-1996).
Awards: 8-Time All-Star (1978, 1981-1986, 1991); A.L. Rookie of the Year (1977).

YEAR	TEAM	LEAGUE	G	AB	R	H	2B	3B	HR	RBI	SB	AVG
1977	BALTIMORE	AL	160	611	81	173	29	2	27	88	0	.283
1978	BALTIMORE	AL	161	610	85	174	32	3	27	95	6	.285
1979	BALTIMORE	AL	159	606	90	179	30	2	25	99	10	.295
1980	BALTIMORE	AL	158	621	100	186	36	2	32	116	7	.300
1981	BALTIMORE	AL	99	378	57	111	21	2	22	78	2	.294
1982	BALTIMORE	AL	151	550	87	174	30	1	32	110	7	.316
1983	BALTIMORE	AL	156	582	115	178	30	3	33	111	5	.306
1984	BALTIMORE	AL	162	588	97	180	26	3	29	110	10	.306
1985	BALTIMORE	AL	156	583	111	173	37	1	31	124	5	.297
1986	BALTIMORE	AL	137	495	61	151	25	1	17	84	3	.305
1987	BALTIMORE	AL	160	618	89	171	28	3	30	91	1	.277
1988	BALTIMORE	AL	161	603	75	171	27	2	28	84	5	.284
1989	LOS ANGELES	NL	160	594	66	147	29	1	20	88	7	.247
1990	LOS ANGELES	NL	155	558	96	184	22	3	26	95	8	.330
1991	LOS ANGELES	NL	153	576	69	150	23	1	19	96	10	.260
1992	NEW YORK	NL	156	551	64	144	37	2	16	93	4	.261
1993	NEW YORK	NL	154	610	77	174	28	1	27	100	2	.285
1994	CLEVELAND	AL	108	433	57	110	21	1	17	76	8	.254
1995	CLEVELAND	AL	113	436	68	141	21	0	21	82	5	.323
1996	CLEVELAND/BALTIMORE	AL	152	566	69	147	21	1	22	79	4	.260
1997	ANAHEIM/LOS ANGELES	AL/NL	55	167	13	37	7	0	3	18	1	.222
CAREER TOTALS			**3026**	**11336**	**1627**	**3255**	**560**	**35**	**504**	**1917**	**110**	**.287**

STAN MUSIAL

"Here stands baseball's perfect warrior. Here stands baseball's perfect knight." — Ford Frick.
      Stan Musial hit the ball the wrong way. Corkscrew stance. Off-balance follow-through. Inside-out swing. But Stan Musial played baseball the right way. Few who saw the Cardinals legend in person thought a better ballplayer existed. Almost half a century after his retirement, Musial remains the face of a Cardinals franchise he helped turn into a dynasty.

Musial began his pro baseball career as a left-handed pitcher in 1938 after signing with the Cardinals. But while playing the outfield due to a shortage of players, Musial permanently damaged his left shoulder while diving for a ball. Musial's manager, Dickie Kerr, suggested that Musial turn to hitting – based on the fact that Musial hit .311 in his part-time outfield duty in 1940. The next year, Musial sailed through the vast Cardinals' minor league system before hitting .426 in a late-season call-up with St. Louis.

In 1942, Musial hit .315 as the Cardinals' everyday left-fielder — one of only two times he would dip under the .330 mark in his first 12 full big league seasons. The Cardinals won the World Series, and the next season Musial won his first of three NL Most Valuable Player awards for leading the Cards back to the World Series, where they lost to the Yankees. Musial and the Cardinals won the World Series again in 1944, and after taking 1945 off to serve in the Navy, Musial won his second MVP in 1946 while leading St. Louis to its third World Series title in five seasons.

He had his greatest offensive season in 1948, hitting a career-high .376 while missing the Triple Crown by just one home run. He won his third and final MVP that year. The next season, Musial finished second in the MVP voting for the first of three straight seasons and played in his sixth All-Star Game. Over the final 14 years of his career, Musial would play in 18 more All-Star Games (two per season from 1959-62).

STANLEY FRANK MUSIAL
"THE MAN"
ST. LOUIS CARDINALS 1941-1963

HOLDS MANY NATIONAL LEAGUE RECORDS, AMONG THEM: GAMES PLAYED 3,026; AT BATS 10,972; HITS 3,630; MOST RUNS SCORED 1,949; MOST RUNS BATTED IN 1951; TOTAL BASES 6,134. LED N.L. IN TOTAL BASES 6 YEARS AND WON SEVEN N.L. BATTING TITLES. MOST VALUABLE PLAYER 1943, 1946, 1948. PLAYED IN 24 ALL-STAR GAMES. LIFETIME BATTING AVERAGE .331.

The Man

Elected To The Hall Of Fame: 1969.
Born: Nov. 21, 1920 in Donora, Pa.
Died: Jan. 19, 2013 in Ladue, Mo.
Height: 6-0. **Weight:** 175.
Threw: Left. **Batted:** Left.
Debut: Sept. 17, 1941.
Final Game: Sept. 29, 1963.
Teams: St. Louis N.L. 1941-44, 1946-63.
Postseason: 3-Time World Series Champion (1942, 1944, 1946); 4 N.L. Pennants (1942-44, 1946). **Awards:** 24-Time All-Star (1943-63); 3-Time N.L. MVP (1943, 1946, 1948).

YEAR	TEAM	LEAGUE	G	AB	R	H	2B	3B	HR	RBI	SB	AVG
1941	ST. LOUIS	NL	12	47	8	20	4	0	1	7	1	.426
1942	ST. LOUIS	NL	140	467	87	147	32	10	10	72	6	.315
1943	ST. LOUIS	NL	157	617	108	220	48	20	13	81	9	.357
1944	ST. LOUIS	NL	146	568	112	197	51	14	12	94	7	.347
1946	ST. LOUIS	NL	156	624	124	228	50	20	16	103	7	.365
1947	ST. LOUIS	NL	149	587	113	183	30	13	19	95	4	.312
1948	ST. LOUIS	NL	155	611	135	230	46	18	39	131	7	.376
1949	ST. LOUIS	NL	157	612	128	207	41	13	36	123	3	.338
1950	ST. LOUIS	NL	146	555	105	192	41	7	28	109	5	.346
1951	ST. LOUIS	NL	152	578	124	205	30	12	32	108	4	.355
1952	ST. LOUIS	NL	154	578	105	194	42	6	21	91	7	.336
1953	ST. LOUIS	NL	157	593	127	200	53	9	30	113	3	.337
1954	ST. LOUIS	NL	153	591	120	195	41	9	35	126	1	.330
1955	ST. LOUIS	NL	154	562	97	179	30	5	33	108	5	.319
1956	ST. LOUIS	NL	156	594	87	184	33	6	27	109	2	.310
1957	ST. LOUIS	NL	134	502	82	176	38	3	29	102	1	.351
1958	ST. LOUIS	NL	135	472	64	159	35	2	17	62	0	.337
1959	ST. LOUIS	NL	115	341	37	87	13	2	14	44	0	.255
1960	ST. LOUIS	NL	116	331	49	91	17	1	17	63	1	.275
1961	ST. LOUIS	NL	123	372	46	107	22	4	15	70	0	.288
1962	ST. LOUIS	NL	135	433	57	143	18	1	19	82	3	.330
1963	ST. LOUIS	NL	124	337	34	86	10	2	12	58	2	.255
CAREER TOTALS			3026	10972	1949	3630	725	177	475	1951	78	.331

HAL NEWHOUSER

"I had a philosophy that I pitched against the pitcher and I did not pitch against the hitters," Hal Newhouser said. "The vast percentage of the time the ball was in my hand, everything was in my favor."

Hal Newhouser's career makes for a nice story of a Detroit native made good with the hometown Tigers, but it was nearly not so. In the summer of 1938, just minutes after Newhouser signed a contract with the Tigers, representatives from the Indians showed up at his family's home offering a larger bonus of $15,000 and a new car. They were too late, though. Newhouser was a Tiger.

Had the Indians arrived at Newhouser's home a little bit earlier, the lefthander would've been given the chance to be roommates with Bob Feller. Instead, Feller and Newhouser's duels became legendary in the baseball lore of both cities. The Indians and Tigers would rearrange their rotations so their aces would face each other, often on a Sunday to spark attendance. The two Hall of Famers squared off 14 times in their careers.

Newhouser was just 19 when he pitched his first full season in the majors in 1940. After the U.S. entered World War II, Newhouser intended to join the armed forces as so many other players did, but a heart murmur made him ineligible for service. So Newhouser kept pitching and hit his stride in 1944.

Newhouser led the American League in wins and strikeouts in 1944, and he captured the league's MVP award. He was even better in 1945, winning the AL's pitching Triple Crown after leading the league in wins, ERA and strikeouts and being named MVP for the second straight year, becoming the first pitcher to win the award in consecutive seasons. He ended the year by winning two games in the 1945 World Series against the Cubs, including Game 7. Newhouser led the AL in ERA again in 1946 and nearly won a third MVP award, finishing second to Ted Williams.

However, after his fourth 20-win season in 1948, Newhouser began experiencing arm troubles and he won just 18 games after his 30th birthday. He briefly rejuvenated his career with none other than the Indians in 1954, serving as a reliever and helping the club win the AL pennant. He went on to a successful scouting career after his playing days, his signings including Dean Chance and Milt Pappas.

HAROLD NEWHOUSER
(PRINCE HAL)
DETROIT, A.L., 1939-1953
CLEVELAND, A.L., 1954-1955
ONLY PITCHER IN MAJOR LEAGUE HISTORY TO WIN BACK-TO-BACK MVP AWARDS (1944-1945). STRIKEOUT KING WITH BLAZING FAST BALL. 207-150 OVER 17 CAMPAIGNS. CONSECUTIVE SEASONS OF 29-9, 25-9 and 26-9 WITH CORRESPONDING ERA'S OF 2.22, 1.81 and 1.94 FROM 1944-1946. HURLED PENNANT-CLINCHER IN 1945 FOLLOWED BY 2 WORLD SERIES VICTORIES OVER CUBS.

Prince Hal

Elected To The Hall Of Fame: *1992.*
Born: *May 20, 1921 in Detroit, Mich.*
Died: *Nov. 10, 1998 in Southfield, Mich.*
Height: *6-2.* **Weight:** *180.*
Threw: *Left.* **Batted:** *Left.*
Debut: *Sept. 29, 1939.*
Final Game: *May 3, 1955.*
Teams: *Detroit A.L. 1939-1953; Cleveland A.L. 1954-1955.*
Postseason: *World Series Champion (1945); 2 A.L. Pennants (1945, 1954).*
Awards: *7-Time All-Star (1942-1948); 2-Time A.L. Most Valuable Player (1944-1945).*

YEAR	TEAM	LEAGUE	G	W	L	SV	SH	IP	H	BB	SO	ERA
1939	DETROIT	AL	1	0	1	0	0	5	3	4	4	5.40
1940	DETROIT	AL	28	9	9	0	0	133.3	149	76	89	4.86
1941	DETROIT	AL	33	9	11	0	1	173	166	137	106	4.79
1942	DETROIT	AL	38	8	14	5	1	183.7	137	114	103	2.45
1943	DETROIT	AL	37	8	17	1	1	195.7	163	111	144	3.04
1944	DETROIT	AL	47	29	9	2	6	312.3	264	102	187	2.22
1945	DETROIT	AL	40	25	9	2	8	313.3	239	110	212	1.81
1946	DETROIT	AL	37	26	9	1	6	292.7	215	98	275	1.94
1947	DETROIT	AL	40	17	17	2	3	285	268	110	176	2.87
1948	DETROIT	AL	39	21	12	1	2	272.3	249	99	143	3.01
1949	DETROIT	AL	38	18	11	1	3	292	277	111	144	3.36
1950	DETROIT	AL	35	15	13	3	1	213.7	232	81	87	4.34
1951	DETROIT	AL	15	6	6	0	1	96.3	98	19	37	3.92
1952	DETROIT	AL	25	9	9	0	0	154	148	47	57	3.74
1953	DETROIT	AL	7	0	1	1	0	21.7	31	8	6	7.06
1954	CLEVELAND	AL	26	7	2	7	0	46.7	34	18	25	2.51
1955	CLEVELAND	AL	2	0	0	0	0	2.3	1	4	1	0.00
CAREER TOTALS			**488**	**207**	**150**	**26**	**33**	**2993**	**2674**	**1249**	**1796**	**3.06**

KID NICHOLS

Charles "Kid" Nichols played 15 seasons in the majors and notched 361 victories over that span, still ranking among the game's all-time winners.

Nichols was an immediate success, and after being signed by Boston in 1889 he won 20 or more games every year for his first 10 seasons, relying almost completely on his fastball throughout his career.

As a rookie, Nichols led the Beaneaters with 27 wins. He also posted a 2.23 ERA to go with 47 complete games and a National League-best seven shutouts. The right-hander notched 30 victories in 1891 when his team won the pennant. In 1892, he went 35-16 winning two games in the league's championship series when they beat Cy Young and the Cleveland Spiders. In total, Nichols helped Boston to five league championships in his first nine seasons with the club.

When the pitching distance went from 50 feet to 60 feet, six inches in 1893 — though it took a toll on his strikeout total — Nichols still went 34-14 and helped the Beaneaters to another title. Nichols led the NL in wins for three straight years from 1896 to 1898 and he won 30 or more games a record seven times, a mark that is likely to stand forever, since the implementation of five-man rotations, pitch counts and inning limits.

Kid found success in 1898 when he posted a 31-12 record. He completed 40 of his 42 starts and had five shutouts, walking only 85 batters in 388 innings. He posted a 2.13 ERA, the second-best of his career.

The righty completed a total of 532 games out of the 562 he started during his time in baseball. He threw more than 300 innings in every season but three, and pitched more than 400 five times.

When his playing days were done, Nichols remained a part of the sport, managing both the Oshkosh Indians of the Wisconsin-Illinois League in 1908 and the Bonham Sliders of the Texas-Oklahoma League in 1914.

CHARLES A.(KID) NICHOLS
RIGHT HANDED PITCHER WHO WON 30 OR MORE GAMES FOR SEVEN CONSECUTIVE YEARS (1891-97) AND WON AT LEAST 20 GAMES FOR TEN CONSECUTIVE SEASONS (1890-99) WITH BOSTON N.L. ALSO PITCHED FOR ST. LOUIS AND PHILADELPHIA N.L. ONE OF FEW PITCHERS TO WIN MORE THAN 300 GAMES, HIS MAJOR LEAGUE RECORD BEING 360 VICTORIES, 202 DEFEATS.

Elected To The Hall Of Fame: 1949.
Born: Sept. 14, 1869 in Madison, Wis.
Died: Apr. 11, 1953 in Kansas City, Mo.
Height: 5-10. **Weight:** 175.
Threw: Right. **Batted:** Both.
Debut: April 23, 1890.
Final Game: May 18, 1906.
Teams: Boston N.L. 1890-1901; St. Louis N.L. 1904-1905; Philadelphia N.L. 1905-1906.
Postseason: N.L. Champion (1892).

YEAR	TEAM	LEAGUE	G	W	L	SV	SH	IP	H	BB	SO	ERA
1890	BOSTON	NL	48	27	19	0	7	424	374	112	222	2.23
1891	BOSTON	NL	52	30	17	3	5	425.3	413	103	240	2.39
1892	BOSTON	NL	53	35	16	0	5	453	404	121	192	2.84
1893	BOSTON	NL	52	34	14	1	1	425	426	118	94	3.52
1894	BOSTON	NL	50	32	13	0	3	407	488	121	113	4.75
1895	BOSTON	NL	48	26	16	1	1	390.7	434	90	148	3.41
1896	BOSTON	NL	49	30	14	1	3	372.3	387	101	102	2.83
1897	BOSTON	NL	46	31	11	3	2	368	362	68	127	2.64
1898	BOSTON	NL	50	31	12	4	5	388	316	85	138	2.13
1899	BOSTON	NL	42	21	19	1	4	343.3	326	82	108	2.99
1900	BOSTON	NL	29	13	16	0	4	231.3	215	72	53	3.07
1901	BOSTON	NL	38	19	16	0	4	321	306	90	143	3.22
1904	ST. LOUIS	NL	36	21	13	1	3	317	268	50	134	2.02
1905	ST. LOUIS/PHILADELPHIA	NL	24	11	11	0	1	190.3	193	46	66	3.12
1906	PHILADELPHIA	NL	4	0	1	0	0	11	17	13	1	9.82
CAREER TOTALS			**621**	**361**	**208**	**17**	**48**	**5067.1**	**4929**	**1272**	**1881**	**2.96**

PHIL NIEKRO

" **C**atching Niekro's knuckeball was great. I got to meet a lot of important people. They all sit behind home plate." — Bob Uecker.

Only 10 of the 17,000-plus men who have played major league baseball played for more seasons than Phil Niekro, who pitched for the Braves, Yankees, Indians, and Blue Jays for 24 seasons. Among pitchers, only Cy Young, Pud Galvin, and Walter Johnson have been on the mound for more innings than Niekro's 5,404—and none of them started their careers prior to the introduction of the live ball in 1920. And Niekro indeed threw a "lively ball." He is perhaps the greatest practitioner of the knuckleball. Another prominent knuckleballer, Tom Candiotti, was Niekro's teammate on the Indians in 1986, and said that talking to "Knucksie" was "like talking to Thomas Edison about light bulbs."

The knuckleball is a notoriously difficult pitch to hit—and to catch. Some posit that Niekro's long minor league career, from 1959 to 1966, was the result of minor league catchers being ill equipped to handle the pitch—though the pitch also helped extend Niekro's big league career.

After brief major league stints in 1964-66, Knucksie stuck in 1967, leading the NL in ERA (at 1.87) and in wild pitches (with 19). He went 23-13 for the Braves in 1969, as they captured the first-ever NL West division title.

On Aug. 5, 1973, Niekro pitched a no-hitter against the Padres.

He and his brother Joe are the all-time leaders in wins by brothers, with 539, topping Jim and Gaylord Perry's 529.

The Niekro brothers tied for the NL lead in wins in 1979, with 21. They faced each other nine times, with Joe holding a slight edge at 5-4. Phil Niekro signed with the Yankees in 1984, and won 16 games that season and the next, winning his 300th game as a Yankee in 1985. He pitched for the Indians in 1986 and '87, finishing up in '87 with brief stints for Toronto and the Braves. From 1994-1997, he managed the women's barnstorming Colorado Silver Bullets.

PHILIP HENRY NIEKRO
MILWAUKEE, N.L. 1964-1965
ATLANTA, N.L. 1966-1983, 1987
NEW YORK, A.L. 1984-1985
CLEVELAND, A.L. 1986-1987
TORONTO, A.L. 1987
PREEMINENT KNUCKLEBALL PITCHER WHOSE OUT-PITCH BAFFLED HITTERS AND LED TO 3,342 STRIKEOUTS, 8th ON ALL-TIME LIST. CAREER RECORD OF 318-274 WITH A 3.35 ERA PLACED HIM 14th IN VICTORIES WITH WINNING PERCENTAGE SIGNIFICANTLY HIGHER THAN THOSE TEAMS FOR WHOM HE PITCHED. TIED WITH CY YOUNG FOR MOST SEASONS, 200 OR MORE INNINGS PITCHED (19) AND LED LEAGUE FOUR TIMES IN THAT DEPARTMENT. NO-HIT SAN DIEGO, AUGUST 5, 1973. WON FIVE GOLD GLOVES AND NAMED TO FIVE ALL-STAR TEAMS.

Knucksie

Elected To The Hall Of Fame: *1997.*

Born: *April 1, 1939 in Blaine, Ohio.*

Height: *6-1.* ***Weight:*** *180.*

Threw: *Right.* ***Batted:*** *Right.*

Debut: *April 15, 1964.*

Final Game: *Sept. 27, 1987.*

Teams: *Milwaukee N.L. 1964-1965; Atlanta N.L. 1966-1983, 1987; New York A.L. 1984-1985; Cleveland A.L. 1986-1987; Toronto A.L. 1987.* ***Postseason:*** *2-Time Playoff Qualifier (1969, 1982).*

Awards: *5-Time All-Star (1969, 1975, 1978, 1982, 1984).*

YEAR	TEAM	LEAGUE	G	W	L	SV	SH	IP	H	BB	SO	ERA
1964	MILWAUKEE	NL	10	0	0	0	0	15	15	7	8	4.80
1965	MILWAUKEE	NL	41	2	3	6	0	74.7	73	26	49	2.89
1966	ATLANTA	NL	28	4	3	2	0	50.3	48	23	17	4.11
1967	ATLANTA	NL	46	11	9	9	1	207	164	55	129	1.87
1968	ATLANTA	NL	37	14	12	2	5	256.7	228	45	140	2.59
1969	ATLANTA	NL	40	23	13	1	4	284.3	235	57	193	2.56
1970	ATLANTA	NL	34	12	18	0	3	229.7	222	68	168	4.27
1971	ATLANTA	NL	42	15	14	2	4	268.7	248	70	173	2.98
1972	ATLANTA	NL	38	16	12	0	1	282.3	254	53	164	3.06
1973	ATLANTA	NL	42	13	10	4	1	245	214	89	131	3.31
1974	ATLANTA	NL	41	20	13	1	6	302.3	249	88	195	2.38
1975	ATLANTA	NL	39	15	15	0	1	275.7	285	72	144	3.20
1976	ATLANTA	NL	38	17	11	0	2	270.7	249	101	173	3.29
1977	ATLANTA	NL	44	16	20	0	2	330.3	315	164	262	4.03
1978	ATLANTA	NL	44	19	18	1	4	334.3	295	102	248	2.88
1979	ATLANTA	NL	44	21	20	0	1	342	311	113	208	3.39
1980	ATLANTA	NL	40	15	18	1	3	275	256	85	176	3.63
1981	ATLANTA	NL	22	7	7	0	3	139.3	120	56	62	3.10
1982	ATLANTA	NL	35	17	4	0	2	234.3	225	73	144	3.61
1983	ATLANTA	NL	34	11	10	0	0	201.7	212	105	128	3.97
1984	NEW YORK	AL	32	16	8	0	1	215.7	219	76	136	3.09
1985	NEW YORK	AL	33	16	12	0	1	220	203	120	149	4.09
1986	CLEVELAND	AL	34	11	11	0	0	210.3	241	95	81	4.32
1987	CLE/TOR/ATL	AL/NL	26	7	13	0	0	138.7	163	66	64	6.30
CAREER TOTALS			**864**	**318**	**274**	**29**	**45**	**5404**	**5044**	**1809**	**3342**	**3.35**

JIM O'ROURKE

The batter who slashed the National League's first hit, Jim O'Rourke played the game professionally past the age of 50 and also served as a manager, umpire and minor league president.

Explaining his longevity, O'Rourke said, "I lived a clean life. I never touched liquor in any form, nor did I ever use tobacco. I always took care of myself. That's the reason I'm playing ball today, and that is the reason why I can enjoy the game."

Nicknamed "Orator Jim" because of a tendency toward lengthy rhetoric, O'Rourke hit .347 in 1884 at the age of 34 – demonstrating his ability to defy time. During his career, he batted .300 or better 13 times and finished with a .310 average.

O'Rourke hit a career-high .362 with the 1877 Boston Red Stockings, leading the National League with an on-base percentage of .407. He scored a league-leading 68 runs in 61 games.

O'Rourke helped New York to its first two league championships in 1888 and 1889. In 1889, he batted .321 with 81 RBI and 33 stolen bases.

In 1890 when a member of the New York Giants of the Players' League, O'Rourke put together a standout season. He batted .360 with a career-high 115 RBI in 111 games and a career-high nine home runs.

O'Rourke continued to play in the minor leagues after hitting .287 as a 43-year-old in 1893 for Washington. At the age of 54, he played one more game in the major leagues with the New York Giants, going 1-for-4 for manager John McGraw.

JAMES H. O'ROURKE
"ORATOR JIM" PLAYED BALL UNTIL HE WAS PAST FIFTY, INCLUDING TWENTY-ONE MAJOR LEAGUE SEASONS. AN OUTFIELDER AND CATCHER FOR THE BOSTON RED STOCKINGS OF 1873, HE LATER WORE THE UNIFORMS OF THE CHAMPIONSHIP PROVIDENCE TEAM OF 1879, BUFFALO, NEW YORK AND WASHINGTON.

Orator Jim

Elected To The Hall Of Fame: 1945.
Born: Sept. 1, 1850 in Bridgeport, Conn.
Died: Jan. 8, 1919 in Bridgeport, Conn.
Height: 5-8. **Weight:** 185.
Threw: Right. **Batted:** Right.
Debut: April 26, 1872.
Final Game: Sept. 22, 1904.
Teams: Middletown, National Association 1872; Boston, National Association 1873-1875; Boston N.L. 1876-1878, 1880; Providence N.L. 1879; Buffalo N.L. 1881-1884; New York N.L. 1885-1889, 1891-1892, 1904; New York, Players' League 1890; Washington N.L. 1893.
Postseason: 2-Time World Series Champions (1888-1889); 2 N.L. Pennants (1888-1889).

YEAR	TEAM	LEAGUE	G	AB	R	H	2B	3B	HR	RBI	SB	AVG
1872	MIDDLETOWN	NA	23	99	25	27	5	0	0	16	1	.273
1873	BOSTON	NA	57	280	79	98	21	2	1	49	9	.350
1874	BOSTON	NA	70	331	82	104	15	8	5	61	11	.314
1875	BOSTON	NA	75	358	97	106	13	7	6	72	17	.296
1876	BOSTON	NL	70	312	61	102	17	3	2	43	NA	.327
1877	BOSTON	NL	61	265	68	96	14	4	0	23	NA	.362
1878	BOSTON	NL	60	255	44	71	17	7	1	29	NA	.278
1879	PROVIDENCE	NL	81	362	69	126	19	9	1	46	NA	.348
1880	BOSTON	NL	86	363	71	100	20	11	6	45	NA	.275
1881	BUFFALO	NL	83	348	71	105	21	7	0	30	NA	.302
1882	BUFFALO	NL	84	370	62	104	15	6	2	37	NA	.281
1883	BUFFALO	NL	94	436	102	143	29	8	1	38	NA	.328
1884	BUFFALO	NL	108	467	119	162	33	7	5	63	NA	.347
1885	NEW YORK	NL	112	477	119	143	21	16	5	42	NA	.300
1886	NEW YORK	NL	105	440	106	136	26	6	1	34	14	.309
1887	NEW YORK	NL	103	397	73	113	15	13	3	88	46	.285
1888	NEW YORK	NL	107	409	50	112	16	6	4	50	25	.274
1889	NEW YORK	NL	128	502	89	161	36	7	3	81	33	.321
1890	NEW YORK	PL	111	478	112	172	37	5	9	115	23	.360
1891	NEW YORK	NL	136	555	92	164	28	7	5	95	19	.295
1892	NEW YORK	NL	115	448	62	136	28	5	0	56	16	.304
1893	WASHINGTON	NL	129	547	75	157	22	5	2	95	15	.287
1904	NEW YORK	NL	1	4	1	1	0	0	0	0	0	.250
CAREER TOTALS			**1999**	**8503**	**1729**	**2639**	**468**	**149**	**62**	**1208**	**229**	**.310**

Mel Ott

During his playing career, longtime New York Giants outfielder Mel Ott was one of the game's most feared sluggers. And according to Hall of Fame manager Leo Durocher, one of the most popular: "I never knew a baseball player who was so universally loved. Why even when he was playing against the Dodgers at Ebbets Field, he would be cheered and there are no more rabid fans than in Brooklyn."

Ott was signed by the Giants as a 16-year-old and would remain with the big league club for the rest of his career (1926-47). Though he didn't play much in the early years, manager John McGraw refused to send him to the minors, stating, "I don't want anyone tinkering with that natural swing."

Giants teammate Fred Lindstrom remarked upon his fellow Hall of Famer's untimely death in 1958, "My first impression was that he couldn't make the grade because of his heavy legs, but through constant play his legs tapered and he became, I think, about the greatest ball player we've ever seen. He was a tremendous credit to baseball and a fine fellow. Baseball will really miss him."

Ott was adored by the hometown Giants fans, and with good reason. A six-time league-leader in homers, he hit 30 or more eight times, while also compiling eight straight seasons with at least 100 runs batted in. Using an unorthodox left-handed swing, in which he lifted his right foot just before he brought his bat around, the compact (5-foot-9, 170 pounds) Ott used the short 257-foot right-field porch at the Polo Grounds as his personal playground — hitting 323 of his then-NL record 511 homers at the park.

A 12-time All-Star, "Master Melvin" ended his 22-season big league career with a .304 batting average, 488 doubles and 1,860 RBI. Lefty O'Doul later said that one of the things that made Ott a great hitter was hard practice: "We used to spend hours, just the two of us, practicing hitting the ball down the right-field foul line. We got so we could keep it fair by just a few inches."

The Boy Wonder, Master Melvin

Elected To The Hall Of Fame: *1951.*
Born: *March 2, 1909 in Gretna, La.*
Died: *Nov. 21, 1958 in New Orleans, La.*
Height: *5-9.* **Weight:** *170.*
Threw: *Right.* **Batted:** *Left.*
Debut: *April 27, 1926.*
Final Game: *July 11, 1947.*
Teams: *New York N.L. 1926-1947.*
Postseason: *World Series Champion (1933); 3 N.L. Pennants (1933, 1936-1937).*
Awards: *12-Time All-Star (1934-1945).*

YEAR	TEAM	LEAGUE	G	AB	R	H	2B	3B	HR	RBI	SB	AVG
1926	NEW YORK	NL	35	60	7	23	2	0	0	4	1	.383
1927	NEW YORK	NL	82	163	23	46	7	3	1	19	2	.282
1928	NEW YORK	NL	124	435	69	140	26	4	18	77	3	.322
1929	NEW YORK	NL	150	545	138	179	37	2	42	151	6	.328
1930	NEW YORK	NL	148	521	122	182	34	5	25	119	9	.349
1931	NEW YORK	NL	138	497	104	145	23	8	29	115	10	.292
1932	NEW YORK	NL	154	566	119	180	30	8	38	123	6	.318
1933	NEW YORK	NL	152	580	98	164	36	1	23	103	1	.283
1934	NEW YORK	NL	153	582	119	190	29	10	35	135	0	.326
1935	NEW YORK	NL	152	593	113	191	33	6	31	114	7	.322
1936	NEW YORK	NL	150	534	120	175	28	6	33	135	6	.328
1937	NEW YORK	NL	151	545	99	160	28	2	31	95	7	.294
1938	NEW YORK	NL	150	527	116	164	23	6	36	116	2	.311
1939	NEW YORK	NL	125	396	85	122	23	2	27	80	2	.308
1940	NEW YORK	NL	151	536	89	155	27	3	19	79	6	.289
1941	NEW YORK	NL	148	525	89	150	29	0	27	90	5	.286
1942	NEW YORK	NL	152	549	118	162	21	0	30	93	6	.295
1943	NEW YORK	NL	125	380	65	89	12	2	18	47	7	.234
1944	NEW YORK	NL	120	399	91	115	16	4	26	82	2	.288
1945	NEW YORK	NL	135	451	73	139	23	0	21	79	1	.308
1946	NEW YORK	NL	31	68	2	5	1	0	1	4	0	.074
1947	NEW YORK	NL	4	4	0	0	0	0	0	0	0	.000
CAREER TOTALS			**2730**	**9456**	**1859**	**2876**	**488**	**72**	**511**	**1860**	**89**	**.304**

SATCHEL PAIGE

The numbers – at least the big league ones – do not do justice to his legend. The stories, however, keep alive the memory of a man who became bigger than the game. Satchel Paige was bigger than mere numbers.

Apocryphal stories surround Paige, who began his professional career in the Negro leagues in the 1920s after being discharged from reform school in Alabama. The lanky 6-foot-3 right-hander quickly became the biggest drawing card in Negro League baseball – able to overpower batters with a buggy-whipped fastball.

Paige, a showman at heart, bounced from team to team in search of the best paycheck, often pitching hundreds of games a year between regular league assignments and barnstorming opportunities. During the 1930s, Paige's stints with Negro National League powerhouse Pittsburgh Crawfords were interrupted by seasons in North Dakota and the Dominican Republic. As he aged, the control he once used to dazzle fans now became his primary weapon as a pitcher.

Bill Veeck signed Paige, 42, for the Indians on July 7, 1948. Two days later, he made his debut for a Cleveland club involved in a tight pennant race. Paige went 6-1 with three complete games and a save and a 2.48 earned run average as Cleveland won the AL pennant in a one-game playoff against Boston, then captured the World Series in six games against the Braves. Paige became the first African-American pitcher to pitch in the World Series when he worked two-thirds of an inning in Game 5.

Paige pitched for the Indians again in 1949, then spent three seasons with the St. Louis Browns. He returned to life in the minors and barnstorming, resurfacing in the majors at 59 in one game with the Athletics. He pitched three shutout innings.

Elected To The Hall Of Fame: 1971.
Born: July 7, 1906 in Mobile, Ala.
Died: June 8, 1982 in Kansas City, Mo.
Height: 6-3. **Weight:** 180.
Threw: Right. **Batted:** Right.
Debut: July 9, 1948.
Final Game: Sept. 25, 1965.
Teams: Negro Leagues 1927-1947; Cleveland A.L. 1948-1949; St. Louis A.L. 1951-1953; Kansas City A.L. 1965.
Postseason: World Series Champion (1948); A.L. Pennant (1948).
Awards: 2-Time All-Star (1952-1953).

YEAR	TEAM	LEAGUE	G	W	L	SV	SH	IP	H	BB	SO	ERA
1927	BIRMINGHAM	NNL	—	5	1	—	2	49.3	42	23	63	3.28
1928	BIRMINGHAM	NNL	—	11	4	—	1	126	103	20	108	2.93
1929	BIRMINGHAM	NNL	—	9	6	—	0	160.3	154	31	167	4.55
1930	BALT./CHI./BIRM.	INDP/NNL	—	10	3	—	3	106.3	80	18	95	3.22
1931	PITT./CLEV.	INDP/NNL	—	1	2	—	1	28.7	22	3	10	3.14
1932	PITTSBURGH	INDP	—	7	4	—	3	103	77	33	77	3.67
1933	PITTSBURGH	NNL	—	4	6	—	0	78	42	11	49	3.81
1934	CUBAN HOD./PITT.	INDP/NNL	—	13	2	—	4	141	96	24	135	2.23
1935	KANSAS CITY	INDP	—	1	1	—	1	21	9	5	25	0.43
1936	PITTSBURGH	NNL	—	5	0	—	1	46	39	4	47	2.93
1940	KANSAS CITY	NAL	—	1	0	—	0	11	6	0	8	0.82
1941	NEW YORK/K.C.	NNL/NAL	—	6	0	—	0	53	36	3	41	3.40
1942	K.C./HOMESTEAD	NAL/NNL	—	6	4	—	2	94.3	60	10	74	2.39
1943	KANSAS CITY	NAL	—	4	5	—	0	56	62	16	46	5.95
1944	KANSAS CITY	NAL	—	6	6	—	4	94	66	14	89	2.30
1945	KANSAS CITY	NAL	—	5	4	—	2	61.7	53	18	70	4.38
1946	KANSAS CITY	NAL	—	5	1	—	2	50	40	7	49	1.98
1947	KANSAS CITY	NAL	—	1	1	—	1	19	7	0	17	0.95
NEGRO LEAGUE TOTALS			—	100	50	—	27	1298.7	994	240	1170	3.22
1948	CLEVELAND	AL	21	6	1	1	2	72.7	61	22	43	2.48
1949	CLEVELAND	AL	31	4	7	5	0	83	70	33	54	3.04
1951	ST. LOUIS	AL	23	3	4	5	0	62	67	29	48	4.79
1952	ST. LOUIS	AL	46	12	10	10	2	138	116	57	91	3.07
1953	ST. LOUIS	AL	57	3	9	11	0	117.3	114	39	51	3.53
1965	KANSAS CITY	AL	1	0	0	0	0	3	1	0	1	0.00
MLB CAREER TOTALS			179	28	31	32	4	476	429	180	288	3.29

JIM PALMER

"When you see an easy thrower like him, you get lulled into believing that the ball is coming up there easy," Angels infielder Dave Chalk once said of Jim Palmer. "It's not. It's coming up there hard and doing all kinds of things. It's amazing how quick the ball gets to you."

Though UCLA offered him a basketball scholarship, Palmer chose instead to sign with the Orioles in 1963. Palmer made his major league debut at age 19 in 1965 and hit a home run in his first career win. The following season Palmer became the youngest pitcher in major league history to throw a complete-game shutout in the World Series, beating Dodgers lefthander Sandy Koufax 6-0 in Game 2 in a series the Orioles would go on to sweep for their first World Series victory in franchise history.

Palmer was one of baseball's premier pitchers in the 1970s, throwing more innings and recording more wins than any other American League pitcher during that decade. Palmer, who spent his entire 19-year career with the Orioles, was a three-time AL Cy Young Award winner and finished in the top five among Cy Young voters eight times. Palmer was the runner-up to Reggie Jackson for AL MVP in 1973, when he led a starting rotation that included Mike Cuellar, Dave McNally and Doyle Alexander. More than just a terrific pitcher, Palmer also fielded his position well, collecting four Gold Glove Awards.

A six-time all-star, Palmer was an excellent postseason pitcher who pitched in six World Series and won three rings, going 8-3 with a 2.61 ERA between the World Series and the ALCS. When Palmer beat the Phillies in Game 3 of the 1983 World Series, he became the first pitcher in major league history to win a World Series game in three different decades. He also threw a no-hitter against Oakland in 1969 and never surrendered a grand slam in his entire career.

Injuries hampered Palmer throughout his career, though he still led the AL in innings pitched four times and complete games once. Palmer threw the ball with a smooth, compact delivery and a high leg kick that helped provide deception, as the ball seemed to jump out of his hand toward home plate.

JAMES ALVIN PALMER
BALTIMORE, A.L., 1965-1984
HIGH-KICKING, SMOOTH-THROWING SYMBOL OF BALTIMORE'S SIX CHAMPIONSHIP TEAMS OF 1960's, 70's AND 80's. IMPRESSIVE NUMBERS INCLUDE 268 WINS WITH .638 PCT., EIGHT 20-WIN SEASONS, 2.86 ERA AND NO GRAND SLAMS ALLOWED OVER ENTIRE 19 YEAR CAREER. INTENSITY WAS TRADEMARK OF 3-TIME CY YOUNG WINNER, WHO COMBINED STRENGTH, INTELLIGENCE, COMPETITIVENESS AND CONSISTENCY TO BECOME ORIOLES' ALL-TIME WINNINGEST HURLER.

Elected To The Hall Of Fame: *1990.*

Born: *Oct. 15, 1945 in New York, N.Y.*

Height: *6-3.* **Weight:** *190.*

Threw: *Right.* **Batted:** *Right.*

Debut: *April 17, 1965.*

Final Game: *May 12, 1984.*

Teams: *Baltimore A.L. 1965-1967, 1969-1984.*

Postseason: *3-Time World Series Champion (1966, 1970, 1983); 6 A.L. Pennants (1966, 1969-1971, 1979, 1983); 8-Time Playoff Qualifier (1966, 1969-1971, 1973-1974, 1979, 1983).*

Awards: *6-Time All-Star (1970-1972, 1975, 1977-1978); 3-Time Cy Young (1973, 1975-1976).*

YEAR	TEAM	LEAGUE	G	W	L	SV	SH	IP	H	BB	SO	ERA
1965	BALTIMORE	AL	27	5	4	1	0	92	75	56	75	3.72
1966	BALTIMORE	AL	30	15	10	0	0	208.3	176	91	147	3.46
1967	BALTIMORE	AL	9	3	1	0	1	49	34	20	23	2.94
1969	BALTIMORE	AL	26	16	4	0	6	181	131	64	123	2.34
1970	BALTIMORE	AL	39	20	10	0	5	305	263	100	199	2.71
1971	BALTIMORE	AL	37	20	9	0	3	282	231	106	184	2.68
1972	BALTIMORE	AL	36	21	10	0	3	274.3	219	70	184	2.07
1973	BALTIMORE	AL	38	22	9	1	6	296.3	225	113	158	2.40
1974	BALTIMORE	AL	26	7	12	0	2	178.7	176	69	84	3.27
1975	BALTIMORE	AL	39	23	11	1	10	323	253	80	193	2.09
1976	BALTIMORE	AL	40	22	13	0	6	315	255	84	159	2.51
1977	BALTIMORE	AL	39	20	11	0	3	319	263	99	193	2.91
1978	BALTIMORE	AL	38	21	12	0	6	296	246	97	138	2.46
1979	BALTIMORE	AL	23	10	6	0	0	155.7	144	43	67	3.30
1980	BALTIMORE	AL	34	16	10	0	0	224	238	74	109	3.98
1981	BALTIMORE	AL	22	7	8	0	0	127.3	117	46	35	3.75
1982	BALTIMORE	AL	36	15	5	1	2	227	195	63	103	3.13
1983	BALTIMORE	AL	14	5	4	0	0	76.7	86	19	34	4.23
1984	BALTIMORE	AL	5	0	3	0	0	17.7	22	17	4	9.17
CAREER TOTALS			**558**	**268**	**152**	**4**	**53**	**3948**	**3349**	**1311**	**2212**	**2.86**

HERB PENNOCK

" I'm going to pitch (Herb) Pennock in spots this season
– the tough ones," said Joe McCarthy, Hall of Fame
Yankees manager.

Pennock saw plenty of tough spots during his 22-year
career. He was a part of three championship teams with the
Yankees and was a perfect 5-0 with a 1.95 ERA in five World
Series trips. He pitched well in the regular season as well,
finishing with a 241-162 record. The lanky left-hander was
the youngest player in the American League when he made
his MLB debut with the Philadelphia Athletics in 1912 at 18
years old. Pennock played sparingly in the first few years of
his career, largely because of the A's star-laden teams. When
Connie Mack split the dynasty up after the 1914 season,
Pennock became the ace. He nearly threw an Opening Day
no-hitter in 1915, but soon found himself on Mack's bad side
and was shipped to the Red Sox midway through the year. In
Boston, Pennock again found himself on an older team and
was seldom used until after he returned from his role with the
Navy in World War I. Upon his return, Pennock went 16-8
with a 2.71 ERA in 1919 for the Red Sox.

Pennock was traded to the Yankees in 1923, heralded
as the final piece that would bring a World Series to the
Bronx. In his first season in New York, Pennock went 19-6,
the best winning percentage in the league, and won two
games and saved another in the Yankees' first World Series
championship. It was the start of a brilliant six-year stretch
for Pennock. From 1923-28, Pennock went 115-57 with a
3.03 ERA. In those six years, he twice led the AL in WHIP,
led baseball in shutouts once and received MVP votes for
three straight seasons. While Pennock was not the most
overpowering pitcher, he prided himself on his command
and rag-arm style, able to throw pitches from many different
release points. After retiring in 1934, Pennock became general
manager of the Philadelphia Phillies and was the architect
behind the 1950 "Whiz Kids" that reached the World Series.
Pennock, however, was not alive to see it. He died of a stroke
in 1948.

HERBERT J. (HERB) PENNOCK
OUTSTANDING LEFT HANDED PITCHER IN
THE A.L.AND EXECUTIVE OF PHILADELPHIA
N.L.CLUB.AMONG RARE FEW WHO MADE
JUMP FROM PREP SCHOOL TO MAJORS.SAW
22 YEARS SERVICE WITH PHILADELPHIA,
BOSTON AND NEW YORK TEAMS IN A.L.
RECORDED 240 VICTORIES,161 DEFEATS,
NEVER LOST A WORLD SERIES GAME,
WINNING FIVE.IN 1927, PITCHED 7⅓
INNINGS WITHOUT ALLOWING HIT IN
THIRD GAME OF SERIES.

The Knight of Kennett Square

Elected To The Hall Of Fame: 1948.
Born: Feb. 10, 1894 in Kennett Square, Pa.
Died: Jan. 30, 1948 in New York, N.Y.
Height: 6-0. **Weight:** 160.
Threw: Left. **Batted:** Both
Debut: May 14, 1912.
Final Game: Aug. 27, 1934.
Teams: Philadelphia A.L. 1912-1915; Boston
A.L. 1915-1917, 1919-1922, 1934; New York
A.L. 1923-1933.
Postseason: 3-Time World Series Champion
(1923, 1927, 1932); 5 A.L. Pennants (1914,
1923, 1926-1927, 1932).

YEAR	TEAM	LEAGUE	G	W	L	SV	SH	IP	H	BB	SO	ERA
1912	PHILADELPHIA	AL	17	1	2	2	0	50	48	30	38	4.50
1913	PHILADELPHIA	AL	14	2	1	0	0	33.3	30	22	17	5.13
1914	PHILADELPHIA	AL	28	11	4	3	3	151.7	136	65	90	2.79
1915	PHILADELPHIA/BOSTON	AL	16	3	6	1	1	58	69	39	31	6.36
1916	BOSTON	AL	9	0	2	1	0	26.7	23	8	12	3.04
1917	BOSTON	AL	24	5	5	1	1	100.7	90	23	35	3.31
1919	BOSTON	AL	32	16	8	0	5	219	223	48	70	2.71
1920	BOSTON	AL	37	16	13	2	4	242.3	244	61	68	3.68
1921	BOSTON	AL	32	13	14	0	1	222.7	268	59	91	4.04
1922	BOSTON	AL	32	10	17	1	1	202	230	74	59	4.32
1923	NEW YORK	AL	35	19	6	3	1	238.3	235	68	93	3.13
1924	NEW YORK	AL	40	21	9	3	4	286.3	302	64	101	2.83
1925	NEW YORK	AL	47	16	17	2	2	277	267	71	88	2.96
1926	NEW YORK	AL	40	23	11	2	1	266.3	294	43	78	3.62
1927	NEW YORK	AL	34	19	8	2	1	209.7	225	48	51	3.00
1928	NEW YORK	AL	28	17	6	3	5	211	215	40	53	2.56
1929	NEW YORK	AL	27	9	11	2	1	157.3	205	28	49	4.92
1930	NEW YORK	AL	25	11	7	0	1	156.3	194	20	46	4.32
1931	NEW YORK	AL	25	11	6	0	1	189.3	247	30	65	4.28
1932	NEW YORK	AL	22	9	5	0	1	146.7	191	38	54	4.60
1933	NEW YORK	AL	23	7	4	4	1	65	96	21	22	5.54
1934	BOSTON	AL	30	2	0	1	0	62	68	16	16	3.05
CAREER TOTALS			**617**	**241**	**162**	**33**	**35**	**3571.2**	**3900**	**916**	**1227**	**3.60**

TONY PÉREZ

One of the national pastime's great run producers, Atanasio "Tony" Pérez Rigal was among the best when it came to driving in big runs for Cincinnati's "Big Red Machine" clubs of the 1970s.

"Pete (Rose) would get his 200 hits, and (Johnny) Bench would do his thing," said former Pérez teammate Pat Corrales. "And Tony would get shoved in the background, driving in his 100 runs every year. You'd see it in the notes at the end of the stories in the paper – 'Oh, by the way, Pérez hit a three-run homer to win the game.'"

Of the 1,652 RBI Pérez collected over his 23-year big league career (1964-86), the slugging first baseman and seven-time All-Star totaled 954 in the '70s, second only to Hall of Famer and former Reds teammate Johnny Bench's 1,013.

"With men in scoring position and the game on the line," said longtime opponent Willie Stargell, "Tony's the last guy an opponent wanted to see."

A native of Cuba, Pérez left a job in a Havana sugar cane factory when he signed a minor league contract with the Reds in 1960. "I ate chicken for a week one time," Pérez said. "It was the only word I knew – chicken, chicken, chicken."

Eventually, Pérez would become a positive influence on those who came afterwards. "(Pérez) was a fatherly type in the clubhouse, especially to the Spanish ballplayers," said longtime Reds teammate Pete Rose. "They looked up to him as well as relating to him through his background and language." By 1967, he had notched the first of seven seasons with 100-or-more RBI as well as earning MVP honors in the 1967 All-Star Game by hitting a game-winning home run in the 15th inning off of future Hall of Famer Jim "Catfish" Hunter. Along the way Pérez compiled nine seasons of at least 20 homers, finishing with a career total of 379. Pérez, who played in five World Series, notched three home runs in the 1975 Fall Classic against the Boston Red Sox, including a two-run shot in the Reds' 4-3 victory in Game 7.

ATANASIO PÉREZ RIGAL
"TONY"
CINCINNATI, N.L., 1964-1976, 1984-1986
MONTREAL, N.L., 1977-1979
BOSTON, A.L., 1980-1982
PHILADELPHIA, N.L., 1983
A CLUTCH PERFORMER THROUGHOUT AN ILLUSTRIOUS 23-YEAR CAREER, HE TORMENTED THE OPPOSITION WITH HIS ABILITY TO CONSISTENTLY DRIVE IN RUNS. HIS COMPOSURE UNDER PRESSURE LED TO 379 HOME RUNS, 505 DOUBLES AND 1652 RBI INCLUDING SEVEN 100-RBI SEASONS AND 954 RBI IN THE 1970s. A CATALYST OF CINCINNATI'S TALENTED BIG RED MACHINE TEAMS DURING THE 1970s, HIS SUBTLE LEADERSHIP AND TIMELY HITTING HELPED PACE THOSE CLUBS TO FIVE DIVISION TITLES, FOUR PENNANTS AND TWO WORLD SERIES CHAMPIONSHIPS.

Elected To The Hall Of Fame: *2000.*

Born: *May 14, 1942 in Camaguey, Cuba.*

Height: *6-2.* **Weight:** *175.*

Threw: *Right.* **Batted:** *Right.*

Debut: *July 26, 1964.*

Final Game: *Oct. 5, 1986.*

Teams: *Cincinnati N.L. 1964-1976, 1984-1986; Montreal N.L. 1977-1979; Boston A.L. 1980-1982; Philadelphia N.L. 1983.*

Postseason: *2-Time World Series Champion (1975-1976); 5 N.L. Pennants (1970, 1972, 1975-1976, 1983); 6-Time Playoff Qualifier (1970, 1972-1973, 1975-1976, 1983).*

Awards: *7-Time All-Star (1967-1970, 1974-1976).*

YEAR	TEAM	LEAGUE	G	AB	R	H	2B	3B	HR	RBI	SB	AVG
1964	CINCINNATI	NL	12	25	1	2	1	0	0	1	0	.080
1965	CINCINNATI	NL	104	281	40	73	14	4	12	47	0	.260
1966	CINCINNATI	NL	99	257	25	68	10	4	4	39	1	.265
1967	CINCINNATI	NL	156	600	78	174	28	7	26	102	0	.290
1968	CINCINNATI	NL	160	625	93	176	25	7	18	92	3	.282
1969	CINCINNATI	NL	160	629	103	185	31	2	37	122	4	.294
1970	CINCINNATI	NL	158	587	107	186	28	6	40	129	8	.317
1971	CINCINNATI	NL	158	609	72	164	22	3	25	91	4	.269
1972	CINCINNATI	NL	136	515	64	146	33	7	21	90	4	.283
1973	CINCINNATI	NL	151	564	73	177	33	3	27	101	3	.314
1974	CINCINNATI	NL	158	596	81	158	28	2	28	101	1	.265
1975	CINCINNATI	NL	137	511	74	144	28	3	20	109	1	.282
1976	CINCINNATI	NL	139	527	77	137	32	6	19	91	10	.260
1977	MONTREAL	NL	154	559	71	158	32	6	19	91	4	.283
1978	MONTREAL	NL	148	544	63	158	38	3	14	78	2	.290
1979	MONTREAL	NL	132	489	58	132	29	4	13	73	2	.270
1980	BOSTON	AL	151	585	73	161	31	3	25	105	1	.275
1981	BOSTON	AL	84	306	35	77	11	3	9	39	0	.252
1982	BOSTON	AL	69	196	18	51	14	2	6	31	0	.260
1983	PHILADELPHIA	NL	91	253	18	61	11	2	6	43	1	.241
1984	CINCINNATI	NL	71	137	9	33	6	1	2	15	0	.241
1985	CINCINNATI	NL	72	183	25	60	8	0	6	33	0	.328
1986	CINCINNATI	NL	77	200	14	51	12	1	2	29	0	.255
CAREER TOTALS			**2777**	**9778**	**1272**	**2732**	**505**	**79**	**379**	**1652**	**49**	**.279**

The Baseball Hall of Fame Almanac

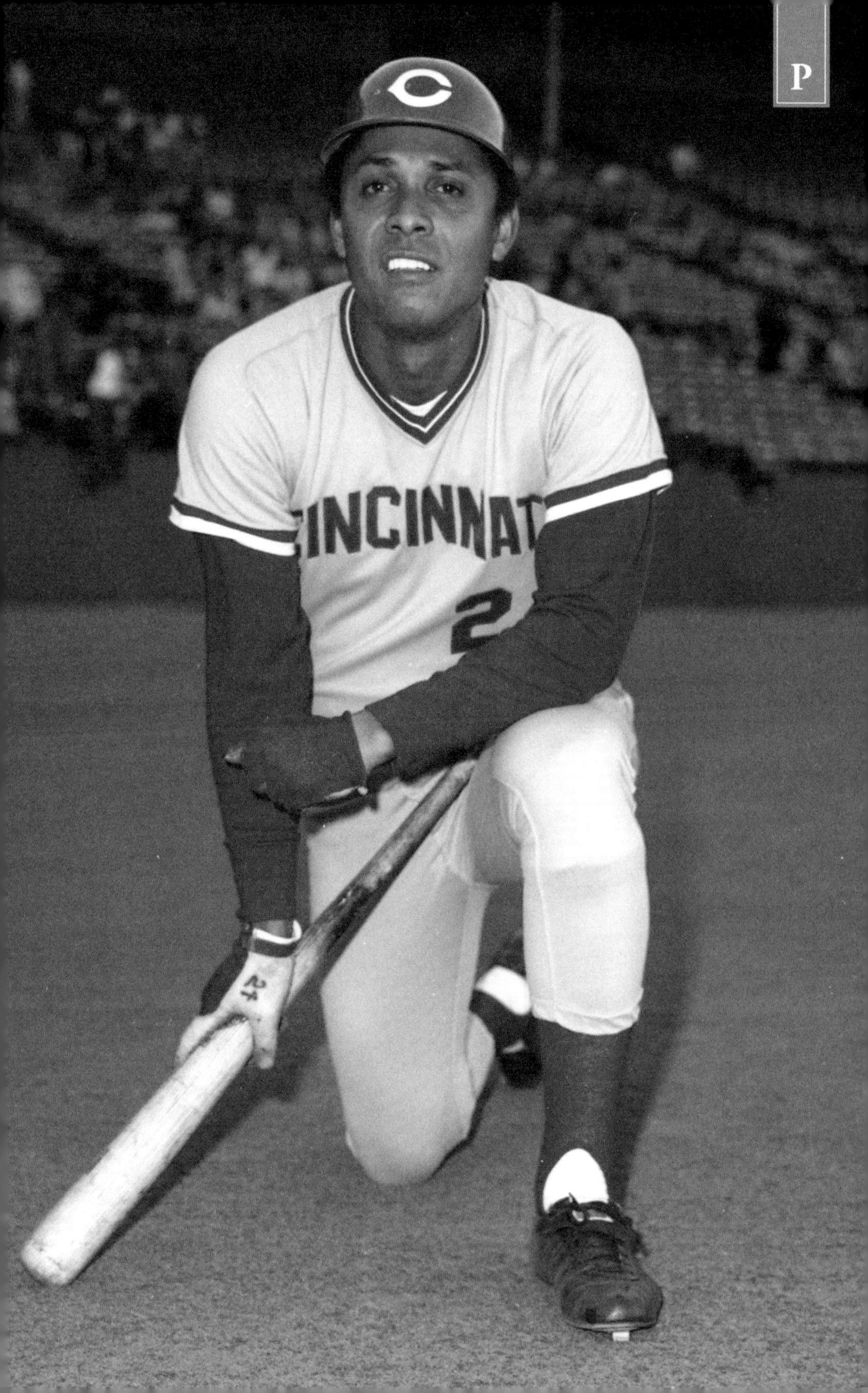

GAYLORD PERRY

"Gaylord was fantastic, simply fantastic. His contributions were even better than the records show, and they show plenty. He was such a great influence on the younger players. Perry was far and away the best pitcher in the American League," said Cleveland Indians President Gabe Paul.

Gaylord Perry was also the best pitcher in the National League. He was the first to win the Cy Young Award in both leagues, winning in 1972 with the Indians and in 1978 with the Padres. He mixed an outstanding repertoire with a spitball, real or imagined. His reputation for doctoring the ball preceded him, and some speculated that it was not so much the spitball itself, as the threat of it which played with opposing batters heads. "I watched Gaylord like a hawk," said umpire Bill Haller. "I've never found anything. I'll tell you what he's got: a good curve, a fine fastball, a good change, and a fine sinker. I'll tell you what Perry is: He's one helluva pitcher, and a fine competitor."

For his part, Perry played to type – he would fidget with his glove, touch his cap, belt, glove, or pockets repeatedly, and play both with the hitters and with his reputation. Despite constant surveillance, he was not ejected for doctoring the ball until 1982, his 21st season. Perry debuted in 1962 with the San Francisco Giants, and had his breakout season in 1966, when he carried a 20-2 record into August, before cooling off to finish 21-8. He pitched a no-hitter at Candlestick Park in 1968, shutting out Bob Gibson 1-0.

Perry was traded to the Indians prior to the 1972 season, and won his first Cy Young Award, leading the AL in wins (24) and complete games (29). He was joined there in 1974 by his brother Jim, who won 215 games to his brother's 314— they trail only the Niekro brothers in total wins, 539 to 529. During their one full season together, they recorded 38 of the team's 77 wins. Gaylord Perry, who pitched for eight teams in 22 years, was traded in 1978 to the Padres, where he won the NL Cy Young Award at age 40, going 21-6. He won his 300th game for Seattle in 1982 at age 43.

Perry, a five-time All-Star and five-time 20-game winner, won 314 games and notched 3,534 strikeouts.

GAYLORD JACKSON PERRY
SAN FRANCISCO, N.L., 1962–1971
CLEVELAND, A.L., 1972–1975
TEXAS, A.L., 1975–1977, 1980
SAN DIEGO, N.L., 1978–1979
NEW YORK, A.L., 1980
ATLANTA, N.L., 1981
SEATTLE, A.L., 1982–1983
KANSAS CITY, A.L., 1983
ACHIEVED PITCHERS' MAGIC NUMBERS WITH 314 WINS AND 3,534 STRIKEOUTS. PLAYING MIND GAMES WITH HITTERS THROUGH ARRAY OF RITUALS ON MOUND WAS PART OF HIS ARSENAL. 20-GAME WINNER 5 TIMES WITH LIFETIME ERA OF 3.10. NO-HIT CARDS FOR GIANTS 9/17/68. OUTSTANDING COMPETITOR. ONLY CY YOUNG WINNER IN BOTH LEAGUES.

Elected To The Hall Of Fame: *1991.*

Born: *Sept. 15, 1938 in Williamston, N.C.*

Height: *6-4.* **Weight:** *205.*

Threw: *Right.* **Batted:** *Right.*

Debut: *April 14, 1962.*

Final Game: *Sept. 21, 1983.*

Teams: *San Francisco N.L. 1962-1971; Cleveland A.L. 1972-1975; Texas A.L. 1975-1977, 1980; San Diego N.L. 1978-1979; New York A.L. 1980; Atlanta N.L. 1981; Seattle A.L. 1982-1983; Kansas City A.L. 1983.*

Postseason: *Playoff Qualifier (1971).*

Awards: *5-Time All-Star (1966, 1970, 1972, 1974, 1979); 2-Time Cy Young (1972, 1978).*

YEAR	TEAM	LEAGUE	G	W	L	SV	SH	IP	H	BB	SO	ERA
1962	SAN FRANCISCO	NL	13	3	1	0	0	43	54	14	20	5.23
1963	SAN FRANCISCO	NL	31	1	6	2	0	76	84	29	52	4.03
1964	SAN FRANCISCO	NL	44	12	11	5	2	206.3	179	43	155	2.75
1965	SAN FRANCISCO	NL	47	8	12	1	0	195.7	194	70	170	4.19
1966	SAN FRANCISCO	NL	36	21	8	0	3	255.7	242	40	201	2.99
1967	SAN FRANCISCO	NL	39	15	17	1	3	293	231	84	230	2.61
1968	SAN FRANCISCO	NL	39	16	15	1	3	290.7	240	59	173	2.45
1969	SAN FRANCISCO	NL	40	19	14	0	3	325.3	290	91	233	2.49
1970	SAN FRANCISCO	NL	41	23	13	0	5	328.7	292	84	214	3.20
1971	SAN FRANCISCO	NL	37	16	12	0	2	280	255	67	158	2.76
1972	CLEVELAND	AL	41	24	16	1	5	342.7	253	82	234	1.92
1973	CLEVELAND	AL	41	19	19	0	7	344	315	115	238	3.38
1974	CLEVELAND	AL	37	21	13	0	4	322.3	230	99	216	2.51
1975	CLEVELAND/TEXAS	AL	37	18	17	0	5	305.7	277	70	233	3.24
1976	TEXAS	AL	32	15	14	0	2	250.3	232	52	143	3.24
1977	TEXAS	AL	34	15	12	0	4	238	239	56	177	3.37
1978	SAN DIEGO	NL	37	21	6	0	2	260.7	241	66	154	2.73
1979	SAN DIEGO	NL	32	12	11	0	0	232.7	225	67	140	3.06
1980	TEXAS/NEW YORK	AL	34	10	13	0	2	205.7	224	64	135	3.68
1981	ATLANTA	NL	23	8	9	0	0	150.7	182	24	60	3.94
1982	SEATTLE	AL	32	10	12	0	0	216.7	245	54	116	4.40
1983	SEATTLE/KANSAS CITY	AL	30	7	14	0	1	186.3	214	49	82	4.64
CAREER TOTALS			**777**	**314**	**265**	**11**	**53**	**5350**	**4938**	**1379**	**3534**	**3.11**

EDDIE PLANK

"Eddie Plank was not the fastest, not the trickiest and not the possessor of the most stuff," Hall of Fame second baseman Eddie Collins said. "He was just the greatest."

For 17 years, Plank staked his claim as one of the best left-handers in baseball history. When he retired in 1917, Plank had won 326 games, then the record for most wins by a lefty, and had a 2.35 career ERA. He still holds the records for most complete games and shutouts by a left-hander.

Plank joined the Philadelphia Athletics in 1901, skipping the minor leagues and coming directly from Gettysburg College. He was immediately successful, winning 17 games his rookie year. While he posted ERAs of 3.31 and 3.30 in his first two years with Philadelphia, they would be the only times Plank's ERA was above 3.00 in his career. By 1903, Plank had become one of the most reliable pitchers in baseball. He went 23-16 with a 2.38 ERA and led the American League in appearances and games started. Plank's best year may have come in 1904 when he went 26-17 with a 2.17 ERA and had seven shutouts.

Plank helped the Athletics to their first World Series appearance in 1905, though they lost to the New York Giants. Plank won two World Series with the Athletics. His 2-5 record in the Fall Classic was more for lack of run support than poor performance. He had a 1.32 ERA in 54 2/3 innings in the World Series.

After the Athletics lost the 1914 World Series to the Boston Braves, A's manager Connie Mack broke up the dynasty. Plank joined the St. Louis Terriers of the Federal League. He won his 300th game Sept. 11, 1915, defeating the Newark Peppers 12-5. Plank won 21 games for the Terriers, the last of eight seasons he reached the plateau. Plank pitched two more seasons for the St. Louis Browns, picking up the final 21 victories of his career. Though he announced his retirement, the New York Yankees traded for him in 1918. Plank remained unswayed, choosing to remain at his farm in Gettysburg, Pa. He spent his retirement as a battlefield tour guide at Gettysburg National Park until he suffered a stroke and died in 1926 at the age of 50.

Elected To The Hall Of Fame: 1946.
Born: Aug. 31, 1875 in Gettysburg, Pa.
Died: Feb. 24, 1926 in Gettysburg, Pa.
Height: 5-11. **Weight:** 175.
Threw: Left. **Batted:** Left.
Debut: May 13, 1901.
Final Game: Aug. 6, 1917.
Teams: Philadelphia A.L. 1901-1914; St. Louis, Federal League 1915; St. Louis A.L. 1916-1917.
Postseason: 2-Time World Series Champion (1911, 1913); 4 A.L. Pennants (1905, 1911, 1913-1914).

YEAR	TEAM	LEAGUE	G	W	L	SV	SH	IP	H	BB	SO	ERA
1901	PHILADELPHIA	AL	33	17	13	0	1	260.7	254	68	90	3.31
1902	PHILADELPHIA	AL	36	20	15	0	1	300	319	61	107	3.30
1903	PHILADELPHIA	AL	43	23	16	0	3	336	317	65	176	2.38
1904	PHILADELPHIA	AL	44	26	17	0	7	357.3	311	86	201	2.17
1905	PHILADELPHIA	AL	41	24	12	0	4	346.7	287	75	210	2.26
1906	PHILADELPHIA	AL	26	19	6	0	5	211.7	173	51	108	2.25
1907	PHILADELPHIA	AL	43	24	16	0	8	343.7	282	85	183	2.20
1908	PHILADELPHIA	AL	34	14	16	1	4	244.7	202	46	135	2.17
1909	PHILADELPHIA	AL	34	19	10	0	3	265.3	215	62	132	1.76
1910	PHILADELPHIA	AL	38	16	10	2	1	250.3	218	55	123	2.01
1911	PHILADELPHIA	AL	40	23	8	4	6	256.7	237	77	149	2.10
1912	PHILADELPHIA	AL	37	26	6	2	5	259.7	234	83	110	2.22
1913	PHILADELPHIA	AL	41	18	10	4	7	242.7	211	57	151	2.60
1914	PHILADELPHIA	AL	34	15	7	3	4	185.3	178	42	110	2.87
1915	ST. LOUIS	FL	42	21	11	3	6	268.3	212	54	147	2.08
1916	ST. LOUIS	AL	37	16	15	3	3	235.7	203	67	88	2.33
1917	ST. LOUIS	AL	20	5	6	1	1	131	105	38	26	1.79
CAREER TOTALS			**623**	**326**	**194**	**23**	**69**	**4495.2**	**3958**	**1072**	**2246**	**2.35**

KIRBY PUCKETT

Few men have played the game of baseball with the youthful enthusiasm of Kirby Puckett. His ever-present smile, leadership skills and outgoing personality made him a fan-favorite in Minnesota.

His clutch skills on the diamond made him one of the best all-around players in the game.

"Kirby Puckett is the kind of player you hope and dream that your franchise will have," said Andy MacPhail, former general manager of the Twins. "He does everything on the field to help you win, and what he does in the clubhouse and the community is remarkable."

Born on March 14, 1960 in Chicago, just a mile from Comiskey Park, Puckett was the youngest of nine children. An All-American third baseman in high school, Puckett received little attention following graduation, but eventually worked his way onto the team at Bradley University.

"He never had a bad day," said former All-Star Frank Thomas. "I don't care how bad things were going on or off the field, Kirby found a way to make you laugh... He was a breath of fresh air in this game."

Drafted by the Minnesota Twins in 1982 as the third over-all pick, Puckett began a relationship with the team he would spend his entire career with. By 1984, he was called up to the big leagues, earning four hits in his major league debut. He finished third in the AL Rookie of the Year voting.

The six-time Gold Glove Award winner was named to 10 consecutive All-Star teams from 1986-1995 and was named MVP of the game in 1993. He finished in the top 10 in MVP voting seven times during his 12-year career. He won two World Series with the Twins in 1987 and 1991. The most memorable performance of his career came in Game 6 in 1991 against the Atlanta Braves when he made a leaping catch against the fence and hit a walk-off homer in the 11th inning to force Game 7.

In 1995, Puckett's career was cut short because of irreversible retina damage in his right eye. He finished with a .318 batting average, 414 doubles, 207 home runs and 1,085 RBI in 1,783 games.

KIRBY PUCKETT
MINNESOTA, A.L., 1984-1995

A PROVEN TEAM LEADER WITH AN EVER-PRESENT SMILE AND INFECTIOUS EXUBERANCE WHO LED THE TWINS TO WORLD SERIES TITLES IN 1987 AND 1991. OVER 12 SEASONS HIT FOR POWER AND AVERAGE, BATTING .318 WITH 414 DOUBLES AND 207 HOME RUNS. ALSO A PROLIFIC RUN PRODUCER, SCORED 1,071 RUNS AND DROVE IN 1,085 IN 1,783 GAMES. A SIX-TIME GOLD GLOVE WINNER WHO PATROLLED CENTER FIELD WITH ELEGANCE AND STYLE, ROUTINELY SCALING OUTFIELD WALLS TO TAKE AWAY HOME RUNS. THE 10-TIME ALL-STAR'S CAREER ENDED ABRUPTLY DUE TO IRREVERSIBLE RETINAL DAMAGE IN HIS RIGHT EYE.

Elected To The Hall Of Fame: *2001.*
Born: *March 14, 1960 in Chicago, Ill.*
Died: *March 6, 2006 in Phoenix, Ariz.*
Height: *5-8.* **Weight:** *178.*
Threw: *Right.* **Batted:** *Right.*
Debut: *May 8, 1984.*
Final Game: *Sept. 28, 1995.*
Teams: *Minnesota A.L. 1984-1995.*
Postseason: *2-Time World Series Champion (1987, 1991); 2 A.L. Pennants (1987, 1991).*
Awards: *10-Time All-Star (1986-1995).*

YEAR	TEAM	LEAGUE	G	AB	R	H	2B	3B	HR	RBI	SB	AVG
1984	MINNESOTA	AL	128	557	63	165	12	5	0	31	14	.296
1985	MINNESOTA	AL	161	691	80	199	29	13	4	74	21	.288
1986	MINNESOTA	AL	161	680	119	223	37	6	31	96	20	.328
1987	MINNESOTA	AL	157	624	96	207	32	5	28	99	12	.332
1988	MINNESOTA	AL	158	657	109	234	42	5	24	121	6	.356
1989	MINNESOTA	AL	159	635	75	215	45	4	9	85	11	.339
1990	MINNESOTA	AL	146	551	82	164	40	3	12	80	5	.298
1991	MINNESOTA	AL	152	611	92	195	29	6	15	89	11	.319
1992	MINNESOTA	AL	160	639	104	210	38	4	19	110	17	.329
1993	MINNESOTA	AL	156	622	89	184	39	3	22	89	8	.296
1994	MINNESOTA	AL	108	439	79	139	32	3	20	112	6	.317
1995	MINNESOTA	AL	137	538	83	169	39	0	23	99	3	.314
CAREER TOTALS			**1783**	**7244**	**1071**	**2304**	**414**	**57**	**207**	**1085**	**134**	**.318**

OLD HOSS RADBOURN

A 19th-Century pitcher who has gained new currency in the 21st Century, Charlie "Old Hoss" Radbourn put together one of baseball's most unbelievable seasons. He's pitching's answer to Hack Wilson, a great player whose one amazing campaign put him into baseball history.

Radbourn had a mercifully short career, considering that in his day, pitchers pitched virtually every day. His statistics are unfathomable by today's standards. In his rookie season, he went 25-11 with a 2.43 ERA in 325⅓ innings, leading the National League with a .694 winning percentage. He made 36 starts, completing 34 of them. He improved on those numbers in 1882 for the Providence Grays, going 33-19 with a 2.11 ERA in 51 starts, leading the league with six shutouts and 201 strikeouts in 466 innings. Then he made 68 starts for the Grays in 1883, going 48-25 with a 2.05 ERA in 632⅓ innings.

That merely set the stage for 1884, when he won 59 games while starting—and completing—73 games. He pitched 678⅔ innings and struck out 441. He didn't just produce quantity, but quality as he led the league with a 1.38 ERA.

Radbourn at first took a back seat to the team's other starting pitcher, Charlie Sweeney, and was suspended without pay in mid-July. But when Sweeney quit the team on July 22, Radbourn came to the team with an offer to pitch every game the rest of the season in exchange for a raise.

There's some dispute whether Radbourn won 59 or 60 games, but he pitched Providence to an 84-28 team record, first place in the NL and a three-game sweep of the 1884 championship series between Providence and the New York Metropolitans of the American Association.

Radbourn was never the same, slumping to 28-21 with a 2.20 ERA in 1885 before moving on to Boston of the NL in 1886. He pitched four seasons there, one for Boston in the Players League in 1890, and wrapped up with Cincinnati in the NL in 1891.

He was elected to the Hall of Fame in 1939.

CHARLIE RADBOURNE
"OLD HOSS"

PROVIDENCE, BOSTON AND CINCINNATI
NATIONAL LEAGUE 1881 TO 1891. GREATEST
OF ALL 19TH CENTURY PITCHERS. WINNING
1884 PENNANT FOR PROVIDENCE, RADBOURNE
PITCHED LAST 27 GAMES OF SEASON, WON
26. WON 3 STRAIGHT IN WORLD SERIES.

Elected To The Hall Of Fame: 1939.
Born: Dec. 11, 1854 in Rochester, N.Y.
Died: Feb. 5, 1897 in Bloomington, Ill.
Height: 5-9. **Weight:** 168.
Threw: Right. **Batted:** Right.
Debut: May 5, 1880.
Final Game: Aug. 11, 1891.
Teams: Providence N.L. 1881-1885;
Boston N.L. 1886-1889; Boston Players'
League 1890; Cincinnati N.L. 1891.
Postseason: World Series Champion
(1884); N.L. Pennant (1884).

YEAR	TEAM	LEAGUE	G	W	L	SV	SH	IP	H	BB	SO	ERA
1881	PROVIDENCE	NL	41	25	11	0	3	325.3	309	64	117	2.43
1882	PROVIDENCE	NL	54	33	19	0	6	466	422	51	201	2.11
1883	PROVIDENCE	NL	76	48	25	1	4	632.3	563	56	315	2.05
1884	PROVIDENCE	NL	75	59	12	2	11	678.7	528	98	441	1.38
1885	PROVIDENCE	NL	49	28	21	0	2	445.7	423	83	154	2.20
1886	BOSTON	NL	58	27	31	0	3	509.3	521	111	218	3.00
1887	BOSTON	NL	50	24	23	0	1	425	505	133	87	4.55
1888	BOSTON	NL	24	7	16	0	1	207	187	45	64	2.87
1889	BOSTON	NL	33	20	11	0	1	277	282	72	99	3.67
1890	BOSTON	PL	41	27	12	0	1	343	352	100	80	3.31
1891	CINCINNATI	NL	26	11	13	0	2	218	236	62	54	4.25
CAREER TOTALS			**527**	**309**	**194**	**3**	**35**	**4527.1**	**4328**	**875**	**1830**	**2.68**

The Baseball Hall of Fame Almanac

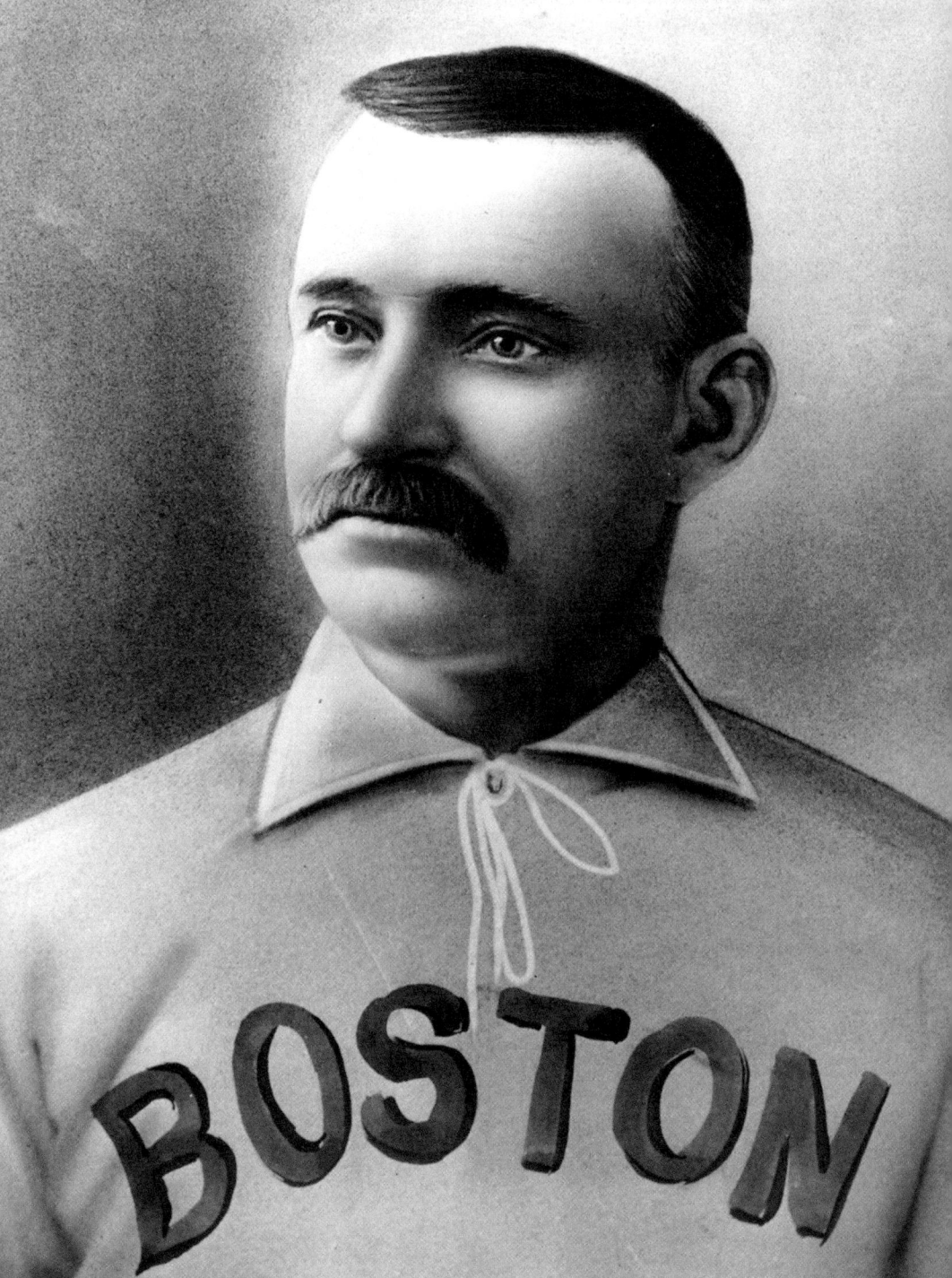

PEE WEE REESE

"Pee Wee didn't want accolades, but he had an ego and he knew that he was an exceptional athlete, and had been blessed with attributes far more important than size. He was brimming with things that made him a leader, one filled with class beyond compare." - Sports Columnist Earl Cox in The Voice-Tribune (08/18/1998)

Pee Wee Reese was the heart and soul of the Dodgers, playing shortstop from 1940-57 (he served in the Navy from 1943-45) in Brooklyn, and for one season in Los Angeles. With Reese, numbers don't tell the whole story. He was a natural leader who was named captain of the team in 1950. He was a 10-time All-Star, and his Dodgers won seven pennants—and one World Series against the Yankees. He never won an MVP award, but eight times he finished in the top 10 in MVP voting.

His nickname came not from stature, but from his childhood days as a marbles champion in Louisville. He broke in with the Dodgers in 1940, became a regular the following year, and by 1942, was leading the league in putouts and assists, and making the first of ten consecutive All-Star appearances.

He was a versatile ballplayer, and his contributions to the team were varied: he led the NL in walks with 104 in 1947, in runs in 1949, and in stolen bases in 1952. Defensively, he led the league four times in putouts, twice in double plays, and once each in fielding percentage and assists.

But his most important action on a baseball field may have been prior to a game. In 1947, the Dodgers were visiting Cincinnati, and the fans and opposing players were getting on rookie Jackie Robinson. Reese calmly walked over to Robinson, put his arm around his teammate's shoulder, and chatted. The gesture is remembered as an important moment in both Robinson's career and the acceptance of African Americans in baseball—and American society.

Earlier, Reese had refused to sign a petition circulating among Dodger teammates concerning Robinson's participation on the team. Jackie's widow, Rachel Robinson, said, "I thought it was a very supportive gesture, and very instinctive on Pee Wee's part. You shouldn't forget that Pee Wee was the captain, and he led the way. Pee Wee was more than a friend. Pee Wee was a good man."

HAROLD HENRY "PEE WEE" REESE
BROOKLYN N.L. 1940-1957
LOS ANGELES N.L. 1958
SHORTSTOP AND CAPTAIN OF GREAT DODGER TEAMS OF 1940's AND 50's. INTANGIBLE QUALITIES OF SUBTLE LEADERSHIP ON AND OFF FIELD, COMPETITIVE FIRE AND PROFESSIONAL PRIDE COMPLEMENTED DEPENDABLE GLOVE, RELIABLE BASE-RUNNING AND CLUTCH-HITTING AS SIGNIFICANT FACTORS IN 7 DODGER PENNANTS. INSTRUMENTAL IN EASING ACCEPTANCE OF JACKIE ROBINSON AS BASEBALL'S FIRST BLACK PERFORMER

Elected To The Hall Of Fame: 1984.
Born: July 23, 1918 in Ekron, Ky.
Died: Aug. 14, 1999 in Louisville, Ky.
Height: 5-10. **Weight:** 160.
Threw: Right. **Batted:** Right.
Debut: April 23, 1940.
Final Game: Sept. 26, 1958.
Teams: Brooklyn N.L. 1940-1942, 1946-1957; Los Angeles N.L. 1958.
Postseason: World Series Champion (1955); 7 N.L. Pennants (1941, 1947, 1949, 1952-1953, 1955-1956).
Awards: 10-Time All-Star (1942, 1946-1954).

YEAR	TEAM	LEAGUE	G	AB	R	H	2B	3B	HR	RBI	SB	AVG
1940	BROOKLYN	NL	84	312	58	85	8	4	5	28	15	.272
1941	BROOKLYN	NL	152	595	76	136	23	5	2	46	10	.229
1942	BROOKLYN	NL	151	564	87	144	24	5	3	53	15	.255
1946	BROOKLYN	NL	152	542	79	154	16	10	5	60	10	.284
1947	BROOKLYN	NL	142	476	81	135	24	4	12	73	7	.284
1948	BROOKLYN	NL	151	566	96	155	31	4	9	75	25	.274
1949	BROOKLYN	NL	155	617	132	172	27	3	16	73	26	.279
1950	BROOKLYN	NL	141	531	97	138	21	5	11	52	17	.260
1951	BROOKLYN	NL	154	616	94	176	20	8	10	84	20	.286
1952	BROOKLYN	NL	149	559	94	152	18	8	6	58	30	.272
1953	BROOKLYN	NL	140	524	108	142	25	7	13	61	22	.271
1954	BROOKLYN	NL	141	554	98	171	35	8	10	69	8	.309
1955	BROOKLYN	NL	145	553	99	156	29	4	10	61	8	.282
1956	BROOKLYN	NL	147	572	85	147	19	2	9	46	13	.257
1957	BROOKLYN	NL	103	330	33	74	3	1	1	29	5	.224
1958	LOS ANGELES	NL	59	147	21	33	7	2	4	17	1	.224
CAREER TOTALS			2166	8058	1338	2170	330	80	126	885	232	.269

JIM RICE

"He had tremendous power, but yet he was an excellent hitter who could hit to the opposite field or go up the middle. Most power hitters have holes. Jim Rice had no big holes," said Hall of Fame relief pitcher Goose Gossage.

When Jim Rice took over as Boston's everyday left fielder in 1975, the Red Sox already had a proud tradition of outfielders patrolling the Green Monster in Fenway Park. Ted Williams spent two decades establishing himself as one of the greatest hitters of all-time before giving way to Carl Yastrzemski, who had a Hall of Fame career himself over a 23-year career with the Red Sox.

With Yastrzemski at first base and designated hitter in 1975, Rice took over in left field at age 22 and led the Red Sox in home runs with 22, finishing third in the American League MVP voting and second in Rookie of the Year voting to teammate Fred Lynn, who also took home the MVP award.

Like Yastrzemski, Rice spent his entire career in Boston, where he proved himself as one of the most dangerous power hitters of his generation. Over a 12-year period from 1975-1986, Rice hit 350 home runs. During that period, only Mike Schmidt and Dave Kingman hit more homers. Rice led the American League in home runs three times and slugging twice during that span.

Rice helped lead Boston to two World Series appearances, and although he didn't play in the '75 World Series due to injury, he hit .333 in seven games against the Mets in 1986.

Rice's best season came in 1978, when he was named the AL's Most Valuable Player. Rice led the major leagues with 46 home runs, becoming the first Red Sox to hit that many home runs in a single season since Jimmie Foxx hit 50 in 1938. No AL hitter had clubbed that many home runs in a single season since Harmon Killebrew swatted 49 for the Twins in 1969.

Rice was more than just a one-dimensional, all-or-nothing slugger. He hit over .300 seven times and ranked among the top 10 in the AL in average six times. An eight-time all-star, Rice finished among the top five in AL MVP voting in six seasons and won two AL Silver Sluggers. Though he wasn't known for his prowess in the field, Rice ranked among the top five AL left fielders in assists 11 times and putouts seven times.

JAMES EDWARD RICE
"JIM"
BOSTON, A.L., 1974-1989

WITH TITANIC STRENGTH AND AN INNATE ABILITY TO HIT TO ALL FIELDS, BATTED .298 WITH 382 HOME RUNS AND 1,451 RBI. ONLY PLAYER WITH THREE STRAIGHT 35-HOME RUN, 100-RBI AND 200-HIT SEASONS. HIT 20 OR MORE HOME RUNS 11 TIMES AND TOTALED EIGHT 100-RBI SEASONS. THE 1978 A.L. MVP, LED LEAGUE IN HOME RUNS (46), RBI (139), HITS (213) AND AN ASTONISHING 406 TOTAL BASES. AN EIGHT-TIME ALL-STAR, LED THE A.L. IN TOTAL BASES FOUR TIMES, HOME RUNS THREE TIMES AND TWICE IN RBI AND SLUGGING PERCENTAGE.

Elected To The Hall Of Fame: 2009.
Born: March 8, 1953.
Height: 6-2. **Weight:** 200.
Threw: Right. **Batted:** Right.
Debut: Aug. 19, 1974.
Final Game: Aug. 3, 1989.
Teams: Boston A.L. 1974-89
Postseason: A.L. Pennant (1986); 2-Time Playoff Qualifier (1986, 1988).
Awards: 8-Time All-Star (1977-1980, 1983-1986); A.L. Most Valuable Player (1978).

YEAR	TEAM	LEAGUE	G	AB	R	H	2B	3B	HR	RBI	SB	AVG
1974	BOSTON	AL	24	67	6	18	2	1	1	13	0	.269
1975	BOSTON	AL	144	564	92	174	29	4	22	102	10	.309
1976	BOSTON	AL	153	581	75	164	25	8	25	85	8	.282
1977	BOSTON	AL	160	644	104	206	29	15	39	114	5	.320
1978	BOSTON	AL	163	677	121	213	25	15	46	139	7	.315
1979	BOSTON	AL	158	619	117	201	39	6	39	130	9	.325
1980	BOSTON	AL	124	504	81	148	22	6	24	86	8	.294
1981	BOSTON	AL	108	451	51	128	18	1	17	62	2	.284
1982	BOSTON	AL	145	573	86	177	24	5	24	97	0	.309
1983	BOSTON	AL	155	626	90	191	34	1	39	126	0	.305
1984	BOSTON	AL	159	657	98	184	25	7	28	122	4	.280
1985	BOSTON	AL	140	546	85	159	20	3	27	103	2	.291
1986	BOSTON	AL	157	618	98	200	39	2	20	110	0	.324
1987	BOSTON	AL	108	404	66	112	14	0	13	62	1	.277
1988	BOSTON	AL	135	485	57	128	18	3	15	72	1	.264
1989	BOSTON	AL	56	209	22	49	10	2	3	28	1	.234
CAREER TOTALS			**2089**	**8225**	**1249**	**2452**	**373**	**79**	**382**	**1451**	**58**	**.298**

SAM RICE

EDGAR CHARLES (SAM) RICE
WASHINGTON, A.L. 1915 TO 1933
CLEVELAND, A.L. 1934
AT BAT 600 OR MORE TIMES EIGHT
DIFFERENT SEASONS. HAD 200 OR MORE HITS
IN EACH OF SIX SEASONS. BATTED .322
FOR 20-YEAR CAREER AND HAD 2987 HITS.
SET A.L. RECORD WITH 182 SINGLES IN
1925. LED A.L. IN NUMBER OF HITS 216
IN 1924 AND 1926. LED A.L. IN PUTOUTS
FOR OUTFIELDERS WITH 454 IN 1920 AND
385 IN 1922.

S am Rice didn't enter the majors until he was 25 years old. He started in the big leagues as a pitcher and developed into a great hitter, with a .322 lifetime average, 2,987 total hits and six seasons with more than 200 hits.

The right fielder batted .299 in his first season and batted over .300 14 times during his 20-year career. Rice was a part of the only three Washington Senators teams that ever won pennants and he holds the franchise records for hits, doubles, triples and runs scored.

In 1920, Rice had 454 putouts, good for the American League record at the time. He led the league in putouts twice and in assists once, and was among the league leaders numerous times. He also topped the circuit in 1920 with 63 stolen bases and was ranked among the top five in that category for eight consecutive seasons.

Rice led the AL in hits in 1924, helping the Senators to their first pennant. They beat the New York Giants to become World Series champions. The following season, Washington once again won the pennant, but lost the Fall Classic in seven games. In that Series, Rice had a .364 average, 12 hits, five runs and three RBI. He had career highs in 1925 in batting average (.350) and hits (227), while scoring 111 runs. Rice had 87 RBI and his 182 singles were a league record until more than half a century later.

Despite his success in the 1925 World Series, he is best remembered for one of the most disputed plays of all time. Rice fell into the stands going after a fly ball, and went out of view. When he emerged with the ball in his glove the umpire called the batter out. He was often asked about the play and generally refused to answer or give any specifics. He wrote a letter to the Hall of Fame about the catch that he requested remain sealed until his death. "I remember trotting back towards the infield carrying the ball for about halfway and then tossed it towards the pitcher's mound (how I wished many times I had kept it)," Rice wrote. "At no time did I lose possession of the ball."

Nearing the end of his career in 1934, Rice signed with Cleveland. In total, he played 543 games over age 40, hitting .321. He retired just 13 hits shy of the 3,000-mark.

Elected To The Hall Of Fame: 1963.
Born: Feb. 20, 1890 in Morocco, Ind.
Died: Oct. 13, 1974 in Rossmoor, Md.
Height: 5-9. *Weight:* 150.
Threw: Right. *Batted:* Left.
Debut: Aug. 7, 1915.
Final Game: Sept. 18, 1934.
Teams: Washington A.L. 1915-1933;
Cleveland A.L. 1934.
Postseason: World Series Champion
(1924); 3 A.L. Pennants (1924-1925, 1933).

YEAR	TEAM	LEAGUE	G	AB	R	H	2B	3B	HR	RBI	SB	AVG
1915	WASHINGTON	AL	4	8	0	3	0	0	0	0	0	.375
1916	WASHINGTON	AL	58	197	26	59	8	3	1	17	4	.299
1917	WASHINGTON	AL	155	586	77	177	25	7	0	69	35	.302
1918	WASHINGTON	AL	7	23	3	8	1	0	0	3	1	.348
1919	WASHINGTON	AL	141	557	80	179	23	9	3	71	26	.321
1920	WASHINGTON	AL	153	624	83	211	29	9	3	80	63	.338
1921	WASHINGTON	AL	143	561	83	185	39	13	4	79	26	.330
1922	WASHINGTON	AL	154	633	91	187	37	13	6	69	20	.295
1923	WASHINGTON	AL	148	595	117	188	35	18	3	75	20	.316
1924	WASHINGTON	AL	154	646	106	216	39	14	1	76	24	.334
1925	WASHINGTON	AL	152	649	111	227	31	13	1	87	26	.350
1926	WASHINGTON	AL	152	641	98	216	32	14	3	76	24	.337
1927	WASHINGTON	AL	142	603	98	179	33	14	2	65	19	.297
1928	WASHINGTON	AL	148	616	95	202	32	15	2	55	16	.328
1929	WASHINGTON	AL	150	616	119	199	39	10	1	62	16	.323
1930	WASHINGTON	AL	147	593	121	207	35	13	1	73	13	.349
1931	WASHINGTON	AL	120	413	81	128	21	8	0	42	6	.310
1932	WASHINGTON	AL	106	288	58	93	16	7	1	34	7	.323
1933	WASHINGTON	AL	73	85	19	25	4	3	1	12	0	.294
1934	CLEVELAND	AL	97	335	48	98	19	1	1	33	5	.293
CAREER TOTALS			**2404**	**9269**	**1514**	**2987**	**498**	**184**	**34**	**1078**	**351**	**.322**

CAL RIPKEN JR.

Longtime manager Joe Torre said, "Cal is a bridge, maybe the last bridge, back to the way the game was played. Hitting home runs and all that other good stuff is not enough. It's how you handle yourself in all the good times and bad times that matters. That's what Cal showed us. Being a star is not enough. He showed us how to be more."

Cal Ripken Jr. was a throwback. He played hard, he played to win, and he played in every game. On May 30, 1982, Ripken began "the streak"— the longest stretch of consecutive games played by anyone in baseball history (2,632), and in the process earned the moniker "Iron Man." Fellow Hall of Fame shortstop Ozzie Smith explained "It is extremely impressive that Cal was able to do something like this while playing shortstop. You have to have size and strength, which he obviously has, you have to have skill and you have to have some luck. I have always thought that shortstops were the best athletes on the field and this just reconfirms that."

A 19-time All-Star and two-time American League Most Valuable Player, Cal Ripken redefined the shortstop position. Traditionally viewed as a position from which you wouldn't expect a lot of offense, Ripken ushered in an era of superstar shortstops that could not only handle the rigors of the position defensively, but regularly hit 20-30 home runs and bat .300.

One of these shortstops, Alex Rodriguez, said of his boyhood idol, "He was a pioneer in many ways. The most underrated thing about him was his defense. The year he went out and made three errors and led the league in double plays, that was awesome. He'll be remembered more for his home runs, RBI and games played, but his defense was something."

It was ultimately Cal Ripken and "the streak" that brought fans back from the dark times of the 1994 baseball strike when on Sept. 6, 1995, baseball's "Iron Man" passed Lou Gehrig's mark of 2,130 consecutive games played. Curt Schilling said, "No one's ever had that aura like he had."

CALVIN EDWIN RIPKEN JR.
"CAL" "IRON MAN"
BALTIMORE, A.L., 1981-2001

ARRIVED AT THE BALLPARK EVERY DAY WITH A BURNING DESIRE TO PERFORM AT HIS HIGHEST LEVEL. DEDICATION AND WORK ETHIC RESULTED IN A RECORD 2,632 CONSECUTIVE GAMES PLAYED FROM MAY 30, 1982 THROUGH SEPTEMBER 19, 1998, EARNING HIM THE TITLE OF BASEBALL'S "IRON MAN" IN 21 SEASONS, COLLECTED 3,184 HITS AND 431 HOME RUNS, AND WAS NAMED TO 19 CONSECUTIVE ALL-STAR TEAMS, WON ROOKIE OF THE YEAR HONORS, TWO MVPS AND TWO GOLD GLOVE AWARDS. HIS ORIOLES WON THE 1983 WORLD SERIES AND HE HIT .336 LIFETIME IN 28 POSTSEASON GAMES.

Iron Man

Elected To The Hall Of Fame: 2007.

Born: Aug. 24, 1960 in Havre de Grace, Md.

Height: 6-4. **Weight:** 200.

Threw: Right. **Batted:** Right.

Debut: Aug. 10, 1981.

Final Game: Oct. 6, 2001.

Teams: Baltimore, A.L. 1981-2001.

Postseason: World Series Champion (1983); A.L. Pennant (1983); 3-Time Playoff Qualifier (1983, 1996-1997).

Awards: 19-Time All-Star (1983-2001); A.L. Rookie of the Year (1982); 2-Time A.L. MVP (1983, 1991).

YEAR	TEAM	LEAGUE	G	AB	R	H	2B	3B	HR	RBI	SB	AVG
1981	BALTIMORE	AL	23	39	1	5	0	0	0	0	0	.128
1982	BALTIMORE	AL	160	598	90	158	32	5	28	93	3	.264
1983	BALTIMORE	AL	162	663	121	211	47	2	27	102	0	.318
1984	BALTIMORE	AL	162	641	103	195	37	7	27	86	2	.304
1985	BALTIMORE	AL	161	642	116	181	32	5	26	110	2	.282
1986	BALTIMORE	AL	162	627	98	177	35	1	25	81	4	.282
1987	BALTIMORE	AL	162	624	97	157	28	3	27	98	3	.252
1988	BALTIMORE	AL	161	575	87	152	25	1	23	81	2	.264
1989	BALTIMORE	AL	162	646	80	166	30	0	21	93	3	.257
1990	BALTIMORE	AL	161	600	78	150	28	4	21	84	3	.250
1991	BALTIMORE	AL	162	650	99	210	46	5	34	114	6	.323
1992	BALTIMORE	AL	162	637	73	160	29	1	14	72	4	.251
1993	BALTIMORE	AL	162	641	87	165	26	3	24	90	1	.257
1994	BALTIMORE	AL	112	444	71	140	19	3	13	75	1	.315
1995	BALTIMORE	AL	144	550	71	144	33	2	17	88	0	.262
1996	BALTIMORE	AL	163	640	94	178	40	1	26	102	1	.278
1997	BALTIMORE	AL	162	615	79	166	30	0	17	84	1	.270
1998	BALTIMORE	AL	161	601	65	163	27	1	14	61	0	.271
1999	BALTIMORE	AL	86	332	51	113	27	0	18	57	0	.340
2000	BALTIMORE	AL	83	309	43	79	16	0	15	56	0	.256
2001	BALTIMORE	AL	128	477	43	114	16	0	14	68	0	.239
CAREER TOTALS			3001	11551	1647	3184	603	44	431	1695	36	.276

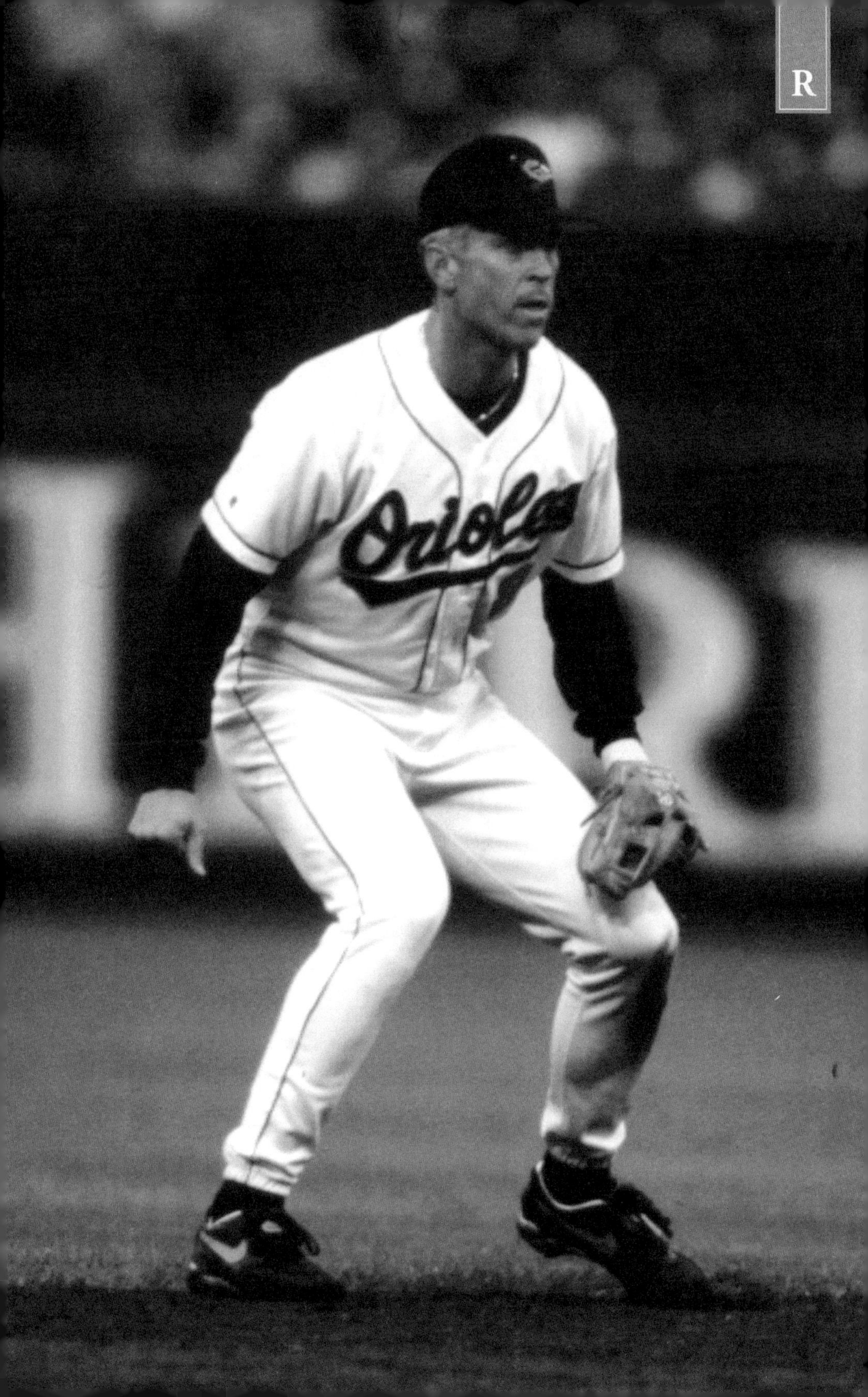
Orioles

EPPA RIXEY

"I finally made it!" Eppa Rixey said in a postcard to his family and friends while visiting Cooperstown after his retirement.

Eppa Rixey was an atypical ball player, coming to the big leagues from the University of Virginia in 1912 with a degree in chemistry. The left-hander's talents were spotted by National League umpire Charles Rigler, who was a part of the baseball and basketball staff at the university, both teams on which Rixey participated. Thanks to Rigler's recommendation, Rixey was brought up to the Philadelphia Phillies without ever having spent any time in the minor leagues. During the offseason, Rixey went back to school to get his master's in chemistry, also studying math and Latin. He fought off the resentment that other players had for his education by engaging in their hazing and standing his ground when initiated.

With the Phillies, the southpaw won a National League pennant in 1915. However, after leaving baseball in 1918 to serve in World War I with the Chemical Warfare Division in Europe, Rixey returned not quite the same ball player he was when he left. After being traded to the Cincinnati Reds before the 1921 season, things turned around for the pitcher. He won 20 or more games in a season three times, racking up eight consecutive winning seasons with his new team. In 1921, Rixey allowed only one home run in the 301 innings he pitched. In 1922, he led the league with 25 wins and between July 24 and August 28, 1932, the hurler threw 27 consecutive scoreless innings.

The 266-251 career record he compiled came while pitching for many second-division teams. During his 21 seasons, Rixey posted a 3.15 lifetime ERA and completed 290 games. He threw 4,494⅔ innings and struck out 1,350 batters. In 1969, he was named the Reds' most outstanding lefty by the fans. He was also later inducted into the Cincinnati Reds Hall of Fame. Rixey's win total stood as the National League record for left-handed pitchers until Warren Spahn topped it in 1959. Always witty, at the time Rixey said that he was glad Spahn beat his record because it was a reminder to everyone that he had set it in the first place.

EPPA RIXEY
PHILADELPHIA, N.L. 1912 TO 1920
CINCINNATI, N.L. 1921 TO 1933
WON 266 LOST 251 PCT. .515 ERA 3.15
SET RECORD FOR MOST VICTORIES BY
LEFT-HANDED PITCHER. LED LEAGUE IN
VICTORIES WITH 25 IN 1922. GAVE ONLY
1082 BASE ON BALLS IN 4494 INNINGS.

Elected To The Hall Of Fame: *1963.*
Born: *May 3, 1891 in Culpeper, Va.*
Died: *Feb. 28, 1963 in Terrace Park, Ohio.*
Height: *6-5.* **Weight:** *210.*
Threw: *Left.* **Batted:** *Right.*
Debut: *June 21, 1912.*
Final Game: *Aug. 5, 1933.*
Teams: *Philadelphia N.L. 1912-1917,*
1919-1920; Cincinnati N.L. 1921-1933.
Postseason: *N.L. Pennant (1915).*

YEAR	TEAM	LEAGUE	G	W	L	SV	SH	IP	H	BB	SO	ERA
1912	PHILADELPHIA	NL	23	10	10	0	3	162	147	54	59	2.50
1913	PHILADELPHIA	NL	35	9	5	2	1	155.7	148	56	75	3.12
1914	PHILADELPHIA	NL	24	2	11	0	0	103	124	45	41	4.37
1915	PHILADELPHIA	NL	29	11	12	1	2	176.7	163	64	88	2.39
1916	PHILADELPHIA	NL	38	22	10	0	3	287	239	74	134	1.85
1917	PHILADELPHIA	NL	39	16	21	1	4	281.3	249	67	121	2.27
1919	PHILADELPHIA	NL	23	6	12	0	1	154	160	50	63	3.97
1920	PHILADELPHIA	NL	41	11	22	2	0	284.3	288	69	109	3.48
1921	CINCINNATI	NL	40	19	18	1	2	301	324	66	76	2.78
1922	CINCINNATI	NL	40	25	13	0	2	313.3	337	45	80	3.53
1923	CINCINNATI	NL	42	20	15	1	3	309	334	65	97	2.80
1924	CINCINNATI	NL	35	15	14	1	4	238.3	219	47	57	2.76
1925	CINCINNATI	NL	39	21	11	1	2	287.3	302	47	69	2.88
1926	CINCINNATI	NL	37	14	8	0	3	233	231	58	61	3.40
1927	CINCINNATI	NL	34	12	10	1	1	219.7	240	43	42	3.48
1928	CINCINNATI	NL	43	19	18	2	3	291.3	317	67	58	3.43
1929	CINCINNATI	NL	35	10	13	1	0	201	235	60	37	4.16
1930	CINCINNATI	NL	32	9	13	0	0	164	207	47	37	5.10
1931	CINCINNATI	NL	22	4	7	0	0	126.7	143	30	22	3.91
1932	CINCINNATI	NL	25	5	5	0	2	111.7	108	16	14	2.66
1933	CINCINNATI	NL	16	6	3	0	1	94.3	118	12	10	3.15
CAREER TOTALS			**692**	**266**	**251**	**14**	**37**	**4494.7**	**4633**	**1082**	**1350**	**3.15**

PHIL RIZZUTO

Longtime shortstop Phil Rizzuto was such an integral part of the New York Yankees' success in the 1940s and 1950s, when the team was winning nine American League pennants and seven World Series titles during his 13 seasons with the club, that fellow Hall of Famer Ted Williams once remarked "if the Red Sox would have had Phil we would have won all those pennants."

"I hustled and got on base and made the double play," Rizzuto said. "That's all the Yankees needed in those days, somebody who could get on base, make the double play and not make too many errors. The other guys did all the work, all the RBIs and home runs."

The diminutive (5-foot-6, 150 pounds) Rizzuto, nicknamed "The Scooter," spent his entire big league career as an excellent-fielding shortstop and deft bunter with the Yankees. After breaking into the lineup in 1941 and becoming an All-Star the next season, he spent the next three years in the Navy.

By 1949 Rizzuto had become an offensive force as well, finishing second in the AL MVP voting after hitting .275 with 110 runs scored. Arguably Rizzuto's best season came in 1950 when won MVP honors after collecting career-highs in hits (200), batting average (.324), on-base percentage (.418), runs (125), home runs (7), walks (92), doubles (36) and slugging average (.439.)

"All the Yankees knew how important he was to the ball club. The heart of the team on defense is up the middle, and there were few better than Phil there," said teammate Gil McDougald. "And he was tough at the plate. He did what had to be done. I saw him even jump up to bunt a ball on a squeeze play, not once but a dozen times, and we scored."

After Rizzuto, a five-time All-Star, finished his playing career in 1956 with a batting average of .273, 1,588 hits, 149 stolen bases, 38 home runs and 563 RBI, he moved directly into the Yankees' broadcast booth.

It was while behind the microphone for the next 40 years that Rizzuto developed a whole new legion of fans with his trademark "Holy Cow" expression and his uniquely amusing style where he often shifted from game action to digressions on non-baseball subjects.

PHILIP FRANCIS RIZZUTO
"SCOOTER"

NEW YORK, A.L., 1941-1942, 1946-1956
OVERCAME DIMINUTIVE SIZE (5'6", 150 LBS) TO ANCHOR SUPERB YANKEE TEAMS WHICH WON 10 PENNANTS AND 8 WORLD SERIES DURING HIS 13 MAJOR LEAGUE SEASONS. OUTSTANDING SHORTSTOP ON FIVE CONSECUTIVE WORLD CHAMPIONSHIP CLUBS. SKILLED BUNTER AND ENTHUSIASTIC BASE RUNNER WITH SOLID .273 LIFETIME BATTING AVERAGE. ALL-STAR FIVE TIMES AND A.L. MVP IN 1950 WHEN HE PEAKED AT .324 WITH 200 HITS AND A .439 SLUGGING PCT.

Scooter

Elected To The Hall Of Fame: 1994.
Born: Sept. 25, 1917 in Brooklyn, N.Y.
Died: Aug. 13, 2007 in West Orange, N.J.
Height: 5-6. **Weight:** 150.
Threw: Right. **Batted:** Right.
Debut: Apr. 14, 1941.
Final Game: Aug. 16, 1956.
Teams: New York A.L. 1941-1942, 1946-1956
Postseason: 7-Time World Series Champion (1941, 1947, 1949-1953 – played on 1956 Yankees but not in World Series); 9 A.L. Pennants (1941-1942, 1947, 1949-1953, 1955).
Awards: 5-Time All-Star (1942, 1950-1953); A.L. Most Valuable Player (1950).

YEAR	TEAM	LEAGUE	G	AB	R	H	2B	3B	HR	RBI	SB	AVG
1941	NEW YORK	AL	133	515	65	158	20	9	3	46	14	.307
1942	NEW YORK	AL	144	553	79	157	24	7	4	68	22	.284
1946	NEW YORK	AL	126	471	53	121	17	1	2	38	14	.257
1947	NEW YORK	AL	153	549	78	150	26	9	2	60	11	.273
1948	NEW YORK	AL	128	464	65	117	13	2	6	50	6	.252
1949	NEW YORK	AL	153	614	110	169	22	7	5	65	18	.275
1950	NEW YORK	AL	155	617	125	200	36	7	7	66	12	.324
1951	NEW YORK	AL	144	540	87	148	21	6	2	43	18	.274
1952	NEW YORK	AL	152	578	89	147	24	10	2	43	17	.254
1953	NEW YORK	AL	134	413	54	112	21	3	2	54	4	.271
1954	NEW YORK	AL	127	307	47	60	11	0	2	15	3	.195
1955	NEW YORK	AL	81	143	19	37	4	1	1	9	7	.259
1956	NEW YORK	AL	31	52	6	12	0	0	0	6	3	.231
CAREER TOTALS			**1661**	**5816**	**877**	**1588**	**239**	**62**	**38**	**563**	**149**	**.273**

ROBIN ROBERTS

Over the course of his career, Robin Roberts was two distinct types of pitcher. Hall of Famer Ralph Kiner described the early part of his career best, when he said "Probably the best fastball I ever saw was Robin Roberts. His ball would rise around six or eight inches, and with plenty on it. And he had great control."

Robin Roberts first toed the rubber for the Philadelphia Phillies at the age of 21 in 1948, against the Pittsburgh Pirates. He walked the first batter he faced on what he described as "four of the wildest pitches you ever saw." Roberts settled down though and struck out the next batter using what would become his signature pitch, the hard rising fastball. Roberts went eight innings exhibiting strong command, but took the hard luck 2-0 loss. He bounced back five days later and earned the first of his 286 career wins, a complete game victory over the Cincinnati Reds.

From 1950-1955, Roberts was arguably the most dominant pitcher in the league recording six straight 20 win seasons, and in 1950 he led the "Whiz Kids" to their first World Series appearance since 1915. Whiz Kids teammate Curt Simmons recalled "He was like a diesel engine. The more you used him, the better he ran. I don't think you could wear him out. The end of the 1950 season, I was in the Army and I think Bob Miller had a bad back. I know Robin had to throw almost every day." As the decade of the 1950's wore on, Roberts lost velocity on his fastball. His precision control allowed him to reinvent himself as the type of finesse pitcher that Hall of Famer Willie Stargell said "looks like the kind of pitcher you can't wait to swing at, but you swing, and the ball isn't where you thought it was."

Roberts retired in 1966. A seven time All-Star, he was inducted into the Baseball Hall of Fame in 1976. Phillies chairman Bill Giles said: "When I think of Robin there is definitely one word that comes quickly to mind: Class. He was a class act both on and off the field. He was definitely one of the most consistent quality pitchers of all time, and the way he lived his life was exemplary. Every young baseball player should model their life after Robin."

ROBIN EVAN ROBERTS
PHILADELPHIA N.L., BALTIMORE A.L.,
HOUSTON N.L., CHICAGO N.L.,
1948-1966
TIRELESS WORKER WHO NEVER MISSED A START
IN DECADE OF THE FIFTIES. WON 286 OVER 19
YEAR CAREER. WON 20 GAMES 6 YEARS IN A ROW
FOR PHILADELPHIA WHIZ KIDS. LED N.L. IN INNINGS
PITCHED, 1951-55 AND IN COMPLETE GAMES, 1952-56.
STARTED 5 ALL-STAR GAMES. MAJOR LEAGUE PLAYER
OF THE YEAR, 1952 AND 1955.

Elected To The Hall Of Fame: 1976.
Born: Sept. 30, 1926 in Springfield, Ill.
Died: May 6, 2010 in Temple Terrace, Fla.
Height: 6-0. **Weight:** 190.
Threw: Right. **Batted:** Both.
Debut: June 18, 1948.
Final Game: Sept. 3, 1966.
Teams: Philadelphia N.L. 1948-1961;
Baltimore A.L. 1962-65; Houston N.L.
1965-66; Chicago N.L. 1966.
Postseason: N.L. Pennant (1950).
Awards: 7-Time All-Star (1950-1956).

YEAR	TEAM	LEAGUE	G	W	L	SV	SH	IP	H	BB	SO	ERA
1948	PHILADELPHIA	NL	20	7	9	0	0	146.7	148	61	84	3.19
1949	PHILADELPHIA	NL	43	15	15	4	3	226.7	229	75	95	3.69
1950	PHILADELPHIA	NL	40	20	11	1	5	304.3	282	77	146	3.02
1951	PHILADELPHIA	NL	44	21	15	2	6	315	284	64	127	3.03
1952	PHILADELPHIA	NL	39	28	7	2	3	330	292	45	148	2.59
1953	PHILADELPHIA	NL	44	23	16	2	5	346.7	324	61	198	2.75
1954	PHILADELPHIA	NL	45	23	15	4	4	336.7	289	56	185	2.97
1955	PHILADELPHIA	NL	41	23	14	3	1	305	292	53	160	3.28
1956	PHILADELPHIA	NL	43	19	18	3	1	297.3	328	40	157	4.45
1957	PHILADELPHIA	NL	39	10	22	2	2	249.7	246	43	128	4.07
1958	PHILADELPHIA	NL	35	17	14	0	1	269.7	270	51	130	3.24
1959	PHILADELPHIA	NL	35	15	17	0	2	257.3	267	35	137	4.27
1960	PHILADELPHIA	NL	35	12	16	1	2	237.3	256	34	122	4.02
1961	PHILADELPHIA	NL	26	1	10	0	0	117	154	23	54	5.85
1962	BALTIMORE	AL	27	10	9	0	0	191.3	176	41	102	2.78
1963	BALTIMORE	AL	35	14	13	0	2	251.3	230	40	124	3.33
1964	BALTIMORE	AL	31	13	7	0	4	204	203	52	109	2.91
1965	BALTIMORE/HOUSTON	AL/NL	30	10	9	0	3	190.7	171	30	97	2.78
1966	HOUSTON/CHICAGO	NL	24	5	8	1	1	112	141	21	54	4.82
CAREER TOTALS			**676**	**286**	**245**	**25**	**45**	**4688.7**	**4582**	**902**	**2357**	**3.41**

BROOKS ROBINSON

Known as "The Human Vacuum Cleaner," Brooks Robinson is regarded as arguably the best defensive third-baseman the game has ever seen – he could make even the most difficult of plays look routine.

Hall of Famer Frank Robinson recalled what it was like to watch his teammate go to work: "He was the best defensive player at any position. I used to stand in the outfield like a fan and watch him make play after play. I used to think, 'WOW, I can't believe this.' "

Robinson began his career with the Baltimore Orioles, the only team he ever played for, in 1955, and for 23 years dazzled fans on the field with his glove. Off the field, he was humble and gracious. Joe Falls of *The Detroit News* pondered "How many interviews, how many questions — how many times you approached him and got only courtesy and decency in return. A true gentleman who never took himself seriously. I always had the idea he didn't know he was Brooks Robinson."

In total, the 18-time All-Star and winner of a record 16 consecutive Gold Glove Awards led the Orioles to six postseasons including two World Series Championships. In 1964, Robinson took home American League MVP honors, putting up the finest offensive season of his career, leading the league with 118 RBI. In 1966, he won the All-Star Game MVP Award despite the American League losing the game, and in 1970, was named the World Series MVP where he batted .429 with two home runs and six RBI.

Robinson retired after the 1977 season and the Orioles wasted no time in retiring his number 5. The Orioles played their last game at Baltimore's Memorial Stadium on October 6, 1991. At the game's conclusion, some of the team's all-time greats were invited to take the field at their position during the closing ceremonies. The first player called to take the field was Brooks Robinson.

He was so beloved in Baltimore that sports writer Gordon Beard wrote "Brooks (Robinson) never asked anyone to name a candy bar after him. In Baltimore, people named their children after him."

BROOKS CALBERT ROBINSON, JR.
BALTIMORE A.L. 1955-1977
ESTABLISHED MODERN STANDARD OF EXCELLENCE FOR THIRD BASEMEN, SETTING MAJOR LEAGUE RECORDS AT HIS POSITION FOR SEASONS (23), FIELDING PCT. (.971), GAMES (2,870), PUTOUTS (2,697), ASSISTS (6,205), AND DOUBLE PLAYS (618). HIT 268 CAREER HOME RUNS. NAMED TO 18 CONSECUTIVE ALL STAR TEAMS. MVP OF 1970 WORLD SERIES. AMERICAN LEAGUE MVP IN 1964.

The Human Vacuum Cleaner

Elected To The Hall Of Fame: *1983.*
Born: *May 18, 1937 in Little Rock, Ark.*
Height: *6-1.* **Weight:** *180.*
Threw: *Right.* **Batted:** *Right.*
Debut: *Sept. 17, 1955.*
Final Game: *Aug. 13, 1977.*
Teams: *Baltimore A.L. 1955-1977*
Postseason: *2-Time World Series Champion (1966, 1970); 4 A.L. Pennants (1966, 1969-1971); 6-Time Playoff Qualifier (1966, 1969-1971, 1973-1974).*
Awards: *18-Time All-Star (1960-1974); A.L. MVP (1964); World Series MVP (1970).*

YEAR	TEAM	LEAGUE	G	AB	R	H	2B	3B	HR	RBI	SB	AVG
1955	BALTIMORE	AL	6	22	0	2	0	0	0	1	0	.091
1956	BALTIMORE	AL	15	44	5	10	4	0	1	1	0	.227
1957	BALTIMORE	AL	50	117	13	28	6	1	2	14	1	.239
1958	BALTIMORE	AL	145	463	31	110	16	3	3	32	1	.238
1959	BALTIMORE	AL	88	313	29	89	15	2	4	24	2	.284
1960	BALTIMORE	AL	152	595	74	175	27	9	14	88	2	.294
1961	BALTIMORE	AL	163	668	89	192	38	7	7	61	1	.287
1962	BALTIMORE	AL	162	634	77	192	29	9	23	86	3	.303
1963	BALTIMORE	AL	161	589	67	148	26	4	11	67	2	.251
1964	BALTIMORE	AL	163	612	82	194	35	3	28	118	1	.317
1965	BALTIMORE	AL	144	559	81	166	25	2	18	80	3	.297
1966	BALTIMORE	AL	157	620	91	167	35	2	23	100	2	.269
1967	BALTIMORE	AL	158	610	88	164	25	5	22	77	1	.269
1968	BALTIMORE	AL	162	608	65	154	36	6	17	75	1	.253
1969	BALTIMORE	AL	156	598	73	140	21	3	23	84	2	.234
1970	BALTIMORE	AL	158	608	84	168	31	4	18	94	1	.276
1971	BALTIMORE	AL	156	589	67	160	21	1	20	92	0	.272
1972	BALTIMORE	AL	153	556	48	139	23	2	8	64	1	.250
1973	BALTIMORE	AL	155	549	53	141	17	2	9	72	2	.257
1974	BALTIMORE	AL	153	553	46	159	27	0	7	59	2	.288
1975	BALTIMORE	AL	144	482	50	97	15	1	6	53	0	.201
1976	BALTIMORE	AL	71	218	16	46	8	2	3	11	0	.211
1977	BALTIMORE	AL	24	47	3	7	2	0	1	4	0	.149
CAREER TOTALS			**2896**	**10654**	**1232**	**2848**	**482**	**68**	**268**	**1357**	**28**	**.267**

FRANK ROBINSON

Frank Robinson had the ability and intensity on the diamond that few possess. Robinson would crowd the plate like he owned it. "Pitchers did me a favor when they knocked me down," he said. "It made me more determined. I wouldn't let that pitcher get me out. They say you can't hit if you're on your back, but I didn't hit on my back. I got up."

He was recognized as one of the most feared baserunners of his era and showed reckless abandon on the base paths. "The baselines belongs to the runner, and whenever I was running the bases, I always slid hard. I wanted infielders to have that instant's hesitation about coming across the bag at second or about standing in there awaiting a throw to make a tag. There are only 27 outs in a ballgame, and it was my job to save one for my team every time I possibly could."

Robinson broke into the National League as a 20-year-old in 1956 and tied a rookie record with 38 home runs en route to NL Rookie of the Year honors. Over the next decade and a half, Robinson was one of the most feared hitters in the game. He won the Triple Crown in 1966 and was the first player in major league history to win the MVP Award in both leagues. A 12-time All-Star, he also took home World Series MVP honors in 1966 and the All-Star Game MVP Award in 1971.

When asked by a fan how he would pitch to Frank Robinson, All-Star pitcher Jim Bouton replied, "Reluctantly." In 1975, as his playing days wound down with the Cleveland Indians, he was named the club's player-manager. He was the first African-American to manage a major league club. He also managed the Giants, Orioles, Expos and Nationals and was named American League Manager of the Year in 1989.

Former Expos and Nationals GM Jim Bowden commented, "I have a lot of respect for Frank Robinson. He has respect for the game of baseball and the way it should be played. I was pleased because he is a man of his word. He said he was going to do something, and he follows up and he does it."

FRANK ROBINSON
CINCINNATI N.L., BALTIMORE A.L., LOS ANGELES N.L., CALIFORNIA A.L., CLEVELAND A.L., 1956-1976
FIRST TO BE CHOSEN MOST VALUABLE PLAYER IN BOTH LEAGUES -- N.L. IN 1961 AND A.L. IN 1966. SET RECORDS BY HITTING HOMERS IN 32 DIFFERENT PARKS AND WITH PAIR OF GRAND-SLAMMERS IN SUCCESSIVE INNINGS IN 1970. FOURTH IN HOMERS (586), FIFTH IN EXTRA BASES ON LONG HITS (2,450), SIXTH IN TOTAL BASES (5,373), ON RETIRING. LED N.L. IN SLUGGING PCT. IN 1960-61-62 AND A.L. IN BATTING, HOMERS, RUNS BATTED IN, TOTAL BASES AND SLUGGING PCT. IN 1966.

Elected To The Hall Of Fame: 1982.
Born: Aug. 31, 1935 at Beaumont, Texas.
Height: 6-1. *Weight:* 183.
Threw: Right. *Batted:* Right.
Debut: April 17, 1956.
Final Game: Sept. 18, 1976.
Teams: Cincinnati N.L. 1956-1965; Baltimore A.L. 1966-1971; Los Angeles N.L. 1972; California A.L. 1973-1974; Cleveland A.L. 1974-1976.
Postseason: 2-Time World Series Champion (1966, 1970); N.L. Pennant (1961); 4 A.L. Pennants (1966, 1969-1971)
Awards: 12-Time All-Star (1956-1957, 1959, 1961-1962, 1965-1967, 1969-1971, 1974); N.L. Rookie of the Year (1956); N.L. Most Valuable Player (1961); A.L. Most Valuable Player (1966); World Series Most Valuable Player (1966).

YEAR	TEAM	LEAGUE	G	AB	R	H	2B	3B	HR	RBI	SB	AVG
1956	CINCINNATI	NL	152	572	122	166	27	6	38	83	8	.290
1957	CINCINNATI	NL	150	611	97	197	29	5	29	75	10	.322
1958	CINCINNATI	NL	148	554	90	149	25	6	31	83	10	.269
1959	CINCINNATI	NL	146	540	106	168	31	4	36	125	18	.311
1960	CINCINNATI	NL	139	464	86	138	33	6	31	83	13	.297
1961	CINCINNATI	NL	153	545	117	176	32	7	37	124	22	.323
1962	CINCINNATI	NL	162	609	134	208	51	2	39	136	18	.342
1963	CINCINNATI	NL	140	482	79	125	19	3	21	91	26	.259
1964	CINCINNATI	NL	156	568	103	174	38	6	29	96	23	.306
1965	CINCINNATI	NL	156	582	109	172	33	5	33	113	13	.296
1966	BALTIMORE	AL	155	576	122	182	34	2	49	122	8	.316
1967	BALTIMORE	AL	129	479	83	149	23	7	30	94	2	.311
1968	BALTIMORE	AL	130	421	69	113	27	1	15	52	11	.268
1969	BALTIMORE	AL	148	539	111	166	19	5	32	100	9	.308
1970	BALTIMORE	AL	132	471	88	144	24	1	25	78	2	.306
1971	BALTIMORE	AL	133	455	82	128	16	2	28	99	3	.281
1972	LOS ANGELES	NL	103	342	41	86	6	1	19	59	2	.251
1973	CALIFORNIA	AL	147	534	85	142	29	0	30	97	1	.266
1974	CALIFORNIA/CLEVELAND	AL	144	477	81	117	27	3	22	68	5	.245
1975	CLEVELAND	AL	49	118	19	28	5	0	9	24	0	.237
1976	CLEVELAND	AL	36	67	5	15	0	0	3	10	0	.224
CAREER TOTALS			**2808**	**10006**	**1829**	**2943**	**528**	**72**	**586**	**1812**	**204**	**.294**

JACKIE ROBINSON

"A life is not important except in the impact it has on other lives," Jackie Robinson once said. The impact Robinson made on Major League Baseball is one that will be forever remembered. On April 15 each season, every team in the majors celebrates Jackie Robinson Day in honor of when he truly broke the color barrier in baseball, becoming the first African-American player in the 20th century to take the field in the big leagues. He opened the door for many others and will forever be appreciated for his contribution to the game.

Robinson stood up for equal rights even before he did so in baseball. He was arrested and court-martialed during training in the Army for refusing to move to the back of a bus. He was eventually acquitted of the charges and received an honorable discharge. He then started his professional baseball career.

The second baseman played for the Kansas City Monarchs as a part of the Negro Leagues until Brooklyn Dodgers general manager Branch Rickey decided he wanted to integrate baseball. Rickey wanted Robinson not only for his talent and style of play, but also because of his demeanor. He knew he was sending him down a tough road and thought Robinson was the man to handle it without fighting back. Robinson endured teammates and crowds who opposed his presence, and threats to himself and his family, with honor and grace.

Robinson joined the Montreal Royals, the Dodgers top farm team, in 1946 and led the International League with a .349 average and also added 40 stolen bases. He earned a promotion to the Dodgers and made his major league debut on April 15, 1947.

"It was the most eagerly anticipated debut in the annals of the national pastime," authors Robert Lipsyte and Peter Levine wrote. "It represented both the dream and the fear of equal opportunity, and it would change forever the complexion of the game and the attitudes of Americans."

At the end of his first season, Robinson was named the Rookie of the Year. He was named the NL MVP just two years later in 1949, when he led the league in hitting with a .342 average and steals with 37, while also notching a career-high 124 RBI. The Dodgers won six pennants in Robinson's 10 seasons, but his contributions clearly extended far beyond the field.

JACK ROOSEVELT ROBINSON
"JACKIE"
BROOKLYN, N.L., 1947-1956

A PLAYER OF EXTRAORDINARY ABILITY RENOWNED FOR HIS ELECTRIFYING STYLE OF PLAY. OVER 10 SEASONS HIT .311, SCORED MORE THAN 100 RUNS SIX TIMES, NAMED TO SIX ALL-STAR TEAMS AND LED BROOKLYN TO SIX PENNANTS AND ITS ONLY WORLD SERIES TITLE. IN 1955, THE 1947 ROOKIE OF THE YEAR, AND THE 1949 N.L. MVP WHEN HE HIT A LEAGUE-BEST .342 WITH 37 STEALS. LED SECOND BASEMEN IN DOUBLE PLAYS FOUR TIMES AND STOLE HOME 19 TIMES. DISPLAYED TREMENDOUS COURAGE AND POISE IN 1947 WHEN HE INTEGRATED THE MODERN MAJOR LEAGUES IN THE FACE OF INTENSE ADVERSITY.

Elected To The Hall Of Fame: 1962.
Born: Jan. 31, 1919 in Cairo, Ga.
Died: Oct. 24, 1972 in Stamford, Conn.
Height: 5-11. **Weight:** 195.
Threw: Right. **Batted:** Right.
Debut: April 15, 1947.
Final Game: Sept. 30, 1956.
Teams: Negro Leagues 1945; Kansas City 1945; Brooklyn N.L. 1947-1956
Postseason: World Series Champion (1955); 6 N.L. Pennants (1947, 1949, 1952-1953, 1955-1956).
Awards: 6-Time All-Star (1949-1954); M.L. Rookie of the Year (1947); N.L. Most Valuable Player (1949).

YEAR	TEAM	LEAGUE	G	AB	R	H	2B	3B	HR	RBI	SB	AVG
1945	KANSAS CITY	NAL	—	58	12	24	4	1	1	—	2	.414
CAREER TOTALS			—	58	12	24	4	1	1	—	2	.414

YEAR	TEAM	LEAGUE	G	AB	R	H	2B	3B	HR	RBI	SB	AVG
1947	BROOKLYN	NL	151	590	125	175	31	5	12	48	29	.297
1948	BROOKLYN	NL	147	574	108	170	38	8	12	85	22	.296
1949	BROOKLYN	NL	156	593	122	203	38	12	16	124	37	.342
1950	BROOKLYN	NL	144	518	99	170	39	4	14	81	12	.328
1951	BROOKLYN	NL	153	548	106	185	33	7	19	88	25	.338
1952	BROOKLYN	NL	149	510	104	157	17	3	19	75	24	.308
1953	BROOKLYN	NL	136	484	109	159	34	7	12	95	17	.329
1954	BROOKLYN	NL	124	386	62	120	22	4	15	59	7	.311
1955	BROOKLYN	NL	105	317	51	81	6	2	8	36	12	.256
1956	BROOKLYN	NL	117	357	61	98	15	2	10	43	12	.275
MLB CAREER TOTALS			1382	4877	947	1518	273	54	137	734	197	.311

JOE ROGAN

Wilber Joe Rogan was not only one of the best pitchers to have played in the Negro Leagues, but he was also one of the best hitters. By not beginning his Negro League career until the age of 27, Rogan got a late start. Nevertheless, he excelled during his 19 seasons with the Kansas City Monarchs, after beginning his baseball career as a part of the Army, playing for a team in the all-black 25th Infantry.

One statistical compilation records the hurler as winning more games than any other in the history of the Negro National League. He went 119-50 in his pitching career, with a 3.68 ERA, completing 128 of the 153 games he started while using his repertoire of curveballs, spitballs, palm balls, forkballs and fastballs to strike out 882.

Splitting his time between the mound and the outfield, Rogan also posted a batting average, at .338. Rogan held a .515 slugging percentage with 45 home runs to go with 99 stolen bases and 361 runs. The slugger also notched 251 RBI, and led the Negro National League with 13 homers in 1922.

Rogan helped the Monarchs win three straight pennants from 1923-1925, and a Negro League World Series championship in 1924. During the championship season, Rogan hit .392 and had an 18-6 record on the mound. In the first Black World Series, he led his team with 13 hits and won two games for Kansas City as the Monarchs took down the Hilldale Daisies.

While Rogan's pitching was often compared to that of Satchel Paige, his son Wilber pointed out that there was at least one difference. "I do know that Satchel needed a designated hitter when he was on the mound," the younger Rogan said of his father. "When dad was on the mound, he was batting cleanup."

WILBER JOE ROGAN
(BULLET)
KANSAS CITY MONARCHS, 1920-38
A VERSATILE PERFORMER WHO WAS EQUALLY SUPERLATIVE AS A PITCHER AND HITTER. UTILIZED A DECEPTIVELY QUICK, NO-WINDUP DELIVERY TO LEAD KANSAS CITY TO FOUR NEGRO NATIONAL LEAGUE TITLES. PITCHING REPERTOIRE INCLUDED A FORKBALL, CURVEBALL AND PALMBALL, AND FEATURED A BLAZING FASTBALL AS AN OUTPITCH. ALSO PLAYED CENTER FIELD, HITTING .343 AS HIS CLUB'S CLEANUP HITTER AND .410 IN WORLD SERIES COMPETITION. PILOTED THE MONARCHS IN THE DUAL ROLE OF PLAYER AND MANAGER FOR SEVERAL SEASONS. SERVED AS AN UMPIRE IN THE NEGRO LEAGUES FOLLOWING PLAYING CAREER.

Bullet

Elected To The Hall Of Fame: *1998.*
Born: *July 28, 1893 in Oklahoma City, Okla.*
Died: *Mar. 4, 1967 in Kansas City, Mo.*
Height: *5-7.* **Weight:** *160.*
Threw: *Right.* **Batted:** *Right.*
Teams: *Negro Leagues 1920-1938; Kansas City 1920-1930; 1933-1935; 1937-1938.*

YEAR	TEAM	LEAGUE	G	AB	R	H	2B	3B	HR	RBI	SB	AVG
1920	KANSAS CITY	NNL	—	146	12	42	5	7	0	—	8	.288
1921	KANSAS CITY	NNL	—	193	21	56	9	8	3	—	16	.290
1922	KANSAS CITY	NNL	—	215	40	85	9	6	13	—	15	.395
1923	KANSAS CITY	NNL	—	209	39	76	12	3	7	—	5	.364
1924	KANSAS CITY	NNL	—	194	37	76	11	6	6	—	6	.392
1925	KANSAS CITY	NNL	—	139	20	53	7	8	?	—	5	.381
1926	KANSAS CITY	NNL	—	147	26	45	8	3	1	—	2	.306
1927	KANSAS CITY	NNL	—	114	15	38	4	3	2	—	0	.333
1928	KANSAS CITY	NNL	—	194	39	67	14	5	3	—	5	.345
1929	KANSAS CITY	NNL	—	264	68	94	16	9	7	—	26	.356
1930	KANSAS CITY	NNL	—	107	26	32	6	0	0	—	5	.299
1933	KANSAS CITY	INDP	—	41	10	13	4	1	1	—	2	.317
1934	KANSAS CITY	INDP	—	31	2	4	2	0	0	—	1	.129
1935	KANSAS CITY	INDP	—	13	0	2	0	0	0	—	0	.154
1937	KANSAS CITY	NAL	—	34	3	10	2	1	0	—	2	.294
1938	KANSAS CITY	NAL	—	20	3	4	1	0	0	—	1	.200
CAREER TOTALS			—	2061	361	697	110	60	45	—	99	.338

YEAR	TEAM	LEAGUE	G	W	L	SV	SH	IP	H	BB	SO	ERA
1920	KANSAS CITY	NNL	—	6	5	—	0	97.7	78	29	84	3.13
1921	KANSAS CITY	NNL	—	12	8	—	2	181	150	57	102	3.38
1922	KANSAS CITY	NNL	—	8	6	—	0	134.3	124	29	91	4.56
1923	KANSAS CITY	NNL	—	16	10	—	4	239.7	209	74	146	4.13
1924	KANSAS CITY	NNL	—	18	6	—	1	204	182	66	115	4.19
1925	KANSAS CITY	NNL	—	17	2	—	5	171.3	137	25	102	2.31
1926	KANSAS CITY	NNL	—	15	5	—	0	149	139	41	77	3.74
1927	KANSAS CITY	NNL	—	16	6	—	3	146.7	130	29	102	3.01
1928	KANSAS CITY	NNL	—	10	2	—	0	114	122	13	52	3.71
1929	KANSAS CITY	NNL	—	0	0	—	0	6.3	7	1	5	4.26
1933	KANSAS CITY	INDP	—	0	0	—	0	1.3	4	0	0	20.25
1935	KANSAS CITY	INDP	—	1	0	—	0	3	5	0	1	9.00
1937	KANSAS CITY	NAL	—	0	0	—	0	5.7	5	0	5	14.29
CAREER TOTALS			—	119	50	—	15	1454	1292	364	882	3.68

EDD ROUSH

"Eddie used to take care of the whole outfield, not just center field," Reds teammate Heinie Groh said. "He was far and away the best outfielder I ever saw."

Edd Roush tends to get overlooked among the great hitters of the 1910s and 1920s, but you'd be hard pressed to find many players who were more productive. Roush broke into the majors in 1913 with the White Sox but didn't establish himself until 1917 with the Reds. In between, he took a two-year detour to play in the Federal League, then began the 1916 season with the New York Giants.

Relegated to a part-time role in New York by manager John McGraw, Roush was traded to the Reds in July 1916 in a deal that sent three future Hall of Famers to Cincinnati: Roush, Christy Mathewson and Bill McKechnie. Roush blossomed in Cincinnati. He captured the National League batting title in his first full season as a Red in 1917 with a .341 average. He won a second batting title in 1919 by hitting .321, which was actually one of the lowest averages of his 12 seasons in Cincinnati. He also played in the 1919 World Series, when the Reds defeated the soon-to-be infamous "Black Sox."

On the field, Roush was well known for playing the game with a hard-nosed style, even by the standards of the era. Growing up on a farm in Indiana, he developed extraordinary strength in his arms and hands, allowing him to wield a 48-ounce bat, one of the heaviest ever used.

Roush used an unusual hitting technique where he would move his feet after the pitcher released the ball, allowing him to adjust his swing and hit the ball to different parts of the field. He firmly believed that hitters shouldn't hesitate to position themselves differently in batter's box depending on the pitcher. He was also an excellent defensive center fielder.

Roush carried his no-nonsense attitude into his dealings with team management. He almost annually held out from spring training while negotiating new contracts with the Reds. Not that Roush missed spring training, which he regarded as a waste of time. He felt he kept himself in shape on his own during the offseason, which was hard to argue with given his production.

EDD J. ROUSH
CHICAGO A.L. 1913
NEW YORK N.L. 1916, 1927 TO 1930
CINCINNATI N.L. 1916 TO 1926, 1931
LEADING N.L. BATTER IN 1917 AND 1919
BATTED .352 IN 1921, .352 IN 1922, .351
IN 1923, .348 IN 1924 BATTED OVER
.300 • 13 SEASONS. LIFETIME BATTING
AVERAGE OF .323. MOST OUTFIELD
PUTOUTS, 410 IN 1920. F.L. 1914 • 1915.

Elected To The Hall Of Fame: 1962.
Born: May 8, 1893 in Oakland City, Ind.
Died: March 21 1988 in Bradenton, Fla.
Height: 5-11. **Weight:** 170.
Threw: Left. **Batted:** Left.
Debut: Aug. 20, 1913.
Final Game: Sept. 27, 1931.
Teams: Chicago A.L. 1913; Indianapolis, Federal League 1914; Newark, Federal League 1915; New York N.L. 1916, 1927-1929; Cincinnati N.L. 1916-1926, 1931.
Postseason: World Series Champion (1919); N.L. Pennant (1919).

YEAR	TEAM	LEAGUE	G	AB	R	H	2B	3B	HR	RBI	SB	AVG
1913	CHICAGO	AL	9	10	2	1	0	0	0	0	0	.100
1914	INDIANAPOLIS	FL	74	166	26	54	8	4	1	30	12	.325
1915	NEWARK	FL	145	551	73	164	20	11	3	60	28	.298
1916	NEW YORK/CINCINNATI	NL	108	341	38	91	7	15	0	20	19	.267
1917	CINCINNATI	NL	136	522	82	178	19	14	4	67	21	.341
1918	CINCINNATI	NL	113	435	61	145	18	10	5	62	24	.333
1919	CINCINNATI	NL	133	504	73	162	19	12	4	71	20	.321
1920	CINCINNATI	NL	149	579	81	196	22	16	4	90	36	.339
1921	CINCINNATI	NL	112	418	68	147	27	12	4	71	19	.352
1922	CINCINNATI	NL	49	165	29	58	7	4	1	24	5	.352
1923	CINCINNATI	NL	138	527	88	185	41	18	6	88	10	.351
1924	CINCINNATI	NL	121	483	67	168	23	21	3	72	17	.348
1925	CINCINNATI	NL	134	540	91	183	28	16	8	83	22	.339
1926	CINCINNATI	NL	144	563	95	182	37	10	7	79	8	.323
1927	NEW YORK	NL	140	570	83	173	27	4	7	58	18	.304
1928	NEW YORK	NL	46	163	20	41	5	3	2	13	1	.252
1929	NEW YORK	NL	115	450	76	146	19	7	8	52	6	.324
1931	CINCINNATI	NL	101	376	46	102	12	5	1	41	2	.271
CAREER TOTALS			**1967**	**7363**	**1099**	**2376**	**339**	**182**	**68**	**981**	**268**	**.323**

RED RUFFING

"That Ruffing is a wonder," Hall of Fame slugger Jimmie Foxx once said. "Always in there winning that important game for you." Indeed, Charles "Red" Ruffing was the epitome of a big-game pitcher. A key right-handed pitcher for seven pennant winners with the Yankees, Ruffing won seven of his nine decisions in World Series play. In his postseason career, Ruffing posted a 2.63 ERA and helped New York win championships in 1932, 1936-39 and 1941. During the Yankees' four consecutive title seasons from 1936-39, Ruffing won at least 20 games each year. Ruffing will forever be identified with the Yankees dynasty, but he actually started his career with the rival Red Sox in 1924. Boston traded him to the Yankees in 1930 for Cedric Durst and $50,000. Ruffing's career blossomed in New York, where sluggers like Babe Ruth and Lou Gehrig gave him plenty of run support.

Born in Granville, Ill., Ruffing lost four of the toes on his left foot in a mining accident as a youth. The accident hastened his transition from the outfield to the mound, but he remained dangerous with a bat in his hands. In 1932, Ruffing threw a complete-game shutout and hit a 10th-inning home run to give the Yankees a 1-0 win against the Washington Senators. In 1935, he led the Yankees in both wins (16) and batting average (.339 in 109 at-bats.) He finished his career with 36 home runs and a .269 batting average. Ruffing was a dominant innings-eater on the mound. He led the American League with 25 complete games in 1928, and led the circuit with five shutouts in 1939. In 1932, he paced the AL with 190 strikeouts.

After missing the 1943 and '44 seasons while serving his country in World War II, Ruffing returned to baseball at the age of 40 in 1945. He spent two more seasons with the Yankees before finishing his playing career with the White Sox in 1947. He returned to the field as the pitching coach for the Mets during their inaugural season of 1962.

CHARLES HERBERT RUFFING
"RED"
BOSTON, A.L. 1924-1930
NEW YORK, A.L. 1930-1946
CHICAGO, A.L. 1947
WINNER OF 273 GAMES.
WON 20 OR MORE GAMES IN EACH OF FOUR
CONSECUTIVE SEASONS, LED IN COMPLETE
GAMES 1928. TIED IN SHUTOUTS 1938-1939.
WON 7 OUT OF 9 WORLD SERIES DECISIONS.
SELECTED FOR ALL STAR TEAMS
1937-1938-1939

Elected To The Hall Of Fame: 1967.

Born: May 3, 1905 in Granville, Ill.

Died: Feb. 17, 1986 in Mayfield Heights, Ohio.

Height: 6-1. **Weight:** 205.

Threw: Right. **Batted:** Right.

Debut: May 31, 1924.

Final Game: Sept. 15, 1947.

Teams: Boston A.L. 1924-1930; New York A.L. 1930-1942, 1945-1946; Chicago A.L. 1947

Postseason: 6-Time World Series Champion (1932, 1936-1939, 1941); 7 A.L. Pennants (1932, 1936-1939, 1941-1942).

Awards: 6-Time All-Star (1934, 1938-1942).

YEAR	TEAM	LEAGUE	G	W	L	SV	SH	IP	H	BB	SO	ERA
1924	BOSTON	AL	8	0	0	0	0	23	29	9	10	6.65
1925	BOSTON	AL	37	9	18	1	3	217.3	253	75	64	5.01
1926	BOSTON	AL	37	6	15	2	0	166	169	68	58	4.39
1927	BOSTON	AL	26	5	13	2	0	158.3	160	87	77	4.66
1928	BOSTON	AL	42	10	25	2	1	289.3	303	96	118	3.89
1929	BOSTON	AL	35	9	22	1	1	244.3	280	118	109	4.86
1930	BOSTON/NEW YORK	AL	38	15	8	1	2	221.7	232	68	131	4.38
1931	NEW YORK	AL	37	16	14	2	1	237	240	87	132	4.41
1932	NEW YORK	AL	35	18	7	2	3	259	219	115	190	3.09
1933	NEW YORK	AL	35	9	14	3	0	235	230	93	122	3.91
1934	NEW YORK	AL	36	19	11	0	5	256.3	232	104	149	3.93
1935	NEW YORK	AL	30	16	11	0	2	222	201	76	81	3.12
1936	NEW YORK	AL	33	20	12	0	3	271	274	90	102	3.85
1937	NEW YORK	AL	31	20	7	0	4	256.3	242	68	131	2.98
1938	NEW YORK	AL	31	21	7	0	3	247.3	246	82	127	3.31
1939	NEW YORK	AL	28	21	7	0	5	233.3	211	75	95	2.93
1940	NEW YORK	AL	30	15	12	0	3	226	218	76	97	3.38
1941	NEW YORK	AL	23	15	6	0	2	185.7	177	54	60	3.54
1942	NEW YORK	AL	24	14	7	0	4	193.7	183	41	80	3.21
1945	NEW YORK	AL	11	7	3	0	1	87.3	85	20	24	2.89
1946	NEW YORK	AL	8	5	1	0	2	61	37	23	19	1.77
1947	CHICAGO	AL	9	3	5	0	0	53	63	16	11	6.11
CAREER TOTALS			**624**	**273**	**225**	**16**	**45**	**4344**	**4284**	**1541**	**1987**	**3.80**

AMOS RUSIE

"You can't hit 'em if you can't see 'em." said Hall of Famer John McGraw about hitting against Amos Rusie's pitching.

In his short but brilliant career, the "Hoosier Thunderbolt" helped revolutionize the game of baseball with his velocity. Perhaps the fastest pitcher of the 1890s, the right-handed Rusie won five National League strikeout titles with the New York Giants in the six seasons from 1890 to '95, both before and after baseball moved the pitching mound in 1893 from 50 feet to its present 60 feet, 6 inches. Rusie struck out 5.4 batters per nine innings in four seasons prior to the switch— and 4.0 per nine in his first five years afterward. But like many hard-throwers past and present, Rusie did not always have the firmest grasp of the strike zone. He led the NL in walks for five straight seasons from 1890 to '94, and his 289 free passes in '90 remain the single-season record. A Rusie fastball once struck Hall of Famer Hughie Jennings in the head and knocked him unconscious for four days.

In Rusie's finest season, 1894, he went 36-13 with a 2.78 ERA—in a year in which the NL average was 5.33—while leading the league in wins, ERA, starts (50) and shutouts (three) as well as both strikeouts (195) and walks (200). Behind the pitching of Rusie, who allowed only one earned run in 18 innings, the '94 Giants defeated the Baltimore Orioles four games to none in the first Temple Cup championship series, which pitted the NL's top team versus the runner-up.

During his time with the Giants, 1890 through '98, Rusie led all big league pitchers with 1,835 strikeouts and a 2.89 ERA, while ranking second in innings pitched (122 behind Kid Nichols) and third in wins (behind Nichols and Cy Young). That was in spite of sitting out all of the 1896 season in a bitter contract dispute with Giants owner Andrew Freedman. The two sides settled in time for Rusie to return to action in 1897, but the effects of arm trouble rendered him unable to pitch during the 1899 and 1900 seasons. New York traded Rusie to the Reds for a 20-year-old Christy Mathewson in December 1900, exchanging one of baseball's most dominant pitchers of the 1890s for one of its best of the early 20th century. Rusie finished with an 8.59 ERA in 22 innings for the 1901 Reds and then called it quits.

The Hoosier Thunderbolt

Elected To The Hall Of Fame: 1977.
Born: May 30, 1871 in Mooresville, Ind.
Died: Dec. 6, 1942 in Seattle, Wash.
Height: 6-1. **Weight:** 200.
Threw: Right. **Batted:** Right.
Debut: May 9, 1889.
Final Game: June 9, 1901.
Teams: Indianapolis N.L. 1889; New York N.L. 1890-1895, 1897-1898; Cincinnati N.L. 1901.

YEAR	TEAM	LEAGUE	G	W	L	SV	SH	IP	H	BB	SO	ERA
1889	INDIANAPOLIS	NL	33	12	10	0	1	225	246	116	109	5.32
1890	NEW YORK	NL	67	29	34	1	4	548.7	436	289	341	2.56
1891	NEW YORK	NL	61	33	20	1	6	500.3	391	262	337	2.55
1892	NEW YORK	NL	65	32	31	0	2	541	410	270	304	2.84
1893	NEW YORK	NL	56	33	21	1	4	482	451	218	208	3.23
1894	NEW YORK	NL	54	36	13	1	3	444	426	200	195	2.78
1895	NEW YORK	NL	49	23	23	0	4	393.3	384	159	201	3.73
1897	NEW YORK	NL	38	28	10	0	2	322.3	314	87	135	2.54
1898	NEW YORK	NL	37	20	11	1	4	300	288	103	114	3.03
1901	CINCINNATI	NL	3	0	1	0	0	22	43	3	6	8.59
CAREER TOTALS			**463**	**246**	**174**	**5**	**30**	**3778.7**	**3389**	**1707**	**1950**	**3.07**

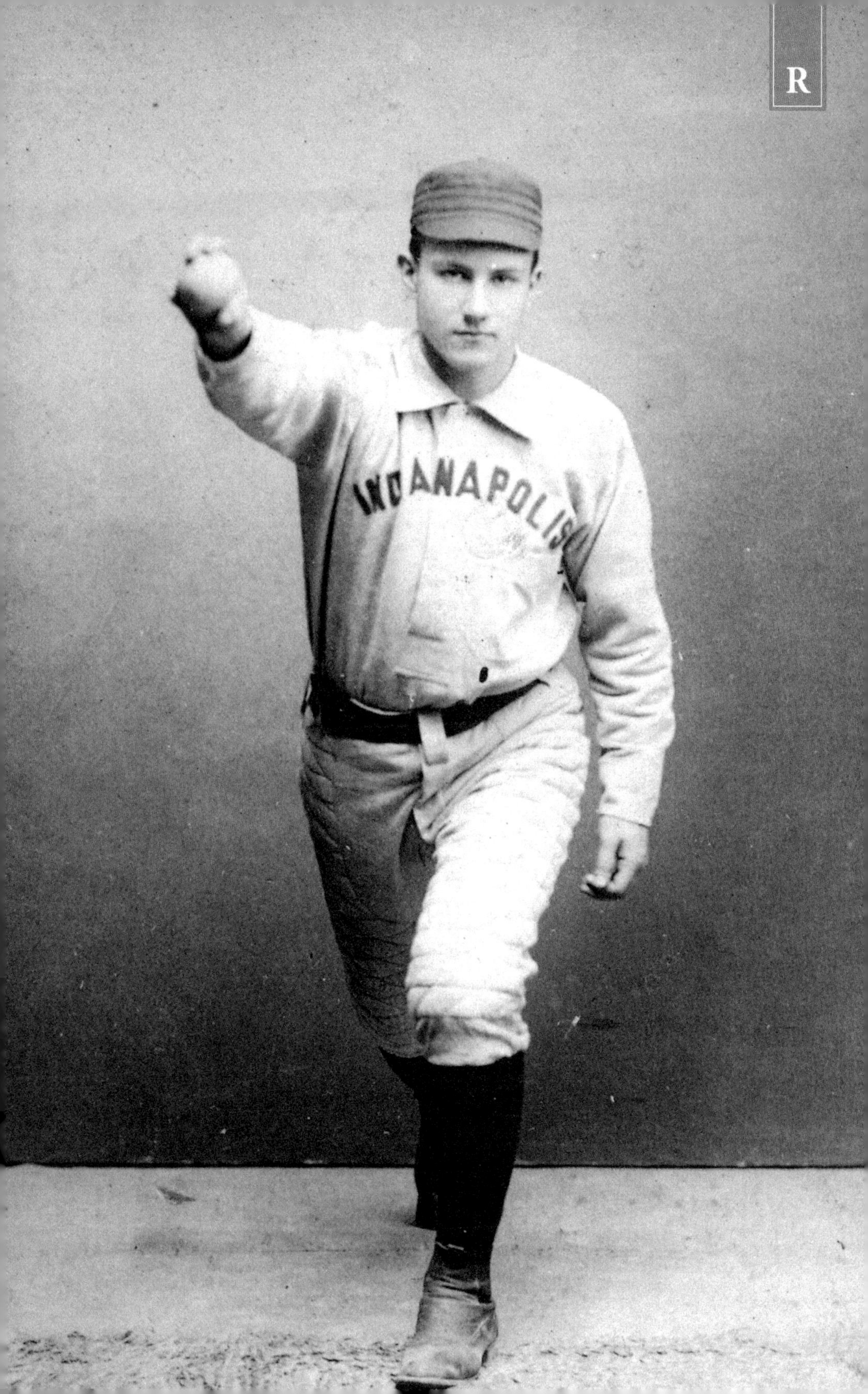
INDIANAPOLIS

BABE RUTH

Sure, Babe Ruth put up monumental statistics during his playing career. But the Bambino was more than numbers, especially to those who knew him, like former teammate Joe Dugan, who once said, "To understand him you had to understand this: He wasn't human."

Sports writer Tommy Holmes, a 1979 J.G. Taylor Spink Award winner, was more succinct: "Some 20 years ago, I stopped talking about the Babe for the simple reason that I realized that those who had never seen him didn't believe me."

Ruth has been called an American original, undoubtedly the game's first great slugger and the most celebrated athlete of his time. Soon after honing his skills at St. Mary's Industrial School for Boys in Baltimore, he came to the big leagues as a lefty hurler with the Red Sox, where he won 89 games in six years while setting the World Series record for consecutive scoreless innings.

Due to his prodigious power, he was shifted to the outfield after his sale to the Yankees in 1920. The Sultan of Swat would lead a powerful and renowned New York squad to seven American League pennants and four World Series titles. Ruth retired in 1935, after a partial season with the Boston Braves, ending his 22-year big league career with 714 home runs, including his remarkable 60 in 1927. His lifetime statistics also include 2,873 hits, 506 doubles, 2,174 runs, 2,213 RBI, a .342 batting average, a .474 on-base percentage, and a .690 slugging percentage.

"It wasn't that he hit more home runs than anybody else," said 1976 Spink Award winner Red Smith, "he hit them better, higher, farther, with more theatrical timing and a more flamboyant flourish."

Among Ruth's other remarkable offensive achievements include leading the league in slugging percentage 13 times, home runs 12 times, bases on balls 11 times, on-base percentage 10 times, runs scored eight times, and runs batted in six times. One of the five in the Baseball Hall of Fame's inaugural class in 1936, Ruth once said, "The fans would rather see me hit one homer to right than three doubles to left."

GEORGE HERMAN (BABE) RUTH
BOSTON-NEW YORK, A.L.; BOSTON, N.L.
1914-1935
GREATEST DRAWING CARD IN HISTORY OF
BASEBALL. HOLDER OF MANY HOME RUN
AND OTHER BATTING RECORDS. GATHERED
714 HOME RUNS IN ADDITION TO FIFTEEN
IN WORLD SERIES.

The Sultan of Swat, Bambino

Elected To The Hall Of Fame: 1936.
Born: Feb. 6, 1895 in Baltimore, Md.
Died: Aug. 16, 1948 in New York, N.Y.
Height: 6-2. **Weight:** 215.
Threw: Left. **Batted:** Left.
Debut: July 11, 1914. **Final Game:** May 30, 1935.
Teams: Boston A.L. 1914-1919; New York A.L. 1920-1934; Boston N.L. 1935.
Postseason: 7-Time World Series Champion (1915-1916, 1918, 1923, 1927-1928, 1932); 10 A.L. Pennants (1915-1916, 1918, 1921-1923, 1926-1928, 1932). **Awards:** 2-Time All-Star (1933-1934); A.L. MVP (1923).

YEAR	TEAM	LEAGUE	G	AB	R	H	2B	3B	HR	RBI	SB	AVG
1914	BOSTON	AL	5	10	1	2	1	0	0	2	0	.200
1915	BOSTON	AL	42	92	16	29	10	1	4	21	0	.315
1916	BOSTON	AL	67	136	18	37	5	3	3	15	0	.272
1917	BOSTON	AL	52	123	14	40	6	3	2	12	0	.325
1918	BOSTON	AL	95	317	50	95	26	11	11	66	6	.300
1919	BOSTON	AL	130	432	103	139	34	12	29	114	7	.322
1920	NEW YORK	AL	142	458	158	172	36	9	54	137	14	.376
1921	NEW YORK	AL	152	540	177	204	44	16	59	171	17	.378
1922	NEW YORK	AL	110	406	94	128	24	8	35	99	2	.315
1923	NEW YORK	AL	152	522	151	205	45	13	41	131	17	.393
1924	NEW YORK	AL	153	529	143	200	39	7	46	121	9	.378
1925	NEW YORK	AL	98	359	61	104	12	2	25	66	2	.290
1926	NEW YORK	AL	152	495	139	184	30	5	47	146	11	.372
1927	NEW YORK	AL	151	540	158	192	29	8	60	164	7	.356
1928	NEW YORK	AL	154	536	163	173	29	8	54	142	4	.323
1929	NEW YORK	AL	135	499	121	172	26	6	46	154	5	.345
1930	NEW YORK	AL	145	518	150	186	28	9	49	153	10	.359
1931	NEW YORK	AL	145	534	149	199	31	3	46	163	5	.373
1932	NEW YORK	AL	133	457	120	156	13	5	41	137	2	.341
1933	NEW YORK	AL	137	459	97	138	21	3	34	103	4	.301
1934	NEW YORK	AL	125	365	78	105	17	4	22	84	1	.288
1935	BOSTON	NL	28	72	13	13	0	0	6	12	0	.181
CAREER TOTALS			**2503**	**8399**	**2174**	**2873**	**506**	**136**	**714**	**2213**	**123**	**.342**

NOLAN RYAN

Two-time National League MVP Dale Murphy called Nolan Ryan "the only pitcher you start thinking about two days before you face him."

Ryan's career spanned four decades and when all was said and done, he retired with 324 wins and a major league-record 5,714 strikeouts.

Ryan's career began with the Mets organization in the mid-1960s, but his commitment to his country, through military reserve service, prevented him from really hitting his stride in New York. It was not until the completion of his military service, and his trade to the California Angels, that the real Nolan Ryan emerged.

During his time with the Angels, he hurled four no-hitters and broke Sandy Koufax's modern-era single-season strikeout record. Reggie Jackson, one of the most dominant sluggers of the generation, explained what it was like to face him. "I love to bat against Nolan Ryan and I hate to bat against Nolan Ryan. It's like ice cream. You may love it, but you don't want it shoveled down your throat by the gallon. I've never been afraid at the plate but Mr. Ryan makes me uncomfortable. He's the only pitcher who's ever made me consider wearing a helmet with an ear flap."

As the 1970s turned into the 1980s, Nolan Ryan returned home to Texas, signing with the Houston Astros and becoming baseball's first one million dollar per year player. The 1980s were a decade of milestones for Nolan Ryan as he passed Walter Johnson's all-time strikeout mark, broke Sandy Koufax major league-record four no-hitters, and struck out the 5,000th batter of his career.

Before hanging up his spikes at age 46, Ryan topped the 300-win mark and hurled a record seventh no-hitter as a member of the Texas Rangers.

The Ryan Express

Elected To The Hall Of Fame: 1999.
Born: Jan. 31, 1947 in Refugio, Texas.
Height: 6-2. **Weight:** 170.
Threw: Right. **Batted:** Right.
Debut: Sept. 11, 1966. **Final Game:** Sept. 22, 1993.
Teams: New York N.L. 1966, 1968-71; California A.L. 1972-79; Houston N.L. 1980-88; Texas A.L. 1989-93.
Postseason: World Series Champion (1969); N.L. Pennant (1969); 5-Time Playoff Qualifier (1969, 1979-1981, 1986). **Awards:** 8-Time All-Star (1972-1973, 1975, 1977, 1979, 1981, 1985, 1989).

YEAR	TEAM	LEAGUE	G	W	L	SV	SH	IP	H	BB	SO	ERA
1966	NEW YORK	NL	2	0	1	0	0	3	5	3	6	15.00
1968	NEW YORK	NL	21	6	9	0	0	134	93	75	133	3.09
1969	NEW YORK	NL	25	6	3	1	0	89.3	60	53	92	3.53
1970	NEW YORK	NL	27	7	11	1	2	131.7	86	97	125	3.42
1971	NEW YORK	NL	30	10	14	0	0	152	125	116	137	3.97
1972	CALIFORNIA	AL	39	19	16	0	9	284	166	157	329	2.28
1973	CALIFORNIA	AL	41	21	16	1	4	326	238	162	383	2.87
1974	CALIFORNIA	AL	42	22	16	0	3	332.7	221	202	367	2.89
1975	CALIFORNIA	AL	28	14	12	0	5	198	152	132	186	3.45
1976	CALIFORNIA	AL	39	17	18	0	7	284.3	193	183	327	3.36
1977	CALIFORNIA	AL	37	19	16	0	4	299	198	204	341	2.77
1978	CALIFORNIA	AL	31	10	13	0	3	234.7	183	148	260	3.72
1979	CALIFORNIA	AL	34	16	14	0	5	222.7	169	114	223	3.60
1980	HOUSTON	NL	35	11	10	0	2	233.7	205	98	200	3.35
1981	HOUSTON	NL	21	11	5	0	3	149	99	68	140	1.69
1982	HOUSTON	NL	35	16	12	0	3	250.3	196	109	245	3.16
1983	HOUSTON	NL	29	14	9	0	2	196.3	134	101	183	2.98
1984	HOUSTON	NL	30	12	11	0	2	183.7	143	69	197	3.04
1985	HOUSTON	NL	35	10	12	0	0	232	205	95	209	3.80
1986	HOUSTON	NL	30	12	8	0	0	178	119	82	194	3.34
1987	HOUSTON	NL	34	8	16	0	0	211.7	154	87	270	2.76
1988	HOUSTON	NL	33	12	11	0	1	220	186	87	228	3.52
1989	TEXAS	AL	32	16	10	0	2	239.3	162	98	301	3.20
1990	TEXAS	AL	30	13	9	0	2	204	137	74	232	3.44
1991	TEXAS	AL	27	12	6	0	2	173	102	72	203	2.91
1992	TEXAS	AL	27	5	9	0	0	157.3	138	69	157	3.72
1993	TEXAS	AL	13	5	5	0	0	66.3	54	40	46	4.88
CAREER TOTALS			**807**	**324**	**292**	**3**	**61**	**5386**	**3923**	**2795**	**5714**	**3.19**

RYNE SANDBERG

"Ryne Sandberg worked harder than any player I've ever seen. A lot of guys with his athletic ability get by on that and have a nice career. Sandberg worked his butt off because he knew it was wrong not to," said Pete Rose.

When Charlie Hustle says you worked harder than anyone else he's seen in a half century in the game, that means you're a pretty hard worker. People may not know that about Sandberg, though, because he was also one to keep his head down and not have much to say. He let his glove, bat, and wheels do the talking.

In 16 seasons, Sandberg played 2,151 games for the Cubs and 13 for the Phillies, who brought him to the big leagues in 1981. He garnered one of his 2,386 hits in a Phillies uniform. Following the 1981 season, they traded him and Larry Bowa to the Cubs for Iván DeJesus, a trade which should get the Cubs off the hook for trading young Lou Brock to the Cardinals for Ernie Broglio.

In his rookie season, third baseman Sandberg hit .271 with 33 doubles and 32 stolen bases, finishing sixth in the league for Rookie of the Year honors. The following season, the Cubs moved him to second base, where his career blossomed.

In 1984, Sandberg led the Cubs to their first postseason play since the 1945 World Series, hitting .314 and leading the league in runs scored with 114, and triples with 19. He also began turning on the ball and chipped in 19 homers on his way to the NL MVP award. He also made his first of 10 consecutive All-Star appearances, and won his second of nine consecutive Gold Glove Awards.

In 1990, Sandberg led the NL in homers with 40, while also leading the league in runs and total bases, driving in 100 runs and stealing 25 bases. He was the first second baseman since Rogers Hornsby in 1925 to lead the NL in homers.

Sandberg finished his career with the highest fielding percentage at second base with .989. He had 15 streaks of 30 or more consecutive errorless games.

At the time of his retirement after the 1997 season, he held the all-time record of 123 consecutive errorless games by a second baseman and also had hit more home runs than any second baseman in baseball history.

RYNE DEE SANDBERG
"RYNO"
PHILADELPHIA, N.L., 1981
CHICAGO, N.L., 1982-1994, 1996-1997
A SURE-HANDED SECOND BASEMAN WITH POWER AND SPEED WHO DIGNIFIED THE GAME WITH HIS PROFESSIONALISM, QUIET LEADERSHIP AND TIRELESS PREPARATION. SET CAREER RECORDS AMONG SECOND BASEMEN FOR HOME RUNS (277 OF 282 OVERALL), FIELDING PERCENTAGE (.989), CONSECUTIVE ERRORLESS GAMES IN A SEASON (90), AND OVER TWO SEASONS (123). EARNED NINE GOLD GLOVES. LED LEAGUE IN RUNS SCORED THREE TIMES. ELECTED TO 10 ALL-STAR TEAMS, AND NAMED NATIONAL LEAGUE MVP IN 1984. HELPED THE CUBS TO TWO DIVISION TITLES, HITTING .385 IN 10 POST-SEASON GAMES.

Ryno

Elected To The Hall Of Fame: *2005.*
Born: *Sept. 18, 1959 in Spokane, Wash.*
Height: *6-1.* **Weight:** *175.*
Threw: *Right.* **Batted:** *Right.*
Debut: *Sept. 2, 1981.*
Final Game: *Sept. 28, 1997.*
Teams: *Philadelphia N.L. 1981;*
Chicago N.L. 1982-1994, 1996-1997.
Postseason: *2-Time Playoff Qualifier*
(1984, 1989).
Awards: *10-Time All-Star (1984-1993);*
N.L. Most Valuable Player (1984).

YEAR	TEAM	LEAGUE	G	AB	R	H	2B	3B	HR	RBI	SB	AVG
1981	PHILADELPHIA	NL	13	6	2	1	0	0	0	0	0	.167
1982	CHICAGO	NL	156	635	103	172	33	5	7	54	32	.271
1983	CHICAGO	NL	158	633	94	165	25	4	8	48	37	.261
1984	CHICAGO	NL	156	636	114	200	36	19	19	84	32	.314
1985	CHICAGO	NL	153	609	113	186	31	6	26	83	54	.305
1986	CHICAGO	NL	154	627	68	178	28	5	14	76	34	.284
1987	CHICAGO	NL	132	523	81	154	25	2	16	59	21	.294
1988	CHICAGO	NL	155	618	77	163	23	8	19	69	25	.264
1989	CHICAGO	NL	157	606	104	176	25	5	30	76	15	.290
1990	CHICAGO	NL	155	615	116	188	30	3	40	100	25	.306
1991	CHICAGO	NL	158	585	104	170	32	2	26	100	22	.291
1992	CHICAGO	NL	158	612	100	186	32	8	26	87	17	.304
1993	CHICAGO	NL	117	456	67	141	20	0	9	45	9	.309
1994	CHICAGO	NL	57	223	36	53	9	5	5	24	2	.238
1996	CHICAGO	NL	150	554	85	135	28	4	25	92	12	.244
1997	CHICAGO	NL	135	447	54	118	26	0	12	64	7	.264
CAREER TOTALS			**2164**	**8385**	**1318**	**2386**	**403**	**76**	**282**	**1061**	**344**	**.285**

RON SANTO

He personified the Chicago Cubs for more than 50 years as a player, a broadcaster and an icon. His legend remains a living monument to his love for the game.

Ron Santo played 14 years for the Cubs and one for the White Sox, defining National League third base play in the 1960s. A talented multi-sport amateur athlete, he first drew the attention of big league scouts in 1958 as a catcher, and he signed with the Cubs in 1959. In his June 26, 1960 major league debut against the Pirates, Santo had three hits and five RBI in a doubleheader sweep. He never appeared in another minor league game. The next season, Santo entrenched himself at third by hitting 23 home runs and driving in 83 runs.

All the while, Santo was harboring a secret. During a routine physical just before his minor league career began, doctors diagnosed Santo with Type 1 juvenile diabetes. At the time, the life expectancy of a juvenile diabetic was thought to be about 25 years. Santo was 18. But he educated himself about the disease and taught himself how to administer insulin injections. He kept his secret until 1971, by which time he was a seven-time All-Star.

On the field, Santo developed into a star at the plate and with the glove. He was named to his first All-Star Game in 1963, and won the first of five straight Gold Glove Awards in 1964. From 1963-70, Santo averaged 29 homers and 105 RBI per season. He also led the NL in walks four times between 1964 and 1968, and paced the league in on-base percentage twice in that same span.

Santo was part of a core group of players – including Hall of Famers Ernie Banks, Ferguson Jenkins and Billy Williams – who led the Cubs back into contention in the late 1960s. In 1969, the Cubs paced the newly created NL East for most of the season before fading in September as the Miracle Mets clinched the title. It would be Santo's best chance at a postseason appearance that would never come.

Santo entered the business world after retiring following the 1974 season, but returned to the Cubs in 1990 as a radio broadcaster, winning over a new generation of fans with his unabashed support of the team. Despite numerous illnesses – including heart bypass surgery and bladder cancer – Santo rarely missed work, even after having both legs amputated due to his diabetes. In 2003, the Cubs retired his No. 10.

Elected to the Hall of Fame: 2012
Born: Feb. 25, 1940 in Seattle, Wash.
Died: Dec. 2, 2010 in Scottsdale, Ariz.
Height: 6-0. **Weight:** 190.
Batted Right, Threw: Right.
Debut: June 26, 1960.
Final Game: Sept. 29, 1974.
Teams: Chicago N.L. 1960-73; Chicago A.L. 1974
Awards: 9-time All-Star (1963-66, 68-69, 71-73); 5-time Gold Glove winner.

YEAR	TEAM	LEAGUE	G	AB	R	H	2B	3B	HR	RBI	SB	BA
1960	CHICAGO	NL	95	347	44	87	24	2	9	44	0	.251
1961	CHICAGO	NL	154	578	84	164	32	6	23	83	2	.284
1962	CHICAGO	NL	162	604	44	137	20	4	17	83	4	.227
1963	CHICAGO	NL	162	630	79	187	29	6	25	99	6	.297
1964	CHICAGO	NL	161	592	94	185	33	13	30	114	3	.313
1965	CHICAGO	NL	164	608	88	173	30	4	33	101	3	.285
1966	CHICAGO	NL	155	561	93	175	21	8	30	94	4	.312
1967	CHICAGO	NL	161	586	107	176	23	4	31	98	1	.300
1968	CHICAGO	NL	162	577	86	142	17	3	26	98	3	.246
1969	CHICAGO	NL	160	575	97	166	18	4	29	123	1	.289
1970	CHICAGO	NL	154	555	83	148	30	4	26	114	2	.267
1971	CHICAGO	NL	154	555	77	148	22	1	21	88	4	.267
1972	CHICAGO	NL	133	464	68	140	25	5	17	74	1	.302
1973	CHICAGO	NL	149	536	65	143	29	2	20	77	1	.267
1974	CHICAGO	AL	117	375	29	83	12	1	5	41	0	.221
CAREER TOTALS			2243	8143	1138	2254	365	67	342	1331	35	.277

LOUIS SANTOP

L ouis Santop has been called "the first of the great Negro League sluggers," and "the first Negro League super-star." Born in Tyler, Texas, Santop was huge for his day, standing 6-foot-4 and weighing in at 240 pounds. Primarily a catcher, he also played the corner infield and outfield positions. He was known as "Big Bertha," after a large piece of German heavy artillery. While he was a gifted slugger who hit mammoth drives in the Dead Ball Era, he also hit for extremely high averages in the upper .300s and lower .400s.

He broke in with the Fort Worth Wonders in 1909, and the following season played with the Philadelphia Giants, where he formed the famous "kid battery" with Dick Redding. For the next four seasons, he caught for the New York Lincoln Giants, where he formed a future Hall of Fame battery with Smokey Joe Williams.

In 1915, he played briefly with the Chicago American Giants, before returning East to play with the Lincoln Giants. The two teams met in the postseason championship, and ended up tied.

He also played in the Black World Series for the Hilldale Daisies in 1921, 1924, and 1925, winning in '21 and '25.

Santop was an outgoing player and an exuberant drawing card, earning as much as $500 per month in the 1910s and 1920s. There are stories of him calling his home run shots, and he often gave pregame throwing exhibitions, throwing a ball over the centerfield fence while standing at the catcher's position, and then crouching and firing repeatedly to each infielder, amazing onlookers with his powerful arm.

He served in the Navy in 1918 and '19.

In exhibitions against white major leaguers, Santop is remembered for having outhit Babe Ruth in a 1920 postseason series, notching three hits against Carl Mays of the Yankees while the Babe recorded none. In a 1917 series, Santop recorded six hits in three games against Chief Bender and Joe Bush.

In the mid-1920s, Santop was replaced at catcher by another future Hall of Famer, Biz Mackey. After a couple of years of pinch hitting duty, he retired and formed his own touring team, the Santop Bronchos.

LOUIS SANTOP
"TOP"
PRE-NEGRO LEAGUES, 1909-1919
NEGRO LEAGUES, 1920-1926
A DURABLE BACKSTOP WITH AN EXCEPTIONALLY STRONG ARM, AND ONE OF BLACK BASEBALL'S MOST POWERFUL BATTERS DURING THE FIRST QUARTER OF THE TWENTIETH CENTURY, HIT FOR AVERAGE AND ALSO CELEBRATED FOR THE DISTANCE HE COULD DRIVE A BASEBALL. A TOP DRAWING CARD DURING HIS PRIME, CAUGHT FOR SOME OF THE BEST TEAMS OF HIS ERA, INCLUDING THE NEW YORK LINCOLN GIANTS, BROOKLYN ROYAL GIANTS, AND HILLDALE DAISIES. FORMED FAMOUS BATTERY WITH SMOKEY JOE WILLIAMS.

Top, Big Bertha

Elected To The Hall Of Fame: *2006.*
Born: *Jan. 17, 1889 in Tyler, Texas.*
Died: *Jan. 6, 1942 in Philadelphia, Pa.*
Height: *6-4. Weight: 240.*
Threw: *Right. Batted: Left.1915*
Teams: *Pre-Negro Leagues 1909-1919; Negro Leagues 1920-1926. Fort Worth 1909; Oklahoma 1909; Philadelphia 1909-1910; Fe 1911; New York 1912; Brooklyn 1916-1919; Hilldale 1918-1926.*

YEAR	TEAM	LEAGUE	G	AB	R	H	2B	3B	HR	RBI	SB	AVG
1911	FE	CUNL	5	14	1	1	0	1	0	2	1	.071
1912	NEW YORK	CNCS	8	21	1	4	1	0	0	3	0	.190
1914	N.Y. LINCOLN GIANTS/NEW YORK	INDP/CNCS	38	151	19	55	5	2	1	29	6	.364
1915	N.Y. LINCOLN STARS	INDP	32	126	19	41	8	1	2	30	0	.325
1916	N.Y. LINCOLN STARS/BROOKLYN	INDP	34	130	27	47	12	7	0	33	6	.362
1917	BROOKLYN	INDP	18	63	18	24	7	1	0	16	6	.381
1918	HILLDALE/BROOKLYN	INDP	17	68	11	28	6	2	1	17	3	.412
1919	BROOKLYN/HILLDALE	INDP	8	28	2	7	0	1	0	2	1	.250
1920	HILLDALE	INDP	—	58	9	16	3	0	0	—	0	.276
1921	HILLDALE	INDP	—	114	28	41	6	2	6	—	4	.360
1922	HILLDALE	INDP	—	24	3	12	3	1	0	—	0	.500
1923	HILLDALE	ECOL	—	133	16	31	3	1	1	—	3	.233
1924	HILLDALE	ECOL	—	218	34	76	10	3	5	—	2	.349
1925	HILLDALE	ECOL	—	30	2	5	1	0	0	—	1	.167
1926	HILLDALE	ECOL	—	31	6	11	1	0	0	—	1	.355
CAREER TOTALS			**—**	**1209**	**196**	**399**	**66**	**22**	**16**	**—**	**34**	**.330**

RAY SCHALK

"If I was a good catcher, it was because I learned from the masters," Ray Schalk said. "I caught pitchers of long experience and they hammered the game into me. I had to learn or lose my job. They made me a star."

A catcher's value can be derived from much more than just his offense, and there's no greater example of this than Ray Schalk. The undersized backstop was a workhorse for the White Sox clubs of the 1910s and 1920s, and he's regarded as the finest defensive catcher of the Dead Ball Era.

Schalk made his big league debut one day before his 20th birthday in August 1912, then took over as the White Sox's everyday catcher in 1913. Schalk's most notable offensive feat was his 30 stolen bases in 1916, establishing a record for catchers that stood until John Wathan broke it in 1982.

Where Schalk really made his name was on defense. Combining his sharp mind for the game with a blue-collar approach, Schalk proved adept at handling a wide variety of pitching styles. A true workhorse, Schalk led the American League in games caught seven times, including his 1920 season when he caught 151 of Chicago's 154 games. His defensive prowess stands out even more since he was doing it at a time when spitballs and other trick pitches were legal. Schalk was also credited with catching four no-hitters in his career, though one of those was taken away when the standards for no-hitters were adjusted in 1991.

Schalk pioneered aspects of the catcher's position often taken for granted. An active part of the infield, he was believed to be the first catcher to back up throws to first base on ground outs or third base on throws from the outfield. He also recorded putouts at every base over the course of his career, even second base, and he led AL catchers in fielding percentage five times.

Schalk was a member of the 1919 Black Sox club, which threw the World Series against the Reds. Schalk himself was clean, and hit .304 in the Series, though he suspected something was amiss when his pitchers kept crossing him up. Schalk always refused to impugn his teammates publicly. Schalk later spent two seasons as a player-manager for the White Sox in 1927-28, followed by a long career coaching in the minor leagues and with Purdue University.

Elected To The Hall Of Fame: *1955.*
Born: *Aug. 12, 1892 in Harvel, Ill.*
Died: *May 19, 1970 in Chicago, Ill.*
Height: *5-9.* ***Weight:*** *165.*
Threw: *Right.* ***Batted:*** *Right.*
Debut: *Aug. 11, 1912.*
Final Game: *Sept. 15, 1929.*
Teams: *Chicago A.L. 1912-1928;*
New York N.L. 1929.
Postseason: *World Series Champion*
(1917); 2 A.L. Pennants (1917, 1919).

YEAR	TEAM	LEAGUE	G	AB	R	H	2B	3B	HR	RBI	SB	AVG
1912	CHICAGO	AL	23	63	7	18	2	0	0	8	2	.286
1913	CHICAGO	AL	129	401	38	98	15	5	1	38	14	.244
1914	CHICAGO	AL	136	392	30	106	13	2	0	36	24	.270
1915	CHICAGO	AL	135	413	46	110	14	4	1	54	15	.266
1916	CHICAGO	AL	129	410	36	95	12	9	0	41	30	.232
1917	CHICAGO	AL	140	424	48	96	12	5	2	51	19	.226
1918	CHICAGO	AL	108	333	35	73	6	3	0	22	12	.219
1919	CHICAGO	AL	131	394	57	111	9	3	0	34	11	.282
1920	CHICAGO	AL	151	485	64	131	25	5	1	61	10	.270
1921	CHICAGO	AL	128	416	32	105	24	4	0	47	3	.252
1922	CHICAGO	AL	142	442	57	124	22	3	4	60	12	.281
1923	CHICAGO	AL	123	382	42	87	12	2	1	44	7	.228
1924	CHICAGO	AL	57	153	15	30	4	2	1	11	1	.196
1925	CHICAGO	AL	125	343	44	94	18	1	0	52	11	.274
1926	CHICAGO	AL	82	226	26	60	9	1	0	32	5	.265
1927	CHICAGO	AL	16	26	2	6	2	0	0	2	0	.231
1928	CHICAGO	AL	2	1	0	1	0	0	0	1	1	1.000
1929	NEW YORK	NL	5	2	0	0	0	0	0	0	0	.000
CAREER TOTALS			**1762**	**5306**	**579**	**1345**	**199**	**49**	**11**	**594**	**177**	**.253**

MIKE SCHMIDT

"If you could equate the amount of time and effort put in mentally and physically into succeeding on the baseball field and measured it by the dirt on your uniform, mine would have been black," Mike Schmidt said.

Michael Jack Schmidt grew up in Dayton, Ohio with a blue-collar work ethic. He carried that mentality onto the baseball field, which helped him get the most of his athletic ability and forever endear him to fans in Philadelphia, where he spent the entirety of his 18-year career.

Schmidt was a second-round pick out of Ohio University in 1971, one pick after George Brett was selected by the Royals. Signed by legendary Phillies scout Tony Lucadello, Schmidt didn't spend long in the minors, making his major league debut on Sept. 12, 1972. Because of that, he took some lumps as a rookie in 1973, hitting just .196. But Schmidt turned things around in a hurry—making the All-Star team in 1974 and never looking back. Schmidt was a 12-time All-Star during his career.

Home runs were Schmidt's calling card at the plate. He led the National League in homers eight times during his career and his 48 home runs in 1980 set the major league record for a third baseman, which he held for 27 years until Alex Rodriguez broke it. On April 18, 1987, Schmidt became the 14th member of the 500 home run club and finished his career with 548.

Along with the power, Schmidt also led the National League in strikeouts four times and retired with the third-most strikeouts in major league history. However, Schmidt drew walks almost as often as he struck out.

In the field, Schmidt was a graceful defender at third base and was occasionally the Phillies' emergency shortstop. Schmidt was a 10-time Gold Glove Award winner and won six Silver Slugger Awards. He was voted the National League's Most Valuable Player in 1980, 1981 and 1986.

The Phillies won the World Series in 1980, beating the Royals in six games, and Schmidt was named World Series MVP.

MICHAEL JACK SCHMIDT
PHILADELPHIA, N.L., 1972-1989
UNPRECEDENTED COMBINATION OF POWER AND DEFENSE WITH UNUSUAL MIXTURE OF STRENGTH, COORDINATION AND SPEED MADE HIM ONE OF THE GAME'S GREATEST THIRD BASEMEN. 7TH ON ALL-TIME LIST WITH 548 HOMERS. HIS 8 HOMERUN TITLES (TIE) BETTERED ONLY BY BABE RUTH. BELTED 40 OR MORE ON 3 OCCASIONS AND TOPPED 30 TEN OTHER TIMES. 48 HOMERUNS IN 1980 MOST EVER BY THIRD BASEMAN. HIT 4 IN ONE GAME IN 1976. 3-TIME MVP WITH 10 GOLD GLOVES FOR FIELDING EXCELLENCE.

Elected To The Hall Of Fame: *1995.*
Born: *Sept. 27, 1949 in Dayton, Ohio.*
Height: *6-2.* ***Weight:*** *195.*
Threw: *Right.* ***Batted:*** *Right.*
Debut: *Sept. 12, 1972.*
Final Game: *May 28, 1989.*
Teams: *Philadelphia N.L. 1972-1989.*
Postseason: *World Series Champion (1980); 2 N.L. Pennants (1980, 1983). 6-Time Playoff Qualifier (1976-1978, 1980-1981, 1983).*
Awards: *12-Time All-Star (1974, 1976-1977, 1979-1984, 1986-1987, 1989); 3-Time N.L. Most Valuable Player (1980-1981, 1986); World Series Most Valuable Player (1980).*

YEAR	TEAM	LEAGUE	G	AB	R	H	2B	3B	HR	RBI	SB	AVG
1972	PHILADELPHIA	NL	13	34	2	7	0	0	1	3	0	.206
1973	PHILADELPHIA	NL	132	367	43	72	11	0	18	52	8	.196
1974	PHILADELPHIA	NL	162	568	108	160	28	7	36	116	23	.282
1975	PHILADELPHIA	NL	158	562	93	140	34	3	38	95	29	.249
1976	PHILADELPHIA	NL	160	584	112	153	31	4	38	107	14	.262
1977	PHILADELPHIA	NL	154	544	114	149	27	11	38	101	15	.274
1978	PHILADELPHIA	NL	145	513	93	129	27	2	21	78	19	.251
1979	PHILADELPHIA	NL	160	541	109	137	25	4	45	114	9	.253
1980	PHILADELPHIA	NL	150	548	104	157	25	8	48	121	12	.286
1981	PHILADELPHIA	NL	102	354	78	112	19	2	31	91	12	.316
1982	PHILADELPHIA	NL	148	514	108	144	26	3	35	87	14	.280
1983	PHILADELPHIA	NL	154	534	104	136	16	4	40	109	7	.255
1984	PHILADELPHIA	NL	151	528	93	146	23	3	36	106	5	.277
1985	PHILADELPHIA	NL	158	549	89	152	31	5	33	93	1	.277
1986	PHILADELPHIA	NL	160	552	97	160	29	1	37	119	1	.290
1987	PHILADELPHIA	NL	147	522	88	153	28	0	35	113	2	.293
1988	PHILADELPHIA	NL	108	390	52	97	21	2	12	62	3	.249
1989	PHILADELPHIA	NL	42	148	19	30	7	0	6	28	0	.203
CAREER TOTALS			**2404**	**8352**	**1506**	**2234**	**408**	**59**	**548**	**1595**	**174**	**.267**

RED SCHOENDIENST

"Red is quite a human being. He treats us like men, lets us play our game and gives our young players confidence," Orlando Cepeda said.

Not many ballplayers have found success on the playing field as well as in the coaching box. Red Schoendienst, however, could do it all. Schoendienst was signed by the Cardinals in 1942. By the next season, Schoendienst was named MVP of the International League and then spent 1944 in the Army, discharged in 1945 for eye problems and a shoulder injury. Despite his injuries, he made the Cardinals club that spring and was their starting left fielder. In his rookie season, he led the National League with 26 stolen bases. The following season, he moved to second base and led the N.L. in fielding percentage, which he would do six more times.

In 1950, he handled 320 consecutive chances without an error, and in 1956 he set an N.L. record with a .9934 fielding percentage at second base, which stood until Ryne Sandberg eclipsed it in 1986. Schoendienst played 11-plus seasons in St. Louis, winning a World Series in 1946. In 1956, he was traded to the New York Giants and then a year later to the Milwaukee Braves, where he would make an immediate impact. Schoendienst led the league with 200 hits in 1957 and helped the team to consecutive pennant wins in 1957-58. He won his second World Series in 1957, the first and only championship the Braves would win in Milwaukee. He suffered multiple injuries in 1958 and missed almost the entire 1959 season fighting tuberculosis, which cost him part of a lung. He signed as a free agent with the Cardinals in 1961, where he finished out his career. He was elected to 10 All-Star Games, hit .300 or higher seven times and finished his career with a .983 fielding percentage. He had a career .289 batting average with 2,449 hits in 19 seasons.

Schoendienst went from coach to manager of the Cardinals in 1965 and went on to hold the longest managerial tenure in club history until Tony La Russa. As manager, he led the team to pennants in 1967 and 1968, won the 1967 World Series and had a .522 winning percentage in 14 seasons. He wore a major league uniform as a player, coach, or manager for seven decades.

ALBERT FRED SCHOENDIENST
"RED"
ST. LOUIS, N.L., 1945-1956, 1961-1963
NEW YORK, N.L., 1956-1957
MILWAUKEE, N.L., 1957-1960
ROOMMATE STAN MUSIAL CREDITED HIM WITH "GREATEST PAIR OF HANDS I'VE EVER SEEN". SLEEK, FAR-RANGING SECOND BASEMAN FOR 18 SEASONS. LED N.L. IN FIELDING AND HIT .300 OR BETTER SEVEN TIMES. WHEN ELECTED IN 1989 HAD WORN MAJOR LEAGUE UNIFORM 45 CONSECUTIVE SEASONS AS PLAYER, COACH AND MANAGER. PILOTING REDBIRDS TO WORLD SERIES IN 1967 AND 1968, 14TH INNING HOMER WON 1950 ALL-STAR GAME FOR N.L.

Elected To The Hall Of Fame: 1989.
Born: Feb. 2, 1923 in Germantown, Ill.
Height: 6-0. **Weight:** 170.
Threw: Right. **Batted:** Both.
Debut: Apr. 17, 1945.
Final Game: July 7, 1963.
Teams: St. Louis N.L. 1945-1956, 1961-1963; New York N.L. 1956-1957; Milwaukee N.L. 1957-1960.
Postseason: 2-Time World Series Champion (1946, 1957); 3 N.L. Pennants (1946, 1957-1958).
Awards: 10-Time All-Star (1946, 1948-1955, 1957)

YEAR	TEAM	LEAGUE	G	AB	R	H	2B	3B	HR	RBI	SB	AVG
1945	ST. LOUIS	NL	137	565	89	157	22	6	1	47	26	.278
1946	ST. LOUIS	NL	142	606	94	170	28	5	0	34	12	.281
1947	ST. LOUIS	NL	151	659	91	167	25	9	3	48	6	.253
1948	ST. LOUIS	NL	119	408	64	111	21	4	4	36	1	.272
1949	ST. LOUIS	NL	151	640	102	190	25	2	3	54	8	.297
1950	ST. LOUIS	NL	153	642	81	177	43	9	7	63	3	.276
1951	ST. LOUIS	NL	135	553	88	160	32	7	6	54	0	.289
1952	ST. LOUIS	NL	152	620	91	188	40	7	7	67	9	.303
1953	ST. LOUIS	NL	146	564	107	193	35	5	15	79	3	.342
1954	ST. LOUIS	NL	148	610	98	192	38	8	5	79	4	.315
1955	ST. LOUIS	NL	145	553	68	148	21	3	11	51	7	.268
1956	ST. LOUIS/NEW YORK	NL	132	487	61	147	21	3	2	29	1	.302
1957	NEW YORK/MILWAUKEE	NL	150	648	91	200	31	8	15	65	4	.309
1958	MILWAUKEE	NL	106	427	47	112	23	1	1	24	3	.262
1959	MILWAUKEE	NL	5	3	0	0	0	0	0	0	0	.000
1960	MILWAUKEE	NL	68	226	21	58	9	1	1	19	1	.257
1961	ST. LOUIS	NL	72	120	9	36	9	0	1	12	1	.300
1962	ST. LOUIS	NL	98	143	21	43	4	0	2	12	0	.301
1963	ST. LOUIS	NL	6	5	0	0	0	0	0	0	0	.000
CAREER TOTALS			**2216**	**8479**	**1223**	**2449**	**427**	**78**	**84**	**773**	**89**	**.289**

The Baseball Hall of Fame Almanac

TOM SEAVER

Perhaps no single player is identified more with one team than "The Franchise" Tom Seaver is with the New York Mets. Seaver helped turn the Mets from loveable losers into formidable foes. Hall of Fame outfielder and Mets broadcaster Ralph Kiner recalled "Tom Seaver was the driving force behind the players, always pushing the team to be better than they were, never letting them settle."

In 1969, the Mets captured their first World Series championship behind the powerful right arm of "Tom Terrific." Seaver took home his first National League Cy Young Award that year, leading the major leagues in victories with 25, which accounted for one quarter of the Mets' wins. Teammate Cleon Jones said "Tom does everything well. He's the kind of man you'd want your kids to grow up to be like. Tom's a studious player, devoted to his profession, a loyal cat, trustworthy - everything a Boy Scout's supposed to be. In fact, we call him 'Boy Scout.' " One year later, Seaver tied a major league record, striking out 19 San Diego Padres, including a record 10 consecutive to end the game.

Seaver was an intelligent pitcher who brought great velocity and pinpoint control with him to the mound. Hall of Famer Hank Aaron said Tom Seaver was "the toughest pitcher I've ever faced." In an ESPN poll, Hall of Famers Bob Gibson, Juan Marichal, Jim Palmer, Nolan Ryan, Steve Carlton, Bert Blyleven, and Don Sutton all said Tom Seaver was the best pitcher of their generation.

From 1967-1977, "The Franchise" was selected to 10 All-Star teams, led the league in strikeouts five times, put together five 20-win seasons, threw five one-hitters and won three Cy Young Awards. Hall of Famer Sparky Anderson, who managed Seaver with the Cincinnati Reds in 1977 and '78, recalled, "My idea of managing is giving the ball to Tom Seaver and sitting down and watching him work."

Tom Seaver no-hit the Cardinals in 1978 and in 1981 became the fifth player in history to record 3,000 strikeouts. In 1985, he returned to New York as a member of the Chicago White Sox and won his 300th major league game at Yankee Stadium.

Tom Terrific, The Franchise

Elected To The Hall Of Fame: 1992.
Born: Nov. 17, 1944 in Fresno, Calif.
Height: 6-1. **Weight:** 195.
Threw: Right. **Batted:** Right.
Debut: April 13, 1967.
Final Game: Sept. 19, 1986.
Teams: New York N.L. 1967-1977, 1983; Cincinnati N.L. 1977-1982; Chicago A.L. 1984-1986; Boston A.L. 1986.
Postseason: World Series Champion (1969); 2 N.L. Pennants (1969, 1973); 3-Time Playoff Qualifier (1969, 1973, 1979).
Awards: 12-Time All-Star (1967-1973, 1975-1978, 1981); N.L. Rookie of the Year (1967); 3-Time N.L. Cy Young (1969, 1973, 1975).

YEAR	TEAM	LEAGUE	G	W	L	SV	SH	IP	H	BB	SO	ERA
1967	NEW YORK	NL	35	16	13	0	2	251	224	78	170	2.76
1968	NEW YORK	NL	36	16	12	1	5	278	224	48	205	2.20
1969	NEW YORK	NL	36	25	7	0	5	273.3	202	82	208	2.21
1970	NEW YORK	NL	37	18	12	0	2	290.7	230	83	283	2.82
1971	NEW YORK	NL	36	20	10	0	4	286.3	210	61	289	1.76
1972	NEW YORK	NL	35	21	12	0	3	262	215	77	249	2.92
1973	NEW YORK	NL	36	19	10	0	3	290	219	64	251	2.08
1974	NEW YORK	NL	32	11	11	0	5	236	199	75	201	3.20
1975	NEW YORK	NL	36	22	9	0	5	280.3	217	88	243	2.38
1976	NEW YORK	NL	35	14	11	0	5	271	211	77	235	2.59
1977	NEW YORK/CINCINNATI	NL	33	21	6	0	7	261.3	199	66	196	2.58
1978	CINCINNATI	NL	36	16	14	0	1	259.7	218	89	226	2.88
1979	CINCINNATI	NL	32	16	6	0	5	215	187	61	131	3.14
1980	CINCINNATI	NL	26	10	8	0	1	168	140	59	101	3.64
1981	CINCINNATI	NL	23	14	2	0	1	166.3	120	66	87	2.54
1982	CINCINNATI	NL	21	5	13	0	0	111.3	136	44	62	5.50
1983	NEW YORK	NL	34	9	14	0	2	231	201	86	135	3.55
1984	CHICAGO	AL	34	15	11	0	4	236.7	216	61	131	3.95
1985	CHICAGO	AL	35	16	11	0	1	238.7	223	69	134	3.17
1986	CHICAGO/BOSTON	AL	28	7	13	0	0	176.3	180	56	103	4.03
CAREER TOTALS			**656**	**311**	**205**	**1**	**61**	**4783**	**3971**	**1390**	**3640**	**2.86**

JOE SEWELL

"When I was a boy I'd walk around with a pocket full of rocks or a Coca-Cola top," Joe Sewell said, "and I can't remember not being able to hit them with a broomstick handle."

Keep your eye on the ball. It's one of the most basic tenets of hitting, stressed from the first time a young player picks up a bat. Joe Sewell took it to another level, though, and it helped pave his way to the Hall of Fame.

Sewell's big league career was born out of one of the game's tragedies. After Indians shortstop Ray Chapman was killed by a pitch from the Yankees' Carl Mays in August 1920, Sewell was called up. The 21-year-old Sewell had played in just 92 minor league games before his big league debut, yet he settled in immediately and helped lead the Tribe to the 1920 World Series title.

Where Sewell really carved out his identity was his ability to get the bat on the ball more consistently than anyone else ever has. Sewell struck out 20 times in 558 at-bats during the 1922 season, and that would be his career high. He never even reached double-digits in strikeouts in any of his last nine seasons. During the 1929 season, Sewell went 115 games between punchouts. He ended his career with a rate of 62.6 at-bats per strikeout.

He had seven seasons in which he recorded over 500 at-bats while striking out less that 10 times. From September 1922 through April 1930, Sewell played in 1,103 consecutive games, the second-longest such streak in history at the time. Sewell was also known for using only a single bat through his entire career, a 40-ouncer he dubbed "Black Betsy."

Hardly a one dimensional player, Sewell led American League shortstops in fielding percentage three times and finished in the top five six times. He shifted to third base in 1929 and, after signing with the Yankees in 1931, was the regular third baseman for the Yankees club that won the 1932 World Series.

Sewell grew up in Alabama and was an accomplished college player with the University of Alabama. In later years, he returned to coach the Crimson Tide baseball team, winning a Southeastern Conference title in 1968. The university renamed its ballpark Sewell-Thomas Stadium in 1978, one year after Sewell's induction to the Hall of Fame.

Elected To The Hall Of Fame: *1977.*
Born: *Oct. 9, 1898 in Titus, Ala.*
Died: *Mar. 6, 1990 in Mobile, Ala.*
Height: *5-6.* **Weight:** *155.*
Threw: *Right.* **Batted:** *Left.*
Debut: *Sept. 10, 1920.*
Final Game: *Sept. 24, 1933.*
Teams: *Cleveland A.L. 1920-1930;*
New York A.L. 1931-1933.
Postseason: *2-Time World Series*
Champion (1920, 1932); 2 A.L.
Pennants (1920, 1932).

YEAR	TEAM	LEAGUE	G	AB	R	H	2B	3B	HR	RBI	SB	AVG
1920	CLEVELAND	AL	22	70	14	23	4	1	0	12	1	.329
1921	CLEVELAND	AL	154	572	101	182	36	12	4	93	7	.318
1922	CLEVELAND	AL	153	558	80	167	28	7	2	83	10	.299
1923	CLEVELAND	AL	153	553	98	195	41	10	3	109	9	.353
1924	CLEVELAND	AL	153	594	99	188	45	5	4	106	3	.316
1925	CLEVELAND	AL	155	608	78	204	37	7	1	98	7	.336
1926	CLEVELAND	AL	154	578	91	187	41	5	4	85	17	.324
1927	CLEVELAND	AL	153	569	83	180	48	5	1	92	3	.316
1928	CLEVELAND	AL	155	588	79	190	40	2	4	70	7	.323
1929	CLEVELAND	AL	152	578	90	182	38	3	7	73	6	.315
1930	CLEVELAND	AL	109	353	44	102	17	6	0	48	1	.289
1931	NEW YORK	AL	130	484	102	146	22	1	6	64	1	.302
1932	NEW YORK	AL	125	503	95	137	21	3	11	68	0	.272
1933	NEW YORK	AL	135	524	87	143	18	1	2	54	2	.273
CAREER TOTALS			**1903**	**7132**	**1141**	**2226**	**436**	**68**	**49**	**1055**	**74**	**.312**

AL SIMMONS

"I wish I had nine players named Al Simmons," Hall of Fame manager Connie Mack said.

Born Aloysius Szymanski in 1902 to Polish immigrants living in Milwaukee, Al Simmons was a slugging left fielder for Connie Mack's fearsome Philadelphia Athletics squads of the late 1920s and early '30s. Simmons was not as celebrated as some of his contemporaries like Babe Ruth, Lou Gehrig or Rogers Hornsby – or even teammates Mickey Cochrane, Lefty Grove and Jimmie Foxx. But at his peak Simmons was one of the most dangerous hitters of the live-ball era.

During his first nine years, from 1924 through 1932, all with Philadelphia, Simmons led all major league batters with 1,796 hits and 343 doubles, while finishing second with 1,156 RBI and fourth behind Ruth, Gehrig and Hack Wilson with 208 home runs. In that time, he batted .358 and slugged .590 across 5,019 at-bats, while finishing as high as second in MVP voting and among the top 10 four other times.

A favorite of Mack and a driving force behind the Athletics' three-time American League pennant winners from 1929 through 1931 – and World Series champions the first two of those years – Simmons won AL batting titles in 1930 (.381) and '31 (.390.) He holds the single-season record for hits by a right-handed batter with 253 in 1925, which he collected in just 153 games.

During a 20-year career, Simmons compiled a .334 batting average, 2,927 hits and 307 home runs, all with an unconventional batting stance that earned him the nickname "Bucketfoot Al" because his stride took him toward third base. Mack sold Simmons to the Chicago White Sox in September 1932. Simmons hit .337 and made a pair of All-Star teams during his first two years in Chicago, and on April 26, 1934, he collected career hit No. 2,000 in his 1,393rd game, making him the fastest player in history to reach that milestone. He turned 33 during the 1935 season, and from that point to the end of his career, Simmons played for seven teams in nine seasons, batting .287 with 67 homers in 2,577 at-bats. Fittingly, he made his final four appearances for Philadelphia in 1944 and joined their coaching staff the following year.

ALOYSIUS HARRY SIMMONS

PLAYED WITH 7 MAJOR LEAGUE CLUBS 1924-1944. STAR WITH PHILA.(A.L.).BATTED .308 TO .392 FROM 1924 TO 1934.LEADING BATTER .381 IN 1930,.390 IN 1931. MOST HITS BY A.L.RIGHT-HANDED BATTER WITH 253,LED LEAGUE RUNS BATTED IN,RUNS SCORED,HITS AND TOTAL BASES SEVERAL SEASONS.HIT 3 HOME RUNS,JULY 15,1932. LIFETIME BATTING AVERAGE .334.

Bucketfoot Al

Elected To The Hall Of Fame: 1953.
Born: May 22, 1902 in Milwaukee, Wis.
Died: May 26, 1956 in Milwaukee, Wis.
Height: 5-11. **Weight:** 190.
Threw: Right. **Batted:** Right.
Debut: April 15, 1924.
Final Game: July 1, 1944.
Teams: Philadelphia A.L. 1924-1932, 1940-1941, 1944; Chicago A.L. 1933-1935; Detroit A.L. 1936; Washington A.L. 1937-1938; Boston N.L. 1939; Cincinnati N.L. 1939; Boston A.L. 1943.
Postseason: 2-Time World Series Champion (1929-1930); A.L. Pennant (1931); N.L. Pennant (1939).
Awards: 3-Time All-Star (1933-1935).

YEAR	TEAM	LEAGUE	G	AB	R	H	2B	3B	HR	RBI	SB	AVG
1924	PHILADELPHIA	AL	152	594	69	183	31	9	8	102	16	.308
1925	PHILADELPHIA	AL	153	654	122	253	43	12	24	129	7	.387
1926	PHILADELPHIA	AL	147	583	90	199	53	10	19	109	11	.341
1927	PHILADELPHIA	AL	106	406	86	159	36	11	15	108	10	.392
1928	PHILADELPHIA	AL	119	464	78	163	33	9	15	107	1	.351
1929	PHILADELPHIA	AL	143	581	114	212	41	9	34	157	4	.365
1930	PHILADELPHIA	AL	138	554	152	211	41	16	36	165	9	.381
1931	PHILADELPHIA	AL	128	513	105	200	37	13	22	128	3	.390
1932	PHILADELPHIA	AL	154	670	144	216	28	9	35	151	4	.322
1933	CHICAGO	AL	146	605	85	200	29	10	14	119	5	.331
1934	CHICAGO	AL	138	558	102	192	36	7	18	104	3	.344
1935	CHICAGO	AL	128	525	68	140	22	7	16	79	4	.267
1936	DETROIT	AL	143	568	96	186	38	6	13	112	6	.327
1937	WASHINGTON	AL	103	419	60	117	21	10	8	84	3	.279
1938	WASHINGTON	AL	125	470	79	142	23	6	21	95	2	.302
1939	BOSTON/CIN.	NL	102	351	39	96	17	5	7	44	0	.274
1940	PHILADELPHIA	AL	37	81	7	25	4	0	1	19	0	.309
1941	PHILADELPHIA	AL	9	24	1	3	1	0	0	1	0	.125
1943	BOSTON	AL	40	133	9	27	5	0	1	12	0	.203
1944	PHILADELPHIA	AL	4	6	1	3	0	0	0	2	0	.500
CAREER TOTALS			**2215**	**8759**	**1507**	**2927**	**539**	**149**	**307**	**1827**	**88**	**.334**

GEORGE SISLER

GEORGE HAROLD SISLER
ST. LOUIS-WASHINGTON A.L.
BOSTON, N.L.•1915-1930
HOLDS TWO AMERICAN LEAGUE RECORDS,
MAKING 257 HITS IN 1920 AND BATTING
.41979 IN 1922. RETIRED WITH MAJOR
LEAGUE AVERAGE OF .341. CREDITED WITH
BEING ONE OF BEST TWO FIELDING FIRST
BASEMEN IN HISTORY OF GAME.

George Sisler was highly thought of as both a person and a ballplayer during his day. A five-tool player before the term came into vogue, Sisler finished his career as one of the game's greatest hitters.

After graduating with a mechanical engineering degree from the University of Michigan in 1915, a rarity for ballplayers at the time, Sisler moved right onto the roster of the St. Louis Browns. Starting his career as a pitcher, he eventually became a first baseman in order to get his powerful left-handed bat in the everyday lineup.

Peerless defensively at first, Sisler also excelled with his 42-ounce bat in hand. In a big league career that lasted 15 seasons, "Gorgeous George" batted over .300 13 times, including league-leading averages of .407 in 1920 and .420 in 1922. His 257 hits during the 1920 campaign remained a modern major league record until Seattle's Ichiro Suzuki broke it in 2004. A skilled base runner as well, he led the league in stolen bases four times.

Baseball great Ty Cobb, an American League rival for many years, once called Sisler "the nearest thing to a perfect ballplayer" he had ever seen.

Sisler claimed that the fact he was once a pitcher helped make him a better hitter. "I used to stand on the mound myself, study the batter and wonder how I could fool him," he said. "Now when I am at the plate, I can the more easily place myself in the pitcher's position and figure what is passing through his mind."

At the height of his success as a baseball player, though, he missed the entire 1923 season due to a sinus infection that produced double vision. He would come back to play another seven seasons, hitting .320 during that span, but even he would acknowledge he was never quite the same hitter.

Ending his career with 2,812 hits and a .340 batting average, Sisler was inducted into the Baseball Hall of Fame in 1939. But because he often played on second-division teams and never had the national stage of a World Series, he was reserved and much less flamboyant that fellow stars of the time like Babe Ruth and Ty Cobb, and as a first baseman was overshadowed by the enormity of Lou Gehrig.

Elected To The Hall Of Fame: *1939.*
Born: *March 24, 1893 in Manchester, Ohio.*
Died: *March 26, 1973 in Richmond Heights, Mo.*
Height: *5-11. Weight: 170.*
Threw: *Left. Batted: Left.*
Debut: *June 28, 1915.*
Final Game: *Sept. 22, 1930.*
Teams: *St. Louis A.L. 1915-1922, 1924-1927; Washington A.L. 1928; Boston N.L. 1928-1930.*
Awards: *A.L. Most Valuable Player (1922).*

YEAR	TEAM	LEAGUE	G	AB	R	H	2B	3B	HR	RBI	SB	AVG
1915	ST. LOUIS	AL	81	274	28	78	10	2	3	29	10	.285
1916	ST. LOUIS	AL	151	580	83	177	21	11	4	76	34	.305
1917	ST. LOUIS	AL	135	539	60	190	30	9	2	52	37	.353
1918	ST. LOUIS	AL	114	452	69	154	21	9	2	41	45	.341
1919	ST. LOUIS	AL	132	511	96	180	31	15	10	83	28	.352
1920	ST. LOUIS	AL	154	631	137	257	49	18	19	122	42	.407
1921	ST. LOUIS	AL	138	582	125	216	38	18	12	104	35	.371
1922	ST. LOUIS	AL	142	586	134	246	42	18	8	105	51	.420
1924	ST. LOUIS	AL	151	636	94	194	27	10	9	74	19	.305
1925	ST. LOUIS	AL	150	649	100	224	21	15	12	105	11	.345
1926	ST. LOUIS	AL	150	613	78	178	21	12	7	71	12	.290
1927	ST. LOUIS	AL	149	614	87	201	32	8	5	97	27	.327
1928	WASHINGTON/BOSTON	AL/NL	138	540	72	179	27	4	4	70	11	.331
1929	BOSTON	NL	154	629	67	205	40	8	2	79	6	.326
1930	BOSTON	NL	116	431	54	133	15	7	3	67	7	.309
CAREER TOTALS			**2055**	**8267**	**1284**	**2812**	**425**	**164**	**102**	**1175**	**375**	**.340**

The Baseball Hall of Fame Almanac

ENOS SLAUGHTER

ENOS BRADSHER SLAUGHTER
"COUNTRY"
ST. LOUIS N.L. 1938-1953
NEW YORK A.L. 1954-1955, 1956-1959
KANSAS CITY A.L. 1955-1956 MILWAUKEE N.L. 1959
HARD-NOSED, HUSTLING PERFORMER WHO PLAYED
THE GAME WITH INTENSITY AND DETERMINATION.
FLAT, LEVEL SWING MADE HIM A LIFETIME .300
HITTER WHO INVARIABLY CAME THROUGH IN
CLUTCH SITUATIONS. EXCELLENT OUTFIELDER WITH
STRONG ARM. DARING BASERUNNER FAMOUS FOR
HIS MAD DASH HOME TO WIN 1946 WORLD SERIES
FOR CARDINALS. BATTED .291 IN 5 WORLD SERIES.

"To be a big league ball player, you have to love the game," Enos Slaughter said. "This is a pretty good game and a pretty swell way to make a living. The conditions in the majors are fine and the money is good. So I say keep yelling and hustling every minute you're in uniform."

Slaughter grew up in Roxboro, N.C., where he earned the nickname, "Country." Though he was a southern gentleman off the field, he was a fierce competitor between the lines and his intensity was often mistaken for brashness or cockiness.

Slaughter began his career with the St. Louis Cardinals in 1938 at the age of 21. He spent 13 seasons with the Cardinals and was a 10-time All-Star. Like many players from his era, Slaughter's career statistics would be better if he hadn't missed three prime seasons (1943-1945) to serve during World War II. During the war, Slaughter was a sergeant in the Army Air Force.

"I wanted to be a pilot," he told author Frederick Turner, "but they said I was color blind. They wanted me to be a bombardier, but I said if I couldn't be the one flying the plane, I'd just as soon not be flying. So, I became a physical education instructor in charge of about 200 troops."

Slaughter didn't skip a beat upon returning to baseball, leading the National League with 130 RBI in 1946 and guiding the Cardinals to a World Series win over the Boston Red Sox.

Aside from his intense, sometimes violent, playing style, Slaughter is best known for his "Mad Dash" in that World Series. In the bottom of the eighth inning of Game 7, the score was tied at 3. Slaughter was on first base with two outs when Cardinals manager Eddie Dyer called for a hit-and-run. Outfielder Harry Walker lined a ball to center field and Slaughter took everyone—including the Red Sox defenders—by surprise when he ran through a stop sign at third base. A rushed throw home by Red Sox shortstop Johnny Pesky allowed Slaughter to score what proved to be the winning run. A statue commemorating Slaughter's Mad Dash slide is outside Busch Stadium.

Country

Elected To The Hall Of Fame: 1985.
Born: April 27, 1916 in Roxboro, N.C.
Died: Aug. 12, 2002 in Durham, N.C.
Height: 5-9. **Weight:** 180.
Threw: Right. **Batted:** Left.
Debut: April 19, 1938.
Final Game: Sept. 29, 1959.
Teams: St. Louis N.L. 1938-1942, 1946-1953; New York A.L. 1954-1959; Kansas City A.L. 1955-1956; Milwaukee N.L. 1959.
Postseason: 4- Time World Series Champion (1942, 1946, 1956, 1958); 2 N.L. Pennants (1942, 1946); 3 A.L. Pennants (1956-1958).
Awards: 10-Time All-Star (1941-1942, 1946-1953).

YEAR	TEAM	LEAGUE	G	AB	R	H	2B	3B	HR	RBI	SB	AVG
1938	ST. LOUIS	NL	112	395	59	109	20	10	8	58	1	.276
1939	ST. LOUIS	NL	149	604	95	193	52	5	12	86	2	.320
1940	ST. LOUIS	NL	140	516	96	158	25	13	17	73	8	.306
1941	ST. LOUIS	NL	113	425	71	132	22	9	13	76	4	.311
1942	ST. LOUIS	NL	152	591	100	188	31	17	13	98	9	.318
1946	ST. LOUIS	NL	156	609	100	183	30	8	18	130	9	.300
1947	ST. LOUIS	NL	147	551	100	162	31	13	10	86	4	.294
1948	ST. LOUIS	NL	146	549	91	176	27	11	11	90	4	.321
1949	ST. LOUIS	NL	151	568	92	191	34	13	13	96	3	.336
1950	ST. LOUIS	NL	148	556	82	161	26	7	10	101	3	.290
1951	ST. LOUIS	NL	123	409	48	115	17	8	4	64	7	.281
1952	ST. LOUIS	NL	140	510	73	153	17	12	11	101	6	.300
1953	ST. LOUIS	NL	143	492	64	143	34	9	6	89	4	.291
1954	NEW YORK	AL	69	125	19	31	4	2	1	19	0	.248
1955	NEW YORK/KANSAS CITY	AL	118	276	50	87	12	4	5	35	2	.315
1956	KANSAS CITY/NEW YORK	AL	115	306	52	86	18	5	2	27	2	.281
1957	NEW YORK	AL	96	209	24	53	7	1	5	34	0	.254
1958	NEW YORK	AL	77	138	21	42	4	1	4	19	2	.304
1959	NEW YORK/MILWAUKEE	AL/NL	85	117	10	20	2	0	6	22	1	.171
CAREER TOTALS			**2380**	**7946**	**1247**	**2383**	**413**	**148**	**169**	**1304**	**71**	**.300**

HILTON SMITH

Hilton Smith is sometimes referred to as the forgotten star of the Negro leagues, a pitcher whose exceptional career is often overshadowed by longtime teammate Satchel Paige. In fact, when the two were with the Kansas City Monarchs, Smith was often called upon to relieve the lanky fireballer after Paige had tossed his obligatory few innings for the adoring fans. But according to many who faced them, Smith was the equal of Paige. Bob Feller even regarded Smith as better.

While Paige's exploits on the field would help him gain induction into the National Baseball Hall of Fame in 1971, Smith, who spent 12 seasons with the powerful Monarchs, would have to wait until 2001 to gain admittance to the game's most exclusive fraternity. The first line of Smith's Hall of Fame plaque may be the main reason he is enshrined in Cooperstown: "A quiet but confidant righthander whose devastating fastball complemented what many regard as the best sweeping curveball in Negro leagues history."

Negro Leagues historian Bob Kendrick once said of the two, "The old-timers would all say that if you were going to hit anything, you better hit it off Satchel because you weren't going to touch Hilton Smith."

This sentiment was shared by many of the players who were contemporaries of the pair. Fellow Hall of Famer Monte Irvin, who played in both the Negro and major leagues, said, "He (Smith) had one of the finest curveballs I ever had the displeasure to try and hit. His curveball fell of the table. Sometimes you knew where it would be coming from, but you still couldn't hit it because it was that sharp. He was just as tough as Satchel was." According to Sammy T. Hughes, "Smith had an excellent curveball in addition to his fast one. And I'd rather face Satchel or anybody who throws the ball hard rather than face a curveball. Because then you've got two pitches to think about." An exasperated Roy Campanella, another Hall of Famer, exclaimed, "My God. You couldn't tell the difference."

Buck O'Neil may have made the most prescient point about the famed duo when he said that you had to be a true baseball fan to know about Smith, but you didn't have to be a baseball fan to know Paige.

HILTON LEE SMITH
NEGRO LEAGUES, 1932-1948

A QUIET BUT CONFIDENT RIGHTHANDER WHOSE DEVASTATING FASTBALL COMPLEMENTED WHAT MANY REGARD AS THE BEST SWEEPING CURVEBALL IN NEGRO LEAGUES HISTORY. AFTER BEGINNING HIS CAREER WITH THE MONROE MONARCHS, WAS CREDITED WITH 20 OR MORE WINS IN EACH OF 12 SEASONS WITH THE KANSAS CITY MONARCHS, INCLUDING A DOMINATING RECORD OF 93-11 FROM 1939 TO 1942. THE SIX-TIME ALL-STAR PITCHED A NO-HITTER VERSUS THE POWERFUL CHICAGO AMERICAN GIANTS IN 1937 AND POSTED A NEAR-PERFECT 25-1 MARK IN 1941. PLAYED ON SEVEN PENNANT WINNERS AND ONE WORLD SERIES CHAMPIONSHIP TEAM.

Elected To The Hall Of Fame: 2001.
Born: Feb. 27, 1907 in Giddings, Texas.
Died: Nov. 18, 1983 in Kansas City, Mo.
Height: 6-2. **Weight:** 180.
Threw: Right. **Batted:** Right.
Teams: Negro Leagues 1932-1948;
Monroe 1932; Kansas City 1937-1948.

YEAR	TEAM	LEAGUE	G	W	L	SV	SH	IP	H	BB	SO	ERA
1932	MONROE	NSL	—	0	0	—	0	0	6	0	2	—
1937	KANSAS CITY	NAL	—	11	3	—	2	115.3	83	14	74	2.65
1938	KANSAS CITY	NAL	—	4	1	—	0	46.3	40	2	38	2.72
1939	KANSAS CITY	NAL	—	4	2	—	1	55.7	40	10	43	2.91
1940	KANSAS CITY	NAL	—	4	3	—	0	51.3	49	9	40	5.26
1941	KANSAS CITY	NAL	—	9	1	—	1	80	51	5	41	2.36
1942	KANSAS CITY	NAL	—	6	3	—	1	69	68	12	42	4.70
1943	KANSAS CITY	NAL	—	1	0	—	1	12	8	1	6	1.50
1944	KANSAS CITY	NAL	—	1	3	—	1	37.3	32	0	12	4.34
1945	KANSAS CITY	NAL	—	2	4	—	1	50.7	51	4	25	4.44
1946	KANSAS CITY	NAL	—	8	2	—	3	84.3	64	13	48	2.24
1947	KANSAS CITY	NAL	—	5	2	—	0	49	57	5	17	4.59
1948	KANSAS CITY	NAL	—	2	1	—	0	21.3	16	4	10	3.80
CAREER TOTALS			**—**	**57**	**25**	**—**	**11**	**672.3**	**565**	**79**	**398**	**3.44**

OZZIE SMITH

"When you're playing you want to be considered the best at what you do," said Ozzie Smith. "I went about doing that, setting myself apart from the rest of the crowd. I didn't want to be one of many, which you certainly are if you're in the norm. But the guys that make it to the Hall of Fame are one of a few."

Known as "The Wizard of Oz," Smith combined athletic ability with acrobatic skill to become one of the greatest defensive shortstops of all time. The 13-time Gold Glove Award winner redefined the position in his nearly two decades of work with the San Diego Padres and St. Louis Cardinals, setting major league records for assists, double plays and total chances.

Smith's talent was evident to those who saw him come up with the Padres in the late 1970s. "Ozzie is the best young infielder I've ever seen," said San Diego manager Roger Craig at the time. "Very soon he's going to be one of the best shortstops in baseball, if not the best." Hall of Fame pitcher Gaylord Perry added, "I saw him as a rookie in San Diego. I was always hoping they would hit the ball his way because I knew then that my trouble was over."

Smith's fame increased after his trade to the Cards, where he helped the team to three National League pennants and one World Series title. While not known for his bat, Smith's offense continued to improve while in St. Louis. In 1985, he got his batting average up to .276 and helped the Cardinals win their second pennant since his arrival. In the NLCS against the Los Angeles Dodgers, with the series tied at two games apiece, Smith faced Tom Niedenfuer with one out in the bottom of the ninth and hit his first career homer batting left-handed (in 3,009 at-bats) to win the game. Smith went on to bat .435 in the Cardinals' six-game triumph and won the NLCS Most Valuable Player Award, but St. Louis lost to the Kansas City Royals in seven games in the World Series.

Smith retired in 1996, the same year the Cardinals retired his number, and in his 19 seasons compiled a .262 batting average, 2,460 hits, 580 stolen bases, and was named to 15 All-Star teams. Smith set the following major league records for his position: most assists (8,375), most double plays (1,590), most total chances accepted (12,624), most years with 500 or more assists (8) and most years leading the league in assists and chances accepted (8).

OSBORNE EARL SMITH
"Ozzie" "The Wizard"
SAN DIEGO, N.L., 1978-1981
ST. LOUIS, N.L., 1982-1996
REVOLUTIONIZED DEFENSIVE PLAY AT SHORTSTOP WITH HIS ACROBATIC FIELDING AND ARTISTIC TURNING OF DOUBLE PLAYS. THE 13-TIME GOLD GLOVE WINNER SET SIX MAJOR LEAGUE FIELDING RECORDS AMONG SHORTSTOPS, INCLUDING MOST ASSISTS, DOUBLE PLAYS AND CHANCES ACCEPTED. AN EFFECTIVE OFFENSIVE PLAYER, HE ACCUMULATED 2,460 HITS AND STOLE 580 BASES. NAMED TO 15 ALL-STAR TEAMS. HIS RELENTLESS PURSUIT OF PERFECTION HELPED LEAD THE CARDINALS TO THREE WORLD SERIES, INCLUDING A 1982 CHAMPIONSHIP. HIS CONGENIAL PERSONALITY, CONSUMMATE PROFESSIONALISM AND TRADEMARK BACK FLIP MADE "THE WIZARD" A FAN FAVORITE.

The Wizard of Oz

Elected To The Hall Of Fame: 2002.

Born: Dec. 26, 1954 in Mobile, Ala.

Height: 5-11. **Weight:** 150.

Threw: Right. **Batted:** Both.

Debut: April 7, 1978.

Final Game: Sept. 29, 1996.

Teams: San Diego N.L. 1978-1981; St. Louis N.L. 1982-1996.

Postseason: World Series Champion (1982); 3 N.L. Pennants (1982, 1985, 1987); 4-Time Playoff Qualifier (1982, 1985, 1987, 1996).

Awards: 15-Time All-Star (1981-1992, 1994-1996).

YEAR	TEAM	LEAGUE	G	AB	R	H	2B	3B	HR	RBI	SB	AVG
1978	SAN DIEGO	NL	159	590	69	152	17	6	1	46	40	.258
1979	SAN DIEGO	NL	156	587	77	124	18	6	0	27	28	.211
1980	SAN DIEGO	NL	158	609	67	140	18	5	0	35	57	.230
1981	SAN DIEGO	NL	110	450	53	100	11	2	0	21	22	.222
1982	ST. LOUIS	NL	140	488	58	121	24	1	2	43	25	.248
1983	ST. LOUIS	NL	159	552	69	134	30	6	3	50	34	.243
1984	ST. LOUIS	NL	124	412	53	106	20	5	1	44	35	.257
1985	ST. LOUIS	NL	158	537	70	148	22	3	6	54	31	.276
1986	ST. LOUIS	NL	153	514	67	144	19	4	0	54	31	.280
1987	ST. LOUIS	NL	158	600	104	182	40	4	0	75	43	.303
1988	ST. LOUIS	NL	153	575	80	155	27	1	3	51	57	.270
1989	ST. LOUIS	NL	155	593	82	162	30	8	2	50	29	.273
1990	ST. LOUIS	NL	143	512	61	130	21	1	1	50	32	.254
1991	ST. LOUIS	NL	150	550	96	157	30	3	3	50	35	.285
1992	ST. LOUIS	NL	132	518	73	153	20	2	0	31	43	.295
1993	ST. LOUIS	NL	141	545	75	157	22	6	1	53	21	.288
1994	ST. LOUIS	NL	98	381	51	100	18	3	3	30	6	.262
1995	ST. LOUIS	NL	44	156	16	31	5	1	0	11	4	.199
1996	ST. LOUIS	NL	82	227	36	64	10	2	2	18	7	.282
CAREER TOTALS			**2573**	**9396**	**1257**	**2460**	**402**	**69**	**28**	**793**	**580**	**.262**

DUKE SNIDER

The Yankees had Mickey Mantle, the Giants had Willie Mays and the Brooklyn Dodgers had "The Duke of Flatbush." At the time when there were three New York baseball teams, the team that had your allegiance was as important in the five boroughs as life itself, and in the 1950s nobody represented Brooklyn baseball more than Duke Snider. Those team rivalries of yesterday live on a half century later with members of that generation. Willie Mays recalled: "Duke was a fine man, a terrific hitter and a great friend, even though he was a Dodger."

Edwin Donald Snider was called Duke his entire life. He got the nickname from his parents as a young boy because of the way he strutted around like he was royalty. On the baseball field, Duke was royalty. He gracefully patrolled centerfield in Brooklyn and was one of the most prolific power hitters of the 1950s, as he hit more home runs and had more RBI in the decade than any other player.

Duke's star seemed to have shone brightest when the pressure was on. In 1949, on the season's final day, he drove in the winning run to clinch the pennant for the Dodgers and in 1955 he led Brooklyn to their one and only World Series victory over the Yankees. In total, Snider hit .286 with 11 home runs and 26 RBI in 36 World Series games, and is the only player to hit at least four home runs in two different Fall Classics.

In 1957, when the Dodgers played their final game in Brooklyn before moving to Los Angeles, it was fitting that Duke hit the last home run ever in Ebbets Field, and ironically, that home run was hit off Robin Roberts. In his career Snider hit 19 home runs off of Roberts—no other batter in major league history has hit that many home runs off of a single pitcher.

Tommy Lasorda, who played with Snider in Brooklyn in 1954 and 1955, said: "I was Duke's teammate and looked up to him with respect. Duke was not only a great player, but he was a great person, too. He loved his family and loved the Dodgers. He was the true Dodger and represented the Dodgers to the highest degree of class, dignity and character."

EDWIN DONALD SNIDER
"DUKE"
BROOKLYN N.L., LOS ANGELES N.L.,
NEW YORK N.L., SAN FRANCISCO N.L.,
1947-1964
HIT 407 CAREER HOME RUNS AND TIED N.L.
RECORD WITH 40 OR MORE ROUND-TRIPPERS
FIVE YEARS IN A ROW. 1953-1957. BATTED .300
OR BETTER SEVEN TIMES IN COMPILING .295
LIFETIME AVERAGE. TOPPED LEAGUE IN SLUGG-
ING PCT. TWICE AND TOTAL BASES THREE TIMES.
FIRST TO HIT FOUR HOMERS IN A WORLD SERIES
TWICE --IN 1952 AND 1955. SET N.L.
RECORD FOR SERIES HOMERS (11).

The Duke of Flatbush

Elected To The Hall Of Fame: 1980.
Born: Sept. 19, 1926 in Los Angeles, Calif.
Died: Feb. 27, 2011 in Escondido, Calif.
Height: 6-0. **Weight:** 179.
Threw: Right. **Batted:** Left.
Debut: April 17, 1947.
Final Game: Oct. 3, 1964.
Teams: Brooklyn N.L. 1947-1957; Los Angeles N.L. 1958-1962; New York N.L. 1963; San Francisco N.L. 1964.
Postseason: 2-Time World Series Champion (1955, 1959); 7 N.L. Pennants (1947, 1949, 1952-1953, 1955-1956, 1959).
Awards: 8-Time All-Star (1950-1956, 1963).

YEAR	TEAM	LEAGUE	G	AB	R	H	2B	3B	HR	RBI	SB	AVG
1947	BROOKLYN	NL	40	83	6	20	3	1	0	5	2	.241
1948	BROOKLYN	NL	53	160	22	39	6	6	5	21	4	.244
1949	BROOKLYN	NL	146	552	100	161	28	7	23	92	12	.292
1950	BROOKLYN	NL	152	620	109	199	31	10	31	107	16	.321
1951	BROOKLYN	NL	150	606	96	168	26	6	29	101	14	.277
1952	BROOKLYN	NL	144	534	80	162	25	7	21	92	7	.303
1953	BROOKLYN	NL	153	590	132	198	38	4	42	126	16	.336
1954	BROOKLYN	NL	149	584	120	199	39	10	40	130	6	.341
1955	BROOKLYN	NL	148	538	126	166	34	6	42	136	9	.309
1956	BROOKLYN	NL	151	542	112	158	33	2	43	101	3	.292
1957	BROOKLYN	NL	139	508	91	139	25	7	40	92	3	.274
1958	LOS ANGELES	NL	106	327	45	102	12	3	15	58	2	.312
1959	LOS ANGELES	NL	126	370	59	114	11	2	23	88	1	.308
1960	LOS ANGELES	NL	101	235	38	57	13	5	14	36	1	.243
1961	LOS ANGELES	NL	85	233	35	69	8	3	16	56	1	.296
1962	LOS ANGELES	NL	80	158	28	44	11	3	5	30	2	.278
1963	NEW YORK	NL	129	354	44	86	8	3	14	45	0	.243
1964	SAN FRANCISCO	NL	91	167	16	35	7	0	4	17	0	.210
CAREER TOTALS			2143	7161	1259	2116	358	85	407	1333	99	.295

WARREN SPAHN

A star on a pitching mound and a hero on the battlefields, Warren Spahn excelled in two far different uniforms. Arguably the greatest southpaw pitcher in big league history, whose 363 triumphs makes him the all-time winningest left-handed hurler in the game, he used his mound mastery to gain admittance into the national pastime's most exclusive club – the National Baseball Hall of Fame – in 1973.

But fellow Hall of Famer Stan Musial had his doubts as to whether Spahn, a major league pitcher until his mid-40s, would ever be honored in Cooperstown, New York, once half-jokingly stating, "I don't think Spahn will ever get into the Hall of Fame. He'll never stop pitching."

Spahn made his big league debut with the Boston Braves in 1942, the same year he would join the Army. Over the next four years he would participate in the Battle of the Bulge and the taking of the bridge at Remagen. A true war hero, he was awarded a Purple Heart for a shrapnel wound, a Bronze Star for bravery and a battlefield commission. Spahn, who returned to the Braves soon after his discharge in 1946, went 21-10 in 1947, the first of 13 seasons in which Spahn, famous for his fluid, high-kicking pitching motion, won at least 20 games, a major league record for a left-handed pitcher. After the Braves moved to Milwaukee prior to the 1953 season, Spahn continued his excellence and the team soon responded by winning pennants in 1957 and 1958. Playing the Yankees in both World Series, Spahn helped Milwaukee capture the 1957 championship, the same year he won his lone Cy Young Award.

As Spahn grew older, his pitching seemed to improve. He won at least 20 games every year from 1956 to 1961, led the league in complete games every year from 1957 to 1963, and in 1963, at age 42, went 23-7 with a 2.60 ERA. In maybe his most memorable pitching performance, Spahn faced off with the Giants' Juan Marichal on July 2, 1963, each hurler pitching shutout ball until Willie Mays hit a home run in the bottom of the 16th inning to give San Francisco the 1-0 victory.

WARREN EDWARD SPAHN
BOSTON N.L., MILWAUKEE N.L.,
NEW YORK N.L., SAN FRANCISCO N.L.,
1942-1965
BECAME FIFTH BIGGEST WINNER IN MAJORS'
HISTORY WITH 363 VICTORIES. MOST
VICTORIES FOR A LEFT-HANDER. WON 20
OR MORE GAMES 13 SEASONS, SIX IN A ROW.
SET ALL-TIME RECORDS FOR YEARS LEADING
LEAGUE IN VICTORIES (8) AND COMPLETE
GAMES (9), ALSO N.L. CAREER HIGHS WITH
665 GAMES STARTED; 5,264 INNINGS;
2,583 STRIKEOUTS. PITCHED NO-HITTER
IN 1960, ANOTHER IN 1961.

Elected To The Hall Of Fame: *1973.*
Born: *Apr. 23, 1921 in Buffalo, N.Y.*
Died: *Nov. 24, 2003 in Broken Arrow, Okla.*
Height: *6-0.* **Weight:** *172.*
Threw: *Left.* **Batted:** *Left.*
Debut: *April 19, 1942.*
Final Game: *Oct. 1, 1965.*
Teams: *Boston N.L. 1942, 1946-1952; Milwaukee N.L. 1953-1964; New York N.L. 1965; San Francisco N.L. 1965.*
Postseason: *World Series Champion (1957); 3 N.L. Pennants (1948, 1957-1958).*
Awards: *17-Time All-Star (1947, 1949-1954, 1956-1959); M.L. Cy Young (1957).*

YEAR	TEAM	LEAGUE	G	W	L	SV	SH	IP	H	BB	SO	ERA
1942	BOSTON	NL	4	0	0	0	0	15.7	25	11	7	5.74
1946	BOSTON	NL	24	8	5	1	0	125.7	107	36	67	2.94
1947	BOSTON	NL	40	21	10	3	7	289.7	245	84	123	2.33
1948	BOSTON	NL	36	15	12	1	3	257	237	77	114	3.71
1949	BOSTON	NL	38	21	14	0	4	302.3	283	86	151	3.07
1950	BOSTON	NL	41	21	17	1	1	293	248	111	191	3.16
1951	BOSTON	NL	39	22	14	0	7	310.7	278	109	164	2.98
1952	BOSTON	NL	40	14	19	3	5	290	263	73	183	2.98
1953	MILWAUKEE	NL	35	23	7	3	5	265.7	211	70	148	2.10
1954	MILWAUKEE	NL	39	21	12	3	1	283.3	262	86	136	3.14
1955	MILWAUKEE	NL	39	17	14	1	1	245.7	249	65	110	3.26
1956	MILWAUKEE	NL	39	20	11	3	3	281.3	249	52	128	2.78
1957	MILWAUKEE	NL	39	21	11	3	4	271	241	78	111	2.69
1958	MILWAUKEE	NL	38	22	11	1	2	290	257	76	150	3.07
1959	MILWAUKEE	NL	40	21	15	0	4	292	282	70	143	2.96
1960	MILWAUKEE	NL	40	21	10	2	4	267.7	254	74	154	3.50
1961	MILWAUKEE	NL	38	21	13	0	4	262.7	236	64	115	3.02
1962	MILWAUKEE	NL	34	18	14	0	0	269.3	248	55	118	3.04
1963	MILWAUKEE	NL	33	23	7	0	7	259.7	241	49	102	2.60
1964	MILWAUKEE	NL	38	6	13	4	1	173.7	204	52	78	5.29
1965	NEW YORK/SAN FRANCISCO	NL	36	7	16	0	0	197.7	210	56	90	4.01
CAREER TOTALS			**750**	**363**	**245**	**29**	**63**	**5243.2**	**4830**	**1434**	**2583**	**3.09**

TRIS SPEAKER

"At the crack of the bat he'd be off with his back to the infield, and then he'd turn and glance over his shoulder at the last minute and catch the ball so easy it looked like there was nothing to it, nothing at all," said Red Sox righthander Smoky Joe Wood.

By the time Tris Speaker turned 21, he was already one of the best center fielders in the game, a player highly regarded for both his work at the plate and in the field. A Texas native, Speaker began his career with the Red Sox, where he had one of the best seasons of his career in 1912. Speaker earned American League MVP honors that year, leading the AL in on-base percentage and carrying Boston to a World Series championship. A tremendous contact hitter who could drive the ball into the gaps and down the line, Speaker led the American League in doubles eight times. Speaker led the Red Sox to another World Series title in 1915, but Boston traded him to the Indians at the start of the 1916 season.

In Speaker's first season with the Indians, he led the AL in average, on-base percentage and slugging. Ty Cobb, Speaker's rival for the greatest center fielder of the Deadball Era, had won five consecutive batting titles before Speaker edged him for the crown by 15 points in 1916. Speaker took over as a player/manager during the 1919 season—a position he held until his final season in Cleveland in 1926—leading the Indians to a 40-21 finish down the stretch. In his first full season as player/manager in 1920, Speaker reached his third and final World Series, helping the Indians capture the championship in seven games over Brooklyn. Speaker was productive well into his later years, posting career-bests in average (.389) and OBP (a league-leading .479) in 1925 at age 37 with Cleveland. He retired at age 40 after the 1928 season.

Speaker earned praise from his peers for his speed, range and arm in the outfield. Speaker was known for playing a shallow center field, which helped him lead AL outfielders in assists three times, while his ability to cover ground on balls hit over his head helped him lead the league in putouts seven times.

TRISTRAM E. (TRIS) SPEAKER
BOSTON (A) 1909 - 15
CLEVELAND (A) 1916 - 26
WASHINGTON (A) 1927
PHILADELPHIA (A) 1928
GREATEST CENTREFIELDER OF HIS
DAY. LIFETIME MAJOR LEAGUE BATTING
AVERAGE OF .344. MANAGER IN 1920
WHEN CLEVELAND WON ITS FIRST
PENNANT AND WORLD CHAMPIONSHIP.

The Grey Eagle

Elected To The Hall Of Fame: 1937.
Born: April 4, 1888 in Hubbard, Texas.
Died: Dec. 8, 1958 in Lake Whitney, Texas.
Height: 5-11. **Weight:** 193.
Threw: Left. **Batted:** Left.
Debut: Sept. 12, 1907.
Final Game: Aug. 30, 1928.
Teams: Boston A.L. 1907-1915; Cleveland A.L. 1916-1926; Washington A.L. 1927; Philadelphia A.L. 1928.
Postseason: 3-Time World Series Champion (1912, 1915, 1920); 3 A.L. Pennants (1912, 1915, 1920).
Awards: A.L. Most Valuable Player (1912).

YEAR	TEAM	LEAGUE	G	AB	R	H	2B	3B	HR	RBI	SB	AVG
1907	BOSTON	AL	7	19	0	3	0	0	0	1	0	.158
1908	BOSTON	AL	31	116	12	26	2	2	0	9	3	.224
1909	BOSTON	AL	143	544	73	168	26	13	7	77	35	.309
1910	BOSTON	AL	141	538	92	183	20	14	7	65	35	.340
1911	BOSTON	AL	141	500	88	167	34	13	8	70	25	.334
1912	BOSTON	AL	153	580	136	222	53	12	10	90	52	.383
1913	BOSTON	AL	141	520	94	189	35	22	3	71	46	.363
1914	BOSTON	AL	158	571	101	193	46	18	4	90	42	.338
1915	BOSTON	AL	150	547	108	176	25	12	0	69	29	.322
1916	CLEVELAND	AL	151	546	102	211	41	8	2	79	35	.386
1917	CLEVELAND	AL	142	523	90	184	42	11	2	60	30	.352
1918	CLEVELAND	AL	127	471	73	150	33	11	0	61	27	.318
1919	CLEVELAND	AL	134	494	83	146	38	12	2	63	19	.296
1920	CLEVELAND	AL	150	552	137	214	50	11	8	107	10	.388
1921	CLEVELAND	AL	132	506	107	183	52	14	3	75	2	.362
1922	CLEVELAND	AL	131	426	85	161	48	8	11	71	8	.378
1923	CLEVELAND	AL	150	574	133	218	59	11	17	130	8	.380
1924	CLEVELAND	AL	135	486	94	167	36	9	9	65	5	.344
1925	CLEVELAND	AL	117	429	79	167	35	5	12	87	5	.389
1926	CLEVELAND	AL	150	539	96	164	52	8	7	86	6	.304
1927	WASHINGTON	AL	141	523	71	171	43	6	2	73	9	.327
1928	PHILADELPHIA	AL	64	191	28	51	22	2	3	30	5	.267
CAREER TOTALS			**2789**	**10195**	**1882**	**3514**	**792**	**222**	**117**	**1529**	**436**	**.345**

WILLIE STARGELL

"Having Willie Stargell on your ball club is like having a diamond ring on your finger," said Chuck Tanner, who managed Stargell with the Pirates from 1977-82.

Willie Stargell was a feared power hitter, and a leader on the field and in the clubhouse during his 21 seasons with the Pittsburgh Pirates, from 1962-1982. Primarily an outfielder, he switched to first base in 1975. In 1964, the left-handed slugger belted 21 home runs, the first of 13 consecutive seasons in which he would hit 20 or more, en route to 475 for his career. He may have hit many more if he had not played the first half of his career in Forbes Field, a spacious ballpark. One source reports that in the park's 62 seasons hosting the Pirates, only 18 balls were hit out of the park—and Stargell notched seven of those. Sparky Anderson noted that, "He's got power enough to hit home runs in any park, including Yellowstone."

In 1971, the Pirates' first full season in Three Rivers Stadium, Stargell led the NL with a career-high 48 home runs, and led the NL again in 1973, with 44. In 1971, Stargell hit .295 and drove in 125 runs, leading the Pirates into the postseason, where they won the World Series against the Baltimore Orioles. The Pirates won six division titles and two World Series during Stargell's time with the club. In 1973, Stargell finished second in the NL MVP voting after hitting .299 while leading the NL in doubles (43) home runs (44), runs batted in (119), and slugging percentage (.646).

Stargell, nicknamed "Pops" was the spiritual father of the 1979 Pirates "We Are Family" team. With Pops handing out "Stargell Stars" to players who'd made great contributions, the team returned to the World Series, and again bested the Orioles in seven games. Stargell swept the MVP awards that year, winning the LCS MVP, the World Series MVP, and sharing the regular season MVP award with Keith Hernandez.

The seven-time All-Star retired following the 1982 season, and left a legacy of winning, leadership, focus, and fun. "It's supposed to be fun," he noted. "The man says 'Play ball,' not 'Work ball,' you know."

WILVER DORNEL STARGELL
"WILLIE"
PITTSBURGH, N.L., 1962 - 1982
INTIMIDATING PRESENCE BETWEEN THE LINES AND CHARISMATIC PATRIARCH IN CLUBHOUSE AND DUGOUT. CRUSHED 475 HOMERS, MANY OF TAPE-MEASURE VARIETY AND HIT MOST BY ANY PLAYER DURING 1970'S. LIKE HIS ROUND-TRIPPERS, HIS 1,540 RBI'S ALSO MOST EVER BY A PIRATE. BATTED .282 OVER 21 SEASONS, ALL WITH PITTSBURGH. SHARED N.L. MVP HONORS IN 1979, AND NAMED MVP IN '79 N.L. CHAMPIONSHIP SERIES AND WORLD SERIES.

Pops

Elected To The Hall Of Fame: 1988.
Born: March 6, 1940 in Earlsboro, Okla.
Died: April 9, 2001 in Wilmington, N.C.
Height: 6-2. **Weight:** 188.
Threw: Left. **Batted:** Left.
Debut: Sept. 16, 1962.
Final Game: Oct. 3, 1982.
Teams: Pittsburgh N.L. 1962-1982.
Postseason: 2-Time World Series Champion (1971, 1979); 2 N.L. Pennants (1971, 1979); 6-Time Playoff Qualifier (1970-1972, 1974-1975, 1979).
Awards: 7-Time All-Star (1964-1966, 1971-1973, 1978); N.L. MVP (1979); World Series MVP (1979).

YEAR	TEAM	LEAGUE	G	AB	R	H	2B	3B	HR	RBI	SB	AVG
1962	PITTSBURGH	NL	10	31	1	9	3	1	0	4	0	.290
1963	PITTSBURGH	NL	108	304	34	74	11	6	11	47	0	.243
1964	PITTSBURGH	NL	117	421	53	115	19	7	21	78	1	.273
1965	PITTSBURGH	NL	144	533	68	145	25	8	27	107	1	.272
1966	PITTSBURGH	NL	140	485	84	153	30	0	33	102	2	.315
1967	PITTSBURGH	NL	134	462	54	125	18	6	20	73	1	.271
1968	PITTSBURGH	NL	128	435	57	103	15	1	24	67	5	.237
1969	PITTSBURGH	NL	145	522	89	160	31	6	29	92	1	.307
1970	PITTSBURGH	NL	136	474	70	125	18	3	31	85	0	.264
1971	PITTSBURGH	NL	141	511	104	151	26	0	48	125	0	.295
1972	PITTSBURGH	NL	138	495	75	145	28	2	33	112	1	.293
1973	PITTSBURGH	NL	148	522	106	156	43	3	44	119	0	.299
1974	PITTSBURGH	NL	140	508	90	153	37	4	25	96	0	.301
1975	PITTSBURGH	NL	124	461	71	136	32	2	22	90	0	.295
1976	PITTSBURGH	NL	117	428	54	110	20	3	20	65	2	.257
1977	PITTSBURGH	NL	63	186	29	51	12	0	13	35	0	.274
1978	PITTSBURGH	NL	122	390	60	115	18	2	28	97	3	.295
1979	PITTSBURGH	NL	126	424	60	119	19	0	32	82	0	.281
1980	PITTSBURGH	NL	67	202	28	53	10	1	11	38	0	.262
1981	PITTSBURGH	NL	38	60	2	17	4	0	0	9	0	.283
1982	PITTSBURGH	NL	74	73	6	17	4	0	3	17	0	.233
CAREER TOTALS			**2360**	**7927**	**1195**	**2232**	**423**	**55**	**475**	**1540**	**17**	**.282**

TURKEY STEARNES

N egro Leagues legend Satchel Paige called Turkey Stearnes "one of the greatest hitters we ever had. He was as good as Josh [Gibson]. He was as good as anybody who ever played ball."

Off the field, Norman "Turkey" Stearnes had a quiet, unassuming personality. Teammate Paul Stevens recalled: "[He was] very quiet. About all he would say were 'yes' and 'no' – he was never a fellow to pop off." But the Tennessee native was far from reserved on the ballfield. He was a five-tool player and five-time All-Star selection to the East-West All-Star Classic. He is said to have earned the nickname "Turkey" because of the unusual way he ran, which resembled that of a turkey, arms flapping and all. Stearnes himself claimed it was because he had a pot belly as a child. Regardless of how the nickname came about, he was widely recognized as one of the game's all-time great players during his career. Negro Leaguer Jim Canada, who played against Stearnes recalled "He hit the ball nine miles. He was a show, people would go to see him play."

Stearnes could beat you in so many ways, whether he was hitting a home run from the third or fourth spot in the line-up, batted lead off and beating out a bunt for a base hit, or tracking down a gapper in left-center field, there was almost nothing he couldn't do on the field.

As with many Negro League stars, Stearnes played for a variety of teams during his career, including the Chicago American Giants with whom he won the Negro Southern League pennant in 1932, and the Negro National League pennant in 1933. It was during his time with the American Giants that Stearnes was selected to play in the first East-West All-Star Game, where he received more votes than any other outfielder.

Negro Leaguer Jimmie Crutchfield described his former teammate as a "quicky-jerky sort of guy who could hit the ball a mile. Turkey had a batting stance that you'd swear couldn't let anybody hit a baseball at all. He'd stand up there looking like he was off balance. But it was natural for him to stand that way, and you couldn't criticize him for it when he was hitting everything they threw at him!"

Elected To The Hall Of Fame: *2000.*
Born: *May 8, 1901 in Nashville, Tenn.*
Died: *Sept. 4, 1979 in Detroit, Mich.*
Height: *5-11.* **Weight:** *175.*
Threw : *Left.* **Batted:** *Left.*
Teams: *Negro Leagues 1923-1941.*
Montgomery 1921, Detroit 1923-1931,
1937; New York 1930; Kansas City 1931,
1934, 1938-1940; Philadelphia 1936;
Chicago 1932-35, 1937-1938.

YEAR	TEAM	LEAGUE	G	AB	R	H	2B	3B	HR	RBI	SB	AVG
1921	MONTGOMERY	INDP	—	18	3	2	0	0	1	—	3	.111
1923	DETROIT	NNL	—	279	70	101	18	14	17	—	17	.362
1924	DETROIT	NNL	—	220	49	77	7	10	8	—	13	.350
1925	DETROIT	NNL	—	354	45	129	24	11	19	—	44	.364
1926	DETROIT	NNL	—	318	25	123	30	8	19	—	39	.387
1927	DETROIT	NNL	—	268	48	96	20	10	19	—	0	.358
1928	DETROIT	NNL	—	314	82	101	17	7	23	—	28	.322
1929	DETROIT	NNL	—	241	60	97	16	4	16	—	36	.402
1930	N.Y. LINCOLN/DET.	INDP/NNL	—	192	45	66	13	13	7	—	24	.344
1931	K.C./DETROIT	NNL	—	169	31	48	8	3	9	—	0	.284
1932	CHICAGO	NSL	—	167	40	51	9	2	5	—	24	.305
1933	CHICAGO	NNL	—	109	24	31	8	2	4	—	4	.284
1934	K.C./CHICAGO	INDP/NNL	—	172	43	60	6	7	8	—	9	.349
1935	CHICAGO	NNL	—	127	35	56	8	4	6	—	23	.441
1936	PHILADELPHIA	NNL	—	136	27	40	2	1	7	—	13	.294
1937	DET./CHICAGO	NAL	—	67	13	18	2	1	2	—	1	.269
1938	K.C./CHICAGO	NAL	—	32	4	6	0	2	0	—	0	.188
1939	KANSAS CITY	NAL	—	74	15	24	4	0	2	—	6	.324
1940	KANSAS CITY	NAL	—	79	14	23	2	1	4	—	8	.291
CAREER TOTALS			—	3336	673	1149	194	100	176	—	289	.344

BRUCE SUTTER

"He's the greatest relief pitcher that I've seen in my 45 years in baseball," were the lofty words Cubs manager Herman Franks used to describe his star closer, Bruce Sutter.

Sutter was on the fringes of professional baseball, a struggling minor league pitcher with an injured arm, until he received a gift that changed his life forever. A new pitch, a split-fingered fastball, was taught to him by a wise, old man of the game, and in a matter of years Sutter took this new weapon and blazed a trail as one of the game's top relief pitchers.

So it was with Sutter when Cubs roving minor league pitching coach Fred Martin stepped into his life in 1973. Martin had been trying to teach Cubs farmhands this new pitch, a derivation of the forkball called the split-fingered fastball, with little success. But he now had an apt pupil in Sutter, who needed something new to keep his big league dream alive. And Sutter took to the pitch, in which the thumb pushes the ball out from between wide-spread fingers, imparting a wicked forward spin to the ball.

By 1977 Sutter was entrenched as the Cubs' closer, finishing with 31 saves garnering the first of six All-Star Game invitations. The Sutter name became known throughout baseball with his remarkable 1979 season, winning the National League Cy Young Award after tying the Senior Circuit record with 37 saves.

Cubs' starting pitchers certainly appreciated seeing Sutter in the bullpen, with Ray Burris once saying, "He was lights out when he came in. As a starter you knew if you got into the seventh or eighth inning that the game was pretty well sealed."

Dealt to the St. Louis Cardinals before the 1981 campaign, Sutter proved to be the missing piece for a championship-caliber club. Not only did he average almost 32 saves over the four seasons he was with the Cards, establishing a NL record for most saves in a season with his 45 in 1984, he also helped the team win the 1982 World Series.

"He had the best makeup of any closer I've ever seen," said Whitey Herzog, the St. Louis manager who had also acquired Sutter. "He just cut the percentages down for me from 27 outs a game to 21." After leaving St. Louis as a free agent, Sutter spent four years with the Braves.

HOWARD BRUCE SUTTER
CHICAGO, N.L., 1976-1980
ST. LOUIS, N.L., 1981-1984
ATLANTA, N.L., 1985-1988

A DOMINANT CLOSER WHO REVOLUTIONIZED THE SPLIT-FINGERED FASTBALL, WHICH CONFOUNDED BATTERS. EARNED 300 SAVES AND POSTED A 2.83 ERA WHILE OFTEN PITCHING TWO OR MORE INNINGS. A SIX-TIME ALL-STAR SELECTION, RANKED AMONG THE TOP TEN IN NATIONAL LEAGUE MVP AND CY YOUNG VOTING FIVE TIMES EACH AND LED THE LEAGUE IN SAVES FIVE TIMES. WON 1979 N.L. CY YOUNG, POSTING 37 SAVES WHILE STRIKING OUT 110, ALLOWING 67 HITS IN 101.1 INNINGS. SAVED TWO GAMES AND RECORDED THE FINAL SIX OUTS FOR THE 1982 WORLD SERIES CHAMPION CARDINALS.

Elected To The Hall Of Fame: 2006.
Born: Jan. 8, 1953 in Lancaster, Pa.
Height: 6-2. *Weight:* 190.
Threw: Right. Batted: Right.
Debut: May 9, 1976.
Final Game: Sept. 9, 1988.
Teams: Chicago N.L. 1976-1980; St. Louis N.L. 1981-1984; Atlanta N.L. 1985-1986, 1988.
Postseason: World Series Champion (1982); N.L. Pennant (1982).
Awards: 6-Time All-Star (1977-1981, 1984); N.L. Cy Young (1979).

YEAR	TEAM	LEAGUE	G	W	L	SV	SH	IP	H	BB	SO	ERA
1976	CHICAGO	NL	52	6	3	10	0	83.3	63	26	73	2.70
1977	CHICAGO	NL	62	7	3	31	0	107.3	69	23	129	1.34
1978	CHICAGO	NL	64	8	10	27	0	98.7	82	34	106	3.19
1979	CHICAGO	NL	62	6	6	37	0	101.3	67	32	110	2.22
1980	CHICAGO	NL	60	5	8	28	0	102.3	90	34	76	2.64
1981	ST. LOUIS	NL	48	3	5	25	0	82.3	64	24	57	2.62
1982	ST. LOUIS	NL	70	9	8	36	0	102.3	88	34	61	2.90
1983	ST. LOUIS	NL	60	9	10	21	0	89.3	90	30	64	4.23
1984	ST. LOUIS	NL	71	5	7	45	0	122.7	109	23	77	1.54
1985	ATLANTA	NL	58	7	7	23	0	88.3	91	29	52	4.48
1986	ATLANTA	NL	16	2	0	3	0	18.7	17	9	16	4.34
1988	ATLANTA	NL	38	1	4	14	0	45.3	49	11	40	4.76
CAREER TOTALS			**661**	**68**	**71**	**300**	**0**	**1042**	**879**	**309**	**861**	**2.83**

GEORGE SUTTLES

George "Mule" Suttles was almost lost to history. As noted in a local *Tuscaloosa (Ala.) News* article following his 2006 induction in the Hall of Fame, "He was born at the start of a century that's passed in a town that no longer exists. He played for teams that have long since folded, in leagues that closed up shop more than 50 years ago." Even so, Suttles' reputation was sufficient to ensure that he would be placed on the Hall of Fame ballot when the time came.

Noted for his soft-spoken personality, Suttles was not known to draw attention to himself. According to teammate Red Moore, "He didn't get the ballyhoo that Satchel (Paige) and Josh (Gibson) got. They were the ones who it seemed all the sports writers put the praise on. Mule Suttles was a powerful hitter. I can't fathom why he didn't get the publicity he got. He didn't do much talking. He wasn't the boastful type. Sometimes the better players get overlooked."

The slugging first baseman and outfielder had a playing career that lasted the entire Golden Era of Negro leagues baseball, from 1921 to 1944. He starred with some of the great squads of segregated baseball, including the Newark Eagles, Chicago American Giants and the Birmingham Black Barons. He boasts a lifetime batting average of .329 and was known for his power. According to Moore, fans and opponents would gather to watch him at batting practice, "They'd come out to see him hit the ball. I can tell you he was a great hitter. He was known for his power. He could really hit the ball a long way. In batting practice he hit some tape-measure balls. He could really hit it for distance."

His skills were so noted by his contemporaries, having been selected to play in five East-West Classic All-Star Games, where in 1933 he knocked the first home run ever hit in the event.

In addition to his baseball skills, Suttles was also known as a good teammate, often serving as a father figure to the younger players. He is fondly remembered by teammates who recall his kind nature and willingness to do anything to help win a game. As noted by Red Moore, "He was kind of a genteel person. He was friendly, but when he was on the field he went to play, he was all business."

GEORGE SUTTLES
"MULE"
NEGRO LEAGUES, 1923-1944

A FIRST BASEMAN AND OUTFIELDER RENOWNED FOR HIS ABILITY TO HIT FOR HIGH AVERAGE WITH PRODIGIOUS POWER SPENT BEST YEARS WITH THE ST. LOUIS STARS, CHICAGO AMERICAN GIANTS AND NEWARK EAGLES, WINNING A CHAMPIONSHIP WITH THE AMERICAN GIANTS IN 1933. PLAYED IN FIVE EAST-WEST ALL-STAR GAMES, HITTING DRAMATIC THREE-RUN HOME RUN TO WIN 1935 CONTEST. AMONG ALL-TIME NEGRO LEAGUES LEADERS IN DOUBLES, HOME RUNS, RBI, SLUGGING PERCENTAGE AND TOTAL BASES.

Mule

Elected To The Hall Of Fame: 2006.
Born: March 31, 1900 in Edgewater, Ala.
Died: July 9, 1966 in Newark, N.J.
Height: 6-3. **Weight:** 215.
Threw: Right. **Batted:** Right.
Teams: Negro Leagues 1923-1944.
Bacharach 1921, Birmingham 1923-1925; St. Louis 1926-1931; Baltimore 1930; Detroit 1932; Washington 1932; Chicago 1929, 1933-1935; Newark 1936-1940, 1942-1944; Indianapolis 1939; New York 1941.

YEAR	TEAM	LEAGUE	G	AB	R	H	2B	3B	HR	RBI	SB	AVG
1921	BACHARACH	INDP	—	4	0	1	0	0	0	—	0	.250
1923	BIRMINGHAM	INDP/NNL	—	127	20	36	4	3	1	—	4	.283
1924	BIRMINGHAM	NNL	—	282	48	96	23	3	4	—	1	.340
1925	BIRMINGHAM	NNL	—	252	37	79	6	4	10	—	9	.313
1926	ST. LOUIS	NNL	—	220	44	86	17	11	15	—	0	.391
1927	ST. LOUIS	NNL	—	67	22	33	6	3	8	—	1	.493
1928	ST. LOUIS	NNL	—	310	70	112	19	11	20	—	5	.361
1929	CHI./ST. LOUIS	NNL	—	269	62	94	26	8	10	—	5	.349
1930	BALT./ST. LOUIS	INDP/NNL	—	145	45	51	9	5	10	—	4	.352
1931	ST. LOIUS	NNL	—	39	7	13	5	0	2	—	0	.333
1932	WASH./DET	EWL	—	75	15	19	7	2	2	—	2	.253
1933	CHICAGO	NNL	—	92	18	25	5	2	3	—	2	.272
1934	CHICAGO	NNL	—	154	18	47	4	2	4	—	3	.305
1935	CHICAGO	NNL	—	109	24	33	5	0	8	—	2	.303
1936	NEWARK	NNL	—	45	9	15	3	0	4	—	1	.333
1937	NEWARK	NNL	—	82	22	29	4	0	5	—	1	.354
1938	NEWARK	NNL	—	89	19	24	1	0	9	—	0	.270
1939	NEWARK	NNL	—	62	12	18	4	0	4	—	0	.290
1940	NEWARK	NNL	—	108	28	30	7	0	5	—	2	.278
1941	NEW YORK	NNL	—	62	10	14	1	0	1	—	0	.226
1942	NEWARK	NNL	—	12	3	5	1	0	2	—	1	.417
1943	NEWARK	NNL	—	5	2	1	0	0	1	—	0	.200
1944	NEWARK	NNL	—	22	5	5	0	1	1	—	0	.227
CAREER TOTALS			—	**2632**	**540**	**866**	**157**	**55**	**129**	—	**43**	**.329**

DON SUTTON

"**M**y mother used to worry about my imaginary friends 'cause I would be out in the yard playing ball," Don Sutton said in his induction speech in 1998. "She worried because she didn't know a Mickey, or a Whitey, or a Yogi, or a Moose, or an Elston, but I played with them every day."

Not only would Sutton get to join his childhood "friends" in the major leagues, Sutton rose to their status in his 23-year career, doubtlessly becoming a player in many children's fantasy backyard games. Sutton went 324-256 and struck out 3,574 batters. His 324 wins rank 14th all-time and he has the seventh most strikeouts. He also ranks in the top 10 in many categories, such as shutouts and games started.

Sutton began his career as a member of the Dodgers' rotation with fellow Hall of Famers Sandy Koufax and Don Drysdale. Sutton helped the Dodgers to five NL pennants. While Sutton never won a Cy Young Award, he was the picture of consistency. He won at least 11 games and had 100 strikeouts in 21 seasons.

Sutton's best season came in 1972 when he went 19-9 and threw nine shutouts. He led the NL with a 0.913 WHIP and made his first All-Star Game. That season was the beginning of a strong five-year stretch for Sutton in which he won 93 games and had a 2.73 ERA. Sutton earned Cy Young votes in all five years. Later in his career, Sutton left the Dodgers and pitched for the Astros, Brewers, Athletics and Angels. He won his 300th game June 18, 1986, pitching for the Angels. He threw a complete game allowing one run on three hits to defeat the Rangers 5-1.

Sutton was known for his durability, never missing his turn in the rotation. He credited his work ethic to watching his father, who was a sharecropper. Sutton said he never saw his father take a day off work, so he didn't want to either.

"Other kids my age were playing for fun," Sutton told *Sports Illustrated* in 1982. "I was playing to get to the big leagues."

DONALD HOWARD SUTTON
LOS ANGELES, N.L., 1966-80, 1988
HOUSTON, N.L., 1981-82
MILWAUKEE, A.L., 1982-84
OAKLAND, A.L., 1985
CALIFORNIA, A.L., 1985-1987
A STALWART ON THE MOUND FOR 23 MAJOR LEAGUE SEASONS, HIS IMPRESSIVE PITCHING RECORD INCLUDES 324 VICTORIES, 3,574 STRIKEOUTS AND A 3.26 ERA. STRIKEOUT TOTAL IS FIFTH BEST ALL-TIME. WHILE WIN TOTAL RANKS TIED FOR 12th. DID NOT MISS A TURN IN THE STARTING ROTATION DUE TO INJURY OR ILLNESS. CONSISTENCY AND MODEL CONTROL LED TO 15 OR MORE WINS IN 12 SEASONS AND 100 OR MORE STRIKEOUTS 21 TIMES. THE RIGHT-HANDER PITCHED IN FOUR WORLD SERIES AND WAS NAMED TO FOUR ALL-STAR TEAMS.

Elected To The Hall Of Fame: *1998.*
Born: *April 2, 1945 in Clio, Ala.*
Height: *6-1.* **Weight:** *185.*
Threw: *Right.* **Batted:** *Right.*
Debut: *April 14, 1966.*
Final Game: *Aug. 9, 1988.*
Teams: *Los Angeles N.L. 1966-1980, 1988; Houston N.L. 1981-1982; Milwaukee A.L. 1982-1984; Oakland A.L. 1985; California 1985-1987.*
Postseason: *5 N.L. Pennants (1974, 1977-78); A.L. Pennant (1982).*
Awards: *4-Time All-Star (1972-73, 1975, 1977).*

YEAR	TEAM	LEAGUE	G	W	L	SV	SH	IP	H	BB	SO	ERA
1966	LOS ANGELES	NL	37	12	12	0	2	225.7	192	52	209	2.99
1967	LOS ANGELES	NL	37	11	15	1	3	232.7	223	57	169	3.95
1968	LOS ANGELES	NL	35	11	15	1	2	207.7	179	59	162	2.60
1969	LOS ANGELES	NL	41	17	18	0	4	293.3	269	91	217	3.47
1970	LOS ANGELES	NL	38	15	13	0	4	260.3	251	78	201	4.08
1971	LOS ANGELES	NL	38	17	12	1	4	265.3	231	55	194	2.54
1972	LOS ANGELES	NL	33	19	9	0	9	272.7	186	63	207	2.08
1973	LOS ANGELES	NL	33	18	10	0	3	256.3	196	56	200	2.42
1974	LOS ANGELES	NL	40	19	9	0	5	276	241	80	179	3.23
1975	LOS ANGELES	NL	35	16	13	0	4	254.3	202	62	175	2.87
1976	LOS ANGELES	NL	35	21	10	0	4	267.7	231	82	161	3.06
1977	LOS ANGELES	NL	33	14	8	0	3	240.3	207	69	150	3.18
1978	LOS ANGELES	NL	34	15	11	0	2	238.3	228	54	154	3.55
1979	LOS ANGELES	NL	33	12	15	1	1	226	201	61	146	3.82
1980	LOS ANGELES	NL	32	13	5	1	2	212.3	163	47	128	2.20
1981	HOUSTON	NL	23	11	9	0	3	158.7	132	29	104	2.61
1982	HOUSTON/MILWAUKEE	NL/AL	34	17	9	0	1	249.7	224	64	175	3.06
1983	MILWAUKEE	AL	31	8	13	0	0	220.3	209	54	134	4.08
1984	MILWAUKEE	AL	33	14	12	0	0	212.7	224	51	143	3.77
1985	OAKLAND/CALIFORNIA	AL	34	15	10	0	1	226	221	59	107	3.86
1986	CALIFORNIA	AL	34	15	11	0	1	207	192	49	116	3.74
1987	CALIFORNIA	AL	35	11	11	0	0	191.7	199	41	99	4.70
1988	LOS ANGELES	NL	16	3	6	0	0	87.3	91	30	44	3.92
CAREER TOTALS			**774**	**324**	**256**	**5**	**58**	**5282.3**	**4692**	**1343**	**3574**	**3.26**

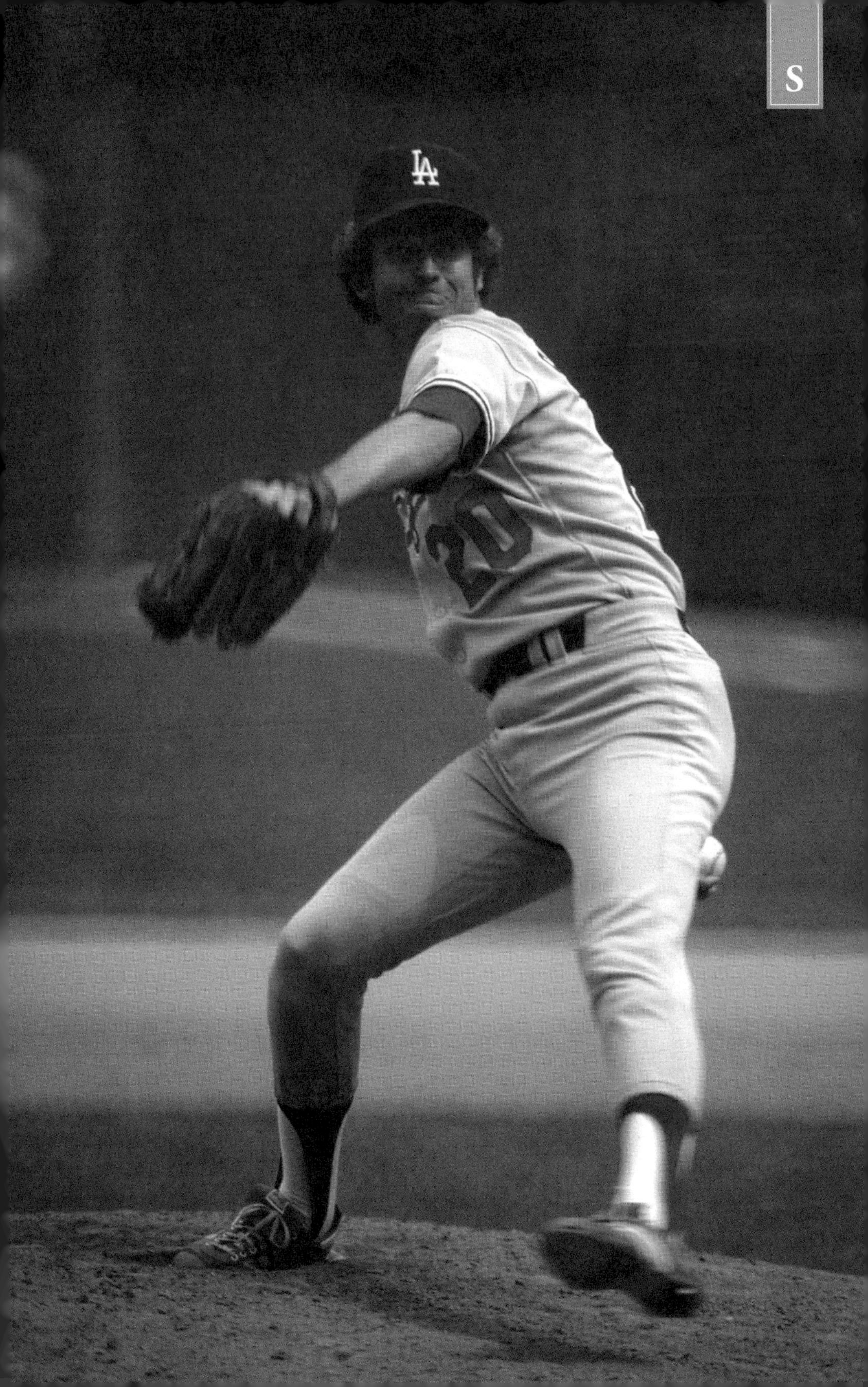

BEN TAYLOR

Belonging to one of the most famous families in black baseball history, Ben Taylor had a career that spanned almost four decades, serving as a premier first baseman and noted manager. Playing along with his brothers C.I., Steel Arm John, and Candy Jim, Ben Taylor starred for a number of teams in the pre-Negro leagues era of 1908 to 1920, and them moved around the various leagues and teams during the Golden Era from 1921 to 1941.

Taylor was a lifetime .300 hitter who maintained a scientific approach to the game. He was noted for his ability to hit to all fields, his execution of the hit-and-run, and became known as "Old Reliable" for both his clutch-hitting and his outstanding defensive play at first base.

He was soft-spoken and well-respected, but his reputation as a teacher was noted by Hall of Famer Buck Leonard who said, "I got most of my learning from Ben Taylor. He helped me when I first broke in with his team. He had been the best first baseman in Negro baseball up until that time, and he was the one who really taught me to play first base."

According to the *Chicago Defender* in 1935, Taylor was described as "a man who has inspired, trained and led baseball teams for many years," and as having "one of the keenest minds in all of baseball and knows the game from all angles."

After his death in 1953, the *Chicago Defender* said simply, "Ben was recognized as one of the great first baseman in Negro baseball. His name is bracketed with that of other top first sackers of that period. He was an excellent fielder and a cracking good hitter from the left side."

As biographer Todd Bolton has noted, Ben Taylor's life can be summed up from 10 words on his gravestone, "A Graceful Player, A Superb Teacher, and A True Gentleman."

BENJAMIN HARRISON TAYLOR
"BEN" "OLD RELIABLE"
PRE-NEGRO LEAGUES, 1908-1919
NEGRO LEAGUES, 1920-1929
A SOFT-SPOKEN AND MODEST TEAM LEADER WHO TRANSITIONED FROM SUCCESSFUL PITCHER TO TOP-FLIGHT DEFENSIVE FIRST BASEMAN AND CLUTCH HITTER. PRODUCTIVE LINE-DRIVE HITTER WHO BATTED OVER .300 WITH REGULARITY, EXCELLING FOR NINE SEASONS WITH INDIANAPOLIS ABCs. COMBINATION OF VAST KNOWLEDGE OF THE GAME, STRONG LEADERSHIP SKILLS AND TEACHING ABILITIES LED TO MANAGING POSITIONS WITH A NUMBER OF NEGRO LEAGUES TEAMS. THE YOUNGEST OF FOUR PROFESSIONAL BASEBALL-PLAYING BROTHERS.

Old Reliable

Elected To The Hall Of Fame: 2006.
Born: July 1, 1888 in Anderson, S.C.
Died: Jan. 24, 1953 in Baltimore, Md.
Height: 6-1. **Weight:** 190.
Threw: Left. **Batted:** Left.
Teams: Pre-Negro Leagues 1908-1919;
Negro Leagues 1920-1929. Habana 1911;
Indianapolis 1914-1922; Atlantic City 1919;
Washington 1923-1924; Harrisburg 1925;
Baltimore 1926-1928; Bacharach 1929.

YEAR	TEAM	LEAGUE	G	AB	R	H	2B	3B	HR	RBI	SB	AVG
1911	HABANA	CUNL	2	4	0	0	0	0	0	0	0	.000
1914	INDIANAPOLIS	INDP	60	216	50	79	23	8	4	53	27	.366
1915	INDIANAPOLIS	INDP/CNCS	80	294	44	91	22	7	1	59	21	.310
1916	INDIANAPOLIS	INDP	41	150	23	47	3	1	0	28	6	.313
1917	INDIANAPOLIS	INDP	57	218	27	64	9	4	0	39	5	.294
1918	INDIANAPOLIS	INDP	39	150	30	48	5	6	2	37	5	.320
1919	ATLANTIC CITY/IND.	INDP	21	79	11	24	4	3	0	12	4	.304
1920	INDIANAPOLIS	NNL	—	169	15	52	8	5	2	—	6	.308
1921	INDIANAPOLIS	NNL	—	196	16	66	8	6	3	—	7	.337
1922	INDIANAPOLIS	NNL	—	194	31	72	13	3	1	—	2	.371
1923	WASHINGTON	INDP	—	20	3	7	2	0	0	—	0	.350
1924	WASHINGTON	ECOL	—	198	32	59	6	2	3	—	3	.298
1925	HARISBURG	ECOL	—	245	36	79	13	5	3	—	0	.322
1926	BALTIMORE	ECOL	—	103	10	26	4	1	0	—	2	.252
1927	BALTIMORE	ECOL	—	108	17	39	4	2	0	—	0	.361
1928	BALTIMORE	ECOL	—	255	30	78	16	3	2	—	4	.306
1929	BACHARACH	ANL	—	55	5	14	2	0	2	—	1	.255
CAREER TOTALS			467	2654	380	845	142	56	23	—	93	.318

BILL TERRY

"He once hit a ball between my legs so hard," Dizzy Dean said, "that my center fielder caught it on the fly backing up against the wall." Bill Terry's big league career almost ended before it began. Once he got his chance. though, Terry became one of the National League's best first baseman of the 1920s and '30s, followed by a highly successful managerial career.

Terry tried to make it as a pitcher in the mid-1910s. He had some fine seasons in the minor leagues, but was never signed by a big league club. He actually got out of professional ball for a time, taking a job with Standard Oil in Memphis. He continued playing for his plant's team though, and in 1922 he was brought to the attention of New York Giants manager John McGraw.

Terry wouldn't join the Giants unless McGraw made it worth his while, and the two would always have a frosty relationship. McGraw eventually relented, and Terry cemented himself as the Giants' everyday first baseman in 1925 when he hit .319.

Terry never batted under .326 in the eight seasons in which he totaled over 500 at-bats. He finished second in the National League in batting three times but only captured a batting title once, when he hit .401 in 1930. He led the Giants in average every year from 1929-35. The lefthanded hitting Terry concentrated on hitting balls up the middle and to left-center. While he did have 20-home run seasons and hit 154 for his career, some observers felt he could've hit more if he had aimed for the short porches down the lines at the Polo Grounds.

Terry succeeded McGraw as the Giants' manager in the middle of the 1932 season. A year later, the 34-year-old managed the Giants to the 1933 World Series title while continuing to be their leading hitter with a .322 average. Terry intended to end his playing career after the 1935 season, but he reversed course in the middle of 1936 and played through severe knee problems, leading the Giants back to the World Series, though they lost to the Yankees. Terry did retire as a player after 1936, but he continued managing the Giants for another five seasons, including another NL pennant in 1937. He had over 800 wins as a manager when his career ended in 1941.

WILLIAM HAROLD TERRY
NEW YORK N.L. 1923 TO 1941

BATTED .401 AND TIED N.L. RECORD FOR
BASE HITS WITH 254 IN 1930. MADE 200 OR
MORE HITS IN SIX SEASONS. RETIRED WITH
LIFETIME BATTING AVERAGE OF .341, A
MODERN N.L. RECORD FOR LEFT-HANDED
BATTERS. MOST VALUABLE PLAYER IN 1930.
SUCCEEDED JOHN McGRAW AS MANAGER IN
1932 AND WON PENNANTS IN 1933-36-37.

Memphis Bill

Elected To The Hall Of Fame: 1954.
Born: Oct. 30, 1898 in Atlanta, Ga.
Died: Jan. 9, 1989 in Jacksonville, Flor.
Height: 6-1. **Weight:** 200.
Threw: Left. **Batted:** Left.
Debut: Sept. 24, 1923.
Final Game: Sept. 22, 1936.
Teams: New York N.L. 1923-1936.
Postseason: World Series Champion (1933); 3 N.L. Pennants (1924, 1933, 1936).
Awards: 3-Time All-Star (1933-1935).

YEAR	TEAM	LEAGUE	G	AB	R	H	2B	3B	HR	RBI	SB	AVG
1923	NEW YORK	NL	3	7	1	1	0	0	0	0	0	.143
1924	NEW YORK	NL	77	163	26	39	7	2	5	24	1	.239
1925	NEW YORK	NL	133	489	75	156	31	6	11	70	4	.319
1926	NEW YORK	NL	98	225	26	65	12	5	5	43	3	.289
1927	NEW YORK	NL	150	580	101	189	32	13	20	121	1	.326
1928	NEW YORK	NL	149	568	100	185	36	11	17	101	7	.326
1929	NEW YORK	NL	150	607	103	226	39	5	14	117	10	.372
1930	NEW YORK	NL	154	633	139	254	39	15	23	129	8	.401
1931	NEW YORK	NL	153	611	121	213	43	20	9	112	8	.349
1932	NEW YORK	NL	154	643	124	225	42	11	28	117	4	.350
1933	NEW YORK	NL	123	475	68	153	20	5	6	58	3	.322
1934	NEW YORK	NL	153	602	109	213	30	6	8	83	0	.354
1935	NEW YORK	NL	145	596	91	203	32	8	6	64	7	.341
1936	NEW YORK	NL	79	229	36	71	10	5	2	39	0	.310
CAREER TOTALS			**1721**	**6428**	**1120**	**2193**	**373**	**112**	**154**	**1078**	**56**	**.341**

SAM THOMPSON

"He was a wonderful friend," former teammate Charlie Bennett said at Sam Thompson's funeral. "No one ever quarrelled with Sam. No one ever knew him with all his strength to be rough or brutal. He was always even-tempered, simple and plain."

During a time when the play was rough and so were many of the players, being recognized as "plain" was complimentary, and only reserved for true gentlemen. Samuel "Big Sam" Thompson spent time over 15 seasons in the major leagues protecting that reputation, also building a name for himself at the plate.

The right fielder's most impressive numbers were the runs he batted in. In 1887, Thompson had 166 total RBI, a record that stood until Babe Ruth broke it 34 years later. Big Sam was the only player in the Dead Ball Era to drive in more than 150 runs in a season, and he did it two times. He currently holds two records in Major League Baseball: his .923 RBI per game are more than any other in the history of baseball; and he also holds the mark for the most RBI in a month with 61. The left-handed hitter did that in August 1894 for the Philadelphia Phillies.

Thompson broke into the big leagues in 1885 with the Detroit Wolverines. In just his second full season in 1887, he had his best year in leading the Wolverines to the National League pennant and a World Series win over the American Association's St. Louis Browns. The slugger batted .372, scored 118 runs, drove in 166 and totaled 203 hits, including 10 home runs.

Between 1889 and 1896, Thompson failed to reach 100 or more RBI only once when he had 90 in 1891. Big Sam became the first player to ever have 20 home runs and 20 stolen bases in the same season when he did it in 1889.

The 6-foot-2, 200-pounder batted a career-high .415 in 1894, even though he missed a month with an injury that required the amputation of his fingertip. He twice led the National League in home runs and three times led the NL in RBI.

Back problems took Thompson out of the game in 1898, though after a decade-long hiatus he made an attempt at coming back, playing in eight games for the Detroit Tigers in 1906.

SAMUEL LUTHER THOMPSON
DETROIT N.L., PHILADELPHIA N.L.
1885 - 1898; DETROIT A.L. 1906
ONE OF THE FOREMOST SLUGGERS OF
HIS DAY. LIFETIME BATTING AVERAGE
.336, BATTED BETTER THAN .400 TWICE.
GREAT CLUTCH HITTER, COLLECTED
200 OR MORE HITS IN A SEASON THREE
TIMES. TOPPED N.L. IN HOME RUNS AND
RUNS BATTED IN TWICE.

Big Sam

Elected To The Hall Of Fame: *1974.*

Born: *March 5, 1860 in Danville, Ind.*

Died: *Nov. 7, 1922 in Detroit, Mich.*

Height: *6-2.* **Weight:** *207.*

Threw: *Left.* **Batted:** *Left.*

Debut: *July 2, 1885.*

Final Game: *Sept. 10, 1906.*

Teams: *Detroit N.L. 1885-1888;*
Philadelphia N.L. 1889-1898; Detroit A.L. 1906.

Postseason: *World Series Champion (1887); N.L. Pennant (1887).*

YEAR	TEAM	LEAGUE	G	AB	R	H	2B	3B	HR	RBI	SB	AVG
1885	DETROIT	NL	63	254	58	77	11	9	7	44	NA	.303
1886	DETROIT	NL	122	503	101	156	18	13	8	89	13	.310
1887	DETROIT	NL	127	545	118	203	29	23	10	166	22	.372
1888	DETROIT	NL	56	238	51	67	10	8	6	40	5	.282
1889	PHILADELPHIA	NL	128	533	103	158	36	4	20	111	24	.296
1890	PHILADELPHIA	NL	132	549	116	172	41	9	4	102	25	.313
1891	PHILADELPHIA	NL	133	554	108	163	23	10	7	90	29	.294
1892	PHILADELPHIA	NL	153	609	109	186	28	11	9	104	28	.305
1893	PHILADELPHIA	NL	131	600	130	222	37	13	11	126	18	.370
1894	PHILADELPHIA	NL	102	451	114	187	32	28	13	147	27	.415
1895	PHILADELPHIA	NL	119	538	131	211	45	21	18	165	27	.392
1896	PHILADELPHIA	NL	119	517	103	154	28	7	12	100	12	.298
1897	PHILADELPHIA	NL	3	13	2	3	0	1	0	3	0	.231
1898	PHILADELPHIA	NL	14	63	14	22	5	3	1	15	2	.349
1906	DETROIT	AL	8	31	4	7	0	1	0	3	0	.226
CAREER TOTALS			**1410**	**5998**	**1262**	**1988**	**343**	**161**	**126**	**1305**	**232**	**.331**

JOE TINKER

"It is impossible to speak of the great deeds which made the Cubs of 1906 the most formidable team in the history of the game without due mention of their peerless shortstop, Joe Tinker," wrote F.C. Lane in *Baseball Magazine*.

Tinker was a standout shortstop who spent 13 full seasons in the major leagues. He is best known for the 11 years he spent with the Chicago Cubs from 1902 to 1912, as a part of one of the best double-play duos of all time, with Johnny Evers. He was a part of the Cubs dynasty that took home four pennants between 1906 and 1910 and two World Series championships in 1907 and 1908.

The speedster began his professional baseball career in 1900 at the age of 19. He hit .290 in the Pacific Northwest League the following year and was purchased by the Cubs to play in the big leagues. During his time with the Cubs, he averaged 28 stolen bases a season. On June 28, 1910, Tinker stole home twice in the same game, an act that in itself has been accomplished less than a dozen times in major league history.

Tinker demonstrated his durability in 1908 when he played in all 157 games when many of his teammates were forced to miss huge parts of the season with injuries. He led the Chicago club with 146 hits, 14 triples, six home runs, 68 RBI and a .391 slugging percentage. Tinker's best season came in his first year as a player-manager, with the Cincinnati Reds in 1913. He had career highs with both a .317 average and a .445 slugging percentage. He also hit 20 doubles, 13 triples and a home run, while his .968 fielding percentage was more than 30 points above the league average.

The shortstop best remembered for anchoring the defense of a team that many consider the greatest of the Dead Ball Era, if not all time, led all National Leaguers at his position in fielding a total of five times. He also led the NL in range factor four times and double plays twice.

Tinker ended his career as a player-manager for the Reds, the Chicago Federals and the Cubs. He later moved on to managing and owning part of the Columbus team in the American Association and then the Orlando Gulls of the Florida State League.

JOSEPH B. TINKER
FAMOUS AS A MEMBER OF ONE OF BASEBALL'S GREATEST DOUBLE PLAY COMBINATIONS-FROM TINKER TO EVERS TO CHANCE. A BIG LEAGUER FROM 1902 THROUGH 1916 WITH THE CHICAGO CUBS AND CINCINNATI REDS AND THE CHICAGO FEDS. MANAGER CINCINNATI 1913 AND CHICAGO N.L.1916. SHORTSTOP ON CUBS' TEAM THAT WON PENNANTS IN 1906,'07 '08 AND 1910.

Elected To The Hall Of Fame: 1946.
Born: July 27, 1880 in Muscotah, Kan.
Died: July 27, 1948 in Orlando, Flor.
Height: 5-9. **Weight:** 175.
Threw : Right. **Batted:** Right.
Debut: April 17, 1902.
Final Game: Sept. 22, 1916.
Teams: Chicago N.L. 1902-1912, 1916; Cincinnati N.L. 1913; Chicago, Federal League 1914-1915.
Postseason: 2-Time World Series Champion (1907-1908); 4 N.L. Pennants (1906-1908, 1910).

YEAR	TEAM	LEAGUE	G	AB	R	H	2B	3B	HR	RBI	SB	AVG
1902	CHICAGO	NL	133	501	55	132	19	5	2	55	27	.263
1903	CHICAGO	NL	124	460	67	134	21	7	2	70	27	.291
1904	CHICAGO	NL	141	488	55	108	12	13	3	41	41	.221
1905	CHICAGO	NL	149	547	70	135	18	8	2	66	31	.247
1906	CHICAGO	NL	148	523	75	122	18	4	1	64	30	.233
1907	CHICAGO	NL	117	402	36	89	11	3	1	36	20	.221
1908	CHICAGO	NL	157	548	67	146	22	14	6	68	30	.266
1909	CHICAGO	NL	143	516	56	132	26	11	4	57	23	.256
1910	CHICAGO	NL	134	473	48	136	25	9	3	69	20	.288
1911	CHICAGO	NL	144	536	61	149	24	12	4	69	30	.278
1912	CHICAGO	NL	142	550	80	155	24	7	0	75	25	.282
1913	CINCINNATI	NL	110	382	47	121	20	13	1	57	10	.317
1914	CHICAGO	FL	126	438	50	112	21	7	2	46	19	.256
1915	CHICAGO	FL	31	67	7	18	2	1	0	9	3	.269
1916	CHICAGO	NL	7	10	0	1	0	0	0	1	0	.100
CAREER TOTALS			**1806**	**6441**	**774**	**1690**	**263**	**114**	**31**	**783**	**336**	**.262**

CRISTÓBAL TORRIENTE

"We have never given [Cristóbal] Torriente the credit he deserved. He did everything well, he fielded like a natural, threw in perfect form, he covered as much field as could be covered; as for batting, he left being good to being something extraordinary," said Hall of Famer Martin Dihigo.

"The Black Babe Ruth" was the nickname Torriente acquired in the fall of 1920. The New York Giants (plus Ruth) visited Torriente's native Cuba for a nine-game series vs. Almendares – Torriente's team. Torriente outhit and out-homered Ruth in the series and the home team won the series by one game.

Torriente was a powerful, stocky centerfielder who possessed all of the five tools: hitting for average and power, fielding, throwing, and running. Torriente came stateside in 1914 to play, appropriately enough, for the Cuban Stars. He also played several seasons in the 'teens for J.L. Wilkinson's "All-Nations" team.

He joined The Chicago American Giants in 1919, helping the team capture the first three Negro National League pennants in 1920-22. He won the league batting title in 1920 and in 1923. He joined the Kansas City Monarchs in 1926, and the next two seasons he spent with the Detroit Stars. He wound up his American career in the early 1930s with Gilkerson's Union Giants, the Atlanta Black Crackers, and the Cleveland Cubs.

Like many players, Torriente had a parallel winter career in the Cuban Winter league. In 13 seasons in his homeland, he hit over .300 11 times, and won two batting titles. His teams won six Cuban championships in those 13 seasons.

He was a left-handed bad ball hitter with dramatic power to all fields, also hitting for gaudy averages, often reported in the high three hundreds and low four hundreds. He was a quick and fast base runner who stole many bases. In center field, his speed seemed odd from such a stocky player, but he covered a lot of ground and had an accurate and powerful arm. He also was an occasional pitcher in the Negro National League, compiling a record of 21-14.

CRISTÓBAL TORRIENTE
"CARLOS"
PRE-NEGRO LEAGUES, 1913-1919
NEGRO LEAGUES, 1920-1928, 1932
A COMPACT AND POWERFUL FIVE-TOOL PLAYER WITH TREMENDOUS EXTRA-BASE POWER TO ALL FIELDS. PLAYED 17 SEASONS OVERALL AND RANKS AMONG ALL-TIME NEGRO LEAGUES LEADERS IN DOUBLES, TRIPLES, SLUGGING PERCENTAGE, TOTAL BASES AND RBI. LED CHICAGO AMERICAN GIANTS TO THREE SUCCESSIVE NEGRO NATIONAL LEAGUE TITLES, 1920-1922. EXCEPTIONAL SPEED AND RANGE ALLOWED HIM TO COVER CENTER FIELD WITH GREAT EASE. PRIOR TO THE FORMATION OF THE NEGRO LEAGUES, STARRED IN HIS NATIVE CUBA. FAMED FOR OUTPLAYING BABE RUTH DURING A NINE-GAME BARNSTORMING SERIES IN 1920.

Elected To The Hall Of Fame: 2006.
Born: Nov. 16, 1893 in Cienfuegos, Cuba.
Died: Apr. 11, 1938 in New York, N.Y.
Height: 5-9. **Weight:** 190.
Threw: Left. **Batted:** Left.
Teams: Pre-Negro Leagues 1913-1919;
Negro Leagues 1920-1928, 1930-1932.
Habana 1912; Almendares 1913-1915;
Cuban Stars 1914-1915; Havana 1916,
1918; Chicago 1919-1925; Kansas City
1916-1917, 1926; Detroit 1927-1928;
Cleveland 1932.

YEAR	TEAM	LEAGUE	G	AB	R	H	2B	3B	HR	RBI	SB	AVG
1912	HABANA	CUNL	28	101	11	26	1	2	1	14	7	.257
1913	ALMENDARES	CMLS	8	32	0	5	1	0	0	3	0	.156
1914	CUBAN STARS/ALM.	INDP/CNCS	38	134	35	52	11	4	2	24	8	.388
1915	CUBAN STARS/ALM.	INDP/CNCS	58	214	43	75	12	4	2	35	15	.350
1916	HAVANA/K.C.	INDP	58	205	37	71	12	2	2	43	7	.346
1917	KANSAS CITY	INDP	15	58	10	16	3	0	0	8	6	.276
1918	HAVANA	INDP	35	128	30	46	4	9	1	26	3	.359
1919	CHICAGO	INDP	41	142	31	46	10	3	3	35	7	.324
1920	CHICAGO	NNL	—	151	21	63	14	7	2	—	7	.417
1921	CHICAGO	NNL	—	168	35	54	4	8	4	—	3	.321
1922	CHICAGO	NNL	—	122	29	33	8	1	6	—	6	.270
1923	CHICAGO	NNL	—	261	69	101	22	5	4	—	12	.387
1924	CHICAGO	NNL	—	254	57	87	24	6	7	—	11	.343
1925	CHICAGO	NNL	—	299	47	79	11	7	9	—	5	.264
1926	KANSAS CITY	NNL	—	296	50	103	19	5	4	—	12	.348
1927	DETROIT	NNL	—	256	30	81	15	2	5	—	5	.316
1928	DETROIT	NNL	—	118	15	38	7	3	1	—	2	.322
1932	CLEVELAND	NSL	—	32	1	8	1	1	0	—	4	.250
CAREER TOTALS			**—**	**2971**	**551**	**984**	**179**	**69**	**53**	**309**	**120**	**.331**

PIE TRAYNOR

"He was a mechanically perfect third baseman," legendary baseball executive Branch Rickey said of Pie Traynor upon his induction into the Hall of Fame. "A man of intellectual worth on the field of play."

Traynor was widely regarded as the premier third baseman of his era—and in 1948 he became the second third baseman elected to the Hall of Fame. Traynor was born and raised in Massachusetts, where he was nicknamed after his favorite dessert as a youth. A scout with the hometown Boston Braves invited Traynor to a tryout, but the scout forgot to notify the Braves' manager, who ordered Traynor off the field.

After starting his professional career as a shortstop for the Portsmouth Truckers of the Virginia League, Traynor was signed by the Pittsburgh Pirates in 1920. He would spend more than a half-century with the Pirates, working as a player, manager, broadcaster and scout.

Traynor became Pittsburgh's full-time third baseman in 1922, then emerged as a star a year later, when he hit .338 with a league-leading 19 triples.

In 1925, Traynor led the Pirates to their first pennant in 16 years. He hit .346 with a home run against the Washington Senators in the World Series, which Pittsburgh won in seven games. He led the Pirates to the pennant again two years later, but they lost the World Series to the New York Yankees.

Though he reached double digits in home runs just once, Traynor was a gifted hitter. Perhaps his best season was 1930, when he hit a career-best .366 and drove in 119 runs.

In 1933, Traynor was selected as a reserve in Major League Baseball's inaugural All-Star Game. The following season was his last as a full-time player, but he served as player-manager until 1937. He retired as manager in 1939, then became a scout for the Pirates.

Traynor took a job in broadcasting in 1944 and became a fixture on the radio for the next 21 years. During this period, he would walk 10 miles round trip from his home to the radio station every day—he never learned to drive, because he found walking to be relaxing and healthy.

HAROLD J. (PIE) TRAYNOR
RATED AMONG THE GREAT THIRD BASEMEN OF ALL TIME, BECAME A REGULAR WITH THE PITTSBURGH N.L. TEAM IN 1922 AND CONTINUED AS A PLAYER UNTIL CONCLUSION OF 1937 SEASON. MANAGED THE PIRATES FROM JUNE, 1934, THROUGH SEPT. 1939. HOLDS SEVERAL FIELDING RECORDS AND COMPILED A LIFETIME BATTING MARK OF .320. ONE OF FEW PLAYERS EVER TO MAKE 200 OR MORE HITS DURING A SEASON, COLLECTING 208 IN 1923.

Elected To The Hall Of Fame: *1948.*
Born: *Nov. 11, 1898 in Framingham, Mass.*
Died: *March 16, 1972 in Pittsburgh, Pa.*
Height: *6-0.* **Weight:** *170.*
Threw: *Right.* **Batted:** *Right.*
Debut: *Sept. 15, 1920.*
Final Game: *Aug. 14, 1937.*
Teams: *Pittsburgh N.L. 1920-1935, 1937.*
Postseason: *World Series Champion (1925); 2 N.L. Pennants (1925, 1927).*
Awards: *2-Time All-Star (1933-1934).*

YEAR	TEAM	LEAGUE	G	AB	R	H	2B	3B	HR	RBI	SB	AVG
1920	PITTSBURGH	NL	17	52	6	11	3	1	0	2	1	.212
1921	PITTSBURGH	NL	7	19	0	5	0	0	0	2	0	.263
1922	PITTSBURGH	NL	142	571	89	161	17	12	4	81	17	.282
1923	PITTSBURGH	NL	153	616	108	208	19	19	12	101	28	.338
1924	PITTSBURGH	NL	142	545	86	160	26	13	5	82	24	.294
1925	PITTSBURGH	NL	150	591	114	189	39	14	6	106	15	.320
1926	PITTSBURGH	NL	152	574	83	182	25	17	3	92	8	.317
1927	PITTSBURGH	NL	149	573	93	196	32	9	5	106	11	.342
1928	PITTSBURGH	NL	144	569	91	192	38	12	3	124	12	.337
1929	PITTSBURGH	NL	130	540	94	192	27	12	4	108	13	.356
1930	PITTSBURGH	NL	130	497	90	182	22	11	9	119	7	.366
1931	PITTSBURGH	NL	155	615	81	183	37	15	2	103	6	.298
1932	PITTSBURGH	NL	135	513	74	169	27	10	2	68	6	.329
1933	PITTSBURGH	NL	154	624	85	190	27	6	1	82	5	.304
1934	PITTSBURGH	NL	119	444	62	137	22	10	1	61	3	.309
1935	PITTSBURGH	NL	57	204	24	57	10	3	1	36	2	.279
1937	PITTSBURGH	NL	5	12	3	2	0	0	0	0	0	.167
CAREER TOTALS			**1941**	**7559**	**1183**	**2416**	**371**	**164**	**58**	**1273**	**158**	**.320**

DAZZY VANCE

"Dazzy Vance could throw a cream puff through a battleship," said former Brooklyn Dodgers teammate Johnny Frederick.

Renowned for his blazing fastball, Vance was the premier strikeout pitcher of the 1920s. He led the National League in strikeouts for seven consecutive seasons from 1922-28, and often he led by wide margins. In 1924, he had more strikeouts than the second- and third-place pitchers combined.

His best season was 1924, when he won the NL MVP award after leading the league in wins (28), ERA (2.16), complete games (30) and strikeouts (262). He beat out fellow Hall of Famer Rogers Hornsby—who hit .424 that season—for the award. He led the league in wins again the next season, during which he also threw a no-hitter against Philadelphia, striking out nine and walking one.

Vance's Dodgers never won a pennant, and in 1933 he was traded to the St. Louis Cardinals, where he joined Dizzy Dean. He was sold to the Reds the following year, but he was waived back to St. Louis in time to win the 1934 World Series as part of the "Gashouse Gang." He finished his career as a reliever back with Brooklyn in 1935.

Vance's career is even more remarkable because he did not break into the major leagues for good until the age of 31 in 1922. He had spent the previous decade pitching mostly in the minor leagues, though he made nine appearances between the Pirates and Yankees in 1915, and two more for the Yankees in 1918. A sore arm was blamed for cutting short his first cracks at the majors.

That soreness became shooting pain after he banged his elbow on a poker table, causing him to have surgery. The procedure cleared up the pain, and also relieved the chronic soreness that had plagued him. He had a strong season for the New Orleans Pelicans of the Southern Association in 1921, but at the age of 30, he was far from a hot prospect. But the Pelicans had a catcher named Hank DeBerry whom the Dodgers wanted, so New Orleans offered DeBerry along with Vance in a package deal for $10,000. The Dodgers took the deal, and Vance won 18 games as a 31-year-old rookie in 1922, en route to a Hall of Fame career.

ARTHUR CHARLES (DAZZY) VANCE
BROOKLYN N.L. 1922 TO 1932, 1935
PITTSBURGH N.L. • NEW YORK A.L.
ST. LOUIS N.L. • CINCINNATI N.L.
FIRST PITCHER IN N.L. TO LEAD IN
STRIKEOUTS FOR 7 STRAIGHT YEARS, 1922 TO
1928. LED LEAGUE WITH 28 VICTORIES IN
1924:22 IN 1925. WON 15 STRAIGHT IN 1924.
PITCHED NO-HIT GAME AGAINST PHILLIES,
1925. MOST VALUABLE PLAYER N.L. 1924.

Elected To The Hall Of Fame: *1955.*
Born: *March 4, 1891 in Orient, Iowa.*
Died: *Feb. 16, 1961 in Homosassa Springs, Fla.*
Height: *6-2.* **Weight:** *200.*
Threw: *Right.* **Batted:** *Right.*
Debut: *April 16, 1915.*
Final Game: *Aug. 14, 1935.*
Teams: *Pittsburgh N.L. 1915; New York A.L. 1915, 1918; Brooklyn N.L. 1922-1932; St. Louis N.L. 1933-1934; Cincinnati N.L. 1934.*
Postseason: *World Series Champion (1934); N.L. Pennant (1934).*
Awards: *N.L. Most Valuable Player (1924).*

YEAR	TEAM	LEAGUE	G	W	L	SV	SH	IP	H	BB	SO	ERA
1915	PITTSBURGH/NEW YORK	NL/AL	9	0	4	0	0	30.7	26	21	18	4.11
1918	NEW YORK	AL	2	0	0	0	0	2.3	9	2	0	15.43
1922	BROOKLYN	NL	36	18	12	0	5	245.7	259	94	134	3.70
1923	BROOKLYN	NL	37	18	15	0	3	280.3	263	100	197	3.50
1924	BROOKLYN	NL	35	28	6	0	3	308.3	238	77	262	2.16
1925	BROOKLYN	NL	31	22	9	0	4	265.3	247	66	221	3.53
1926	BROOKLYN	NL	24	9	10	1	0	169	172	58	140	3.89
1927	BROOKLYN	NL	34	16	15	1	2	273.3	242	69	184	2.70
1928	BROOKLYN	NL	38	22	10	2	4	280.3	226	72	200	2.09
1929	BROOKLYN	NL	31	14	13	0	1	231.3	244	47	126	3.89
1930	BROOKLYN	NL	35	17	15	0	4	258.7	241	55	173	2.61
1931	BROOKLYN	NL	30	11	13	0	2	218.7	221	53	150	3.38
1932	BROOKLYN	NL	27	12	11	1	1	175.7	171	57	103	4.20
1933	ST. LOUIS	NL	28	6	2	3	0	99	105	28	67	3.55
1934	CINCINNATI/ST. LOUIS	NL	25	1	3	1	0	77	90	25	42	4.56
1935	BROOKLYN	NL	20	3	2	2	0	51	55	16	28	4.41
CAREER TOTALS			**442**	**197**	**140**	**11**	**29**	**2966.7**	**2809**	**840**	**2045**	**3.24**

ARKY VAUGHAN

JOSEPH FLOYD VAUGHAN
"ARKY"
PITTSBURGH N.L. 1932-1941
BROOKLYN N.L. 1942-1948
AMONG HALL OF FAME SHORTSTOPS, HIS .318
LIFETIME BATTING AVERAGE IS SECOND ONLY TO
HONUS WAGNER'S .329. LED LEAGUE WITH .385 IN
1935. HOMERED TWICE IN 1941 ALL-STAR GAME.
FANNED ONLY 276 TIMES IN 6622 CAREER AT-BATS.
POLISHED FIELDER AND ACCOMPLISHED BASE
RUNNER, LEADING N.L. WITH 20 STOLEN BASES IN
1943.

Arky Vaughan was the premier shortstop of his era and one of the best in baseball history. He hit .300 or better in each of his first 10 major league seasons—all with the Pittsburgh Pirates—and led the National League in runs and triples three years apiece, as well as stolen bases once.

Vaughan was born in Arkansas, and although his family moved to Fullerton, Calif., when he was an infant, he was nicknamed "Arky" when he was a child because he spoke with an Arkansas accent, picked up from his family.

He was a noted high school athlete who received interest from colleges for his football talent, but he signed a baseball contract with the minor league Wichita Aviators in 1931. He hit .338 for the Aviators, then joined the Pirates in 1932 at the age of 20.

Vaughan rose to stardom quickly, and played in his first of nine straight All-Star Games in 1934. He hit .364 in his career in midsummer classics, highlighted by a two-homer, four-RBI game in 1941. That performance was overshadowed by Ted Williams' game-winning home run in the ninth inning.

Vaughan's best season was 1935, when he led the NL in batting, slugging and on-base percentage. His .385 average that year was the highest in the 20th century for a National League shortstop.

Vaughan was traded to the Brooklyn Dodgers in late 1941, and though he led the NL in runs and stolen bases in 1943, he was never as great a player as he was in Pittsburgh. He clashed with fiery manager Leo Durocher in 1943 and sat out the next three years. He said the absence was so he could devote his time to his California farm in support of the war effort.

After Durocher's suspension from baseball for the 1947 season, Vaughan returned to the Dodgers and hit .325 in 64 games as a 35-year-old. He retired from the majors for good after the 1948 season. Vaughan died in 1952 at the age of 40, when a sudden storm capsized his fishing boat on a lake near his California home. Vaughan tried to save his companion, who could not swim, and they both drowned. He was inducted into the Hall of Fame by the Veterans Committee in 1985.

Elected To The Hall Of Fame: 1985.
Born: March 9, 1912 in Clifty, Ark.
Died: Aug. 30, 1952 in Eagleville, Calif.
Height: 5-10. **Weight:** 175.
Threw: Right. **Batted:** Left.
Debut: April 17, 1932.
Final Game: Sept. 22, 1948.
Teams: Pittsburgh N.L. 1932-1941;
Brooklyn N.L. 1942-1943, 1947-1948.
Postseason: N.L. Pennant (1947).
Awards: 9-Time All-Star (1934-1942).

YEAR	TEAM	LEAGUE	G	AB	R	H	2B	3B	HR	RBI	SB	AVG
1932	PITTSBURGH	NL	129	497	71	158	15	10	4	61	10	.318
1933	PITTSBURGH	NL	152	573	85	180	29	19	9	97	3	.314
1934	PITTSBURGH	NL	149	558	115	186	41	11	12	94	10	.333
1935	PITTSBURGH	NL	137	499	108	192	34	10	19	99	4	.385
1936	PITTSBURGH	NL	156	568	122	190	30	11	9	78	6	.335
1937	PITTSBURGH	NL	126	469	71	151	17	17	5	72	7	.322
1938	PITTSBURGH	NL	148	541	88	174	35	5	7	68	14	.322
1939	PITTSBURGH	NL	152	595	94	182	30	11	6	62	12	.306
1940	PITTSBURGH	NL	156	594	113	178	40	15	7	95	12	.300
1941	PITTSBURGH	NL	106	374	69	118	20	7	6	38	8	.316
1942	BROOKLYN	NL	128	495	82	137	18	4	2	49	8	.277
1943	BROOKLYN	NL	149	610	112	186	39	6	5	66	20	.305
1947	BROOKLYN	NL	64	126	24	41	5	2	2	25	4	.325
1948	BROOKLYN	NL	65	123	19	30	3	0	3	22	0	.244
CAREER TOTALS			**1817**	**6622**	**1173**	**2103**	**356**	**128**	**96**	**926**	**118**	**.318**

Rube Waddell

"He had more stuff than any pitcher I ever saw," legendary manager Connie Mack once said about Rube Waddell.

Mack knew that as well as anyone. As Waddell's manager with the Philadelphia A's starting in 1902, Mack helped the young left-hander harness his electric fastball, devastating curveball and baffling screwball. Waddell posted the first of four consecutive 20-win seasons that year, and led the American League in strikeouts from 1902-07. On July 1, 1902, Waddell became the first pitcher in modern major league history to strike out the side on nine pitches. In 1903, Waddell struck out 302 batters – 115 more than the runner up. The following year, he fanned 349, to lead the league by 110. In 1905, Waddell won the AL's pitching Triple Crown, leading the league with 27 wins, 287 strikeouts and a 1.48 ERA. He was instrumental in the early growth of the game, as one of its first real drawing cards and one of its first celebrities, as biographer Alan Howard Levy wrote.

As dominant as Waddell was on the mound, he might have been just as notorious for his unpredictable behavior off the field. Born in Bradford, Pa., Waddell earned the nickname "Rube" – a term commonly used to refer to farmboys – because he was a big, fresh kid. Waddell had a habit of leaving the dugout in the middle of games to follow passing fire trucks to fires. He performed as an alligator wrestler in the offseason, and also played professional football in the first National Football League, as a fullback for the Philadelphia Athletics in 1902. Newspapers of the time referred to Waddell as "eccentric." Others called him "screwball" or "nutsy." Waddell also battled alcoholism for much of his adult life.

Waddell's drinking led to constant battles with his managers and scuffles with teammates, and after the 1907 season the A's sold him to the St. Louis Browns for $5,000. He posted another strong season in 1908, and Browns owner Robert Hedges hired him as a hunter over the next two winters to try to keep him out of trouble. He was released in 1910 and never pitched another major league game. He died of tuberculosis four years later, at the age of 37.

GEORGE EDWARD WADDELL
"RUBE"
COLORFUL LEFTHANDED PITCHER WHO WAS IN BOTH LEAGUES, BUT WHO GAINED FAME AS A MEMBER OF THE PHILADELPHIA A.L. TEAM, WON MORE THAN 20 GAMES IN FIRST FOUR SEASONS WITH THAT CLUB AND COMPILED MORE THAN 200 VICTORIES DURING MAJOR LEAGUE CAREER. WAS NOTED FOR HIS STRIKEOUT ACHIEVEMENTS.

Elected To The Hall Of Fame: 1946.
Born: Oct. 13, 1876 in Bradford, Pa.
Died: Apr. 1, 1914 in San Antonio, Texas.
Height: 6-1. **Weight:** 196.
Threw: Left. **Batted:** Right.
Debut: Sept. 8, 1897.
Final Game: Aug. 1, 1910.
Teams: Louisville N.L. 1897, 1899; Pittsburgh N.L. 1900-1901; Chicago N.L. 1901; Philadelphia A.L. 1902-1907; St. Louis A.L. 1908-1910.

YEAR	TEAM	LEAGUE	G	W	L	SV	SH	IP	H	BB	SO	ERA
1897	LOUISVILLE	NL	2	0	1	0	0	14	17	6	5	3.21
1899	LOUISVILLE	NL	10	7	2	1	1	79	69	14	44	3.08
1900	PITTSBURGH	NL	29	8	13	0	2	208.7	176	55	130	2.37
1901	PITTSBURGH/CHICAGO	NL	31	14	16	0	0	251.3	249	75	172	3.01
1902	PHILADELPHIA	AL	33	24	7	0	3	276.3	224	64	210	2.05
1903	PHILADELPHIA	AL	39	21	16	0	4	324	274	85	302	2.44
1904	PHILADELPHIA	AL	46	25	19	0	8	383	307	91	349	1.62
1905	PHILADELPHIA	AL	46	27	10	0	7	328.7	231	90	287	1.48
1906	PHILADELPHIA	AL	43	15	17	0	8	272.7	221	92	196	2.21
1907	PHILADELPHIA	AL	44	19	13	0	7	284.7	234	73	232	2.15
1908	ST. LOUIS	AL	43	19	14	3	5	285.7	223	90	232	1.89
1909	ST. LOUIS	AL	31	11	14	0	5	220.3	204	57	141	2.37
1910	ST. LOUIS	AL	10	3	1	1	0	33	31	11	16	3.55
CAREER TOTALS			**407**	**193**	**143**	**5**	**50**	**2961.1**	**2460**	**803**	**2316**	**2.16**

The Baseball Hall of Fame Almanac

HONUS WAGNER

Hall of Fame skipper John McGraw called Honus Wagner "the nearest thing to a perfect player no matter where his manager chose to play him." Honus Wagner played 21 seasons, primarily with his hometown Pittsburgh Pirates, and was the total package. He could hit for average and power and could change the dynamics of a game on the base paths and in the field–he played every position on the diamond in his major league career except for catcher.

Nicknamed "The Flying Dutchman," a reference to his German heritage, Wagner had a bit of an awkward look about him. But in this case, looks were deceiving. "The Flying Dutchman" was one of the best hitters and better athletes the game has ever seen. He gripped the bat with his hands inches apart and went the other way on outside pitches or slid his hands together in a more traditional grip and pulled pitches down the line. He was a smart player who could adjust his game to fit the situation. Burleigh Grimes, who as a youngster was a teammate of Wagner, recalled, "One day he was batting against a young pitcher who had just come into the league. The catcher was a kid, too. A rookie battery. The pitcher threw Honus a curveball, and he swung at it and missed and fell down on one knee. Looked helpless as a robin. I was kind of surprised, but the guy sitting next to me on the bench poked me in the ribs and said, 'Watch this next one.' Those kids figured they had the old man's weaknesses, you see, and served him up the same dish — as he knew they would. Well, Honus hit a line drive so hard the fence in left field went back and forth for five minutes."

During the first decade of the 20th century no player was more dominant than Wagner. He led the majors in hits, runs doubles, total bases, extra-base hits, runs batted in, stolen bases, batting average, on-base percentage and slugging percentage. John McGraw stated his feelings on the game's greatest player unequivocally when he said, "You can have your Cobbs, your Lajoies, your Chases, your Bakers, but I'll take Wagner as my pick of the greatest."

The Flying Dutchman

Elected To The Hall Of Fame: *1936.*
Born: *Feb. 24, 1874 in Chartiers, Pa.*
Died: *Dec. 6, 1955 in Carnegie, Pa.*
Height: *5-11.* **Weight:** *200.*
Threw : *Right.* **Batted:** *Right.*
Debut: *July 19, 1897.*
Final Game: *Sept. 17, 1917.*
Teams: *Louisville N.L. 1897-1899;*
Pittsburgh N.L. 1900-1917.
Postseason: *World Series Champion (1909); 2 N.L. Pennants (1903, 1909).*

YEAR	TEAM	LEAGUE	G	AB	R	H	2B	3B	HR	RBI	SB	AVG
1897	LOUISVILLE	NL	62	242	38	81	18	4	2	39	20	.335
1898	LOUISVILLE	NL	151	588	80	176	29	3	10	105	27	.299
1899	LOUISVILLE	NL	148	575	100	196	45	13	7	114	37	.341
1900	PITTSBURGH	NL	135	527	107	201	45	22	4	100	38	.381
1901	PITTSBURGH	NL	140	549	101	194	37	11	6	126	49	.353
1902	PITTSBURGH	NL	136	534	105	176	30	16	3	91	42	.330
1903	PITTSBURGH	NL	129	512	97	182	30	19	5	101	46	.355
1904	PITTSBURGH	NL	132	490	97	171	44	14	4	75	53	.349
1905	PITTSBURGH	NL	147	548	114	199	32	14	6	101	57	.363
1906	PITTSBURGH	NL	142	516	103	175	38	9	2	71	63	.339
1907	PITTSBURGH	NL	142	515	98	180	38	14	6	82	53	.350
1908	PITTSBURGH	NL	151	568	100	201	39	19	10	109	35	.354
1909	PITTSBURGH	NL	137	495	92	168	39	10	5	100	24	.339
1910	PITTSBURGH	NL	150	556	90	178	34	8	4	81	20	.320
1911	PITTSBURGH	NL	130	473	87	158	23	16	9	89	26	.334
1912	PITTSBURGH	NL	145	558	91	181	35	20	7	102	21	.324
1913	PITTSBURGH	NL	114	413	51	124	18	4	3	56	22	.300
1914	PITTSBURGH	NL	150	552	60	139	15	9	1	50	23	.252
1915	PITTSBURGH	NL	156	566	68	155	32	17	6	78	22	.274
1916	PITTSBURGH	NL	123	432	45	124	15	9	1	39	11	.287
1917	PITTSBURGH	NL	74	230	15	61	7	1	0	24	5	.265
CAREER TOTALS			**2794**	**10439**	**1739**	**3420**	**643**	**252**	**101**	**1733**	**723**	**.328**

BOBBY WALLACE

RODERICK J. WALLACE
CLEVELAND-ST. LOUIS-CINCINNATI N. L.
ST. LOUIS A.L. - 1894 TO 1918
ONE OF LONGEST CAREERS IN MAJOR
LEAGUES. OVER 60 YEARS AS PITCHER,
THIRD-BASEMAN, SHORTSTOP, MANAGER,
UMPIRE AND SCOUT. ACTIVE AS PLAYER
FOR 25 YEARS. SET A.L. RECORD FOR
CHANCES IN ONE GAME AT SHORTSTOP, 17,
JUNE 10, 1902. RECOGNIZED AS ONE OF
GREATEST SHORTSTOPS. PITCHED FOR
CLEVELAND IN 1896 TEMPLE CUP SERIES.

Bobby Wallace made his major league debut in 1894, taking the mound for the Cleveland Spiders. In a few short years, he evolved into one of the best shortstops the game has ever seen. He pitched for a starting rotation that included Cy Young and in his first full season he won 12 of his 26 decisions. Though his pitching wasn't overwhelmingly impressive to the team's management, the level of athleticism he displayed was enough for them to start giving him chances at other positions.

Wallace played the outfield as much as he took the mound by his third year in Cleveland, and he eventually turned into a regular infielder. The versatile player's best season came in 1897 when he batted .335 with 173 hits in 130 games while playing third base full time. He drove in a team-leading 112 runs, scored 99 runs, and hit 33 doubles and 21 triples. He was moved from the hot corner to the middle infield, first spending time at second base before getting a chance at shortstop. In 1901, Wallace led all shortstops in chances per game, assists and double plays, and was still a threat at the plate, batting .324 over the duration of the season.

Wallace made more plays per game than any other shortstop who played at least 600 games during the first decade of the major leagues, including players like Wagner, Joe Tinker and George Davis. He led the American League in assists twice in his career, and fielding percentage three times. In 1902 he set a league record for the most chances in a game with 17. He also finished in the top 10 in RBI eight times in his career. Because of his smart style of play and his remarkable defensive skills, Wallace was able to play the game until he was 44 years old.

Elected To The Hall Of Fame: 1953.
Born: Nov. 4, 1873 in Pittsburgh, Pa.
Died: Nov. 3, 1960 in Torrance, Calif.
Height: 5-8. **Weight:** 170.
Threw: Right. **Batted:** Right.
Debut: Sept. 15, 1894.
Final Game: Sept. 2, 1918.
Teams: Cleveland N.L. 1894-1898; St. Louis N.L. 1899-1901, 1917-1918; St. Louis A.L. 1902-1916.

YEAR	TEAM	LEAGUE	G	AB	R	H	2B	3B	HR	RBI	SB	AVG
1894	CLEVELAND	NL	4	13	0	2	1	0	0	1	0	.154
1895	CLEVELAND	NL	30	98	16	21	2	3	0	10	0	.214
1896	CLEVELAND	NL	45	149	19	35	6	3	1	17	2	.235
1897	CLEVELAND	NL	130	516	99	173	33	21	4	112	14	.335
1898	CLEVELAND	NL	154	593	81	160	25	13	3	99	7	.270
1899	ST. LOUIS	NL	151	577	91	170	28	14	12	108	17	.295
1900	ST. LOUIS	NL	126	485	70	130	25	9	4	70	7	.268
1901	ST. LOUIS	NL	134	550	69	178	34	15	2	91	15	.324
1902	ST. LOUIS	AL	133	494	71	141	32	9	1	63	18	.285
1903	ST. LOUIS	AL	135	511	63	136	21	7	1	54	10	.266
1904	ST. LOUIS	AL	139	541	57	149	29	4	2	69	20	.275
1905	ST. LOUIS	AL	156	587	67	159	25	9	1	59	13	.271
1906	ST. LOUIS	AL	139	476	64	123	21	7	2	67	24	.258
1907	ST. LOUIS	AL	147	538	56	138	20	7	0	70	16	.257
1908	ST. LOUIS	AL	137	487	59	123	24	4	1	60	5	.253
1909	ST. LOUIS	AL	116	403	36	96	12	2	0	35	7	.238
1910	ST. LOUIS	AL	138	508	47	131	19	7	0	37	12	.258
1911	ST. LOUIS	AL	125	410	35	95	12	2	0	31	8	.232
1912	ST. LOUIS	AL	100	323	39	78	14	5	0	31	3	.241
1913	ST. LOUIS	AL	55	147	11	31	5	0	0	21	1	.211
1914	ST. LOUIS	AL	26	73	3	16	2	1	0	5	1	.219
1915	ST. LOUIS	AL	9	13	1	3	0	1	0	4	0	.231
1916	ST. LOUIS	AL	14	18	0	5	0	0	0	1	0	.278
1917	ST. LOUIS	NL	8	10	0	1	0	0	0	2	0	.100
1918	ST. LOUIS	NL	32	98	3	15	1	0	0	4	1	.153
CAREER TOTALS			**2383**	**8618**	**1057**	**2309**	**391**	**143**	**34**	**1121**	**201**	**.268**

ED WALSH

"Big Ed Walsh. Great, big, strong, good-looking fellow," Hall of Famer Sam Crawford said. "He threw a spitball. I think that ball disintegrated on the way to the plate, and the catcher put it back together again. I swear, when it went past the plate, it was just the spit went by."

Two achievements in particular speak to the right-hander's dominance at the turn of the 20th century: his lifetime ERA of 1.82, the lowest of all time, and his 40-win season for the 1908 Chicago White Sox. Walsh won 195 times in a 14-year career. Among modern era pitchers, 1901 to present, only contemporary Addie Joss at 1.89 registered a career ERA below the 2.00 mark. As to the latter accomplishment, Walsh is the last pitcher to top 40 wins in a season, with only Christy Mathewson (37 wins in 1908) and Walter Johnson (36 in 1913) coming anywhere close.

Walsh stood 6-foot-1 and weighed 193 pounds and by his own estimate he threw his outstanding spitball, taught to him by teammate Elmer Stricklett, about 90 percent of the time. He broke in with the White Sox as a 22-year-old rookie in 1904 and worked as a spot starter (21 times) and reliever (19 relief appearances) for two seasons before ascending to ace of the White Sox in 1906. Chicago's "Hitless Wonder" club of '06 rode Walsh all the way to a World Series championship against the cross-town Cubs. Walsh won both of his Series starts, allowing seven hits and six runs (only one earned) in 15 innings. He struck out 17 Cubs batters.

For seven seasons, from 1906 through '12, no pitcher in the game was more durable than Walsh, and few were as effective. He paced all of baseball with 268 starts (an average of more than 38 per year), 2,526 ⅓ innings (nearly 361 per year) and 1,540 strikeouts during those seven seasons—and ranked third with 89 relief outings and 33 saves.

Beginning in 1913 Walsh struggled with arm injuries, later recalling: "My arm would keep me awake till morning with a pain I had never known before." He appeared in just 33 games and pitched 190 2/3 innings in the five seasons from 1913 though '17, earning his release from the White Sox in December '16 and retiring after one partial season with the Boston Braves.

EDWARD ARTHUR WALSH
"BIG ED"
OUTSTANDING RIGHTHANDED PITCHER OF CHICAGO A.L. FROM 1904 THROUGH 1916. WON 40 GAMES IN 1908 AND WON TWO GAMES IN THE 1906 WORLD SERIES. TWICE PITCHED AND WON TWO GAMES IN ONE DAY, ALLOWING ONLY ONE RUN IN DOUBLEHEADER AGAINST BOSTON ON SEPT. 29, 1908. FINISHED BIG LEAGUE PITCHING CAREER WITH BOSTON N.L. IN 1917.

Big Ed

Elected To The Hall Of Fame: 1946.
Born: May 14, 1881 in Plains, Pa.
Died: May 26, 1959 in Pompano Beach, Flor.
Height: 6-1. **Weight:** 193.
Threw: Right. **Batted:** Right.
Debut: May 7, 1904.
Final Game: Sept. 11, 1917.
Teams: Chicago A.L. 1904-1916; Boston N.L. 1917.
Postseason: World Series Champion (1906); A.L. Pennant (1906).

YEAR	TEAM	LEAGUE	G	W	L	SV	SH	IP	H	BB	SO	ERA
1904	CHICAGO	AL	18	6	3	1	1	110.7	90	32	57	2.60
1905	CHICAGO	AL	22	8	3	0	1	136.7	121	29	71	2.17
1906	CHICAGO	AL	41	17	13	2	10	278.3	215	58	171	1.88
1907	CHICAGO	AL	56	24	18	4	5	422.3	341	87	206	1.60
1908	CHICAGO	AL	66	40	15	6	11	464	343	56	269	1.42
1909	CHICAGO	AL	31	15	11	2	8	230.3	166	50	127	1.41
1910	CHICAGO	AL	45	18	20	5	7	369.7	242	61	258	1.27
1911	CHICAGO	AL	56	27	18	4	5	368.7	327	72	255	2.22
1912	CHICAGO	AL	62	27	17	10	6	393	332	94	254	2.15
1913	CHICAGO	AL	16	8	3	1	1	97.7	91	39	34	2.58
1914	CHICAGO	AL	8	2	3	0	1	44.7	33	20	15	2.82
1915	CHICAGO	AL	3	3	0	0	1	27	19	7	12	1.33
1916	CHICAGO	AL	2	0	1	0	0	3.3	4	3	3	2.70
1917	BOSTON	NL	4	0	1	0	0	18	22	9	4	3.50
CAREER TOTALS			**430**	**195**	**126**	**35**	**57**	**2964.1**	**2346**	**617**	**1736**	**1.82**

LLOYD WANER

"The Pirates took Lloyd Waner to spring training in 1927, mostly just to look at him a little closer," Lloyd's brother, Paul Waner, said in "The Glory of Their Times." "They never thought he could possibly make the team 'cause Lloyd only weighed about 130 pounds then. He was only 20 years old, and was even smaller than me."

Waner was born in Harrah, Okla. in 1906 and started his professional career with the San Francisco Seals in 1925, where he was teammates with his brother. After six games with the Seals the following year, Lloyd asked for his release and joined the Pittsburgh Pirates. He reached the majors with the Pirates in 1927, joining his brother in the team's outfield, and hit .355. He led the National League with 133 runs scored. Paul Waner—nicknamed "Big Poison"—won the MVP that year and Lloyd—dubbed "Little Poison"—finished sixth in the voting.

Of his 1,993 major league games played, Waner spent 1,803 of them with the Pirates.

The nickname fit because Lloyd stood just 5-foot-9 and 150 pounds. He was known for his good eye at the plate. Only three times in the majors did he strike out more than 15 times in a season. Waner was an All-Star in 1938. He had four 200-hit seasons and led the National League in hits in 1931. He had very good speed and was an excellent defensive center fielder.

Waner was elected to the Hall of Fame by the Veterans Committee in 1967 and passed away on July 22, 1982.

"He is a better player than me and can spot me 25 feet and then beat me in a sprint," Paul Waner said. "A batter's got to knock a fly over the fence to keep him from reaching it, and he doesn't miss 'em either."

LLOYD JAMES WANER
"LITTLE POISON"
PITTSBURGH N.L., BOSTON N.L.,
CINCINNATI N.L., PHILADELPHIA N.L.,
BROOKLYN N.L. 1927-1945
MADE 223 HITS IN 1927 FIRST YEAR
WITH PITTSBURGH INCLUDING 198 SINGLES,
A MODERN MAJOR LEAGUE RECORD.
LED N.L. IN MOST SINGLES 1927-1928-1929-1931.
LIFE TOTAL 2459 HITS. BATTING AVERAGE .316.
WITH BROTHER PAUL,"BIG POISON"
STARRED IN PITTSBURGH OUTFIELD
1927-1940

Little Poison

Elected To The Hall Of Fame: 1967.
Born: Mar. 16, 1906 in Harrah, Okla.
Died: July 22, 1982 in Oklahoma City, Okla.
Height: 5-9 **Weight:** 150.
Threw: Right. **Batted:** Left.
Debut: Apr. 12, 1927.
Final Game: Sept. 16, 1945.
Teams: Pittsburgh N.L. 1927-1941, 1944-1945; Boston N.L. 1941; Cincinnati N.L. 1941; Philadelphia N.L. 1942; Brooklyn N.L. 1944.
Postseason: N.L. Pennant (1927).
Awards: All-Star (1938).

YEAR	TEAM	LEAGUE	G	AB	R	H	2B	3B	HR	RBI	SB	AVG
1927	PITTSBURGH	NL	150	629	133	223	17	6	2	27	14	.355
1928	PITTSBURGH	NL	152	659	121	221	22	14	5	61	8	.335
1929	PITTSBURGH	NL	151	662	134	234	28	20	5	74	6	.353
1930	PITTSBURGH	NL	68	260	32	94	8	3	1	36	3	.362
1931	PITTSBURGH	NL	154	681	90	214	25	13	4	57	7	.314
1932	PITTSBURGH	NL	134	565	90	188	27	11	2	38	6	.333
1933	PITTSBURGH	NL	121	500	59	138	14	5	0	26	3	.276
1934	PITTSBURGH	NL	140	611	95	173	27	6	1	48	6	.283
1935	PITTSBURGH	NL	122	537	83	166	22	14	0	46	1	.309
1936	PITTSBURGH	NL	106	414	67	133	13	8	1	31	1	.321
1937	PITTSBURGH	NL	129	537	80	177	23	4	1	45	3	.330
1938	PITTSBURGH	NL	147	619	79	194	25	7	5	57	5	.313
1939	PITTSBURGH	NL	112	379	49	108	15	3	0	24	0	.285
1940	PITTSBURGH	NL	72	166	30	43	3	0	0	3	2	.259
1941	PITTSBURGH/BOSTON/CINCINNATI	NL	77	219	26	64	5	1	0	11	1	.292
1942	PHILADELPHIA	NL	101	287	23	75	7	3	0	10	1	.261
1944	BROOKLYN/PITTSBURGH	NL	34	28	5	9	0	0	0	3	0	.321
1945	PITTSBURGH	NL	23	19	5	5	0	0	0	1	0	.263
CAREER TOTALS			**1993**	**7772**	**1201**	**2459**	**281**	**118**	**27**	**598**	**67**	**.316**

PAUL WANER

"I may have got (Paul) Waner out, but I never fooled him," said Hall of Fame pitcher Burleigh Grimes For 14 seasons, brothers Paul and Lloyd Waner were synonymous with Pittsburgh Pirates baseball. Paul "Big Poison" Waner patrolled right field for the Pirates from 1926 through '40, while younger brother Lloyd, known as "Little Poison," manned center for all but one of those seasons. Led by the Waners, the Pirates of the 1920s and '30s consistently ranked among the National League's top run-scoring outfits, with ample contributions coming from a pair of Hall of Fame infielders: third baseman Pie Traynor at the beginning of the Waners' tenure and shortstop Arky Vaughan at the end. Paul and Lloyd Waner combined to strike 5,611 hits, the most ever by brothers and more even than successful brother trios like Felipe, Matty and Jesus Alou (5,094 hits) and Joe, Dom and Vince DiMaggio (4,853 hits.)

Even in an era of high offensive production, Paul Waner stood out from the crowd. Though he hit just 113 career home runs, the left-handed hitting Waner, who finished his 20-year career with 3,152 hits and a .333 lifetime average, was more than a singles hitter. Just the seventh player in history to collect 3,000 hits, Waner's total still ranks 17th all time, while his 605 doubles (11th all time) and 191 triples (10th) also score highly. As a sophomore, he batted .380 in 1927 to claim his first of three batting titles and his only MVP award. He also led the NL with 131 RBI and 237 hits in '27, a pennant-winning year for the Pirates that ended at the hands of the "Murderer's Row" New York Yankees. Waner also collected NL batting titles in 1934 (.362) and '36 (.373).

Few players were as well-rounded as Waner was at his peak. During his time in Pittsburgh, from 1926 through '40, he batted .340 and led all players with 2,868 hits, 558 doubles and 187 triples. Released by the Pirates in December 1940, Waner bounced from the Brooklyn Dodgers to the Boston Braves to the New York Yankees during his final five seasons. He gained entrance to the Hall of Fame in 1952, his sixth year on the ballot; brother Lloyd joined him as a Veterans Committee selection in '67.

PAUL GLEE WANER
(BIG POISON)
PITTSBURGH-BROOKLYN-BOSTON,N.L.
NEW YORK,A.L.
1926-1945
LEFT HANDED HITTING OUTFIELDER BATTED
.300 OR BETTER 14 TIMES IN NATIONAL
LEAGUE.ONE OF SEVEN PLAYERS EVER TO
COMPILE 3,000 OR MORE HITS. SET MODERN
N.L.RECORD BY COLLECTING 200 OR MORE
HITS EIGHT SEASONS.MOST VALUABLE PLAYER
IN 1927 AND FOUR TIMES SELECTED FOR
ALL STAR GAME.

Big Poison

Elected To The Hall Of Fame: *1952.*
Born: *Apr.16, 1903 in Harrah, Okla.*
Died: *Aug. 29, 1965 in Sarasota, Flor.*
Height: *5-8.* **Weight:** *153.*
Threw: *Left.* **Batted:** *Left.*
Debut: *Apr. 13, 1926.*
Final Game: *Apr. 26, 1945.*
Teams: *Pittsburgh N.L. 1926-1940;*
Brooklyn N.L. 1941, 1943-1944; Boston
N.L. 1941-1942; New York A.L. 1944-1945.
Postseason: *N.L. Pennant (1927).*
Awards: *4-Time All-Star (1933-1935,*
1937); N.L. Most Valuable Player (1927).

YEAR	TEAM	LEAGUE	G	AB	R	H	2B	3B	HR	RBI	SB	AVG
1926	PITTSBURGH	NL	144	536	101	180	35	22	8	79	11	.336
1927	PITTSBURGH	NL	155	623	114	237	42	18	9	131	5	.380
1928	PITTSBURGH	NL	152	602	142	223	50	19	6	86	6	.370
1929	PITTSBURGH	NL	151	596	131	200	43	15	15	100	15	.336
1930	PITTSBURGH	NL	145	589	117	217	32	18	8	77	18	.368
1931	PITTSBURGH	NL	150	559	88	180	35	10	6	70	6	.322
1932	PITTSBURGH	NL	154	630	107	215	62	10	8	82	13	.341
1933	PITTSBURGH	NL	154	618	101	191	38	16	7	70	3	.309
1934	PITTSBURGH	NL	146	599	122	217	32	16	14	90	8	.362
1935	PITTSBURGH	NL	139	549	98	176	29	12	11	78	2	.321
1936	PITTSBURGH	NL	148	585	107	218	53	9	5	94	7	.373
1937	PITTSBURGH	NL	154	619	94	219	30	9	2	74	4	.354
1938	PITTSBURGH	NL	148	625	77	175	31	6	6	69	2	.280
1939	PITTSBURGH	NL	125	461	62	151	30	6	3	45	0	.328
1940	PITTSBURGH	NL	89	238	32	69	16	1	1	32	0	.290
1941	BROOKLYN/BOSTON	NL	106	329	45	88	10	2	2	50	1	.267
1942	BOSTON	NL	114	333	43	86	17	1	1	39	2	.258
1943	BROOKLYN	NL	82	225	29	70	16	0	1	26	0	.311
1944	BROOKLYN/NEW YORK	NL/AL	92	143	17	40	4	1	0	17	1	.280
1945	NEW YORK	AL	1	0	0	0	0	0	0	0	0	—
CAREER TOTALS			2549	9459	1627	3152	605	191	113	1309	104	.333

JOHN M. WARD

"Players have been bought, sold and exchanged as though they were sheep instead of American citizens." – John Montgomery Ward said.

Ward was a bright child who attended Penn State University at the age of 13. But tragedy struck the following year, when both of Ward's parents died and he was forced to quit school and support himself. He tried to make it as a traveling salesman, but quit after two weeks and discovered baseball.

He played on semipro teams for a few years and did odd jobs on the side before his big break came with the Providence Grays in 1878. That year, as an 18-year-old pitcher, he led the National League with a 1.51 ERA on his way to a 22-13 season over 37 starts and 334 innings. In 1880, Ward was the second pitcher in baseball history to throw a perfect game.

Babe Ruth wasn't the only Hall of Famer that was known for pitching and hitting. Ward was a pitcher and outfielder for his first seven seasons before a nagging arm injury forced a move over to shortstop and second base for the next 11 years.

Ward acted as a player-manager, managing parts of seven seasons. He attended law school in the offseason and earned a law degree from Columbia in 1885 and a political science degree in 1886.

He put the degrees to good use by fighting for players' rights and set up the first-ever players union in 1885, challenging the player reserve clause, which bound players to one team for long periods of time. In 1887, he reportedly talked Giants owner John Day into signing Negro League pitcher George Stovey, but when other owners and players complained, Day backed off.

Ward retired from baseball at age 34 to continue with his legal career. He represented baseball players against the National League and later acted as president of the Boston Braves franchise. He died in 1925 and was elected to the Hall of Fame by the Veterans Committee in 1964.

JOHN MONTGOMERY WARD
1878 – 1894
PITCHING PIONEER WHO WON 158,
LOST 102 GAMES IN SEVEN YEARS.
PITCHED PERFECT GAME FOR PROVIDENCE
OF N. L. IN 1880.
TURNED TO SHORTSTOP AND MADE 2,151 HITS.
MANAGED NEW YORK AND BROOKLYN IN N.L.
PRESIDENT OF BOSTON, N. L. 1911-1912.
PLAYED IMPORTANT PART IN ESTABLISHING
MODERN ORGANIZED BASEBALL.

Elected To The Hall Of Fame: *1964.*
Born: *Mar. 3, 1860 in Bellefonte, Pa.*
Died: *Mar. 4, 1925 in Augusta, Ga.*
Height: *5-9.* **Weight:** *165.*
Threw: *Right.* **Batted:** *Left.*
Debut: *July 15, 1878.*
Final Game: *Sept. 29, 1894.*
Teams: *Providence N.L. 1878-1882; New York N.L. 1883-1889, 1893-1894; Brooklyn, Player's League 1890; Brooklyn N.L. 1891-1892.*
Postseason: *2-Time World Champions (1888-1889); 2 N.L. Pennants (1888-1889).*

YEAR	TEAM	LEAGUE	G	AB	R	H	2B	3B	HR	RBI	SB	AVG
1878	PROVIDENCE	NL	37	138	14	27	5	4	1	15	0	.196
1879	PROVIDENCE	NL	83	364	71	104	9	4	2	41	0	.286
1880	PROVIDENCE	NL	86	356	53	81	12	2	0	27	0	.228
1881	PROVIDENCE	NL	85	357	56	87	18	6	0	53	0	.244
1882	PROVIDENCE	NL	83	355	58	87	10	3	1	39	0	.245
1883	NEW YORK	NL	88	380	76	97	18	7	7	54	0	.255
1884	NEW YORK	NL	113	482	98	122	11	8	2	51	0	.253
1885	NEW YORK	NL	111	446	72	101	8	9	0	37	0	.226
1886	NEW YORK	NL	122	491	82	134	17	5	2	81	36	.273
1887	NEW YORK	NL	129	545	114	184	16	5	1	53	111	.338
1888	NEW YORK	NL	122	510	70	128	14	5	2	49	38	.251
1889	NEW YORK	NL	114	479	87	143	13	4	1	67	62	.299
1890	BROOKLYN	PL	128	561	134	188	15	12	4	60	63	.335
1891	BROOKLYN	NL	105	441	85	122	13	5	0	39	57	.277
1892	BROOKLYN	NL	148	614	109	163	13	3	1	47	88	.265
1893	NEW YORK	NL	135	588	129	193	27	9	2	77	46	.328
1894	NEW YORK	NL	138	549	102	146	12	5	0	79	39	.266
CAREER TOTALS			**1827**	**7656**	**1410**	**2107**	**231**	**96**	**26**	**869**	**540**	**.275**

MICKEY WELCH

M ichael "Mickey" Welch became the third pitcher in baseball history to reach 300 wins on July 28, 1890 against Pittsburgh. The only two hurlers that preceded him were Pud Galvin and Timothy Keefe.

The right-hander relied on an assortment of off-speed pitches to keep him effective on the mound, and taking time to understand the players he was throwing to. "I studied the hitters and I knew how to pitch to all of them," Welch said. "I had a pretty good fastball, but I depended chiefly on a change of pace and an assortment of curveballs."

Over his first big league season with the Troy Haymakers in 1880, Welch went 34-30 and threw a total of 574 innings. When the franchise moved to New York in 1883, he pitched the first game in the original Polo Grounds in New York City. Welch also played 38 games in the outfield that season.

In 1884, Welch completed 62 of his 65 starts, winning 39 games and fanning a career-high 345 batters. On Aug. 28, 1884, he struck out the first nine Cleveland Blues batters he faced, a record that has yet to be matched in the major leagues.

He was able to utilize his array of pitches en route to becoming a nine-time 20-plus game winner. His best season was in 1885 when he won 44 games, including seven shut-outs. From July 18 to Sept. 4 of that year, Welch notched 17 consecutive victories with four shutouts and five one-run games. He completed each of the 55 games he started that year and posted a 1.66 ERA.

Teamed up with Keefe, the pair won 76 games for the New York Giants during the 1885 season. Keefe was the only pitcher in the league to have a better ERA than Welch, at 1.58. Together, the duo was responsible for 61 of New York's wins in 1888, bringing their team to its first pennant. The Giants were once again league champions when Welch went 27-12 in 1889.

Welch recorded 41 shutouts in his career, and he remains among the baseball leaders in complete games with 525 and in innings with 4,802. Not only was he effective on the mound, but Welch also hit for decent numbers as a pitcher. He had 492 career hits, and 93 of them were doubles. Welch was also the first ever major league pinch hitter. On Aug. 10, 1889, he batted for teammate Hank O'Day in the bottom of the fifth inning.

MICHAEL FRANCIS WELCH
"SMILING MICKEY"
TROY N.L. 1880·1882
NEW YORK N.L. 1883·1892
CREDITED WITH MORE THAN 300 VICTORIES
DURING 13 SEASONS IN MAJORS. WON 17
GAMES IN A ROW IN 1885 WHILE COMPILING
44·11 RECORD FOR LEAGUE·LEADING .800
WINNING PERCENTAGE. TOPPED 30·VICTORY
TOTAL IN FOUR YEARS.

Smiling Mickey

Elected To The Hall Of Fame: 1973.
Born: July 4, 1859 in Brooklyn, N.Y.
Died: July 30, 1941 in Concord, N.H.
Height: 5-8. **Weight:** 160.
Threw: Right. **Batted:** Right.
Debut: May 1, 1880.
Final Game: May 17, 1892.
Teams: Troy N.L. 1880-1882; New York N.L. 1883-1892.
Postseason: 2-Time World Champions (1888-1889); 2 N.L. Pennants (1888-1889).

YEAR	TEAM	LEAGUE	G	W	L	SV	SH	IP	H	BB	SO	ERA
1880	TROY	NL	65	34	30	0	4	574	575	80	123	2.54
1881	TROY	NL	40	21	18	0	4	368	371	78	104	2.67
1882	TROY	NL	33	14	16	0	5	281	334	62	53	3.46
1883	NEW YORK	NL	54	25	23	0	4	426	431	66	144	2.73
1884	NEW YORK	NL	65	39	21	0	4	557.3	528	146	345	2.50
1885	NEW YORK	NL	56	44	11	1	7	492	372	131	258	1.66
1886	NEW YORK	NL	59	33	22	0	1	500	514	163	272	2.99
1887	NEW YORK	NL	41	22	15	0	2	346	339	91	115	3.36
1888	NEW YORK	NL	47	26	19	0	5	425.3	328	108	167	1.93
1889	NEW YORK	NL	45	27	12	2	3	375	340	149	125	3.02
1890	NEW YORK	NL	37	17	14	0	2	292.3	268	122	97	2.99
1891	NEW YORK	NL	22	5	9	1	0	160	177	97	46	4.28
1892	NEW YORK	NL	1	0	0	0	0	5	11	4	1	14.40
CAREER TOTALS			**565**	**307**	**210**	**4**	**41**	**4802**	**4588**	**1297**	**1850**	**2.71**

WILLIE WELLS

The only woman elected to the National Baseball Hall of Fame, Effa Manley, called Willie Wells "The finest shortstop, black or white." Wells played in an era where the color of his skin kept him out of the Major Leagues, but Wells had a very successful career in baseball's Negro leagues and Canada, as well as Mexico and Cuba where he played against white major leaguers. It was during his time in Mexico that he was christened with the nickname "El Diablo." Because of his unbelievable play at the shortstop position the players in the Mexican League began to say "don't hit it to shortstop because 'El Diablo' plays there." Cool Papa Bell recalled "The shortstops I've seen, Wells could cover ground better than any of them. Willie Wells was the greatest shortstop in the world"

During his 20-plus year career on the diamond, Wells was the epitome of a "five-tool player." He could hit for average and power, run and was a tremendous defensive shortstop with an accurate arm. Tigers Hall of Fame second baseman Charlie Gehringer called him "the kind of player you always wanted on your team, he played the way all great players play – with everything he had."

Wells was selected to play in the annual East-West All-Star Game eight times, despite the fact that the game didn't begin until 1933, and Wells had already played nine full seasons of pro ball. He also led the Chicago American Giants to back-to-back pennants in two different leagues, capturing the Negro Southern League title in 1932 and then the inaugural pennant of the new Negro National League the following season. Wells was also part of the Newark Eagles famed "million dollar infield" in the late 1930s alongside future Hall of Famers Mule Suttles and Ray Dandridge.

Wells was also a mentor to younger players, including Jackie Robinson and Monte Irvin. Irvin recalled, "Wells showed me everything he knew. We talked about hitting – he was a really good curve ball hitter – about moving around on different pitchers, especially left-handers, moving up in the box, moving back, trying to throw the pitcher off, trying to take a peek back to see how the catcher is holding his target in a close game."

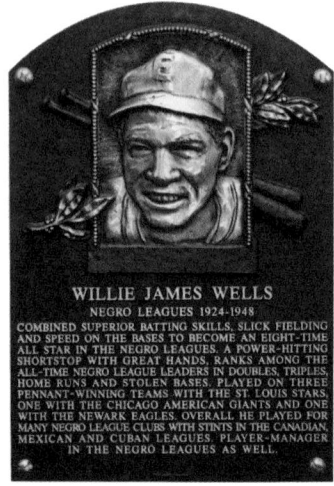

WILLIE JAMES WELLS
NEGRO LEAGUES 1924-1948
COMBINED SUPERIOR BATTING SKILLS, SLICK FIELDING AND SPEED ON THE BASES TO BECOME AN EIGHT-TIME ALL STAR IN THE NEGRO LEAGUES. A POWER-HITTING SHORTSTOP WITH GREAT HANDS, RANKS AMONG THE ALL-TIME NEGRO LEAGUE LEADERS IN DOUBLES, TRIPLES, HOME RUNS AND STOLEN BASES. PLAYED ON THREE PENNANT-WINNING TEAMS WITH THE ST. LOUIS STARS, ONE WITH THE CHICAGO AMERICAN GIANTS AND ONE WITH THE NEWARK EAGLES. OVERALL, HE PLAYED FOR MANY NEGRO LEAGUE CLUBS WITH STINTS IN THE CANADIAN, MEXICAN AND CUBAN LEAGUES. PLAYER-MANAGER IN THE NEGRO LEAGUES AS WELL.

El Diablo

Elected To The Hall Of Fame: *1997.*
Born: *Aug. 10, 1905 in Austin, Texas.*
Died: *Jan. 22, 1989 in Austin, Texas.*
Height: *5-8.* **Weight:** *160.*
Threw: *Right.* **Batted:** *Right.*
Teams: *Negro Leagues 1924-1948. St. Louis 1924-1931; Chicago 1929, 1933-1935; Kansas City 1932; Detroit 1932; Homestead 1932, 1937; Newark 1936-1939, 1942, 1945; Birmingham 1941; New York 1945-1946; Baltimore 1946; Indianapolis 1947; Memphis 1948.*

YEAR	TEAM	LEAGUE	G	AB	R	H	2B	3B	HR	RBI	SB	AVG
1924	ST. LOUIS	NNL	—	151	24	44	12	3	1	—	0	.291
1925	ST. LOUIS	NNL	—	270	60	75	14	7	6	—	8	.278
1926	ST. LOUIS	NNL	—	183	35	60	11	3	7	—	3	.328
1927	ST. LOUIS	NNL	—	239	53	81	15	1	16	—	3	.339
1928	ST. LOUIS	NNL	—	326	84	119	28	6	23	—	14	.365
1929	ST. LOUIS/CHI.	NNL	—	261	73	93	13	7	19	—	18	.356
1930	ST. LOUIS	NNL	—	181	60	76	18	0	10	—	7	.420
1931	ST. LOUIS	NNL	—	35	6	12	2	1	0	—	3	.343
1932	KANSAS CITY/DETROIT/HOMESTEAD	IND./EWL/EWL	—	144	24	39	5	5	2	—	2	.271
1933	CHICAGO	NNL	—	100	21	30	2	1	1	—	5	.300
1934	CHICAGO	NNL	—	146	22	29	6	3	0	—	6	.199
1935	CHICAGO	NNL	—	146	44	52	10	3	4	—	11	.356
1936	NEWARK	NNL	—	45	11	12	0	0	2	—	0	.267
1937	NEWARK)/HOMESTEAD	NNL/NNL	—	93	23	27	1	1	2	—	2	.290
1938	NEWARK	NNL	—	96	15	28	3	3	2	—	1	.292
1939	NEWARK	NNL	—	59	13	11	1	0	1	—	2	.186
1941	BIRMINGHAM	NAL	—	1	0	0	0	0	0	—	0	.000
1942	NEWARK	NNL	—	127	31	48	10	0	3	—	3	.378
1945	NEWARK/N.Y	NNL	—	67	10	19	6	0	0	—	1	.284
1946	BALTIMORE/N.Y.	NNL	—	135	14	40	7	1	1	—	1	.296
1947	INDIANAPOLIS	NAL	—	11	1	5	0	1	0	—	0	.455
1948	MEMPHIS	NAL	—	8	5	5	2	1	0	—	0	.625
CAREER TOTALS			—	**2824**	**629**	**905**	**166**	**47**	**100**	—	**90**	**.320**

ZACK WHEAT

"One of the grandest guys ever to wear a baseball uniform, one of the greatest batting teachers I have ever seen, one of the truest pals a man ever had and one of the kindliest men God ever created," Casey Stengel said of Wheat.

After growing up in Missouri, Wheat made his major league debut in 1909. He played 19 season in the major leagues, 18 of which came with Brooklyn, though he finished his career in 1927 with the Philadelphia Athletics, a team that featured six other eventual Hall of Famers.

At 5-foot-10 and 170 pounds, Wheat batted left-handed and threw right-handed. The outfielder hit over .300 14 times in his career, led the National League in batting in 1918, and finished with a .317 career batting average. He was also known for being a graceful outfielder with a strong arm.

Wheat's Brooklyn teams were mostly bad, but he did play in two World Series in 1916 and 1920, though his team lost both of them. Wheat, who was nicknamed "Buck," spent the first part of his career in the dead-ball era and his best season during that timeframe was in 1914, when he hit .319/.377/.452 with 26 doubles, 9 triples and 9 home runs. He finished ninth in the MVP voting that year. Zack got to play with his younger brother, Mack, from 1915 to 1919. Wheat was elected to the Hall of Fame by the Veteran's Committee in 1959 and passed away in 1972.

"The idea of being in the Hall of Fame still hasn't sunk in," Wheat said after learning of his induction. "I wonder if I would have been any good with the live ball today." Once described as "170 pounds of scrap iron, rawhide and guts," Wheat was a model of consistency during a 19-year career, spent mostly with the Brooklyn clubs of the National League. Wheat's soft-spoken demeanor off the field belied a competitive fierceness on the diamond. Considered an intelligent ballplayer with impressive defensive skills, Wheat vexed his opponents the most with line-drive hitting, which netted 2,884 career hits. Beloved by the fans in Brooklyn, Wheat was remembered by Casey Stengel as "the only great ballplayer who was never booed."

Elected To The Hall Of Fame: 1959.
Born: May 23, 1888 in Hamilton, Mo.
Died: Mar. 11, 1972 in Sedalia, Mo.
Height: 5-10. **Weight:** 170.
Threw: Right. **Batted:** Left.
Debut: Sept. 11, 1909.
Final Game: Sept. 21, 1927.
Teams: Brooklyn N.L. 1909-1926; Philadelphia A.L. 1927.
Postseason: 2 N.L. Pennants (1916, 1920).

YEAR	TEAM	LEAGUE	G	AB	R	H	2B	3B	HR	RBI	SB	AVG
1909	BROOKLYN	NL	26	102	15	31	7	3	0	4	1	.304
1910	BROOKLYN	NL	156	606	78	172	36	15	2	55	16	.284
1911	BROOKLYN	NL	140	534	55	153	26	13	5	76	21	.287
1912	BROOKLYN	NL	123	453	70	138	28	7	8	65	16	.305
1913	BROOKLYN	NL	138	535	64	161	28	10	7	58	19	.301
1914	BROOKLYN	NL	145	533	66	170	26	9	9	89	20	.319
1915	BROOKLYN	NL	146	528	64	136	15	12	5	66	21	.258
1916	BROOKLYN	NL	149	568	76	177	32	13	9	73	19	.312
1917	BROOKLYN	NL	109	362	38	113	15	11	1	41	5	.312
1918	BROOKLYN	NL	105	409	39	137	15	3	0	51	9	.335
1919	BROOKLYN	NL	137	536	70	159	23	11	5	62	15	.297
1920	BROOKLYN	NL	148	583	89	191	26	13	9	73	8	.328
1921	BROOKLYN	NL	148	568	91	182	31	10	14	85	11	.320
1922	BROOKLYN	NL	152	600	92	201	29	12	16	112	9	.335
1923	BROOKLYN	NL	98	349	63	131	13	5	8	65	3	.375
1924	BROOKLYN	NL	141	566	92	212	41	8	14	97	3	.375
1925	BROOKLYN	NL	150	616	125	221	42	14	14	103	3	.359
1926	BROOKLYN	NL	111	411	68	119	31	2	5	35	4	.290
1927	PHILADELPHIA	AL	88	247	34	80	12	1	1	38	2	.324
CAREER TOTALS			**2410**	**9106**	**1289**	**2884**	**476**	**172**	**132**	**1248**	**205**	**.317**

DEACON WHITE

Deacon White stopped playing big league baseball in the 19th Century. But his accomplishments still shine bright on the National Pastime – and now in Cooperstown as a member of the Hall of Fame.

Born Dec. 7, 1847, James Laurie White played for Forest City of Cleveland (1871-1872), the Red Stockings of Boston (National Association 1873-1875, National League 1877), Chicago White Stockings (1876), Cincinnati Red Stockings (1878-1880), Buffalo Bisons (National League 1881-1885, Players' League 1890), Detroit Wolverines (1886-1888) and Pittsburgh Pirates (1889).

At one time in White's professional career, he played all nine positions on the field, including two appearances pitching. He primarily played third base and catcher and is considered one of the best barehanded catchers of his time.

White was a standout catcher in a catcher-important era. Catchers did not use any equipment and were positioned much farther back from the pitcher than in modern baseball. Just catching the ball was considered an advantage, but White could catch and throw runners out.

White was 42 during his last season and had been the oldest player in the league for his last four seasons. He was also one of the first ever players to be voted an MVP and earned the honor in 1875 when his Red Stockings went 71-8.

At the end of his career, White had a career batting average of .312, 2,067 hits in just 1,560 games and 988 RBIs. He led his league in batting average twice and RBI three times.

White becomes the oldest player elected to the Hall of Fame – having a birthday that predates any other player enshrined in Cooperstown.

JAMES LAURIE WHITE
"DEACON"

Elected To The Hall of Fame: 2013
Born: Dec. 7, 1847 at Caton, NY
Died: July 7, 1939 at Aurora, IL
Height: 5-11. **Weight:** 175
Threw: Right. **Batted:** Left
Debut: May 4, 1871
Final Game: Oct. 4, 1890
Teams: Cleveland N.A. 1871-72; Boston N.A. 1873-75; Chicago N.L. 1876; Boston N.L. 1877; Cincinnati N.L. 1878-80; Buffalo N.L. 1881-85; Detroit N.L. 1886-88; Pittsburgh N.L. 1889; Buffalo P.L. 1890
Postseason: World Series championship 1887

YEAR	TEAM	LEAGUE	G	AB	R	H	2B	3B	HR	RBI	SB	BA
1871	CLEVELAND	NA	29	146	40	47	6	5	1	21	2	.322
1872	CLEVELAND	NA	22	109	21	37	2	2	0	22	0	.339
1873	BOSTON	NA	60	311	79	122	17	8	1	77	19	.392
1874	BOSTON	NA	70	352	75	106	5	7	3	52	1	.301
1875	BOSTON	NA	80	371	76	136	23	3	1	60	2	.367
1876	CHICAGO	NL	66	303	66	104	18	1	1	60		.343
1877	BOSTON	NL	59	266	51	103	14	11	2	49		.387
1878	CINCINNATI	NL	61	258	41	81	4	1	0	29		.314
1879	CINCINNATI	NL	78	333	55	110	16	6	1	52		.330
1880	CINCINNATI	NL	35	141	21	42	4	2	0	7		.298
1881	BUFFALO	NL	78	319	58	99	24	4	0	53		.310
1882	BUFFALO	NL	83	337	51	95	17	0	1	33		.282
1883	BUFFALO	NL	94	391	62	114	14	5	0	47		.292
1884	BUFFALO	NL	110	452	82	147	16	11	5	74		.325
1885	BUFFALO	NL	98	404	54	118	6	6	0	57		.292
1886	DETROIT	NL	124	491	65	142	19	5	1	76	9	.289
1887	DETROIT	NL	111	449	71	136	20	11	3	75	20	.303
1888	DETROIT	NL	125	527	75	157	22	5	4	71	12	.298
1889	PITTSBURGH	NL	55	225	35	57	10	1	0	26	2	.253
1890	BUFFALO	PL	122	439	62	114	13	4	0	47	3	.260
20 YRS	**20 YRS**	**20 YRS**	**1560**	**6624**	**1140**	**2067**	**270**	**98**	**24**	**988**	**70**	**.312**

HOYT WILHELM

"I got to messing with the (knuckleball) in high school," Hoyt Wilhelm said. "I started to see that the ball was doing something. I figured it was my only ticket to the big leagues, 'cause I couldn't throw hard, and I knew if I was going to play ball, I'd have to make it some other way."

There was nothing usual about Wilhelm's path to the Hall of Fame. For one, he spent most of his big league career coming out of the bullpen, becoming the first reliever ever enshrined. For another, he didn't make his major league debut until he was 29 years old, and he pitched until he was nearly 50. Finally, he didn't blaze his way to Cooperstown with overpowering fastballs or knee-bending curveballs, instead relying almost exclusively on his darting, unpredictable knuckleball.

Wilhelm's big league career nearly ended before it began. While serving in the Army during World War II, shrapnel from a German artillery blast struck Wilhelm in the back and right hand. He received the Purple Heart for his actions and he would pitch his entire career with that piece of metal still lodged in his back. Wilhelm spent seven seasons in the minors before getting to the majors with the New York Giants in 1952. He'd been a starter in several seasons during his minor league career, but Giants manager Leo Durocher moved him to the bullpen. All Wilhelm did was lead the National League in ERA and appearances as a rookie.

A few years later, Orioles manager Paul Richards gave Wilhelm the chance to be starter again after he came over from the Indians in August 1958. In just his third start for Baltimore, Wilhelm threw a no-hitter against the Yankees on Sept. 20, striking out eight. He remained in the Orioles rotation in 1959 and won the AL's ERA title, though he moved back to the bullpen again the following season. Wilhelm settled in as the premier relief pitcher in an era dominated by pitching. He posted ERAs under 2.00 in five consecutive seasons from 1964-68 with the White Sox, doing all of it after his 40th birthday.

Elected To The Hall Of Fame: 1985.

Born: July 26, 1922 in Huntersville, N.C.

Died: Aug. 23, 2002 in Sarasota, Flor.

Height: 6-0. **Weight:** 190.

Threw: Right. **Batted:** Right.

Debut: Apr. 18, 1952.

Final Game: July 10, 1972.

Teams: New York N.L. 1952-1956; St. Louis N.L. 1957; Cleveland A.L. 1957-1958; Baltimore A.L. 1958-1962; Chicago A.L. 1963-1968; California A.L. 1969; Atlanta N.L. 1969-1970, 1971; Chicago N.L. 1970; Los Angeles N.L. 1971-1972.

Postseason: World Series Champion (1954): N.L. Pennant (1954).

Awards: 8-Time All-Star (1953, 1959, 1961-1962, 1970).

YEAR	TEAM	LEAGUE	G	W	L	SV	SH	IP	H	BB	SO	ERA
1952	NEW YORK	NL	71	15	3	11	0	159.3	127	57	108	2.43
1953	NEW YORK	NL	68	7	8	15	0	145	127	77	71	3.04
1954	NEW YORK	NL	57	12	4	7	0	111.3	77	52	64	2.10
1955	NEW YORK	NL	59	4	1	0	0	103	104	40	71	3.93
1956	NEW YORK	NL	64	4	9	8	0	89.3	97	43	71	3.83
1957	ST. LOUIS/CLEVELAND	NL/AL	42	2	4	12	0	58.7	54	22	29	4.14
1958	CLEVELAND/BALTIMORE	AL	39	3	10	5	1	131	95	45	92	2.34
1959	BALTIMORE	AL	32	15	11	0	3	226	178	77	139	2.19
1960	BALTIMORE	AL	41	11	8	7	1	147	125	39	107	3.31
1961	BALTIMORE	AL	51	9	7	18	0	109.7	89	41	87	2.30
1962	BALTIMORE	AL	52	7	10	15	0	93	64	34	90	1.94
1963	CHICAGO	AL	55	5	8	21	0	136.3	106	30	111	2.64
1964	CHICAGO	AL	73	12	9	27	0	131.3	94	30	95	1.99
1965	CHICAGO	AL	66	7	7	20	0	144	88	32	106	1.81
1966	CHICAGO	AL	46	5	2	6	0	81.3	50	17	61	1.66
1967	CHICAGO	AL	49	8	3	12	0	89	58	34	76	1.31
1968	CHICAGO	AL	72	4	4	12	0	93.7	69	24	72	1.73
1969	CALIFORNIA/ATLANTA	NL	52	7	7	14	0	78	50	22	67	2.19
1970	ATLANTA/CHICAGO	NL	53	6	5	13	0	82	73	42	68	3.40
1971	ATLANTA/CHICAGO	NL	12	0	1	3	0	20	12	5	16	2.70
1972	LOS ANGELES	NL	16	0	1	1	0	25.3	20	15	9	4.62
CAREER TOTALS			**1070**	**143**	**122**	**227**	**5**	**2254.1**	**1757**	**778**	**1610**	**2.52**

BILLY WILLIAMS

The first line of text on Billy Williams' National Baseball Hall of Fame plaque may sum up the long-time Chicago Cubs leftfielder the best: "Soft-spoken, clutch performer was one of the most respected hitters of his day."

Over an 18-season big league career (1959-76), 16 spent with the Cubs, Williams had 2,711 hits, a .290 batting average, 426 home runs, hit 20 or more home runs 13 straight seasons, and once held the National League record for consecutive games played with 1,117.

"Billy Williams is the best hitter, day-in and day-out, that I have ever seen," said longtime Cubs teammate Don Kessinger. "He's unbelievable. He didn't hit for just one or two days, or one or two weeks. He hit all the time."

But even in his autobiography, Williams acknowledged the perception of his career, writing, "People say I'm not an exciting player. I go out there and catch the ball and hit the ball and play the game like it should be played."

A longtime opponent, Joe Torre, explained, "He leads his club with his bat and just the way he plays. I think he knows if he blows his stack, he might affect a lot of the young kids, and Billy feels that kind of responsibility to his teammates, and it carries over."

Fellow Hall of Famer Lou Boudreau, a longtime Cubs broadcaster, said, "If he's worried, he never shows it. It helps him mentally at the plate. I don't think he allows outside matters to affect him once that game gets underway."

Though Williams may have been overshadowed, he was not unrecognized, with six All-Star Game selections, the NL Rookie of the Year Award in 1961, and *The Sporting News* player of the year in 1972, when he led the league with a .333 batting average while also hitting 37 home runs and driving in 122 runs.

"The leader of the Cubs is, of all people, the quiet man of the clubhouse, Billy Williams," wrote Chicago sports columnist Bill Gleason. "Billy Williams, who seldom speaks in a voice that can be heard beyond his own cubicle, who wouldn't say 'Rah! Rah!' if (Cubs owner) Phil Wrigley promised him a $10,000 bonus for each 'Rah!' is the man to whom the Cubs look for leadership."

BILLY LEO WILLIAMS
CHICAGO, N.L., 1959 - 1974
OAKLAND, A.L., 1975 - 1976
SOFT-SPOKEN, CLUTCH PERFORMER WAS ONE OF MOST RESPECTED HITTERS OF HIS DAY. BATTED SOLID .290 OVER 18 SEASONS SOCKING 426 HOME RUNS. HIT 20 OR MORE HOMERS 13 STRAIGHT SEASONS. 1961 N.L. ROOKIE OF YEAR. 1972 N.L. BATTING CHAMPION WITH .333. HELD N.L. RECORD FOR CONSECUTIVE GAMES PLAYED WITH 1117.

Elected To The Hall Of Fame: *1987.*
Born: *June 15, 1938 in Whistler, Ala.*
Height: *6-1.* **Weight:** *175.*
Threw: *Right.* **Batted:** *Left.*
Debut: *Aug. 6, 1959.*
Final Game: *Oct. 2, 1976.*
Teams: *Chicago N.L. 1959-1974;*
Oakland A.L. 1975-1976.
Postseason: *Playoff Qualifier (1975).*
Awards: *6-Time All-Star (1962, 1964-1965, 1968, 1972-1973); N.L. Rookie of the Year (1961).*

YEAR	TEAM	LEAGUE	G	AB	R	H	2B	3B	HR	RBI	SB	AVG
1959	CHICAGO	NL	18	33	0	5	0	1	0	2	0	.152
1960	CHICAGO	NL	12	47	4	13	0	2	2	7	0	.277
1961	CHICAGO	NL	146	529	75	147	20	7	25	86	6	.278
1962	CHICAGO	NL	159	618	94	184	22	8	22	91	9	.298
1963	CHICAGO	NL	161	612	87	175	36	9	25	95	7	.286
1964	CHICAGO	NL	162	645	100	201	39	2	33	98	10	.312
1965	CHICAGO	NL	164	645	115	203	39	6	34	108	10	.315
1966	CHICAGO	NL	162	648	100	179	23	5	29	91	6	.276
1967	CHICAGO	NL	162	634	92	176	21	12	28	84	6	.278
1968	CHICAGO	NL	163	642	91	185	30	8	30	98	4	.288
1969	CHICAGO	NL	163	642	103	188	33	10	21	95	3	.293
1970	CHICAGO	NL	161	636	137	205	34	4	42	129	7	.322
1971	CHICAGO	NL	157	594	86	179	27	5	28	93	7	.301
1972	CHICAGO	NL	150	574	95	191	34	6	37	122	3	.333
1973	CHICAGO	NL	156	576	72	166	22	2	20	86	4	.288
1974	CHICAGO	NL	117	404	55	113	22	0	16	68	4	.280
1975	OAKLAND	AL	155	520	68	127	20	1	23	81	0	.244
1976	OAKLAND	AL	120	351	36	74	12	0	11	41	4	.211
CAREER TOTALS			**2488**	**9350**	**1410**	**2711**	**434**	**88**	**426**	**1475**	**90**	**.290**

JOE WILLIAMS

JOSEPH WILLIAMS
"SMOKEY" "CYCLONE"
NEGRO LEAGUES, 1910 – 1932

A STAR PITCHER IN THE EARLY DAYS OF THE NEGRO LEAGUES. THE LANKY RIGHT-HANDER WITH THE SMOOTH, OVERHAND DELIVERY, WAS DESTINED FOR GREATNESS WITH HIS PINPOINT CONTROL, EFFECTIVE CHANGE OF PACE PITCH AND FASTBALL THAT TRAVELED WITH EXCEPTIONAL VELOCITY. PLAYING FOR SEVERAL TEAMS, THE NEW YORK LINCOLN GIANTS (1911–23) AND THE HOMESTEAD GRAYS (1925–32) WERE THE PRIMARY BENEFICIARIES OF HIS ACCOMPLISHMENTS. THE EASY-GOING TEXAN ROUTINELY REACHED DOUBLE-DIGITS IN STRIKEOUTS IN A GAME AND ON AUGUST 7, 1930, HE STRUCK OUT 27 MONARCHS IN A 12-INNING CONTEST. VOTED THE TOP PITCHER IN NEGRO LEAGUES HISTORY IN A 1952 POLL CONDUCTED BY THE PITTSBURGH COURIER.

"If you have ever witnessed the speed of a pebble in a storm you have not even then seen the equal of the speed possessed by this wonderful Texan Giant," wrote longtime Negro leagues owner Frank Leland of Smokey Joe Williams. "He is the King of all pitchers hailing from the Lone Star State and you have but to see him once to exclaim, 'That's a Plenty!'"

Williams was one of the most feared Negro Leagues pitchers in the first part of the 20th century, a tall Texan known for his fastball, smooth motion and great control. One of black baseball's great drawing cards, the talented right-hander with the broad shoulders would shine for more than two decades for a number of teams, including the Chicago American Giants, New York Lincoln Giants and Homestead Grays.

"Someone gave me a baseball at an early age and it was my companion for a long time. I carried it in my pocket and slept with it under my pillow," Williams once said. "I always wanted to pitch."

Once called "the mighty man of baseball," Williams excelled in a segregated game, but when given the opportunity he faced and was often victorious over the years against such big league stalwarts as Walter Johnson, Grover Cleveland Alexander, Chief Bender, Rube Marquard, Waite Hoyt, Jeff Tesreau, Eddie Rommel, Jesse Barnes and Rube Walberg.

"If I was going to pick a man to throw hard, I'd have to pick Joe Williams," said former Negro leagues pitcher Sam Streeter. "I'd pick him over all of them. They talk about Satchel (Paige) and them throwing hard, but I think Joe threw harder. It used to take two catchers to hold him. By the time the fifth inning was over, that catcher's hand would be like that, all swollen up. He'd have to have another catcher back there the rest of the game."

According to Williams, he learned to hold something back. "If I throw them really hard, they won't see them at all."

In one of his most oft-mentioned performances, Williams, in a 1930 game on a dimly lit field, struck out 27 Kansas City Monarchs while giving up a single hit in a 12-inning, 1-0 victory. The opposing pitcher, Chet Brewer, fanned 19.

Smokey

Elected To The Hall Of Fame: *1999.*
Born: *April 6, 1885 in Seguin, Texas.*
Died: *Feb. 25, 1951 in New York, N.Y.*
Height: *6-4.* **Weight:** *190.*
Threw: *Right.* **Batted:** *Right.*
Teams: *Negro Leagues 1910-1932;*
Habana 1911; Fe 1912; New York
1912, 1914-1921, 1923, 1925;
Homestead 1928-1930.

YEAR	TEAM	LEAGUE	G	W	L	SV	SH	IP	H	BB	SO	ERA
1911	HABANA	CUNL	21	10	7	—	0	155	117	66	80	3.08
1912	FE/NEW YORK	CUNL/CNCS	28	10	9	—	1	173.3	145	62	109	4.52
1914	NEW YORK	INDP	9	4	3	—	1	59.7	61	16	37	4.68
1915	NEW YORK	INDP	7	6	1	—	0	55.7	49	10	34	3.88
1916	NEW YORK	INDP	9	5	2	—	1	63.3	66	17	41	2.98
1917	NEW YORK	INDP	10	8	0	—	1	81	68	28	53	2.89
1918	NEW YORK	INDP	16	10	6	—	0	134.7	128	32	93	2.87
1919	NEW YORK	INDP	11	8	2	—	2	85.7	71	19	79	3.36
1920	NEW YORK	INDP	—	0	1	—	0	8	9	0	0	6.75
1921	NEW YORK	INDP	—	0	0	—	0	0.7	2	0	1	0.00
1923	NEW YORK	ECOL	—	3	5	—	0	64	59	1	27	6.75
1925	NEW YORK	ECOL	—	1	0	—	0	16.3	14	2	9	3.86
1928	HOMESTEAD	ECOL	—	3	1	—	0	22	16	2	12	1.64
1929	HOMESTEAD	ANL	—	3	4	—	0	69.3	78	13	38	4.41
1930	HOMESTEAD	INDP	—	6	5	—	1	86	63	15	66	3.77
CAREER TOTALS			**—**	**84**	**52**	**—**	**7**	**1186**	**1063**	**303**	**726**	**3.79**

TED WILLIAMS

Ted Williams always knew what he wanted. Others could debate who was the best all-around player in baseball history. Williams was a hitter. "All I want out of life is that when I walk down the street folks will say, 'There goes the greatest hitter that ever lived,'" Williams said.

Babe Ruth and Hank Aaron may have been better power hitters. You could argue that the graceful Joe DiMaggio or Willie Mays was a better all-around player. If you're talking about the greatest hitter that ever stepped into the batters box, the discussion begins with the long-time Red Sox left fielder. Williams wrote the book on hitting; his "The Science Of Hitting" disproves the adage that great hitters can't teach hitting. He won six batting titles, but that doesn't really explain his mastery at the plate. Thanks to an excellent batting eye, Williams led the American League in on-base percentage seven straight years and 12 times overall. His .482 career on-base percentage is the best of all time. And he wasn't just doing it with walks and singles. Williams led the AL in home runs four times, and his .634 career slugging percentage is second to only Ruth.

He did all of it despite missing most of five seasons due to military service. He learned to fly fighter planes during World War II, working as an instructor from 1943-1945. He was recalled to duty in 1952 during the Korean War, and he served in Korea for more than a year, flying combat missions in a Marine fighter jet. That missed time explains why the game's greatest hitter didn't reach 3,000 hits. After missing the all-star game as a rookie, Williams was an all-star in every non-military interrupted season of the rest of his career. In his final season, 1960, as a 41-year-old, he hit .316 with 29 home runs. His body may have been slowing down, but his ability to hit never left.

THEODORE SAMUEL WILLIAMS
"TED"
BOSTON RED SOX A.L. 1939 - 1960
BATTED .406 IN 1941. LED A.L. IN BATTING
6 TIMES; SLUGGING PERCENTAGE 9 TIMES;
TOTAL BASES 6 TIMES; RUNS SCORED 6 TIMES;
BASES ON BALLS 8 TIMES. TOTAL HITS 2654
INCLUDED 521 HOME RUNS. LIFETIME BATTING
AVERAGE .344; LIFETIME SLUGGING AVERAGE
.634. MOST VALUABLE A.L. PLAYER 1946 & 1949.
PLAYED IN 18 ALL STAR GAMES, NAMED PLAYER
OF THE DECADE 1951 - 1960.

The Splendid Splinter

Elected To The Hall Of Fame: 1966.

Born: Aug. 30, 1918 in San Diego, Calif.

Died: July 5, 2002 in Inverness, Flor.

Height: 6-3. **Weight:** 205.

Threw: Right. **Batted:** Left.

Debut: Apr. 20, 1939.

Final Game: Sept. 28, 1960.

Teams: Boston A.L. 1939-1942, 1946-1960.

Postseason: A.L. Pennant (1946).

Awards: 17-Time All-Star (1940-1942, 1946-1951, 1953-1960); 2-Time A.L. Most Valuable Player (1946, 1949).

YEAR	TEAM	LEAGUE	G	AB	R	H	2B	3B	HR	RBI	SB	AVG
1939	BOSTON	AL	149	565	131	185	44	11	31	145	2	.327
1940	BOSTON	AL	144	561	134	193	43	14	23	113	4	.344
1941	BOSTON	AL	143	456	135	185	33	3	37	120	2	.406
1942	BOSTON	AL	150	522	141	186	34	5	36	137	3	.356
1946	BOSTON	AL	150	514	142	176	37	8	38	123	0	.342
1947	BOSTON	AL	156	528	125	181	40	9	32	114	0	.343
1948	BOSTON	AL	137	509	124	188	44	3	25	127	4	.369
1949	BOSTON	AL	155	566	150	194	39	3	43	159	1	.343
1950	BOSTON	AL	89	334	82	106	24	1	28	97	3	.317
1951	BOSTON	AL	148	531	109	169	28	4	30	126	1	.318
1952	BOSTON	AL	6	10	2	4	0	1	1	3	0	.400
1953	BOSTON	AL	37	91	17	37	6	0	13	34	0	.407
1954	BOSTON	AL	117	386	93	133	23	1	29	89	0	.345
1955	BOSTON	AL	98	320	77	114	21	3	28	83	2	.356
1956	BOSTON	AL	136	400	71	138	28	2	24	82	0	.345
1957	BOSTON	AL	132	420	96	163	28	1	38	87	0	.388
1958	BOSTON	AL	129	411	81	135	23	2	26	85	1	.328
1959	BOSTON	AL	103	272	32	69	15	0	10	43	0	.254
1960	BOSTON	AL	113	310	56	98	15	0	29	72	1	.316
CAREER TOTALS			**2292**	**7706**	**1798**	**2654**	**525**	**71**	**521**	**1839**	**24**	**.344**

VIC WILLIS

Victor G. "Vic" Willis spent only 13 seasons in major league baseball, but he managed to notch 249 wins along the way. He also had 50 shutouts and a 2.63 lifetime ERA. Of the 471 games he started, he completed 388 of them.

His first season in the game was with the Boston Beaneaters in 1898. He won 25 games that year, and played an important role in helping his team win the pennant. Willis had his best season in 1899 when he had a 27-8 record, and posted a 2.50 ERA. He threw 342.2 innings for the Beaneaters, and led the National League with the fewest hits allowed per nine innings. He also had the only no-hitter of his career on August 7. Willis was the last pitcher to throw a no-hitter in the 19th century.

In 1901 the right-hander had a 20-17 record and finished fourth in the league in ERA. He also pitched more than 300 innings. The following season he completed a league-high 45 games, and he threw 410 innings, the fifth-highest total in modern major league history. He also led the league with 225 strikeouts. From 1903 to 1905, his ERA was 3.02, and twice he posted a mark of under 3.00. Willis had developed into the foundation of Boston's staff when he was traded to the Pirates following that stretch.

In Pittsburgh he averaged more than 22 wins per season and fewer than 12 losses, consistently pitching around 300 innings a year. He started his tenure with his new team with three straight shutouts to begin the 1906 season. During his four years with the Pirates, Willis went 89-46 with a 2.08 ERA, despite pitching for another team with offensive troubles. In 1909 Willis went 22-11, winning 11 straight games at one point during the season. He played a key role in the team's 110 total victories that season, helping the Pirates get to the Fall Classic and become World Series champions.

He had long fingers, which allowed him to throw a very unique and sharp curveball. Local media outlets penned Willis as almost impossible to hit.

The "Delaware Peach" won more than 20 games a total of eight times in his career. When Willis retired, he followed his love for the game and continued to participate in baseball, managing a semi-pro team and coaching at the youth and college level.

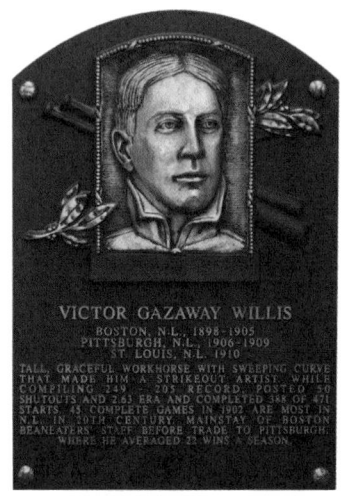

Elected To The Hall Of Fame: *1995.*

Born: *Apr. 12, 1876 in Cecil County, Md.*

Died: *Aug. 3, 1947 in Elkton, Md.*

Height: *6-2.* **Weight:** *185.*

Threw: *Right.* **Batted:** *Right.*

Debut: *Apr. 20, 1898.*

Final Game: *Sept. 5, 1910.*

Teams: *Boston N.L. 1898-1905;*
Pittsburgh N.L. 1906-1909; St. Louis
N.L. 1910.

Postseason: *World Series Champion*
(1909); N.L. Pennant (1909).

YEAR	TEAM	LEAGUE	G	W	L	SV	SH	IP	H	BB	SO	ERA
1898	BOSTON	NL	41	25	13	0	1	311	264	148	160	2.84
1899	BOSTON	NL	41	27	8	2	5	342.7	277	117	120	2.50
1900	BOSTON	NL	32	10	17	0	2	236	258	106	53	4.19
1901	BOSTON	NL	38	20	17	0	6	305.3	262	78	133	2.36
1902	BOSTON	NL	51	27	20	3	4	410	372	101	225	2.20
1903	BOSTON	NL	33	12	18	0	2	278	256	88	125	2.98
1904	BOSTON	NL	43	18	25	0	2	350	357	109	196	2.85
1905	BOSTON	NL	41	12	29	0	4	342	340	107	149	3.21
1906	PITTSBURGH	NL	41	23	13	1	6	322	295	76	124	1.73
1907	PITTSBURGH	NL	39	21	11	1	6	292.7	234	69	107	2.34
1908	PITTSBURGH	NL	41	23	11	0	7	304.7	239	69	97	2.07
1909	PITTSBURGH	NL	39	22	11	1	4	289.7	243	83	95	2.24
1910	ST. LOUIS	NL	33	9	12	3	1	212	224	61	67	3.35
CAREER TOTALS			**513**	**249**	**205**	**11**	**50**	**3996**	**3621**	**1212**	**1651**	**2.63**

HACK WILSON

LEWIS ROBERT WILSON
"HACK"
NEW YORK N.L., CHICAGO N.L.,
BROOKLYN N.L., PHILADELPHIA N.L.,
1923-1934
ESTABLISHED MAJOR LEAGUE RECORD OF 190
RUNS BATTED IN AND NATIONAL LEAGUE HIGH
OF 56 HOMERS IN 1930. LED OR TIED FOR N.L.
HOMER TITLE FOUR TIMES. COMPILED LIFETIME
.307 BATTING AVERAGE AND DROVE IN 100 OR
MORE RUNS SIX YEARS. HIT TWO HOMERS IN
INNING IN 1925 AND THREE IN GAME IN 1930.

L ewis R. "Hack" Wilson played in major league baseball for 12 seasons, finishing his career with a lifetime .307 average, 244 home runs and 1,063 RBIs.

Though his tenure in baseball was relatively short, he hit the ball well enough to be remembered. He captured four home run titles during his time with the Chicago Cubs. In 1929, he finished third in the league with 39, and he was just getting started.

One year later he had his best season and one of the greatest in major league history, launching 56 long balls, a National League record that stood for 68 years. He also notched 191 RBIs, still the all-time major league record, with a .356 batting average. In his season of highlights, he also had a .723 slugging percentage, and he walked 105 times.

His RBI record actually stood at 190 until later research found a run that had been attributed to Charlie Grimm actually belonged to Wilson, changing the record to 191. Wilson's RBI total puts him ahead of fellow Hall of Famers Lou Gehrig who had 184, Hank Greenberg with 183 and Jimmie Foxx who had 175. No player has gotten within 25 RBIs of his mark since 1938. Wilson also reached his mark in 1930 without ever hitting a grand slam.

Wilson drove in more than 100 runs in six of his 12 seasons, and though he is not widely remembered for his home run records, he led the league for three consecutive seasons. Though hitting 56 home runs in a season isn't as rare now as it once was, for more than 120 years, from 1876 to 1998, no National Leaguer outside of Wilson was able to it.

The center fielder had both 25- and 27-game hitting streaks in his career, and he once hit for the cycle. In 1927 he led the league's outfielders with 400 putouts.

Wilson lived the life of a popular athlete and made one of baseball's highest salaries during the years of the Depression.

Elected To The Hall Of Fame: *1979.*
Born: *Apr. 26, 1900 in Ellwood City, Pa.*
Died: *Nov. 23, 1948 in Baltimore, Md.*
Height: *5-6.* **Weight:** *190.*
Threw: *Right.* **Batted:** *Right.*
Debut: *Sept. 29, 1923.*
Final Game: *Aug. 25, 1934.*
Teams: *New York N.L. 1923-1925;*
Chicago N.L. 1926-1931; Brooklyn N.L.
1932-1934; Philadelphia N.L. 1934.
Postseason: *2 N.L. Pennants (1924,*
1929).

YEAR	TEAM	LEAGUE	G	AB	R	H	2B	3B	HR	RBI	SB	AVG
1923	NEW YORK	NL	3	10	0	2	0	0	0	0	0	.200
1924	NEW YORK	NL	107	383	62	113	19	12	10	57	4	.295
1925	NEW YORK	NL	62	180	28	43	7	4	6	30	5	.239
1926	CHICAGO	NL	142	529	97	170	36	8	21	109	10	.321
1927	CHICAGO	NL	146	551	119	175	30	12	30	129	13	.318
1928	CHICAGO	NL	145	520	89	163	32	9	31	120	4	.313
1929	CHICAGO	NL	150	574	135	198	30	5	39	159	3	.345
1930	CHICAGO	NL	155	585	146	208	35	6	56	191	3	.356
1931	CHICAGO	NL	112	395	66	103	22	4	13	61	1	.261
1932	BROOKLYN	NL	135	481	77	143	37	5	23	123	2	.297
1933	BROOKLYN	NL	117	360	41	96	13	2	9	54	7	.267
1934	BROOKLYN/PHILADELPHIA	NL	74	192	24	47	5	0	6	30	0	.245
CAREER TOTALS			**1348**	**4760**	**884**	**1461**	**266**	**67**	**244**	**1063**	**52**	**.307**

JUD WILSON

According to outfielder Ted Page, "Wilson was strong enough to go bear huntin' with a switch." None other than the great Satchel Paige considered him to be among the best hitters he ever faced, Ernest Judson Wilson was known throughout the Negro leagues as "Boojum" because of the sound of his hits bouncing off outfield walls. One article stated that he was "probably the hardest hitter Negro baseball has seen."

Quick-tempered and fearless, Wilson terrorized pitchers with his hitting and umpires with his reputation for arguing almost every call. He was wide-shouldered and short-legged, standing only 5-foot-8 inches tall, weighing 195 pounds, and batting left-handed, he played in both the American Negro leagues and the Cuban Winter League, following a stint with the U.S. Army during World War I.

From the early 1920s through the end of World War II, Wilson starred for some of the greatest teams in all of black baseball, including the Baltimore Black Sox, Homestead Grays, Pittsburgh Crawfords and Philadelphia Stars. He regularly batted over .300 and is considered to be among the top-five hitters for average in the Negro leagues. His career batting average is believed to be around .339 in the Negro leagues and above .370 in the winter leagues.

Wilson had adequate defensive skills at third base, often using his chest to stop hard-hit balls, and at bat, he would crowd the plate, thereby ensuring that he was often playing hurt. However, he was known for playing through the many injuries and for a fierce competitive drive that he used to incite teammates to work harder, and to drive opponents to distraction.

His numerous altercations with umpires and opponents ensured his reputation would precede him at every stop. There were no pitchers who wanted to face him and few umpires that wanted to call balls and strikes against him. Having played against all the great black pitchers, and many of the white stars in exhibition games, Wilson made it perfectly clear, he just did not like pitchers, regardless of their color.

ERNEST JUDSON WILSON
"JUD" "BOOJUM"
NEGRO LEAGUES, 1922-1945

A HARD-NOSED, FIERY COMPETITOR WHO EXCELLED IN THREE DECADES, AS A FIRST AND THIRD BASEMAN WITH THE BALTIMORE BLACK SOX, HOMESTEAD GRAYS AND PHILADELPHIA STARS. FEARED AND RESPECTED BATTER WHO TERRORIZED PITCHERS BY HITTING OVER .350 DURING CAREER, INCLUDING SEVERAL SEASONS OVER .400. CAPTAINED RENOWNED 1931 HOMESTEAD GRAYS AND PLAYED ON FOUR CHAMPIONSHIP TEAMS. NAMED TO THREE EAST-WEST ALL-STAR TEAMS AND STARRED IN THE CUBAN WINTER LEAGUE.

Boojum

Elected To The Hall Of Fame: 2006.
Born: Feb. 28, 1896 in Remington, Va.
Died: June 24, 1963 in Washington, D.C.
Height: 5-8. **Weight:** 195.
Threw: Right. **Batted:** Left.
Teams: Negro Leagues 1922-1945. Baltimore 1922-1930; Homestead 1931-1932, 1940-1945; Pittsburgh 1932, 1936; Philadelphia 1933-1939; New York Cubans 1936.

YEAR	TEAM	LEAGUE	G	AB	R	H	2B	3B	HR	RBI	SB	AVG
1922	BALTIMORE	INDP	—	32	5	12	2	0	0	—	4	.375
1923	BALTIMORE	ECOL	—	108	18	32	7	1	1	—	1	.296
1924	BALTIMORE	ECOL	—	192	31	70	10	1	3	—	3	.365
1925	BALTIMORE	ECOL	—	161	30	57	12	1	5	—	7	.354
1926	BALTIMORE	ECOL	—	124	36	43	8	2	3	—	20	.347
1927	BALTIMORE	ECOL	—	124	28	50	9	2	1	—	0	.403
1928	BALTIMORE	ECOL	—	194	60	82	21	3	12	—	17	.423
1929	BALTIMORE	ANL	—	90	20	31	3	0	3	—	8	.344
1930	BALTIMORE	INDP	—	144	36	56	12	1	2	—	1	.389
1931	HOMESTEAD	INDP	—	140	42	56	7	5	3	—	0	.400
1932	PITT./HOMESTEAD	INDP/EWL	—	107	19	34	7	0	0	—	2	.318
1933	PHILADELPHIA	INDP	—	76	17	21	2	0	1	—	1	.276
1934	PHILADELPHIA	NNL	—	219	38	76	6	1	4	—	3	.347
1935	PHILADELPHIA	NNL	—	189	37	65	10	1	10	—	3	.344
1936	N.Y./PITT./PHIL.	NNL	—	135	19	37	3	2	3	—	1	.274
1937	PHILADELPHIA	NNL	—	74	9	22	3	2	0	—	0	.297
1938	PHILADELPHIA	NNL	—	94	15	22	0	1	3	—	0	.234
1939	PHILADELPHIA	NNL	—	84	15	25	4	1	2	—	0	.298
1940	HOMESTEAD	NNL	—	81	14	22	4	0	0	—	0	.272
1941	HOMESTEAD	NNL	—	77	18	36	7	2	0	—	0	.468
1942	HOMESTEAD	NNL	—	90	13	23	2	1	1	—	0	.256
1943	HOMESTEAD	NNL	—	140	13	39	8	3	0	—	0	.279
1944	HOMESTEAD	NNL	—	34	1	8	2	0	0	—	0	.235
1945	HOMESTEAD	NNL	—	33	5	11	0	0	1	—	0	.333
CAREER TOTALS			—	**2742**	**539**	**930**	**149**	**30**	**58**	—	**71**	**.339**

DAVE WINFIELD

Dave Winfield is the only athlete in history to be drafted by four different leagues, but in the end he chose Major League Baseball over the NFL, the ABA and the NBA.

The outfielder didn't spend a single day in the minor leagues, and he began his career with the Padres. Winfield found success even when his team did not. In 1979, he had 118 RBI in a season when the Padres scored just 603 runs. He had 34 home runs, 27 doubles, 10 triples and a .308 average. He scored 97 runs, stole 15 bases and drew more walks than strikeouts. He was also the best defensive right fielder in the National League, winning the Gold Glove Award that year, and adding another the following season.

From San Diego, he moved to New York in 1981 where he found much success. In 1982 he launched a career-high 37 long balls. He followed with 116 RBI in 1983. The following season he hit a career mark with a .340 batting average. His accomplishments were evident during his entire stint with New York. Five more Gold Glove Awards were also added to his total before he left the team.

Playing for the Angels, on June 24, 1991, he became the oldest player to hit for the cycle, at the age of 39. Winfield became a member of the Blue Jays as a free agent following the 1991 season. Despite being more than 40 years old, he batted .290 with 26 home runs and 108 RBI. He led Toronto to their first World Series win with a run-scoring double in the top of the 11th inning of Game 6 to take the championship against the Atlanta Braves. Then he went back to his hometown and played for the Twins. He collected his 3,000th career hit with Minnesota in 1993.

His career ended after he spent 46 games playing for the Indians in 1995. Winfield was a 12-time All-Star selection who amassed 3,110 hits, 465 home runs and 1,833 RBI.

DAVID MARK WINFIELD
SAN DIEGO, N.L., 1973-1980, NEW YORK, A.L., 1981-1990
CALIFORNIA, A.L., 1990-1991, TORONTO, A.L., 1992
MINNESOTA, A.L., 1993-1994, CLEVELAND, A.L., 1995
A COMPLETE PLAYER WHO INTIMIDATED THE OPPOSITION WITH HIS IMMENSE STATURE, POWER, AGGRESSIVE BASERUNNING AND DOMINANT DEFENSE. ADVANCED DIRECTLY FROM COLLEGE TO THE MAJOR LEAGUES. THE 12-TIME ALL-STAR COMPILED 3,110 HITS, 465 HOME RUNS, 1,833 RBI AND A .283 CAREER AVERAGE. THE MULTITALENTED OUTFIELDER, RENOWNED FOR LONG STRIDES AND A ROCKET ARM, EARNED SEVEN GOLD GLOVE AWARDS. AMONG ALL-TIME LEADERS IN HITS, RBI, GAMES, DOUBLES, EXTRA BASE HITS, TOTAL BASES AND PUTOUTS. HIS 11TH INNING, TWO-OUT DOUBLE IN GAME SIX CLINCHED TORONTO'S 1992 WORLD SERIES TITLE.

Elected To The Hall Of Fame: 2001.
Born: Oct. 3, 1951 in St. Paul, Minn.
Height: 6-6. **Weight:** 220.
Threw: Right. **Batted:** Right.
Debut: June 19, 1973.
Final Game: Oct. 1, 1995.
Teams: San Diego N.L. 1973-1980; New York A.L. 1981-1988, 1990; California A.L. 1990-1991; Toronto A.L. 1992; Minnesota A.L. 1993-1994; Cleveland A.L. 1995.
Postseason: World Series Champion (1992); 2 A.L. Pennants (1981, 1992). 2-Time Playoff Qualifier (1981, 1992).
Awards: 12-Time All-Star (1977-1988).

YEAR	TEAM	LEAGUE	G	AB	R	H	2B	3B	HR	RBI	SB	AVG
1973	SAN DIEGO	NL	56	141	9	39	4	1	3	12	0	.277
1974	SAN DIEGO	NL	145	498	57	132	18	4	20	75	9	.265
1975	SAN DIEGO	NL	143	509	74	136	20	2	15	76	23	.267
1976	SAN DIEGO	NL	137	492	81	139	26	4	13	69	26	.283
1977	SAN DIEGO	NL	157	615	104	169	29	7	25	92	16	.275
1978	SAN DIEGO	NL	158	587	88	181	30	5	24	97	21	.308
1979	SAN DIEGO	NL	159	597	97	184	27	10	34	118	15	.308
1980	SAN DIEGO	NL	162	558	89	154	25	6	20	87	23	.276
1981	NEW YORK	AL	105	388	52	114	25	1	13	68	11	.294
1982	NEW YORK	AL	140	539	84	151	24	8	37	106	5	.280
1983	NEW YORK	AL	152	598	99	169	26	8	32	116	15	.283
1984	NEW YORK	AL	141	567	106	193	34	4	19	100	6	.340
1985	NEW YORK	AL	155	633	105	174	34	6	26	114	19	.275
1986	NEW YORK	AL	154	565	90	148	31	5	24	104	6	.262
1987	NEW YORK	AL	156	575	83	158	22	1	27	97	5	.275
1988	NEW YORK	AL	149	559	96	180	37	2	25	107	9	.322
1990	NEW YORK/CALIFORNIA	AL	132	475	70	127	21	2	21	78	0	.267
1991	CALIFORNIA	AL	150	568	75	149	27	4	28	86	7	.262
1992	TORONTO	AL	156	583	92	169	33	3	26	108	2	.290
1993	MINNESOTA	AL	143	547	72	148	27	2	21	76	2	.271
1994	MINNESOTA	AL	77	294	35	74	15	3	10	43	2	.252
1995	CLEVELAND	AL	46	115	11	22	5	0	2	4	1	.191
CAREER TOTALS			**2973**	**11003**	**1669**	**3110**	**540**	**88**	**465**	**1833**	**223**	**.283**

EARLY WYNN

One of the greatest hitters of all time, Ted Williams, once called fellow Hall of Famer Early Wynn "the toughest pitcher I ever faced." Undoubtedly, the Splendid Splinter's sentiment was shared by many big league hitters for more than two decades. Wynn combined his physical gifts with intimidation and determination to overcome early struggles and become one of the most dominant players of his era.

"Since the first time I saw my father play semipro ball in Alabama, it has been my greatest ambition and desire to be a big league ballplayer," Wynn once said. It was during Wynn's early years with the Senators that he began to gain a reputation for meanness on the mound, exemplified by his willingness to knock down a batter if the occasion warranted. Among his famous quotes concerning this subject are: "A pitcher has to look at the hitter as his mortal enemy," "A pitcher will never be a big winner until he hates hitters," and "I've got a right to knock down anybody holding a bat."

After eight seasons with mediocre Washington teams, in which he had a 72-87 mark, Wynn was traded with first baseman Mickey Vernon to the Indians prior to 1949. The move to Cleveland, where he teamed up with Bob Feller, Bob Lemon and Mike Garcia to give the team one of baseball's great pitching rotations, proved fortuitous for Wynn. But after compiling a 163-100 record for the Indians from 1949-57, he was traded to the White Sox. In 1959, at age 39, Wynn led the league in wins (22), was named the Cy Young Award winner, and helped pitch the White Sox to the 1959 pennant. Wynn finished the 1962 season with 299 career wins, but was released by the White Sox after the season. After signing with the Indians, the 43-year-old posted his 300th win on July 13, 1963, becoming the 14th hurler in major league history to achieve the milestone. Wynn finished his big league pitching with a record of 300-244, 2,334 strikeouts in 4,564 innings, and had a 3.54 ERA. He won at least 20 games in a season five times, was named an All-Star every season from 1955-60.

EARLY WYNN
"GUS"
WASHINGTON A. L., CLEVELAND A. L.,
CHICAGO A. L. 1939 - 1963
WINNER OF 300 MAJOR LEAGUE GAMES. SET
RECORD BY PITCHING 23 YEARS IN MAJORS.
GAINED 20 OR MORE VICTORIES FIVE TIMES
AND LED A. L. IN EARNED-RUN AVERAGE IN
1950. LEADER IN INNINGS PITCHED THREE
SEASONS AND IN STRIKEOUTS TWICE. TIED
FOR MOST VICTORIES WITH 23 IN 1954 AND
LED LEAGUE WITH 22 WINS AT AGE 39 IN
1959 TO EARN CY YOUNG AWARD.

Gus

Elected To The Hall Of Fame: 1972.

Born: Jan. 6, 1920 in Hartford, Ala.

Died: Apr. 4, 1999 in Venice, Flor.

Height: 6-0. **Weight:** 190.

Threw: Right. **Batted:** Both.

Debut: Sept. 13, 1939.

Final Game: Sept. 13, 1963.

Teams: Washington A.L. 1939, 1941-1944, 1946-1948; Cleveland A.L. 1949-1957, 1963; Chicago A.L. 1958-1962.

Postseason: 2 A.L. Pennants (1954, 1959).

Awards: 7-Time All-Star (1947, 1955-1960); M.L. Cy Young (1959).

YEAR	TEAM	LEAGUE	G	W	L	SV	SH	IP	H	BB	SO	ERA
1939	WASHINGTON	AL	3	0	2	0	0	20.3	26	10	1	5.75
1941	WASHINGTON	AL	5	3	1	0	0	40	35	10	15	1.58
1942	WASHINGTON	AL	30	10	16	0	1	190	246	73	58	5.12
1943	WASHINGTON	AL	37	18	12	0	3	256.7	232	83	89	2.91
1944	WASHINGTON	AL	33	8	17	2	2	207.7	221	67	65	3.38
1946	WASHINGTON	AL	17	8	5	0	0	107	112	33	36	3.11
1947	WASHINGTON	AL	33	17	15	0	2	247	251	90	73	3.64
1948	WASHINGTON	AL	33	8	19	0	1	198	236	94	49	5.82
1949	CLEVELAND	AL	26	11	7	0	0	164.7	186	57	62	4.15
1950	CLEVELAND	AL	32	18	8	0	2	213.7	166	101	143	3.20
1951	CLEVELAND	AL	37	20	13	1	3	274.3	227	107	133	3.02
1952	CLEVELAND	AL	42	23	12	3	4	285.7	239	132	153	2.90
1953	CLEVELAND	AL	36	17	12	0	1	251.7	234	107	138	3.93
1954	CLEVELAND	AL	40	23	11	2	3	270.7	225	83	155	2.73
1955	CLEVELAND	AL	32	17	11	0	6	230	207	80	122	2.82
1956	CLEVELAND	AL	38	20	9	2	4	277.7	233	91	158	2.72
1957	CLEVELAND	AL	40	14	17	1	1	263	270	104	184	4.31
1958	CHICAGO	AL	40	14	16	2	4	239.7	214	104	179	4.13
1959	CHICAGO	AL	37	22	10	0	5	255.7	202	119	179	3.17
1960	CHICAGO	AL	36	13	12	1	4	237.3	220	112	158	3.49
1961	CHICAGO	AL	17	8	2	0	0	110.3	88	47	64	3.51
1962	CHICAGO	AL	27	7	15	0	3	167.7	171	56	91	4.46
1963	CLEVELAND	AL	20	1	2	1	0	55.3	50	15	29	2.28
CAREER TOTALS			**691**	**300**	**244**	**15**	**49**	**4564**	**4291**	**1775**	**2334**	**3.54**

CARL YASTRZEMSKI

It's not easy following in Ted Williams' footsteps, but that's exactly what Carl Yastrzemski had to do as a rookie for Boston in 1961. Williams' final season was in 1960 and Yaz stepped right in as a 21-year-old rookie in 1961.

Yastrzemski was raised in Southampton, N.Y. by Polish parents on a family potato farm. He briefly attended Notre Dame on a basketball scholarship before signing a professional baseball contract with the Red Sox for $100,000.

Originally a second baseman in the minors, Yaz moved to left field when Williams vacated the spot for the 1961 season. He was solid but unspectacular in his first two seasons, but really broke out in 1963 when he made his first all-star game and led the league with a .321 batting average.

Yastrzemski was well-known for his batting stance, in which he held his bat high in the air, giving his swing a large, dramatic arc, and more power at the plate. In his later years, he adjusted his stance and held the bat lower. He was also known for modifying his batting helmets by enlarging the right ear hole for comfort and removing part of the right ear flap for better vision of the ball as it was being pitched.

Yastrzemski spent his entire 23-year career in Boston, where he was a 18-time All-Star and seven-time Gold Glove winner. In 1967, he won the American League Triple Crown, becoming just the 13th player to lead his respective league in batting average, home runs and RBIs. Yaz was named the American League MVP that year as well.

Yastrzemski led the league in hitting three times during his career, and in 1979 he became the first American League player to record more than 3,000 hits and more than 400 home runs. "I'm most proud of that," Yastrzemski said. "Not (Ted) Williams, not (Lou) Gehrig, not (Joe) DiMaggio did that. They were Cadillacs and I'm a Chevrolet."

CARL MICHAEL YASTRZEMSKI
"YAZ"
BOSTON, A.L., 1961-1983
SUCCEEDED TED WILLIAMS IN FENWAY'S LEFT FIELD IN 1961 AND RETIRED 23 YEARS LATER AS ALL-TIME RED SOX LEADER IN 8 CATEGORIES. PLAYED WITH GRACEFUL INTENSITY IN RECORD 3,308 A.L. GAMES. ONLY A.L. PLAYER WITH 3,000 HITS AND 400 HOMERS. 3-TIME BATTING CHAMPION. WON MVP AND TRIPLE CROWN IN 1967 AS HE LED RED SOX TO "IMPOSSIBLE DREAM" PENNANT.

Yaz

Elected To The Hall Of Fame: *1989.*
Born: *Aug. 22, 1939 in Southampton, N.Y.*
Height: *5-11.* **Weight:** *175.*
Threw: *Right.* **Batted:** *Left.*
Debut: *Apr. 11, 1961.*
Final Game: *Oct. 2, 1983.*
Teams: *Boston A.L. 1961-1983.*
Postseason: *2 A.L. Pennants (1967, 1975); 2-Time Playoff Qualifier (1967, 1975).*
Awards: *18-Time All-Star (1963, 1965-1979, 1982-1983); A.L. Most Valuable Player (1967).*

YEAR	TEAM	LEAGUE	G	AB	R	H	2B	3B	HR	RBI	SB	AVG
1961	BOSTON	AL	148	583	71	155	31	6	11	80	6	.266
1962	BOSTON	AL	160	646	99	191	43	6	19	94	7	.296
1963	BOSTON	AL	151	570	91	183	40	3	14	68	8	.321
1964	BOSTON	AL	151	567	77	164	29	9	15	67	6	.289
1965	BOSTON	AL	133	494	78	154	45	3	20	72	7	.312
1966	BOSTON	AL	160	594	81	165	39	2	16	80	8	.278
1967	BOSTON	AL	161	579	112	189	31	4	44	121	10	.326
1968	BOSTON	AL	157	539	90	162	32	2	23	74	13	.301
1969	BOSTON	AL	162	603	96	154	28	2	40	111	15	.255
1970	BOSTON	AL	161	566	125	186	29	0	40	102	23	.329
1971	BOSTON	AL	148	508	75	129	21	2	15	70	8	.254
1972	BOSTON	AL	125	455	70	120	18	2	12	68	5	.264
1973	BOSTON	AL	152	540	82	160	25	4	19	95	9	.296
1974	BOSTON	AL	148	515	93	155	25	2	15	79	12	.301
1975	BOSTON	AL	149	543	91	146	30	1	14	60	8	.269
1976	BOSTON	AL	155	546	71	146	23	2	21	102	5	.267
1977	BOSTON	AL	150	558	99	165	27	3	28	102	11	.296
1978	BOSTON	AL	144	523	70	145	21	2	17	81	4	.277
1979	BOSTON	AL	147	518	69	140	28	1	21	87	3	.270
1980	BOSTON	AL	105	364	49	100	21	1	15	50	0	.275
1981	BOSTON	AL	91	338	36	83	14	1	7	53	0	.246
1982	BOSTON	AL	131	459	53	126	22	1	16	72	0	.275
1983	BOSTON	AL	119	380	38	101	24	0	10	56	0	.266
CAREER TOTALS			**3308**	**11988**	**1816**	**3419**	**646**	**59**	**452**	**1844**	**168**	**.285**

CY YOUNG

Cy Young left a legacy as a pitcher that is unlikely to ever be matched.

The right-hander won 511 games during his tenure in baseball, almost 100 more than any other pitcher in history. He recorded 30 victories on five occasions and won more than 20 games 15 times.

Young's best season came in 1901 when he led in strikeouts, wins and ERA. It was the first year of the American League and he set the bar high, winning its Triple Crown. In 1903 he won two games in the first modern World Series, helping Boston to victory. On May 5, 1904, Young pitched the first perfect game of the 20th century, a day he considered to be his greatest. The pitcher totalled three no-hitters throughout his time in the sport. He still holds the records for most career innings pitched (7,356), games started (815) and complete games (749). He is fourth all-time with 76 career shutouts.

Young threw his first no-hitter was on Sept. 18, 1897. He had one walk and his team committed four errors (one was originally ruled a hit, but Cleveland's third baseman sent a note to the press box after the eighth inning indicating that he had actually made an error, so the ruling on the field was changed). Young considered the game to be a one-hitter, despite a valiant effort from his teammate. In 1908, he pitched his third no-hitter and was the oldest man to ever accomplish the feat, at 41 years and three months old. His record lasted 82 years until Nolan Ryan threw a no-no in 1990 at the age of 43. Young led his league in victories on five occasions, in 1892, 1895, and from 1901 to 1903, and finished second two more times. In 1892 he reached a career-high in wins with 36.

He led the league in ERA twice (1.93 in 1892 and 1.62 in 1901). For 19 straight years, the right-handed pitcher was in the top 10 in the AL for number of innings pitched. In 14 of those seasons, he was among the top five finishers. Young did not throw two consecutive incomplete games until he was already 10 years into his baseball career.

Cyclone

Elected To The Hall Of Fame: *1937.*
Born: *Mar. 29, 1867 in Gilmore, Ohio.*
Died: *Nov. 4, 1955 in Newcomerstown, Ohio.*
Height: *6-2.* **Weight:** *210.*
Threw: *Right.* **Batted:** *Right.*
Debut: *Aug. 6, 1890.*
Final Game: *Oct. 6, 1911.*
Teams: *Cleveland N.L. 1890-1898; St. Louis N.L. 1899-1900; Boston A.L. 1901-1908; Cleveland A.L. 1909-1911; Boston N.L. 1911.*
Postseason: *N.L. Pennant (1892); World Series Champion (1903); A.L. Pennant (1903).*

YEAR	TEAM	LEAGUE	G	W	L	SV	SH	IP	H	BB	SO	ERA
1890	CLEVELAND	NL	17	9	7	0	0	147.7	145	30	39	3.47
1891	CLEVELAND	NL	55	27	22	2	0	423.7	431	140	147	2.85
1892	CLEVELAND	NL	53	36	12	0	9	453	363	118	168	1.93
1893	CLEVELAND	NL	53	34	16	1	1	422.7	442	103	102	3.36
1894	CLEVELAND	NL	52	26	21	1	2	408.7	488	106	108	3.94
1895	CLEVELAND	NL	47	35	10	0	4	369.7	363	75	121	3.26
1896	CLEVELAND	NL	51	28	15	3	5	414.3	477	62	140	3.24
1897	CLEVELAND	NL	46	21	19	0	2	335.7	391	49	88	3.78
1898	CLEVELAND	NL	46	25	13	0	1	377.7	387	41	101	2.53
1899	ST. LOUIS	NL	44	26	16	1	4	369.3	368	44	111	2.58
1900	ST. LOUIS	NL	41	19	19	0	4	321.3	337	36	115	3.00
1901	BOSTON	AL	43	33	10	0	5	371.3	324	37	158	1.62
1902	BOSTON	AL	45	32	11	0	3	384.7	350	53	160	2.15
1903	BOSTON	AL	40	28	9	2	7	341.7	294	37	176	2.08
1904	BOSTON	AL	43	26	16	1	10	380	327	29	200	1.97
1905	BOSTON	AL	38	18	19	0	4	320.7	248	30	210	1.82
1906	BOSTON	AL	39	13	21	2	0	287.7	288	25	140	3.19
1907	BOSTON	AL	43	21	15	2	6	343.3	286	51	147	1.99
1908	BOSTON	AL	36	21	11	2	3	299	230	37	150	1.26
1909	CLEVELAND	AL	35	19	15	0	3	294.3	267	59	109	2.26
1910	CLEVELAND	AL	21	7	10	0	1	163.3	149	27	58	2.53
1911	CLEVELAND/BOSTON	AL/NL	18	7	9	0	2	126.3	137	28	55	3.78
CAREER TOTALS			**906**	**511**	**316**	**17**	**76**	**7356**	**7092**	**1217**	**2803**	**2.63**

ROSS YOUNGS

Though the career of Royce M. "Ross" Youngs was ended prematurely, he made an impact on the baseball world during the time he was able to spend in the league.

Youngs made his major league debut in 1917 with the New York Giants. His first full season came in the following year, and he was sixth in the league with a .302 batting average.

The left-handed hitter finished his career with a .322 lifetime average and batted over .300 for seven straight seasons, including reaching an average of more than .350 twice. He scored 100-plus runs on three occasions and led National League outfielders in assists three times.

Youngs had his best season in 1920 when he finished second in the NL batting race to Rogers Hornsby, with a .351 average. At just 23 years old, he collected 204 hits, scored 92 runs, had 27 doubles, 14 triples and six home runs. He also notched 78 RBI and walked 75 times. He had a .427 on-base percentage and was third-best in the league with a .477 slugging mark. On May 11 of his season of highlights, Youngs had three triples in one game against the Redlegs, tying a modern major league record.

Youngs helped his team get to the World Series four years in a row, from 1921 to 1924, and the Giants won the Fall Classic twice, in 1921 and 1922. He became the first player to get two hits in one inning in a Series game in 1921. Youngs had a triple and a double in the Giants' eight-run seventh inning in Game 3 against the Yankees.

The outfielder's career ended in 1926 when he was diagnosed with a kidney disorder. He died at the early age of 30. A plaque was installed at the Polo Grounds in 1928 to honor him.

"A brave untrammelled spirit of the diamond, who brought glory to himself and his team by his strong, aggressive, courageous play," the plaque read. "He won the admiration of the nation's fans, the love and esteem of his friends and teammates, and the respect of his opponents. He played the game."

One of the colleagues Youngs had the biggest effect on was his manager John McGraw. Until his own death in 1934, McGraw kept only two framed photos in his office at the Polo Grounds, one of Christy Mathewson and the other of Youngs.

ROSS MIDDLEBROOK YOUNGS
"PEP"
NEW YORK N.L. 1917·1926
STAR RIGHT FIELDER OF CHAMPION GIANTS OF 1921·22·23·24 WHEN HE BATTED .327, .331, .336, AND .356 COMPILED LIFETIME AVERAGE OF .322, TOPPING .300 IN NINE OF TEN YEARS. TWICE MADE 200 OR MORE HITS IN A SEASON, LED LEAGUE IN DOUBLES IN 1919 AND RUNS SCORED IN 1923, LED N.L. OUTFIELDERS IN ASSISTS TWICE AND TIED ONCE.

Pep

Elected To The Hall Of Fame: *1972.*
Born: *Apr. 10, 1897 in Shiner, Texas.*
Died: *Oct. 22, 1927 in San Antonio, Texas.*
Height: *5-8.* **Weight:** *162.*
Threw: *Right.* **Batted:** *Left.*
Debut: *Sept. 25, 1917.*
Final Game: *Aug. 10, 1926.*
Teams: *New York N.L. 1917-1926.*
Postseason: *2-Time World Series Champion (1921-1922); 4 N.L. Pennants (1921-1924).*

YEAR	TEAM	LEAGUE	G	AB	R	H	2B	3B	HR	RBI	SB	AVG
1917	NEW YORK	NL	7	26	5	9	2	3	0	1	1	.346
1918	NEW YORK	NL	121	474	70	143	16	8	1	25	10	.302
1919	NEW YORK	NL	130	489	73	152	31	7	2	43	24	.311
1920	NEW YORK	NL	153	581	92	204	27	14	6	78	18	.351
1921	NEW YORK	NL	141	504	90	165	24	16	3	102	21	.327
1922	NEW YORK	NL	149	559	105	185	34	10	7	86	17	.331
1923	NEW YORK	NL	152	596	121	200	33	12	3	87	13	.336
1924	NEW YORK	NL	133	526	112	187	33	12	10	74	11	.356
1925	NEW YORK	NL	130	500	82	132	24	6	6	53	17	.264
1926	NEW YORK	NL	95	372	62	114	12	5	4	43	21	.306
CAREER TOTALS			**1211**	**4627**	**812**	**1491**	**236**	**93**	**42**	**592**	**153**	**.322**

ROBIN YOUNT

"He could do everything. He never stopped hustling. He was what a ballplayer is supposed to be," Bob Uecker said.

After one season in the New-York Penn League, Robin Yount joined the Milwaukee Brewers as their 18-year-old shortstop in 1974. A steady hitter and a fine fielder, he led the AL in games in 1976 and in doubles in 1980. He led the league in putouts, total chances, and double plays in 1976.

Yount emerged in 1982, as he hit .331, the first of six times he would top the .300 mark. He led the AL in hits (210), doubles, (46), and slugging (.578). In addition, he hit 29 home runs, drove in 114 runs, scored 129 runs, hit 12 triples and swiped 14 bases. He won the Gold Glove Award at shortstop and was named the league's Most Valuable Player. He made the All-Star team in 1980, 1982, and 1983.

He led the Brewers into the postseason for a second consecutive year, and performed very well in the 1982 World Series, hitting .414 with 12 hits, three doubles, a homer and six RBI. The Brewers lost to the Cardinals in seven games. His career postseason batting average was .344, with 22 hits in 17 games. Yount became a centerfielder after mid-career shoulder surgery in 1985. He won his second AL MVP award in 1989, joining Stan Musial and Hank Greenberg as the only other Hall of Famers to win the award at two different positions. That season, Yount hit .318, with 103 runs-batted-in, 101 runs scored, 21 home runs, 38 doubles, 9 triples and 19 stolen bases. Yount led the league in fielding percentage once at each position. He garnered his 3,000th career hit in 1992, the 17th player in major league history to reach that hallowed plateau. He retired after the 1993 season with a career .285 batting average, 3,142 hits, 1,632 runs scored, 583 doubles, 126 triples, 251 home runs, 1,406 RBI, and 271 stolen bases.

"Robin is everything good about the game of baseball. He set an example every day he went on the field," said Phil Garner, who played against Yount early in his career, and managed him in his final two seasons. Teammate Pete Vuckovich added, "He was special. He came to play every day and genuinely loved the game."

ROBIN R. YOUNT
MILWAUKEE, A.L., 1974 – 1993

A PROLIFIC HITTER WITH A STOIC DEMEANOR WHO WAS EQUALLY GRACEFUL AT SHORTSTOP AND IN CENTER FIELD. ONE OF THREE PLAYERS TO EARN MVP HONORS AT TWO POSITIONS. HIT .300 SIX TIMES, 40 DOUBLES FOUR TIMES. 20 HR FOUR TIMES AND SCORED 100 RUNS FIVE TIMES. EXCEPTIONAL CONDITIONING AND EXTRAORDINARY WORK ETHIC MADE HIM A BASTION OF CONSISTENCY AND DURABILITY FOR 20 SEASONS. AN EVERY DAY MAJOR LEAGUER AT AGE 18.

Elected To The Hall Of Fame: 1999.
Born: Sept. 16, 1955 in Danville, Ill.
Height: 6-0. Weight: 165.
Threw: Right. Batted: Right.
Debut: Apr. 5, 1974.
Final Game: Oct. 3, 1993.
Teams: Milwaukee A.L. 1974-1993.
Postseason: A.L. Pennant (1982);
2-Time Playoff Qualifier (1981-1982).
Awards: 3-Time All-Star (1980, 1982-1983); 2-Time A.L. Most Valuable Player (1982, 1989).

YEAR	TEAM	LEAGUE	G	AB	R	H	2B	3B	HR	RBI	SB	AVG
1974	MILWAUKEE	AL	107	344	48	86	14	5	3	26	7	.250
1975	MILWAUKEE	AL	147	558	67	149	28	2	8	52	12	.267
1976	MILWAUKEE	AL	161	638	59	161	19	3	2	54	16	.252
1977	MILWAUKEE	AL	154	605	66	174	34	4	4	49	16	.288
1978	MILWAUKEE	AL	127	502	66	147	23	9	9	71	16	.293
1979	MILWAUKEE	AL	149	577	72	154	26	5	8	51	11	.267
1980	MILWAUKEE	AL	143	611	121	179	49	10	23	87	20	.293
1981	MILWAUKEE	AL	96	377	50	103	15	5	10	49	4	.273
1982	MILWAUKEE	AL	156	635	129	210	46	12	29	114	14	.331
1983	MILWAUKEE	AL	149	578	102	178	42	10	17	80	12	.308
1984	MILWAUKEE	AL	160	624	105	186	27	7	16	80	14	.298
1985	MILWAUKEE	AL	122	466	76	129	26	3	15	68	10	.277
1986	MILWAUKEE	AL	140	522	82	163	31	7	9	46	14	.312
1987	MILWAUKEE	AL	158	635	99	198	25	9	21	103	19	.312
1988	MILWAUKEE	AL	162	621	92	190	38	11	13	91	22	.306
1989	MILWAUKEE	AL	160	614	101	195	38	9	21	103	19	.318
1990	MILWAUKEE	AL	158	587	98	145	17	5	17	77	15	.247
1991	MILWAUKEE	AL	130	503	66	131	20	4	10	77	6	.260
1992	MILWAUKEE	AL	150	557	71	147	40	3	8	77	15	.264
1993	MILWAUKEE	AL	127	454	62	117	25	3	8	51	9	.258
CAREER TOTALS			**2856**	**11008**	**1632**	**3142**	**583**	**126**	**251**	**1406**	**271**	**.285**

JOHN J McGRAW

The
MANAGERS

WALTER ALSTON

Always displaying a calm, professional demeanor, Walter Alston managed the Brooklyn and Los Angeles Dodgers for 23 seasons – on 23 one-year contracts – winning seven National League pennants and four World Series championships, including Brooklyn's only title in 1955. His squads won 2,040 games.

Alston, born Dec. 1, 1911, was named Manager of the Year six times and won a record seven All-Star Games. He helped to establish a legacy of Dodger greatness, which led many of his former players to become successful managers. He was elected to the Hall of Fame in 1983, and died on Oct. 1, 1984.

Elected To The Hall Of Fame: 1983.

Born: Dec. 1, 1911 in Venice, Ohio.

Died: Oct. 1, 1984 in Oxford, Ohio.

Teams: Brooklyn N.L. 1954-1957; Los Angeles N.L. 1958-1976.

SPARKY ANDERSON

George "Sparky" Anderson was the first manager in history to win World Series championships in both the American and National leagues, with the Detroit Tigers and Cincinnati Reds. His career totals include 2,194 victories, two Manager of the Year awards, five league pennants and three World Series crowns.

Anderson's heavy use of the bullpen staff earned him the nickname "Captain Hook." Known for his jovial disposition, and prone to hyperbole, he once said of Willie Stargell, "He's got power enough to hit home runs in any park, including Yellowstone."

Captain Hook

Elected To The Hall Of Fame: 2000.

Born: Feb. 22, 1934 in Bridgewater, S.D.

Died: Nov. 4, 2010 in Thousand Oaks, Calif.

Teams: Cincinnati N.L. 1970-1978; Detroit A.L. 1979-1995.

LEO DUROCHER

Light-hitting but slick-fielding Leo Durocher spent 17 years playing shortstop in the majors, but he is most remembered for his 24 years at the helm of the Brooklyn Dodgers, New York Giants, Chicago Cubs and Houston Astros.

Brilliant yet controversial, Durocher focused his clubs completely on winning. "As long as I've got a chance to beat you, I'm going to take it," Durocher once said. And he did win: 2,008 games, three pennants and the 1954 World Series for the Giants, their first championship since 1933. "The Lip" was named Manager of the Year by the *Sporting News* in 1939, 1951 and 1954.

Elected To The Hall Of Fame: *1994.*
Born: *July 27, 1905 at West Springfield, MA.*
Died: *October 7, 1991 at Palm Springs, CA.*
Teams: *Brooklyn N.L. 1939-1946, 1948; New York N.L. 1948-1955; Chicago N.L. 1966-1972; Houston N.L. 1972-1973*

NED HANLON

Ned Hanlon was a smart and influential manager, winning five pennants in seven years from 1894 to 1900. A fine major league outfielder for 13 seasons, Hanlon was respected for his base running and leadership as a player. Hanlon's teams in Baltimore and Brooklyn perfected rough, aggressive "inside baseball," favoring bunts, base stealing and defense. Some of Hanlon's players, including Hughie Jennings, Wilbert Robinson and John McGraw became successful managers. Connie Mack once stated, "I always rated Ned Hanlon as the greatest leader baseball ever had. I don't believe any man lived who knew as much baseball as he did."

Elected To The Hall Of Fame: *1996.*
Born: *August 22, 1857 at Montville, CT.*
Died: *April 14, 1937 at Baltimore, MD.*
Teams: *Pittsburgh N.L. 1889, 1891; Pittsburgh, Player's League 1890; Baltimore N.L. 1892-1898; Brooklyn N.L. 1899-1905; Cincinnati N.L. 1906-1907*

BUCKY HARRIS

When Bucky Harris, "The Boy Wonder," took over the helm of the lowly Washington Senators as a 27-year-old player-manager in 1924, he promptly led the team to its first two American League pennants and a 1924 World Series title, also hitting two homers and batting .333 in the Fall Classic. Harris' playing days ended in 1931 with the Detroit Tigers, but his managerial career continued until 1956 with the Tigers, Senators, Boston Red Sox, Philadelphia Phillies and New York Yankees. He won his second championship with the Yankees in 1947. Harris was the fourth manager to win 2,000 games and finished his career with 2,158 victories.

The Boy Wonder

Elected To The Hall Of Fame: 1975. **Born:** November 8, 1896 at Port Jervis, NY. **Died:** November 8, 1977 at Bethesda, MD. **Teams:** Washington A.L. 1924-1928, 1935-1942, 1950-1954; Detroit A.L. 1929-1933, 1955-1956; Boston A.L. 1934; Philadelphia N.L. 1943; New York A.L. 1947-1948

WHITEY HERZOG

A lifetime in baseball helped manager Dorrel "Whitey" Herzog adapt his clubs to the modern game played on artificial turf, resulting in consistent success. After brief managerial posts in Texas and California, his Kansas City Royals and St. Louis Cardinals of the 1970s and '80s played "Whitey Ball," focusing on aggressive base running, sparkling defense and a strong bullpen. Herzog won three division titles in five years with Kansas City, and a trio of pennants and the 1982 World Series with the Cardinals. Managing for 18 big league seasons (1973 to 1990), Herzog retired with a record of 1,281-1,125.

Elected To The Hall Of Fame: 2010. **Born:** November 9, 1931 at New Athens, IL **Teams:** Texas A.L. 1973; California A.L. 1974; Kansas City A.L. 1975-1979; St. Louis N.L. 1980-1990

MILLER HUGGINS

Shrewd is the word best used to describe Miller Huggins. A smart second baseman who always found a way to get on base, the 5-foot-6-inch "Hug" forged a 13-year major league career as a player with the St. Louis Cardinals and Cincinnati Reds.

He became better known for managing the Cardinals and New York Yankees for 17 seasons, leading the Bronx Bombers to their first six pennants and three World Series championships, effectively beginning the Yankees dynasty. In 1932, a monument to the "Mighty Mite" was dedicated and placed in center field at Yankee Stadium in his memory.

Mighty Mite

Elected To The Hall Of Fame: 1964.
Born: March 27, 1878 at Cincinnati, OH.
Died: September 25, 1929 at New York, NY.
Teams: St. Louis N.L. 1913-1917; New York A.L. 1918-1929

TOMMY LASORDA

After more than 60 years in the organization, Tommy Lasorda remains the embodiment of Dodger Blue. Lasorda, won 1,599 games, two World Series and two more National League pennants while managing the Los Angeles Dodgers from 1976-1996.

Lasorda got his start in pro baseball at the age of 18 as a southpaw pitcher when he signed with the Phillies. He made his major league debut in 1954 with the Dodgers, then worked as a scout and minor league manager before joining Walter Alston's staff in 1973. When Alston retired in 1976, Lasorda took the reins. After retiring in 1996, Lasorda has remained a Dodgers adviser.

Elected To The Hall Of Fame: 1997.
Born: September 22, 1927 at Norristown, PA.
Teams: Los Angeles N.L. 1976-1996

AL LOPEZ

Al Lopez's career in professional baseball began at age 16, when he signed with his hometown Class D Tampa team, and he eventually spent 19 years behind the plate for Brooklyn, Pittsburgh, Cleveland and the Boston Braves, breaking Gabby Hartnett's record for games caught. It was as a manager, though, that Lopez's star shone brightest.

In his 15 full seasons as manager, Lopez's teams finished lower than second only three times and never with a losing record. Although he never won a World Series, he's one of only a handful of managers to manage 2,000 games whose career winning percentage exceeded the .580 mark.

Elected To The Hall Of Fame: 1977.
Born: August 20, 1908 at Tampa, FL.
Died: October 30, 2005 at Tampa, FL.
Teams: Cleveland A.L. 1951-1956; Chicago A.L. 1957-1965, 1968-1969

CONNIE MACK

Connie Mack won five World Series titles, a record nine American League pennants and 3,731 games, nearly 1,000 more than any other manager in history.

Still, "The Tall Tactician" is best remembered as a dignified leader who donned a business suit to dispense wisdom to a generation of players. "You're born with two strikes against you, so don't take a third one on your own," Mack was fond of stating to his clubs. Though his entrance to baseball came by playing catcher for 11 seasons, in 1901 Mack assumed control of the Philadelphia Athletics, the team he would lead for the next 50 years.

The Tall Tactician

Elected To The Hall Of Fame: 1937.
Born: December 22, 1862 at East Brookfield, MA.
Died: February 8, 1956 at Philadelphia, PA.
Teams: Pittsburgh N.L. 1894-1896; Philadelphia A.L. 1901-1950

JOE MCCARTHY

Joe McCarthy, the New York Yankees manager of the 1930s and early-1940s, finished his 24-year major league career with an all-time best winning percentage of .615 to go along with 2,125 wins. McCarthy's teams won nine pennants—one with the Chicago Cubs and the rest with the Yankees, including seven World Series championships, four of them consecutively from 1936 to 1939. Six times his teams won 100 or more games in a season, never finishing out of the first division. "I don't know where he learned all his psychology about ballplayers. He could handle almost anybody," claimed former Yankees outfielder Tommy Henrich.

Elected To The Hall Of Fame: 1957.
Born: April 21, 1887 at Philadelphia, PA.
Died: January 13, 1978 at Buffalo, NY.
Teams: Chicago N.L. 1926-1930; New York A.L. 1931-1946; Boston A.L. 1948-1950

JOHN MCGRAW

"There has been only one manager, and his name is John McGraw," Hall of Fame manager Connie Mack once declared. McGraw was a fiery third baseman for the Baltimore Orioles in the 1890s, but he achieved much more recognition as an innovative, autocratic field manager. In his 31 years at the helm of the New York Giants, McGraw's teams won 10 pennants, finished second 11 times and won three World Series titles. "Little Napoleon" finished his career with 2,763 managerial wins. As a player, he was credited with helping to develop the hit-and-run, the "Baltimore chop," the squeeze play and other strategic moves.

Little Napoleon

Elected To The Hall Of Fame: 1937.
Born: April 7, 1873 at Truxton, NY.
Died: February 25, 1934 at New Rochelle, NY.
Teams: Baltimore N.L. 1899, Baltimore A.L. 1901-1902; New York N.L. 1902-1932

BILL McKECHNIE

Known for his expertise of pitching and defense, Bill McKechnie became a highly successful manager after an 11-year playing career and was the first skipper to win pennants with three different National League clubs – the Pittsburgh Pirates (1925), St. Louis Cardinals (1928) and Cincinnati Reds (1939 and 1940).

Former pitcher Johnny Vander Meer said of McKechnie, "He knew how to hold on to a one- or two-run lead better than any other manager." In 1925 and 1940, "Deacon" led his clubs to World Series victories; and he was also named Manager of the Year on two separate occasions (1937 and 1940).

Elected To The Hall Of Fame: *1962.*
Born: *August 7, 1886 at Wilkinsburg, PA.*
Died: *October 29, 1965 at Bradenton, FL.*
Teams: *Newark, Federal League 1915; Pittsburgh N.L. 1922-1926; St. Louis N.L. 1928-1929; Boston N.L. 1930-1937; Cincinnati N.L. 1938-1946*

WILBERT ROBINSON

Wilbert Robinson rose to prominence as a catcher for the savvy, hard-nosed Baltimore Orioles of the 1890s. In 1892, he lashed a record seven hits in a nine-inning game. Robinson moved on to coach with the New York Giants, but after a falling out with long-time friend and Giants manager John McGraw, Robinson left to become manager of the rival Brooklyn franchise. During his tenure, the Dodgers were nicknamed the "Robins" in his honor. Affectionately dubbed "Uncle Robbie" thanks to an easygoing and fatherly attitude, the long-time Brooklyn manager guided his team to two National League pennants.

Uncle Robbie

Elected To The Hall Of Fame: *1945.*
Born: *June 29, 1864 at Boston, MA.*
Died: *August 8, 1934 at Atlanta, GA.*
Teams: *Baltimore A.L. 1902; Brooklyn N.L. 1914-1931.*

FRANK SELEE

Watchmaker Frank Selee was one of the most successful managers in the history of the National League. Though he lacked major league playing experience, Selee led the Boston Beaneaters to five pennants in 12 seasons. He was the architect behind the Chicago Cubs' rise to prominence in the early 1900s, before illness forced him to retire prematurely. Selee, an impeccable judge of talent, was adept at handling personalities. Historian David Nemec described Selee as having "a flair for bending players acquired from here, there and everywhere. [He was] a master at putting together a team better than the sum of its parts."

Elected To The Hall Of Fame: 1999.
Born: October 26, 1859 at Amherst, NH.
Died: July 5, 1909 at Denver, CO.
Teams: Boston N.L. 1890-1901; Chicago N.L. 1902-1905

BILLY SOUTHWORTH

Billy Southworth spent 13 seasons as an outfielder and 13 as a National League manager. Respected by his players, Southworth skippered the St. Louis Cardinals for seven seasons, averaging 101 wins a season between 1941 and 1945. He won three pennants with the Redbirds, along with World Series titles in 1942 and 1944.

During his six-year stint as manager of the Boston Braves, Southworth brought the perennial league doormats their first pennant in 34 years during the 1948 season. Southworth finished with a 1,044-704 record, the fifth-best winning percentage (.597) of all time.

Elected To The Hall Of Fame: 2008.
Born: March 9, 1893 at Harvard, NE.
Died: November 15, 1969 at Columbus, OH.
Teams: St. Louis N.L. 1929, 1940-45; Boston N.L. 1946-51

Casey Stengel

Casey Stengel's remarkable 54-year professional career included 14 years playing the outfield and 25 years managing in the major leagues. Always colorful and wildly popular, Stengel reached unparalleled success with the New York Yankees, winning 10 pennants and seven World Series titles from 1949 to 1960.

An astute judge of talent who often platooned players and juggled his pitchers, he was equally admired for "Stengelese," his own brand of double-talk, which made him one of the most quoted people in baseball history. "The Yankees don't pay me to win every day – just two out of three," he once declared.

Elected To The Hall Of Fame: 1966.
Born: July 30, 1890 at Kansas City, MO.
Died: September 29, 1975 at Glendale, CA.
Teams: Brooklyn N.L. 1934-1936; Boston N.L. 1938-1943; New York A.L. 1949-1960; New York N.L. 1962-1965

Earl Weaver

Earl Weaver's Orioles teams included plenty of talent, but he had a knack for shaping them into winning teams, guiding a dynastic Orioles group that won three consecutive pennants beginning in 1969, and took home a World Series championship in 1970. His teams also won the division in 1973 and '74, and the pennant in 1979.

Weaver's Orioles teams were known for pitching, defense and the three-run homer. For his career, he posted a winning percentage of .583—ninth on the all-time list. "On my tombstone, just write: 'The sorest loser that ever lived.'"

The Earl of Baltimore

Elected To The Hall Of Fame: 1996.
Born: August 14, 1930 at St. Louis, MO.
Died: January 19, 2013 at sea
Teams: Baltimore A.L. 1968-1982, 1985-1986

DICK WILLIAMS

He specialized in turning losers into winners, and Dick Williams did it often enough to earn a place in Cooperstown. After a 13-year big league playing career that ended in 1964, Williams got his first major league managing job with the Red Sox in 1967, leading the team to the American League pennant. He took over the Oakland Athletics in 1971 and led them to three AL West titles and two World Series championships in three seasons. After a stint with the Angels, he turned the Expos into consistent winners before heading for San Diego, where he led the Padres to their first NL Pennant in 1984. He finished his career with 1,571 wins.

Elected To The Hall Of Fame: *2008.*
Born: *May 7, 1929 at St. Louis, MO.*
Died: *July 7, 2011 at Las Vegas, NV.*
Teams: *Boston A.L. 1967-69; Oakland A.L. 1971-73; California A.L. 1974-76; Montreal N.L. 1977-81; San Diego N.L. 1982-85; Seattle A.L. 1986-88*

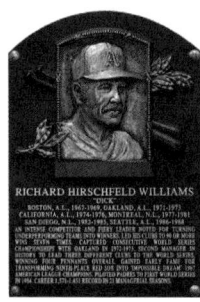

KENESAW MOUNTAIN LANDIS
BASEBALL'S FIRST COMMISSIONER

The
EXECUTIVES

ED BARROW

Ed Barrow was an excellent judge of baseball talent and responsible for the creation of the game's greatest dynasty, the New York Yankees. The team's chief executive used wise trades, outright player purchases and a budding farm system to put together teams that won 14 pennants and 10 World Series championships – including five Series sweeps – between 1921 and 1945.

An accomplished manager, Barrow led the 1918 Boston Red Sox to a World Series title before ending his field career in 1920 to join New York's front office. In 1919, he made the historic decision to convert Babe Ruth from pitcher to outfielder.

Elected To The Hall Of Fame: 1953.
Born: May 10, 1868 at Springfield, IL.
Died: December 15, 1953 at Port Chester, NY.

MORGAN BULKELEY

A respected member of the Connecticut business community and a former amateur baseball player, Morgan Bulkeley became involved in baseball as an executive with the National Association's Hartford Dark Blues in 1874. With the creation of the National League in 1876, Bulkeley agreed to serve as its first president, where he helped clean up the image of the game by targeting illegal gambling, drinking and fan rowdiness. He would later serve as mayor of Hartford, governor of Connecticut, and then as a United States Senator.

Elected To The Hall Of Fame: 1937.
Born: December 26, 1837 at East Haddam, CT.
Died: November 6, 1922 at Hartford, CT.

ALEXANDER CARTWRIGHT

Alexander Cartwright is often referred to as "The Father of Modern Baseball." Cartwright was a founding and influential member of the Knickerbocker Base Ball Club of New York City, baseball's first organized club. He played a key role in formalizing the first published rules of the game, including the concepts of foul territory, the distance between bases, three-out innings, nine-member teams with fixed batting orders, and the elimination of retiring baserunners by throwing batted baseballs at them. In 1849, Cartwright traveled west, sowing the seeds of baseball all the way to California and subsequently Hawaii.

The Father of Modern Baseball

Elected To The Hall Of Fame: 1938.
Born: Apr. 17, 1820 at New York, NY.
Died: July 12, 1892 at Honolulu, HI.

HENRY CHADWICK

A pioneer of early baseball, Henry Chadwick influenced the game by wielding a pen, not a bat. A renowned journalist, he developed the modern box score, introduced statistics such as batting average and the concept of earned and unearned runs, wrote numerous instructional manuals on the game, and edited multiple baseball guides.

He was an influential member of baseball's early rules committees, and his tireless work and devoted love for the game greatly aided in popularizing baseball during its infancy.

Elected To The Hall Of Fame: 1938.
Born: October 5, 1824 at Exeter, England.
Died: April 20, 1908 at Brooklyn, NY.

HAPPY CHANDLER

A U.S. Senator and former governor of Kentucky, Albert "Happy" Chandler succeeded Kenesaw Mountain Landis as commissioner in 1945, guiding Major League Baseball through its historic integration when Jackie Robinson broke the color barrier in 1947.

Though he served just one six-year term, Chandler upheld Landis' model as an authoritarian with honesty and respect, suspending players for leaving for the Mexican League, and banning Leo Durocher for one year for a series of actions. Chandler established a now common practice of six umpires on the field for World Series games.

Elected To The Hall Of Fame: 1982.
Born: July 14, 1898 at Corydon, KY.
Died: June 15, 1991 at Versailles, KY.

CHARLIE COMISKEY

C harles Comiskey experienced success as a player, manager and owner for a half century. He became player-manager of the American Association's St. Louis Browns at age 24 in 1883 and won four consecutive pennants from 1885 to 1888.

He was one of the founders of the upstart American League in 1901 and owned the Chicago White Sox for 31 years, winning four pennants. In 1910, he built famed Comiskey Park, an impressive steel and concrete structure that lasted 80 years.

The Old Roman, Commy

Elected To The Hall Of Fame: 1939.
Born: August 15, 1859 at Chicago, IL.
Died: October 26, 1931 at Eagle River, WI.

CANDY CUMMINGS

Often cited as the inventor of the curveball, Candy Cummings' stellar pitching career was well established when professional baseball began.

Cummings had an impressive 1875 season, winning 35 games, including seven shutouts, and compiling a 1.60 ERA. He was also the first major leaguer to start, complete and win both games of a doubleheader when he turned the trick on Sept. 9, 1876.

Elected To The Hall Of Fame: *1939.*
Born: *October 18, 1848 at Ware, MA.*
Died: *May 16, 1924 at Toledo, OH.*

BARNEY DREYFUSS

An innovative team owner and policy maker, Barney Dreyfuss was one of the most highly regarded executives in organized baseball. During his career, he merged his Louisville Colonels with the Pittsburgh Pirates to form a National League powerhouse, was one of the original advocates of a commissioner's office in baseball, helped to establish the modern World Series and was the Senior Circuit's first vice president. As president of the Pirates from 1900 until his death in 1932, Dreyfuss led Pittsburgh to six pennants, two World Series and 21 finishes of third place or better.

Elected To The Hall Of Fame: *2008.*
Born: *February 23, 1865 at Freiburg, Grand Duchy of Baden [Germany].*
Died: *February 5, 1932 at Pittsburgh, PA.*

RUBE FOSTER

A player, manager, owner, commissioner and unsurpassed visionary, Rube Foster was one of baseball's greatest renaissance men. In his youth, Foster was a star pitcher of the deadball era. Later, as owner-manager of the Chicago American Giants, the burly Texan instilled in his players the daring, aggressive, yet disciplined, style of play for which the Negro leagues became famous. Saying, "I cannot let such talent go to waste a day longer," Foster founded the first successful Negro league, the Negro National League, in 1920. It flourished until the Great Depression, and demonstrated that baseball with African-American ownership and players could succeed.

Elected To The Hall Of
Fame: 1981.
Born: September 17, 1879
at Calvert, TX.
Died: December 9, 1930 at
Kankakee, IL.

FORD FRICK

Ford Frick worked as a sportswriter and broadcaster before becoming the National League President in 1934. As president, he provided the official support necessary to establish the Baseball Hall of Fame in Cooperstown. When opposition arose to Jackie Robinson playing in the majors in 1947, Frick warned potential strikers that they would "be barred from baseball even though it means the disruption of a club or a whole league." Frick became Commissioner in 1951, serving in that post for 14 seasons and overseeing relocation, expansion and the transition from radio to television, which broadened coverage of the game.

Elected To The Hall Of
Fame: 1970.
Born: December 19, 1894
at Wawaka, IN.
Died: April 8, 1978 at
Bronxville, NY.

WARREN GILES

Baseball must always keep pace with the times," Warren Giles said upon retiring after 18 years as National League president. Although he respected tradition, Giles refused to be bound by old practices. Serving from 1951 to 1969, Giles oversaw one of the most significant and dynamic eras in league history. He addressed franchise relocation, expansion and the construction of new stadiums during his tenure. Giles began his 51-year baseball career in 1919 as a minor league club president, and ran the Cincinnati Reds from 1937 to 1951, a profitable tenure that included pennants in 1939 and 1940.

Elected To The Hall Of Fame: *1979.*
Born: *May 28, 1896 at Tiskilwa, IL.*
Died: *February 7, 1979 at Cincinnati, OH.*

PAT GILLICK

Pat Gillick built it – again and again and again – and at every stop, they came: victories, fans and championships. In 27 seasons as a general manager, Gillick's teams advanced to the postseason 11 times and finished with 20 winning records.

Gillick was a left-handed pitcher who moved into front office work in 1963 and became GM of the Blue Jays in 1978, winning back-to-back World Series championships in 1992-93. He took over as the Orioles' GM in 1996, then landed with the Mariners in 2000. He took over as Phillies GM in 2006. Two years later, the Phillies gave Gillick his third World Series title as a GM.

Elected To The Hall Of Fame: *2011.*
Born: *Aug. 22, 1937 at Chico, CA.*

CLARK GRIFFITH

Clark Griffith was a baseball pioneer his entire life. In 1901, "The Old Fox" became a player-manager for the Chicago White Sox in the new American League, leading them to the pennant. Griffith managed until 1920, when he became the Washington Senators' principal owner after being a part-owner since 1912. Innovative with limited finances, he won three pennants, set up one of the first farm teams, hired entertainers for fans and signed many Cuban players. "He was the greatest humanitarian who ever lived, and the greatest pillar of honesty baseball ever had," said Bobo Newsom. "I never played for a better man."

The Old Fox

Elected To The Hall Of Fame: 1946.
Born: November 20, 1869 at Clear Creek, MO.
Died: October 27, 1955 at Washington, D.C.

WILL HARRIDGE

Will Harridge – who worked for the American League for 48 years – started out as a ticket agent for the Wabash Railroad Company, where he handled booking and transportation for A.L. teams and umpires. In 1911, he was hired as personal secretary for A.L. president and founder Ban Johnson before becoming league secretary in 1927. Elected A.L. president in 1931, Harridge served in that capacity until his retirement in 1958, later serving on the board of directors. During his record 28-year tenure, he presided over the birth of the All-Star Game in 1933 and maintained prosperity for the league.

Elected To The Hall Of Fame: 1972.
Born: October 16, 1881 at Chicago, IL.
Died: April 9, 1971 at Evanston, IL.

WILLIAM HULBERT

In a meeting led by Chicago White Stockings owner William Hulbert on Feb. 2, 1876, at the Grand Central Hotel in New York City, the National League was founded. Hulbert stressed clean play in the embryonic circuit, banning drinking, gambling and all forms of rowdiness. Upon his death in 1882, future Hall of Fame member Albert Spalding wrote of the silver-tongued executive, "I ask all living professional Base Ball players to join me in raising our hats to the memory of William A. Hulbert, the man who saved the game."

Elected To The Hall Of Fame: 1995.
Born: October 23, 1832 at Burlington Flats, NY.
Died: April 10, 1882 at Chicago, IL.

BAN JOHNSON

Ban Johnson was an ambitious, driven leader who was instrumental in catapulting the minor-league Western League into a status on par with the established National League. Renaming the loop the American League and paring it down from 11 clubs to eight, no detail was too small for the autocratic A.L. czar. Johnson was also a major force on the pre-commissioner, three-man National Commission. Fellow Hall of Famer Branch Rickey once opined that Johnson's "contribution to the game is not closely equaled by any other single person or group of persons."

Elected To The Hall Of Fame: 1937.
Born: January 5, 1865 at Norwalk, OH.
Died: March 28, 1931 at St. Louis, MO.

BOWIE KUHN

A lawyer by trade, Bowie Kuhn's baseball odyssey went from working the scoreboard at Washington's Griffith Stadium to becoming Major League Baseball's fifth commissioner in 1969. During his 15-year tenure, baseball experienced dramatic increases in attendance, salaries, revenue and franchise values. While steering the game through labor strife and the establishment of free agency, Kuhn introduced night baseball to the World Series, expanded television coverage and instituted divisional play in each league.

Elected To The Hall Of Fame: *2008.*
Born: *October 28, 1926 at Takoma Park, MD.*
Died: *March 15, 2007 at Jacksonville, FL.*

KENESAW LANDIS

Kenesaw Mountain Landis was elected as baseball's first commissioner on Nov. 12, 1920. A strict disciplinarian, Landis helped restore public confidence in baseball following the scandal of the 1919 "Black Sox." The former U.S. district judge banned eight Chicago White Sox players for life, despite their acquittal in a court of law. Landis often utilized the "absolute power" granted him by the owners to ensure the game's integrity.

Elected To The Hall Of Fame: *1944.*
Born: *November 20, 1866 at Millville, OH.*
Died: *November 25, 1944 at Chicago, IL.*

LARRY MACPHAIL

L arry MacPhail was one of baseball's great inno-
vators, introducing night baseball to the major
leagues, along with airplane travel and regular
broadcast coverage of his team's games. MacPhail
also initiated pension plans and helped develop and
promote the use of protective batting helmets. He laid
the foundation for a Cincinnati Reds World Series
championship team before taking the reigns of the
Brooklyn Dodgers and New York Yankees.

**Elected To The Hall Of
Fame:** *1978.*
Born: *February 3, 1888 at
Cass City, MI.*
Died: *October 1, 1975 at
Miami, FL.*

LEE MACPHAIL

I n spite of his father Larry's warnings not to follow
in his footsteps, Lee MacPhail began his career as a
baseball executive in 1941 as business manager for the
minor league team in Reading, Pa. The Yankees hired him
as director of player personnel in 1948. He joined the
Baltimore Orioles as general manager from 1958-1965,
building the team that won the 1966 World Series. He
became the chief administrative assistant to Commissioner
William Eckert in November 1965, and returned to New
York to serve as GM before becoming American League
President from 1974-83. He served as president of the
Major League Player Relations Committee from 1984-85.

**Elected To The Hall Of
Fame:** *1998*
Born: *October 25, 1917 at
Nashville, TN.*
Died: *Nov. 8, 2012 at
Delray Beach, FL.*

EFFA MANLEY

Co-owner and business manager of the Newark Eagles from 1936 to 1948, Effa Manley was noted for running one of the most professional organizations in the Negro leagues. Using her position with Newark to crusade for civil rights, Manley made the Eagles a social force off the field and a baseball force on it, as the club was usually a top-division team and won the Negro League World Series in 1946. With the sale of Monte Irvin to the New York Giants, Manley established that major league clubs should respect the contracts of the Negro leagues by offering financial compensation.

Elected To The Hall Of Fame: *2006.*
Born: *March 27, 1897 at Philadelphia, PA.*
Died: *April 6, 1981 at Los Angeles, CA.*

WALTER O'MALLEY

Walter O'Malley is among the most influential baseball team owners of the last half of the 20th Century. He was a persuasive and visionary businessman who altered the big league landscape with seismic force by moving his Brooklyn Dodgers to Los Angeles. Thwarted in attempts to replace an outdated Ebbets Field, O'Malley led baseball's geographic expansion west after the 1957 season by relocating his team to California, while convincing the New York Giants to follow suit. Under O'Malley's ownership, the Dodgers became the "gold standard" of baseball franchises, winning 11 pennants and four World Series titles.

Elected To The Hall Of Fame: *2008.*
Born: *October 9, 1903 at New York, NY.*
Died: *August 9, 1979 at Rochester, MN.*

ALEX POMPEZ

The son of Cuban immigrants, Alejandro "Alex" Pompez owned the Cuban Stars of the Eastern Colored League, and later the New York Cubans of the Negro National League. Following the demise of the Negro leagues, Pompez was a scout for the New York and San Francisco Giants for 25 years, working to enable Caribbean players to enter the major leagues. He helped sign stars such as Orlando Cepeda, Juan Marichal and the Alou brothers. With his expertise on African-American baseball history, he was asked to serve on the Hall of Fame's Committee on Negro Leagues in 1971.

Elected To The Hall Of Fame: 2006.
Born: May 14, 1890 at Key West, FL.
Died: March 14, 1974 at New York, NY.

CUM POSEY

As a player, manager and owner, Cumberland "Cum" Posey was the driving force behind the Homestead Grays, one of the most successful teams in Negro leagues history, for 35 years. Posey's business acumen and organizational skills made the Grays a perennial powerhouse and money-making machine. Skilled at talent evaluation and development, Posey's teams produced a number of future Hall of Famers. Homestead split its "home" games between Pittsburgh and Washington, D.C., regularly drawing 25,000 to 30,000 fans at Forbes Field and Griffith Stadium. His teams won eight of nine Negro National League pennants from 1937 to 1945, including three championships.

Elected To The Hall Of Fame: 2006.
Born: June 20, 1890 at Homestead, PA.
Died : March 28, 1946 at Pittsburgh, PA.

Branch Rickey

ranch Rickey spent half a century as a baseball visionary. With the St. Louis Cardinals in the 1920s and 1930s, Rickey invented the modern farm system, promoting a new way of training and developing players. After joining the Brooklyn Dodgers, Rickey became the first executive to challenge baseball's color line when he signed Jackie Robinson, who would become the major leagues' first African-American player in the 20th century in 1947. When Robinson asked Rickey if he was looking for a Negro who was afraid to fight back, Rickey replied, "No. I'm looking for a ballplayer with the guts enough not to."

The Mahatma

Elected To The Hall Of Fame: 1967.
Born: December 20, 1881 at Flat, OH.
Died: December 9, 1965 at Colombia, MO.

Jacob Ruppert

he greatest sports dynasty in American history began with a second-division team. Jacob Ruppert changed all that when he bought the New York Yankees in 1915.

Within a decade, Ruppert had built Yankee Stadium, acquired Babe Ruth and won the first of the franchise's record 27 World Series titles.

Ruppert guided the Yankees to 10 AL pennants and seven World Series titles before his death on Jan. 13, 1939. As the 71-year-old Ruppert lay dying, Ruth visited him in the hospital. "It was the only time in his life he ever called me 'Babe' to my face," said Ruth.

Elected To The Hall Of Fame: 2013
Born: Aug. 5, 1867 at New York, NY.
Died: Jan. 13, 1939 at New York, NY.
Teams: Owner, New York Yankees, 1915-1939

AL SPALDING

Albert G. Spalding, the premier pitcher of the 1870s, led the league in victories in each of his six full seasons. His 47 victories in 1876 led the Chicago White Stockings to the inaugural National League championship. In 1877, he turned his boundless energies to the sporting goods business and also to his executive role with the White Stockings, where he gained renown as the era's top promoter of baseball as the national game. "The genius of our institutions is democratic," Spalding maintained. "Baseball is a democratic game."

Elected To The Hall Of Fame: 1939.
Born: September 2, 1850 at Byron, IL.
Died: September 9, 1915 at San Diego, CA.

BILL VEECK

Bill Veeck, owner of the Cleveland Indians, St. Louis Browns and Chicago White Sox, broke attendance records with ingenious promotions, outrageous door prizes and interactive fan participation. An inveterate hustler and energetic maverick, he introduced the concept of honoring fans, Bat Day, fireworks, exploding scoreboards, player names on uniforms and even a 3-foot-7-inch player, Eddie Gaedel. "I try not to break the rules, but merely test their elasticity," Veeck said. He also signed the American League's first African-American player – Larry Doby in 1947 – and its oldest rookie, 42-year-old Satchel Paige in 1948.

Elected To The Hall Of Fame: 1991.
Born: February 9, 1914 at Chicago, IL.
Died: January 2, 1986 at Chicago, IL.

GEORGE WEISS

After serving 13 years in the minor leagues, George Weiss moved into the New York Yankees front office in 1932 and remained active in the game until 1971. Noted for developing a wide-ranging farm system, which produced the talent driving the Yankees' dominance, Weiss' clubs captured 19 American League pennants and 15 World Series titles from 1932 to 1960. Weiss was considered an astute evaluator of talent – a rival executive once said, "I never made a single deal with him. He was too smart."

Elected To The Hall Of Fame: 1971.
Born: June 23, 1894 at New Haven, CT.
Died: August 13, 1972 at Greenwich, CT.

SOL WHITE

King Solomon "Sol" White was one of the early pioneers of black baseball, participating in the game as a player, manager and historian. His distinguished playing career included five seasons with teams in integrated minor leagues, where he compiled a .356 batting average. During the 1890s, White was a member of the top independent black teams. In 1902, he helped found the powerhouse Philadelphia Giants, a team for which he served as player-manager through the 1909 season. In 1907, he authored "Sol White's Official Base Ball Guide," the earliest-known work on the topic and the seminal piece of early African-American baseball history.

Elected To The Hall Of Fame: 2006.
Born: June 12, 1868 at Bellaire, OH.
Died: August 26, 1955 at Central Islip, NY.

J.L. WILKINSON

A native Iowan, J.L. Wilkinson was the innovative creator and owner of the Kansas City Monarchs, the longest-running franchise in Negro National League history. His teams won an unprecedented 17 pennants as well as two Colored World Series. Wilkinson is credited with developing the first successful lighting system for night games – five years before Major League Baseball played its first night game in 1935. His Monarchs supplied the once-segregated major leagues with more players than any other black ballclub. Prior to the Monarchs, he owned one of the first all-girls barnstorming teams, as well as the multi-ethnic All-Nations squad.

Elected To The Hall Of Fame: *2006.*
Born: *May 14, 1878 at Perry, IA.*
Died: *August 21, 1964 at Kansas City, MO.*

GEORGE WRIGHT

George Wright was an accomplished cricket player who helped transform baseball into the national pastime. Wright was a star on the first all-professional team, the 1869 Cincinnati Red Stockings. In addition to possessing excellent hitting skills, Wright revolutionized the role of the shortstop. Hall of Famer Jim O'Rourke said, "George Wright never had any equal as a fielder, baserunner and batsman, combined with heady work of a quality never accredited to any ball tosser. All his qualifications taken together, he was really in a class by himself."

Elected To The Hall Of Fame: *1937.*
Born: *January 28, 1847 at New York, NY.*
Died: *August 21, 1937 at Boston, MA.*

HARRY WRIGHT

Legendary baseball promoter Henry Chadwick once wrote, "There is no doubt that Harry Wright is the father of professional base ball playing." William Henry "Harry" Wright organized, managed and played centerfield for baseball's first all-professional team, the famed 1869 Cincinnati Red Stockings. Wright first played baseball with the New York Knickerbockers and later guided the Boston Red Stockings to four straight National Association pennants (1872-1875) and National League titles in 1877 and 1878. According to Chadwick, Wright was "the most experienced, skillful and successful manager of a base ball team in the professional fraternity."

Elected To The Hall Of Fame: *1953.*
Born: *January 10, 1835 at Sheffield, England.*
Died: *October 3, 1895 at Atlantic City, NJ.*

TOM YAWKEY

Thomas Austin Yawkey purchased the struggling Boston Red Sox in 1933 and dedicated the next 44 years to building a model franchise, capturing American League pennants in 1946, '67 and '75. A popular leader in Boston, Yawkey was beloved by his players and the fans, and was a leader among owners.

Ted Williams once said, "He had a heart as big as a watermelon. I loved the man from the bottom of my heart. He was unselfish, fair, sincere and honest." Yawkey said, "I was always taught to help others; that those of us fortunate enough to be born with abundance should do what we can for those who are not."

Elected To The Hall Of Fame: *1980.*
Born: *February 21, 1903 at Detroit, MI.*
Died: *July 9, 1976 at Boston, MA.*

ROBERT CAL HUBBARD
UMPIRE
AMERICAN LEAGUE 1936-1951

The UMPIRES

AL BARLICK

A World War II Coast Guard veteran who entered the umpiring field because of a coal mining strike, Al Barlick served as a National League umpire for 28 seasons, breaking in at age 25.

With seven All-Star games and seven World Series assignments, he developed a reputation for hustle, stern demeanor and a strict, but fair, interpretation of the rules. Renowned for a booming voice, decisive hand signals and a superb knowledge of the rules, Barlick was also active in forming the umpires' union and was a leader in their drive for better pay and respect.

Elected To The Hall Of Fame: *1989.*
Born: *April 2, 1915 at Springfield, IL.*
Died: *December 27, 1995 at Springfield, IL.*

NESTOR CHYLAK

C onsidered the model umpire of the post-war era, Nestor Chylak was a skillful arbiter who earned the respect of players and managers alike during his 25-year major league career.

The longtime American League crew chief worked five All-Star Games, three League Championship Series and five World Series. During service in the U.S. Army in World War II, he nearly lost his eyesight in the Battle of the Bulge after being struck by shrapnel from an exploding shell. His courage merited the prestigious Silver Star and Purple Heart.

Elected To The Hall Of Fame: *1999.*
Born: *May 11, 1922 at Olyphant, PA.*
Died: *February 17, 1982 at Dunmore, PA.*

Jocko Conlan

Jocko Conlan became an umpire by accident when Red Ormsby was overcome by the heat while umpiring a 1935 game between the Chicago White Sox and St. Louis Browns. Conlan, an outfielder with the White Sox, was asked to fill in. The following year, Conlan launched his new career. A polka-dot tie, balloon chest protector and quick grin became his trademarks. Conlan won the respect of players and managers alike with his hustle, accuracy and fairness. He umpired in five World Series.

Elected To The Hall Of Fame: *1974.*
Born: *December 6, 1899 at Chicago, IL.*
Died: *April 16, 1989 at Scottsdale, AZ.*

Tom Connolly

An umpire for 35 years during the roughest era in baseball history, Englishman Tom Connolly gained players' respect as an impartial and fair-minded arbiter. Connolly umpired in the National League for three years before switching to the new American League in 1901, where he would stay for 32 years. Connolly was a calm and dignified disciplinarian who once went 10 consecutive seasons without ejecting a player. He umpired in the first modern World Series in 1903 and in eight overall.

Elected To The Hall Of Fame: *1953.*
Born: *December 31, 1870 at Manchester, England.*
Died: *April 28, 1961 at Natick, MA.*

BILLY EVANS

Athletic and educated, Billy Evans was only 22 when he joined the American League umpire crew in 1906, becoming the youngest major league umpire in history. Working six World Series during a 22-year career, Evans was lauded for fairness and superior integrity. Evans once said, "The umpire must be firm and insistent on his dignity but must not be officious." Besides being an umpire, Evans was an accomplished sportswriter. He also later served as a front office executive for the Cleveland Indians, Boston Red Sox and Detroit Tigers.

Elected To The Hall Of Fame: 1973.
Born: February 10, 1884 at Chicago, IL.
Died: January 23, 1956 at Miami, FL.

DOUG HARVEY

A methodical, authoritative umpire in the National League for more than three decades, Doug Harvey became so revered that players, managers and even fellow umpires dubbed him "god." Harvey joined the Senior Circuit's umpiring crew in 1962, the last umpire hired in the big leagues who did not attend umpire school. Working 4,673 games over 31 years, 18 as crew chief, Harvey often drew assignments to the game's biggest events, including six All-Star Games, nine National League Championship Series and five World Series.

God

Elected To The Hall Of Fame: 2010.
Born: March 13, 1930 at South Gate, CA.

CAL HUBBARD

Big, tough and smart, Cal Hubbard was one of the game's most respected umpires and was selected to call four World Series and three All-Star games. Hubbard had perhaps the strongest eyesight in sports, but a hunting accident damaged his vision, cutting short his career. He then supervised umpires and devised new ways to position them. Hubbard was a great athlete, included in the Pro Football Hall of Fame's first induction class and listed as the most feared lineman of his time. He remains the only man to be enshrined in both the Pro Football and Baseball Halls of Fame.

Elected To The Hall Of Fame: *1976.*
Born: *October 31, 1900 at Keytesville, MO.*
Died: *October 17, 1977 at Gulfport, FL.*

BILL KLEM

Colorful and flamboyant, Bill Klem brought dignity and respect to his profession. Known as "The Old Arbiter," he umpired almost exclusively behind the plate his first 16 years because of his superior ability to call balls and strikes. Klem was among the first to use arm signals to coincide with his calls. Proof of his skill and universal respect were his 18 World Series assignments. Klem umpired from 1905 to 1941 and then served as chief of National League umpires. When honored at the Polo Grounds on Sept. 2, 1949, he declared: "Baseball to me is not a game; it is a religion."

The Old Arbiter

Elected To The Hall Of Fame: *1953.*
Born: *February 22, 1874 at Rochester, NY.*
Died: *September 16, 1951 at Miami, FL.*

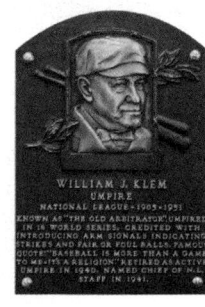

BILL McGOWAN

Bill McGowan was an exception to the old adage that fans don't pay to see the umpire. He introduced a colorful umpiring style with aggressive body gestures that bordered on the pugnacious. Yet McGowan ejected very few players. His enthusiasm never waned over 30 American League seasons, while his hustle and skill commanded the players' respect. In 1933, McGowan was selected to be a member of the umpiring crew that worked the initial All-Star Game. He was an iron man among umpires – not missing an inning for 16 years, spanning 2,541 consecutive games.

Elected To The Hall Of Fame: 1992.
Born: January 18, 1896 at Wilmington, DE.
Died: December 9, 1954 at Silver Spring, MD.

HANK O'DAY

A player, manager, umpire and scout for over 40 years in the National League, Hank O'Day served the league in many capacities, but it was as an umpire where O'Day made his greatest mark.

O'Day made his major league debut in 1884 as a pitcher for the Toledo Blue Stockings and ended his playing career in 1893 in the minors. He became a National League umpire in 1895 and umpired the first modern World Series in 1903 and 10 World Series overall. He took a break from umpiring to manage the Reds in 1912 and Cubs in 1914 but otherwise umpired through the 1927 season.

Elected To The Hall Of Fame: 2013
Born: July 8, 1859 at Chicago, IL
Died: July 2, 1935 at Chicago, IL
Umpire: National League 1888-89, 1893, 1895-1911, 1913, 1915-27; Players' League 1890

The
APPENDIX

Rules for Election to the National Baseball Hall of Fame by Members of the Baseball Writers' Association of America

1. Authorization: By authorization of the Board of Directors of the National Baseball Hall of Fame and Museum Inc., the Baseball Writers' Association of America is authorized to hold an election every year for the purpose of electing members to the Natwional Baseball Hall of Fame from the ranks of retired baseball players.

2. Electors: Only active and honorary members of the BBWAA, who have been active baseball writers for at least 10 years, shall be eligible to vote. They must have been active as baseball writers and members of the Association for a period beginning at least 10 years prior to the date of election in which they are voting.

3. Eligible Candidates: Candidates to be eligible must meet the following requirements:

(A) A baseball player must have been active as a player in the major leagues at some time during a period beginning 20 years before and ending five years prior to election.

(B) Player must have played in each of 10 Major League championship seasons, some part of which must have been within the period described in 3 (A).

(C) Player shall have ceased to be an active player in the Major Leagues at least five calendar years preceding the election but may be otherwise connected with baseball.

(D) In case of the death of an active player or a player who has been retired for less than five full years, a candidate who is otherwise eligible shall be eligible in the next regular election held at least six months after the date of death or after the end of the five-year period, whichever occurs first.

(E) Any player on Baseball's ineligible list shall not be an eligible candidate.

4. Method of Election:

(A) BBWAA screening committee: A screening committee consisting of baseball writers will be appointed by the BBWAA. This screening committee shall consist of six members, with two members to be elected at each Annual Meeting for a three-year term. The duty of the screening committee shall be to prepare a ballot listing in alphabetical order eligible candidates who (1) received a vote on a minimum of five percent of the ballots cast in the preceding election or (2) are eligible for the first time and are nominated by any two of the six members of the BBWAA screening committee.

(B) Electors may vote for as few as zero and as many as 10 eligible candidates deemed worthy of election. Write-in votes are not permitted.

(C) Any candidate receiving votes on 75 percent of the ballots cast shall be elected to membership in the National Baseball Hall of Fame.

5. Voting: Voting shall be based upon the player's record, playing ability, integrity, sportsmanship, character, and contributions to the team(s) on which the player played.

6. Automatic Elections: No automatic elections based on performances such as a batting average of .400 or more for one year, pitching a perfect game or similar outstanding achievement shall be permitted.

7. Time of Election: The duly authorized representatives of the BBWAA shall prepare, date and mail ballots to each elector no later than the 15th day of January in each year in which an election is held. The elector shall sign and return the completed ballot within 20 days. The vote shall then be tabulated by the duly authorized representatives of the BBWAA.

8. Certification of Election Results: The results of the election shall be certified by a representative of the Baseball Writers' Association of America and an officer of the National Baseball Hall of Fame and Museum Inc. The results shall be transmitted to the Commissioner of Baseball. The BBWAA and National Baseball Hall of Fame and Museum Inc. shall jointly release the results.

9. Amendments: The Board of Directors of the National Baseball Hall of Fame and Museum, Inc. reserves the right to revoke, alter or amend these rules at any time.

Rules For Election For Managers, Umpires, Executives And Players For Pre-Integration Era Candidates To The National Baseball Hall Of Fame

Name: The Pre-Integration Era Committee shall refer to the electorate that considers retired Major League Baseball players no longer eligible for election by the Baseball Writers' Association of America, along with managers, umpires and executives, whose greatest contributions to the game were realized from the 1876-1946 era.

Membership: The Pre-Integration Era Committee shall consist of 16 members, including members of the National Baseball Hall of Fame, executives, and veteran media members. The Chairman of the Board of Directors of the National Baseball Hall of Fame and Museum Inc. shall act as the non-voting chairman of the committee and shall act as non-voting Secretary of the Committee.

Method of Appointment: The Hall of Fame's Board of Directors shall appoint the Committee.

Term: Each appointee is to serve for a renewable term, with the Committee scheduled to meet on a cycle of once every three years.

Time and Place of Election: Beginning in 2012, an election for Pre-Integration Era candidates shall be held every three years at the Major League Baseball Winter Meetings. A quorum will consist of three-fourths of the total membership of the committee. Proxies are permitted in emergency situations only. In the absence of a quorum, a conference call with absent committee members will be permitted.

Eligible Candidates: Eligible candidates must be selected from managers, umpires, executives and players, who meet following criteria related to their classification: Players who played in at least 10 major league seasons, who are not on Major League Baseball's ineligible list, and have been retired for 21 or more seasons; managers and umpires with 10 or more years in baseball and retired for at least five years (candidates who are 65 years or older are eligible six months following retirement); executives retired for at least five years. Active executives 65 years or older are eligible for consideration.

Those whose careers entailed involvement in multiple categories will be considered for their overall contribution to the game of Baseball; however, the specific category in which these individuals shall be considered will be determined by the role in which they were most prominent. In those instances when a candidate is prominent as both a player and as a manager, executive or umpire, the BBWAA-appointed Historical Overview Committee shall determine that individual's category as a player, as a manager or as an umpire or as an executive/pioneer. Those designated as players must fulfill the requirements above.

Any person designated by the Office of the Commissioner of Major League Baseball as ineligible shall not be an eligible candidate.

Screening Committee: The BBWAA-appointed Historical Overview Committee shall serve as the Screening Committee and consist of 10-12 representatives. The Committee shall identify 10 candidates for the Pre-Integration Era Ballot.

Ballot Size: The final Pre-Integration Era Ballot shall consist of 10 candidates.

Voting: The Committee shall consider all 10 candidates and voting shall be based upon the individual's record, ability, integrity, sportsmanship, character and contribution to the game. Electors may vote for as few as zero and as many as four eligible candidates deemed worthy of election. Write-in votes are not permitted.

Number to be Elected: All candidates receiving votes on at least 75% of ballots cast will earn election.

Minutes/Certification: The Committee shall keep minutes of its meetings, one copy of which is to be placed on file at the National Baseball Hall of Fame and Museum Inc. The results of the election shall be certified by the Secretary of the Committee.

Amendments: The Board of Directors of the National Baseball Hall of Fame and Museum Inc. reserves the right to revoke, alter or amend these rules at any time.

RULES FOR ELECTION FOR MANAGERS, UMPIRES, EXECUTIVES AND PLAYERS FOR GOLDEN ERA CANDIDATES TO THE NATIONAL BASEBALL HALL OF FAME

Name: The Golden Era Committee shall refer to the electorate that considers retired Major League Baseball players no longer eligible for election by the Baseball Writers' Association of America, along with managers, umpires and executives, whose greatest contributions to the game were realized from the 1947-1972 era.

Membership: The Golden Era Committee shall consist of 16 members, including members of the National Baseball Hall of Fame, executives, and veteran media members. The Chairman of the Board of Directors of the National Baseball Hall of Fame and Museum, Inc. shall act as the non-voting chairman of the committee and shall act as non-voting Secretary of the Committee.

Method of Appointment: The Hall of Fame's Board of Directors shall appoint the Committee.

Term: Each appointee is to serve for a renewable term, with the Committee scheduled to meet on a cycle of once every three years.

Time and Place of Election: Beginning in 2011, an election for Golden Era candidates shall be held every three years at the Major League Baseball Winter Meetings. A quorum will consist of three-fourths of the total membership of the committee. Proxies are permitted in emergency situations only. In the absence of a quorum, a conference call with absent committee members will be permitted.

Eligible Candidates: Eligible candidates must be selected from managers, umpires, executives and players, who meet following criteria related to their classification: players who played in at least 10 major league seasons, who are not on Major League Baseball's ineligible list, and have been retired for 21 or more seasons; managers and umpires with 10 or more years in baseball and retired for at least five years (candidates who are 65 years or older are eligible six months following retirement); executives retired for at least five years. Active executives 65 years or older are eligible for consideration.

Those whose careers entailed involvement in multiple categories will be considered for their overall contribution to the game of Baseball; however, the specific category in which these individuals shall be considered will be determined by the role in which they were most prominent. In those instances when a candidate is prominent as both a player and as a manager, executive or umpire, the BBWAA-appointed Historical Overview Committee shall determine that individual's category as a player, as a manager or as an umpire or as an executive/pioneer. Those designated as players must fulfill the requirements above.

Any person designated by the Office of the Commissioner of Major League Baseball as ineligible shall not be an eligible candidate.

Screening Committee: The BBWAA-appointed Historical Overview Committee shall serve as the Screening Committee and consist of 10-12 representatives. The Committee shall identify 10 candidates for the Golden Era Ballot.

Ballot Size: The final Golden Era Ballot shall consist of 10 candidates.

Voting: The Committee shall consider all 10 candidates and voting shall be based upon the individual's record, ability, integrity, sportsmanship, character and contribution to the game. Electors may vote for as few as zero and as many as five eligible candidates deemed worthy of election. Write-in votes are not permitted.

Number to be Elected: All candidates receiving votes on at least 75 percent of ballots cast will earn election.

Minutes/Certification: The Committee shall keep minutes of its meetings, one copy of which is to be placed on file at the National Baseball Hall of Fame and Museum Inc. The results of the election shall be certified by the Secretary of the Committee.

Amendments: The Board of Directors of the National Baseball Hall of Fame and Museum Inc. reserves the right to revoke, alter or amend these rules at any time.

Rules For Election For Managers, Umpires, Executives And Players For Expansion Era Candidates To The National Baseball Hall Of Fame

Name: The Expansion Era Committee shall refer to the electorate that considers retired Major League Baseball players no longer eligible for election by the Baseball Writers' Association of America, along with managers, umpires and executives, whose greatest contributions to the game were realized from the 1973 to the present era.

Membership: The Expansion Era Committee shall consist of 16 members, including members of the National Baseball Hall of Fame, executives, and veteran media members. The Chairman of the Board of Directors of the National Baseball Hall of Fame and Museum Inc. shall act as the non-voting chairman of the committee and shall act as non-voting Secretary of the Committee.

Method of Appointment: The Hall of Fame's Board of Directors shall appoint the Committee.

Term: Each appointee is to serve for a renewable term, with the Committee scheduled to meet on a cycle of once every three years.

Time and Place of Election: Beginning in 2010, an election for Expansion Era candidates shall be held every three years at the Major League Baseball Winter Meetings. A quorum will consist of three-fourths of the total membership of the committee. Proxies are permitted in emergency situations only. In the absence of a quorum, a conference call with absent committee members will be permitted.

Eligible Candidates: Eligible candidates must be selected from managers, umpires, executives and players, who meet following criteria related to their classification: Players who played in at least 10 major league seasons, who are not on Major League Baseball's ineligible list, and have been retired for 21 or more seasons; managers and umpires with 10 or more years in baseball and retired for at least five years (candidates who are 65 years or older are eligible six months following retirement); executives retired for at least five years. Active executives 65 years or older are eligible for consideration.

Those whose careers entailed involvement in multiple categories will be considered for their overall contribution to the game of Baseball; however, the specific category in which these individuals shall be considered will be determined by the role in which they were most prominent. In those instances when a candidate is prominent as both a player and as a manager, executive or umpire, the BBWAA-appointed Historical Overview Committee shall determine that individual's category as a player, as a manager or as an umpire or as an executive/pioneer. Those designated as players must fulfill the requirements above.

Any person designated by the Office of the Commissioner of Major League Baseball as ineligible shall not be an eligible candidate.

Screening Committee: The BBWAA-appointed Historical Overview Committee shall serve as the Screening Committee and consist of 10-12 representatives. The Committee shall identify 12 candidates for the Expansion Era Ballot.

Ballot Size: The final Expansion Era Ballot shall consist of 12 candidates.

Voting: The Committee shall consider all 12 candidates and voting shall be based upon the individual's record, ability, integrity, sportsmanship, character and contribution to the game. Electors may vote for as few as zero and as many as five eligible candidates deemed worthy of election. Write-in votes are not permitted.

Number to be Elected: All candidates receiving votes on at least 75 percent of ballots cast will earn election.

Minutes/Certification: The Committee shall keep minutes of its meetings, one copy of which is to be placed on file at the National Baseball Hall of Fame and Museum Inc. The results of the election shall be certified by the Secretary of the Committee.

Amendments: The Board of Directors of the National Baseball Hall of Fame and Museum Inc. reserves the right to revoke, alter or amend these rules at any time.

NATIONAL BASEBALL HALL OF FAME MEMBERS (306)

YEAR-BY-YEAR

1936
Cobb, Tyrus R. (Ty)
Johnson, Walter P.
Mathewson, Christopher (Christy)
Ruth, George H. (Babe)
Wagner, John P. (Honus)

1937
Bulkeley, Morgan G.
Johnson, Byron Bancroft (Ban)
Lajoie, Napoleon (Nap)
Mack, Cornelius A. (Connie)
McGraw, John J.
Speaker, Tristram E. (Tris)
Wright, George
Young, Denton T. (Cy)

1938
Alexander, Grover C. (Pete)
Cartwright, Alexander J.
Chadwick, Henry

1939
Anson, Adrian C. (Cap)
Collins, Edward T.
Comiskey, Charles A.
Cummings, William A. (Candy)
Ewing, William (Buck)
Gehrig, Henry Louis (Lou)
Keeler, Willie H. (Wee Willie)
Radbourn, Charles G. (Old Hoss)
Sisler, George H.
Spalding, Albert G.

1942
Hornsby, Rogers

1944
Landis, Kenesaw M.

1945
Bresnahan, Roger P.
Brouthers, Dennis (Dan)
Clarke, Fred C.
Collins, James J.
Delahanty, Edward J.
Duffy, Hugh
Jennings, Hugh A.
Kelly, Michael J. (King)
O'Rourke, James H.
Robinson, Wilbert

1946
Burkett, Jesse C.
Chance, Frank L.
Chesbro, John D. (Jack)
Evers, John J.
Griffith, Clark C.
McCarthy, Thomas F.
McGinnity, Joseph J.
Plank, Edward S.
Tinker, Joseph B.
Waddell, George E. (Rube)
Walsh, Edward A.

1947
Cochrane, Gordon S. (Mickey)
Frisch, Frank F.
Grove, Robert M. (Lefty)
Hubbell, Carl O.

1948
Pennock, Herbert J.
Traynor, Harold J. (Pie)

1949
Brown, Mordecai
Gehringer, Charles L.
Nichols, Charles A. (Kid)

1951
Foxx, James E.
Ott, Melvin T. (Mel)

1952
Heilmann, Harry E.
Waner, Paul G.

1953
Barrow, Edward G.
Bender, Charles A. (Chief)
Connolly, Thomas H.
Dean, Jay H. (Dizzy)
Klem, William J.
Simmons, Aloysius H. (Al)
Wallace, Roderick J. (Bobby)
Wright, William H. (Harry)

1954
Dickey, William M.
Maranville, Walter J. (Rabbit)
Terry, William H.

1955
Baker, John Franklin (Home Run)
DiMaggio, Joseph P.
Hartnett, Charles L. (Gabby)
Lyons, Theodore A.
Schalk, Raymond W.
Vance, Arthur C. (Dazzy)

1956
Cronin, Joseph E.
Greenberg, Henry B. (Hank)

1957
Crawford, Samuel E.
McCarthy, Joseph V.

1959
Wheat, Zachariah D.

1961
Carey, Max, G.
Hamilton, William R.

1962
Feller, Robert W.A.
McKechnie, William B.
Robinson, Jack R.
Roush, Edd J.

1963
Clarkson, John G.
Flick, Elmer H.
Rice, Edgar C. (Sam)
Rixey, Eppa

1964
Appling, Lucius B. (Luke)
Faber, Urban C. (Red)
Grimes, Burleigh A.
Huggins, Miller J.
Keefe, Timothy J.
Manush, Henry E. (Heinie)
Ward, John Montgomery

1965
Galvin, James F. (Pud)

1966
Stengel, Charles D. (Casey)
Williams, Theodore S.

YEAR-BY-YEAR

1967
Rickey, Wesley Branch
Ruffing, Charles H. (Red)
Waner, Lloyd J.

1968
Cuyler, Hazen S. (Kiki)
Goslin, Leon A. (Goose)
Medwick, Joseph M.

1969
Campanella, Roy
Coveleski, Stanley
Hoyt, Waite C.
Musial, Stanley F.

1970
Boudreau, Louis
Combs, Earle B.
Frick, Ford C.
Haines, Jesse J.

1971
Bancroft, David J. (Beauty)
Beckley, Jacob P.
Hafey, Charles J. (Chick)
Hooper, Harry B.
Kelley, Joseph J.
Marquard, Richard W. (Rube)
Paige, Leroy R. (Satchel)
Weiss, George M.

1972
Berra, Lawrence P. (Yogi)
Gibson, Joshua
Gomez, Vernon L. (Lefty)
Harridge, William
Koufax, Sanford (Sandy)
Leonard, Walter F. (Buck)
Wynn, Early
Youngs, Royce M. (Ross)

1973
Clemente Walker, Roberto
Evans, William G.
Irvin, Monford (Monte)
Kelly, George L.
Spahn, Warren E.
Welch, Michael F. (Mickey)

1974
Bell, James T. (Cool Papa)
Bottomley, James L.
Conlan, John B. (Jocko)
Ford, Edward C. (Whitey)
Mantle, Mickey C.
Thompson, Samuel L.

1975
Averill, Howard Earl
Harris, Stanley R. (Bucky)
Herman, William J.
Johnson, William J. (Judy)
Kiner, Ralph M.

1976
Charleston, Oscar M.
Connor, Roger
Hubbard, Robert Cal
Lemon, Robert G.
Lindstrom, Frederick C.
Roberts, Robin E.

1977
Banks, Ernest
Dihigo Llanos, Martín
Lloyd, John H. (Pop)
Lopez, Alfonso R.
Rusie, Amos W.
Sewell, Joseph W.

1978
Joss, Adrian (Addie)
MacPhail, Leland S. (Larry)
Mathews, Edwin L.

1979
Giles, Warren C.
Mays, Willie H.
Wilson, Lewis R. (Hack)

1980
Kaline, Albert W.
Klein, Charles H.
Snider, Edwin D. (Duke)
Yawkey, Thomas A.

1981
Foster, Andrew (Rube)
Gibson, Robert
Mize, John R.

1982
Aaron, Henry L. (Hank)
Chandler, Albert B. (Happy)
Jackson, Travis C.
Robinson, Frank

1983
Alston, Walter E.
Kell, George C.
Marichal Sánchez, Juan A.
Robinson, Brooks C.

1984
Aparicio Montiel, Luis E.
Drysdale, Donald S.
Ferrell, Richard B.
Killebrew, Harmon C.
Reese, Harold H. (Pee Wee)

1985
Brock, Louis C.
Slaughter, Enos B. (Country)
Vaughan, Joseph F. (Arky)
Wilhelm, James Hoyt

1986
Doerr, Robert P.
Lombardi, Ernest N.
McCovey, Willie L.

1987
Dandridge, Raymond E.
Hunter, James A. (Catfish)
Williams, Billy L.

1988
Stargell, Wilver D. (Willie)

1989
Barlick, Albert Joseph
Bench, Johnny L.
Schoendienst, Albert F. (Red)
Yastrzemski, Carl M.

1990
Morgan, Joe L.
Palmer, James A.

1991
Carew, Rodney C.
Jenkins, Ferguson A. (Fergie)
Lazzeri, Anthony M.
Perry, Gaylord J.
Veeck, William L.

1992
Fingers, Roland G. (Rollie)
McGowan, William A.
Newhouser, Harold (Hal)
Seaver, George T. (Tom)

1993
Jackson, Reginald M.

1994
Carlton, Steven N.
Durocher, Leo
Rizzuto, Phillip F.

1995
Ashburn, Don Richard (Richie)
Day, Leon
Hulbert, William
Schmidt, Michael J.
Willis, Victor G.

1996
Bunning, James
Foster, William H.
Hanlon, Edward H. (Ned)
Weaver, Earl S.

1997
Fox, Jacob N. (Nellie)
Lasorda, Thomas C.
Niekro, Philip H.
Wells, Willie J.

1998
Davis, George S.
Doby, Lawrence E. (Larry)
MacPhail, Leland S. (Lee)
Rogan, Wilber J. (Bullet)
Sutton, Donald H.

1999
Brett, George H.
Cepeda Pennes, Orlando M.
Chylak, Nestor L.
Ryan, Lynn Nolan
Selee, Frank G.
Williams, Joe (Smokey)
Yount, Robin R.

2000
Anderson, George L. (Sparky)
Fisk, Carlton E.
McPhee, John A. (Bid)
Pérez Rigal, Atanasio (Tony)
Stearnes, Norman T. (Turkey)

2001
Mazeroski, Williams S.
Puckett, Kirby
Smith, Hilton
Winfield, David M.

2002
Smith, Osborne Earl (Ozzie)

2003
Carter, Gary E.
Murray, Eddie C.

2004
Eckersley, Dennis L.
Molitor, Paul L.

2005
Boggs, Wade
Sandberg, Ryne

2006
Brown, Raymond
Brown, Willard
Cooper, Andy
Grant, Franklin
Hill, Pete
Mackey, James R. (Biz)
Manley, Effa
Méndez, José
Pompez, Alejandro (Alex)
Posey, Cumberland (Cum)
Santop, Louis
Sutter, Bruce
Suttles, George (Mule)
Taylor, Ben
Torriente, Cristóbal
White, Solomon
Wilkinson, J.L.
Wilson, Ernest (Jud)

2007
Gwynn, Anthony K. (Tony)
Ripken Jr., Calvin E. (Cal)

2008
Dreyfuss, Barney
Gossage, Richard (Goose)
Kuhn, Bowie
O'Malley, Walter
Southworth, Billy
Williams, Richard (Dick)

2009
Gordon, Joseph L.
Henderson, Rickey N.H.
Rice, James E.

2010
Dawson, Andre N.
Harvey, Harold D. (Doug)
Herzog, Dorrel N.E. (Whitey)

2011
Alomar, Roberto
Blyleven, Bert
Gillick,Pat

2012
Larkin, Barry
Santo, Ron

2013
O'Day, Henry (Hank)
Ruppert, Jacob
White, James (Deacon)

2014
Cox, Robert (Bobby)
Glavine, Tom
La Russa, Anthony (Tony)
Maddux, Greg
Thomas, Frank
Torre, Joe

Pitchers *(74)*

Pete Alexander
Chief Bender
Bert Blyleven
Mordecai Brown
Raymond Brown
Jim Bunning
Steve Carlton
Jack Chesbro
John Clarkson
Andy Cooper
Stan Coveleski
Leon Day
Dizzy Dean
Martin Dihigo
Don Drysdale
Dennis Eckersley
Red Faber
Bob Feller
Rollie Fingers
Whitey Ford
Bill Foster
Pud Galvin
Bob Gibson
Tom Glavine
Lefty Gomez
Goose Gossage
Burleigh Grimes
Lefty Grove
Jesse Haines
Waite Hoyt
Carl Hubbell
Catfish Hunter
Ferguson Jenkins
Walter Johnson
Addie Joss
Tim Keefe
Sandy Koufax
Bob Lemon
Ted Lyons
Greg Maddux
Juan Marichal
Rube Marquard
Christy Mathewson
Joe McGinnity
José Méndez
Hal Newhouser
Kid Nichols
Phil Niekro
Satchel Paige
Jim Palmer
Herb Pennock
Gaylord Perry
Eddie Plank
Charles Radbourn

Eppa Rixey
Robin Roberts
Bullet Rogan
Red Ruffing
Amos Rusie
Nolan Ryan
Tom Seaver
Hilton Smith
Warren Spahn
Bruce Sutter
Don Sutton
Dazzy Vance
Rube Waddell
Ed Walsh
Mickey Welch
Hoyt Wilhelm
Joe Williams
Vic Willis
Early Wynn
Cy Young

Catchers *(16)*

Johnny Bench
Yogi Berra
Roger Bresnahan
Roy Campanella
Gary Carter
Mickey Cochrane
Bill Dickey
Buck Ewing
Rick Ferrell
Carlton Fisk
Josh Gibson
Gabby Hartnett
Ernie Lombardi
Biz Mackey
Louis Santop
Ray Schalk

First Basemen *(21)*

Cap Anson
Jake Beckley
Jim Bottomley
Dan Brouthers
Orlando Cepeda
Frank Chance
Roger Connor
Jimmie Foxx
Lou Gehrig
Hank Greenberg
George Kelly
Harmon Killebrew
Buck Leonard
Willie McCovey
Johnny Mize

Eddie Murray
Tony Pérez
George Sisler
Mule Suttles
Ben Taylor
Bill Terry

Second Baseman *(20)*

Roberto Alomar
Rod Carew
Eddie Collins
Bobby Doerr
Johnny Evers
Nellie Fox
Frankie Frisch
Joe Gordon
Frank Grant
Charlie Gehringer
Billy Herman
Rogers Hornsby
Nap Lajoie
Tony Lazzeri
Bill Mazeroski
Bid McPhee
Joe Morgan
Jackie Robinson
Ryne Sandberg
Red Schoendienst

Third Basemen *(16)*

Frank Baker
Wade Boggs
George Brett
Jimmy Collins
Ray Dandridge
Judy Johnson
George Kell
Fred Lindstrom
Eddie Mathews
Paul Molitor
Brooks Robinson
Ron Santo
Mike Schmidt
Pie Traynor
Deacon White
Jud Wilson

Shortstops *(24)*

Luis Aparicio
Luke Appling
Dave Bancroft
Ernie Banks
Lou Boudreau
Joe Cronin
George Davis

Travis Jackson
Hughie Jennings
Barry Larkin
Pop Lloyd
Rabbit Maranville
Pee Wee Reese
Cal Ripken Jr.
Phil Rizzuto
Joe Sewell
Ozzie Smith
Joe Tinker
Arky Vaughan
Honus Wagner
Bobby Wallace
John Ward
Willie Wells
Robin Yount

Left Fielders (21)

Lou Brock
Jesse Burkett
Fred Clarke
Ed Delahanty
Goose Goslin
Chick Hafey
Rickey Henderson
Monte Irvin
Joe Kelley
Ralph Kiner
Heinie Manush
Joe Medwick
Stan Musial
Jim O'Rourke
Jim Rice
Al Simmons
Willie Stargell
Zack Wheat
Billy Williams
Ted Williams
Carl Yastrzemski

Center Fielders (23)

Richie Ashburn
Earl Averill
Cool Papa Bell
Willard Brown
Max Carey
Oscar Charleston
Ty Cobb
Earle Combs
Joe DiMaggio
Larry Doby
Hugh Duffy
Billy Hamilton
Pete Hill

Mickey Mantle
Willie Mays
Kirby Puckett
Edd Roush
Duke Snider
Tris Speaker
Turkey Stearnes
Cristóbal Torriente
Lloyd Waner
Hack Wilson

Right Fielders (24)

Hank Aaron
Roberto Clemente
Sam Crawford
Kiki Cuyler
Andre Dawson
Elmer Flick
Tony Gwynn
Harry Heilmann
Harry Hooper
Reggie Jackson
Al Kaline
Willie Keeler
King Kelly
Chuck Klein
Tommy McCarthy
Mel Ott
Sam Rice
Frank Robinson
Babe Ruth
Enos Slaughter
Sam Thompson
Paul Waner
Dave Winfield
Ross Youngs

Designated Hitter (1)

Frank Thomas

Managers (23)

Walter Alston
Sparky Anderson
Bobby Cox
Leo Durocher
Rube Foster
Ned Hanlon
Bucky Harris
Whitey Herzog
Miller Huggins
Tony La Russa
Tommy Lasorda
Al Lopez
Connie Mack
Joe McCarthy

John McGraw
Bill McKechnie
Wilbert Robinson
Frank Selee
Billy Southworth
Casey Stengel
Joe Torre
Dick Williams
Earl Weaver

Umpires (10)

Al Barlick
Nestor Chylak
Jocko Conlan
Tom Connolly
Billy Evans
Doug Harvey
Cal Hubbard
Bill Klem
Bill McGowan
Hank O'Day

Executives (33)

Ed Barrow
Morgan Bulkeley
Alexander Cartwright
Henry Chadwick
Happy Chandler
Charles Comiskey
Candy Cummings
Barney Dreyfuss
Rube Foster
Ford Frick
Warren Giles
Pat Gillick
Clark Griffith
Will Harridge
William Hulbert
Ban Johnson
Bowie Kuhn
Kenesaw Landis
Larry MacPhail
Effa Manley
Walter O'Malley
Alex Pompez
Cumberland Posey Jr.
Branch Rickey
Jacob Ruppert
A.G. Spalding
Bill Veeck
George Weiss
J. L. Wilkinson
Sol White
George Wright
Harry Wright
Tom Yawkey

DID YOU KNOW?

An estimated average 15,000 fans annually attend Hall of Fame Induction Ceremonies. In 2007, an estimated 75,000 fans packed Cooperstown, honoring the Hall of Fame induction of Cal Ripken Jr. and Tony Gwynn and setting a Hall of Fame Weekend attendance record.

■ When the All-Star Game debuted on July 6, 1933 in Chicago, the National Baseball Hall of Fame and Museum in Cooperstown, N.Y., was not yet a part of the American lexicon. But for 17 players, both managers and two umpires, Cooperstown – and immortality – would become a part of their future. Of the 30 players that appeared in that first All-Star Game, 17 – eight from the National League and nine from the American League – would one day be elected to the Hall of Fame. The NL box score featured future Hall of Famers Frankie Frisch, Chick Hafey, Gabby Hartnett, Carl Hubbell, Chuck Klein, Bill Terry, Pie Traynor and Paul Waner, while future Hall of Famers who appeared in the game for the AL included Earl Averill, Joe Cronin, Rick Farrell, Lou Gehrig, Charlie Gehringer, Lefty Gomez, Lefty Grove, Babe Ruth and Al Simmons. The teams were managed by future Hall of Famers Connie Mack (AL) and John McGraw (NL), with future Hall of Fame umpires Bill Klem and Bill McGowan at first and second base, respectively.

■ A total of 571 ballots were cast by Baseball Writers' Association of America Hall of Fame voters in 2014, marking the 12th time that more than 500 ballots have been cast: (also: 515-2001; 506-2004; 516-2005; 520-2006; 545-2007; 543-2008; 539-2009; 539-2010; 581-2011; 573-2012; 569-2013). At least 400 ballots have been cast in every election since 1986. Voting privileges are extended to those BBWAA members meeting their organization's Hall of Fame voting qualifications and in good standing with the BBWAA. Voters can select from zero to 10 names on their Hall of Fame ballot. Votes on 75 percent of all ballots cast are necessary for election.

■ 2014 marked the 70th Hall of Fame election held by the Baseball Writers' Association of America. Starting in 1936, the BBWAA has elected someone 62 times and on eight occasions it did not elect anyone (1945, 1946, 1950, 1958, 1960, 1971, 1996, 2013). On nine occasions, no election was held (1940, 1941, 1943, 1944, 1957, 1959, 1961, 1963, 1965). The BBWAA membership has elected from zero to five candidates in each of its 70 elections. The BBWAA has voted in one player more than any other quantity (26 times).

■ Through 2014, the Hall of Fame is composed of 306 elected members. Included are 211 former major league players, 28 executives, 35 Negro Leaguers, 22 managers and 10 umpires. The Baseball Writers' Association of America has elected 115 candidates to the Hall while the veterans committees (in all forms) has chosen 162 deserving candidates (96 major leaguers, 28 executives, 19 managers, 10 umpires and nine Negro Leaguers). The defunct "Committee on Negro Baseball Leagues" selected nine men between 1971-77 and the Special Committee on Negro Leagues in 2006, elected 17 Negro leaguers.

■ Through 2014, 47 players have been elected to the Hall of Fame in their first year of eligibility (13 pitchers, seven RF, six LF, four CF, five SS, three 2B, five 3B, two 1B, one DH and one catcher; position based on where electee played the majority of his big league games). Other than the inaugural Hall of Fame election in 1936, 1999 is the only year where as many as three first-year candidates were elected at once.

■ Including the Class of 2014, there are 48 Hall of Famers who spent their entire careers with one team. 2012 inductee Barry Larkin is the most recent addition to that list. The others: Luke Appling, Ernie Banks, Johnny Bench, George Brett, Roy Campanella, Roberto Clemente, Earle Combs, Bill Dickey, Joe DiMaggio, Bobby Doerr, Don Drysdale, Red Faber, Bob Feller, Whitey Ford, Lou Gehrig, Charlie Gehringer, Bob Gibson, Tony Gwynn, Carl Hubbell, Travis Jackson, Walter Johnson, Addie Joss, Al Kaline, Sandy Koufax, Bob Lemon, Ted Lyons, Mickey Mantle, Bill Mazeroski, Bid McPhee, Stan Musial, Mel Ott, Jim Palmer, Kirby Puckett, Pee Wee Reese, Jim Rice, Cal Ripken Jr., Phil Rizzuto, Brooks Robinson, Jackie Robinson, Mike Schmidt, Willie Stargell, Pie Traynor, Bill Terry, Ted Williams, Carl Yastrzemski, Robin Yount and Ross Youngs.

PHOTO CREDITS

George C. Burke: **Elmer Flick** (Page 169). **John Cordes: Paul Molitor** (Page 325); **Nolan Ryan** (Page 389). **Charles M. Conlon: Frank Baker** (Page 39); **Tom Connolly** (Page 527); **Sam Crawford** (Page 121); **Joe Cronin** (Page 123); **Bill Dickey** (Page 139); **Billy Evans** (Cover, Page 528); **Johnny Evers** (Page 155); **Frankie Frisch** (Page 179); **Chick Hafey** (Page 209); **Jesse Haines** (Page 211); **Rogers Hornsby** (Page 227); **Miller Huggins** (Page 500); **Joe Medwick** (Page 319); **Eddie Plank** (Page 353); **Sam Rice** (Page 363); **Joe Sewell** (Page 405); **Tris Speaker** (Page 421); **Ed Walsh** (Page 455); **Paul Waner** (Page 459). **George Dorrill: Mordecai Brown** (Page 71). **Carl J. Horner: Jimmy Collins** (Page 111). **Webster Jeffrey: Harry Wright** (Page 524). **Brad Mangin: Dennis Eckersley** (Page 153); **Barry Larkin** (Page 275); **Greg Maddux** (Page 13); **Frank Thomas** (Page 15).

Doug McWilliams: **Rod Carew** (Page 83); **Ray Dandridge** (Page 127); **Catfish Hunter** (Page 233); **Reggie Jackson** (Page 237); **Joe Morgan** (Page 327); **Phil Niekro** (Page 337); **Jim Palmer** (Page 345); **Tony Perez** (Page 349); **Brooks Robinson** (Page 373); **Ryne Sandberg** (Page 391); **Ron Santo** (Page 393); **Mike Schmidt** (Page 399); **Willie Stargell** (Page 423); **Billy Williams** (Page 473); **Robin Yount** (Cover, Page 495). **Anthony Neste: Steve Carlton** (Page 87); **Don Sutton** (Page 431). **G. Frank E. Pearsall: Henry Chadwick** (Page 509). **PhotoFile: Lou Brock** (Page 67); **Roy Campanella** (Page 81); **Don Drysdale** (Page 149); **Harmon Killebrew** (Page 265); **Mickey Mantle** (Page 293); **Willie Mays** (Cover, Page 307). **Rich Pilling: Cal Ripken Jr.** (Page 365); **Bruce Sutter** (Page 427).

Michael Ponzini: **Roberto Alomar** (Page 27); **George Brett** (Page 65). **Richard Raphael: Johnny Bench** (Page 49); **Rollie Fingers** (Page 165); **Tom Seaver** (Page 403). **Lou Sauritch: Bert Blyleven** (Page 55); **Wade Boggs** (Page 57); **Gary Carter** (Page 89); **Andre Dawson** (Page 131); **Carlton Fisk** (Page 167); **Tony Gwynn** (Page 207); **Doug Harvey** (Page 528); **Rickey Henderson** (Page 219); **Jim Rice** (Page 361); **Dave Winfield** (Page 485). **Herman Seid: Lou Boudreau** (Page 61). **William M. Vander Weyde: Fred Clarke** (Page 99). **Ben Van Houten: Pat Gillick** (Page 513). **Louis Van Oeyen: Earle Combs** (Page 113); **Stan Coveleski** (Page 119); **Lefty Gomez** (Page 191); **Napoleon Lajoie** (Page 273). **Don Wingfield: Luis Aparicio** (Page 31); **Ernie Banks** (Page 43); **Whitey Ford** (Page 171).

ON THE COVER

Front (clockwise from upper left): Bobby Cox, Billy Evans, Cool Papa Bell, Sandy Koufax, Buck Leonard, Robin Yount, Al Simmons, Willie Mays.

Back (clockwise from upper left): Leo Durocher, Nester Chylak, Mickey Welsh, Monte Irvin, Barney Dreyfuss, Joe Gordon, Tony La Russa, Satchel Paige.

STATISTICS

Statistics provided by Baseball-Reference.com. There are no formal or official statistics from the various Negro Major Leagues. Statistics included on these pages were produced by the Negro League Researchers and Authors Group as part of a major study on African-American baseball history. These numbers were compiled from box scores found in more than 120 newspapers and other resources, and include only league-sanctioned games from 1920 through 1954 for which there is a viable box score. Exhibition games and other related events are not included. There are many seasons and games where no useable information has been found, so these figures are not included. Different publications have attempted to rebuild the Negro Leagues' statistics, each of which established different criteria for inclusion, so numbers may vary greatly from source to source.